Women and Revolution in Africa, Asia, and the New World

Edited by Mary Ann Tétreault

University of South Carolina Press

Published in Columbia, South Carolina, by the
University of South Carolina Press

Manufactured in the United States of America

Library of Congress Cataloging-in-Publication Data

Women and revolution in Africa, Asia, and the New World / edited by
Mary Ann Tétreault
p. cm.
Includes bibliographical references and index.
ISBN 1–57003–016–2
1. Women in politics—History. 2. Revolutions—History.
I. Tétreault, Mary Ann, 1942–
HQ1236.W6364 1995
305.42—dc20 94–18706

This book is dedicated to the women whose efforts to free themselves and their people have been erased and forgotten.

We remember you.

Contents

Women and Revolution in Africa, Asia, and the New World

I

Introduction

Chapter 1

Women and Revolution:

A Framework for Analysis

Mary Ann Tétreault

In *Political Order in Changing Societies*, Samuel Huntington defines revolution as "a rapid, fundamental, and violent domestic change in the dominant values and myths of a society, in its political institutions, social structure, leadership, and government activity and policies."[1] Most of the academic literature dealing with revolutions concentrates on their social origins, their particular or generic progress as coherent sets of events, and their consequences for state structure, political institutions, class relations, and the international system.[2] When individuals and families are examined in the context of revolution it is generally as representatives of their class[3] or, in recent studies by scholars whom Lawrence Stone calls "revisionists," as single consciousnesses acting and reacting in a unique immediate environment.[4] The connection between revolution and family structure itself is seldom the focus of analysis,[5] though studies of the family frequently examine the intersection of politics and family life.[6]

In this essay and in this volume, revolution is considered primarily from the perspectives of women and families. Taking Huntington's definition literally, there is no more fundamental context for values and myths than the family that produces human beings as physical and social creatures.[7] In Marxian terms, the family reproduces the social relations of production: it rears the new generation to conform to a particular political economy and the social arrangements that underpin that economy. Both structures are targets of revolutionary transformation. Why and how do families produce individuals who challenge the structures rather than conform to them?

The family also provides the basic model for a domestic context. International relations theorists such as Kenneth Waltz, assert that international politics and domestic politics vary radically because each one is characterized by a different method of social control.[8] Actors in the international system strive autonomously for status and power among themselves, constrained only by the actions of other, similarly (though not equally) autonomous actors. Domestic politics is mediated by the state which monopolizes the legitimate use of coercion. State power reduces the autonomy of all other domestic actors. It makes them, to varying but always significant degrees, subservient to the state that can command their resources, and dependent upon the state for protection from one another and from other states. This distinction is mirrored in analyses that compare the public space of domestic political action to the private space of the household. As described by Hannah Arendt,[9] the public space is filled with autonomous men of action, striving among themselves for status and glory. Within the private space, hidden from the public arena, the head of the household, who monopolizes the legitimate use of coercion, directs the rest of the inhabitants to produce for his needs in return for his protection and a place in the household community. The analogy between international and domestic politics and power relations in the public and private spaces informs theories about each set of relationships and reinforces assumptions that these theories are fundamentally correct.

Women have been more closely associated with the family than men in most cultures. The family and the state are interdependent social forms. They are organized along parallel lines but their interests frequently conflict. States mobilize instrumental resources in the form of men and wealth generated by families. Aspirants to the overthrow of states and regimes must compete with them for these resources. Unless a revolution can topple an old regime within a very short period of time, its ultimate triumph depends upon successful appeals to women and families to supply resources to nourish it. As primary producers, women are essential for a sustained challenge to the state to be successful. However, their cooperation is not free. In this volume we examine the contexts of alliances between revolutionary movements and women, and assess the rewards of cooperation for women and families under victorious post-revolutionary regimes.

DEFINING REVOLUTION

Revolution as an analytical category is itself problematic. In the earliest writings of western philosophers, revolutions are treated as events that transform domestic political relations but are the products rather than the causes of the social order. Aristotle, who wrote extensively about revolutions in ancient city-states, looked at changes in political structures as normal outcomes of conflicts among social groups whose relative rise and decline change the number and character of the hands on the levers of power.[10] Aristotle did not regard revolution as producing novelty nor did he regard it as altering, in any fundamental way, the role of the state or the social structure over which it presides, even though the nature or stability of a regime may be affected by the qualities of a social structure. For example, Aristotle writes that oligarchy and mass rule often alternate in the absence of a middle class that could support a stable democracy. Among eastern philosophies, both Hinduism and Confucianism explain revolution as part of a cyclical process analogous to birth, growth, degeneration, and decay. Again, novelty and changes of state are absent from these models.

In contrast, later writers see among the outcomes of revolution the dawning of a new age characterized by the appearance of new men and new relationships among human beings. New age references make their first appearances in Western political thought with the spread of Christianity through the Mediterranean world. Many Christian new age thinkers wrote and spoke extensively about reordering gender relations as part of what they saw as a revolutionary transformation initiated by Christ, and women were prominent in burgeoning Christian sects. Struggles to control the church were often fought on formal lines drawn by considerations of gender and sexuality in the new age.[11] The adoption of virginity as a Christian ideal challenged the state by threatening its resource base, jeopardizing the continued reproduction of persons as well as household formation and economic productivity. The Augustinian counter-revolution rescinded the expansion of freedom for women that some early Christians had found in the teachings of Christ.[12] It reimposed the authority of the state and the now separate but still institutional church, mediated by a male priesthood and male heads of household, over production and reproduction. This model of revolution, mobilizing women with the promise of freedom followed by counter-revolution reimposing controls on women's productivity and reproductivity for the benefit of men and states, is widely observable in the modern world.

Nineteenth- and twentieth-century writers on revolution, whose ideas were shaped by the rationalist values of the Enlightenment rather than by religious ideologies, explain revolutionary transformation as a logical result of the structural changes fueled by modernization.[13] Examples of this can be found in *The Communist Manifesto* by Karl Marx and Friedrich Engels, which develops a scientific theory of revolution based on dialectical materialism, and in Vladimir Lenin's writings on imperialism that project an external international arena, and an internal domestic arena as jointly responsible for changes leading to revolution. These and other modern students of revolution also project the vision of a new age, a recreation of the individual and the structure of social life, as important and valued outcomes of revolution. Such visions of a new age are not confined to scholars. In seventeenth-century England and eighteenth-century North America and France, modern revolutionaries made attempts as strenuous as those devised by members of the early Christian sects and the later molders of the new Soviet man to create social and ideological structures that would cement the gains of their revolutions in patterns they hoped would survive political and moral backsliding.[14]

Many modern studies of revolution focus on social groups and classes rather than on ideologies or psychologies. Some of these studies examine modernization as a cause of revolution, although the connection between modernization and revolution may be viewed differently and few of these studies consider women as a separate category of participants in revolutionary transformation. For example, Huntington proposes two ways to categorize revolutions, both dominated by domestic considerations.[15] The Eastern pattern is generated by the struggle of new men produced by economic modernization against a strongly entrenched governing class dominated by traditional elites. Although the new men control significant resources, the old elites shut them out of political participation. This forces the new men into the periphery, where they build bases from which to challenge the legitimacy and power of the central government. The relative strength of the old regime requires that it be overthrown through violent means, a process that may take a long time to accomplish in spite of Huntington's inclusion of speed as a characteristic of revolutions. In Western revolutions, the central government collapses rapidly as the result of its inability to respond to the demands of a modernizing economy and its associated new classes.

Huntington sees Western revolutions as relatively nonviolent. His judgment is contested by Barrington Moore who argues that Western revolutions only look less brutal because the violence that accompanies them is spread out over long periods of time and is accomplished more by apparently natural processes, such as starvation and exposure, than by force of arms on fields of battle.[16] Like Huntington, however, Moore develops an essentially domestic theory of revolutions as the outcome of the modernization process. He argues that the differences in the regimes they generate are due to differences in their class bases. Bourgeois revolutions are shaped primarily by commercial classes and result in liberal democracies. Elite revolutions, often called "revolutions from above," are created by alliances between capitalists and modernizing elements within the old regime. They result in fascist systems. Peasant-based revolutions, whatever the nature of other participating groups, give rise to communist states. Moore stresses that the makers of revolution and the beneficiaries of revolution are seldom the same people, and that every transition to industrialization has been pushed by a ruthless minority.[17]

Theda Skoçpol treats revolution as proceeding from domestic and international political, economic, and social conditions. She is most interested in social revolutions, "basic transformations of a society's state and class structures . . . accompanied and partly carried through by class-based revolts from below."[18] This kind of revolution corresponds to some degree to Huntington's Eastern pattern and Moore's communist revolutions. But Skoçpol's explicit inclusion of an international dimension places her theory of revolutions firmly in the context of world historical time and of a state that is one among others of its kind. Interstate competition for power and wealth is grounded in the ability of the participants to command domestic resources. Thus the state is the pivot around which interstate competition and intrastate resource transfers occur. External pressures can force a state to extract more resources from its population in order to remain competitive internationally, but these pressures may also affect the state's ability to crush internal dissent if there are not enough resources to go around. Successful rebellion against such a state results either in eventual accommodation to a new class within the elite—a political revolution in Skoçpol's terms—or to a growing vulnerability to peasant revolts that simultaneously bring down an old regime and destroy its social bases—a social revolution.

Huntington, Moore, and Skoçpol explain the origins and outcomes of revolution in terms of class relations, the nature and adaptability of state institutions, and the position of the state among other states. In seeking primary causes of successful revolutions, these models discount motivation, ideology, and other individually based phenomena that register losses of legitimacy in the Weberian sense. Yet, if a solely structural focus is used in the study of revolutions, we lose an important explanation, not simply of the process by which revolutionary groups are mobilized, but also of the particular structure, especially the fine structure, of post-revolutionary society—the new age. Although theorists such as Tocqueville justifiably believe that the old regime structures of state and society have a remarkable ability to persist into the new age,[19] revolutions both require and make possible fundamental change in at least some of these structures. This, after all, is how we define revolution. The content of revolutionary ideologies, from the rationalism of the French to the Islamic fundamentalism of the Iranians, shapes not only the social and political structures of the new age but, more importantly, the grounds upon which its political battles are fought: the terms of discourse that define structural and political power in post-revolutionary societies.

This political discourse is embedded in normative and positive theories about political and social systems. A new age order is least susceptible to challenge when these theories are congruent, that is, when the mechanisms or patterns of order they postulate as natural or preferred are similar to each other.[20] When this occurs, the propositions of these theoretical systems resonate in a hegemonic ideology, the dominant interpretation of empirical observations of real systems.[21] The symmetry among normative beliefs, positive theory, and a hegemonic ideology is an integral element in a new age order and becomes the "problematique" of the theories generated during its dominance.[22] Thus, the survival of revolutionary ideology is contingent on social change, just as social change expressed in new institutions is contingent on some vision of a just or desirable social order. If a post-revolutionary regime cannot or will not make or mediate changes in social structures congruent with revolutionary ideology and practice, the system transformation effected by the revolution will unravel.

From this perspective, revolutions are attempts to guide the process of political change along a preferred path of system transformation. This is not to say that revolutions actually achieve any or all of the outcomes desired by revolutionaries. Revolutions are neither unitary nor static. Different participants hope for different outcomes or different emphases among a set of shared goals. These emphases and even the goals themselves change as individuals and groups rise or are destroyed over the course of the conflict. Outcomes are as much or more dependent upon resources and the composition of the coalitions that support new regimes. But despite their dependence on material means and particular casts of characters, revolutions are as much struggles over symbols—theoretical concepts—as struggles over political and economic power. The resulting disruption of congruence allows alternative models—different arrangements of symbols—to be developed, and opens a political space in which they can be manipulated and made concrete through the development of new structures and institutions. The culmination of this process is a new problematique, a new set of theories, and a new symmetry. The demands of congruence are also constrained by material reality and the persistence of particular human relationships, explaining the high degree of continuity between pre- and post-revolutionary social orders.

GENDER AS CLASS, FAMILY AS STRUCTURE

Two issues must be examined before a discussion of women and revolution can proceed. The first is the question of gender as class: do women and men have different interests based solely on gender? On the one hand, women are perceived to be biologically bound to human reproduction in ways that men are not. The physical facts of pregnancy and lactation are often translated theoretically as embedding women, through their biological role, in the private subsistence economy of the household.[23] Women have rarely been viewed as agents in the public exchange economy of the polis. Indeed, Claude Lévi-Strauss argues that women themselves are status markers and commodities in pre-modern exchange orders.[24] The personification of women as human individuals or as members of the social groups into which we categorize men is thereby blurred or even negated. On the other hand, women and men could have substantially similar interests related to their social class and factors such as regional ties, ethnicity, and religion. Some of the rhetoric of the black civil rights movement in the United States calls upon black women to repudiate feminist alliances with white, generally middle-class women, and devote their activities to the pursuit of their true interests as oppressed black women in alliance with oppressed black men.[25] But despite this rhetoric, history is replete with evidence of gender as class underlying social orders. Scholars from a variety of disciplinary and ideological perspectives have found evidence of gender class consciousness in patriarchal societies.[26] But while men often see themselves as a gender class, women seldom do. The reasons for this are chiefly structural, located in marriage and the family as social institutions.

Marriage in many cultures is arranged so that female partners face structural disadvantages even where formal oppressive institutions such as polygyny are absent. For example, social mores often prescribe an age difference in spouses favoring men; property arrangements generally favor men; education, social activities and linkages, and political rights also favor men. Biology reflects this social inequality: on the average, men are larger than women. Even more restricting, women bear physical evidence of sexual experience while men do not, allowing virginity to be used to guarantee the restricted rearing and therefore the ignorance of a new bride. In parts of the Mediterranean world even today, a woman who is suspected of not being a virgin when she marries is killed by male kinsmen,[27] reinforcing the power of patriarchy through deterrence. The outcome of these marriages is often a modal marriage pairing between a larger, older, better educated, richer, sexually experienced, and legally favored man, and a smaller, younger, less well educated, propertyless, inexperienced, and socially and legally less well protected woman. The structural disadvantages make it difficult for the weaker partner to assert herself, much less to protect herself from exploitation and violence. The persistence of structural inequality in marriage is visible in most cultures including many where women's political rights are nominally protected by law.[28]

Women are also not a new class in the sense that the term is used to identify groups of men whose roles and interests did not exist before modernization and the theories and problematiques it gave rise to. New men are important agents of system transformation—their resources enable them to reorder systems in which they are denied suitable access to public space.[29] Like new men, women are also restricted from the public arena but have fewer resources than new men to help them break in. When new men make revolutions they may mobilize women as auxiliaries, but such women do not have a distinct political identity in their own right and thus hold little claim on the new order for status, power, or justice.

Family structure affects whether women can develop a gender class consciousness. It also mediates the connection between the family and the larger society that makes the family effective or ineffective as a locus of revolutionary activity. In the next section, I will describe two ideal types of family structure, the privatized family and the socially embedded family, and assess both types of families' potential as agents of revolutionary transformation. Here I would like to indicate the mechanism by which family structure impinges on gender class consciousness among women.

Structures that isolate adult women from one another, especially from their generational peers, reduce the potential for gender class consciousness among women. The classical example is the nuclear family with a mother who does not work outside the home.[30] Its utility for the support of patriarchy is part of the reason why it is so idealized in philosophical and political polemics (see the discussion of Rousseau below). A family structure that alienates as well as isolates is the traditional Japanese family described by Ruth Benedict in *The Chrysanthemum and the Sword*.[31] Here, the son brings his wife to the patriarchal home where she is isolated both from society and from him by her mother-in-law. The isolation of the Japanese wife continues even in modern nuclear families today through social proscriptions against "well-side chat," female generational peers gathering together for anything other than prescribed and supervised occasions.[32] Such family structures, that isolate and block the development of gender class consciousness among women, are poor agents of revolutionary transformation.

The importance of family and family ideology in a society is directly connected to the role of the family as the primary agent of socialization. The family reproduces not simply the biological individual but also the social relations of politics and production. The patriarchal family is characteristic of hierarchical societies and authoritarian regimes. It is not so much that men in such a society are given women to repress to make up for their own repression, as that these men live with the remembrance of their cherished mothers as female models of powerlessness and submission.[33] Perhaps such men learn to hate women because their mothers could not protect them, and then they learn to hate themselves for their own acquiescence to those in authority.[34]

SOCIETY, FAMILY, AND REVOLUTION

Although many scholars believe that one can talk about changes in the status of groups of men without considering the structure of the family and its place in society, few would argue that changes in the status of women can be considered this way. This is partly because of male gender class consciousness and its resultant relegation of women and families to the status of environmental factors affecting—or not affecting—conflicts among men. It is also part of the rhetorical struggle to identify the family with a social and cultural system that reflects the values of individuals and groups contending for political, economic, and private power in public space. Theories about the origin of the family from the Genesis myth to the more formal arguments of scholars are embedded in deeply held beliefs about the nature of woman as separate from the nature of man and the place of the family in the moral order.[35] These theories also reflect assumptions about the role of the family in society. Roughly speaking, analysts fall into two groups with respect to the latter issue, those who think that the structure of the family is not connected to the structure of the social order, and those who believe that it is.

Rousseau, for example, who believed that modern society corrupted human nature, looked back to a state of nature predating civilization to determine the basic nature of man, woman, and human society. He postulated the existence of three stages of social development. The first was an original, sexually egalitarian state of nature where men and women lived identical lives as self-sufficient, unattached individuals who reproduced the species as the result of random sexual encounters. The second stage resulted from what Rousseau calls the first revolution, which might be defined as the domestication of women. This stage was based on the social equality of patriarchal nuclear families living in relative isolation from one another. Within this family, there was a complete division of labor between the sexes resulting in the economic dependence of women on men. Rousseau's third stage followed the great revolution, the invention of agriculture and metallurgy. This revolution produced a division of labor among men and, as a result, was the origin of social inequality in Rousseau's sense—that is, social inequality among men.[36] It is the division of labor that is the key to inequality, but Rousseau ignores its effects in the second stage. Here, where women are totally dependent on and subservient to men while each man is equal to and independent of all other men, Rousseau found the ideal, egalitarian society. Analytically, Rousseau separated the family from "particular social and economic arrangements and power relationships,"[37] making women irrelevant to considerations of political and social change.

Engels was also concerned about social inequality. His discussion of the origin of the family was intended to show how capitalism degraded human relationships and put women in bondage. Unlike Rousseau's, Engels's state of nature was based on the notion of an original organic unity of family and society, the gens.[38] In these early human groups, men and women did not pair off into nuclear families but lived communally. Lineage was traced through the mother, the only parent whose biological connection to the child was unambiguous. This primitive society was imagined to have been classless and egalitarian with respect to gender. Engels believed that women instituted "the pairing family" that, together with the development of a more complex economy, ended the egalitarian Eden.[39] Humanity's "lowest interests—base greed, brutal appetites, sordid avarice, selfish robbery of the common wealth" precipitated "a fall from the simple moral greatness of the old gentile society."[40] These lowest interests led to the development of private property which isolated individual pairing families as men in these families seized and held property for themselves. Men overthrew traditional kinship forms in order to keep their property to themselves and transmit it to their sons. As a result, women were subjugated, slavery was instituted, and economic classes developed. And to perpetuate "this growing cleavage of society into classes [and] also the right of the possessing class to exploit the non-possessing . . . [t]he state was invented."[41]

Social scientists have shown us that both of these models of the natural family are idealizations and over-generalizations. Family and kinship patterns differ across cultures as well as within cultures over time. Spike Peterson's work on families in ancient Greece and Mesopotamia demonstrates that their evolving structure is tied to the historical event of the formation of the state. She argues that Athenian family structure has been reified as the state of nature to most Western political philosophers, such as Rousseau, even though the developed patriarchy of Athenian high culture came from antecedents that dispute its position as the paradigm of the family in the state of nature.[42] K. J. Dover's examination of Greek homosexuality also challenges the natural qualities of family life in ancient Greece, tying the legal and ideological construction of intimate personal relationships to the military requirements of Greek city states.[43]

In his study of the evolution of the family in England from the sixteenth through the eighteenth centuries, Stone also finds explicit connections between the state and family structure. He argues that the patriarchal family in England was fostered by the mutual interests of an absolutist state and post-reformation sects. Both encouraged the development of psychological and physical boundaries between the nuclear family, where the father was "a legalized petty tyrant," and kin, neighbors, and other elements in civil society likely to challenge the control of the population by the authoritarian state or the authoritarian sect.[44] Stone sees family life prior to the early modern period as relatively permeable to the demands of kin and civil society though, unlike Christine Gailey who studied the transition of Tongan Islands society from a kinship to a kingship system, he does not regard the previous kin-based society as especially supportive of women or even of what we might recognize as family life: "The closest analogy to a sixteenth-century home is a bird's nest."[45]

Most analysts who see family structure and political forms in society as contingent do not believe that such contingency is constant. Some family forms are closely integrated with larger social, political, and economic patterns, while others are much less dependent on or connected to macrolevel structures. Stone finds multiple family forms coexisting within the same political economy, a function mostly of social class and how different classes are integrated into it. He believes that family form is also influenced by individual situations and temperaments.[46] The analyses of Rousseau and Engels indicate that the degree of contingency between the family and the political community may well be a function of the extent to which the family as an institution or groups of families in practice are privatized in any given society.

The ideal family of the liberal Rousseau reflects its problematique as a vision of extreme privatization, while that of the socialist Engels embodies a communitarian vision. Rousseau's ideal family exists outside of society and thus is both irrelevant and impermeable to revolutionary transformation. To Engels, both the original communal family and the more recent patriarchal family are linked to the overall organization of the economy and society, a general proposition that Peterson and Stone would probably agree with. But as Eli Zaretsky argues, the connection between society and the bourgeois family, intensely private and socially isolated, more closely resembles the family-society relationship postulated by Rousseau rather than the one envisioned by Engels.[47] The traditional family might be a point at which revolutionary transformation can be initiated but Zaretsky believes that this is not true for the modern family.

The bourgeois family form is itself an outgrowth of capitalism, and thus a product of modernization. This family and its intimacy represent the ultimate in privatization, a private personal life severed from the public sphere.[48] Zaretsky traces its beginnings to sixteenth-century England where the family, including nonrelated workers, replaced the manor as the basic economic unit of production. Although some new style families were made up of members of the nobility and merchant capitalists, their "most revolutionary sectors came from the class of small producers working their own property." The appearance of the bourgeois family gave rise to a new ideology of the family "linked with the newly emerging ideas of private property and individualism."[49]

Although its economic relations differentiated the bourgeois family from family forms under feudalism, it is the insulation of the bourgeois family from the rest of society that is its dominant characteristic. Toward the end of the sixteenth century, in England and the Netherlands, the middle-class family and its home began to be separated from work, the workplace, and nonfamily members employed in the family business.[50] This sequestering produced a pattern of gender relations analogous to that of the *oikos* of ancient Greece, within which elite men conducted their private lives and many women their entire lives.[51] However, the nature of the public sphere differed radically between these two patterns. In the world of ancient Greece, the public sphere was the place where men created their personal identities by defining themselves politically in terms of other men. In the society developing around capitalism, however, the public sphere was increasingly dominated by the economy external to the household. Here, only a few elite men could define themselves in terms of other men, while the vast majority of participants in this public sphere became faceless laborers whose successes or failures went generally unnoticed. As a result, home and family in the modern period increasingly formed the bases of a private life composed of personal relationships. In this intimate space, men create their personal identities psychologically by defining themselves in terms of other men—and women.

This development had a number of social consequences that bore heavily upon middle- and upper-class women. It kept these women in their homes, away from the contaminating influences of the public life of economic and political competition.[52] It reinforced the idealization of autonomy over community as a social and political virtue at the same time that the nation-state began to take shape in Europe as a political form.[53] Family privatization can thus be seen as part of the new problematique associated with theories of sovereignty and possessive individualism.[54] It reinforced and corresponded to the normative belief that conflict based on competition is the primary mode by which human beings interact in public realms such as the national economy or interstate relations.[55]

The bourgeois family changed the relationship between husband and wife from one oriented around the contractual formalities involved in conveying property and ensuring the paternity of offspring to one rooted in romantic love and personal regard.[56] Like the move to patriarchalism in the sixteenth century, this change in husband and wife relationships added to male autonomy by loosening further the ties of kinship and contract that bound men to their extended families. In contrast, the autonomy of women was reduced by downgrading kinship as a source of economic and emotional support. Meanwhile, the isolation of women in privatized families increased their husbands' control of their lives. At the same time, however, the nuclear family provided an environment within which women could have egalitarian relationships with men rather than the hierarchical relationships characteristic of the extended patriarchal family. Out of the control of fathers, sexuality offered couples mutual satisfaction and psychic independence from the extended family and the external order.[57]

By the end of the nineteenth century, the bourgeois family had enshrined voluntary marriage based on mutual affection as a social ideal.[58] But the substitution of private desires for social constraints did not stop there. The ideology of privatization became more extreme. Its social manifestations as cut-throat competition and political separatism were rhetorically transformed into economic individualism and self determination. By the end of the twentieth century, this trend was clearly manifest at the level of the family, evident in declining marriage rates, high divorce rates, and widespread sexual abuse of women and children, a process that Carroll Smith-Rosenberg would attribute to the decline of the bourgeois family rather than to its developmental continuation.[59] The social supports that gave rise to the bourgeois family are weakened when privatization becomes so extreme that it erases the infrastructure of family life. This privatization results not in increased freedom for everyone but only for increased male independence from family obligations. Ironically, the social results feed American conservative critiques of liberalism and are used to justify calls for a state-supported neopatriarchal social order.[60]

The bourgeois family also has macrosocial deficiencies. As Zaretsky points out, the privatized family resists revolutionary transformation by attenuating the connection between the individual and society. Disappointment and failure are personal, internalized, and attributed to flaws in the individual rather than to the effects of unjust or oppressive social structures. The burdens of failure are carried primarily by the family, and often disproportionately by the mother.[61] Neither state nor society bears responsibility for the results of family ineffectiveness and pathology, which are falsely, but firmly, regarded as independent of the social order. This belief undercuts the legitimacy of attempts to connect family pathology to political and economic forces, and discourages dissatisfied persons and families from organizing to change anything but their own individual situations.[62]

However, the potential impact of the bourgeois family on politics can be viewed positively as well as negatively. This family's relative insulation from state and society allow it to reproduce novel sets of social and political relations, both by reducing the access of outside forces to the socialization of children and by permitting deviant—for example, egalitarian—family relationships to flourish relatively unmolested. Thus, the bourgeois family may support social transformation at other levels because it is the most likely point at which the three-fold symmetry underlying stable social systems can be challenged, structurally as well as ideologically. The children of unconventional families become liminal adults who, for various reasons, do not fit comfortably into the categories defined by the status quo. Such persons are, in Lynn Hunt's view, the intelligent instruments of lasting social change.[63]

Yet the privatized family can also be a dead end, a black hole absorbing energy that could otherwise be used to transform society. Its deviance can be authoritarian rather than democratic. Its isolation can be atomization, making it a poor arena for political mobilization. States support privatized family forms because it is in their interest.[64] Atomized families, like atomized workers, are at a structural disadvantage when making demands on the state.[65] In this situation, one strategy for revolutionary movements, in a society where the privatized family dominates, is to create new civil structures to compensate for kinship and community networks inadvertently lost in the process of modernization or purposely destroyed by an authoritarian state. The Christian base community is an example of such a strategy.

Revolutions that neglect the kin and community aspects of social organization are unlikely to affect family life or women's roles directly. They are more likely to result in broadened elite competition, a political revolution in Skoçpol's terms, than in significant social change. However, family forms based on contract rather than affection, which are embedded in extensive social and economic networks, encourage political mobilization at this level. Here individual and family are explicitly as well as implicitly connected to the larger society, and social rather than personal determinants form the basis of marriage, child custody, and the distribution of property. The congruence between relationships within the family and relationships in the larger society provides a point of leverage from which revolutionary groups can challenge the state. In addition, because the family is not simply a private affair but rather the locus of the socialization that produces cosmic, economic, and political structures and then becomes part of all of them, revolutionary transformation necessarily affects family life and women's roles as well as politics and the economy as a whole. It is revolutionized families or communities that produce the next generation who will either succeed or fail at preserving and extending what the revolution accomplished.

Where the mobilization of families and family members is a rational revolutionary strategy, it is likely to be pursued. Such a strategy would be difficult to apply where the family is privatized (atomized rather than autonomous) and dispersed through a political economy organized by class (an economically defined unit) rather than by kinship or community (socially defined units). Not only is there no direct linkage between the privatized family and the political economy—where class is the organizing principle of society—but the separate mobilization of women simultaneously alienates men who would otherwise find their class interests coinciding with revolutionary goals. This problem also afflicts the mobilization of women in traditional societies. However, if it is true that Western revolutions proceed from rather than to a collapse of the state, then it is the absence of linkages between state and society, and within civil society, that underlies this pattern. Western revolutions depend upon the collapse of the center to succeed because effective mobilization at the periphery is unlikely.[66] This supports Huntington's assertion that revolutions do not occur in liberal democratic societies, but his explanation, which relies on the democratic structure of the liberal state, is less compelling than one that includes consideration of the extreme privatization characteristic of liberal societies.[67]

WOMEN AND REVOLUTION

Although women have participated in revolutionary movements in all societies, not all of these movements addressed directly the problems of women in pre-revolutionary society or attempted to resolve these problems in post-revolutionary political and social constitutions and institutions. Women's liberation movements formed part of the English revolutions of the seventeenth century and the American and French revolutions at the end of the eighteenth century, but in none of these revolutions did post-revolutionary regimes "remember the ladies" by defining their rights or protecting their interests independently of the interests of their male relations.[68]

The socialist revolutions of the twentieth century are often contrasted favorably with the liberal revolutions of the past as models of women's as well as men's liberation.[69] However, the evidence here is mixed at best. The Russian revolution at first liberated women rhetorically and in reality, but policies liberalizing marriage and access to abortion were soon reversed under Stalin. Women in the communist countries of Eastern Europe experienced a similar pattern of gender oppression, including the denial of nontraditional jobs to women.[70] The Nicaraguan revolution, which arguably featured a greater rate of military participation by women than any other, still resulted in the subordination of women's interests to state interests even though a vast improvement in the autonomy and status of women took place. Despite the rhetoric, communist women are still not equal to communist men and, ironically, the privatization of family life characteristic of modern capitalist societies also occurs under socialist regimes.[71]

How then can we evaluate the interaction of women and revolutionary movements in order to capture the contribution of women and families to the success of a particular revolution and the success of that revolution in improving the situations of women and families? Three sets of issues must be addressed. First, the structure of the pre-revolutionary society must be analyzed with respect to the relative position of women and men. Was gender a basis for discrimination under the old regime? Gailey, like Peterson, argues that all states rest on a foundation consisting of gender hierarchy as well as class stratification, and that "[t]he subordination of women . . . emerges as an integral part of the emergence of . . . the state."[72] If the subordination of women and other social groups is a foundation of state formation, all revolutions against state based regimes have the potential to liberate women from men as well as to liberate men from one another. However, because revolutions also result in the strengthening of state institutions, the continued subordination of women and other previously exploited social groups after revolutionary transformation may be structurally favored.

Second, the relationship between family, society, and the pre-revolutionary state also must be analyzed. What were the customs and laws affecting marriage and family life, including sexuality, reproduction, custody, property ownership, and inheritance, and how were these customs and laws enforced? The answers to these questions allow us to see the degree of penetration into social and kinship structures by the state, and to determine whether and how the linkage between state and society enabled civil organization to challenge state power. The relationship between family structure and the structure of a pre-revolutionary political economy is a variable requiring us to analyze pre-revolutionary family forms and the autonomy of women as revolutionary actors.

Autonomous female participation in revolutions underlies the legitimacy of post-revolutionary demands for women's liberation. This notion goes back at least to the Renaissance and the writings of Bruni and Machiavelli that idealized an army of citizen-soldiers: "it is the possession of arms which makes a man a full citizen, capable of, and required to display, the multiple versatility and self-development which is the crown of citizenship."[73] Mary Lou Kendrigan regards military service as a major avenue for the achievement of political equality by disadvantaged groups in society.[74] A parallel argument could be made about the legitimacy of group demands after a revolution: what any group gets is at least in part a function of what that group is perceived to have earned by the blood of its members. Do women as women hold up half the sky or does the individual woman hold up her man? If the latter, is it only he and his group who are entitled to claim a share of the victory, or are she and hers entitled as well?[75]

A third concern deals with the rhetorical and symbolic bases of legitimacy. Rhetorical commitment to female equality is necessary to legitimate women's liberation in post-revolutionary society.[76] Such legitimacy, because it rests upon the perception that women as well as men have paid the price of victory, requires that the achievements of women be integrated with other revolutionary myths, and that women share authority over them. A related set of issues deals with symbolic and objective outcomes. After the revolution, do women as well as men have the liberty to participate in public life (the outcome that Hannah Arendt identifies as the primary aim of revolution)? Does this participation result in the creation of institutions and the development of policies that protect women and children from subjugation to the wishes of individual men as well as the state? The connection between women's liberation and institutions that are responsive to the needs of women and families is evident from history: freedom for men alone has never been sufficient to protect the interests or the persons of women and children.[77] Consideration of these questions allows one to evaluate a revolution as a successful movement to liberate persons as compared to a successful movement to alter the social bases of political and economic power or the form and structure of support for a regime.

WHAT WE CAN LEARN BY STUDYING WOMEN AND REVOLUTION

The study of women and revolution is interesting and important both normatively and analytically. Normatively, women, as human beings whose social role is always defined at least in part by their reproductive capabilities, experience revolution and its outcomes differently from men. To classify revolutions so that their microsocial impacts may be ignored in the analysis of paradigm cases reflects a philosophical bias that is not simply sexist but also rigidly masculinist and ahistorical. Interest groups (i.e., groups with a professional or class connection to the political economy) are commonly treated as units of analysis in the study of both political and social revolutions by scholars from the right as well as the left. However, the impact of community on revolutionary movements is less frequently pursued in studies of political revolutions and connections between women's roles, family structure, and either political or social revolutions are rarely explored.[78] The members of revolutionary groups who are consumers and sometimes even producers of this literature, and who use it to envision concrete possibilities for themselves, encourage women to subordinate their interests as women to their interests as members of an economic class or particular subculture in the course of their participation in revolutionary movements. But encouraging such interests over female gender interests also supports reaction. For example, in societies where there is a strong middle class, the force of middle-class women as a counter-revolutionary social group may be especially strong.

While the privatization of the family (a major arena in the life of nearly every woman in every society) continues, the interplay between family, society, and political economy remains underexamined. Karl Polanyi's belief, that modernization is a social and economic process that takes place at the level of family and community as well as the nation, warns us not to ignore these relationships.[79] The privatization of the family, like other aspects of modernization, breaks the integral connection of unit to society and reduces the role of family and community as structural constraints on the power of political and economic regimes.

Another connection between women, families, and political transformation that should be explored through a systematic study of women and revolution is a hypothesis already noted, that state formation necessarily results in the repression of women. If this is correct, revolutionary transformation cannot liberate women unless it also constrains state power. The relationship between state power and the oppression of women is often construed from another perspective: Charles Fourier once wrote that the "extension of *privileges* to women is the general principle of all social progress."[80] Both constructions imply that the state is an extension of the power of men and posit a direct connection between the level of women's liberation and the effectiveness of constitutional restraints on state power.

The revolutionary potential of the bourgeois family should also be an object of research and analysis. Despite Zaretsky's concern, that privatization has made the family irrelevant to social transformation, I believe that the role of women and the structure of the family are keys that can open an entirely new way to imagine and achieve revolutionary transformation in the modern world. The privatization that isolates the state from responsibility for the family is an advantage if it also insulates the family from state manipulation and control and preserves it as a base from which to challenge state power. Families may form the units of a newly constituted civil structure capable of challenging the state directly. Christian base communities in Latin America and women's committees in the Palestinian Intifada joined families into socially organized bases for defense against and attacks upon repressive states. A similar mechanism can be seen in the organization of political opposition against the Kuwaiti regime during suspensions of domestic civil rights. Here the norm that protects the Kuwaiti home from state intervention also protects it as the locus of political gatherings organized to oppose the state and its policies.[81]

Families may challenge state power less directly by disturbing the congruence between theories and the social structures that form their problematiques. Change in either introduces new terms of discourse that may also be applied to change the others. Stone described how the state used congruence to support absolutism by fostering the development of the patriarchal family as a mirror image of itself. Macrostructures, such as the international system and the nation-state, are based firmly on this pattern of dominance and submission, supported by the illusion that "dominance rests on values [that are] universal, eternal, and exclusive."[82] The hegemony of this value system is challenged when it becomes possible to see that dominance is none of these things. Egalitarian family forms that subjugate neither women nor children refute the claim to universality underpinning dominance at other levels of society. Transformation of the family from an authoritarian to an egalitarian unit promises to cut new paths toward multiple patterns of autonomy and community, increasing the number of vulnerable points at which critics can challenge the status quo.[83] Attacks on egalitarian families by statists demonstrate that the state and other structures of dominance are vulnerable to such a challenge.[84]

CONCLUSIONS

The normative and analytical concerns reflected in feminist theory and its impact on the choice of research problems and approaches are not confined to women's issues as these are defined by the political and scholarly mainstream. Feminism as a philosophical and intellectual framework challenges traditions that relegate women and families to the realm of nature that exists to be subjugated and exploited. Feminists, along with other post-modern analysts, are engaged in the search for "alternative conceptualizations of human community at levels both below and beyond that of the modern state."[85] The examination of the role of women in revolution is directly concerned with enlarging our understanding of human community in the context of the modern or modernizing state. As such, it is a subject whose pursuit can expand the terms of political discourse beyond the trap of perpetual conflict to include possibilities for the recreation of international as well as domestic society.

The case studies in this collection explore the role of women in revolutions and liberation movements in Africa, Asia (somewhat broadly defined), and the New World. The authors have considered the parts women played in revolutionary movements, and have evaluated the outcomes of revolutions with respect to the status and power of women as a class defined by gender in post-revolutionary politics. The topics covered in each chapter reflect the particular circumstances surrounding the revolution that is its special concern, and the availability of information about the revolution and its aftermath. Each author was free to incorporate different theories to explain the events that are recounted. Feminist theories and theories that focus on variables other than gender are liberally represented throughout this volume.

The preparation of the case studies took place over four years, and most were presented on panels at professional meetings. We have borrowed theories and insights from one another over the course of the project, which unfolded like an irregularly convened seminar with a growing cast of participants. Every chapter benefitted from repeated critical evaluations and revisions. A few chapters were published elsewhere during the stately course of the preparation of this volume. External review constituted an additional source of critical evaluation. But in spite of all the criticisms and rewriting, the case studies remain the expressions of the theoretical visions and empirical analyses of their authors, and reflect the authors' scholarly ideals and their normative and substantive concerns.

This project was originally much more limited in scope. The framework paper was prepared for the 1988 annual meeting of the Southern Political Science Association and four case studies based upon it were scheduled to be delivered at the 1989 annual meeting of the International Studies Association (ISA). The genesis of both panels was a request by a colleague at the University of Kentucky, Chung In Moon, who had asked me to provide an opportunity for a young protege of his, Kyung Ae Park, to "do some work on women."

This request came at a time when I was reaching the culmination of a personal odyssey whose objective was to make sense of the experiences of the Vietnam generation. As part of this project I developed a course on the Vietnam war, along with scores of other American professors about my age who also found themselves, at about the same time, ready to think about Vietnam again. I taught this course three times to large groups of interested students. A number of them had fought in Vietnam and brought their intense memories of the country, its people, and their experiences with both into my classroom. Over this period, I conceived a strong desire to travel to Vietnam, to see it for myself. When Chung In made his request, I was making plans for this trip and, as a result, focused my research agenda around the subject of Vietnamese women and their experiences.

At the same time, I organized a panel on women and their participation in revolutionary movements in east Asia for the 1989 ISA meeting in London. The panel was fascinating. Our original papers were sketchy but, in the process of putting them together, we realized that there was more work to be done than we had had time or space to deal with. We decided to organize additional panels, both to elaborate on the findings in the original papers and to invite additional participants who could tell us about other revolutions.

Our second and third panels included Latin Americanists and West Asianists. The following year, I sought participants who could write about African cases as well. Meanwhile, I spent the spring of 1990 on a Fulbright fellowship in Kuwait, studying Kuwait's pro-democracy movement and other manifestations of the vast social changes that oil money had inaugurated in that country. This pushed us to broaden our conception of revolution. Soon we had expanded our focus to three continents and movements that might be defined as rebellions or nationalist movements rather than as revolutions in the strict sense of Huntington's definition—elements of which Huntington himself ignores when they become inconvenient.

The volume that you hold is the result of the expansion of our conceptions of this project over the past several years. We did not want to be limited by too narrow a conceptualization, either of what we were studying—women and revolution—or of where we might find it. As a result, rather than concentrating on exclusive definitions and frameworks, our intention is to be inclusive on both counts as well as strongly empirical. If we are successful, readers will not only be able to draw their own conclusions, but also to develop their own definitions and frameworks for future work in this field.

NOTES

1. Samuel Huntington, *Political Order in Changing Societies* (New Haven: Yale University Press, 1968), 264.

2. For modern examples see ibid.; Crane Brinton, *The Anatomy of Revolution* (New York: Vintage Books, 1956); Hannah Arendt, *On Revolution* (New York: Viking Press, 1963); Theda Skoçpol, *States and Social Revolutions* (Cambridge: Cambridge University Press, 1979); Barrington Moore, Jr., *Social Origins of Dictatorship and Democracy: Lord and Peasant in the Making of the Modern World* (Boston: Beacon Press, 1966); Jack A. Goldstone, *Revolution and Rebellion in the Early Modern World* (Berkeley: University of California Press, 1992); Ted Robert Gurr, *Why Men Rebel* (Princeton: Princeton University Press, 1970); Eric R. Wolf, *Peasant Wars of the Twentieth Century* (New York: Harper and Row, 1969); Nikki

R Keddie, *Roots of Revolution: An Interpretive History of Modern Iran* (New Haven: Yale University Press, 1981), and many others. Of course, Marx and Tocqueville in the nineteenth century wrote about revolution using similarly macrolevel units of analysis.

3. For example, see Lynn Hunt, *Politics, Culture, and Class in the French Revolution* (Berkeley: University of California Press, 1985).

4. Lawrence Stone, "The Revolution Over the Revolution," *The New York Review*, 11 June 1992. Stone concentrates particularly on the work of Conrad Russell.

5. Exceptions include Carol R. Berkin and Clara M. Lovett, eds., *Women, War and Revolution* (New York: Holmes and Meyer, 1980); Joan B. Landes, *Women and the Public Sphere in the Age of the French Revolution* (Ithaca: Cornell University Press, 1988); and Lynn Hunt, *The Family Romance of the French Revolution* (Berkeley: University of California Press, 1992).

6. See, for example, Lawrence Stone, *The Family, Sex, and Marriage in England, 1500–1800* (New York: Harper and Row, 1977); Georges Duby, *The Knight, the Lady, and the Priest: The Making of Modern Marriage in Medieval France*, trans. Barbara Bray (New York: Pantheon Books, 1983); Carroll Smith-Rosenberg, *Disorderly Conduct: Visions of Gender in Victorian America* (New York: Oxford University Press, 1985); Susan Moller Okin, *Justice, Gender, and the Family* (New York: Basic Books, 1989).

7. This thesis is explored at length in Hunt, *The Family Romance of the French Revolution*.

8. Kenneth N. Waltz, *Theory of International Politics* (Reading, Mass: Addison-Wesley, 1979), chap. 5.

9. Hannah Arendt, *The Human Condition: A Study of the Central Dilemmas Facing Modern Man* (Garden City: Doubleday Anchor, 1959), 24–34, 50–65, 73–79, 84–89, 102–10.

10. *Aristotle's Politics*, trans. Hippocrates G. Apostle and Lloyd P. Gerson (Grinnell, Iowa: Peripatetic Press, 1986).

11. Elaine Pagels, *Adam, Eve, and the Serpent* (New York: Random House, 1988); Peter Brown, *The Body and Society: Men, Women and Sexual Renunciation in Early Christianity* (New York: Columbia University Press, 1988).

12. Pagels, *Adam, Eve, and the Serpent*, chap. 5.

13. Examples can be found in Huntington, *Political Order in Changing Societies*; Moore, *Social Origins of Dictatorship and Democracy*; Skoçpol, *States and Social Revolutions*; and Walt W. Rostow, *Politics and the Stages of Growth* (Cambridge: Cambridge University Press, 1971). Karl Polanyi's analysis of modernization in *The Great Transformation* (New York: Farrar and Rinehart, 1944), sees domestic political conflict as the inevitable outcome of industrial capitalism, but Polanyi does not deal with revolutions as such in this work.

14. Hunt, *Politics, Culture, and Class in the French Revolution*, chaps. 2–3; David I. Kertzer, *Ritual, Politics, and Power* (New Haven: Yale University Press, 1988), chap. 8.

15. Huntington, *Political Order in Changing Societies*, chap. 5.

16. *Social Origins of Dictatorship and Democracy*, 426.

17. Ibid., 428-29, 506.

18. Skoçpol, *States and Social Revolutions,* 4.

19. Alexis de Tocqueville, *The Old Regime and the French Revolution,* trans. Stuart Gilbert (Garden City: Doubleday Anchor, 1955).

20. The harmonization of normative and positive theory with a dominant ideology is discussed in many works on the physical sciences. See, for example, Cynthia Eagle Russett, *Darwin in America: The Intellectual Response, 1865–1912* (San Francisco: W. H. Freeman, 1976); Stephen Jay Gould, *The Mismeasure of Man* (New York: Norton, 1981); and the essays in part three of Evelyn Fox Keller, *Reflections on Gender and Science* (New Haven: Yale University Press, 1985). Jean Bethke Elshtain has also noted this tendency in political theory. See "Sovereignty, Identity, Sacrifice," in *Gendered States: Feminist Re(Visions) of International Relations Theory,* ed. V. Spike Peterson (Boulder, Colo: Lynne Rienner, 1992).

21. Louis Althusser, "Ideology and Ideological State Apparatuses: (Notes Toward an Investigation)," in *Lenin and Philosophy and Other Essays,* trans. Ben Brewster (New York: Monthly Review Press, 1971); Eric R. Wolf, *Europe and the People Without History* (Berkeley: University of California Press, 1982), 83, 389.

22. The term "problematique" is used following Robert Cox to mean a historically conditioned awareness of certain problems and issues that guide the translation of reality into theory. See Robert W. Cox, "Social Forces, States and World Orders: Beyond International Relations Theory," *Millennium* 10 (Summer 1981).

23. Susan Moller Okin, *Women in Western Political Thought* (Princeton: Princeton University Press, 1979); also Okin, *Justice, Gender, and the Family;* and Jill K. Conway, Susan C. Bourque, and Joan W. Scott, "Introduction: The Concept of Gender," *Daedalus* 116 (Fall 1987). However, this is not meant to imply that all women actually mother or that men are not also biologically bound to reproduction.

24. With marriage being the model pattern for exchange. See Claude Lévi-Strauss, *The Elementary Structures of Kinship,* rev. ed., trans. James Haile Bell et al. (Boston: Beacon Press, 1969), 480–83.

25. See the essays by Fran Sanders, Abbey Lincoln, Kay Lindsey, Toni Cade [Bambera], Gail Stokes, and Jean Carey Bond and Pat Peery in *The Black Woman,* ed. Toni Cade [Bambera] (New York: Signet, 1970). Also recall the words of Stokely Carmichael about women in the civil rights movement: "The position of women in the movement is prone (sic)." This example of men as a class working to dilute or destroy the sense of women as a class was painfully evident during the confirmation hearings of U.S. Supreme Court Justice Clarence Thomas in the fall of 1991.

26. See, for example, Stone, *The Family, Sex and Marriage In England;* or Christine Ward Gailey, *Kinship to Kingship: Gender Hierarchy and State Formation in the Tongan Islands* (Austin: University of Texas Press, 1987).

27. Nawal El-Saadawi, *The Hidden Face of Eve,* trans. Sherif Hetata (London: Zed Press, 1980); Germaine Tillion, *The Republic of Cousins: Women's Oppression in Mediterranean Society,* 9th ed., trans. Quintin Hoare (London: Al Saqi Books,

1983).

28. Okin, *Justice, Gender, and the Family*, chap. 7.

29. Mary Ann Tétreault, *The Kuwait Petroleum Corporation* (Westport, Conn: Quorum Books, forthcoming), chap. 4.

30. Betty Friedan, *The Feminine Mystique* (New York: Dell, 1963).

31. Ruth Benedict, *The Chrysanthemum and the Sword: Patterns of Japanese Culture* (New York: Meridian, 1946).

32. Interviews by the author with Japanese families in Kitakyushu, Japan, June 1989.

33. Hisham Sharabi, *Neopatriarchy: A Theory of Distorted Social Change in Arab Society* (New York: Oxford University Press, 1988).

34. Jane Jacquette, letter to the author.

35. Joseph Campbell believes that the Genesis myth is unique in equating "woman" with "sinner" and thus separating life from goodness. Joseph Campbell with Bill Moyers, *The Power of Myth* (New York: Doubleday, 1988), 45–48. A discussion of the considerable literature on creation myths and their transformation at that point when state formation replaces kinship structures can be found in V. Spike Peterson, "An Archaeology of Domination: Historicizing Gender and Class in Early Western State Formation," Ph.D. diss., American University, Washington, D.C., August 1988.

36. Most of Rousseau's discussion of the development of the family can be found in *A Dissertation On the Origin and Foundation of the Inequality of Mankind,* and in *Emile,* Rousseau's novel about a "natural" man in the civilized world. His assumptions regarding the ideal pattern of sexual roles within the family are analyzed by Susan Moller Okin in "Rousseau's Natural Woman," *Journal of Politics* 41 (May 1979) and in *Women in Western Political Thought,* especially chaps. 5–8.

37. Okin, "Rousseau's Natural Woman," 402.

38. Friedrich Engels, *The Origin of the Family, Private Property, and the State* (New York: Penguin Books, 1884/1985).

39. Ibid., 78–83.

40. Ibid., 131.

41. Ibid., 141.

42. Peterson, "An Archeology of Domination."

43. K. J. Dover, *Greek Homosexuality* (London: Duckworth, 1978), 200–2.

44. Stone, *The Family, Sex and Marriage,* 7, 123–40.

45. Ibid.

46. Stone's discussion of the impact of temperament can be found in ibid., chap. 11. Stone organizes his work into comparative analyses of dominant family forms within several social classes through each section of his book.

47. Eli Zaretsky, *Capitalism, the Family, and Personal Life,* rev. ed. (New York: Perennial Library, 1986).

48. Arendt, *The Human Condition,* 46, 188. This description of the bourgeois family is also reflected in Robert N. Bellah et al., *Habits of the Heart: Individualism and Commitment in American Life* (New York: Perennial Library, 1986), and in Peter Gay, *The Bourgeois Experience: Victoria to Freud,* vol. 1,

Education of the Senses (New York: Oxford University Press, 1984), and vol. 2, *The Tender Passion* (New York: Oxford University Press, 1986).

49. Zaretsky, *Capitalism, the Family, and Personal Life*, 23.

50. Stone, *The Family, Sex and Marriage*, chaps. 5–6; Witold Rybczynski, *A Short History of an Idea: Home* (New York: Viking, 1986), chap. 3.

51. Peterson, "An Archeology of Domination," 180–85.

52. Elizabeth Janeway, *Man's World, Woman's Place: A Study in Social Mythology* (New York: Delta Books, 1971). Even the great liberal feminist John Stuart Mill idealized the bourgeois family and the sequestering of women within it as "essential for humanity." (Quoted in Okin, *Women in Western Political Thought*, 226.)

53. Hanna Fenichel Pitkin, *Fortune is a Woman: Gender and Politics in the Thought of Niccòlo Machiavelli* (Berkeley: University of California Press, 1984), 19–22.

54. John Gerard Ruggie, "Continuity and Transformation in the World Polity: Toward a Neorealist Synthesis," in *Neorealism and its Critics*, ed. Robert O. Keohane (New York: Columbia University Press, 1986), 142–48.

55. Pitkin, *Fortune is a Woman*. Although his analysis does not include gender relations, Ruggie also looks at the substitution of possessive individualism at the individual and state levels for the communitarian ethic of the medieval period as forming a system of congruent beliefs underlying the operation of the modern world system of competitive nation-states. Ruggie, "Continuity and Transformation in the World Polity," 142–45.

56. Stone, *The Family, Sex and Marriage*, chap. 6; Gay, *Education of the Senses*, chap. 6.

57. William Irwin Thompson, *The Time Falling Bodies Take to Light: Mythology, Sexuality and the Origins of Culture* (New York: St. Martin's Press, 1981); Sharabi, *Neopatriarchy*, 32–48.

58. Page Smith, *Daughters of the Promised Land* (Boston: Little Brown, 1971), 41–47; Gay, *The Tender Passion*, 100–6.

59. Smith-Rosenberg, *Disorderly Conduct*, 51.

60. See, for example, George Gilder, *Sexual Suicide* (New York: Quadrangle Books, 1973).

61. Zaretsky, *Capitalism, the Family, and Personal Life*, 90–94.

62. This is evident in the most successful national movement in the United States to attack family pathologies that express themselves as substance abuse, Alcoholics Anonymous and such related organizations as Alanon, Alateen, and Narcotics Anonymous. For a defense of this private attack on family pathology expressed as substance abuse, see A. Lawrence Chickering, "Denial Hardens the Drug Crisis," *Wall Street Journal*, 25 July 1988, 16. Although Chickering is criticizing statist attacks on the drug problem, he dismisses the connection between substance abuse and the political economy as less important and less susceptible to change than individual attitudes. In contrast, the thrust of feminist analysis of domestic violence is to take it out of the model of private and personal pathology and into the public domain. See, for example, Elizabeth H. Pleck, *Domestic Tyranny: The Making of Social Policy Against Family Violence*

from Colonial Times to the Present (New York: Oxford University Press, 1987).

63. Hunt, *Politics, Culture, and Class in the French Revolution*, chap. 6.

64. This point is emphasized by both Peterson and Stone.

65. Alfred Stepan, "State Power and the Strength of Civil Society in the Southern Cone of Latin America," in *Bringing the State Back In*, eds. Peter B. Evans, Deitrich Rueschemeyer, and Theda Skoçpol (New York: Cambridge University Press, 1979).

66. The privatization of social life to decrease challenges to oppressive regimes is discussed in ibid., 322–23.

67. Huntington, *Political Order in Changing Societies*, 275. The argument I make here is foreshadowed by Walter Dean Burnham in *Critical Elections and the Mainsprings of American Politics* (New York: Norton, 1970). Burnham denies that the paradigm liberal state, the United States, adjusts smoothly to demands for inclusion by new groups, the argument that Huntington uses to explain the absence of revolution in democratic states. Burnham finds repeated attempts by excluded groups to mount social revolutions in the United States, but points to the successful atomization of such groups as preventing achievement of their programmatic goals. The judgment that American liberalism has strangled American democracy can also be found in Mary G. Dietz, "Context is All: Feminism and Theories of Citizenship," *Daedalus* 116 (Fall 1987): 16.

68. The letter of Abigail Adams to her husband John, written during the deliberations on the U.S. constitution, asks that he "remember the ladies" by denying their husbands "unlimited power" over them. See Alice S. Rossi, ed., *The Feminist Papers: From Adams to de Beauvoir* (New York: Columbia University Press, 1973), 10–11. Stone notes that English feminists took the rhetoric of the English revolutions, specifically their rejection of Divine Right of Kings and passive obedience to the state, as bases for their arguments supporting women's liberation. ("The Results of the English Revolutions of the Seventeenth Century," in *Three British Revolutions, 1641, 1688, 1776*, ed. J. G. A. Pocock (Princeton: Princeton University Press, 1980), 71.) One of the most famous contemporary analyses supporting women's liberation, Mary Wollstonecraft's *Vindication of the Rights of Women*, is evidence both of women's desires that revolutionary outcomes be extended to women—and the lack of such any such desires on the part of male revolutionaries.

69. Valentine M. Moghadam, "Revolution, Culture and Gender: Notes on 'the Woman Question' in Revolutions," paper presented at the Twelfth World Congress on Sociology, 1990.

70. Hilda Scott, *Does Socialism Liberate Women?* (Boston: Beacon Press, 1974); Maxine Molyneux, "Mobilization Without Emancipation? Women's Interests, the State, and Revolution in Nicaragua," *Feminist Studies* 11 (Summer 1985): 229.

71. Scott, *Does Socialism Liberate Women?*, especially chap. 9; Sondra Hale, "Transforming Culture or Fostering Second-Hand Consciousness? Women's Front Organisations and Revolutionary Parties—The Sudan Case," in *Arab Women: Old Boundaries, New Frontiers*, ed. Judith E. Tucker (Bloomington: Indiana University Press, 1993), 152; Sonia Kruks, Rayna Rapp, and Marilyn B. Young, "Introduction," in *Promissory Notes: Women in the Transition to Socialism*

(New York: Monthly Review Press 1989), 10–11.

72. Gailey, *Kinship to Kingship*, xi. Also see Peterson, *An Archeology of Domination*.

73. J. G. A. Pocock, *The Machiavellian Moment: Florentine Political Thought and the Atlantic Republican Tradition* (Princeton: Princeton University Press, 1975), 90.

74. Mary Lou Kendrigan, "Citizenship, Gender Roles, and Military Service," paper presented at the annual meeting of the Midwest Political Science Association, Chicago, April 1986.

75. Kendrigan argues that blood sacrifice is the only valid ticket entitling a group to admission to power, an argument rejected by Gailey. Gailey's concept of "gender hierarchy" posits the existence not simply of the social oppression of women as a class but also the ideological suppression of values associated with women and the association of values attributed to maleness with social power. The argument I make here takes the androcentric perspective that women's blood payments are entitlements to power, but this is not normatively preferable to a gender neutral entitlement to liberty as the result of revolutionary transformation.

76. See the discussion by Hunt on the importance of rhetoric in reconstituting regimes after revolutions in *Politics, Culture, and Class in the French Revolution*, 20–24; also Molyneux, "Mobilization Without Emancipation?" 229.

77. John Stuart Mill and Harriet Taylor Mill, *On the Subjection of Women* (New York: Fawcett Books, 1869/1971); Okin, *Women in Western Political Thought*.

78. In two notable exceptions, Barrington Moore looked at communal relations and community structures in his analysis of political and social revolutions. For example, he considered the structure and role of the family farm in the American midwest as an element in the conflict leading to the Civil War, to him the real American revolution. Lynn Hunt examined kinship and community networks in her structural and motivational analyses of the new men of the French revolution and their role in political and social transformation.

79. Polanyi, *The Great Transformation*.

80. Quoted in Zaretsky, *Capitalism, the Family, and Personal Life*, 67, emphasis added.

81. Mary Ann Tétreault, "Kuwait's Democratic Reform Movement," *Middle East Executive Reports* 13 (October 1990): 16–17; and "Civil Society in Kuwait: Protected Spaces and Women's Rights," *Middle East Journal* 47 (Spring 1993): 277–81.

82. Lester Edwin J. Ruiz, "Theology, Politics, and the Discourse of Transformation," *Alternatives* 13 (April 1988): 161.

83. Bradley Klein, "After Strategy: The Search for a Post-Modern Politics of Peace," *Alternatives* 13 (July 1988): 312–13.

84. Michael Rogin, *Ronald Reagan, The Movie, and Other Episodes in Political Demonology* (Berkeley: University of California Press, 1987), 200–5, 240–45, 293–95.

85. Klein, "After Strategy," 313.

II

Africa

Chapter 2

Women and Revolution in Mozambique

A Luta Continua

Kathleen Sheldon

Mozambique, on Africa's southeastern coast, was a Portuguese colony until 1975 when the country won its independence after more than a decade of armed struggle. During the course of that struggle *Frente de Libertação de Moçambique* (the Front for the Liberation of Mozambique, FRELIMO) developed a socialist program of reforms. One of the most publicized aspects of that program was the attention paid to women's liberation. Mozambican women have been portrayed as part of an international feminist vanguard, in part because of the presence of the *Organização da Mulher Moçambicana* (Organization of Mozambican Women, OMM). Yet OMM statutes, themselves, contradict the idea of Mozambican women being in the vanguard, stating that OMM's purpose was "to guarantee the implementation of women's emancipation *as defined by the Frelimo Party*" (my emphasis).[1] OMM was the recognized voice for women in the government as well as in

---

Earlier versions of portions of this chapter appeared in Kathleen Sheldon, "Working Women in Beira, Mozambique," Ph.D. diss., University of California, Los Angeles, 1988; and in Sheldon, "'To Guarantee the Implementation of Women's Emancipation as Defined by the Frelimo Party': The Women's Organization in Mozambique," Working Paper no. 206, Women in International Development, Michigan State University, 1990. I would like to thank the Organization of Mozambican Women (OMM) for supporting my research, in particular by allowing me to attend their provincial meeting in Beira in September 1983.

FRELIMO, which became the ruling party following independence. This legitimacy gave OMM a strong opening to push for women's needs, "to guarantee the implementation of women's emancipation." But the qualifying phrase "as defined by the FRELIMO party," acknowledged the organization's subordinate relation to the male-dominated FRELIMO party. It allowed male leaders to segregate and even ignore the demands of women. Social issues, especially those dealing with marriage and the family, were commonly considered to be OMM's responsibility. This approach proved inadequate to the monumental task of changing power relations between men and women, as OMM was relegated to (and accepted) an advisory rather than policymaking position.

A frequently quoted source demonstrating FRELIMO's commitment to women is a 1973 speech by Samora Machel, a FRELIMO leader and Mozambique's first president after independence. In it he said, "The liberation of women is a fundamental necessity for the Revolution, the guarantee of its continuity and the precondition for its victory."[2] Since then, much of the attention given to Mozambican women has focused on their political involvement.[3] Mozambique continued to incorporate women and gender issues into its socialist practice though the results were complex and diverse. This essay examines women in Mozambique's history, the efforts to introduce reforms in women's social position, and the persistence of patriarchal attitudes. The specific course of Mozambique's history includes Portuguese colonialism, continuing destitution (Mozambique is commonly listed as the world's poorest country), and a years-long war of destabilization that exacerbated the problems inherent in bringing about lasting change in gender relations.

WOMEN IN PRECOLONIAL MOZAMBIQUE

The Mozambican approach to emancipating women is rooted in the Mozambican analysis of women's oppression, which incorporated evidence from both precolonial and colonial history. Samora Machel's speech on women's liberation cited several sources of women's oppression, including polygamy and *lobolo* (bridewealth). This official Mozambican explanation of gender inequality describes the capitalist system of labor exploitation as the basis for such practices:

> To possess women is to possess workers, unpaid workers, workers whose entire labour power can be appropriated without resistance by the husband. . . . What is more important is that compared with, say, the slave, who is also a source of wealth and an unpaid

> worker, the woman offers her owner two added advantages. She is a source of pleasure and above all, she produces other workers, she produces new sources of wealth.[4]

Machel concluded that the solution depended on women uniting to improve their situation, though he emphasized the role of FRELIMO in formulating the line and "methods of struggle."[5] His comments are corroborated by recent research on women in southern Africa. Describing the complex interrelationship between marriage and women's productive and reproductive labor, the research concludes that "these societies were based upon the appropriation of women's labour by men."[6]

The few early sources on women in precolonial and colonial Mozambique focus on southern Mozambique and patrilineal societies such as the Thonga and the Valenge.[7] Later researchers built on this earlier work,[8] but their conclusions about southern Mozambique cannot be extended to all of Mozambique because, although the patrilineal societies in the south incorporated *lobolo* into their marital and social arrangements, northern Mozambicans were more often matrilineal and practiced polygyny. Swahili communities along the northern coast had an Islamic patrilineal social system. Many traditional marital and social practices persisted after independence, especially in rural areas, despite government opposition to their continuation. Although the term traditional lacks historic precision, it is commonly used by Mozambicans to refer to activities, such as initiation rites, which are rooted in precolonial Mozambican rural experience.[9] Referring to practices such as *lobolo* as traditional does not mean that they have always played the same role throughout time or throughout Mozambique. On the contrary, there have been important changes historically and there are regional variations to such practices.

Lobolo is a marriage payment from the husband-to-be and his family to the woman's family, understood as compensating them for rearing their daughter, and as cementing kin relations between the two families. Whether paid in cash, goods, or services, *lobolo* contains the "idea of domination of the will and interests of the woman by those of the man," and also brings the concept of ownership into parent/child relations.[10] Cattle were a common medium of exchange in precapitalist southern Africa, giving rise to the phrase "cattle beget children," a comment that captures much of the local understanding of the role of *lobolo* in developing lineages.[11] *Lobolo* was sometimes turned over to a son for his own *lobolo* payment, so that the income the family gained from a daughter was used to finance a wife for a son. Recent complaints focus on the increasing cash component and inflated value of *lobolo* prices, but evidence shows that cash entered into such transactions as early as the 1870s, when Mozambican men first migrated to work in South Africa's mines.[12] Some parents arranged marriages between their young daughters and older men with the necessary *lobolo*, another aspect criticized by FRELIMO.

That women felt oppressed by this marriage system was demonstrated in their response to missionaries at the turn of the century. Many women escaped from unhappy marriages by converting and affiliating themselves with mission centers. Court records also indicate that cases brought against run-away wives and stolen women were frequently the result of disputes arising from male attempts to control female kin. It appears that such cases involved women trying to free themselves from desperate situations.[13]

Information from precolonial northern Mozambique is more elusive. The Makonde and Makua, the major ethnic groups in the north, were matrilineal. Their marriage practices allowed polygyny, as did the Swahili communities along the coast. The actual extent of polygamous marriages is impossible to know, though various observers described polygamy as a common practice.[14] OMM described polygamy as oppressive to women, though many women felt it was an acceptable and even beneficial form of social organization. The expectation that all adult women would marry and have children contributed to this compliance, as a polygamous marriage was preferable to no marriage.

Initiation rites were also described as oppressive to women in traditional societies. A 1983 OMM discussion document presented information on the specific activities in the rites. While there were variations from province to province, the following elements were common: teaching domestic duties; instilling respect for adults; transmitting rules of hygiene; and teaching sexual education "in the spirit of [a woman] submitting herself to her husband's will."[15] In some regions these rites included tattooing, genital mutilation, and artificial defloration. According to OMM's official interpretation, the general consequence for girls was to learn to be wives under the domination of their husbands. At the same time, many women experienced the rituals as a time for women to gather as women; it was one of the few recognized social activities where women's knowledge and power was allowed to flourish.

There is evidence that women enjoyed only limited political and religious power in precolonial societies. In the Gaza kingdom in the south, women of the royal family held some power, though primarily they acted as checks on male power in the provincial areas distant from the king.[16] But more generally women were seen as commodities to be owned, as indicated by the use of the same word for slave and for wife.[17] That men felt a need to control women in very direct ways indicated the centrality of women's productive and reproductive labor to the basic organization of these societies. Women's social position was fundamental to the general political, religious, and economic organization of the society.[18]

In some areas women held local religious authority, though practices observed in the late nineteenth and early twentieth centuries may have developed in response to men leaving rural villages to work for wages.[19] In northern Mozambique, there were no large centralized political entities comparable to the Gaza kingdom; social control was exerted through village assemblies. The inextricable intertwining of religion and politics in these societies may have given older women with medicoreligious knowledge the opportunity to wield power. Nonetheless, village meetings in northern Mozambique were mainly attended by men and usually presided over by a male chief, though examples of women chiefs do exist.[20]

While it is difficult to draw conclusions based on such spatially and temporally dispersed information, it is clear that women did not have regular access to formal positions in the ruling structures of their societies in any region. Informal sources of female power, based perhaps on women's central role in agricultural production as well as their religious contributions, are still to be discovered and analyzed. Women were subordinate to men in precolonial Mozambican societies, and this was perpetuated through the specific local organization of marriage and women's labor.

WOMEN IN COLONIAL MOZAMBIQUE

FRELIMO's analysis of women's liberation recognized the confluence of traditional practices that kept women under the control of male family members, with the demands of Portuguese colonialism that deepened women's oppression.[21] Portugal, during the early part of the century, was not a strong colonial power and relied on outside capital, primarily British, to finance the development of Mozambique's infrastructure through large, ostensibly Portuguese, companies which were granted charters to govern large areas of Mozambique.[22] After 1928, Portugal itself was ruled by António Salazar's fascist "personalized autocracy" which imposed strict controls over much of the country's social and economic life.[23] Salazar's imperialist aims included the total control of Portugal's colonies by Lisbon, the exploitation of those colonies' resources for the benefit of Portuguese capitalists (not foreign investors), and a civilizing role that involved a close alliance with the Catholic Church.[24] These goals were unattainable given Portugal's poverty, so the civilizing duties were turned over in part to the Catholic Church, which was given the responsibility for educating the African population. The Church imposed fees and other restrictions on all Africans; as a result, the illiteracy rate for black Mozambicans was over 95 percent. But even in this dismal situation, girls faced greater difficulties in obtaining a formal education. In 1970, only 9 percent of Mozambicans had completed primary school, a proportion that included twice as many males (511,032) as females (246,587).[25]

One of the most disgraceful aspects of Portuguese rule was the system of forced labor (*chibalo*). *Chibalo* referred to a variety of low paid and unpaid work, based on forced recruitment or contract, and administered by either private companies or the state. Forms of coercion included prison labor, contract labor, and compulsory work for the state on such projects as railway lines and roads. *Chibalo* extended to the mandatory cultivation of rice and sisal and, most notoriously, cotton for export to Portugal's textile industry.[26] This burden fell to both men and women, although men were often able to leave to work in neighboring countries. Less mobile women not only were forced to grow inedible cotton but, in order to meet their quotas, they were forced to neglect their own food production.[27]

Historic and current testimony indicates how women suffered from forced labor and forced cotton cultivation. Some sources report that women were coerced into performing *chibalo* when their husbands were absent, that girls as young as fifteen were forced to work on roads and plantations, and that the sexual abuse of women was common.[28] One woman from Angoche in the north described in detail her contribution to a six-month forced road construction project probably undertaken in the 1940s. She asserted that few in Angoche escaped the house to house recruitment. Work began at 6 A.M. and lasted until 5 P.M., with a break for lunch which workers brought from home. Women cleared the fields while men pulled out tree trunks and leveled the land. Those who resisted were beaten.[29] Similar scenarios were recounted by workers throughout the country.

Land expropriation was also a source of oppression. Portuguese settlers claimed the best land along the southern rivers for themselves and because of this, women remaining in rural areas faced increased work, having to carry water greater distances and farm less fertile soil. At the same time there were fewer able bodies in the villages to assist with these burdens because many men left to work for wages.[30]

The post-World War II period was marked by a rapid increase in the number of white Portuguese settlers in Mozambique, the development of local industries, and the expansion of private investment. Throughout the 1940s and 1950s, Portugal negotiated contracts to supply African labor to South Africa and Southern Rhodesia (now Zimbabwe). This dependence was made permanent by the construction of roads and railways that led from Mozambican coastal cities to the interior of neighboring countries.

Beginning in the 1940s, women migrated to Lourenço Marques, the capital (now called Maputo), in greatly increasing numbers. Marriages were damaged by long-term separations; in addition, women could not depend on the return of their husbands. Some women sought waged work to repay the *lobolo* and end unhappy marriages resulting from long separations and also from early arranged marriages to unwanted older men. Women also left husbands who beat them or who were too old or ill to support them properly.[31] The combination of greater difficulties in the rural areas, the desire to repay *lobolo* and free themselves from burdensome marriages, and the possibility of waged work in Lourenço Marques, stimulated women to migrate to urban areas.[32] The colonial authorities viewed this influx as a serious social problem, in common with colonial rulers in other parts of Africa who viewed rural life as the African norm, and who tried to control and restrict African urbanization. The majority of the women working in industry in Lourenço Marques were single heads-of-households supporting minor children.[33] Because their skills were limited and the number of job openings was still small, many turned to illegal activities such as beer brewing or prostitution. An increase in tourism from South Africa and Rhodesia, and the presence of sailors at the port of Lourenço Marques, also contributed to this development. Residents of neighborhoods in Maputo confirmed that women came into the city with no legally marketable skills, learned to say a few words in Portuguese and "I love you" in English, and began work as prostitutes.[34]

The accelerated pace of colonial settlement and industrialization in the 1950s and 1960s did not bring appreciable benefits to women. Almost all waged jobs went to men, including domestic service, nursing, and teaching—three positions which in other world regions are commonly filled by women. Though a few women in the first half of the century were able to work at the docks or in garment or tobacco manufacturing, until the cashew processing factories opened in the 1950s, the number of women working for a wage was never more than a few hundred.[35]

The cashew factories became the most prominent site of female employment. The majority of cashew workers were women,[36] and the majority of female wage earners were cashew workers.[37] The pay was low and, further restraining women's possibilities for earning a living wage, the colonial Governor General of Mozambique issued a ruling in 1961 that limited the industrial wages of adult African women to 55 percent of the wages of African men.[38] Despite wage discrimination, women generally preferred work in the cashew factories to domestic service. Not only were they subject to long hours, low pay, and arbitrary discipline in domestic service, but female servants were the target of sexual harassment and attack by male household members.[39]

Africans resisted the brutality of Portuguese rule throughout the colonial era. Direct resistance could bring severe punishment, and many Mozambicans tried to avoid drawing the negative attention of the Portuguese rulers.[40] The most common means of resistance was a male option, as workers travelled to neighboring countries where conditions were comparatively better. In 1960, it was estimated that five hundred thousand Mozambicans were living and working outside Mozambique.[41]

Inside Mozambique, people resorted to small-scale labor actions such as sabotage, petty theft, slowdowns, and strikes.[42] Resistance at Sena Sugar Estates included pretending illness, stealing chalk and falsely marking tools to indicate a day's work completed, and currying favor with African overseers, all of which minimized discovery and therefore punishment.[43] Perhaps the largest action occurred in Buzi in 1947. Seven thousand women organized a strike and refused to accept or plant cotton seeds, claiming they had no time to cultivate cotton as their men were already working on nearby sugar plantations. Their partial victory exempted pregnant women and mothers of more than four children from planting cotton.[44] Songs collected by Leroy Vail and Landeg White testify to women's dissatisfaction with their position. One woman's work song, expressing her sorrow about cultivating cotton, her husband's maltreatment on a sugar plantation, and the forced separation of husbands and wives, was marked by the refrain, "I suffer, my heart is weeping."[45] Intellectuals also wrote about the abuses of colonial rule and sometimes organized groups that worked for reforms. Some were based in urban Mozambique, especially Lourenço Marques, while others—mostly men, although Noémia de Sousa made an important contribution with her poetry[46]—had gone to be educated in Lisbon. There they found themselves part of a growing anti-colonial movement which included people from Portugal's other African colonies, Angola and Guinea-Bissau.

As in other colonized countries, the impact of Portuguese colonialism on Mozambican women was contradictory. Some women took advantage of new, though limited, opportunities in education and work, and found ways to leave oppressive family situations. Yet the majority of women faced greater burdens in their agricultural work and greater stress in their family lives, as colonialism led to arbitrary laws, forced labor, and the disruption of older kin obligations and connections without introducing a viable alternative.

THE LIBERATION STRUGGLE

Portugal's colonies were not part of the general move toward independence for Africa in the early 1960s, but groups from several different regions of Mozambique pushed for Portugal's withdrawal from their country. In 1962 these groups merged to form FRELIMO, and attempted to subsume their different political approaches under the shared desire for liberation from Portugal. Throughout the 1960s, there were internal struggles over the political direction of FRELIMO. Some activists supported a narrowly nationalist approach based in part on traditional political structures, while others developed a socialist politics that proposed new political arrangements.[47] Promises to emancipate women were part of attempts to develop a movement for independence with local resonance. Generally, those who rejected a revolutionary socialist transformation and supported the traditional power of local chiefs also rejected a role for women in the struggle. Control over women's labor and reproduction were central to the rural patriarchy, and changes in women's participation in society threatened the political and economic power of the older male rulers.

The armed struggle against Portuguese colonialism began in northern Mozambique in 1964. Initially women were only marginally involved and were excluded from guerrilla training. At that time, FRELIMO did not have a "coherent ideological position on gender issues," but women joined in response to their experience of colonialism.[48] Once active, women became more aware of their position as women within the armed struggle. When they complained about their absence from combat and positions of authority, the leadership responded. One result was a statement from FRELIMO's Central Committee in 1966 that "condemned the tendency which exists among many male members of FRELIMO to systematically exclude women from the discussion of problems related to the Revolution, and to limit them to executing tasks." The document went on to encourage the inclusion of women in the activities of FRELIMO at all levels.[49]

There is evidence that women engaged in combat in a battle near Niassa in 1965, though FRELIMO officially opposed such activity.[50] The 1966 formation of the Women's Detachment at the instigation of activist women marked the formal entry of women into armed struggle. Yet women continued to be denied advancement within FRELIMO's ranks. As Eduardo Mondlane stated in his history of the struggle in Mozambique, "nobody [that is, no *men*] had thought of making women officers" until women themselves raised the issue in 1968. After women raised the issue, they were considered as candidates for leadership roles within the army.[51] Hundreds underwent guerrilla training, with an unknown number advancing to positions of authority.

Available evidence illustrates a variety of ways in which women supported and participated in the armed struggle. Machel's speech to the First Conference of Mozambican Women in 1973 catalogued the contributions of women in the revolutionary army to those attending the conference: transporting equipment, mobilizing the population, feeding guerrillas, working clandestinely, working as teachers and nurses in camps in Tanzania, and fighting "alongside the men, their comrades in arms."[52] Josina Machel, the heroine of the Mozambican revolution, was also a leader in agitating for a stronger role for women at the top levels of FRELIMO. She was personally involved in the education of recruits, and in organizing orphanages as the need grew with the toll of war. In a report on the role of women, she mentioned women's military role, but emphasized the political activities of women in educating and mobilizing the population.[53] Another activist, "Mamana" Laurina Mandima, described being denied access to military training in 1969. She subsequently had six months of military training in the FRELIMO camp at Nachingwea, Tanzania. She engaged in some military activity, but was eventually assigned to work in an orphanage in Cabo Delgado.[54] Reports of women's roles in the revolution refer to military activity, but it is clear that this was a minor part of their contribution to the armed struggle. Even so, the work done by women was recognized for its centrality in furthering the struggle. It was not simply dismissed as women's work. Women themselves reported that they were integral to the struggle, as in this statement made by Josina Machel:

> Before the struggle, even in our society women had an inferior position. Today in FRELIMO the Mozambican woman has a voice and an important role to play; she can express her opinions; she is free to say what she likes. She has the same rights and duties as any militant because she is Mozambican, because in our party there is no discrimination based on sex.[55]

Yet women continued to face restrictions in gaining leadership roles; the Executive and Central Committees of FRELIMO apparently continued as all-male political bodies at least until independence.[56]

There was a contradiction in the perception of women's role in Mozambican society. Women's work continued to be separate from men's, particularly since men rarely took responsibility for child care and food preparation. While some women were active militarily, their foremost contribution was in traditionally female roles as suppliers of food and caretakers of children. These endeavors were an important part of the victory that finally came in 1975, but did little to expand women's political power.

In 1974, Portugal's wars in Africa returned to Lisbon, when disaffected troops staged a coup and ended decades of fascist government. Negotiations with the new Portuguese government brought a year of transition and, finally, independence for Mozambique in 1975. In the next sections, women's participation in politics in independent Mozambique will be discussed, with a separate focus on agricultural policy.

WOMEN IN MOZAMBICAN POLITICS

There are two intersecting aspects to women's involvement in Mozambican politics: one is their role in the primary political structures of the nation, and the other is the work and efforts of the women's organization, OMM. In Mozambique, women continue to promote women's needs within a male-dominated government and party.

Until 1990 FRELIMO was the only party in a one party state, so there was a great deal of overlap between the party and the government. Party leaders often held both elected and appointed seats in the government. In both party and government, women were noticeable for their absence from leadership positions, whether elected or appointed. Graça Machel has been the only woman minister in Mozambique. Following her resignation as minister of education in January 1989, no other women have served at the ministerial level, though Salomé Moiane, for many years the national director of OMM, was named as deputy minister for foreign affairs in January 1991. Despite Moiane's involvement, none of the twenty-one ministries was headed by a woman or directly charged with women's issues.[57]

OMM was originally designed to bring women into the fight for liberation, not to raise fundamental questions about gender inequality. Structured by FRELIMO as an arm of FRELIMO, the document announcing OMM's formation made the relationship between them very clear: "To liberate herself, a woman must assume and creatively live the political line of FRELIMO."[58] The irony was that because the FRELIMO leadership was dominated by men, gender issues were sidestepped and women's programs ignored.

The official policy towards women in Mozambique following independence derived from the orthodox Marxist view that women would be emancipated when they supported themselves economically. A section of the resolution from the OMM's second conference in 1976 stated that "the idle woman is not involved in collective production. . . . She is an individualist with narrow horizons. . . . She is an excellent victim for reactionary ideas." To combat this problem, OMM advocated involving women in collective production, and encouraged all women to raise their "cultural, scientific and technical level."[59] This supported the orthodox Marxist view that involvement in collective work, either waged work or communal or cooperative farming arrangements, was a key element in women's eventual liberation.

Women in independent Mozambique benefitted from positive legal supports, including a constitutional guarantee of equal rights, and legislation guaranteeing them maternity leave of sixty days with pay and time off during working hours to nurse infants. Daycare centers were a national priority and were present in many work places. The development of rural agricultural cooperatives and the availability of work on state farms increased rural women's job opportunities and improved their access to legal supports. The continuing poverty and lack of opportunities for paid work, however, undermined the actual consequences of such legislation. For instance, the laws cited above did not apply to the majority of Mozambican women, who were engaged in agricultural work on individual family plots. They applied only to women working for a wage.[60]

There have been some attempts to bring more women into government, and statistics indicate that this has met with limited success. In Mozambique, as in other countries, the largest proportion of women in the government are found at the local level and fewer women at the national level. Unlike other countries, however, women in Mozambique seem to have easier access to elected than to appointed positions. FRELIMO's Fourth Party Congress in 1983 slightly increased the proportion of women on the Central Committee. The outgoing Central Committee had five women among its sixty-seven members. The new Central Committee was doubled in size to 130 seats, and 14 women were elected. All positions were filled by election by the congress delegates, but elected positions clearly owed a great deal to suggestions made by those already in the leadership. Four of the new female members were long-time activists who had been part of the Women's Detachment during the armed struggle.[61]

The 1986 national elections resulted in about 25 percent female representation at the district, city, and provincial levels, and 16 percent female representation in the national People's Assembly (the 249 delegates included 39 women).[62] The electoral system in Mozambique was a pyramidal structure, where the mass electorate voted for local representatives, local assemblies voted for representatives to the next level, and so on. Voters were given a list of candidates approved by the party and could vote against a candidate by crossing that name off. Although the distinction between elected and appointed positions was murky at all levels, gaining appointed positions at the top levels of government has been more elusive for women than becoming candidates for the election itself.

It remains to be seen how effective these women in government will be in raising women's or gender issues as insiders. At independence, a controversy over nationality was resolved in such a way as to suggest the influence of the newly elected women. The nationality law decreed that women who married foreigners would lose their Mozambican citizenship, while men married to foreigners would not. Many people felt that this was patently unfair. The issue was raised at the OMM conference in 1984 only to be dismissed by then President Samora Machel. In 1988, however, the People's Assembly changed the law to remove this discrimination against women. Women who were affected in the past may simply declare their situation to the authorities in order to regain Mozambican citizenship.[63]

The process by which FRELIMO controlled OMM policy became clearer during the preparations for the OMM's Extra-Ordinary Conference, held in November 1984. The preparations began at meetings held throughout the country in rural villages, urban neighborhoods, and work places. The discussion topics included both traditional forms of oppression (polygamy, *lobolo,* and initiation rites) and contemporary problems such as divorce, family relations, single mothers, and the general situation of women in modern Mozambican society. The national organization provided an outline to guide discussion, though participants did not feel constrained to adopt the official line. People at meetings all over Mozambique spoke of their own experiences in defense of some traditional customs and did not simply criticize these customs according to official expectations.[64]

The final document from the November 1984 conference praised OMM's role in advancing Mozambican women, but included little substantive policy change. In some cases, such as the controversial issue of initiation rites, the document called for further study. But the nuclear family was maintained as the fundamental unit of society and relations within the family were not questioned. In what appeared to be a compromise statement, the document called for "each family [to] make an effort to create a new equilibrium based on equality of duties and rights in carrying out the functions of each one of its members, as father and head of the family, as mother and housewife."[65] Although in preliminary documents and discussion women were quite outspoken about the need for men to take on their share of housework and child care, this was omitted from the final document.[66]

Ironically, the women's organization succumbed to traditional social expectations about women's role. OMM projects included teaching newly urbanized women how to care for their apartments, and how to crochet and sew infant clothes to sell for income. These activities involved women in the socialist endeavor of developing Mozambique without raising more disturbing questions about gender inequality and power relations.

Other problems added to the desperate straits of Mozambicans in the 1980s. Mozambique has suffered immeasurably from a war fomented by South Africa, which funded and trained Renamo (Mozambican National Resistance). Renamo has been responsible for widespread rural devastation and a near total breakdown of rural production and distribution. This war made organized agricultural production difficult if not impossible, and was also responsible for a surge of immigrants to the cities.[67] Women in the rural areas have been particularly affected by the war due to their responsibility for food cultivation and preparation, and their continuing primary role in child care. The large numbers of refugees and the disruption of basic agricultural production in many parts of the country made it clear that women were suffering the brunt of the destabilization.[68]

Women active in OMM were especially targeted by Renamo, as in the case of Teresa Liquice in Cheringoma, Sofala province. Despite the murder of her husband and son, the destruction of her home, and her own sexual assault by Renamo, she continued as district secretary of OMM, and worked to draw attention to women's unique suffering. As she reported, "it's important to note that . . . the largest number of people displaced by the war are women and children . . . there are at least 5,000 women and children here [in a refugee camp]."[69] In such an extreme situation it took women of uncommon courage to continue their activities on behalf of other suffering women. One of OMM's achievements was the training of ten thousand women in the militias formed to combat Renamo.[70]

In 1987, Mozambique implemented an economic restructuring program based on conditions imposed by the World Bank and International Monetary Fund (IMF) for acquiring loans. In order to repay its foreign debt, the currency was devalued and austerity measures introduced. It appeared that these outside agencies were involved in policymaking.[71] The cuts in the government's ability to provide services meant that many sectors that had supported women, such as child care centers and health services, were adversely affected.

Restructuring also affected OMM severely. Because of mandated increases in salary levels, OMM was forced to reduce its staff, especially outside the capital. In Beira, the second largest city in Mozambique, OMM could pay only two staff members to organize a city of nearly half a million residents in 1989. OMM projects, such as sewing cooperatives, could not afford to continue to pay salaries to all those who were cooperative members, and the costs of supplies such as cloth, thread, and sewing machines became prohibitive.

Further developments concerning women's involvement in national politics became evident in August 1989, when FRELIMO held its Fifth Party Congress. At that meeting delegates decided to end the definition of the party as a Marxist-Leninist organization, establish a clearer division between party and government, make provisions for multi-party elections, and shift to a mass party rather than a vanguard party formation.

Women's representation at the party congress (29 percent) was double their representation at the 1983 congress,[72] and a larger proportion than female party membership. A FRELIMO document prepared for the 1989 congress expressed concern at the low percentage of female members—in 1989 women accounted for only 25 percent of Frelimo members, a decrease from 30 percent in 1983. More women were members of FRELIMO (51,659 in 1989, up from 33,000 in 1983), but their relative weight had decreased.[73] Many women chose to belong to OMM without also belonging to FRELIMO: OMM counted 281,000 members in 1989.[74]

Though some OMM members had hoped that a woman would be elected to the Political Bureau, the ruling body of FRELIMO, those elected at the 1989 congress were still all men. This was finally changed at the Sixth FRELIMO Party Congress in August 1991. Deolinda Guezimane, a long-time activist and veteran of the Women's Detachment, was the first woman elected to the Political Bureau. The Sixth Congress also marked the first time that secret ballots were used in electing members of the Central Committee; in combination with what was called positive discrimination for women—members were obliged to vote for a minimum number of female candidates—the number of women on the Central Committee rose to an unprecedented level. Fifty-seven women became Central Committee members, a full 36 percent of the total 160 members.[75]

FRELIMO's concern with increasing party membership resulted in a program in 1989 to create a mass party by extending membership to groups previously excluded, including property owners, religious activists, and polygamists.[76] FRELIMO justified this strategy by asserting that potential members should be analyzed within their own cultural contexts; if a man had more than one wife but was treating them all fairly, then polygamy alone should not be a prohibition against his FRELIMO membership. As polygamy had been one of the first oppressive practices denounced by FRELIMO and OMM, this party-building strategy seemed to conflict with the party's official position on women in Mozambique. One OMM national leader spoke to me in 1989 about the advantages of a polygamous relationship for women (a woman knows where her husband is, co-wives can cooperate in their work), and concluded by saying that the earlier anti-polygamy position had been premature.

It may be that the war forced FRELIMO to investigate Renamo's attraction for rural Mozambicans. Some evidence suggests that Renamo appealed strongly to disgruntled local (male) leaders.[77] It is possible that FRELIMO leaders believed that they could temper their socialism by admitting property owners, and their commitment to other social changes by admitting polygamists and religious activists. Undoubtedly some rural men resented FRELIMO's stand on polygamy; whether a revision in membership policy will be sufficient to change their attitudes toward FRELIMO's leadership is not known.

The connection of polygamy to particular rural social and economic structures made it difficult to abolish without a deeper social transformation. There are no reliable statistics, but women I spoke with indicated that urban residents and people with some education tended to be monogamous. The new membership policy, however, demonstrated the limitations of a politics that did not include broader gender issues when discussing immediate practical reforms: in this case, the expansion of FRELIMO membership appears to appeal to men, and traditional men at that, while requiring women's continued subordination.

At the least this decision illustrates internal contradictions in FRELIMO, which discussed women's declining role in the party in its central committee report, yet in the same report introduced a policy that clearly favored male over female membership. One explanation is the strength of patriarchal attitudes among male leaders in FRELIMO, who apparently see traditional men as more valuable potential recruits than women. The extension of FRELIMO membership to polygamous men demonstrates a further reliance on male ideas and a decline in the influence of OMM, whose leaders had to try to explain the situation after the decision had been made.

Further changes came in November 1990, when Mozambique introduced a new constitution that legalized multi-party elections, established expanded political rights and freedoms, and proposed a new reliance on market forces in the economy.[78] Some observers believe that these changes—including the protection of civil liberties such as the right to strike, and freedom of the press, assembly, and religion—have opened a space for organizing. In 1990 and 1991 numerous workers went on strike, farmers in agricultural cooperatives became quite active, and religious activists took a leading role in organizing for change.[79]

While it is still not clear how women will be affected by these changes, there are specific new policies that impact OMM. OMM, along with other organizations, was proclaimed an autonomous organization, no longer dependent on FRELIMO for its political direction. At the Fourth National Conference of OMM in November 1990, OMM adopted a new set of statutes that established OMM as an independent organization with membership open to all women, whether they agree with FRELIMO's politics or not. The organization will no longer focus on implementing Frelimo policy, but will emphasize legislation that will extend women's rights. While this new formation allows for greater political freedom, OMM faces serious problems in funding. In the past OMM's daily operations were supported by FRELIMO. OMM's Fourth National Conference discussed the financial issue at length, with OMM leaders arguing for more self-funding efforts and a greater reliance on volunteer staff.[80] Finding private funding or relying on membership dues in a time of extreme economic difficulty seems problematic at best.

There can be no clear conclusion regarding Mozambican women and politics in the 1980s and early 1990s. There have been important changes that could bring either advances or reversals in women's positions. While there have been obvious gains in the numbers of women involved in the political arena, the continuation of war and extreme poverty have forced FRELIMO to make difficult decisions and have placed some new obstacles to the realization of women-centered policies.

AGRICULTURAL POLICY

Because women in Mozambique have historically contributed extensively to agricultural labor and production, the impact of national agricultural policy on women was notable. The goal of developing communal work organizations included women as well as men. Because of the educational and other constraints on them, women had few options for supporting their families other than agriculture. Yet the media in Mozambique focus attention on the situation of working women, partly to encourage women to join in that more visible contribution to national development. The emphasis on women entering formerly male sectors of the economy has also been characteristic of Western writings about Mozambican women where their participation in this part of the economy is treated as a measure of their emancipation. Female tractor drivers gained prominence, and were highlighted in an article on women working at the Mafambisse sugar processing complex outside of Beira.[81] Despite the importance of such women for propaganda purposes, they are clearly in the minority in Mozambique, and they are not easily accepted by everyone in the society. There are many stories of men opposing their wives' waged work or political activity. I met one woman in Maputo in 1989 whose husband had cut off her nose when his demands that she remain home were not met. While most men are not so violent, it is generally understood that men prefer that their wives attend full-time to housework and child care.[82]

Women's main area of work continued to be agriculture. The 1980 census reported a total of 187,862 urban women active economically with 132,173 of them working in agriculture, primarily as unpaid producers. In contrast, only 55,951 of the 370,913 working men were based in agriculture.[83] Women not only lacked the necessary education for most urban waged jobs, they also faced opposition from their husbands. In war-torn and poverty-stricken Mozambique, there was no possibility to expand industry, or the economy in general, so that women could find increased options for work. While women wanted to work for a wage, for financial necessity as well as for personal fulfillment, they faced continuing social barriers despite the supportive laws.

Mozambique's agricultural policies have been extensively analyzed, especially the failure of post-independence plans to develop the rural areas through the establishment of communal villages, cooperatives, and state farms.[84] These plans derived in part from a desire to eliminate some of the uncertainties inherent in individual small-scale farming, and not simply from a blind adherence to socialist theories about agriculture.

Communal villages were designed to establish individual farmers in more centralized settlements, to facilitate delivery of services, and to assist in forming collective productive units or cooperatives. Some of the services directly alleviated women's daily burden of work, for example, when digging wells in a settled village reduced the time spent collecting water. A centralized settlement also made it easier to offer literacy classes, and to mobilize women into OMM.[85] The long-term goal of organizing communal villages was to have rural producers involved in collective production, though the formation of communal villages was bureaucratically separate from the development of producer collectives. Communal villages and producer collectives could exist separately, though often the collectives were part of a communal village. Generally, communal villages relied on continued individual agricultural production. A 1976 resolution on communal villages called them the backbone of development policy but did not specify how individual families were to be integrated into the village organization.[86] Local initiative and self-reliance were at the core of the policy.

In 1977, still referring to communal villages as the "chosen strategy," the state sector was declared the "dominant and decisive" sector.[87] This reflected the perception that the most efficient response to a growing rural food crisis was to develop centralized state farms on the abandoned colonial rural enterprises. Because employment for women on the state farms was usually limited to seasonal and part-time positions, this policy excluded the bulk of women's agricultural work. Funding was channeled into the state farms, and cooperatives and small farmers were left with almost no material support from the government. A FRELIMO Central Committee report showed that only 2 percent of all agricultural funding went to cooperatives between 1977 and 1982.[88] The role of women in the rural cooperatives displayed a marked regional variation that derived from colonial era experiences. In the south, where men regularly left Mozambique to work in South Africa, rural cooperatives appeared to be almost entirely female. In the center and north of the country, the Portuguese had employed local male labor on tea, sugar, copra (coconut), and sisal plantations. There, fewer cooperatives were established, and women played a lesser role in them.

Official policy favoring large state farms worked to women's detriment. State farms offered some opportunities for women to earn wages, but it is difficult to find accurate figures reporting the extent of female employment on these farms. Regional data indicate a higher rate of female employment on state farms in the south.[89] Stephanie Urdang observed in 1980 that one section of Moamba State Farm, in southern Mozambique, employed only about 200 women in a work force of 1,850; the number of women working on state farms in northern Mozambique was still lower (and most women working on these farms were single). Urdang presents evidence that married women faced opposition from their husbands, who expected them to maintain the family fields while the husbands earned wages.[90] State farms were not a realistic source of employment for women who remained responsible for most of the daily work on individual family farms.

These attempts at restructuring agriculture were neither economically successful nor popular with those who should have benefitted from them. The communal villages and cooperatives did not become strong centers of production, and the state farms performed poorly. Family production relying heavily on women's labor remained central to food production in Mozambique, but it was denied the financial and bureaucratic support necessary for success and growth. In retrospect it is easy to criticize these policies for their inattention to rural realities or for their failure to take into account the variety of rural social formations. But, despite these variations, women in all regions generally performed the labor that provided food for their families. The absence of women from participation in rural development planning was a serious strategic error, and certainly contributed to the current food production crisis brought on by continuing war and drought.[91]

In the 1980s, the Mozambican government began a campaign of "Green Zones" in the urban areas, partially in response to Renamo's disruption of food supplies going from the rural areas to the cities. Part of the Green Zones structure included cooperatives for agricultural production, and some of these, especially in the south, have become centers for women's political power. Maputo's Green Zones are famous for the strength of their women-dominated cooperatives, with up to 90 percent of cooperative members being female.[92] Women worked without pay at first. The cooperatives still do not always pay a living wage to members, but cooperative members can purchase harvested food at low cost and also have access to amenities such as day care centers and literacy classes organized by the cooperatives. Many cooperative members cultivate personal garden plots as well as contribute several hours each day to the cooperative fields.

In Beira, the Green Zones were generally not organized into cooperatives and most women worked as individuals. The Women's Project within the Office of Green Zones for Beira has received

UNICEF support for courses directed at women who work in the Green Zones fields. The program offers classes in literacy, basic arithmetic, agriculture, and health; women attend afternoon classes after working in their fields in the morning. In addition to information, the Green Zones office supplies seeds, hoes, and other materials to the women who participate.[93] While admirable, this program suffered from the many shortages afflicting the whole society; for example, the teachers at a child care center associated with the program went without pay for long periods of time, and the children's food was limited to *massa*, the local maize porridge. Women hesitated to become involved as they could not be sure that their children would be well cared for in the center.[94]

In the late 1980s and early 1990s a struggle over the use of urban land continued between female farmers and those who wanted to build residences or factories. Those who tried to deprive the cooperatives of their land claimed that the women did not know how to use it properly. Celina Cossa, the national president of the União Geral de Cooperativistas (General Union of Cooperativists, UGC), spoke out repeatedly for the rights of farming women.[95] In 1989, at the Fifth Party Congress of FRELIMO she called attempts to take over cooperative land a form of banditry. Speaking to a UGC conference in 1990, Cossa was explicit about the attitudes of some entrepreneurs toward the cooperative women:

> Some people, arguing as ever that we are illiterate, incapable, ignorant and above all, almost all women, sum it up by saying that we don't know how to manage our property, our land. . . . As poor people, we feel the need to unite and work together in cooperatives.[96]

President Joaquim Chissano responded by supporting the contribution made by the cooperative women to the nation's political and productive effort. He said, "we are aware that there are those who want to kill the cooperative movement. But we know that the cooperatives do not merely produce food. They also develop men and women, they liberate men and women."[97]

The cooperative union has become a vehicle for raising issues central to rural women, as well as to urban women engaged in agriculture. Perhaps because it was not conceived of as a women's organization, the cooperative union is not plagued by gender segregation as is OMM. While women were vulnerable as urban farmers, they found that their access to agricultural land was protected through membership in the cooperatives. It is also significant that the strongest advocates of the political and social importance of agricultural cooperatives are now urban women, and not the rural men envisioned in earlier formulations of cooperative strategies.

Given the centrality of agriculture to almost all Mozambican women, it is not surprising that their political weight is concentrated in agricultural cooperatives. Through the cooperative union they acted as peasants with agricultural interests though their special situation as women also shaped their efforts. When OMM celebrated fifteen years of existence in March 1988, a focal point of the festival in Maputo was "an agricultural exhibition . . . set up to demonstrate the potential of the 'green zones' . . . around Maputo city, which have been developed chiefly by women."[98] The leading role of women in the cooperative movement may contribute to changing the attitudes of agricultural policy planners as they acknowledge that women's agricultural work needs to be centrally integrated into future development strategies for a successful outcome.

CONCLUSION

As Mozambique enters the 1990s, it faces a combination of issues that are difficult to disentangle, especially in terms of the impact on women's position in society and possibilities for the future. These include the continuing war with Renamo, economic restructuring, and changes in government policies as free market economic measures are expanded. These events have had different effects on different segments of Mozambican society, though women appear to be bearing the brunt of increased instability and poverty. Some elite women and men who have access to education and capital may be successful, but the vast majority of Mozambicans are poorer and hungrier than they were at independence. New possibilities for political organizing autonomously of FRELIMO may make it easier for OMM to raise questions of gender equality, but it may not have the resources to exploit them effectively.[99]

Women in Mozambique have a long history of political subordination despite their central role in the agricultural economy. Colonialism and the increasing connection of local Mozambican societies to the international capitalist economy increased women's work without improving their political status. FRELIMO's policies for liberating women were not simply the result of its socialist program but were devised in recognition of the history of the oppression of women in Mozambican societies. The continuing limitations to women's progress in Mozambique include deeply rooted patriarchal attitudes among male leaders and a limited vision of gender equality among some female leaders. Yet the initial steps that have been taken, including legal supports for women that lay a foundation for future struggles, are exceedingly important. Despite the lack of an official gender analysis, these programs may contribute to future female empowerment.

NOTES

1. Frelimo, Departamento de Trabalho Ideológico, *Estatutos e Programa da OMM* (Maputo: FRELIMO, n.d.), 7.

2. Samora Machel, "The Liberation of Women is a Fundamental Necessity for the Revolution," in his *Mozambique: Sowing the Seeds of Revolution* (London: Committee for Freedom in Mosambique, Angola and Guiné, 1974), 21–36, quote on 24.

3. Sylvia Hill, "Lessons from the Mozambican Women's Struggle," *Transafrica Forum* 2, no. 1 (1983): 77–90; Sonia Kruks, "Mozambique: Some Reflections on the Struggle for Women's Emancipation," *Frontiers* 7, no. 2 (1983): 32–41; and "Mozambique: Mobilizing Women," *Isis International Bulletin* 19 (1981): 17–20.

4. Machel, "The Liberation of Women," 27.

5. Ibid., 25, 32.

6. Jeff Guy, "Gender Oppression in Southern Africa's Precapitalist Societies," in *Women and Gender in Southern Africa to 1945*, ed. Cherryl Walker (London: James Currey, 1990), 33–47, quote on 33.

7. Henri A. Junod, *The Life of a South African Tribe*, 2 vols. (New Hyde Park, N.Y.: University Books, 1962; first published in 1912); E. Dora Earthy, *Valenge Women: The Social and Economic Life of the Valenge Women of Portuguese East Africa* (London: Frank Cass, 1968; first published in 1933); and Augusto Cabral, *Raças, Usos e Costumes dos Indigenas do Districto de Inhambane* (Lourenço Marques: Imprensa Nacional, 1910).

8. For instance, see Jeanne Penvenne, "Making Our Own Way: Women Working in Lourenço Marques, 1900–1933," Boston University African Studies Center, Working Paper no. 114 (1986); and Sherilynn Young, "Fertility and Famine: Women's Agricultural History in Southern Mozambique," in *The Roots of Rural Poverty in Central and Southern Africa* , ed. Robin Palmer and Neil Parsons (Berkeley: University of California Press, 1977), 66–81. A useful overview of the colonial political economy, including some discussion of women, is in Otto Roesch, "Migrant Labour and Forced Rice Production in Southern Mozambique: The Colonial Peasantry of the Lower Limpopo Valley," *Journal of Southern African Studies* 17, no. 2 (1991): 239–70.

9. Gita Honwana Welch, Francesca Dagnino, and Albie Sachs, "Transforming the Foundations of Family Law in the Course of the Mozambican Revolution," *Journal of Southern African Studies* 12, no. 1 (1985): 60–74, discussion of use of traditional on 61; reprinted in Albie Sachs and Gita

Honwana Welch, *Liberating the Law: Creating Popular Justice in Mozambique* (London: Zed Books, 1990), 64–85.

10. Gita Honwana Welch, "Lobolo," Tese de Licenciatura, Faculdade de Direito, Universidade Eduardo Mondlane (1983), 2; a revised version, co-authored with Albie Sachs, was published as "The Bride Price, Revolution, and the Liberation of Women," *International Journal of the Sociology of Law* 15 (1987): 369–92.

11. Adam Kuper, *Wives for Cattle: Bridewealth and Marriage in Southern Africa* (London: Routledge and Kegan Paul, 1982), 10.

12. Sherilynn Young, "Women in Transition: Southern Mozambique 1975–1976, Reflections on Colonialism, Aspirations for Independence," paper presented at the Conference on the History of Women, College of St. Catherine, Minn., 1977, 3; and Roesch, "Migrant Labour and Forced Rice Production," 249–50.

13. Young, "Women in Transition," 4–5; for related regional evidence, see Sandra Burman, "Fighting a Two-Pronged Attack: The Changing Legal Status of Women in Cape-Ruled Basutoland, 1872–1884," in Walker, *Women and Gender in Southern Africa*, 48–75.

14. Abel dos Santos Baptista, *Monografia Etnográfica sobre os Macuas* (Lisbon: Agência Geral do Ultramar, 1951), 54; Great Britain, Naval Intelligence Division, Geographical Section, *A Manual of Portuguese East Africa* (London: HMSO, 1920), 93–94; and Jorge Dias, Margaret Dias, and M. Viegas Guerreiro, *Os Macondes de Moçambique*, 4 vols. (Lisbon: Junta de Invesstigações do Ultramar, 1964–1970).

15. Organização da Mulher Moçambicana, Gabinete Central de Preparação da Conferencia Extraordinária, "Temas-base para Discussão: Ritos de Iniciação" (Maputo: typescript, 1983); also see Earthy, *Valenge Women*, 109–136.

16. Young, "Women in Transition," 3.

17. Ibid., 3.

18. Edward A. Alpers, "State, Merchant Capital, and Gender Relations in Southern Mozambique to the End of the Nineteenth Century: Some Tentative Hypotheses," *African Economic History* 13 (1984): 23–55.

19. Sherilynn Young, "What Have They Done with the Rain?: 20th Century Transformation in Ceremonial Practice and Belief in Southern Mozambique," presented at the 1978 Annual Meeting of the African Studies Association; Martha B. Binford, "Julia: An East African Diviner," in *Unspoken Worlds: Women's Religious Lives in Non-Western Cultures*, ed. Nancy A. Falk and Rita M. Gross (San Francisco: Harper and Row, 1980), 3–21; and see Earthy, *Valenge Women*, for a description of women who held a variety of religious roles in the southern province of Gaza in the 1920s. These included women possessed by spirits (200–7), and *nyamusoros*, which Earthy translates as "priestesses."

20. J. Gus Liebenow, *Colonial Rule and Political Development in Tanzania: the Case of the Makonde* (Evanston, Ill.: Northwestern University Press, 1971), 54.

21. For discussion of women during the late colonial period, including an analysis of women's pages in Mozambican newspapers, see Isabel Casimiro, "Transformação nas Relações Homem/Mulher em Moçambique 1960–1974," M.A. thesis, Universidade Eduardo Mondlane, 1986.

22. Leroy Vail, "Mozambique's Chartered Companies: The Rule of the Feeble," *Journal of African History* 17, no. 3 (1976): 389–416.

23. The phrase is from John Marcum, "The People's Republic of Angola: A Radical Vision Frustrated," in *Afro-Marxist Regimes: Ideology and Public Policy*, ed. Edmond J. Keller and Donald Rothchild (Boulder: Lynne Reiner, 1987), 67–83, quote on 68; see also Alan K. Smith, "The Idea of Mozambique and its Enemies, c. 1890–1930," *Journal of Southern African Studies* 17, no. 3 (1991): 496–524.

24. For further detail, see Allen Isaacman and Barbara Isaacman, *Mozambique: From Colonialism to Revolution, 1900–1982* (Boulder: Westview, 1983), 39.

25. Anton Johnston, *Education in Moçambique 1975–1984* (Stockholm: Swedish International Development Authority, 1984), 16–22; and Isaacman and Isaacman, *Mozambique*, 49–53.

26. For evidence of the economic marginality of the early years of cotton cultivation, see M. Anne Pitcher, "Sowing the Seeds of Failure: Early Portuguese Cotton Cultivation in Angola and Mozambique, 1820–1926," *Journal of Southern African Studies* 17, no. 1 (1991): 43–70.

27. Allen Isaacman et al., "'Cotton is the Mother of Poverty': Peasant Resistance to Forced Cotton Production in Mozambique, 1938–1961," *International Journal of African Historical Studies* 13, no. 4 (1980): 581–615, reference to women resisting on 603; Leroy Vail and Landeg White, "'Tawani, Machambero!': Forced Cotton and Rice Growing on the Zambezi," *Journal of African History* 19, no. 2 (1978): 239–63. The distribution of cotton seed to women in order to keep the men free for work on the sugar plantations is mentioned on 248.

28. E. A. Ross, *Report on Employment of Native Labor in Portuguese Africa* (New York: Abbott Press, 1925), 40–41, 45–46; Alpheus Manghezi, "Interviews with Mozambican Peasant Women," in *Third World Lives of Struggle*, ed. Hazel Johnson and Henry Bernstein (London: Heinemann, 1982), 164–72; and Leroy Vail and Landeg White, "Forms of Resistance: Songs and Perceptions of Power in Colonial Mozambique," *American Historical Review* 88, no. 4 (1983): 883–919.

29. "Fatima Jamal: Recordando a Infância de Angoche," *Tempo* 626 (10 October 1982): 49–51. See also the interview with Martha Chissano in Manghezi, "Interviews with Mozambican Peasant Women," 165–66.

30. Young, "Women in Transition," 8–9.

31. Sheldon, "Working Women," 241–47.

32. Penvenne, "Making Our Own Way," 8–9.

33. Jeanne Penvenne, "Here Everyone Walked with Fear: The Mozambican Labor System and the Workers of Lourenço Marques, 1945–1962," in *Struggle for the City: Migrant Labor, Capital, and the State in Urban Africa*, ed. Frederick Cooper (Beverly Hills: Sage, 1983), 151.

34. Hilário Matusse, "Chamanculo: Memórias de um Bairro," *Tempo* 682 (6 November 1983): 22–28; and Hilário Matusse, "Mafalala: Fronteira entre a Cidade e o Subúrbio, O Passado," *Tempo* 685 (27 November 1983): 14–19.

35. Penvenne, "Here Everyone Walked with Fear," 151.

36. In 1956, three-quarters of the 1,672 cashew factory employees in Lourenço Marques were women. Penvenne, "Here Everyone Walked with

Fear," 131–66, see 149.

37. In 1958, 63.4 percent of the 2,176 employed women in Lourenço Marques worked at the cashew factory Caju Industrial. Maria da Silva, *As Missões Católicas Femininas*, Estudos de Ciências Politicas e Sociais No. 37 (Lisbon: Junta de Investigações do Ultramar, 1960), 56. This study was concerned with the "grave social and moral problem" of these working women, as 1,127 of the 1,308 cashew workers "lived without a man," yet only 425 did not have children.

38. "New Trends and Concepts in Mozambique African Labor," U.S. Foreign Service Despatch, 6 February 1961; this is part of a set of Department of State documents obtained by Allen Isaacman under the Freedom of Information Act. Edward A. Alpers brought this to my attention.

39. Penvenne, "Here Everyone Walked with Fear," 152.

40. "The Situation in the Territories under Portuguese Administration Since January 1961," *Presence Africaine* 17, no. 45 (1963): 177–96.

41. Ruth First, *Black Gold: The Mozambican Miner, Proletarian and Peasant* (New York: St. Martin's Press, 1983), 15; M. Newitt, "Migrant Labour and the Development of Mozambique," in *The Societies of Southern Africa in the 19th and 20th Centuries*, University of London, Institute of Commonwealth Studies, Collected Seminar Papers no. 17 (1974): 67–76; Edward A. Alpers, "'To Seek a Better Life': The Implications of Migration from Mozambique to Tanganyika for Class Formation and Political Behavior," *Canadian Journal of African Studies* 18, no. 2 (1984): 367–88; and Peter Scott, "Migrant Labor in Southern Rhodesia," *Geographical Review* 44, no. 1 (1954): 29–48; Isaacman and Isaacman, *Mozambique*, 64.

42. Jeanne Penvenne, "Labor Struggles at the Port of Lourenço Marques, 1900–1933," *Review: Journal of the Fernand Braudel Center* 8, no. 2 (1984): 249–85.

43. Judith Head, "Opressão Colonial e Formas de Luta dos Trabalhadores: O Caso da Sena Sugar Estates," *Não Vamos Esquecer!* 1, no. 2/3 (1983): 39–44.

44. Isaacman and Isaacman, *Mozambique*, 66.

45. Vail and White, "'Tawani Machambero,'" and "Forms of Resistance," song cited on 896.

46. Four of her most cited poems are available in English in Margaret Dickinson, ed., *When Bullets Begin to Flower* (Nairobi: East African Publishing House, 1972).

47. Barry Munslow, *Mozambique: the Revolution and its Origins* (London: Longman, 1983) contributes a thorough discussion of these events.

48. Allen Isaacman and Barbara Isaacman, "The Role of Women in the Liberation of Mozambique," *Ufahamu* 13, no. 2–3 (1984): 128–85, quote and other information on 142–43.

49. *Mozambique Revolution* 27 (October–December 1966): 3–5, cited in Isaacman and Isaacman, "The Role of Women," 158.

50. *Mozambique Revolution* 21 (September 1965): 7, cited in ibid., 156.

51. Eduardo Mondlane, *The Struggle for Mozambique* (London: Penguin, 1969), 186.

52. Machel, "The Liberation of Women," 21–22; also see Munslow,

Mozambique, 123–24; and Isaacman and Isaacman, "The Role of Women."

53. Josina Machel, "The Role of Women in the Revolution," in *The Mozambican Woman in the Revolution* (Richmond, B.C.: LSM Information Center, 1974), 5–8, reprinted from *Mozambique Revolution* 41 (1969).

54. António César, "Quando o Marido Mobiliza a Companheira Para a Frente," *Diário de Moçambique,* 10 January 1983, 8; also see his "A Fome Não Mata o Patriotismo," *Diário de Moçambique,* 31 January 1983, 4, 7, for testimony from an activist in the Women's Detachment.

55. Mondlane, *Struggle,* 186.

56. I did not find a single list of committee members, and there was no mention elsewhere of female members of these groups. One prominent woman, Graça Simbine, later Graça Machel, was the only woman named as a minister in 1975 when FRELIMO named a Council of Ministers for the independent government. That list of ministers stated whether those named had been on the Central or Executive Committee during the armed struggle; Graça Simbine was not listed as a member of either committee.

57. "Chissano Appoints New Ministers," *Mozambiquefile* 175 (1991): 3–4.

58. "Organização da Mulher Moçambicana," in João Reis and Armando Pedro Muiuane, eds., *Datas e Documentos da História da FRELIMO* (Maputo: Imprensa Nacional de Moçambique, 1975, 2d ed.), 311–25, quote on 316.

59. "Mozambican Women's Conference," *People's Power* 6 (1977): 5–26, quote on 13.

60. Barbara Isaacman and June Stephen, *Mozambique: Women, the Law and Agrarian Reform* (Addis Ababa: United Nations Economic Commission for Africa, 1980), especially 29–65 on civic rights and family law, and 67–95 on rural women. For more detail, see Stephanie Urdang, *Rural Transformation and Peasant Women in Mozambique* (Geneva: International Labour Office, 1986); and Sonia Kruks and Ben Wisner, "The State, the Party and the Female Peasantry in Mozambique," *Journal of Southern African Studies* 11, no. 1 (1984): 106–27.

61. "Special Issue: Fourth Congress of the Frelimo Party," *AIM Information Bulletin* 82 (1983): 34–35.

62. "The Newly Elected People's Assembly Meets in its First Session," *AIM Information Bulletin* 127 (1987): 5.

63. "New Legislation Approved," *AIM Information Bulletin* 138 (1988): 4.

64. For more on this meeting, see Signe Arnfred, "Women in Mozambique: Gender Struggle and Politics," *Review of African Political Economy* 41 (1988): 5–16; "Pelo Sucesso da Sua Conferência, Mulher Moçambicana Saúda Partido Frelimo," *Domingo,* 2 December 1984, 1; and Joseph Hanlon, *Mozambique: The Revolution Under Fire* (London: Zed Books, 1984), 169.

65. "Mozambican Women Plan a Strategy for Emancipation," *AIM Information Bulletin* 101 (1984): 1–4; "The General Resolution Passed by the Extra-Ordinary Conference of the OMM (Mozambican Women's Organization) in Maputo, November 6–11, 1984," Supplement to *AIM Information Bulletin* 104 (1984): 5.

66. Organização da Mulher Moçambicana, Gabinete Central da Preparação de Conferência Extraordinária da O.M.M., Provincia de Sofala, untitled report

prepared for Extra-Ordinary Conference (Beira: typescript, 1984), 33–36.

67. The impact of the war on women is discussed in Stephanie Urdang, *And Still They Dance: Women, War, and the Struggle for Change in Mozambique* (New York: Monthly Review, 1989).

68. Hilário Matusse, "Guerra e Fome Retardam Libertação da Mulher," *Tempo* 860 (5 April 1987): 27–31; and "7 de Abril: Data Assinalada com Espírito de Luta," *Tempo* 861 (12 April 1987): 4–8.

69. "Women in Desperate Situation in Inhaminga," *AIM Information Bulletin* 140 (1988): 11.

70. Partido Frelimo, *Relatório do Comité Central ao V Congresso* (Maputo: CEGRAF, 1989), 133.

71. Joseph Hanlon, *Mozambique: Who Calls the Shots?* (Bloomington: Indiana University Press, 1991).

72. "Who Was There?" *Mozambiquefile* 157 (1989): 9.

73. Partido Frelimo, *Relatório do Comité Central ao V Congresso*, 32.

74. Ibid., 134.

75. "Frelimo Sixth Congress," *Mozambiquefile* 182 (1991): 4–9.

76. Partido Frelimo, *Relatório do Comité Central ao V Congresso*, 51.

77. Alex Vines, *Renamo: Terrorism in Mozambique* (Bloomington: Indiana University Press, 1991), 73–119.

78. The new constitution was published as an insert to *Mozambiquefile* 174 (1991).

79. Judith Marshall, "Resisting Adjustment in Mozambique: The Grassroots Speak Up," *Southern Africa Report* 7, no. 1 (1991): 3–8.

80. "Mozambican Women at the Crossroads," *Mozambiquefile* 174 (1991): 4–6.

81. António César, "Mulheres-Tractoristas: Quebram-se os Tabus," *Diário de Moçambique*, 30 December 1982, 8–9; and Stephanie Urdang, "What Women Driving Tractors Can Prove," *New African* (May 1981): 18–19.

82. Also see Stephanie Urdang, "The Last Transition? Women and Development," in John S. Saul, ed., *A Difficult Road: The Transition to Socialism in Mozambique* (New York: Monthly Review, 1985), 347–88, especially 372.

83. Conselho Coordenador de Recenseamento, *1° Recenseamento Geral da População: Informação Pública* (Maputo: Conselho Coordenador de Recenseamento, 1983), 34.

84. Helena Dolny, "The Challenge of Agriculture," in Saul, *A Difficult Road*, 211–52; Otto Roesch, "Peasants and Collective Agriculture in Mozambique," in *The Politics of Agriculture in Tropical Africa*, ed. Jonathan Barker (Beverly Hills, Calif.: Sage, 1984), 291–316; and Marc Wuyts, "Money, Planning and Rural Transformation in Mozambique," *Journal of Development Studies* 22, no. 1 (1985): 190–207. Two dissertations that examine these issues are Merle Bowen, "'Let's Build Agricultural Producer Cooperatives': Socialist Agricultural Development Strategy in Mozambique 1975–1983," Ph.D. diss., University of Toronto, 1986; and Otto Roesch, "Socialism and Rural Development in Mozambique: The Case of Aldeia Comunal 24 de Julho," Ph.D. diss., University of Toronto, 1986.

85. Urdang, *Rural Transformation and Peasant Women*, 54–72.

86. Roesch, "Peasants and Collective Agriculture," 294.

87. Roesch, "Peasants and Collective Agriculture," 295, quoting official Frelimo documents.

88. Partido Frelimo, *Relatório do Comité Central ao IV Congresso* (Maputo: Imprensa Nacional, 1983), 32.

89. Urdang, *Rural Transformation and Peasant Women*, 78–90.

90. Ibid., 79–90.

91. Regarding the absence of women from agricultural planning in Africa in general, see Dolores Koenig, "Old Stereotypes, New Stereotypes: The Realities for Africa's Women Farmers," *Transafrica Forum* 4, no. 4 (1987): 17–34; and Anita Spring, "Women Farmers and Food in Africa: Some Considerations and Suggested Solutions," in *Food in Sub-Saharan Africa*, ed. Art Hansen and Della E. McMillan (Boulder: Lynne Reiner, 1986), 332–48.

92. For more on the Green Zones cooperatives in Maputo, see Anna Maria Gentili, "Donne e Lavoro: Il Movimento Cooperativo Delle *Zonas Verdes* di Maputo," *Africa* (Rome) 44, no. 1 (1989): 1–24; and Anneke Mulder, "The Participation of Women in the Agricultural Cooperatives in Maputo, Mozambique," M.Sc. thesis, University of London, 1988.

93. This information is from a discussion with Nelton Guta, director of the Women's Project of the Beira Green Zones Office, 15 August 1989.

94. Kathleen Sheldon, "*Creches, Titias*, and Mothers: Working Women and Child Care in Mozambique," in *African Encounters with Domesticity*, ed. Karen T. Hansen (New Brunswick, N.J.: Rutgers University Press, 1992), 290–309.

95. Joaquim Salvador, "Uma Camponesa Presidente que Sabe o Que Quer: Entrevista com Celina Cossa da União das Cooperativas," *Tempo* 802 (23 February 1986): 13–16; Judith Marshall, "Life on the Frontline: Mozambique Diary," *Southern Africa Report* 3, no. 4 (1988): 7–9; Arnfred, "Women in Mozambique," 15–16.

96. Cited in Marshall, "Resisting Adjustment in Mozambique," 7.

97. "Peasant Land Being Stolen by Private Farmers," *Mozambiquefile* 153 (1989): 16, and "Cooperatives Fighting a Double War," *Mozambiquefile* 157 (1989): 13.

98. "Women's Role Reevaluated as OMM Celebrates Fifteen Years," *AIM Information Bulletin* 141 (1988): 7–9.

99. "Relatório do Gabinete Central á IV Conferência Nacional da O.M.M." (Maputo: typescript, 1990). In this report about the preparations for OMM's fourth national conference, the primary difficulty mentioned was "a lack of financial and material means" to complete their work (13).

Chapter 3

"This, too, is a Way of Fighting"

Rural Women's Participation in Zimbabwe's Liberation War

Sita Ranchod-Nilsson

In 1980, after more than a decade of protracted guerrilla warfare, the former colony of Southern Rhodesia became the independent country of Zimbabwe. The liberation war in Zimbabwe has attracted scholarly attention for a number of reasons, including the highly publicized participation of African women in the armed struggle. Large numbers of African women joined liberation movements, underwent military training together with men, and fought side by side with them during the war. A number of women held positions of authority in the military command structure and the general staff. According to some estimates, by the middle of the war (about 1977) between one-quarter and one-third of the thirty thousand Zimbabwe African National Liberation Army (ZANLA) guerrillas were women and thousands of

---

This chapter is based on data collected for my unpublished Ph.D. dissertation, "Gender Politics and National Liberation: Women's Participation in the Liberation of Zimbabwe," Northwestern University, 1992. The research was supported, in part, by a grant from the National Science Foundation and a Woodrow Wilson Women's Studies Research grant. Because the liberation war was still a sensitive topic of discussion almost a decade after it ended, all of the rural women I interviewed were guaranteed anonymity as a condition of speaking with me. Thus, interviews will be designated by the date and number which correspond to the time and place of the interview. All of the interviews, unless otherwise noted, were conducted by the author with the invaluable assistance of Gladys Mukwedeya and Rose Mazena. In addition, I am indebted to Karen Tranberg Hansen for comments on earlier drafts of this work.

other women lived and worked in the camps in nonmilitary capacities.[1] But female combatants were not the only women to participate in the liberation war; rural African women who stayed in the countryside during the war also put themselves at tremendous risk to support local guerrilla forces. In addition to sustaining the forces with food and other supplies, rural women provided the guerrillas with valuable information and logistical assistance. The support of rural African women was, in fact, crucial to guerrilla efforts in the countryside.

Because women played such significant roles in the liberation war one might expect to find that the war was an important watershed or catalyst for changing women's positions in Zimbabwean society. However, more than ten years after independence, the changes in women's lives have not been as dramatic as one might expect. In part this reflects the broader politics of the liberation war; even though, arguably, the leadership and some of the dominant values of society changed, the liberation war in Zimbabwe was not a revolution which brought about fundamental changes in political institutions, social structures, and government activity.[2] Rather, the war is most often described in terms of peasant nationalism. Because the majority of the population lived in the countryside it is not surprising that the agenda of the peasants and the guerrillas during the rural mobilization was dominated by grievances associated with the land policies and agricultural practices of the white settler government. Inside the country these grievances were interwoven with a strong sense of cultural nationalism that was expressed through African religion.[3] In a broad sense, the program or ideology of rural mobilization did not emphasize gender issues. This lack of emphasis on gender may account, at least in part, for the lack of transformation in women's circumstances after independence.

Yet, at the local level, the war did unleash class, generation, lineage, and gender tensions within the peasantry, tensions that became entangled with, and ultimately helped to shape, the program of the war. Although contemporary debates on peasant participation in the war tend to focus on the extent to which the guerrillas actually had support from the peasants,[4] these conflicts within the peasantry also illuminate the complexities of the nationalist struggle at the local level, specifically the complexities of rural women's agendas.

This chapter examines rural women's participation in the liberation war at the local level. I suggest that rural women did not participate in the war simply as a result of being mobilized by groups of guerrillas who went into the rural areas to politicize the masses and gain their support. In fact, there is little evidence that this process included a consistent message about changing women's circumstances during the war, or after independence. Rather, rural African women had their own agendas that were rooted in the rapid reconfiguration of gender relations that had taken place during the relatively brief colonial period. The grievances they took to the guerrillas reveal their class circumstances as African peasant farmers in a white settler state. Interwoven with these grievances were complaints, framed in the context of household relations, against African male authorities, particularly their husbands. These household matters, too often dismissed as private family concerns, reveal how race, class, gender, and generation shaped rural women's lives and their agendas for change during the war. These domestic concerns were central to women's consciousness of their own circumstances as peasants and, during the liberation war, were central to the rural mobilization.

The material presented here is based primarily on my collection and analysis of the experiences of rural women in Wedza district. Because my information comes from one district, any generalizations about women's participation in other areas of the country, unless otherwise noted, are speculative and require further research. While there is perhaps no area of the country that can be described as having a typical experience during the liberation war, some exceptional features of Wedza district and its experience of the war should be noted. First, Wedza district is overwhelmingly dominated by the Shona people, who make up approximately 80 percent of the population of Zimbabwe. Throughout this chapter, allusions to African cultural practices refer only to the Shona.[5] Second, only guerrilla units from ZANLA were active in the district, so discussions of the ideology and program of the liberation forces refer only to the Zimbabwe African National Union (ZANU) or their military wing, ZANLA.[6] And finally, I found no evidence that female combatants ever operated in Wedza district, even though (after 1976) women did operate in many other parts of the country. It is likely that this situation influenced the gender ideology of the guerrilla groups operating in the area.

The first section of this chapter provides a brief overview of the ways in which colonial practices changed existing gender meanings and shaped conflicts between African men and women. From the turn of the century, through the early years of the armed struggle, the European settler's manipulation of gender relations among Africans exacerbated and reconfigured the nature of domestic conflicts. The next section describes the guerrillas' arrival in Wedza district and focuses specifically on the ways that women participated in the rural mobilization. The third section highlights the role of domestic conflict during the rural mobilization, paying particular attention to the issues raised by women and the guerrillas' responses. I conclude this chapter by suggesting some reasons why the gender transformation that began at the local level during the liberation war was never completed or fully carried out after independence.

GENDER CONFLICT AND COLONIAL RULE

During more than eighty years of European domination (1890–1972), Southern Rhodesia underwent rapid changes associated with capitalist transformation. Because the outcomes of household negotiations—struggles—between African men and women both shaped and were shaped by this transformation, gender relations permeated interstices of social and economic change in the colony. Incorporation into expanding markets, creation and codification of African customary laws, colonial education, and increased demands for labor placed men and women in very different positions in a highly stratified society. Within African households, decisions regarding production and the allocation of resources and labor were negotiated over time. The outcomes of these negotiations, or struggles, shaped a number of *a priori* conditions of capitalist transformation involving the composition of the wage labor force, the retention of land and productive/reproductive capacities, and the maintenance of the cultural autonomy of African social systems.[7]

One of the premises of the argument presented here is that the policies and practices of European settlers in Southern Rhodesia fundamentally reshaped gender relations among Africans. That is not meant to imply that prior to colonial conquest Africans lived in an idyllic state where men and women were equals; rather, the claim is that differences that existed in what men and women did and how their actions were valued in society were not only exacerbated under colonialism, but were in fact reconfigured in ways that were clearly disadvantageous for African women.[8]

While generalizations about the very broad epoch referred to as pre-colonial history may be misleading, it is necessary to establish some broad parameters for gender relations among Africans prior to European settlement before discussing how these relations were reconfigured under colonialism. Prior to permanent European settlement in the late nineteenth century, Shona society was characterized by a strict gender-based division of labor in which women were responsible for most of the agricultural work, with the exception of clearing fields, as well as for providing for household subsistence needs. Men were responsible for clearing the fields, controlling accumulated wealth, usually in the form of cattle, and directing family labor. Women in pre-colonial society could gain status through the institution of bridewealth (*lobola*). More than just an exchange of wealth for a wife, *lobola* created a broad network of reciprocal relations between kin groups to ensure the continuation of patrilineal lines and good treatment of daughters and wives. Women could also gain status with age through the accumulation of gifts, particularly cattle (associated with motherhood) or through accumulation from trading, either of the agricultural surplus from fields that were allocated to them by their husbands or fathers, or from hand-crafted items such as pottery and baskets. As in many other areas of Africa, gender relations among the Shona were characterized by male dominance. Women did not hold formal responsibility for community or household decision-making, although they could wield considerable influence as wives, healers, and spirit mediums.[9] In some circumstances a woman could hold the position of chief if, for example, there were no male lineage members to inherit the position. While women were, overall, subordinate to men, their skills in agriculture and handicrafts, and their responsibilities for child-rearing and household subsistence commanded respect and protection.

When European settlers, under the auspices of the British South African Company, entered the territory that would become Southern Rhodesia, they were primarily interested in finding mineral deposits comparable to earlier discoveries on the Witwatersrand in South Africa. After two decades of disappointments, the settlers turned their attention toward obtaining wealth through agriculture. By then African farmers, particularly among the Shona, had seized opportunities presented to them by the new markets that had grown up around European towns and mining settlements. According to Robin Palmer, "it proved possible, and obviously preferable, for the Shona to meet their tax commitments through the sale of foodstuffs and cattle rather than becoming migrant labourers."[10] Since the early part of this century, first the British South African Company administration and then, after the attainment of internal self-government in 1923, the European settler government in Southern Rhodesia, had promulgated policies of African land alienation in order to eliminate competition from Africans, control agricultural markets, and ensure adequate supplies of cheap African labor.

Africans resisted colonial policies and practices intended to undermine peasant agriculture. The resistance of rural households to men leaving their homes to work for wages on mines and farms was particularly fierce. One way in which they fought to maintain peasant agriculture was to increase agricultural production in order to meet the increasing tax obligations. As the primary agricultural producers, women were key not only to the emergence of an African peasantry, but also to this strategy of rural resistance. To help men escape the necessity of going to work for wages, women's agricultural burden was greatly increased during a period in which agricultural returns fell sharply.[11] In many cases, the work burden became too heavy to bear and women from poor peasant households fled to towns and missions to escape the harsh conditions of rural life. But African male authorities, who needed women's labor for agriculture, did not accept the departure of their wives and daughters. They demanded that the colonial authorities intervene to force the women to return.[12] In response colonial authorities saw an opportunity to placate African men, who had many other grievances, including low agricultural prices, by strengthening their control over African women. Thus, an unlikely alliance between these two groups sought to control African wives and daughters by increasing male authority over women in the recently codified African customary law which already reflected Western biases toward male authority.[13] At the same time, the few positions of authority that did exist for women in rural communities, midwifery, traditional healing, and artistry, were undercut by the introduction of Western medicine and manufactured goods.

After the passage of the Land Apportionment Act (LAA) in 1930, the main issue of contention, between colonial officials and Africans, shifted from the control of African women to the control of land.[14] The LAA divided the colonial territory between Africans and Europeans. Although Europeans made up only 3 percent of the population, the LAA gave them control over more than half of the land in Southern Rhodesia—almost all of it located in the most fertile areas. This legislation provided a blueprint for a system of unequal, racially-based, land distribution that remained relatively unchanged until independence. African access to land was greatly restricted and control of women's labor did not guarantee levels of production sufficient to avoid working for wages.

The new focus on land did not mean that turmoil in African households had dissipated. On the contrary, limited access to land meant that day-to-day survival became increasingly difficult and that household negotiations over resources and labor intensified. Indeed, in an examination of civil cases concerning domestic matters such as divorce, child custody, the return of *lobola* or household goods, and seduction, historian Teresa Barnes found that during the 1930s "increased economic difficulties . . . seem to have greatly intensified domestic struggle."[15] In these cases, gender struggles were directly linked to broader changes in the colonial political economy. Restricted educational and economic opportunities (particularly the dwindling access to land) greatly altered relations between men and women within African households. African women, in particular, became less autonomous as they lost access to land where they could grow their own crops and to the surplus they had enjoyed as the result of trading agricultural goods or crafts. At the same time, African women's responsibilities grew as many struggled to maintain their households' agricultural livelihoods in the countryside, while increasing numbers of men left these households to work for wages in towns. These circumstances contributed to household conflicts over the growing shortages of resources and authority in household decision-making.

Following World War II, Southern Rhodesia experienced a period of rapid economic growth in commercial agriculture and manufacturing. At the same time, record levels of European immigration, returning ex-servicemen, and population growth in the Native Reserves combined to create pressures for land reorganization. The Native Land Husbandry Act of 1951 (NLHA) created a system of individualized land tenure in the reserves that forced landless African men into a permanent urban labor pool. African opposition to the act was fierce since the NLHA completely disregarded customary claims to communal land. Colonial government policies (including forced population resettlement, the imposition of particular cultivation practices, and mandatory cattle destocking) led to increased support for African nationalists who politicized the issues surrounding African land rights.

Household negotiations between men and women were again strained as rural household incomes fell by approximately 13 percent.[16] African women struggled to maintain their households in the face of growing male labor migration and increasing oppression by government policies and African men. The high cost of implementing the NLHA and African opposition to individualized land tenure, forced methods of cultivation, and forced resettlement caused the government to abandon the act in the early 1960s. However, the unequal land distribution, codified in the LAA, remained unchanged throughout this more than thirty-year period.

Prior to the NLHA, Wedza district was relatively underpopulated by Native Affairs Department standards. Wedza district is located approximately 170 kilometers southeast of Salisbury, the capital city, now called Harare, in an area that enjoys relatively favorable agricultural conditions. By the early 1950s, people from the overpopulated Tribal Trust Land (TTL) of Soswe in neighboring Makoni were relocated to the Wedza TTL. By the end of the decade, implementation of the NLHA further exacerbated the already crowded conditions and rural survival became increasingly difficult.[17] The burden of these problems fell on the women, who had difficulty raising crops for sale on small pieces of land without fertilizers, new agricultural technologies, or entitlements to the cash incomes earned by their migrant husbands, fathers, or sons. An agricultural extension officer who had worked in Wedza district during the 1960s told me that "[w]hen I came here I found that many men were employed in towns. Only women were left on the land to supervise agricultural production." Of the farmers who attended his extension courses, "three quarters were women."[18]

Despite their growing responsibility for agricultural production, women in Wedza had little control over household decision-making, particularly those decisions that involved spending money. Even when women acquired cash from selling crops, garden vegetables, or craft items, they were seldom permitted to keep the money or make decisions about how the money would be spent. One woman explained,

> We were afraid because if the husbands found out that you had some money you would be in trouble because after the sale of the crops he took all the money and so where would you say you got the other money from? The husbands did all the buying and women could not go to a shop to buy anything they liked.[19]

Women were in a very difficult situation. Despite the fact that their migrant husbands did not send enough money home to support their families or to send their children to school, these women were still forbidden by their husbands to take employment that would remove them from the household. These conflicts came into sharp focus when the homecraft club movement began in the rural areas during the 1950s and 1960s.

The homecraft club movement was part of a broad range of community development policies adopted by the Southern Rhodesian government in 1962.[20] In response to deteriorating conditions in the rural areas and a growing threat from spreading African nationalist movements, the community development approach sought to expand the notion of rural development, increase local input in determining local development needs, and devolve limited power to local governments.[21] The government's policy of community development specifically targeted women as agents of progress within local communities. J. Holleman, one of the contributors to the community development approach in Southern Rhodesia, wrote that, "the pace of social advancement of many Africans will be set not by themselves but by their wives. It may not be as fast as many would like to see it, since Eve is essentially a traditionalist."[22] According to his view, rural women retarded progress through their attachment to backward practices of housekeeping and child-rearing. Thus, by educating Eve in Western notions of housewifery, one could ensure that progress and increased prosperity would come to African rural communities.

One way to involve women in community development was through the women's club movement. There were a number of women's voluntary organizations in Southern Rhodesia. Some were affiliated with churches. Others, such as the Federation of African Women's Clubs (FAWC), relied on district administrators' wives and wives of other state administrators to guide the clubs in their formation and programs. The FAWC, which grew to be the largest of the voluntary organizations teaching homecraft skills in Southern Rhodesia, began shortly after World War II. European women, together with a few African women, cooperated to teach "simple rules of health and some of the domestic skills to the very backward African women, to try to combat the dreadful child mortality rate and prevent such diseases as malaria, dysentery, trachoma, and kwashiorkor."[23] This, too, reflected the assumption that African women were both the cause of and the potential solution to problems actually caused by the racially biased political economy.

The women's clubs were popular among rural women because they provided an opportunity for adult education. The clubs taught skills intended to improve individual homes, but women were quick to utilize these new skills to gain resources that they desperately needed, especially cash. Women's clubs also offered a forum in which women could develop a sense of group consciousness among themselves. In a society where opportunities for women to meet, either socially or in the context of agricultural work, had decreased over time, the clubs provided women an opportunity to get together, discuss common problems, and develop strategies of accommodation (and occasionally resistance) to the increasing demands placed upon them.[24]

In Wedza district, women responded enthusiastically to these programs despite the resistance, and in some cases the outright hostility, of their husbands. Men were suspicious of the clubs and reluctant to hand over money to buy materials necessary for the sewing and needlecraft work. But financial hardship or the desire to monopolize household resources were not the only reasons African men objected to their wives attending the clubs. In some accounts of male resistance to women attending the clubs, the ideology of male control over women's mobility and sexuality is revealed. One woman said,

> These husbands refused us from going to the clubs because they were ignorant. They did not know that if a wife went to the club she got knowledge. They wanted wives to stay home and do housework only. They said that if you wanted to go somewhere, it was laziness, or maybe you wanted to chat unproductively with other women or maybe you were going for prostitution. That, then, caused misunderstandings in the home. If you insisted that he should allow you sometimes, he wanted to beat you.[25]

Another woman described the concerns of men in similar terms,

> Men refused their wives from attending clubs because they said that they did not see any reason why they should go to clubs. Sometimes some men refused the wives from going out for courses saying that they wanted to go for prostitution.[26]

Eventually most women were able to overcome male resistance to their participation in the clubs. They did this by convincing their husbands, either individually or collectively, that the clubs would actually benefit men because the quality of their homes would improve as a result of the skills taught at the clubs. Nevertheless, the conflicts between men and women during the early years of the club movement in Wedza district illuminate areas of conflict within rural African households. For example, at the clubs women also developed strategies to keep some cash from their husbands. One woman told me,

> women complained that their husbands didn't give them money. In the clubs they were taught how to sew clothes and sell them for pocket money. They would show the husband a quarter of the money and hide the rest.[27]

Although the government's community development policy did not succeed in improving overall conditions in rural areas, or in appeasing African demands for greater participation in economic and political affairs, it was a turning point for women in Wedza district. The clubs promoted group consciousness and cooperation among women, giving them the courage to speak out in their homes, and helping them to develop organizational and leadership skills which later became invaluable to the rural mobilization during the war. The domestic conflicts brought on by the club movement in Wedza district suggest that the struggle to shift the balance of domestic power was initiated by women and began long before the liberation forces and their mobilization programs became entrenched in the district in 1976.

RURAL MOBILIZATION IN WEDZA DISTRICT

Wedza district did not become fully embroiled in the war until 1976. ZANLA was the only force operating in the area and the fighters remained a constant presence in the district from 1976 until 1980. Prior to the guerrillas' arrival in the district most local women had heard about the war that was being waged in the northeastern part of the country. Some African women had been involved in the nationalist organizations in the district during the open nationalist period (1950–1961), or had children or brothers who had left school for the camps in Mozambique. But more often, they had heard of the guerrillas as *gandangas*, or terrorists, strange people with tails.[28] Women in the homecraft clubs learned about the war and what the guerrillas were saying about African oppression under colonialism from their children when the children came home from boarding schools during holidays.[29]

Throughout Wedza district, women's accounts of their first meetings with the guerrillas were remarkably similar. Initially they were called by the guerrillas to a mobilization meeting, a *pungwe*,[30] in their village. At the *pungwe* the guerrillas explained that they had come to liberate African people from white settlers and colonial rule. They recounted grievances against the white government which involved lost lands, lack of education, inadequate employment opportunities, and racial discrimination. The guerrillas often referred to themselves as the children of the parents at the *pungwe*, or the children of Zimbabwe. They also asked, or even demanded, that the villagers support them by providing food, money, supplies, and information. The following account from a woman who first attended a *pungwe* shortly after the guerrillas arrived in the district is typical:

> They explained a lot of things and then we started to realize how oppressed we were and that our lives could be better than they were. . . . Because we agreed with them in what they were fighting for they then told us that they needed our help. We were to fight

> together. We were to fight by providing them food, clothes, shoes because the guerrillas did a lot of walking and running.[31]

The behavior of the guerrillas and the reactions of the people were not entirely uniform. They varied significantly based on the geographic location of the village and the period during which the villagers first came into contact with the guerrillas. The terrain of Wedza is comprised of gentle, rolling hills. In the center of the district is a very large hill, known as Wedza mountain, with dense foliage, several caves, and an abandoned iron mine. For the duration of the war in Wedza, there were several bases located around Wedza mountain. People from the nearby villages had early contact with the guerrillas, whom they mostly described in favorable terms. By contrast, villages located near the Wedza township where the Rhodesian soldiers had their camp did not have regular contact with the guerrillas until the very end of the war. In these villages people mainly discussed their fear of the guerrillas and the difficulty of being caught in between the soldiers and the guerrillas. In three of the villages I visited, initial contact with the guerrillas had been accompanied by the death of some village people who were branded as "sellouts"—those alleged to have given information about the guerrillas to the security forces.[32] People in these villages also expressed fear when discussing the war.

Regardless of the nature of the relations between the guerrillas and the villagers, each village was responsible for organizing a support committee. Usually comprised of a chairperson, secretary, treasurer, security officer, organizer, logistics representative, and political commissar, these committees coordinated the support activities of village members to make sure that the guerrillas at local bases were fed and supplied. The committees kept careful records of household contributions. They were also responsible for identifying potential sellouts and making sure that villagers attended *pungwes*. Attendance at *pungwes*, held from one to three times per week, and contributions of food, clothing, money, and other supplies, were by no means voluntary. Failure to do either of these things raised the risk of being branded a sellout.

Both women and men participated on the village committees. For most women, this was their first experience of participating in an organization with political authority at the village level.[33] In several villages, the women in charge of village committees during the war had also been leaders in their local women's clubs. In one Wedza mountain village, women claimed that the communication skills they had developed in the women's clubs helped to make their donation committee very successful:

> Here in our area which was used as a base . . . the work seems to have been done by women. . . . In the next village the committee leaders were men. There was a difference in the way they operated and the way we did. Men failed to communicate properly so the people did not give them food to feed the comrades. If they did not get the food the comrades did not have anything to eat for the day. If that happened everybody in the village was called and beaten by the comrades. It never happened here in our base.[34]

In general, women saw their participation on the committees as a significant way of supporting the liberation war despite the hardships that accompanied it. The following two women, from different villages, give their reasons for supporting the guerrillas, or, as they were more commonly known, the boys or the comrades:

> We helped the boys because of what they had told us. So women tried their best even if they did not have money they had to try hard to get the money in order to help the comrades who were fighting to free us. Those with working husbands also bought whatever was wanted because sometimes they brought lists of what they wanted. . . . We did that whole-heartedly because we felt that these boys were fighting for a good cause to free us.[35]

> During the war we talked about ways of doing things for the comrades. For instance if one was sent to buy bread or cigarettes for the comrades one had to be vigilant in walking. There were problem during the war. Sometimes we gave chicken to the *mujibas* (teenagers who travelled with the guerrillas and acted as their liaisons with the rural population) but we were afraid . . . in case the soldiers came. We were not afraid of comrades, they were like our friends.[36]

All the women I spoke with who had lived in the district during that time claimed to have participated in the war. Every one of the women said she had given food, clothing, blankets, or cash to village donation committees. One of the main tasks of women in Wedza was to provide and cook food for the guerrillas, although when *chimbwidos* (female *mujibas*) were available, they seem to have been responsible for cooking.[37] This was no easy task in the district because of the continual presence of Rhodesian soldiers camping at the Wedza township. To avoid the attention of the soldiers, women devised ingenious ways of smuggling supplies to the guerrilla bases, cleverly disguising their support of the guerrillas as the women went about their daily tasks. Two women, from different villages, describe how they carried guns to the comrades:

> Women could carry these parcels as if we were coming from a long journey. Sometimes on our way back we looked for firewood and if we met soldiers they just thought we had gone to fetch firewood.[38]

> There is one incident when the soldiers passed by this road and the comrades were in this house. The comrades ran away and left their guns in the house. Mrs. ——— wrapped the guns in blankets and then carried the blankets in the dish pretending as if she was going to wash. Then she took the guns to the comrades.[39]

Women hid food and supplies under their clothing or disguised these items as babies, which women in Zimbabwe carry bundled on their backs. Secured with a piece of cloth or a towel, food and other supplies could easily be disguised and carried. Even in the presence of Rhodesian security forces, women would transport supplies in this way:

> As for going to the shops, we would select three women. One would be carrying a [real] baby and the other two would have the baby carrier and nappies to carry bread and cigarettes. Then on the way back, the one with the baby would walk first and the other two with supplies would follow behind.[40]

Another woman made use of the baby disguise in this way:

> Sometimes even when the soldiers were patrolling all over, sometimes the mother would get into the house, prepare the *sadza* [thick cornmeal porridge] for the comrades, maybe the comrades would be hiding somewhere. She would then carry the *sadza* as a baby to go and feed the comrades and that is a way of fighting.[41]

Women also lent their clothing to the guerrillas so that, disguised, the guerrillas could move around even during the day. There were also several accounts of guerrillas donning women's clothing to work in the fields with women.[42]

Initially women were not suspected of helping the guerrillas. However, soon after their arrival in Wedza, the Rhodesian soldiers became aware of the ways in which women were supporting the guerrillas. Thereafter women were routinely subjected to very harsh treatment by the Security Forces that included beatings, rape, and electric shock.[43]

With the exception of women from those villages contacted toward the very end of the war, and the three villages where guerrillas had initially killed people accused of selling out, women spoke in relatively favorable terms about the guerrillas. Local men also spoke of the close relationship between women and the comrades with a definite air of exclusion. According to a young woman who was a *chimbwido* in Wedza, "men were complaining that women wanted their boyfriends with the guns."[44] None of the women I spoke with said that they knew of sexual relations between guerrillas and rural adult women.

Rural women supported the guerrillas' agenda for a number of reasons. Because African women were primarily responsible for agricultural and household subsistence in the countryside, they could identify with guerrilla claims that they were fighting for lost lands and an end to economic hardship. When asked about their grievances prior to the war, women repeatedly cited problems having to do with agriculture, education, employment, and racial and gender discrimination.[45] They spoke of the lack of educational opportunities for themselves and for their children, as well as the inferior education generally provided to blacks. The women described their grievances over the lack of employment opportunities, low wages for Africans, and white privileges.

The complaints most often relayed by the women involved the ways in which they saw themselves as oppressed by agricultural policies. As the primary agricultural producers within their households, women had to deal directly with the effects of land shortages, forced cultivation, lack of extension services, and discriminatory pricing policies. They complained about shortages of land and the fact that they could not plow wherever they wanted, especially in the *vleis* or watershed areas where they wanted to plant rice. They also complained about low grain prices, particularly the discriminatory practice of routinely assigning African maize low grades, so that it would bring less in the market than European-grown maize. Many women also mentioned the lack of transportation to take their crops to markets and their lack of knowledge about and the availability of fertilizers. The following exchange illustrates how women related these agricultural issues to their own oppression:

Q: Were women oppressed before the war?
A: Yes, very much. The government was oppressing women

mostly. Also, our husbands were oppressing us.

Q: How?

A: The government was oppressing us through low prices for selling maize and no transport. Also we were not allowed to sell to the GMBs [Grain Marketing Board], that was only for whites. If I could take ground nuts, I was just given $1.50 a bucket. This was coming from the government. This was oppression of women because they did the agricultural work.[46]

In conveying their grievances rural women reveal how class and gender are interwoven. In addition to complaints about state policies, African women identified African men as contributing to women's oppression. In discussions about the lack of educational facilities women complained that men did not allow their daughters or wives to attend school because of the men's fear that their daughters or wives would become prostitutes.[47] Some men refused to give their wives permission to work for wages for the same reason. Women also complained that the cash earnings from agriculture, even from crops such as groundnuts that are traditionally women's crops, were confiscated by their husbands. One woman described the role of husbands in their wives' oppression as follows:

> Even our husbands were oppressors. I mean these men in trousers, they oppressed us. They did not allow women to get employed even if a woman was educated. The second thing is that if a woman got any money the husbands demanded half of it. They did not want women to use their money as they saw fit.[48]

Thus, rural African women's own accounts of their grievances prior to the liberation war suggest that gender concerns played an integral part in shaping their agendas during the war.

DOMESTIC STRUGGLES AND RURAL MOBILIZATION IN WEDZA

Earlier, I discussed the nature of gender struggle under colonial rule. By the time the war began, there were few formal mechanisms to adjudicate domestic disputes. Regardless of whether women appealed to the courts of headmen and chiefs, or the Native commissioner's courts, disputes were seldom resolved in women's favor. Divorce laws greatly favored men, since the laws required a partial or complete return of *lobola* and gave custody of the children to the husband. In addition, women received no marital property in divorce settlements.

There was little a native commissioner could do to stop a man from abusing his wife, or to make sure that a man provided adequate support for his wife (or wives) and children. In cases where it was impossible to return *lobola,* or where headmen and chiefs were not trusted by their subject populations, women had few avenues of recourse. Furthermore, during the war, the loyalties of many headmen and all native commissioners were suspect, because of their connections with the Rhodesian government. Hence, rural dwellers minimized their contact with them in order to avoid falling under suspicion of being sellouts.

As the guerrillas established their authority in rural areas, they were confronted with local problems they had not anticipated. Women went to them with domestic problems involving, among other things, lack of financial support from their husbands, domestic abuse, jealousy over husbands' extramarital affairs, and unwanted divorces. In their advice and intervention, the guerrillas were very sympathetic to women. One male ex-combatant, who operated in districts located in the northeastern part of the country, described the situation this way:

> A woman would come to me and say, comrade, I think that my husband is not giving me all of the money, [or] he is doing this to me. And, I would call in on the husband and just try and straighten him out. We eventually became their advisors in any domestic problems.[49]

The guerrillas also discovered domestic problems while gathering donations from villagers. For example, in two different villages women knew of a case where a man had married two wives and had twelve children between them. He left these wives and married a third woman. When the guerrillas came and saw the first two wives living in poverty, they told the man to pack his things and go back to his wives straight away.[50]

The guerrillas' attempts to resolve domestic disputes varied over time and from village to village. In some cases, the guerrillas spoke privately with the husband; in other cases they spoke with the husband and wife together. Sometimes the disputes were discussed publicly at *pungwes*. In some cases the guerrillas reasoned with men, threatened them, and even beat them. Women occasionally expressed fears that the guerrillas would kill their husbands although I never located any evidence of a man who had been killed in this context.

None of the women I interviewed recounted her own experience of taking a domestic dispute to the guerrillas, but women did discuss incidents of this nature that occurred in their villages or at the nearby bases. One former *chimbwido*, who lived in a base camp in Wedza, described incidents that she had witnessed:

> They [the comrades] took the man, and if he didn't understand, they didn't use their hands, they said the woman should revenge him with a whip. Then they said [to the couple] shake your hands and go home in peace. These things only happened for a short time. When the husbands saw that they would be beaten, they stopped.[51]

The following are typical examples from other accounts:

> There was a certain case of a man from Chingwedera area, who for a long time had a dispute with his wife. The man had a shop at Dendenyore and he no longer wanted his wife so she went to the elders to report this matter. They knew that this matter could be settled by the comrades, so they went to find them. The man was told to go back and live in a better way of life than he did before. He was asked whether he wanted a divorce—if he had said yes, they would have killed him. He said he didn't want a divorce and went to his wife. This dispute was settled privately but she knew because she used to organize the cooking at the base.[52]

> A woman would go to the comrades and complain that she was not getting enough support. The husband would be called by the comrades and be asked but because he would be afraid of being beaten up or killed he tried to defend himself politely and then was told to give money to the wife. He gave the wife some money there and then. Then the comrades told the man that they would send people to watch him to see whether he was giving her enough. From that day the man changed his attitude and started to look after his wife.[53]

Evidence from other sources suggests that the guerrillas' involvement in domestic disputes was not isolated to Wedza district. In Mutoko district, in the northeastern part of the country, Kriger found that guerrillas told men to stop "beating their wives, cease drinking, terminate extra-marital affairs, marry women whom they had impregnated, [and] desist from divorcing."[54] Guerrillas would come through a village at night and hear a woman crying because she was being beaten and would then beat the husband. According to Kriger's informants, women began reporting their husbands to the comrades and the husbands would be publicly beaten. The novella *Woman in*

Struggle, by Irene Ropa Rinopfuka Mahamba, recounts the story of Nyevenutsai, a young woman being forced by her family to follow the custom of *chimutsa mapfihwa*, replacing a dead female relative in marriage. Nyevenutsai runs away to a favorite uncle, an educated headmaster, who calls on the guerrillas to adjudicate the conflict. Nyevenutsai is freed from her obligation to marry her dead aunt's husband and eventually travels to Mozambique to join the liberation struggle (Mahamba 1984). Mahamba's fiction draws on popular consciousness that guerrillas supported women in domestic disputes. These examples suggest that guerrilla involvement in settling domestic disputes was widespread. Even women who did not take disputes to the guerrillas probably perceived that the guerrillas supported women.

Wives who did not report their husbands to the guerrillas out of fear that the husbands would be beaten or killed, still benefitted from the new public knowledge that the guerrillas supported the claims of women. Such support lent legitimacy to women's claims about domestic issues. Two women who provided support for the guerrillas at the same base on Wedza mountain explained the new position of women in this way:

> The women were very happy because when the comrades came and told the men not to beat their wives it was a relief to them. If ever a husband beat a wife he was in trouble. Whatever we asked, the men gave us.[55]

> Things have changed because the comrades politicized a lot about women's position. Some men said that if a wife was working it was the fault of the man who had allowed her to work and that he had allowed her to be a prostitute. Women were not allowed to go to school because she would be a prostitute. This was not true but the men were suspicious . . . but now because they see what we are doing and that they were wrong, they have changed. They now respect us . . . the comrades used to say that we are all the same with equal brains. Even at jobs, a woman can do the same job like men and that they should earn the same amount of money. Even during the war we all fought side by side, both men and women, boys and girls.[56]

Guerrilla support for the claims of women contributed to the legitimacy of the guerrillas' movement in Wedza district where their agenda also included support for grievances over land, education, employment, and racial discrimination. In a village near Wedza mountain, where women were particularly active in supporting the guerrillas, one woman explained, "we did not support the comrades because they made life between us and our husbands easier . . . that was only part of the reasons for supporting them."[57]

If the guerrillas gained legitimacy by supporting the claims of women in domestic disputes, one also has to consider why they chose this particular strategy, especially since it placed them at odds with rural African men. There are several strategic reasons why the guerrillas chose to support the claims of women. First, particularly during the early stages of the war, women were immune to suspicion and could carry information and supplies for the guerrillas without harassment. Yet, to do this the women had to be mobile, and male objections about women traveling had to be squelched. The Rhodesia forces, however, soon became aware that women were aiding the guerrilla forces. As the war intensified, rural women and *chimbwidos* put themselves at even greater risk to provide food, domestic services, and intelligence to guerrillas. One woman described a task she carried out:

> I went as far as Kwenda Mission to collect some money from teachers for the comrades. That was unheard of long back, that a woman could go that far. I hid the money in my underpants all the way from Kwenda. It was a lot of money. This was what we are talking about, it liberated women mostly.[58]

Second, women made up the majority of the permanent population in the rural areas. Among the women I interviewed, more than half had husbands who were working outside the district prior to the war.[59] In order to meet the constant guerrilla demands for money and goods (including blue jeans, shoes, and watches) and thus ensure the safety of their families, many of these men continued to work during the war. Because the guerrillas were dependent on rural women for food, information, and occasionally places to hide, they had to address the problems that were brought to them by those women. Finally, to the extent that the guerrilla program represented a kind of cultural nationalism, rural women were perhaps fighting for the return of a status perceived to have been theirs prior to colonialism.[60]

African women in Wedza district believe that their participation was integral to the success of the liberation war. In many instances women saw their provision of domestic care as their way of fighting. The African women in Wedza clearly had their own agenda for change which they raised with the groups of guerrillas who began to enter the district in 1976. Their active participation in shaping the nationalist agenda at the local level raised gender issues within households and, to a lesser extent, within communities and the nation, in ways that had not been anticipated by the liberation movements.

CONCLUSION

ZANU/ZANLA not only recognized women's participation in the struggle but, during the last several years of the war, made an explicit commitment to women's liberation. At the first ZANU Women's Seminar in May 1979, Robert Mugabe, then President of ZANU and now President of Zimbabwe, made the connection between national liberation and women's emancipation clear when he said "the national struggle . . . especially at its highest level, when it became armed national struggle, became as much a process towards the liberation of the nation as towards the emancipation of women."[61]

Despite recognition of women's participation in the liberation struggle and claims to support their emancipation, the new government's policies affecting women can, at best, be described as ambiguous. After independence women's concerns were to be addressed by the newly created Ministry of Cooperatives and Women's Affairs under the direction of the highest ranking woman in the liberation movement, Comrade Teurai Ropa Nhongo. Other women, such as Fay Chung and Opah Chamu Muchinguri, held cabinet positions. Soon after independence, the government passed several pieces of legislation intended to improve the status of women, including the 1982 Legal Age of Majority Act[62] and the 1985 Matrimonial Causes Act.[63] Despite an angry backlash that has vitiated its effectiveness, the legislation remains on the books. In addition, changes in health care and education began to address women's concerns at the local level.

During the same period, the government also took action leaving few doubts about women's place as second-class citizens. For example, on several occasions the government initiated police sweeps to rid urban centers of so-called prostitutes and vagrants. In October 1983, numerous women suspected of being prostitutes were arrested in Operation Cleanup. According to the Women's Action Group, "flats occupied by single women were raided and women 'roaming' the streets were arrested and taken away. There appeared to be no discrimination. Old women, young mothers with babies on their backs, girls of eleven and twelve years old were included in this sweep,"[64] whose effects were often brutalizing. Women who were arrested reported being raped, insulted, and humiliated while in custody. In addition, many who were arrested lost their jobs, were evicted from their homes, and were stigmatized by their communities and coworkers. Even women who were not detained or harassed in the round-up got the message that, for them, independence had prescribed limits. Despite vehement protests against Operation Cleanup, the government launched similar campaigns in 1985, 1987, and 1988. Government policies that discriminate against women indirectly include state policies on land resettlement which assign land primarily to male household heads.[65]

How is it possible to reconcile these two images of women in Zimbabwe? On the one hand, women are celebrated for their participation in the liberation struggle, which appeared to embrace women's liberation as one of its goals. On the other hand, legislation to improve the status of women is met with hostility, while the government rounds up innocent women for questionable reasons. Is this case yet another example of a revolutionary movement embracing women's issues during the struggle only to return to the status quo of women's oppression after independence?

While that may, in part, be true, I suggest it is also true that the experiences and goals of different groups of African women who participated in the war were very different and even contradictory. On the one hand, women combatants, who were most often young and childless when they joined the liberation movements, expected that their war-time experiences of relative equality with men would be continued under the new government. On the other hand, rural women, who were often older and had children, wanted continued support for their status and household responsibilities. Because ZANLA tried to fit in with local norms during the war, competing and contradictory expectations with regard to gender ideology were raised during that period. These clashing expectations proved difficult to reconcile after independence was achieved.

NOTES

1. These figures are taken from Gay Seidman, "Women in Zimbabwe: Postindependence Struggles," *Feminist Studies* 10, no. 3 (1984): 419–40; and Olivia Muchena, "Zimbabwe: It Can Only be Handled by Women," in *Sisterhood is Global*, ed. Robin Morgan (New York: Anchor, 1984), 725–55, respectively. The figures may be overstated by the inclusion of women who were living in the camps as refugees or in capacities other than as military personnel (personal communication, Norma Kriger, 1989).

2. There is broad consensus that the liberation war in Zimbabwe was not a revolution, although some argue that within the movement there were, at

various points, possibilities of creating a movement which would bring about social revolution. For example, Astrow argues that the rank-and-file military forces and their supporters inside the country were thwarted by the petty bourgeois interests of the nationalist leadership. Andre Astrow, *Zimbabwe: A Revolution That Lost Its Way?* (London: Zed, 1983).

3. See for example, David Lan, *Guns and Rain* (Berkeley: University of California Press, 1985). Based on his extensive fieldwork in Dande, Lan argues that spirit mediums, who form a vital link between dead ancestors and local political authorities, provided the guerrillas with legitimacy during the liberation war. See also Terence Ranger, *Peasant Consciousness and Guerrilla War in Zimbabwe* (Berkeley: University of California Press, 1985). Ranger uses the involvement of spirit mediums to develop his argument about the role of cultural nationalism in Zimbabwe's liberation war.

4. See for example, Astrow, *Zimbabwe*; Lan, *Guns and Rain*; Ranger, *Peasant Consciousness and Guerrilla War*; Norma Kriger, *Peasant Perspectives on Zimbabwe's War of Liberation* (Cambridge: Cambridge University Press, 1991); and Norma Kriger, "The Zimbabwean War of Liberation: Struggles Within the Struggle," *Journal of Southern African Studies* 14, no. 2 (1988): 304–22.

5. The Ndebele people, who live mainly in the southwestern and western regions of the country, make up approximately 20 percent of the population.

6. A high degree of international involvement, class division among Africans and, to a certain extent, the politicization of ethnic differences led to deep factions and changing alliances among several liberation movements. However, toward the end of the war there were two main movements, the Zimbabwe African National Union (ZANU) and the Zimbabwe African People's Union (ZAPU), and their military wings, the Zimbabwe African National Liberation Army (ZANLA) and the Zimbabwe African People's Army (ZIPRA), respectively. The fact that only ZANU/ZANLA was operative in Wedza district in no way implies that ZANU/ZANLA were the only ones who fought the war. That is clearly not the case. Recent research focuses on the war in Matabeleland. See, for example, Richard Werbner, *Tears of the Dead: The Social Biography of an African Family* (Edinburgh: Edinburgh University Press, 1991).

7. A detailed exposition of this argument in the South African case is provided by Belinda Bozzoli, "Marxism, Feminism and South African Studies," *Journal of Southern African Studies* 9, no. 2 (1983): 139–71.

8. Janet Bujra, "Urging Women to Redouble Their Efforts: Class, Gender and Capitalist Transformation in Africa," in *Women and Class in Africa*, ed. Claire Robertson and Iris Berger, (New York: Africana Publishing Co., 1986), 117–40; Martin Chanock, "Making Customary Law: Men, Women and Courts in Northern Rhodesia," in *African Women and the Law: Historical Perspectives*, ed. Margaret Jean Hay and Marcia Wright (Boston: Boston University Papers on Africa VII, 1982), 53–67; Margot Lovett, "Gender Relations, Class Formation and the Colonial State in Africa," in *Women and the State in Africa*, ed. Jane Parpart and Kathleen Staudt (Boulder, Colo: Lynne Rienner, 1989), 23–46; Jean O'Barr, "Pare Women: A Case of Political Involvement," *Rural Africana* 29 (1976): 121–34.

9. In Shona society, spirit mediums form a link between communities and dead ancestors who are supposed to watch over them. The spirit medium can thus exercise considerable political power. For detailed analyses of the role of spirit mediums in Zimbabwe, see Lan, *Guns and Rain*; and Michael Bourdillion, *The Shona People* (Gweru: Mambo Press, 1987), especially chapters 9 and 10.

10. Robin Palmer, "The Agricultural History of Rhodesia," in *The Roots of Rural Poverty in Central and Southern Africa*, ed. Robin Palmer and Neil Parsons (Berkeley: University of California Press, 1977), 228. For other work on the struggle of Africans to retain the peasant option in Southern Rhodesia see Ian Phimister, "Peasant Production and Underdevelopment in Southern Rhodesia 1890–1914," in *The Roots of Rural Poverty in Central and Southern Africa*, 225–67; Ian Phimister, *An Economic and Social History of Zimbabwe 1890–1948* (London: Longman, 1988); Ranger, *Peasant Consciousness and Guerrilla War in Zimbabwe*; Elizabeth Schmidt, "Ideology, Economics, and the Role of Shona Women in Southern Rhodesia, 1899–1939," Ph.D. diss., University of Wisconsin, Madison, 1987.

11. Phimister, *An Economic and Social History of Zimbabwe 1890–1948*, 205.

12. This argument is made by Schmidt in "Ideology, Economics, and the Role of Shona Women in Southern Rhodesia, 1899–1939."

13. The colonial codification of African customs, known as African customary law, provided the basis for adjudicating civil cases among Africans throughout colonial Africa. But what passed as custom was subject to interpretation by those who had vested interests, particularly in the area of family law which included marriage, divorce, inheritance, and child custody and property rights in marriage. Elizabeth Schmidt, "Men, Women and the Law in Colonial Zimbabwe 1890–1939," *Journal of Southern African Studies* 16, no. 4 (1990): 626. According to Chanock, African customary law was heavily biased toward the male elite and coincided with the "moral predilections and administrative purposes" of colonial officials. Previously flexible practices were turned into inflexible rules that bolstered male domination. Chanock, "Making Customary Law: Men, Women and Courts in Northern Rhodesia."

14. For an expanded version of this argument as it applies to Makoni district, see Terence Ranger, "Women in the Politics of Makoni District, Zimbabwe, 1890–1980," unpublished paper, 1982.

15. Teresa Barnes, "African Female Labour and the Urban Economy of Colonial Zimbabwe with Special Reference to Harare, 1920–1939," M.A. thesis, University of Zimbabwe, 1987, 39.

16. See Michael Bratton, *Beyond Community Development* (London: Catholic Institute for International Relations, 1978), 15.

17. The actual implementation of the NLHA in Wedza occurred between 1959–1962. Documents from the Wedza District Commissioner's office for this period were destroyed (National Archives of Zimbabwe, Oral/256 1986, interview with Francis and Miriam Staunton).

18. Interview with Agritex Extension Officer Matatu, 20 February 1989.

19. Interview #47, 31 January 1989.

20. The shift in development policy paralleled a general shift in

development policy undertaken by colonial powers after World War II.

21. For an expanded discussion of community development in Southern Rhodesia see Bratton, *Beyond Community Development*; and N. D. Mutizwa-Mangiza, "Community Development in Pre-independence Zimbabwe," supplement to *Zambezia*, 1985.

22. National Archives of Zimbabwe 163/44/32, 1958.

23. National Archives of Zimbabwe 3078/659, 1970.

24. See James Scott, *Weapons of the Weak: Everyday Forms of Peasant Resistance* (New Haven, Conn.: Yale University Press, 1985).

25. Interview #47, 31 January 1989.

26. Interview #49, 11 February 1989.

27. Interview #41, 1 February 1989.

28. The term *magandanga* literally means "wild people who live in the bush." According to Ranger, the use of the term by the Security Forces effectively conveyed the idea that "the bush [was] a source of danger and illegitimate violence and [it] offered one way of situating unknown young men with guns who operated out of caves in hills." Terence Ranger, "Bandits and Guerrillas: The Case of Zimbabwe," in *Banditry, Rebellion and Social Protest in Africa*, ed. Donald Crummey (Portsmouth: Heinemann, 1986), 379.

29. Interview #42, 15 February 1989.

30. A *pungwe* was a mobilization session that was held by guerrilla unit. During the war, these sessions were most often held at night, often lasting all night. Attendance by entire villages was compulsory, with occasional exceptions made only for the very sick or the very elderly.

31. Interview #47, 31 January 1989.

32. Those who were accused of being sellouts by villagers, or more often by the young teenagers, known as *mujibas*, who travelled with the guerrillas, were subject to very harsh treatment and even death at the hands of the guerrillas. For accounts of what happened to those accused of being sellouts see David Caute, *Under the Skin: The Death of White Rhodesia* (Evanston, Ill.: Northwestern University Press, 1983); Shimmer Chinodya, *Harvest of Thorns* (Portsmouth: Heinemann, 1989); Kriger, *Peasant Perspectives on Zimbabwe's War of Liberation*; Bruce Moore-King, *White Man, Black War* (Harare: Baobab, 1988).

33. There are several accounts of female chiefs in the early part of the century, all of whom were replaced by men under the colonial state. Otherwise women were completely excluded from the *dare*, the village political council, and largely excluded from elected local councils in the 1950s.

34. Interview #49, 11 February 1989.

35. Interview #47, 31 January 1989.

36. Interview #48, 14 February 1989.

37. *Mujibas* also refers to young men and young women who travelled with guerrilla units and acted as their liaisons in rural communities. However, since there were some gender-based divisions in the tasks carried out by the youth, it is also common to see references to *mujibas* referring to young men, and *chimbwidos*, referring to young women.

38. Interview #48, 14 February 1989.

39. Interview #49, 11 February 1989.
40. Interview #48, 14 February 1989.
41. *Sadza* is the staple food in Zimbabwe. Interview #49, 11 February 1989.
42. The type of support outlined above has been documented in other guerrilla struggles. For Algeria, see Franz Fanon, *The Wretched of the Earth* (New York: Grove Press, 1963); and David Gordon, *Women of Algeria* (Cambridge: Cambridge University Press, 1972). For Guinea-Bissau, see Stephanie Urdang, *Fighting Two Colonialisms* (New York: Monthly Review Press, 1979); and "Women in National Liberation Movements," in *African Women South of the Sahara*, ed. Margaret Jean Hay and Sharon Stichter (New York: Longman, 1984), 156–69. For Kenya, see Donald L. Barnett and Karari Njama, *Mau Mau from Within* (New York: Monthly Review Press, 1966); and Tabitha Kanongo, *Squatters and the Roots of Mau Mau 1905–1963* (Nairobi: Heinemann, 1987). And for Vietnam, see Arlene Eisen, *Women and Revolution in Vietnam* (London: Zed, 1984).
43. See, for example, Julie Fredrikse, *None But Ourselves: Masses vs. Media in the Making of Zimbabwe* (New York: Penguin, 1982), especially chapters 3 and 6; and Miriam Staunton, ed., *Mothers of the Revolution* (Harare: Baobab, 1991), especially chapters 9 and 10 that refer to Wedza district.
44. Interview #44, 17 February 1989.
45. With the exception of gender discrimination, these issues have been identified as part of the peasant agenda by Ranger in *Peasant Consciousness and Guerrilla War*; by Lan in *Guns and Rain*; by Astrow in *Zimbabwe*; and by Ibbo Mandaza in his introduction to *Zimbabwe: The Political Economy of Transition 1980–1986* (Harare: Codesria, 1986).
46. Interview #15, 11 February 1989.
47. The term prostitute as it is used in Zimbabwe seems to have ambiguous and shifting meanings which range from a woman who sells sexual services for money to a woman who is living alone and is financially independent. For a discussion of this issue see Women's Action Group, "Women of Zimbabwe Speak Out: Report and Recommendations of the Workshop Organised by Women's Action Group" (Harare: Women's Action Group, 1984).
48. Interview #48, 14 February 1989.
49. Interview #52 in Harare, 20 November 1988.
50. Interviews #11, 7 December 1988; and #33, 1 February 1989.
51. Interview #44, 14 February 1989.
52. Interview #35, 8 December 1988.
53. Interview #49, 11 February 1989.
54. See Kriger, "The Zimbabwean War of Liberation: Struggles within the Struggle," 377.
55. Interview #49, 11 February 1989.
56. Interview #41, 11 February 1989.
57. Interview #48, 14 February 1989.
58. Interview #49, 11 February 1989.
59. No statistics on male labor migration were kept by the government prior to independence. Several studies of African households in Wedza communal

lands (formerly TTL) yield differing figures. In a 1982 study, Callear found that 41 percent of households surveyed had the male head of household working outside the communal area and remitting income. Diane Callear, "The Social and Cultural Factors Involved in Production by Small Farmers in Wedza Communal Area, Zimbabwe," Report no. 178, Division for the Study of Development (Paris: UNESCO, 1982). In a 1985 study for Agritex, Truscott found that just over half of the men reporting considered themselves migrating workers. Kate Truscott, "The Wedza Project: Its Impact on Farmer Households, Agricultural Production and Extension," Wedza Evaluation no. 10 (Harare: Agritex, 1985). In my own research, 63 percent of the women who were married prior to 1976 had husbands working away from home. All of these figures are low when compared to the census figures from 1962 which indicated that 82 percent of the population of the TTLs consisted of women and children. Central Statistical Office, "Final Report of the April/May Census of Africans in Southern Rhodesia" (Salisbury: Central African Statistical Office, 1962), 7.

60. I make this argument in detail in "Gender Politics and National Liberation," especially chapter 5.

61. Robert Mugabe, "Women's Liberation in the Zimbabwean Revolution," opening address to the Zimbabwe African National Union (ZANU) Women's Seminar, Xai-Xai, Mozambique, 21 May 1979, 22.

62. The 1982 Legal Age of Majority Act (LAMA) confers the status of legal major on all persons once they reach the age of eighteen. This act was particularly significant for women who had previously been defined as legal minors requiring male guardianship under customary law. See Joyce Kazembe, "The Women Issue," in *Zimbabwe: The Political Economy of Transition 1980–1986*, ed. Ibbo Mandaza (Harare: Codesria, 1986), 377–404.

63. The 1985 Matrimonial Causes Act stipulates that in the event of divorce, marital property will be divided by the courts. This benefitted women who previously often received no more than kitchen utensils in divorce settlements. See Kazembe, "The Women Issue."

64. Women's Action Group, "Women Speak Out," 1.

65. There are two types of resettlement schemes. Model A is distributed to individual household heads to the exclusion of married women. Although widows and divorced women with children are eligible to apply, their numbers are small. If a woman is divorced while living on a Model A scheme, she loses her right to stay. Model B resettlement schemes are production cooperatives where land is communally held. Since these schemes are based on individual, not household, membership, women can hold their own membership rights. However, Model B schemes are generally underfunded and involve a smaller number of people. See Susan Jacobs, "Zimbabwe: State, Class and Gendered Models of Land Resettlement," in *Women and the State in Africa*, 161–84.

Chapter 4

"Men in Our Country Behave Like Chiefs"

Women and the Angolan Revolution

Catherine V. Scott

In the 1970s, it was often argued that the second wave of African socialism would usher in an era of genuinely revolutionary politics. The 1975 grants of independence to the former Portuguese colonies (Angola, Guinea-Bissau, and Mozambique), guerrilla struggle in Zimbabwe, and radicalization of the anti-apartheid movement in South Africa, led many to make claims about the distinctiveness of these newly emerging regimes. Many Africanists began referring to them as Afro-Marxist or Afro-Communist to distinguish them from earlier African socialist regimes such as those in Tanzania, Ghana, and Guinea, and to emphasize the nationalist flavor of their Marxism: eclectic ideologies, flexible organizational structures, and pragmatic leadership.[1]

In the effort to distinguish Afro-Marxist regimes from their African socialist counterparts, the determination to create vanguard parties, the primacy of class struggle, and affinities with the Soviet bloc were viewed as significant. An often overlooked, but important, aspect of the new revolutions was the conditions they created for debates about women and gender in post-colonial society. In Angola, the embrace of Marxism-Leninism and the battle against colonial rule put pressure on the male-dominated leadership of the *Movimento Popular de Libertação de Angola* (Popular Movement for the Liberation of Angola, MPLA) to address the woman question in the post-independence period.

Transitions to socialism in the periphery are fraught with obstacles. Weak economies, rudimentary political organizations, and the fragile and recent attainment of political consciousness among workers and peasants are the legacies of oppressive colonial rule. External destabilization has been a feature of virtually every third world revolution, and perhaps the most devastating war has been waged against Angola. Since Angola gained independence in November 1975, South African- and United States-backed *União Nacional para a Independência Total de Angola* (National Union for the Total Independence of Angola, UNITA) forces have engaged the MPLA in battle. This war has killed five hundred thousand, produced fifty thousand orphans, and denied approximately seven million of the country's ten million people access to clean water and basic health care.[2] Under such conditions gender and class struggle are usually assigned to the future: "First defense, then peace, and socialism later."[3]

The resource expenditure required to defend the revolution explains an obvious impulse to postpone gender and class struggles in the Angolan revolution indefinitely. Nevertheless, despite the continuous destabilization, an attempted coup in 1977, and the death of MPLA leader Agostinho Neto in 1979, there have been achievements that, along with the setbacks and contradictions, deserve examination. These achievements include attempts to lay the foundations for new forms of democratic participation as well as finding different ways to establish a new political system that pays more than lip service to egalitarianism. Gender issues have played a role in these new formulations. The MPLA has consistently supported an expanded role for women in education and production, two areas in which progress is regarded as necessary in order to defend the revolution.

Yet in some respects, Bie Nio Ong is right to argue that "inadequate theoretical conceptualization" has plagued the Angolan formulation of gender issues, much as it has in other revolutions that have taken place in the twentieth century.[4] Women's structural location within the household has usually been ignored by state leaders, while legal changes and women's contributions to national defense have been considered sufficient for bringing about transformations in gender relations. However, to characterize what Maxine Molyneux terms the productivist bias of social revolutions simply as a case of inadequate conceptualization about the role of women in society seems to beg the question.[5] Why is such a conceptualization so inadequate? The argument here is that prevailing conceptions of the public and private spheres in Angola's and other third world revolutions are rooted in a Marxist tradition that shares, with liberalism, the tendency to cordon off the private, while treating the public as a place women and men enter to achieve political equality. In this framework, male dominance within the household is portrayed as natural. Women benefit from revolution to the extent that they are able to take advantage of civil and political rights conferred in the public sphere—an ability limited by social class and rural residence.

The contradictions of the Angolan revolution have more complicated origins than inadequate conceptualization. They can be traced to an international and domestic interest in maintaining women's subordination through state structures and policies that consistently work to subordinate the household in relation to masculine power. In the case of the MPLA, official commitment to Marxism-Leninism overlays an ambivalence about women's liberation that is rooted in a nationalist impulse to maintain rural support and preserve tradition, a term laden with implications for gender relations. This is not to say that male state leaders consciously and purposefully pursue the interests of men at all times. A useful distinction can be made between the masculinist power of the state and the power of men by characterizing the former as "the multiple dimensions of socially constructed masculinity" that shape gender relations, and the latter as the power of specific men over the lives of women.[6] Masculine power realized through both the state and opposition movements is the basis of UNITA's support in Angola. Ironically, UNITA has used the limited threat of women's liberation espoused by the MPLA to solidify its support among men in the south central portion of Angola. UNITA's appeals to tradition signify discomfort with any transformation of gender relations and help explain the organization's attractiveness in the rural areas, at least in the 1970s.

GENDER AND WEST CENTRAL AFRICA TO THE 1920S

The fact that there are three major ethnic groups in Angola complicates our understanding of gender relations before the arrival of Europeans. The Kongo reside in the northern part of the country. The Mbundu live in the central part, including the area around the capital of Luanda. The Ovimbundu live in the central highlands in the south central portion of Angola. Smaller ethnic groups such as the Cokwe and Ganguela live in the east.

In general, in Angolan pre-capitalist societies, the fundamental division of labor was based on gender and age, with wives and children subordinate to married men/homestead heads.[7] Despite this, women at times were able to exercise political power. For example, although the Mbundu "endowed their networks of political positions with masculine symbolism and associations," Queen Nzinga achieved power over them in the seventeenth century.[8] Among the Kongo during the eighteenth century, women wielded some authority as office-holders or as the head wives of noblemen, although they were subordinate to men of their own age. Women also participated in the council of elders and were actively involved in community events such as healing, initiation, and funerals.[9]

This limited evidence we have about women in the pre-colonial and the early colonial periods shows that their status among the major groups of Angola was, of course, complicated and varied. Despite the fact that women in some societies (e.g., among the Kongo) were able to exercise political power, most women were firmly subordinated to the household head. This pattern intensified during the colonial period. The homestead, the family, male property rights, and patriarchal authority structured relationships in the rural areas. Polygyny and brideprice were widespread. On the eve of independence in Angola, these basic features of rural life were still important in many areas of the country, despite the profound changes introduced by colonial capitalism. Farmer and farmer-herder communities, defined by "a variety of precapitalist modes of production," and in general marked by gender stratification and inequality, provided a context that shaped the contours of nationalist politics.[10]

The increasing importance of the slave trade in the nineteenth century also disrupted Angolan societies. Most of the slaves sold to Europe were male. As a consequence, women began to play a much larger role in the domestic slave system. The introduction of new crops, such as groundnuts, often increased women's labor, and as ruling elites attempted to consolidate power and compete with external and internal opponents, women's workloads producing crops invariably increased.[11]

During the nineteenth century the changing relationship between the household and the colonial economy was characterized by an increasing flow of resources derived from trade in crops and slaves to men. Men increasingly dominated the trading system—traditional avenues of power for women were closed.[12] Striking alliances with Europeans became more important than marriage and lineage politics among the Kongo. As a result, more slave than free wives were acquired because slavery was less complicated and expensive. As more and more women were recruited into the domestic slave system, elite women's status declined. Slave women were vulnerable because they had no relatives to protect their interests.[13] With the shift from trade to agricultural production in the 1920s in the central highlands, men became more heavily involved in maize production, previously considered women's work.[14]

COLONIALISM, NATIONALISM, AND THE STATUS OF WOMEN

Although the effect of Portuguese colonialism was not uniform, cash crop production, forced and contract labor, the gradual destruction of local trade networks, and the growth of migrant wage labor, represent a pattern of exploitation common in peripheral and dependent colonial economies. In the mid-nineteenth century, coffee, palm oil, and groundnut crops were introduced in order to benefit Portugal and fuel its bourgeois revolution.[15] Forced labor was used to build a very rudimentary infrastructure, and pacification of the countryside was pursued in order to establish claims against competing European powers.[16] The weakness of the Portuguese economy led to concession grants to other foreign interests in, for example, diamond mining.[17]

The late nineteenth and early twentieth centuries were a period of fairly extensive missionary activity, particularly by Baptists in the north (among the Bakongo), and by Congregationalists in south central Angola (among the Ovimbundu). Missionary education provided upward mobility for Angolans throughout the colonial period and contributed to the spread of nationalism. The Portuguese blamed the Protestant missions for the uprisings in 1961 that created the conditions for a guerrilla war.[18] The extensive network of Congregationalist mission schools, hospitals, and social organizations "eventually [became] the nucleus for an alternate, Ovimbundu-controlled structure" under UNITA.[19]

Beginning in the early 1950s, the Portuguese government pursued, with renewed vigor, its intent to increase white settler migration from its 1950 level of slightly less than 2 percent of the population.[20] The government's plan was accomplished through the encouragement of planned rural settlements and by providing relatively demanding jobs in the civil service and in commerce. Settler monopoly of jobs in the service sector (as waiters, taxi and bus drivers, and bank clerks) blocked an important avenue of mobility for male Angolans.[21]

Portuguese colonial policy in the 1930s favored settler farmers who resorted to forced labor to work on their large-scale enterprises. This dramatically enlarged the male migrant labor pool.[22] The concomitant displacement from the land, the spread of contract labor, and slack male migration to coffee farms and diamond mines in the north, disrupted family life in rural areas and increased the burdens on rural women. At the same time, this situation undoubtedly gave peasant women more control over household resources and allowed them to engage in trade, although economic opportunities remained limited. Under some circumstances, colonialism loosened patriarchal control. Renewed male attempts to control women's labor in the face of declines in slave trading when the European demand for slaves had ceased, could be averted through flight to the towns, where work could be found in the service sector, including prostitution. Some women earned enough money to escape marriage, allowing them more control over their own sexuality.[23]

Sustained political opposition emerged in the 1920s, at first among *mestiços* (the offspring of Portuguese and African marriages) and *assimilados* (Africans who had achieved assimilated status). By 1960 there were approximately fifty thousand *mestiços* in the country, with fifteen thousand residing in Luanda.[24] *Assimilados* had to demonstrate a certain level of missionary education and prove that they were model citizens. By 1950, *assimilados* numbered approximately thirty thousand in an African population of four million. *Assimilados* founded the Angolan Communist Party in 1955.[25] After various organizational changes, the MPLA was formed in 1956. The continued dominance of male *mestiços* and *assimilados* in leadership positions has been a source of conflict since the MPLA's inception. Many believed that *mestiços* and *assimilados* wielded excessive influence within the party and were contemptuous of rural black Angolans.

Two other nationalist organizations emerged with separate bases of support, ideological orientations, external alliances, and political strategies. The *Frente Nacional Libertação de Angola* (Front for the National Liberation of Angola, FNLA), led by Holden Roberto and based in the rural north of Angola, was formed in 1973 from the merger of two older nationalist organizations. Its predecessors' strong appeal to tradition was evident in their attempts, throughout the 1950s, to convince the United Nations to recognize the Kongo Kingdom and bring it under U.N. trusteeship.[26] UNITA was formed in 1966 as a result of Jonas Savimbi's disgruntlement with Roberto's leadership of the MPLA and the strength of his own ambition. Savimbi argued that an alliance with the MPLA was impossible because ethnic groups from the central and southern portions of the country were not represented in the leadership of the MPLA.[27] Its precarious position in the resulting three-way competition for power, forced UNITA to appeal to Portuguese settlers, South Africa, and eventually to the Portuguese secret police at the close of independence negotiations to try and force the MPLA to hold elections.[28]

Angolan nationalist politics was wracked by constant

intraorganizational conflict and the three-way competition that took place in a context of extensive colonial repression. By my own count, between January 1960 and June 1975, there were at least thirteen instances of various groups within the MPLA, FNLA, UNITA, and among the Portuguese working for either the formation of a common front or for agreements, accords, and pledges to end hostilities. The extensive policing system of the Portuguese, complemented by a vast informer network, competition among Africans as a result of state-imposed legal distinctions, and growing rural/urban divisions, ensured that attempts to create an effective oppositional strategy would face formidable obstacles.

MPLA ideology during the pre-independence struggle was marked by increasing radicalization, contradiction, and self-criticism over its weakness on the peasant question. The launching of the guerrilla struggle in 1961 led to the first of many reorganizations intended to broaden its urban base. The movement held a party conference in December 1962, and created a number of mass organizations, including the *Organização das Mulheres de Angola* (Organization of Angolan Women, OMA) to increase its ability to operate among the peasantry in the rural areas.[29] Women received combat training and took part in the guerrilla struggle. Angola Women's Day (March 2) commemorates the day five female guerrillas were murdered by the FNLA in 1967. Women also took part in literacy training and cooperative work in the rural areas, and were elected to village committees (institutions created to counteract the power of chiefly authority).

For its part, the MPLA focused on mobilizing peasants reacting to the social dislocation and disruption of rural life resulting from colonial rule and war. It did not lay a foundation for a revolution in gender relations. For example, village elders were usually able to maintain control of elected village councils with tacit MPLA approval, and in 1962 the leadership mounted an effort to win support among the peasantry through an appeal to tradition.[30] The MPLA perspective is clear in leader Viriato da Cruz's observation that Portuguese rule had torn two million Africans from their social and geographic surroundings. He said that the 1961 rebellion should be viewed as "the result of the irreversible blow dealt to traditional African structures by the market economy introduced under the Portuguese colonial administration."[31]

Continued factional conflict impaired the movement's ability to pursue sustained mobilization in the countryside where most women resided. Unlike the *Frente de Libertação de Moçambique* (Front for the Liberation of Mozambique, FRELIMO), its counterpart in Mozambique, the MPLA was unable to carry out sustained transformation of the rural areas under its control during the war. Growing evidence of disorganization and discord within the MPLA led the Russians to withdraw their support in 1972 and 1973.[32] Daniel Chipenda, the organizer of MPLA forces in the eastern region, and one of several military leaders who had accused the exile leadership of incorrect strategy, defected in 1974 and took several thousand supporters with him.[33] By early 1974 MPLA eastern operations were limited to "sporadic mine and ambush incidents."[34]

THE STATUS OF WOMEN IN THE POST-INDEPENDENCE PERIOD

When Angola achieved independence, Portuguese civil servants, farmers, traders, and plantation owners fled the country, taking as much of the capital and machinery as they could carry and sabotaging what was left behind. Cities and towns experienced immediate food shortages because of the collapse of trading networks, while production of maize and cassava for the market declined precipitously.[35] Rural to urban migration increased dramatically, with severe housing shortages and unemployment the result.

The Angolan government estimated that the South African offensive of 1975–1976, aimed at ousting the MPLA government, caused six billion dollars in damage to the economy. By 1981, the United Nations estimated that 712,000 people had been displaced by the war.[36] By 1987, President dos Santos estimated that the conflict had inflicted twelve billion dollars in damage to the economy.[37]

In addition to the dislocation caused by repeated South African attacks (whose forces became increasingly willing openly to join forces with UNITA in the early 1980s), the MPLA was dramatically shaken by an attempted coup, led by Nito Alves, in May 1977. Alves had been the leader of the First Military Region during the colonial war and a loyal supporter of Neto during the Neto-Chipenda contest.[38] Interior Minister in the newly independent government, Alves was in charge of organizing people's power committees and MPLA executive commissions in the provinces.[39] He packed these various structures with his own followers, called "Nitistas," and was accused of factionalism at the October 1976 and May 1977 Central Committee meetings. After the May 1977 meeting the attempted coup took place. Its effects upon the party, and its associated institutions, were devastating. Thousands of party members were purged and opposition was uncovered within the youth organization, the army, and the trade union.[40] Thus, constant war and party struggles provide the challenging context in which the changes in women's status have occurred. It is useful to keep in mind the obstacles faced in attempts at transformation in third world socialist states: "the uneven nature of the transition means that even at best, the process of social emancipation is likely to be of an incomplete and limited nature."[41]

During the struggle for national liberation women occupied only a few leadership positions within the MPLA, usually because they were connected to powerful men in the movement. For example, Deolinda Rodriguez de Almeida was elected a member of the newly constituted executive committee that was formed after Viriato da Cruz's ouster in 1962. She was a cousin of Agostinho Neto and had studied in mission schools in Angola and at Drew University in the United States.[42] She was murdered on 2 March 1967, by FNLA forces, and is considered an important heroine of the revolution. Ruth Neto, the head of the OMA, is the wife of Agostinho Neto. Ruth Lara, the wife of Lucio Lara, a founder of the MPLA and one of its leading members, was a member of the Central Committee Secretariat until the early 1980s.

Women have also participated in the newly constituted political institutions—there are four women on the Central Committee, seventeen in the National Assembly (elected in 1980 and 1985), one hundred female deputies in provincial assemblies, and an unknown number of female municipal and communal commissioners.[43] While in many respects this is impressive, direct political participation by women is proportionately lower than in Mozambique, in part because national and provincial assembly elections were postponed until 1980 because of the security situation and the attempted coup by Alves.[44] Thus, for example, whereas 6,291 women were elected to local assemblies in Mozambique in 1977, the MPLA still has only provincial-level elections and has yet to open up any important local avenue for women's participation.

Membership in the OMA increased from 351,590 in 1979 to 1,014,988 in 1983.[45] Its tasks have been defined through a series of national assemblies held since independence and the Congress of 1983. The theme of the 1978 assembly was to carry out the tasks of reconstruction elaborated at the 1977 MPLA Congress; in 1979 the focus was on Angolan children in an effort to coincide with the U.N. Year of the Child.[46]

Women have also been involved in coffee harvests and have been recruited into trade unions. My comparison of FRELIMO and MPLA press treatment of women's issues in the late 1970s and early 1980s, especially exhortations to combat feudal practices such as brideprice, showed much less coverage of these issues by the MPLA.[47] Wolfers and Bergerol confirm this by noting that the OMA has chosen to avoid open opposition to such issues because of fears that this would evoke hostility from traditionalists.[48]

In agriculture, women have undoubtedly suffered from a government policy that has officially favored cooperatives, but in practice has not allocated the resources to make them work. With stepped-up attacks from UNITA and South Africa, resources have become even scarcer. The effects of male absence because of war have certainly been felt—250,000 women work in approximately 3,500 peasant associations (cooperatives in the initial stages of formation), 35,000 work in approximately 300 cooperatives, and 50,747 work in the coffee sector.[49] Lack of state support of the peasant associations has caused a drift away from them and toward subsistence agriculture on private plots.[50] In the early 1980s, one observer described an "ancient world of barter trade" existing in the rural areas between private traders and peasant producers, providing a precarious survival for female-headed households.[51]

Women have benefited from an expansion of educational opportunities. The colonial legacy had left an estimated 85 percent of the population illiterate, so the new government gave priority to literacy campaigns. The OMA reported that in 1984, 42.7 percent of the 673,968 newly literate people were women (that is 288,163 women). By 1977, primary school enrollment had increased to one million from five hundred thousand in 1973 (of whom a third were Portuguese).[52] Enrollment in secondary schools increased from 72,000 (of whom four-fifths were Portuguese) to 105,000 over the same period.[53] Although no data are available, women are probably included in this figure—although their ability to attend school is constrained by daily involvement in farming and domestic tasks, and by the fact that most secondary schools are located in the towns.

The MPLA has been less successful in challenging the colonial inheritance in education which, in 1977, was described as "profoundly reactionary," depriving Angolans of their own past, and "producing a petty bourgeoisie which was ideologically, politically, socially, and culturally dependent on the stereotypes of the colonizing power."[54] Birmingham found a striking continuity in education into the post-independence period: "Learning by rote seems to have survived at all levels of education."[55]

POST-INDEPENDENCE ANALYSIS OF THE WOMAN QUESTION

Socialist revolutionaries have relied upon Engels's *Origin of the Family, Private Property, and the State* and Lenin's *On the Emancipation of Women* to develop positions on the status of women in their societies.[56] Both of these works emphasize the importance of engaging women in production outside the domestic sphere, and involving them in public activity. But they neglect any analysis of the possible persistence of patriarchal attitudes in post-revolutionary societies. Analysis of representative MPLA documents makes it clear that the party applied a similar analysis in a mechanical way. For example, at the First Party Congress in December 1977, the OMA was characterized as "an organization of all Angolan women, which fights for their complete emancipation and for their involvement in the tasks of the revolution and the building of socialism."[57] The document elaborates development plans for the future yet women's roles in the household economy are ignored while strengthening the worker/peasant alliance, forming rural cooperatives to raise the standard of living of the peasantry, and attaining production targets, are presented as key elements in the modernization of the country.[58]

Documents from the 1983 OMA Congress display similar ambiguities and contradictions. On the one hand, they argue that "women's struggle for liberation must be seen as part of the more general struggle against capitalism . . . and never as an isolated struggle directed against men." A familiar argument of leaders of revolutions, this dampens attempts to discuss and question household relations. However, the OMA Congress also recognized the importance of gender relations in the household, pointing out that "men in our country behave like chiefs with absolute and unlimited powers,"[59] and recognizing that the persistence of *macho* attitudes and authoritarian behavior within the household are an important dimension of women's oppression. Yet, at the same time the Congress argued that "only changes in productive relations will bring about changes in the family."[60]

Two other important themes emerged in the Congress's analysis of gender relations. The first is the portrayal of women as passive victims, "doubly oppressed by capitalist society and family tradition."[61] In the Report of the Central Committee to the First Party Congress, women are defined as "one of the strata of our population who have greatly suffered from the vicissitudes of colonial exploitation and capitalist mentality that dominated our country."[62] This assumes that women in

Angola constitute a homogeneous group with identical strategic and practical interests regardless of class, ethnic, racial, or religious location.[63] Furthermore, presenting women as an "extreme and telling example of the marginalization of the periphery"[64] is a classic formulation made by dependency theorists which has serious political consequences for women. This presentation renders the household itself unworthy of analysis as the site of immutable, traditional, and ignorant cultural practices and social relations. The site of oppression is shifted from the household to colonial public policies and the impersonal forces of capitalism, both of which are alone responsible for leaving women powerless victims. This doubly oppressed approach to the analysis of gender puts discussion of male domination within the household off limits. It implies that the only approach to women's liberation is through their participation in the public sphere which has been revolutionized by an enlightened male leadership. Portraying women as victims also helps validate the party's definition of the meaning of modernity and development, which emphasizes the liberating potential of advanced technology, heavy industry, and bureaucratic rationalization. Such a construction of modernity and tradition as polar opposites inextricably links women with tradition, ignorance, and backwardness.

A second, and related theme of the OMA report is its consistent tendency to define the household as a drag on women's ability to participate in the tasks of national reconstruction. The document recognizes the household division of labor as a fundamental problem, but there is no discussion of the way in which male domination imposes the double burden, and no recognition of the inevitable male resistance that would accompany full-fledged attempts to collectivize childcare and agricultural production.[65] Ong notes this contradictory approach in the OMA discussion of fertility and motherhood. While it is argued that women should have the right to choose motherhood freely, men's power in imposing their sexuality upon women is not discussed.[66] The Congress's injunction to wage a struggle against underdevelopment rather than male dominance precludes a full treatment of the division of labor within the household and the sexual exploitation of women by men, presenting the two issues as mutually exclusive rather than related.

Official ambivalence about gender relations highlights the complex role that tradition plays in efforts to forge a national identity. Tradition is often called upon to demonstrate that Africans were not the passive recipients of European colonialism. Queen Nzinga is regarded as a heroine because she never fully accepted Portuguese rule—although she is also an anomaly because of her sex and outsider status.[67] The Bailundu and Bie kingdoms remain powerful symbols of heroic (male) Ovimbundu resistance to colonialism.[68] Savimbi's grandfather participated in the 1902 Bailundu war against the Portuguese, and occupies an important place in Ovimbundu traditions of resistance, which revere men who resisted colonial rule.[69]

Tradition, however, is also often denigrated in nationalist and Marxist-Leninist discourse, and is linked to women's natural habitat, the household. Rhetorically, the household is presented as an obstacle to women's ability to undertake socially useful work.[70] Underlying this dichotomy between household and socially useful work is what Christine Di Stefano has termed a constitutional inability of Marxism to "see women's reproductive labor and its derivatives as human labor."[71] Embedded in Marx's and other revolutionaries' approaches to understanding human labor is an emphasis on the conscious, rational, and planned dimension of human activity that only takes place outside the household. Thus Marxist and Marxist-Leninist shortcomings in the analysis of the household cannot be addressed by simply adding reproduction and women's labor into the analysis of human labor. As Di Stefano puts it, "Marx's epistemological commitment to the area of 'production' commits him to an ontological reality which is detectably masculine, not merely male."[72] A different conception of human labor would recognize women not as victims, but rather as engaged in productive, conflictual, and historically different forms of human labor often situated within, but not limited to, the household.

SAVIMBI'S BACKLASH

Colonialism, capitalism, war, and economic dislocation and upheaval have influenced gender relations in Africa, so much so that a sex war is currently underway throughout the continent.[73] Struggles over the control of resources, the increase in poor female-headed households, urban/rural migration, and growing class differences have produced male anxiety, expressed discursively and symbolically, over changes in gender relations. It is ironic to note that UNITA's success can be partly attributed to its implicit recognition of the increasing tension and conflict within the household and over women's status. While UNITA has undoubtedly served external interests (the United States and South Africa) and has reflected some Ovimbundu fears of ethnic dominance, it has increasingly moved away from its Maoist ideology toward efforts to reconstruct Ovimbundu traditional institutions and an African nationalist ideology with distinctively conservative tendencies. Even during the period when UNITA officially courted the Chinese and espoused a Maoist ideology, Savimbi insisted on the importance of respecting the traditions of the peasantry. Savimbi assiduously cultivated the persona of a traditional or tribal leader, which "set him at odds with the *dirigiste* and anti-religious trends within the MPLA."[74] In 1979, Savimbi stated:

> My own doctrine is this: why don't we go back to our African roots and analyze them? It is true that we have to work for progress, and in modern times we cannot apply all our traditions without changing them or adjusting them, but we have to keep an *essence* of our values in order to remain a people with an identity.[75]

Stockwell noted that Savimbi's leadership style was a "throwback to the great tribal leaders of Africa"; his name among some Ovimbundu in the 1980s was *Sekulu da Paz* (Elder of Peace).[76]

Savimbi's and UNITA's cause are often portrayed in heroic terms by Western journalists sympathetic to their efforts.[77] In 1977, Leon Dash, a *Washington Post* reporter, spent seven-and-a-half months with UNITA guerrillas and carried out several interviews with Jonas Savimbi and high-ranking members of the movement. Dash argued that "much of the UNITA guerrillas' success in garnering the support of a large number of peasants grew out of their ability to meld strong tribal traditions with their modern-day struggle."[78] Richard Harwood, another *Washington Post* reporter, noted the boost in morale provided by rallies that married "traditional African rituals with UNITA's ideological goals."[79] Dash reports Savimbi arguing that even though tribalism is divisive it is also "the lifeblood of Africa," thus defending the movement's deferential treatment of chiefs and elders of non-Ovimbundu tribes in an effort to win them to UNITA's cause.[80] Dash argues that affinity for tradition, "an emotional attachment to kinship, tribe, and the Angolan south," rather than ideology, kept the guerrillas fighting under such trying conditions.[81] One lieutenant colonel Dash interviewed said that he fought to remove all foreigners from Angola because "they want to end our way of life. We will lose our heritage."[82]

Savimbi and the UNITA leadership believe that the basic structure of Ovimbundu villages can be used as a model of development in the south central region of the country, and that Ovimbundu representatives can effectively adapt to other structures in non-Ovimbundu areas.[83] In 1983, Bridgland was led on a tour of UNITA held territory where villagers were told by UNITA's Chief of Staff that "the MPLA has been teaching children not to respect their parents."[84]

Bridgland recorded murmurs of approval from villagers and rumbles of approval from "the old men when he [Puna] said he would later hold a meeting restricted to village elders."[85]

At UNITA's Fourth Congress, in March 1977, the concept of Negritude was adopted to differentiate the movement's black nationalist ideology from Marxism and the multiracialism of the MPLA. In addition, UNITA-controlled areas of Angola were declared to be the Black African and Socialist Republic of Angola, to reinforce African traditions and build opposition to MPLA cosmopolitanism. Harwood described Miguel Puna, the secretary-general of UNITA, as "an African chauvinist, a peasant down to his bones, a man contemptuous of Western-style intellectuals."[86]

UNITA's ideology reflects an implicit concern with gender relations and effectively taps into sentimental and romantic notions of African tribal life and women's role within it. Although there are female and child guerrillas, their roles, from Dash's account, remain largely associated with traditional female work of preparing food and celebrating military victories. Harwood reported on all-male battalions.[87] Dash discusses a captain who was reluctant to sit in judgment on a case where two women were accused of witchcraft: "He is a Ganguela, all of the people involved were Ovimbundu, and he was not sure he knew all of the Ovimbundu rules governing witchcraft."[88] He wound up releasing the women, but instructed their accusers to defer to the local chief in such matters, thus abdicating any responsibility for challenging prevailing social practices and sanctioning continued male authority over and persecution of women. In 1983, UNITA's minister of justice, Smart Chata, told Bridgland that UNITA's policy was to "encourage people to maintain their culture . . . we incorporate that culture into our political structures."[89]

As UNITA and Savimbi increasingly turned toward forced recruitment for the army, Savimbi was accused of killing rivals. Collaboration with South Africa was patently obvious, and the movement became even less concerned with presenting a coherent alternative ideology. However, it is important to note the extent to which UNITA continued to rely upon traditional constructions of Ovimbundu life in its efforts to garner support. Deference toward village elders and male seniority were key elements in UNITA's fashioning of a counter discourse on African liberation. The appeals to tradition undoubtedly had resonance among village men who had lost their power because of colonialism, war, and the spread of capitalism, and who found the MPLA's ideology a threat to their already declining hegemony.

The conservative and utopian images of tribal life discussed by Savimbi and other UNITA leaders portrayed an idealized image about traditional African families that, at an implicit level, revolved around conceptions of appropriate gender roles. These attempts to revive an African (and particularly Ovimbundu) past resemble efforts on the part of some African-American nationalists "to invent an African past to suit their own conservative agenda on gender and sexuality."[90] UNITA's efforts to do the same found, at least initially, a receptive audience among men who were rapidly losing their material basis of dominance, and who sought to maintain patriarchal control by behaving like chiefs. By comparison, the MPLA's ideology certainly looks progressive. It possesses, however, its own ambivalences and silences about the sources of women's oppression. The persistence of male dominance in the household, the failure to recognize women's varying interests across class and ethnic lines, and the failure to give gender the prominence given class, regionalism, and religion all demonstrate a blind spot in the MPLA's ideology, a blind spot which has been recognized by numerous critics of official Marxism and Marxism-Leninism. But perhaps the most significant lesson of twentieth-century revolutions is that simply adding women to Marxist-Leninist formulations of liberation and development is problematic. Indeed, most revolutionary documents of the twentieth century demonstrate that ideas about liberation have been constructed in opposition to the perceived backwardness of the household, to which women (as doubly oppressed victims) are bound. Savimbi's efforts to glorify and reinforce this construction demonstrate the dangers inherent in reviving traditions based on the complementary roles of men and women. Official Marxism's successes in affirmative action for women in the public sphere need to be accompanied by a rethinking of the concept of human labor, reproduction, and the contradictory and changing nature of the household.

CONCLUSION

The Angolan revolution demonstrates that masculinist constructions of the public and private spheres are not unique to liberal tradition. For the male-dominated leadership of the MPLA, the private sphere of the household—into which all Angolan women, regardless of ethnicity or class, are placed—is something to be acted upon through the introduction of enlightened state policy. In state formulations, women are relegated to a distant past; they remain enmeshed in feudal practices while the public realm is the present, inhabited by forward-looking men. Linear progress from these political constructions of female backwardness to male modernity is only possible through the rationalization of factory labor and capital accumulation (i.e., moving beyond the household). In order to garner support for state policies, party leaders also tread warily around patriarchal control in the rural areas. Support is tenuous because aspects of Marxist-Leninist policy pose a threat to male dominance. The household becomes a contested terrain as a result of these contradictions as counter-revolutionary groups hold out the promise of a return to tradition, a code for unfettered male control over women. Under such conditions, feminist struggle to undo the political constructions of public and private is necessary in order to recast the debate about gender and revolution.

NOTES

1. See for example, Carl G. Rosberg and Thomas M. Callaghy, eds., *Socialism in Sub-Saharan Africa: A New Assessment* (Berkeley: Institute of International Studies, 1979), 1–13; David Ottaway and Marina Ottaway, *Afrocommunism* (New York: Holmes and Meier, 1980); and Crawford M. Young, *Ideology and Development in Africa* (New Haven: Yale University Press, 1982).

2. Vicki R. Finkel, "Brothers in Arms," *Africa Report* 37 (1992): 63–64.

3. Carlos Vilas, "War and Revolution in Nicaragua," in *Socialist Register*, ed. Ralph Miliband, Leo Panitch, and John Saville (London: Merlin Press, 1988), 185.

4. Bie Nio Ong, "Women and the Transition to Socialism in Sub-Saharan Africa," in *Africa: Problems in the Transition to Socialism*, ed. Barry Munslow (London: Zed Press, 1986), 72.

5. Maxine Molyneux, "Women in Socialist Societies: Problems of Theory and Practice," in *Of Marriage and the Market: Women's Subordination Internationally and Its Lessons*, ed. Kate Young, Carol Wolkowitz, and Roslyn McCullagh (London: Routledge and Kegan Paul, 1984), 59.

6. Wendy Brown, "Finding the Man in the State," *Feminist Studies* 18 (1992): 14.

7. Jeff Guy, "Analyzing Pre-Capitalist Societies in Southern Africa," *Journal of Southern African Studies* 14 (1987): 21. Although Guy treats Southern African societies his ideas have wider applicability.

8. Joseph Miller, "Nzinga of Matamba in New Perspective," *Journal of African History* 16 (1975): 202.

9. John Thornton, *The Kingdom of the Kongo: Civil War and Transition, 1614–1718* (Madison: University of Wisconsin Press, 1983), 48.

10. Franz Wilhelm-Heimer, *The Decolonization Conflict in Angola: An Essay in Political Sociology* (Geneva: Institute for International Studies, 1979), 9.

11. Susan Herlin Broadhead, "Slave Wives, Free Sisters: Bakongo Women and Slavery, c. 1700–1850," in *Women and Slavery in Africa*, ed. Claire C. Robertson and Martin A. Klein (Madison: University of Wisconsin Press, 1983),

177.

12. E. Frances White, "Women of Western and Western Central Africa," in *Restoring Women to History: Teaching Packets for Integrating Women's History into Courses on Africa, Asia, Latin America and the Caribbean, and the Middle East* (Bloomington: Organization of American Historians, 1988), 82; Broadhead, "Slave Wives, Free Sisters,"176.

13. White, "Women of Western and Western Central Africa," 83.

14. Linda M. Heywood, "The Growth and Decline of African Agriculture in Central Angola," *Journal of Southern African Studies* 13 (1987): 357.

15. W. G. Clarence-Smith, "The Myth of Uneconomic Imperialism: The Portuguese in Angola," *Journal of Southern African Studies* 5 (1979): 170.

16. Malyn Newitt, *Portugal in Africa: The Last Hundred Years* (London: Longman, 1981), 20, 50.

17. Ibid., 75.

18. John Marcum, *The Revolution in Angola*, vol. 1, *The Anatomy of an Explosion* (Boston: MIT Press, 1969), 147.

19. Linda Heywood, "UNITA and the Ethnic Nationalism in Angola," *Journal of Modern African Studies* 27 (1989): 50.

20. Gerald Bender and Stanley P. Yoder, "Whites in Angola on the Eve of Independence: The Politics of Numbers," *Africa Today* 21 (1976): 28.

21. Wilhelm-Heimer, *The Decolonization Conflict in Angola*, 12.

22. Heywood, "The Growth and Decline of African Agriculture in Central Angola," 370.

23. White, "Women of Western and Western Central Africa," 88.

24. Marcum, *The Revolution in Angola*, vol. 1, 18.

25. Ibid., 5.

26. Ibid., 62.

27. John Marcum, *The Revolution in Angola*, vol. 2, *Exile Politics* (Boston: MIT Press, 1978), 166.

28. Wilhelm-Heimer, *The Decolonization Conflict in Angola*, 31.

29. Marcum, *The Revolution in Angola*, vol. 2, 29–30.

30. Don Barnett and Ron Harvey, *The Revolution in Angola: Life Histories and Documents* (Indianapolis: Bobbs Merrill, 1972), 24; Movimento Popular de Libertação de Angola, *First National Conference of the Popular Movement for the Liberation of Angola* (Luanda: MPLA, 1962), 12.

31. Marcum, *The Revolution in Angola*, vol. 1, 120.

32. Ibid., vol. 2, 201.

33. Ibid., 204.

34. Anthony Wilkinson, "Angola and Mozambique: The Implications of Local Power," *Survival* 16 (1974): 218.

35. M. R. Bhagavan, *Angola's Political Economy, 1975–1985* (Uppsala: Scandinavian Institute for African Studies, 1986), 19.

36. Ibid., 76.

37. Anthony Pazzanita, "The Conflict Resolution Process in Angola," *Journal of Modern African Studies* 29 (1991): 96.

38. David Birmingham, "The 27th of May: A Note on the Abortive Coup

Attempt in Angola," *African Affairs* 77 (1978): 555.

39. Paul Fauvet, "The Rise and Fall of Nito Alves," *Review of African Political Economy* 9 (1978): 93.

40. Catherine V. Scott, "Political Development in Afromarxist Regimes: An Analysis of Angola and Mozambique," Ph.D. diss., Emory University, 1986, 96.

41. Molyneux, "Women in Socialist Societies," 58.

42. Marcum, *The Revolution in Angola*, vol. 1, 254.

43. Organização das Mulheres de Angola (OMA), *Angolan Women Building the Future*, trans. Margaret Holness (London: Zed Press, 1984), 109.

44. Scott, "Political Development in Afromarxist Regimes," 123, 126.

45. Ibid., 136; OMA, *Angolan Women Building the Future*, 96.

46. OMA, *Angolan Women Building the Future*, 94.

47. Scott, "Political Development in Afromarxist Regimes," 94.

48. Michael Wolfers and Jane Bergerol, *Angola in the Frontline* (London: Zed Press, 1983), 126.

49. Scott, "Political Development in Afromarxist Regimes," 154; OMA, *Angolan Women Building the Future*, 109.

50. Wolfers and Bergerol, *Angola in the Frontline*, 140.

51. Bhagavan, *Angola's Political Economy, 1975–1985*, 140.

52. Wolfers and Bergerol, *Angola in the Frontline*, 114; Keith Somerville, *Angola: Politics, Economy, and Society* (London: Frances Pinter, 1986), 154.

53. Somerville, *Angola*, 154.

54. Movimento Popular de Libertação de Angola (MPLA), *First Congress of the MPLA: Report to the Central Committee* (Luanda: MPLA, 1977), 13.

55. David Birmingham, "Angola Revisited," *Journal of Southern African Studies* 15 (1988): 10.

56. Molyneux, "Women in Socialist Societies," 64.

57. MPLA, *First Congress of the MPLA*, 13.

58. Ibid., 32.

59. OMA, *Angolan Women Building the Future*, 62.

60. Ibid., 54.

61. Ibid., 39.

62. Ibid., 35.

63. Maxine Molyneux, "Mobilization without Emancipation? Women's Interests, the State, and Revolution," in *Transition and Development: Problems of Third World Socialism*, ed. Richard R. Fagen, Carmen Diana Deere, and Jose Luis Coraggio (New York: Monthly Review Press, 1986), 284.

64. Jane S. Jaquette, "Women and Modernization Theory: A Decade of Feminist Criticism," *World Politics* 39 (1982): 273.

65. OMA, *Angolan Women Building the Future*, 42.

66. Ong, "Women and the Transition to Socialism in Sub-Saharan Africa," 85.

67. Miller, "Nzinga of Matamba in New Perspective," 213, 216.

68. Marcum, *The Revolution in Angola*, vol. 1, 103.

69. Heywood, "UNITA and Ethnic Nationalism," 50.

70. OMA, *Angolan Women Building the Future*, 34.

71. Christine Di Stefano, "Masculine Marx," in *Feminist Interpretations and Political Theory*, ed. Mary Lyndon Shanley and Carole Pateman (University Park: Pennsylvania State University Press, 1991), 157.

72. Ibid., 158.

73. Ann Whitehead, "Food Crisis and Gender Conflict in the African Countryside," in Henry Bernstein et al., *The Food Question: Profits vs People* (London: Earthscan, 1990), 58.

74. Fred Bridgland, *Jonas Savimbi: A Key to Africa* (New York: Paragon House Publishers, 1986), 68.

75. Ibid., 290.

76. John Stockwell, *In Search of Enemies: A CIA Story* (New York: W. W. Norton, 1978), 140; Heywood, "UNITA and Ethnic Nationalism," 57.

77. Elaine Windrich, *The Cold War Guerrilla: Jonas Savimbi, the U.S. Media, and the Angolan War* (Westport, Conn.: Greenwood Press, 1992); see also William Minter, "Behind the UNITA Curtain," *Africa Report* 35 (1990): 45–49.

78. Leon Dash, "Ambushing an Unwary Enemy," *Washington Post*, 7 August 1977, A24.

79. Richard Harwood, "Guerrillas Demonstrate High Morale," *Washington Post*, 22 July 1981, A15.

80. Dash, "Ambushing an Unwary Enemy," A24.

81. Leon Dash, "What Leads Guerrillas to Fight On?" *Washington Post*, 9 August 1977, A8.

82. Ibid.

83. Heywood, "UNITA and Ethnic Nationalism," 60–61.

84. Bridgland, *Jonas Savimbi*, 365.

85. Ibid.

86. Richard Harwood, "Angola Rebels' Precious Jewels," *Washington Post*, 21 July 1981, A8.

87. Richard Harwood, "Rebel Goal: An End to Foreign Control," *Washington Post*, 20 July 1983, A8.

88. Leon Dash, "Politics Taught by Fable," *Washington Post*, 11 August 1981, A8.

89. Bridgland, *Jonas Savimbi*, 413.

90. E. Frances White, "Africa on My Mind: Gender, Counter-Discourse, and African-American Nationalism," *Journal of Women's History* 2 (1990): 75.

III

Asia

Chapter 5

Women and Revolution in Vietnam

Mary Ann Tétreault

Vietnam's Confucian tradition displays revolution as a normal, cyclical process, that restores an ideally imagined status quo ante. The state is believed to participate in the same ethical system of virtuous conduct as society (and the families that comprise it); a ruler then demonstrates righteousness by presiding over domestic tranquility.[1] The loss of this tranquility for any reason signifies a personal moral deficiency in the ruler. Domestic turmoil shows that the "mandate of Heaven," the correspondence between the ruler's rectitude and the cosmology of the universe, has been lost.[2] During such times, the Vietnamese look for a new leader whose moral stature promises to restore harmony.

The occupation and pacification of Vietnam by the French undermined this Confucian order.[3] French dominance of Vietnamese rulers meant one of two things; either the world was wrong and the virtuous Vietnamese should withdraw from public life to set a moral example for their peers, or Vietnamese conceptions of "the way," the proper ordering of society, needed to be reexamined. Both strategies opened Vietnam to penetration by Western ideas—those who withdrew had no program for change and those who looked for other answers ranged widely for them. As a result, Confucian ideas about social hierarchies were challenged.

Vietnamese intellectuals often used gender as a model for analyzing conditions in Vietnam under colonialism.[4] Censorship prevented an open political discourse that might criticize the regime. Thus "debates on women became primary vehicles for arguing about topics that could not be addressed forthrightly."[5] Both conservatives and radicals used women as symbols in their analyses. Conservatives argued that colonialism caused social change and corruption. Wanting to preserve the national essence, they took refuge in a neo-Confucianism that emphasized the family as the foundation of society and female subordination as the foundation of the family.[6] Radicals adopted the image of Camille as the talisman of their revolution against both the colonial "father" in France and "the Vietnamese paterfamilias at home."[7] They invited the Vietnamese to see women as one of many oppressed groups in their society, and revolution as the way to liberate them all. "This tendency to generalize grievances cannot be overemphasized. Without it, the Vietnamese would never have been able to mount a sophisticated mass attack on French rule."[8]

Vietnamese revolutionaries did more than use gender as a code through which to discuss the penetration of their society by the French. They appealed directly to women to participate in the struggle to liberate their country, promising them in return equal political, social, and economic rights and status under a new regime. These appeals attracted women who felt oppressed by the old regime. Even though Vietnamese legends glorify female heroes like Trieu Au and the Trung sisters, the status of women in Vietnamese society from the Han invasions in the third century C.E. to the establishment of the Democratic Republic of Vietnam (DRVN) in 1954 was always formally and informally subordinate to men.[9]

Women's status declined most rapidly during what Vietnamese call the feudal period. It began in 939, after Ngo Quyen expelled the Chinese and organized an independent state modeled more closely on the Chinese cultural pattern than the Vietnamese had been willing to tolerate when they still lived under direct Chinese rule.[10] Vietnamese legal systems, beginning with the Ly Code in the eleventh century, embedded male domination and female subordination in laws permitting such things as forced marriages, the immolation of the king's wives upon his death, and polygamy. Although women's status did improve briefly during the Hung Dynasty, it declined under subsequent kings.[11]

French missionaries first visited Vietnam in the seventeenth century. Systematic colonial penetration did not begin until the early nineteenth century, during the reign of Gia Long whose legal code was extraordinarily repressive with respect to the status of women.[12] French colonial policy prescribed the "preservation of old traditions, respect for Viet Nam's ancestral customs and usages."[13] Although the French imported their own penal code and imposed new land tenure and tax laws,[14] they retained most Gia Long social regulations. The Gia Long system served French economic interests. French investors took advantage of legal wage discrimination to pay female employees of colonial enterprises less than male employees.[15] French businessmen also profited from the prostitution of Vietnamese women, institutionalized under Gia Long laws regulating the status of concubines.[16]

In the early twentieth century, proposals for women's formal education began to be made by Vietnamese intellectuals and women were invited to attend public lectures at a short-lived but influential school in Hanoi.[17] Initial French support for female education among the upper classes weakened once women joined the anti-colonial movement. Women's books—even cookbooks—often featured advertisements for overtly anti-colonial publications, and women's educational and social groups evolved into fora for the public discussion of national issues.[18] Vietnamese intellectuals also vacillated in their recognition of women's oppression and their support for women's rights. None advocated raising women's status by changing the law. Even Marxists "failed to get the point entirely" by acquiescing in the conservative assumption that women belonged in the home, finding in their own analyses women's inborn "feminine strengths such as virtue, patience, and loyalty."[19] Polygamy remained legal throughout Vietnam during French rule, and was not even nominally abolished in the south until 1958.[20]

WOMEN, THE FAMILY, AND REVOLUTION IN VIETNAM

The traditional Vietnamese family was patriarchal and authoritarian. Its relationship to the structure of society increased the value of women as a target group for political mobilization. The family was the economic unit of Vietnamese society. Polygamy in Vietnam, as in other societies, underpinned a subsistence economy dependent on the labor of women—wives, daughters, concubines, and mostly female servants.[21] As forced labor, these women worked because men made them, either through private coercion or by resorting to community sanctions against uncooperative behavior.[22] In families where affection and consent motivated labor, women worked so that the family unit could survive.[23] For the revolution to succeed, women had to be motivated to work not simply for themselves and their children, but for the movement and its army. Many observers have remarked upon the mobilization of women by the revolution, and the reciprocal effect of this mobilization on the status of women in Vietnam, especially in the north.[24]

Women's political mobilization was mediated by the Women's Union, established under the auspices of the Indochinese Communist Party (ICP) in 1930. The focus of the Women's Union, like its name, has changed several times since its founding. What did not change was its role as the Party organization responsible for the political mobilization, education, and representation of Vietnamese women. It is organized at every level of society beginning with the village. Virtually every woman who has held a position of authority in the Vietnamese government has been a member of the Women's Union.[25] The Women's Union was one of the functional organizations established to build a social base for the ICP. From its inception, the ICP took a stronger line favoring women's liberation than any other group seeking to lead either the revolution or Vietnamese society as a whole.[26] The statement of Party principles made shortly after the ICP was founded listed the liberation of women as the Party's tenth—and last—goal.[27] Women's liberation was part of the generalization of grievances that permitted a broad-based assault on the colonial regime. In Ho Chi Minh's words, "women are half the people. If women are not free then the people are not free."[28]

The ICP recognized the importance of women by sending Nguyen Thi Minh Khai to represent the Party at the Seventh International Congress in Moscow in 1935.[29] Female workers and peasants took part from the beginning of the upsurge of revolutionary activity following the foundation of the ICP, and women carried the bulk of the supplies destined for the secret bases of the revolutionaries.[30] Some women became revolutionary martyrs: Nguyen Thi Minh Khai was captured and guillotined by the French in 1941.

The ICP was a key component of the Viet Minh, the united front coalition of Vietnamese formed by Ho Chi Minh in 1941 to combat the Japanese. The Japanese formally ended the French colonial administration in 1945. That August, during the confusion at the end of World War II, Ho moved into Hanoi and proclaimed the establishment of the Democratic Republic of Vietnam. Women were policymaking members of the Viet Minh throughout the period, and a female Viet Minh leader, Nguyen Khoa Dieu Hong, took a public role during the August Revolution, making an appeal for national salvation to an enthusiastic crowd at a large rally. The Viet Minh offered more than words to Vietnamese women. Women who previously had no rights to land were given a share of land in the areas taken over as the revolution proceeded in the countryside.[31] In 1946, the new constitution proclaimed the economic and political equality of women and men, defined the rights of women within the family, and provided for female suffrage. Vietnamese women voted for the first time in their history on 6 January 1946, sending ten women to the chamber of deputies, 2.5 percent of the total.[32]

During the French war (1946–1954), women assumed larger roles in local communities. Some engaged in combat, mostly as members of small bands of commandos. In the early 1950s, about 840,000 female guerrillas operated in the north and some 140,000 in the south.[33] Women also engaged in local "struggle" movements, community mobilization, intelligence gathering, and the transport of *materiél*. The latter was especially critical when main force units were engaged. The Dan Cong labor battalions ferried supplies to the front. Two-thirds of the Dan Cong were women.[34] During the battle of Dien Bien Phu, the Dan Cong transported virtually everything needed by the attackers on their backs or balanced on bicycles, moving through the monsoon rains which made using motor vehicles impossible.[35]

The quality of the revolution changed after partition in 1954, and the role of women with it. Cochinchina, the most recently settled area of the country, was also the region that had been most deeply penetrated by the French and thus most affected—socially and economically—by colonialism. The greater wealth of the southern population and the looser structure of its rural life made villagers in the south harder to organize against the regime than villagers in the economically marginal northern and central sections of the country.[36] Prior to partition, the Communist Party in the south faced strong competition for the role of chief organizer of the nationalist opposition, primarily from the Catholic Church and the syncretic sects.[37]

The new DRVN regime in the north was more interested in building its institutions and rebuilding its economy than in fighting a revolution in the south. The stability of the DRVN itself was threatened in 1957 as scattered local uprisings and a full-scale revolt in Nghe An province were mounted against a harsh land reform policy.[38] These uprisings and an internal struggle for control of the party contributed to the lack of involvement by the DRVN in the southern movement before 1960.[39]

Southern opponents of the U.S.-backed, Roman Catholic, Ngo Dinh Diem regime were quiet, waiting for the elections promised in the 1954 Geneva Accords which they expected would provide them with a bloodless victory. But in 1955, Diem announced that the elections would not take place and increased his efforts to liquidate his regime's opponents. The southern insurgency resumed in 1957.[40] As the armed sects were decimated by Diem's army and police and the Catholic Church became more closely identified with the regime, the mostly communist Viet Minh, with its mostly Buddhist values and its emphasis on incorporating women into the struggle against Diem, assumed the dominant position in the continuation of the revolution in the south.[41]

Madame Nhu, Diem's sister-in-law, sought to counter the Viet Minh's appeal to women by forming her own women's groups, the Women's Solidarity Movement, which David Halberstam describes as "an apparatus for family espionage," and the Paramilitary Girls, whom Madame Nhu referred to as her "little darlings."[42] But like other organizations formed by the Diem regime to mobilize popular support, these were not very effective. The regime was too Catholic and too brutal in its suppression of its domestic opponents to appeal to peasants in the countryside.[43] Still the size and reach of the Viet Minh contracted during this time because of the low level of assistance it received from the north, the growing militarization of Diem's regime, and economic and military assistance to Diem from the United States.

The material poverty of Diem's opposition dictated reliance on "people's war" as a strategy. This required mobilizing the whole population against "My-Diem," the government of the south assisted throughout the period by U.S. military and economic aid. People's war tactics included strikes, community action against local civilian and military officials, sabotage, and, most important of all, political struggle—intense and repeated attempts to persuade neutrals or partisans on the other side to join the revolution.[44] The emphasis on political and ideological issues was intended not simply to convert opponents but also to support partisans; the southern revolutionaries were "remarkably committed, tough people, and their personal and political lives were largely inseparable."[45] U.S. troops, for whom ideology meant attachment to "the big PX," could not understand why their enemies were such good fighters. Many attributed the bravery of the enemy to drugs.[46] Political motivation was critical for the success of the southern revolutionaries who had minimal resources and lived under constant fear of exposure and death. Northern party leaders were much more secure because they controlled the government and society in their half of the country.

> [W]hile the same men led the Party, its members in the north and south were becoming increasingly distinctive in terms of their local Party's internal life and styles of existence. Southern Revolutionaries were highly motivated and devoted, informal, and

> forced to make correct decisions quickly. . . . Party leaders in the south assumed ever-greater responsibilities . . . and were . . . in much closer contact with the masses. . . . To be a Party member in the North was a social asset and a . . . source of authority. . . . [I]ts huge size . . . offered ambitious people the possibility of abusing power.[47]

Differences in the nature and the salience of the conflict from south to north shaped the conduct of the post-1954 war in each half of the country. In the south, the success of the revolution was a literal matter of life and death. In the north, the southern insurgency took second place to the desire to consolidate the regime, build the economy, and gain political power in the DRVM. Once U.S. bombing of the north began, the interests of northern and southern party members converged, but their different situations affected the way they mobilized their resources, including women.

U.S. bombing threatened the infant economy of the north, already crippled by an economic boycott imposed by the United States. Women's activities during this phase of the war were critical to its eventual success and women, in turn, increased their autonomy in villages where patriarchal relationships had begun to be reasserted and reinforced as the new regime consolidated itself after the failure of its land reform program.[48] As more men went into the armed forces after the mid-1960s, women became the majority of workers in many rural villages. In 1967, government regulations encouraging and even mandating women's participation in decision-making positions went into effect.[49] Industrialization in the north after 1954 had proceeded similarly to industrialization in other socialist developing countries, concentrating on heavy industry and collectivized agriculture. When the U.S. bombing campaigns began in 1965, about half of the country's industrial infrastructure was still composed of small forges or a few machine tools located in huts or caves in the countryside.[50] U.S. bombing encouraged further decentralization. Though it reduced overall efficiency, decentralization ensured the continued production of needed *materiél* despite the heavy bombing which reduced substantially the production from the centralized factories owned by the state.

The feminization of agriculture partly reversed the post-1957 weakening of party commitment to collectivization because women were among the most likely villagers to eschew family-based work to join cooperatives.[51] This halted, for a time, the reversion to patriarchy—the family farm—in many villages. The state's role in agriculture expanded as farmers became more dependent on chemical fertilizers and mechanical equipment, such as pumps to flood and drain rice fields. Even so, local initiatives remained strong. Production responsibility was vested more in production brigades, essentially hamlet-sized working groups, rather than in village leaders.[52] And a free market in agricultural products existed throughout the war, despite vacillations in government policy toward it.[53] Food production remained stable from 1965, the first year of extensive bombing of the north, through 1972, when direct participation in the war by U.S. troops officially ended. In agriculture as in industry, the basic organization of production remained highly decentralized and structurally resistant to disruption from the bombing.

The reliance of the DRVN on a pre-modern organization of its economy in order to decentralize sufficiently to preserve its productive capacity was mirrored in the reliance of the southern revolutionaries on the pre-modern structures of family and village to disperse and conceal personnel engaged in revolutionary activities. Vo Nguyen Giap, the leading general of the northern forces, said that "until the war in the south [I] knew nothing about 'people's war'"[54] even though the earlier anti-French phases of the revolution had depended heavily upon underground political action and popular mobilization. In the south after 1954, the distinction between friend and enemy was existentially, as well as tactically, unclear—and the war itself was not conventional in any sense.

The villages formed the main arena in which people's war was fought and peasants were the group that each side tried to win over. Many peasants, presumed by the Viet Minh to be the natural constituency of the revolution, were confused and frightened by the conflict. Unclear as to which side was right (given the pain inflicted by each)[55] and the inability of either to take permanent control in most of the country, many peasants preferred to wait until one side or the other should capture the Mandate of Heaven.[56] Yet without peasant help, Viet Minh cadres would suffer massive casualties and the revolution would melt away, not only because of lack of support from the north but, more crucially, because of physical elimination of southerners committed to continuing the struggle against Diem.[57]

The extent of domestic repression by Diem weakened the Viet Minh and threatened it with extinction.

> As early as January, 1956, police-state measures directed against *anyone* who disagreed with the prevailing edicts of the Diem regime forced all opposition into the agonizing choice of self-

> imposed exile (if rich), total silence (if less fortunate and thus forced to remain in Viet-Nam), or armed resistance.[58]

At the same time, the repression sparked massive resistance throughout the population. In January 1960, after Communist Party leaders finally decided to authorize a resumption of armed struggle in the south, a series of demonstrations by thousands of peasant women began in Ben Tre province under the leadership of Nguyen Thi Dinh.[59] Reacting to large-scale indiscriminate killing and looting by government troops, the unarmed women had large numbers and the moral authority of passive resistance; government forces were stymied in their desire to drive the women away and the district chief was eventually forced to accede to their demands. Following these demonstrations, various local and regional groups, along with individuals who had opposed Diem, formed the National Liberation Front.[60] The NLF membership was eclectic. At first even the Cao Dai and the Hoa Hao, the two largest religious sects, belonged to the organization which embraced virtually all of the old Viet Minh coalition as well as three southern political parties, members of ethnic minority groups, students, farmers, and intellectuals.[61]

The NLF was a formidable force in the southern countryside for two reasons. One was its land reform policy which was far more appealing to Vietnamese peasants than the indifferently applied program of the U.S.-backed Diem regime.[62] The other was its policy of building on real and symbolic family relationships to sustain its cadres.[63] Frances Fitzgerald describes this as the "children of the people" strategy. It meant that NLF cadres would depend upon village residents to protect them and in turn would obey their wishes. Unlike the representatives of the Diem government, the NLF reversed the normal hierarchy of family and nation. The villagers became the "parents" and the cadres their "children." The NLF had to be accommodating because it depended upon villagers for sustenance and concealment. Unlike their opponents, NLF members could not exploit the population from the relative safety of national or provincial capitals, or from behind a wall of native soldiers and foreign military and civilian advisors.[64] Even where the cadre had no blood relationship to the local inhabitants, appealing to them as father or mother often evoked a protective response. Nguyen Thi Dinh wrote of an instance when she had been arrested, beaten, and threatened with rape. She saw an old woman outside the hut where she was being held and shouted to her: "Mother, I've been arrested, please come in and ask them to release me so I can go back to my child." The old woman came in and pretended that Madame Dinh was her daughter, enabling both women to escape when the soldiers were called away to reinforce another unit.[65]

NLF strategy relied on the fact that many of the original cadres sent to the villages were local residents and most of the families they appealed to for help were either their own or had relatives in the revolution.[66] Where cadres were strangers, the NLF utilized other techniques to foster a family feeling between its members and local villagers. For example, the NLF retained the old Viet Minh practice of organizing older women in the villages into Foster Mothers' Associations whose members were charged with serving as surrogate mothers to young guerrillas "who were away from home for perhaps the first time in their lives."[67]

Yet there were limits to this strategy. Not all villages could be supplied with local cadres. Also, strangers were looked at suspiciously, at least at first. This problem was aggravated by high levels of attrition in 1963 to 1964 and by the wholesale replacement of local cadres with strangers who frightened villagers.[68] Despite their reputation, not all cadres behaved like children of the village. Some showed favoritism, were disrespectful of the elderly, or committed crimes against the population.[69] Offenders were rejected by villagers but, unlike villager rejection of government troops, this was the result of specific offenses rather than general hostility.[70] When offenders were removed after their superiors became aware of their conduct, support for the NLF increased. But as attrition levels rose, some cadres were returned to villages where they had alienated members of the population.[71] The resulting alienation of the villagers was aggravated by the bombing the NLF drew from U.S.-GVN forces. Bombing weakened the faith of the local population that the NLF would prevail—it showed that the Mandate of Heaven had not descended on them.[72] Even so, the ability of the NLF to hold or reclaim villages in the south, and the tendency of villagers to protect individuals they knew against outsiders, enabled the children of the people strategy to save many of the regime's opponents from destruction.

When the NLF strategy was successful, cadres found refuge and built bases throughout the countryside from which they ambushed and harassed their enemies and recruited new members. Throughout the war in the south, large areas of the countryside were unsafe for government troops, especially at night. The NLF also formed alternative village political systems throughout rural South Vietnam, where local populations paid increasingly onerous taxes to the NLF.[73]

This dual sovereignty period even supported underground societies located near U.S. military bases.[74]

The children of the people strategy can be thought of as resting on the cultural symbol of the nurturing mother. Another cultural symbol underpinned the legitimacy of the "Long-Haired Army," a term coined by the Diem regime to describe the women who had participated in the series of uprisings in Ben Tre province. It gradually came to stand for all women fighting for the NLF. Madame Dinh's heroic role resonated with old legends of female heroes who had risen in the past to fight off occupying forces. This traditional female model for the Vietnamese was the antithesis of the nurturing mother who stayed in the background in a supporting role.

Madame Dinh was made a general of the People's Liberation Armed Forces (PLAF) based on her credentials as a co-founder of the NLF and the leader of the Ben Tre uprising. Her position also reflected the significance of women in the PLAF; Arlene Eisen reports that about 40 percent of the PLAF regimental commanders were women.[75] As in the north, most women served in local and regional guards rather than in the national forces. Thus, the PLAF was only a small segment of the total number of female forces engaged in revolutionary activity:

> The regular forces were not very large but services, self-defense, and the guards were very large and mostly women. [In the south] . . . more women than men participated in the war. In enemy occupied areas, the women were very important because if we wanted to send troops we needed places for them to stay, and to provide for them. After the women got ready we could send troops in. All the supplies were carried by women. The forces that we sent in first to survey an area were women. Our struggle was carried with two principles, first, military, and second, uprising. There women played a very important part.[76]

The extensive participation by women in the revolution in the south was reflected in the high rates of female casualties. Le Tan Danh reports that from 1954 to 1965, female revolutionaries in the south suffered 250,000 deaths, 40,000 disabilities as the result of torture, and 36,000 imprisonments.[77] Nguyen Van Luong, president of the People's Committee of Binh Tri Thien province, tells of casualties from a broader perspective:

> The majority of the women now in the work force now are married. Most are not married who took part in the war. After 30

> years of war, many could not marry. In many cases couples just married and went to the war. Afterward, they are too old to have children.[78]

Women also shared in the civilian leadership of the NLF and the People's Revolutionary Government (PRG). Memoirs of the period, such as Truong Nhu Trang's 1985 book, note instances when women took part in policymaking and planning and suffered the consequences of their activities when they were taken prisoner by the southern regime.[79] But despite their bravery and ubiquity in the movement, women had a difficult time gaining the respect of their male peers. They were not recruited to be cadres until the male pool was depleted by high casualties.[80] Eisen believes that women in the north occupied a higher status than their sisters in the south because the southern branch of the Women's Union was an illegal organization, retarding both the mobilization of women and the education of men.[81] Although some male party leaders from below the seventeenth parallel acknowledge the contributions of women to the success of the revolution in the south, Women's Union leaders from the south remain more cynical than their northern sisters about the extent of women's liberation in Vietnam.[82] This may be because women in the south exercised more authority during the war than northern women. They were more aware of the extremity of the situation that was needed to give them their opportunity.

SYMBOLS AND STATUS

The cultural symbols of the nurturing mother and the heroine who leads the people to expel the foreign invader are both interpreted as models of female autonomy in writings about the revolution by Vietnamese men and women. Unlike analytical forms of discourse traditional in the west which emphasize abstract concepts and data,[83] analytical discourse in Vietnam uses role models and personalization to convey values as well as information. These symbols show multiple messages: the bravery of the Vietnamese people, the totality of national mobilization, and the extent of sacrifice demanded by the revolution.

Symbols featuring women were also used to mock or impeach the enemy. The most ubiquitous cartoon from the revolution is probably a poster that shows a small Vietnamese peasant woman holding a rifle on a large U.S. pilot and marching him off. This is an ambiguous symbol from a feminist perspective in that the weakness of the woman is the core of the message about the impotence of the enemy. Female revolutionaries also appear on postage stamps, such as the commemorative issued in 1969 to honor the women of the Ben Tre uprising and their leader, Nguyen Thi Dinh. Here the symbol memorializes a female leader at a crucial moment in the history of the revolution. The most famous of the war memorials which have been built all over the country also features a female figure. It is in downtown Hanoi and marks one of the sites of the 1972 Christmas bombing. The figures of a woman and a child are used to personalize the destruction of the bombing of civilians. Here, also, the use of a female symbol carries a mixed message, the sort of "women and children" cliche common in situations where the home front and the war front are depicted as gender-specific sites. Despite the ambiguity of some of the symbols, however, the depiction of women in art dealing with their revolutionary roles tends to affirm their agency rather than their victimization—or their status as helpers of the real revolutionaries.

The integration of these symbols into the cultural life of the nation is something else altogether, however. In the Museum of the Revolution in Hanoi, which boasts the most extensive collection of photographs and artifacts from the revolutionary period, little in the collection features or even includes women. Women have a separate museum but, as Americans know from our own historical experience, separate is not equal. The most thorough integration of women's and men's pictures and artifacts occurs in the War Crimes Museum in Ho Chi Minh City, but this is an ambiguous situation in which to celebrate gender equality as it memorializes victims, not agents. The largest photograph from the American war is of the heaps of mostly female bodies left after the massacre at My Lai.

Although the symbolic representation of Vietnamese female revolutionaries shows agency and power, these symbols are not accorded equal status with those representing male revolutionary experiences. As a result, memories of women's contributions to the revolution are fading faster than memories of men's contributions. A similar mechanism can be seen in the Truong memoirs. Women in the photographs are seldom identified by name and only a few are discussed in the text, often in the context of victimization. The destruction of much of the NLF infrastructure during the Tet offensive, antagonism between the two halves of the ideologically and geographically divided party, and the experientially divided consciousnesses of the interpreters of the past, make the NLF a shadowy institution to the present generation. The status and contributions of the women in its ranks are the faintest of shadows left behind.

SUBSTANCE AND STATUS

La femme a une place importante, un grand rôle dans le mouvement, révolutionnaire, tout comme depuis plusieurs décennies, elle a participé activement au mouvement révolutionnaire dans son ensemble.[84]

This 1959 statement reflects the position of the leadership of the revolution with respect to the importance of women to the movement. The post-revolutionary regime did honor its promise to elevate the status of women in the new order. But despite great gains, the status and power of women in Vietnam today still compare unfavorably to the status and power of men.

Education is one of the success stories of the post-revolutionary regime. Before the revolution, 95 percent of the whole population and 98 percent of the female population was illiterate.[85] During the 1984–1985 school year, almost 12.5 million children attended primary and secondary school.[86] Despite the poverty of the educational system, the commitment of the regime to equal education for women and minorities prevents a strategy of allocating resources to male over female students, or to ethnic Vietnamese over minority students. In 1986, 50 percent of all primary and secondary school children were female, and 9 percent of the total school population was made up of ethnic minorities.[87] However, many fewer women than men attend university where there are far fewer female than male faculty members. In 1984, 43 percent of the students in colleges and universities were women, up from 39 percent in 1982.[88] By 1987, 27 percent of college and university faculties were female and women held 11 percent of the doctor of science degrees. Female professionals in Vietnam, as elsewhere, face more family responsibilities than their male colleagues, impeding their progress upward through the hierarchies of their institutions.[89] But few have the chance to compete. On a 1988 visit to universities in Hanoi, Hue, Dalat, and Saigon, I observed that none of these institutions included women on their faculties above the level of lecturer and none had female administrators.

The Women's Union has pushed for policies to mitigate structural impediments to women's professional success in universities and scientific communities in Vietnam. In December 1984, responding to a study identifying structural problems of female professionals, the National Assembly adopted a resolution written by the Women's Union proposing affirmative remedies to deal with discrimination in education and employment. Among the reforms was the introduction of a limit on the percentage of male students permitted to train in fields where a shortage of women in the labor force already exists to increase the proportion, number, and quality of women available for these jobs.[90] The Women's Union also uses propaganda to improve opportunities for women, spotlighting difficulties faced by female scientists and featuring stories about them in its publications.

Women make up 52 percent of the population and 60 percent of the work force in Vietnam, a fact explained by the high death rate among adult males during thirty years of war.[91] Despite the dearth of men, a gender division of labor is evident. Female workers in Vietnam are disproportionately represented in light industry and the "helping" professions, and few hold executive positions in either state-run or local firms.[92] In all cases, the proportions of women in executive positions are much lower than the proportions of women in other fields and, like higher education profiles, they reflect structural impediments to female advancement.

In agriculture, the revolution's emphasis on women's rights to land and the need to employ female managers on cooperative farms during the war countered to some extent the effects of persisting male domination. In a study of the Yen So cooperative located outside Hanoi, Jayne Werner reports that men returning from the war in 1975 recognized the competence of the women who had run the coop in their absence and accepted their continuance in managerial roles.[93] When I visited this coop in 1988, women continued to occupy leadership positions. However, I also found evidence of a gender division of labor. Women were concentrated in jobs considered light work, and in those paying piece rates such as in embroidery and carpet factories.[94] Only men pumped water, considered heavy work, as the coop changed over from fish farming, which it does for half the year, to rice cultivation. Heavy work earns the same salary as light work, but those who do it work fewer hours per week. The net effect of the gender division of labor at Yen So is a shorter work week for most men, giving them more time for study and leisure activities than most of the women.

The limits to women's liberation in agricultural areas are highlighted by Francois Houtart and Genevieve Lemercinier in their study of the Hai Van cooperative, located in the Ha Nam Binh province in the Red River Delta. The majority of its population is Catholic. More women than men are engaged in agricultural labor, jobs with lower status in the community. However, the shift from family farming to collective farming created a larger social space for women, most of whom now go to work every day outside the home and do their work, agricultural or other, in the company of persons to whom they are not related. Before, women worked in the fields for their families or sold produce in the markets, but otherwise were confined to their homes, forbidden an independent social existence and participation in local political and social organizations. Now, even though women in Hai Van are less involved than men in the management of the cooperative, their friendships and social lives extend beyond their families.

These sketches indicate limits to the emancipation of rural women, limits reinforced by the reinstatement of patriarchal control in the villages retained even after 1986 when other aspects of the economy were reformed.[95] The power of family heads over family members underlies recent widespread breakdown of cooperation in village and work brigades and the continued exploitation of women in rural areas. Even though studies show that rural as well as urban wives today have more autonomy than their counterparts before the revolution, Vietnamese women are still oppressed by a patriarchal social and economic system.

Other changes in family life in Vietnam were intended to raise the status of women. The 1980 constitution, which replaced the constitution written by the victors of the August Revolution, reaffirmed the state's commitment to the equality of women and men in every aspect of Vietnamese society (Article 63). In 1959, the first family law, seeking an explicit reversal of the discrimination against women embodied in the Gia Long code, was passed. In 1986, a new family law extended women's rights in areas that earlier legislation had neglected. Vietnam's family law reflects a democratic ethic in gender relations. Article 12 guarantees each spouse the right to choose her or his profession and to engage in social and political activities. Article 10 repudiates the unequal burdens of household chores and child care: "The spouses have equal duties and rights in all fields of family life." The law guarantees joint control of common property and requires joint consent to economic transactions—for example, both spouses must sign to take out a loan. It provides additional protection for women over and above what is provided for men, recognizing that women are the usual victims of family violence and other "social evils." In response to the upsurge of divorce in Vietnam today,[96] the law permits a pregnant woman to seek a divorce but denies that right to her husband until one year after the delivery of their child (Article 41). Each party to a divorce is entitled to one-half of the common property of the marriage regardless of whether he or she worked outside the home, and either may request alimony on the basis of need (Articles 42 and 43). The law also reflects the contemporary unequal sex ratio in the population of childbearing ages by legitimizing children born out of wedlock (Article 31). In general, the new family law looks like the old one except that it makes the protection of family members "more concrete."[97]

The Women's Union, which drafted the 1986 family law, has special obligations under it. If a union member knows that a husband is abusing his wife, she must intervene even if the wife does not make a formal complaint. If necessary, she must get "respected people" to intervene as well. Should the husband continue his abusive behavior, the Woman's Union must find a temporary shelter for the woman and request legal intervention. Husbands convicted of wife-abuse (and presumably wives convicted of husband-abuse) may receive jail sentences.[98] The special role of the Women's Union gives strength to Vietnam's family law. In the absence of community structures obliged to intervene against abuse, no law can be effective in protecting victims of family violence. The provisions mandating equal treatment counter traditional social norms which predispose judges to rule in favor of husbands in cases of divorce and custody.

The family law states that family planning is a state goal and that spouses are duty-bound to practice it. The most widely used form of family planning in Vietnam is the intrauterine device (IUD), which is dispensed free of charge and, in 1988, carried with it a bounty of 500 dong for the woman. There are also rewards for sterilization, but for a tubal ligation a woman receives only ⅔ of the amount a man receives for a vasectomy.[99] Although the state exhorts citizens to limit their families, implementation of Vietnam's "two-child policy" is limited to bounties, propaganda campaigns, and programs for maternal and child health. Abortion is legal in Vietnam but it is seldom used as a means of birth control; it tends to be confined to cases where birth defects are expected and, even here, women are reluctant to have them.[100] Despite the general absence of coercion in family planning policy, urban families tend to conform to the two-child ideal. In the countryside, especially in areas facing labor shortages, larger families are common. However, at Yen So, where the average family has between three and four children, the coop planning commission chief, a woman, reports that women are required to get IUDs after the birth of their second child.[101]

A major problem linked to the resuscitation of patriarchal authority in the midst of modernization is child neglect. A function of changing life and work patterns—the disappearance of three-generation families at the same time that more and more women choose or are forced to work outside the home—child neglect has been identified by native and foreign scholars as a plague in rural as well as urban areas.[102] The new family law attempts to deal with this by declaring that both parents have equal responsibility for rearing their children but, in practice, fathers spend less time with children than mothers and working mothers have less time for their children than mothers who stay at home. At the Yen So coop, I saw a number of working mothers who had their small children with them, but this is just another form of neglect as the mothers could not pay attention to the children and do their work at the same time.

Politics, the military, and the church tend to be the last bastions of male domination in all societies—Vietnam is no exception. Women have never held more than a few positions in the political leadership of the DRVN or the PRG. For example, women made up at most 17 percent of the central committee of the PRG in 1965,[103] despite their crucial role in the resumption of the southern insurgency and their large numbers among guerrillas and main forces fighting in the south. This is unfortunate as the revolutionary period was the high point of women's representation on central committees. Women headed five ministries in 1982, but only three in 1986, although women made gains during this period with respect to their representation on provincial people's councils and committees.[104] Women have been a minority in the National Assembly throughout the history of the DRVN. Their proportion rose from a low of 2.5 percent in the first (1946) assembly to 32.3 percent in the assembly elected in 1975.[105] In the three subsequent elections, the proportion of victorious women dropped, falling to 17.5 percent after the 1987 election.[106]

Nguyen Thi Binh explained the decline in the proportion of women elected to the assembly in 1976 and 1981 as the result of a heavier residue of feudal attitudes in the south.[107] The disappointing election results in 1987 were mitigated by the greater visibility of women in positions of leadership in the assembly. Women held no commission presidencies in the 1981 assembly, but in the 1987 assembly women held three out of seven—the presidencies of legislative, social, and external affairs. A woman was also chosen to head Vietnam's delegation to the United Nations. The decline in Vietnamese women's electoral fortunes coincides with the disappearance from public life of the "grand old women" of the revolution. Both trends reduce women's political authority and the legitimacy of their claims to positions of importance in the national government. A counter-trend shows an increasing number of women holding leadership positions at the provincial level but, despite decentralization and increased local autonomy, the overall position of women in the political power structure of Vietnam is declining.

CONCLUSIONS

Vietnamese women responded in large numbers to appeals by revolutionary leaders to join in the struggle to free Vietnam from colonial rule and establish a socialist state committed to women's liberation. In return, from the earliest days of the August Revolution, the post-revolutionary government enshrined women's rights in its constitutions and laws. Ironically, given the greater level of integration of women and men in fighting forces in the south as compared to the north, reunification stalled women's progress in electoral politics. Still, the government has continued to reinforce and expand legal protection of women and families, and the rights of women to an education enabling them to compete successfully with men in the job market. State and Party officials refer to the Women's Union as a powerful influence on policy, which itself raises the status of women and contributes to the legitimacy of their claims for social and political equality.

Legal intervention has characterized state policy to incorporate gains for women into social and political frameworks, providing remedies for women whose personal situations revert to feudal forms. However, the decision of the regime to reinstate patriarchy in return for rural support also reinstated structural impediments to the realization of women's rights enshrined in Vietnam's constitutions and laws. These impediments are reinforced by gender inequality in the symbolic construction of the revolutionary past and memories of women's participation in the revolution, and are excused as persistent legacies of Confucian—or Confucianesque—social and cultural patterns. However, they undermine gains made by the revolution.

In his analysis of the French revolution, Alexis de Tocqueville concluded that post-revolutionary France was not greatly dissimilar from the society of the *ancien regime*. Theda Skoçpol's analysis of three great revolutions—the French, the Russian, and the Chinese—comes to a similar conclusion.[108] Social revolutions make great changes in class relations and in the relative power of the state as opposed to society. Yet there are vast continuities between pre- and post-revolutionary societies and cultures. Over time, these can challenge novel social arrangements and keep old notions of legitimacy and old patterns of social relations alive, even when the identities of the groups occupying the various positions in the patterns have changed. The Vietnam experience demonstrates how these continuities are constructed. Revolutionaries pay tremendous attention to who gets to run the state after the shooting is over. They compose a "state class" of persons who have limited means for achieving high levels of status and power other than as their deserts from revolutionary success.[109] After 1954, the leadership in north Vietnam was concerned with maintaining, consolidating, and gaining power for itself. It was less concerned with maintaining, consolidating, and gaining power for the opponents of the southern regime, or for women and other marginal groups in the north who had supported the revolution but offered few resources to support men struggling for dominance in the new state. By ignoring the southern revolutionaries for so long, the DRVN contributed to the divergence in ideology, culture, experience, and identification that has made the reintegration of the country so difficult and so painful. By ignoring women, it ensured the continuation and strengthening of social groups and structures that undermine the legitimacy, power, and reach of the post-revolutionary state.

Conservatives and radicals believe that a harmony between personal life and larger social structures is necessary for long-term stability. English conservatives tried to restrict women's personal freedom as part of a strategy to stave off Jacobinism and class conflict which they feared would break out in England in imitation of the revolution in France. They believed that preservation of the patriarchal family would protect the broader social and political status quo.[110] Some may doubt the logic or truth of this assumption, yet its opposite is visible in post-revolutionary Vietnam. Failure to overthrow the patriarchal family along with the old regime validated the positions of conservatives who, from the beginning, wanted no more from the revolutionary process than the removal of the French. This validation keeps Vietnamese women and families in private space, retarding the development of social policy that could make women's paper liberties realizable in practice. It also maintains a social structure that challenges the authority of the state to command resources and pursue its own interests.

The paucity of women in important positions in government and industry in Vietnam today demonstrates the failure of the regime to consolidate the cultural as opposed to the class and political gains made by the revolution. It is also indicative of a structural contradiction in the consideration of gender as analogous to class. Women's interests as women may and often do conflict with their economic class interests, group interests, and even their personal situations. Catholic and middle-class women under Diem's regime joined Madame Nhu's organizations even though Diem had abolished polygamy, reluctantly, only in 1958 and did not enforce the new law after it was passed. Women adjust to the desires of husbands and in-laws in socialist rural communes even when this means that they must work longer hours than men and neglect their infants in the process. The organization of women as a revolutionary class and expectations that they will be consistent in the pursuit of their class interests thus defined is borne out by events only in a minority of cases.

This helps to explain why gains made by women during periods of revolutionary upheaval tend to erode over time. Women themselves fail to maintain solidarity with one another, and men, from their positions of structural superiority, place obstacles in the paths even of the ones who try. Though few women favor gender-class identity over other identities, most men do. The recurrence of patriarchy as a mode of social control in rural villages in Vietnam after 1957 and throughout the country after reintegration in 1975 provides strong evidence of the ease with which men can adjust their ideological prisms to block out inconsistencies arising from the pursuit of male gender-class interests. It also reflects the extent to which control over women is a measure of male success, both as a source of economic gain and as a counter in status competition. As in China, economic liberation has intensified the rate of female exploitation. Recently the sale of female children into prostitution has become widespread again in Vietnam.

This basic difference in the expression of gender in social organization, coupled to the political compromises that are routinely made in order for a new regime to entrench itself, keep social structures that oppress women alive and well despite the massive upheavals in political control and class structure that revolutionary transformation brings about. Even gains in legal protection made by women through participation in revolutionary movements may be more fragile than corresponding gains made by men. Women are uniquely vulnerable to the revival or resurgence of social patterns whose locus in society and connection to a shared past make them seem innocuous or even irrelevant to male members of the state class. Yet the longevity of the political changes brought about by revolutions is a hostage to these remnants of the past whose power rests in their ability to control people and other resources independently of the state. A revolution that fails to liberate women, leaving their fate to the whims of despots in the private sphere, also fails to protect the liberation of men from assault and erosion when these despots leave their houses to seize control in the public sphere.

NOTES

1. David G. Marr, *Vietnamese Tradition on Trial, 1920–1945* (Berkeley: University of California Press, 1981), 58–59.

2. Frances Fitzgerald, *Fire In the Lake: The Vietnamese and the Americans in Vietnam* (Boston: Little, Brown, 1972), 30.

3. Marr, *Vietnamese Tradition on Trial*, 60.

4. Ibid., 228–29.

5. Hue-Tam Ho Tai, *Radicalism and the Origins of the Vietnamese Revolution* (Cambridge: Harvard University Press, 1992), 91.

6. Ibid., 92.

7. Ibid., 90.

8. Marr, *Vietnamese Tradition on Trial*, 235.

9. Ibid., 191–99; Mai Thi Tu and Le Thi Nham Tuyet, *Women in Viet Nam* (Hanoi: Foreign Languages Publishing House, 1978), 30–31.

10. Mai and Le, *Women in Viet Nam*, 31–32.

11. Ibid., 46–48.

12. Ibid., 48–59.

13. Ibid., 93.

14. Nancy Wiegersma, *Vietnam: Peasant Land, Peasant Revolution: Patriarchy and Collectivity in the Rural Economy* (New York: St. Martin's Press, 1988), 68–84; Stanley Karnow, *Vietnam: A History* (New York: Viking Press, 1983), 114.

15. Mai and Le, *Women in Viet Nam*, 101.

16. Ibid., 104; Bernard B. Fall, *Street Without Joy* (New York: Schocken Books, 1972), 131–32.

17. Marr, *Vietnamese Tradition on Trial*, 200.

18. Ibid., 217–18.

19. Ibid., 242–43.

20. Fall, *Street Without Joy*, 131.

21. V. Spike Peterson, "An Archaeology of Domination: Historicizing Gender and Class in Early Western State Formation," Ph.D. diss., American University, 1988, 173–75.

22. See, for example, Le Ly Hayslip, with Jay Wurts, *When Heaven and Earth Changed Places: A Vietnamese Woman's Journey from War to Peace* (New York: Doubleday, 1989), 20–22.

23. Mai Thi Tu, "The Vietnamese Woman, Yesterday and Today," *Vietnamese Studies* 10 (1978): 15.

24. See, for example, Gerard Chaliand, *The Peasants of North Vietnam* (Baltimore: Penguin Books, 1969).

25. Mai and Le, *Women in Viet Nam*, 119; Arlene Eisen, *Women and Revolution in Viet Nam* (London: Zed Books, 1984), 119–34.

26. Marr, *Vietnamese Tradition on Trial*, 235–36; Douglas Pike, *Vietcong: The Organization and Techniques of the National Liberation Front of South Vietnam* (Cambridge: MIT Press, 1966), 174.

27. Mai and Le, *Women in Viet Nam*, 112–13; Wiegersma, *Vietnam*, 94.

28. The exact wording of this quote varies from source to source. This is the

version told to me by Duong Thi Duyen, secretary for Western Affairs of the Vietnam Women's Union, on 4 January 1988 in Hanoi.

29. Eisen, *Women and Revolution in Viet Nam*, 87.

30. Pike, *Vietcong*, 178; Mai and Le, *Women in Viet Nam*, 118, 124.

31. Eisen, *Women and Revolution in Viet Nam*, 97; Francois Houtart and Genevieve Lemercinier, *Hai Van: Life in a Vietnamese Commune* (London: Zed Books, 1984), 165.

32. Eisen, *Women and Revolution in Viet Nam*, 244.

33. Mai and Le, *Women in Viet Nam*, 101, 161.

34. Ibid., 163.

35. Douglas Pike uses this as evidence that women were exploited by male communist revolutionaries, for whom they were merely "the water buffalo[es] of the Revolution." Pike, *Vietcong*, 178.

36. Samuel L. Popkin, *The Rational Peasant: The Political Economy of Rural Society in South Vietnam* (Berkeley: University of California Press, 1979), 230.

37. Ibid., 184–85; Fitzgerald, *Fire in the Lake*, 155; Bernard B. Fall, *Viet-Nam Witness, 1953–1966* (New York: Praeger, 1976), 141–59.

38. Eric R. Wolf, *Peasant Wars of the Twentieth Century* (New York: Harper and Row, 1969), 191.

39. Wiegersma, *Vietnam*, 202; R. B. Smith, *An International History of the Vietnam War: Revolution Versus Containment, 1955–1961* (New York: St. Martin's Press, 1983), 93–99.

40. Fall, *Viet-nam Witness*, 169–89.

41. Neil Sheehan, *A Bright Shining Lie: John Paul Vann and America in Vietnam* (New York: Random House, 1988), 122.

42. David Halberstam, *The Making of a Quagmire: America and Vietnam During the Kennedy Era*, rev. ed. (New York: Knopf, 1988), 24–28.

43. Sheehan, *A Bright Shining Lie*, 101–5.

44. Frank Denton, "Volunteers for the Viet Cong," Rand Corporation Memorandum RM-5647-ISA/ARPA, 1968, ix; Tam Vu, "People's War Against Special War," *Vietnamese Studies* 11 (n.d.): 50–55, 64–66.

45. Gabriel Kolko, *Anatomy of a War: Vietnam, the United States, and the Modern Historical Experience* (New York: Pantheon, 1985), 270; also, W. P. Davison and J. J. Zasloff, "Profile of Viet Cong Cadres," Rand Corporation Memorandum RM-4983-1-ISA/ARPA, 1968; Konrad Kellen, "A View of the VC: Elements of Cohesion in the Enemy Camp in 1966–1967," Rand Corporation Memorandum RM-5462-1-ISA/ARPA, 1969; Nguyen Thi Dinh, "No Other Road to Take," recorded by Trans Huong Nam, trans. Mai Elliott, Data Paper 102, Southeast Asia Program, Cornell University, 1976.

46. Charles C. Moskos, Jr., *The American Enlisted Man: The Rank and File in Today's Military* (New York: Russell Sage Foundation, 1970), 152.

47. Kolko, *Anatomy of a War*, 269.

48. Wiegersma, *Vietnam*, 166–67.

49. Ibid., 157–58.

50. Kolko, *Anatomy of a War*, 266.

51. Wiegersma, *Vietnam*, 159–60, 179.

52. Ibid., 161.

53. Kolko, *Anatomy of a War*, 265–66.

54. Fitzgerald, *Fire in the Lake*, 140.

55. For example, see Hayslip, *When Heaven and Earth Changed Places*, 94–97.

56. Fitzgerald, *Fire in the Lake*, 150–57; Rand Corporation, *Viet Cong Infrastructure in South Vietnamese Villages*, Rand Vietnam Interview Series PIE, Interim Reports 1965–1966, Santa Monica, 1972. This *attentisme* is very clear in the Rand interviews. Questioners asked many defectors and captives what percentage of their villages supported the NLF and what percentage did not. NLF supporters were generally reported as a positive number: 3 or 10 or 30 percent of the villages the respondents came from. The remainder of the village populations were almost never judged to be GVN supporters, however. They were described as neutral.

57. Denton, "Volunteers for the Viet Cong"; Nguyen Thi Dinh, "No Other Road to Take," 61–62.

58. Fall, *Viet-nam Witness*, 138, emphasis in original.

59. Nguyen Thi Dinh, "No Other Road to Take," 62–74.

60. Wiegersma, *Vietnam*, 203.

61. Mai Elliott, "Translator's Introduction," to Nguyen Thi Dinh, "No Other Road to Take," 11–13; Pike, *Viet Cong*, 82–84.

62. Jeffrey Race, *War Comes to Long An* (Berkeley: University of California Press, 1972).

63. Rand Corporation, *Viet Cong Infrastructure.*

64. Fitzgerald, *Fire in the Lake*, 157–64.

65. Nguyen Thi Dinh, "No Other Road to Take," 74.

66. Rand Corporation, *Viet Cong Infrastructure*; Hayslip, *When Heaven and Earth Changed Places*; Nguyen Thi Dinh, "No Other Road to Take."

67. William Andrews, *The Village War: Vietnamese Communist Revolutionary Activities in Dinh Tuong Province, 1960–1964* (Columbia: University of Missouri Press, 1973), 77.

68. Rand Corporation, *Viet Cong Infrastructure.*

69. Ibid.; see also Hayslip, *When Heaven and Earth Changed Places.*

70. Konrad Kellen, "A View of the VC: Elements of Cohesion in the Enemy Camp in 1966–1967," Rand Corporation Memorandum RM 5462-1-ISA/ARPA, 1969, 9–10.

71. Rand Corporation, *Viet Cong Infrastructure.*

72. Ibid.

73. Ibid.

74. The term "dual sovereignty" comes from Charles Tilly, "Does Modernization Breed Revolution?" *Comparative Politics* 5 (1973). The juxtaposition of NLF and U.S. bases is described in Tom Mangold and John Penycate, *The Tunnels of Cu Chi* (New York: Berkeley Books, 1986).

75. Eisen, *Women and Revolution in Viet Nam*, 105.

76. Nguyen Van Luong, interview with the author, 6 January 1988, in Hue.

77. Le Han Danh, "The Long-Haired Army," *Vietnamese Studies* 10 (1966): 61-62.

78. Interview with the author.

79. Truong Nhu Tang, *A Viet Cong Memoir* (New York: Vintage Books, 1985), 110–11, 118–21, 130.

80. Rand Corporation, *Viet Cong Infrastructure.*

81. Eisen, *Women and Revolution in Viet Nam,* 123.

82. Compare the views of southerner Nguyen Thi Dinh as reported in the *Christian Science Monitor,* 4 November 1987 (at the time she was president of the Women's Union), and those of northerner Duong Thi Duyen, another top official of the Women's Union, revealed in an interview with me on 4 January 1988. In the interview, Madame Duyen attributed the relative lack of women important economic and political positions in Vietnam to the absence of education for such a long period, something that should have affected men at least as much as women. She saw the drop in the number of women elected to the National Assembly in 1987 as a failure by the Women's Union to campaign effectively. Madame Dinh, in contrast, was reported as believing that the inferior position of women in post-revolutionary Vietnam was the result of men clinging to their outmoded Confucian values—and privileges.

83. Henry Kissinger, *American Foreign Policy,* exp. ed. (New York: Norton, 1974), 48–49.

84. The statement was made by Le Duan, then general-secretary of the Workers Party, and is cited in Nguyen Thi Dinh, "La Loi Sur le Mariage et la Famille et L'emancipation de la Femme," *Bulletin de Droit* 1 (1987): 4.

85. Nguyen Thi Binh, interview by a delegation from the United States-Indochina Reconciliation Project, in Hanoi, 1986. Transcript available from USIRP, Philadelphia, mimeo. Madame Binh was education minister at the time. Also, Hoang Xuan Sinh, "Participation of Women and Their Emancipation through the Development of Education and Science in Viet Nam," *Women of Vietnam* 1 (1987): 1.

86. Interview with Nguyen Thi Binh.

87. Ibid.

88. Le Thi, "Vietnamese Women Advance Under Socialism," *Women of Vietnam* 2 (1987).

89. Ibid., 27.

90. Le Thi, "Vietnamese Women Advance Under Socialism," 18.

91. Interview by the author, 4 January 1988, in Hanoi.

92. See (no author), "Woman Workforce in Vietnam," *Women of Vietnam* 2 (1987): 5; (no author), "Women's Participation in State Administration and Economic Management," *Women of Vietnam* 4 (1987): 22–23.

93. Eisen, *Women and Revolution in Viet Nam,* 143–44.

94. Wiegersma reports the same pattern in other northern coops prior to the reintegration of the country (*Vietnam,* 162–63) and throughout the country afterwards (ibid., 221–24).

95. Wiegersma, *Vietnam,* 243.

96. Nuoc Van, "The Changes and Noteworthy Problems in Vietnamese Family Life," *Women of Vietnam* 4 (1987): 22–23.

97. Interview with Duong Thi Duyen.

98. Ibid.

99. Interviews by the author with members of the staff of Tu Do Hospital, Ho Chi Minh City, 16 January 1988.

100. Ibid.

101. Interview with Nguyen Thi Thuc, at Yen So outside of Hanoi, 3 January 1988.

102. See, for example, Houtart and Lemercinier, *Hai Van*, 107; Nuoc Van, "The Changes and Noteworthy Problems"; and Wiegersma, *Vietnam*, 245.

103. This figure was calculated from the list presented in Nguyen Huu Tho, "Personalities of the Liberation Movement of South Vietnam," Commission of External Relations of the NLF, mimeo, n.d., and represents a high estimate even though the list is not complete. A full list may have included additional women as well as additional men. However, the list omits the secret leaders of the NLF discussed in Pike, *Viet Cong*, 216–17, and alluded to in Truong Nhu Trang, *A Viet Cong Memoir*. Trang identifies himself as one of these secret members of the NLF leadership. It is unlikely that any of the secret members was female as the secrecy itself was a function of the high position in either the government of South Vietnam or in a major private corporation that these NLF leaders held. None of these positions was occupied by a woman.

104. "Women's Participation in State Administration and Economic Management," 27.

105. Eisen, *Women and Revolution in Viet Nam*, 244.

106. Ibid., 246; interview with Doang Thi Duyen.

107. Eisen, *Women and Revolution in Viet Nam*, 246.

108. Theda Skoçpol, *States and Social Revolutions* (Cambridge: Cambridge University Press, 1979).

109. Ibid., 164–67.

110. Claudia L. Johnson, *Jane Austin: Women, Politics, and the Novel* (Chicago: University of Chicago Press, 1988). For a discussion of the revolutionaries and their efforts to harmonize politics and everyday life according to a new pattern, see Lynn Hunt, *Politics, Culture, and Class in the French Revolution* (Berkeley: University of California Press, 1984).

Chapter 6

Women and Revolution in China

The Sources of Constraints on Women's Emancipation

Kyung Ae Park

Earlier studies of women in post-revolutionary China portrayed a remarkable improvement in women's social position. They took the optimistic view that orthodox Marxism as an ideology, and the Chinese Communist Party (CCP) as its instrument, had made sweeping accomplishments in liberating women.[1] Many believed that changes for women were one of the greatest miracles of the Chinese revolution. Since the late 1970s, however, the optimism has gradually dissipated. Recent studies have advanced the critical view that the Chinese socialist regime has failed to address the "woman issue."[2] Many conclude that Chinese women have not been liberated in any fundamental way and that the CCP has not given a strong and sufficient commitment to women's liberation. This chapter explores various sources of constraints on women's emancipation in China. Using ideological, historical, and developmental perspectives, it also addresses such issues as women's status in the pre-revolutionary society, women's role in and their contribution to the revolution, and the relationship between the socialist revolution and women's status in the post-revolutionary society.

THE IDEOLOGICAL CONSTRAINT

In the tradition of classical Marxist theory, particularly the theory of Friedrich Engels, women's liberation is a natural consequence of socialist revolution. Engels said: "The first requisite for the emancipation of women is that all women participate again in social labor; to achieve this, individual families are no longer required to be the units of the social economy."[3] This ultimate emancipation of women ensues as the full-fledged classless society is built. Sexual equality results from economic liberation, and women's participation in economic production outside the home leads to their full emancipation. Mao embraced this idea when he said: "Only when a class society no longer exists and cumbersome labor and agriculture have been made automatic and mechanized, will it be possible to realize equality between the sexes."[4] As one scholar points out, Chinese women were told that "they would not be fully equal with men until China had achieved a communist society," confronting them with the fact that "their real equality had been postponed until the millennium."[5]

Based on this basic tenet of Marxist theory, attempts to organize the masses around women's issues are seen as selfish and divisive to class solidarity. Only bourgeois women confine themselves to the woman question. Women in China should pursue the equality of men and women together rather than focusing on their status as women. Accordingly, feminism, which places women's concerns first, is evil and counter-revolutionary. Many leftist women as well as men opposed feminism as being selfish and bourgeois, and viewed women's problems as peripheral to the proletarian struggle. One of the most influential women during the revolutionary period, Xing Jiangyou, opposed feminists' struggle, and another revolutionary heroine, Cai Chang, also denounced feminism. According to Cai Chang, as a result of feminism:

> Work suffers setbacks, the masses' experience isn't studied. Further feminism is putting on airs and insulting people . . . without giving aid to women's work. . . . This kind of subjectivism and formalism which lacks the masses' point of view on the way of work, especially in the area of women's work, means that in the long run feminists are not able to penetrate the masses of women.[6]

This ideological constraint discouraged the women's liberation movement in China, and may help explain why the campaign to liberate Chinese women from traditional oppression has been left to the CCP whose goals and strategies have been defined by men.

THE HISTORICAL CONSTRAINT

One aspect of the historical constraint on women's emancipation in China is that the strategy of the Chinese communist revolution was based on the peasantry rather than on the urban proletariat. As the

CCP was forced to retreat to rural areas after the 1927 massacre, the party mobilized the peasants and relied on them for a successful revolution. This has exerted an enormous impact on Chinese women because the CCP's efforts to change women's position encountered strong resistance from conservative peasants.

Ideological constraints and peasant resistance reduced female participation in the revolutionary process and led to the exclusion of women from most leadership positions. Their participation in the revolution was so marginal that female leaders could not mobilize popular support to change the status of Chinese women after the revolution. For centuries, Confucian principles had organized Chinese society in an elaborate social hierarchy in which women consistently lagged behind men. Throughout life, a woman remained subordinate to men: in youth, she followed the authority of her father; when married, she obeyed her husband; after her husband's death, she was subject to her son. Women were powerless and dependent, both at home and in society. They suffered from female infanticide, foot-binding, and arranged marriages. They could not own property or work outside the home. Widows were not allowed to remarry, and were often expected to commit suicide to show loyalty to their husbands. Except for a small group of women from important families, all Chinese women suffered from these traditional patterns of oppression.

During the nineteenth century, as a result of Western influence, sporadic attempts were made to improve women's lot, particularly by educated, upper-class women. The women's movement gained momentum by the early twentieth century, especially after the 1911 revolution that ended the one-thousand-year-old feudal system. Women supported the establishment of a republic hoping that the new republic would pass legislation to improve their position in society. Chiu Chin, who was from a wealthy family, was an early upper-class feminist. She started the first feminist newspaper and became the first woman to die for the revolution. Following the 1911 revolution, women's groups formed a Woman Suffrage Alliance, asking that political equality between men and women be included in the Provisional Constitution. When their efforts failed, angry supporters actually stormed the parliament demanding women's political rights, but the Alliance failed to gain substantial support.

During the 1919 May Fourth Movement, which began as an anti-imperialist campaign protesting concessions of Chinese sovereignty by the allies at the end of the World War I, demands for women's rights quickly spread among the female population. This gave birth to feminist groups such as the Association for the Collective Advancement of Women and the Association for the Promotion of Women's Education.[7] These women demanded the right to own property, be educated, marry freely, vote, and run for office. All forms of feudal oppression, including the traditional family, came under heavy attack and, by 1922, educated upper-class feminists had developed additional feminist organizations on a national scale: the Women's Suffrage Organization focused on women's political rights and the Women's Rights League demanded legal equality between the sexes.[8]

In the meantime, the CCP was formed in 1921. The second CCP Congress, held in 1922, issued a proclamation for women's rights and established a special women's bureau. It appointed Xing Jiangyou as the first woman member of the CCP Central Committee (CC) in the second Congress and, in 1923, appointed her the first director of the new women's bureau.[9] The CCP was keenly aware of women's oppression. Mao himself wrote several essays on women and the family, and favored reforms in this area. As the CCP and the nationalist Kuomintang (KMT) formed the first United Front (1923–1927) against the warlord government, they set up a Women's Department headed by He Xingning of the KMT. The department formed women's unions and set up union locals in the countryside to educate and mobilize women. They began to celebrate International Women's Day, 8 March, in 1924. During this period, prominent CCP women like Xing Jiangyou, Cai Chang (Xing's sister-in-law), and Deng Yingchao (Zhou Enlai's wife) helped organize over 1.5 million women into the Women's Department. Urban feminists and revolutionaries worked together to train rural recruits and, according to Kay Ann Johnson, for the first and last time, politically independent women's organizations advocated such issues as marriage reform.[10]

The coalition between the CCP and the KMT broke apart during the "white terror" in 1927. The KMT forced the CCP out of the urban areas and executed more than a thousand female activists, including Xing Jiangyou, as suspected communists.[11] After the split, the KMT, largely in response to bourgeois pressure, adopted a legal code in 1930 that guaranteed women equal inheritance rights and, in 1933, revised the criminal code to provide for freedom of marriage and monogamy. Yet, with the New Life Movement in 1934 calling for a revival of Confucian values, little effort was made to enforce the new codes. While many urban women still supported the KMT, KMT female activists such as He Xingning and Song Qingling, the widow of Sun Yat-sen, eventually turned to women's groups sponsored by the CCP.

The CCP had been forced to retreat to the countryside following its defeat, where the women's movement had no base and women's equality became obscured. In 1928, the sixth CCP Congress's resolution on the Peasants' Movement recognized that failure to win over the women in the villages would result in the failure of the agrarian revolution.[12] To mobilize women as a major revolutionary force, the CCP began to organize women's associations again and appointed Deng Yingchao as the director of the Women's Department. The Constitution of the Soviet Republic of Jiangxi, adopted in 1931, expressly stated that the purpose of the government was "to guarantee the thorough emancipation of women," and to create the conditions for women's participation in the "social, economic, and political and cultural life of the entire society."[13] The CCP also experimented with reforms of the marriage law and a land reform law granting women important property and economic rights. Under its first marriage law in 1931, women were entitled to free choice in marriage, divorce, and child custody. In addition, a political and economic quota system for women was established so that "every local party should do its best to reach the goal set up by the Central Committee which requires that women comrades in the movement should occupy one-third to two-thirds of the party positions."[14] During the Jiangxi Soviet, women gained favorable legislation designed to enhance their lot; undoubtedly these measures aroused widespread resistance from peasant men.

As the KMT encircled the Jiangxi revolutionary base, the CCP began its Long March in 1934, arriving at Yenan in 1936. Meanwhile, at the Zunyi meeting in January 1935, Mao established himself as the CCP chair. But the party's policy toward women was marked by inconsistency. The Sino-Japanese War required women to leave their homes for production activities, yet the conservative tradition of Yenan made this difficult. During the second United Front (1937–1945) against Japan, the CCP was forced to retreat from policies which exposed men and women to the idea of promoting women's rights. Land and family reform policies were relaxed while attacks on that trend were criticized as divisive. After the defeat of Japan in 1945, however, the CCP reinstituted land and marriage reforms in the liberated zones and, in 1948, issued a new resolution encouraging women to struggle against their inferior status.[15] The well-known "speak bitterness" sessions were organized and, for the first time, women were encouraged to express their anger in public. As one scholar put it, "women, who for most of their lives had been required to stay indoors, denied all forms of social contact, were to be seen . . . dragging well-known women-oppressors to the women's headquarters and forcing out of them unheard-of public self-criticisms and often giving them revengeful floggings."[16]

Although the Chinese women's movement greatly expanded women's rights in economic, social, and political arenas, women's participation in the revolution was not significant enough to affect women's status in post-revolutionary Chinese society. From the first CCP Congress in 1921 to the seventh in 1945, only two women were named as full members of the Central Committee (Xing Jiangyou in 1922 and Cai Chang in 1928 and 1945).[17] Women who did manage to rise in the party hierarchy were confined to the Women's Department which was given a low priority in party activity, and thus power in it meant little.[18] Suzette Leith indicated that only about twenty women were influential in the communist movement in the 1920s.[19]

Women's participation in the military, one of the most vital sources of CCP leadership, was virtually nil. In his theory of social inequality, Gerhard Lenski identifies three sources of power influencing inequality in society: the power of property, the power of position, and the power of force.[20] Chinese women during the revolution never gained the power of force, although they were granted some economic and political rights. There were revolutionary heroines and fighters, but only about fifty out of the over fifty thousand who joined the Long March were women.[21] A 2,000-member armed Women's Independence Battalion was organized in 1933 yet, except for a handful of commanders and veteran revolutionaries such as Zhang Qinqiu and Tao Wanrong, most of the women were young and inexperienced.[22] Although they were allowed to join the army, as Janet Salaff and Judith Merkle pointed out, they neither fought nor gained control of the means of coercion which could have guaranteed their power.[23] Given the fact that the CCP and the People's Liberation Army (PLA) were virtually identical in the early years of the CCP, it is clear that leadership during the revolutionary period was monopolized by men.

In accounting for the absence of female leadership and power during the revolutionary period, one historical event deserves special attention: the "white terror" of 1927. After this, the CCP was forced to abandon its urban proletarian strategy as it was pushed into the countryside. The new peasant-based strategy challenged liberal policies promoting women's rights because male peasants who felt their patriarchal rights were threatened vigorously resisted such policies. They feared losing their purchased wives and their property. Their conservatism and their interests made free-choice marriage, divorce, female equality, and women's roles outside the home intolerable. From the party's viewpoint, urban working women who shared the economic oppression of capitalism with men were easily organized into the class struggle. Peasant women, who saw their oppression as a sexist practice, were not.[24]

The shift to a peasant base for the revolution clouded the future of female emancipation. Many studies of Chinese women emphasize the relationship between kinship structure and women's oppression, and view the patriarchal family as the real source of inequality between men and women.[25] But instead of abolishing patriarchal, patrilineal, and patrilocal organization to achieve gender equality, these studies argue that the regime actually reinforced these structures to mobilize a male peasant base. According to Judith Stacey, the communists deliberately "rescued peasant family life from the precipice of destruction"[26] to avoid alienating rural patriarchs whose support was crucial. Instead of creating a new democratic family, the CCP presided over the emergence of a new democratic patriarchy. Land reform democratized patriarchy as land ownership was transferred from an elite class of patriarchs to a vast number of poor male peasants. Agricultural collectivization was organized around existing kinship clusters, further securing patriarchy. The CCP's collaboration with the peasants made it difficult to launch a frontal attack on the patriarchal family. Whenever there was a conflict between women's rights and poor peasants, the CCP chose the latter. Kay Ann Johnson and Phyllis Andors agree with Stacey that the CCP never had a strong commitment to women's emancipation.[27] They view the low priority given to gender equality as intentional because male peasants' support was so crucial to revolutionary success.

This historical legacy constrained women's leadership and participation during the revolution, and also shaped the setting within which women's rights were handled afterward. As Salaff and Merkle note, women were not organized as women during the revolutionary period. The absence of a women's power bloc resulted in a post-revolutionary "star system" promoting individual women as "symbols of the fulfillment of revolutionary promises rather than making a substantial commitment to end the oppression of women *as a category*."[28]

THE DEVELOPMENTAL CONSTRAINT

The liberation of women in China is also bound to the process of political development. In China, as developmental goals have changed over the years, policies concerning women have been adjusted to help the regime achieve those goals and enhance its legitimacy. Women's issues have been subordinated to developmental interests and their relative importance has changed over the years to accommodate China's development. To examine how China's development process[29] has constrained women's emancipation, I will apply a paradigm of political development as a framework. Han S. Park's paradigm of political development draws on Maslow's concept of need-hierarchy which states that human needs are ordered systematically according to their relative urgency for the survival of the organism and the social community.[30] Thus, a given level of need does not emerge as the primary motivational basis of an individual's behavior until she or he is satisfied with, and is confident of, her or his continued ability to meet prior levels of need.

Under these assumptions, Park conceptualizes a needs hierarchy of political demands upon a regime: (1) survival, (2) belongingness, (3) leisure, and (4) control. The most essential requirement in this hierarchy is physical survival—that is, adequate food, shelter, clothing, and security from physical threat. Once this most fundamental need is met, a person will pursue the next need—psychological belongingness. This encompasses a desire for subjectively meaningful interpersonal relationships, including family ties, friendships, and membership in a larger political community. After survival is assured and the need to belong is satisfied, human beings strive for leisure. After people feel that they have enough leisure, they pursue more resources, seeking relative gratification in relation to other people and satisfying their need to control.

Although human needs have an incremental structure, all needs may not be satisfied for every person. This happens only if lower level needs are well secured and maintained. If this is not the case, one might be forced to recoup resources to satisfy a more basic need before seeking the satisfaction of higher level needs. Thus, the process of satisfying all human needs is not necessarily unilinear.

The political dimensions of corresponding human needs also constitute hierarchical stages. At the lowest level, the need for survival is manifest most often when a new nation-state is formed or a new regime in an already existing nation-state is emerging. Such times are often characterized by internal instability and/or external warfare. Thus, the very survival of the members of the society may be endangered. Under these conditions, people naturally seek a regime which can most effectively restore social stability and normal economic activity, irrespective of the type of government. The regime's task in this stage is referred to as "regime formation." In the second stage, in order to cope with the belongingness need, the governmental task focuses on the integration of the political system. As people's needs shift from survival to belongingness, a regime seeks to build ideological consensus on policies and policy orientations. It is during this stage that a regime appeals most strongly to the sentiments, beliefs, and other normative qualities of the governed. If it succeeds in political integration, and serious challenges to basic survival for the majority continue to be avoided or repelled, members of the society turn to material acquisition and leisure. The government, in turn, contributes to this rising expectation for leisure activities by fostering industrialization and other forms of resource expansion. But as people seek relative gratification, the government has no way of satisfying everyone in society—for the gratification of one requires the deprivation of another. In this zero-sum situation, the government's role is to manage social competition and conflict and try to ameliorate its effects.

This conceptual scheme was developed as a paradigm of political development. If these needs are universal and provide the motivational basis of human behavior in all societies, they constitute the basis upon which a regime can build its legitimacy. This hierarchy of needs will be applied to analyze the Chinese case.

The Regime Formation Period (1949–1953)

Proclaiming the People's Republic of China on October 1, 1949, Mao Zedong declared the principal tasks of the new nation to be the consolidation of the socialist regime and the establishment of order under CCP authority. To ensure the basic survival needs of the population, the regime conducted a comprehensive land survey and reform. Aiming to rehabilitate agricultural productivity and eventually collectivize agriculture, the regime, by 1952, had confiscated about 47 million hectares of land and eliminated the landlord class.

The communist revolution was also intended to change the traditional social structure, liberating those oppressed under the traditional society. The new regime incorporated this task into the regime formation process, identifying family law and land reform as keys to social change and instituting the marriage law and the land reform law of 1950. The marriage law emphasized equal rights and the right to free-choice marriages and divorce. It explicitly rejected "the arbitrary and compulsory feudal marriage system, which is based on the superiority of man over woman."[31] It ended arranged marriages, polygamy, concubinage, buying and selling of women, child betrothal, and infanticide. It granted men and women rights to divorce, remarriage, property, and inheritance. The land reform law granted women equal allotments of land. The Chinese government reported that in the beginning, sixty million women acquired land equally with men in central and eastern China alone.[32] More than three million CCP cadres were trained to implement the new laws. In addition, a mass organization for women, the All China Democratic Women's Federation, was established in April 1949 to unite the women's movement under the CCP.

The marriage law was strongly resisted by both men and older women. It came to be known as the divorce law, and resulted in an estimated seventy thousand to eighty thousand suicides and murders of women between 1950 and 1953. Although the campaign was seen as a key to changing the old social structure, establishing a new order, and winning significant popularity for the regime among women, the militant policy also threatened the family as an institution and thereby threatened the regime's stability. The 1953 Government Administration Council's Directive Concerning the Thorough Enforcement of the Marriage Law noted that the death of women "is not only an offense against the equality of the rights of women and their freedom of marriage, but it also affects solidarity among the people, and it badly affects national production and construction and the whole social order."[33] As a result of the severity of popular reactions, the government chose to relax its tactic, and encouraged mediation to resolve family problems.

The First Five Year Plan (1953–1957) and the Great Leap Forward (1958–1960)

The regime formation period in China was primarily a time of economic rehabilitation designed to resume pre-war productivity in agriculture and industry. Economic reconstruction was such a high priority for the survival of the regime that it tolerated some private enterprise during this period in order to avoid disrupting agricultural production by applying excessively drastic socialist measures (see table 6.1). Mao stated in 1945, "China's greatest postwar need is economic development. . . . Neither the farmer nor the Chinese people as a whole are ready for socialism. They will not be ready for a long time to come. It will be necessary to go through a long period of private enterprise, democratically regulated."[34] In 1947, Mao further said, "Even after the country-wide victory of the revolution, it will still be necessary to permit the existence for a long time of a capitalist sector of the economy."[35]

In 1953, the Chinese leadership prepared to launch its major effort to achieve political integration. Ideology plays a very important role at this stage of development. It is a mechanism by which a government tries to institutionalize a belief system upon which the people's sense of belongingness and their loyalty to the regime can be built. A regime provides a program of socialization and political integration to generate

Table 6.1
Socialist Transformation in Industry, 1949–1953

	Industry (share of gross industrial product, without handicrafts)				
		State-capitalistic enterprise			
Year	State enterprise	Total	Mixed state-private firms	Private firms with state contracts	Private enterprise
1949	34.7	9.5	2.0	7.5	55.8
1950	45.3	17.8	2.9	14.9	36.9
1951	45.9	25.4	4.0	21.4	28.7
1952	56.0	26.9	5.0	21.9	17.1
1953	57.5	28.5	5.7	22.8	14.0

Source: Abstracted from Willy Kraus, *Economic Development and Social Change in the People's Republic of China* (New York: Springer-Verlag, 1982), 42.

a belief system that can be shared by most members of the society and can bind them together psychologically. Ideology provides a common political belief system, the psychological basis for the individual's sense of belongingness in the broader political community.

Having consolidated its regime, the leadership, which had up to then been fairly tolerant of private enterprise, accelerated the nationalization of the remaining private industries as well as trade and transportation, and collectivized agriculture through cooperatives. Its goal, the socialist transformation of ownership of the means of production, became reality by the end of the First Five Year Plan (1953–1957). By 1958, 98 percent of peasant households belonged to cooperatives, and the share of retail trade turnover by private trading firms had declined sharply to 2.7 percent of the total.[36]

The government also attempted to mobilize intellectuals and other elite groups fearing that, if alienated, they could serve as a counter-ideological force and pose a persistent impediment to regime-led political integration. Chinese policies to win the support and cooperation of the intellectuals were typified by the slogan, "let a hundred flowers bloom, let a hundred schools of thought contend," under the assumption that the socialist construction of a rich and powerful China could not flourish if only one flower bloomed alone, no matter how beautiful that flower might be.[37] Freedom of independent thinking and debate was guaranteed at least temporarily by the "hundred flowers" doctrine. Even demonstrations and strikes protesting government policies were regarded as legitimate.

However, many of the flourishing ideas and cultural activities of the intellectuals turned out to be a broad wave of anti-communist criticism which did not remain within the boundaries of acceptable diversity. Fearing instability for the system itself, the regime changed its integration strategy. As the attempt to integrate mass belief systems through mobilizing intellectuals failed, the regime inaugurated the Great Leap Forward (GLF) to strengthen political integration through the revolutionary ardor of the masses. Intellectuals were attacked, and ideological education and political consciousness were given renewed emphasis.

During this political integration period, the focus of women's policy also shifted, from achieving equality and liberation from traditional oppression to Engels's liberation through labor. The purpose was to connect women's emancipation to the regime's task of building a socialist China. Through a socialist ideology that could be shared by both men and women, people's belief systems could be integrated and the goal of the regime at this stage achieved. The regime claimed that women had already achieved liberation because the groundwork for equality had been laid in the law. Women were told to turn their energies to productive work to help build socialist China. However, the regime admitted that housework would not be socialized for many years, despite Lenin's dictum that although participation in labor is a necessary condition of female emancipation, real emancipation will begin "only where and when an all-out struggle begins against this petty housekeeping, or rather when its wholesale transformation into a large-scale socialist economy begins."[38] The Chinese leadership merely encouraged women to keep a balance between housework and productive labor.

After the launching of the GLF, housework began to be socialized through mess halls, nurseries, and laundries in the communes to free women for productive labor. By 1958, women accounted for more than one-half of the agricultural labor force. At the same time, women's participation in public and political affairs was encouraged:

> Women's federations must assist the cooperatives in training women backbone elements so that a woman director or deputy director is appointed in every cooperative and a woman chief or

> deputy chief is found in every production squad. Women members, women deputy chiefs, women technicians and women bookkeepers should be increased and promoted every year in the management committees and control committees of the cooperatives.[39]

The eighth CCP Congress convened in 1956. It named four women to be full members of the CC and an additional four as alternates. This was a significant increase because from the first to the seventh Congress, only two women had been named as full members of the CC. The same trend was found at lower levels: local female deputies to the People's Congress doubled to 20 percent from 1951 to 1956; two-thirds of the Agricultural Producers' Cooperatives (APCs) had female deputies or full directors in 1957.[40] Women were encouraged to take on more economic, social, and political roles in an effort to integrate the society through socialist ideology. Although the socialization of housework remained limited, and women had to take on double burdens, they could acquire economic independence through paid labor, become socially active, and hold responsible public positions, all new nontraditional roles.

The Adjustment Phase (1961–1965)

The GLF's efforts to achieve political integration failed. Socialist values and ideas were vigorously implemented but the economic consequences were catastrophic. Exacerbated by the sudden withdrawal of Soviet technicians from China, the first signs of trouble appeared in November 1958. By then, it was apparent that the communes had not attained the desired objectives. Peasant intransigence was blamed for harvest losses estimated at 1.5 million yuan. High absenteeism crippled production. Peasants complained about living quarters, low wages, poor and inadequate food, and the breaking up of the traditional solidarity of the family. Peasants in Honan, for example, attributed 30 percent of the food shortage crisis of that time to natural disaster and 70 percent to human factors.[41] In the fall of 1959, grain production fell to 250 million tons from 375 million tons in 1958, and continued to fall in 1960. Industrial production declined 42 percent from 1960 to 1961, and very severe food shortages swept the country.[42]

At the same time, the drastic reorganization of conventional social structures necessitated by collectivization placed great stress on the extended family system, creating additional turmoil and instability. Social instability and political unrest were further aggravated by the discontent of many party leaders such as Liu Shaoqi and Deng Xiaoping who, in the wake of the collapse of the GLF, criticized Mao's integration strategy and the way the government had implemented revolutionary ideals. By 1960, the deterioration of economic conditions in general and the agrarian depression in particular made Mao's leadership position precarious, threatening the very foundation of the regime. Mao was forced to recognize the gravity of the economic situation and accept the inevitability of dismantling the GLF. By 1960, adjusted targets and efforts ended the GLF.

The first goal of adjustment was to restore the social stability vital to the survival of the regime. To secure basic needs and regime stability, the leadership attached primary importance to the development of agriculture. Confronted with acute food shortages which had spread to the cities, the Central Work Conference of 1960 abandoned "walking on two legs" (the simultaneous development of industry and agriculture), adopting a more realistic formulation. The "agriculture first" policy mobilized all available resources to support agriculture—the "foundation" of the national economy. Industry was shifted to the status of the "leading factor." Thus, "all the people to agriculture and food grains" became a nationwide slogan in 1960.

This reverse development[43] which set the regime back to the first stage inevitably changed policy concerning women. With the deterioration of the economy, the first institutional reforms to be relinquished were the socialized services that freed women for labor outside the home. To shore up the stability of the regime, stable family life was reemphasized and women were encouraged to serve the nation as homemakers and not as production heroines. Women's magazines featured articles on choosing a husband, rearing children, and doing housework.[44]

THE GREAT PROLETARIAN CULTURAL REVOLUTION (1966–1970)

As the chaos of the GLF diminished and the regime recovered its stability, Mao tried to reverse the retreat from socialism in another massive campaign—the Great Proletarian Cultural Revolution (GPCR, CR hereafter). Originating in the Socialist Education Movement (SEM) initiated at the tenth CC plenum held in September 1962, the CR was intended to push Chinese society toward greater integration. Popular reactions to the GLF had convinced Mao that it was necessary to emphasize political education to eliminate the remnants of any Confucian norms and values. Mao was proud of Chinese culture but

Confucian norms such as family-oriented rather than state-oriented authority, and the belief that man should obey rather than dominate the forces of nature, were viewed as detrimental to the complete reorganization of society under socialism. During the GLF, collectivization beyond the extended family had met serious mass resistance. Thus Mao believed it necessary to change the mentality of the Chinese people, and the CR, launched in 1966, was designed to do just that.

The CR had a profound impact on policy concerning women. To integrate China, it was necessary to eliminate the gaps between intellectual and physical work, workers and peasants, the city and the countryside, and men and women. A pamphlet entitled *Between Husband and Wife* argued that the husband-wife relationship was "first of all comradely relations" and that feelings between spouses are "primarily revolutionary sentiments."[45] Husbands were urged to change their traditional values and behavior becoming new types of men who would prepare for the demands of a new society by regarding their wives as revolutionary comrades. Men and women were encouraged to do the same type of work, wear the same clothes, use the same title—"comrade" instead of Mr. or Mrs.—and allow a woman's surname to be the family name.[46]

At the same time, "reactionary bourgeois authorities" in the party, such as Liu Shaoqi and Tung Pien (senior editor of *Women of China*), were severely attacked for taking the "capitalist road" by advocating the special interests of women. Liu was accused of emphasizing sex distinction and neglecting the political work of women as a revolutionary force in the class struggle. Tung Pien was denounced as a "black gang element":

> [Her views] were intended to create ideological confusion so that women cadres and women staff and workers would be intoxicated with the small heaven of motherhood, bearing children, and managing family affairs, and sink into the quagmire of the bourgeois "theory of human nature," forgetting class struggle and disregarding revolution. This is an echo of the reactionary themes advocated by modern revisionism, such as "feminine tenderness," "mother love" and "human sentiments."[47]

Women's magazines attacked traditional marriage norms and re-stressed women's participation in the economic and political sector, describing women as equal revolutionary agents.

The renewed emphasis on political and economic work by women resulted in increased female leadership positions. The ninth Congress of the CCP in 1969 adopted quotas for female party membership. Female full members of the CC increased to 7.6 percent from 4.2 percent in the previous congress,[48] and the first two women were named to the Politburo: Jiang Qing (Mao's wife) and Yeh Chun (Lin Biao's wife). Even though their rise was attributed to marriage rather than to their independent political achievements, in the lower echelons of power women increasingly assumed leadership positions based on their political activities and their reputations as successful workers. During 1966–1973, one-fourth of all party recruits were female.[49]

Consolidation and the Gang of Four (1971–1976)

The second great effort to promote political integration was also a disaster. Mao himself acknowledged that "the Great Cultural Revolution wreaked havoc after I approved Nieh Yuan-tzu's big-character poster. . . . I myself had not foreseen that as soon as the Peking University poster was broadcast (on June 1, 1966) the whole country would be thrown into turmoil. . . . Since it was I who caused the havoc, it is understandable if you have some bitter words for me."[50] As a consequence of the continued struggle between the mostly young Red Guards who sought power and the old guards of the party who resisted them, many cities experienced great chaos. As party and governmental institutions disintegrated, and the chaos of the CR penetrated all segments of society, the security and safety of people's daily lives were endangered. Once again, regime stability, the most basic need of a political community, was at stake. In response, the post-CR leadership replaced the frightening ideological storm with a pragmatism emphasizing the forces of production rather than ideological activism, urging the consolidation of the socioeconomic base and the restoration of law and order. The dominant theme of the CR, "politics can overrule everything else," was repudiated as a fallacy cynically promoted by "swindlers like Liu Shaoqi."

As the CR subsided in the early 1970s, regime stabilization became more visible. During 1973–1976, however, the extreme left Gang of Four sparked a new cultural revolution. With its 1973 "Campaign to Criticize Lin Biao and Confucius," the regime itself pursued the unfinished task of the CR—to erase Confucian values from the mentality of the Chinese people through political education. Lin Biao, like Liu Shaoqi, was attacked for imposing Confucian norms on the masses to undermine the proletarian dictatorship and restore China to the capitalist road. The campaign soon spread to women's issues, arguing that incorrect Confucian theory had imposed the three obediences on women (to fathers, husbands, and sons), and that this

Confucian male supremacy principle was responsible for the oppression of, and discrimination against, women. Women were urged to participate in the campaign in order to guarantee its success. They were mobilized into nationwide study groups to identify and criticize the origins of their oppression and thus to enhance their consciousness. It was argued that as long as women themselves subscribed to Confucian ideology, equality between men and women would not be possible. Although women "hold up half the sky," according to *Women of China*, "without self-awareness a woman will be unwilling to fly though the sky is high."[51] The campaign stressed that not only women but also men should stop believing and living as though women were men's slaves:

> Men comrades should offer to share a portion of the household chores from the standpoint of equality, to enable women comrades to participate properly in social revolution and social construction.[52]

The tenth CCP Congress (1973) featured another increase in female membership on the CC: twenty full members (10%) and twenty-one alternates (16%), the most since the first Congress in 1921. The same trend marked the National People's Congress (NPC) which convened in 1975. Twenty-three percent of the deputies were women compared to 12 percent in the first (1954) and second (1959) NPCs, and 18 percent in the third (1964). The number of female members of standing committees (forty-two) was also the highest at 25 percent.

Great Leap into Resource Expansion

With the death of Mao Zedong and the subsequent purge of the Gang of Four in October 1976, calls for a new cultural revolution came to a halt. China's third attempt at integration had failed, and a pragmatic new leadership brought rapid change in all policy areas. The ambitious program of the "Four Modernizations" was intended to go beyond recovering economic losses caused by the "sabotage and interference" of the Gang. China now launched itself into the third stage of political development—resource expansion. To achieve rapid industrialization, the new leadership opted for resource expansion despite the incomplete integration of the political system.[53] The negative results of previous integration strategies explain why the Chinese leadership shifted to concentrate less on political integration and more on industrialization. Thus, the leadership modified its ideological stance toward market socialism by combining a market mechanism with state planning to facilitate industrialization without necessarily following the road of socialist integration.

Since 1978, the Chinese regime has introduced reforms throughout the economy. It has granted more autonomy to enterprises, integrated market forces with the state plan, decentralized foreign trade activities, and introduced a system of contract responsibility in agriculture. Although many reforms resulted in troublesome consequences and suffered from factional disputes between radical reformists (associated with Zhao Ziyang) and conservative reformists (such as Li Peng), after the Tiananmen Square incident in June 1989 the new general secretary, Jiang Zemin, announced that there would be no change in policy. Radical measures such as price reform were delayed, but there were no fundamental changes in reform principles.

The implications of these new policies for women are double-tiered. Although women would benefit from overall economic progress, the agricultural contract responsibility system and the expansion of sideline production emphasize the family as an economic unit. As many recent studies point out,[54] this has driven rural women back into the household. Under the contract system, an individual household is allotted communal land for cultivation through a long-term contract with the production team that assigns production quotas to member farmers. After submitting the amount specified in its contract, the household may retain the surplus for personal consumption or sale. The mobilization of labor under rural heads of household means that rather than being independent wage earners, rural women work at home. They receive no wages, are socially and economically less active, are ineligible for welfare benefits awarded to state workers, and are subordinate to male heads of household. This system also reinforces the preference for male children for the labor force and, along with the one-child-family policy, encourages female infanticide in the countryside. Furthermore, the demise of agricultural communes reversed the socialization of housework and increased the double burdens on women. In rural areas, young school girls are reported to leave school early to help with housework and child care.[55]

In urban areas, although women benefit from increased employment opportunities, enterprises have become reluctant to hire female workers since the introduction of competition. Competition was previously prohibited since it was regarded as a capitalist concept; now it is encouraged in order to motivate enterprises to reform and reorganize. This shift to competition directly affects women who are assumed to be less productive due to absences related to maternity and child care, and more costly due to paid maternity leave and expenses for women's welfare facilities. The new job contract system threatens women with the prospect of unemployment. According to a 1987 poll of 660 enterprises, 64 percent of their planned layoffs of industrial laborers were projected to be women.[56] In Shanghai, 70 to 80 percent of the unemployed youth in 1984 were women.[57] Women were even blamed for causing urban unemployment, and eliminating women from the work force was often proposed as a solution.[58] In recruitment, some work units required higher examination scores for women than for men to qualify for the same job.[59] Women were also encouraged to quit their jobs voluntarily while receiving 60–70 percent of their salary and to take prolonged maternity leaves which grant 75 percent of salary but no fringe benefits, bonuses, or special subsidies.[60] With the increase in the number of household enterprises and the spread of "putting out," in which enterprises contract with women to work in their homes, increasing numbers of women are engaged in home-based production activities. Thus, industrial reform has adversely affected women's status as enterprises are granted more discretion to discriminate against women.

In the political arena, the twelfth party congress in 1982 elected one woman, Chen Muhua, as an alternate member of the Political Bureau and another, Hao Jianxiu, to the CC Secretariat. The thirteenth congress in 1987 elected no woman to either political body. When asked about this, former General Secretary Zhao Ziyang replied, "It was the hope of us all that some female comrades would join the Political Bureau, but none were elected. However, this doesn't mean we have adjusted our policies on women."[61] Still, women's representation in the CC has continuously decreased from 7 percent in 1977 to 5.1 percent in 1987. From the fourth (1975) to the seventh (1988) NPC, the percentage of female deputies fell from 23 percent to 20 percent. Female representation on standing committees fell from 25 percent in 1975 to 9 percent in 1983 (the sixth NPC). Though this trend was reversed in 1988, when women held 12 percent of standing committee memberships, a decline in the number of women in leading bodies at the county and township levels was also evident.[62]

In some ways the new industrialization policies have created a more positive context supporting women's activities outside the home. They expanded economic opportunities for women, especially in urban areas. At the end of 1986, of sixty-two million urban women of working age (16–54), fifty-one million were in the labor force.[63] The figure can be compared to rates for the United States (54 percent), Great Britain (35.7), France (33.3), and West Germany (32.7). Urban women workers and staff members in 1986 increased by 50 percent over 1978 and accounted for 36.6 percent of the total work force. There were six million enterprises in rural areas of China in 1987, and half of their 64 million employees were women. Today, one out of three advanced researchers in science and technology is a woman and, in the Chinese Academy of Sciences, where there was only one female member before 1982, fifteen women had received that honor by 1986.

The number of single-child families increased following the introduction of the population management responsibility system, which offers women the possibility of fewer household chores and more free time for outside activities. At the same time, there has been renewed attention to freedom of marriage and the property rights of women under the marriage law of 1980 and the inheritance law of 1986. In 1985, China opened the No. 8 Legal Counselling Office of the Dongcheng District in Beijing giving legal assistance to women and children, the first office in China to be devoted exclusively to women's rights. It was reported that today 70 percent of divorces are initiated by women in contrast to the feudal marriage system where only men could initiate divorce. It is even argued that "an increase [in the divorce rate] as such is not inherently bad; in encouraging freedom of marriage, China includes freedom to divorce. It is vital to women's emancipation."[64] Thus China's entry into the resource expansion stage created both adverse consequences and new opportunities for women.

CONCLUSION

Women's emancipation in China has been continuously constrained by ideological, historical, and developmental factors. However, the prospect for the future is not necessarily gloomy. As China progresses toward a more industrialized society, some of these constraints are likely to be alleviated. China has already modified its ideology to adopt market socialism. The stringent ideology that requires women to wait for their emancipation until the country achieves a full-fledged socialist state is also likely to be modified to become more tolerant of feminist goals and activities. At the same time, the basis of the historical constraints, China's patriarchal kinship structure, is also undergoing change. As Stacey points out, rural cooperatives were initially organized around natural villages where most households were related through male members; kin relationships contributed to collectivization and, in turn, collectivization strengthened patriarchy.[65] Because the current contract responsibility system signals a clear departure from collective farming, it could eventually weaken traditional ties among village members. Moreover, with increasingly open competition, income inequalities are rising among families in the villages which are gradually becoming competitors rather than parts of a collective unit. This could weaken patrilineal kinship solidarity and thus the most important structural threat to women's rights. Finally, as China becomes more industrialized, women themselves will benefit from increasing prosperity, although this hope is tinged by the increasingly explicit discrimination against women accompanying reform. The developmental constraint can be expected to continue to persist.

Women's self-consciousness can also be expected to increase when China is ready to move into the next stage of development—conflict management—intended to accommodate the esteem and self-actualization needs of the individual. In fact, there is already a rise in female activism in China, affected by the more relaxed political atmosphere and increasing exposure to Western feminist ideas. Emily Honig and Gail Hershatter noted the appearance of "feminist outcries," women's magazines, and autonomous grass-roots women's organizations such as women's studies groups and women's professional associations in the mid-1980s.[66] The increasingly outspoken All-China Women's Federation advocates women's rights and speaks out against the abuse of women and anti-woman discrimination in the workplace. In 1986, for the first time in China, the organization even sponsored a conference on theories in women's studies.

After the Tiananmen Square incident, enthusiasm for women's studies and public discussion of gender discrimination did not disappear. In June 1990, the Sino-American Conference on Women's Issues was held in Beijing. In March 1991, the Women-Development-Media Seminar was held under the auspices of UNESCO, at which various problems including women's disadvantaged position resulting from China's reforms and open-door policy were discussed.[67] Although these developments represent an emergence of feminist consciousness, they have not developed into an organized women's movement.[68] The vast majority of Chinese women residing in rural areas have yet to achieve feminist self-consciousness. The conflict management developmental stage could encourage the emergence of more autonomous feminist groups and a political, economic, and social environment more favorable to women. When China's ideological, historical, and developmental legacies are overcome, and women themselves demand change, the movement and campaigns for women's emancipation will be more meaningful, and their effect more salient.

NOTES

1. See Jack Belden, *China Shakes the World* (New York: Monthly Review, 1970); and Claudia Broyelle, *Women's Liberation in China* (New York: Atlantic Highlands, 1977). This optimistic view was also shared by many committed

feminists such as Linda Gordon, Sheila Rowbotham, Ruth Sidel, and Gloria Steinem. See Sue Gronewold, "Women in China: A Revolution of Their Own?" *Trends in History* 4, no. 1 (1985): 28.

2. See, for example, Phyllis Andors, *The Unfinished Liberation of Chinese Women, 1949–1980* (Bloomington: Indiana University Press and Wheatsheaf Books, 1983); Elisabeth Croll, *Feminism and Socialism in China* (New York: Schocken Books, 1980); Kay Ann Johnson, *Women, the Family and Peasant Revolution in China* (Chicago: University of Chicago Press, 1983); Judith Stacey, *Patriarchy and Socialist Revolution in China* (Berkeley: University of California Press, 1983); and Margery Wolf, *Revolution Postponed: Women in Contemporary China* (Stanford: Stanford University Press, 1985).

3. Phyllis Andors, "Social Revolution and Woman's Emancipation: China During the Great Leap Forward," *Bulletin of Concerned Asian Scholars* 7, no. 1 (January–March 1975): 35.

4. Shelah Leader, "The Emancipation of Chinese Women," *World Politics* 26, no. 1 (October 1973): 65.

5. Ibid., 66.

6. Mariam Frenier, "Aids and Barriers to Feminism in Modern China: The Effects of War and Economic Change on the Rate of Advance of Chinese Women's Status," *International Journal of Women's Studies* 1, no. 3 (1978): 274–75.

7. Suzette Leith, "Chinese Women in the Early Communist Movement," in *Women in China: Studies in Social Change and Feminism*, ed. Marylyn B. Young (Ann Arbor: Center for Chinese Studies, University of Michigan, 1973), 48.

8. Ibid., 49.

9. Xing was very critical of a bourgeois women's movement and criticized that most feminist groups did not include lower-class women. See ibid., 51.

10. See Johnson, *Women, the Family and Peasant Revolution.*

11. Judith Stacey, "When Patriarchy Kowtows: The Significance of the Chinese Family Revolution for Feminist Theory," *Feminist Studies* 2, no. 2–3 (1975): 75.

12. Joan Maloney, "Women in the Chinese Communist Revolution: The Question of Political Equality," in *Women, War, and Revolution*, ed. Carol Berkin and Clara Lovett (New York: Holmes and Meier Publishers, 1980), 167.

13. Ibid., 170.

14. Chinese Communist Party Soviet Central Committee, "May Work Report and the Women's Movement," in Frenier, "Aids and Barriers to Feminism," 279.

15. Stacey, "When Patriarchy Kowtows," 77.

16. Anita Chan, "Rural Chinese Women and the Socialist Revolution: An Inquiry into the Economics of Sexism," *Journal of Contemporary Asia* 4, no. 2 (1974): 198–99.

17. Cai Chang's rise to the CC was assumed to be owed more to her husband, Li Fuchuan, a life long friend of Mao's and one of the founders of the CCP, than to her own work, although she was an active worker in the women's movement during the Jiangxi and Yenan periods. See Maloney, "Women in the Chinese Communist Revolution," 178.

18. Leith, "Chinese Women in the Early Communist Movement," 67.

19. Ibid., 66.

20. Gerhard Lenski, *Power and Privilege: A Theory of Social Stratification* (New York: McGraw-Hill, 1966).

21. Janet Weitzner Salaff and Judith Merkle, "Women in Revolution: The Lessons of the Soviet Union and China," *Berkeley Journal of Sociology* 15 (1970): 182.

22. *Women of China* (October 1986): 27.

23. Salaff and Merkle, "Women in Revolution," 182.

24. Leith, "Chinese Women in the Early Communist Movement," 65.

25. For example, Andors, *The Unfinished Liberation of Chinese Women*; Stacey, *Patriarchy and Socialist Revolution*; and Johnson, *Women, the Family and Peasant Revolution.*

26. Stacey, *Patriarchy and Socialist Revolution*, 108.

27. Johnson, *Women, the Family and Peasant Revolution*; and Andors, *The Unfinished Liberation of Chinese Women.*

28. Salaff and Merkle, "Women in Revolution," 190 (emphasis added).

29. For an account of Chinese political development, see Han Shik Park and Kyung Ae Park, *China and North Korea: Politics of Integration and Modernization* (Hong Kong: Asian Research Service, 1990).

30. Han S. Park, *Human Needs and Political Development: A Dissent to Utopian Solutions* (Cambridge: Schenkman Publishing Co., 1984). For a comparative discussion of the paradigm and other development theories, see chaps. 1, 2, and 3.

31. Stacey, "When Patriarchy Kowtows," 81.

32. Katie Curtin, "Women and the Chinese Revolution," *International Socialist Review* 35, no. 3 (March 1974): 25.

33. Leader, "The Emancipation of Chinese Women," 62.

34. Willy Kraus, *Economic Development and Social Change in the People's Republic of China* (New York: Springer-Verlag, 1982), 13.

35. Ibid., 15.

36. State Statistical Bureau, ed., *Ten Great Years: Statistics of the Economic and Cultural Achievements of the People's Republic of China* (Beijing: Foreign Languages Press, 1960), 40.

37. Speech by Lu Dingyi, director of the propaganda section of the Central Committee, 20 May 1956.

38. V. Lenin, "A Great Beginning," in *The Emancipation of Women: From the Writings of V.I. Lenin* (N.Y.: International Publishers, 1966), 63–64, in Phyllis Andors, "A Look at the Present Socio-Economic and Political Context of the Changing Role of Women and the Family in China," *The Australian and New Zealand Journal of Sociology* 12, no. 1 (1976): 23.

39. National Women's Federation Draft for Realizing the "National Program for Agriculture," *NCNA*, 8 March 1956, in Andors, "Social Revolution," 35.

40. Curtin, "Women and the Chinese Revolution," 34.

41. Byung-Joon Ahn, "The Political Economy of the People's Commune in China: Changes and Continuities," *Journal of Asian Studies* 34, no. 3 (May 1975): 634.

42. Joint Economic Committee, Congress of the U.S., *Chinese Economy: Post-Mao* (Washington, D.C.: U.S. Government Printing Office, 1978), 208.

43. For more about reverse development, see Park, *Human Needs and Political Development*, 85–92.

44. Salaff and Merkle, "Women in Revolution," 188. *Women of China* printed such articles as "Engag[ing] in Enterprises is Like Flying Kites Under the Bed," "Women Live for the Purpose of Raising Children," and "Women Should Do More Family Duties."

45. Leader, "The Emancipation of Chinese Women," 70.

46. Wen Lang Li, "Changing Status of Women in Mainland China," *Issues and Studies* 24, no. 3 (March 1988): 124.

47. Cited in Salaff and Merkle, "Women in Revolution," 187.

48. Maloney, "Women in the Chinese Communist Revolution," 173.

49. Ibid., 172.

50. Mao Zedong, "Talk to Leaders of the Center," 21 July 1966, in Stuart Schram, *Mao Tse-tung: Unrehearsed Talks and Letters 1956–1971* (London: Penguin Books, 1974), 253.

51. Elisabeth Croll, "A Recent Movement to Redefine the Role and Status of Women," *The China Quarterly* 71 (Spring 1977): 592.

52. From the *Guangming People's Daily*, 8 July 1973, in Andors, "A Look at the Present Socio-Economic and Political Context," 25.

53. The fragile political integration stage could invite a reverse development as demonstrated in the Tiananmen Square incident.

54. See studies in Susan Williams O'Sullivan, "Traditionalizing China's Modern Women," *Problems of Communism* 34 (November–December, 1985), n. 2; Elisabeth Croll, *Chinese Women Since Mao* (New York: M. E. Sharpe, 1983); and Emily Honig and Gail Hershatter, *Personal Voices: Chinese Women in the 1980s* (Stanford: Stanford University Press, 1988).

55. Wolf, *Revolution Postponed*, 126–133.

56. *Beijing Review* 31, no. 44 (31 October–6 November 1988): 19.

57. Honig and Hershatter, *Personal Voices*, 246.

58. Ibid., 252.

59. Ibid., 245.

60. Ibid., 253–54.

61. *Beijing Review* 31, no. 10 (7–13 March 1988): 27.

62. Ibid., 27.

63. *Beijing Review* 30, no. 41 (12 October 1987): 23.

64. *Beijing Review* 31, no. 21 (23–29 May 1988): 24–25.

65. Stacey, *Patriarchy and Socialist Revolution*, 211.

66. See Honig and Hershatter, *Personal Voices*, chapter 9.

67. *Women of China*, July 1991, 18-19.

68. Honig and Hershatter, *Personal Voices*, 325.

Chapter 7

Women and Revolution in South and North Korea

Kyung Ae Park

Studies of the position of women in society disagree on the type of social system most conducive to the emancipation of women. The Western liberal modernization perspective predicts that industrialization will remove traditional constraints on women, changing the traditional sexual division of labor and thereby fostering women's liberation. The widespread subordination or marginalization of women in capitalist societies is interpreted as a deviation from Western norms of equality, freedom, and justice, and is explained by history: the fruits of modernization have primarily benefitted men because only men worked in the public sphere while women were confined to the domestic sphere. The problem of sexual inequality is presumed solvable within the capitalist system through reforms such as legal and attitudinal changes: women can be liberated by being integrated into the process of modernization and the public sphere of capitalist structures.

The Marxist perspective views the roots of sexual inequality, like other forms of social inequality including class hierarchy, as occurring in the institution of private property. Private property depends upon the family institution to preserve wealth through inheritance in the

---

An earlier version of this paper was presented at the 1990 meeting of the American Political Science Association in San Francisco. I would like to thank Cindy Kobayashi, Gerry Kosasa-Terry, Marta Savigliano, and Mary Ann Tétreault for helpful comments.

paternal line. In the bourgeois family, a woman is the property of her husband. Her responsibilities include unpaid domestic production and reproduction. Hence, according to this perspective, wives are the proletariat exploited by bourgeois husbands. Accordingly, the oppression of women is a structural problem that cannot be solved within capitalism. The subordination of women can only be ended by a socialist revolution that will eventually free women from unpaid domestic labor and integrate them into social production.

The socialist system of North Korea and the capitalist system of South Korea are ideal laboratories in which to examine the two perspectives in an empirical context. This chapter analyzes how different patterns of social change have affected Korean women's position by comparing the status of women in North and South Korea. A number of issues will be addressed, including the status of women in traditional society; women's roles in, and their contributions to, the revolutionary changes in their respective societies; the relationship between the socialist revolution and women's status in post-revolutionary North Korea; and the relationship between capitalist economic development and women's status in South Korea.

North Korea is an extremely closed system and a dearth of data severely limits any study of that country. Few earlier studies touched on the subject of women. Of those that did, most were short accounts of fact-finding trips to North Korea. As one scholar notes, information on North Korean women is "conspicuous by its absence in most studies on women in post-revolutionary societies."[1] The present study is based mainly on North Korean sources, including a women's magazine, the speeches of President Kim Il Sung, newspapers, and other government publications. South Korean government sources were also consulted.

KOREAN WOMEN BEFORE 1945

In traditional Korean society, women lived under a social system where kinship and patriarchal orders dictated their daily lives. Before the Yi Dynasty (1392–1910) when neo-Confucianism was adopted as the official ideological basis of social organization, women appeared to have had more freedom and legal rights and to have enjoyed a higher status,[2] although this did not mean that women were treated as equals to men. During the Shilla period (fourth century–918) three queens ruled. Shilla women had the right to be heads of families. During the Koryo period (918–1392), equal property inheritance between men and women was a common practice and women's remarriage was socially acceptable. Confucian ideology, which was firmly entrenched during the Yi Dynasty, severely restricted women's freedom. Gender segregation began at the age of seven. Men stayed in the outer part of the house (*sarangchae*) while women stayed in the inner part (*anchae*). Adhering to a rigid hierarchical order based on age, sex, and class, the society encouraged women to follow Confucian ideals and to attain Confucian virtues. A virtuous woman obeyed men throughout her life: in youth, she obeyed her father; when married, she obeyed her husband; if her husband died, she was subject to her son. Confucius's teachings also set forth the "seven evils" (*chilgo Chiak*) justifying the expulsion of a wife from the household: disobeying parents-in-law, bearing no son, committing adultery, jealousy, carrying a hereditary disease, garrulousness, and larceny.[3] Women were powerless, dependent, and suffered from patriarchal oppression.

During the nineteenth century, however, various movements altered the traditional social system. New schools of thought, such as *Silhak* (practical learning) and *Tonghak* (Eastern learning), coupled with Western influence through Christianity, advocated human rights and the equality of people regardless of social class or gender,[4] the improvement of women's status, and universal education. Toward the end of the Yi Dynasty, missionaries supported women's education. The first modern school for women, *Ewha Haktang*, was established in 1886. Ironically, during this time, Western-educated men were more likely to emphasize the need for women's education than were women.[5] Male intellectuals, such as So Chae Pil and Yun Chi Ho, advocated women's liberation through the activities of their organization, the Independence Club, and the first nongovernmental newspaper, *Tongnip Shinmun*.

Encouraged by these reform movements, the first Korean women's rights organization, *Chanyang-hoe*, was organized in 1898, and issued the first declaration of women's rights in Korea:

> Why should our women live on what their husbands earn as if fools, confining themselves to their deep chambers all their lives and subjecting themselves to regulations imposed by their husbands? In enlightened countries, both men and women are equal. Women's skills and principles are equal to those possessed by their husbands. . . . We are going to establish a girl's school with the aim of making women equal to men.[6]

Led by upper-class widows, *Chanyang-hoe* promoted women's education. The government responded, although slowly, establishing the first public girls' school, Hansong Girls' High School, in 1908. In 1899, another women's rights group, *Yo-u-hoe* (Association of Women

Friends), was organized. It staged the first sit-in demonstration by women to protest customs such as concubinage. During the early twentieth century, numerous women's organizations were formed. They were soon suppressed by the Japanese after the annexation of Korea in 1910 because female activists were also involved in independence movements.

After that, until the liberation of Korea in 1945, the women's movement was primarily devoted to gaining the nation's independence rather than to feminist concerns. Several underground patriotic women's organizations were formed, including the *Yosong Aeguk Tongji-hoe* (Patriotic Women's League) and the *Taehan Aeguk Buin-hoe* (Korean Patriotic Women's Society). They collected funds for resistance campaigns and inspired anti-Japanese sentiments among their members. Although women's political activities were founded on the independence movement, some religious and civic organizations engaged in feminist work to improve women's social and economic position.[7] These included organizations established by socialist women who advocated women's emancipation over economic independence under a socialist system. The *Kyungsung Yoja Chongnyon Dongmaeng*, in particular, advocated revolutionary class struggle to achieve women's liberation by organizing proletarian women. The founders of these groups included wives of the leaders of the Korean communist movement.[8]

Female participation in the independence movement did not affect women's status in post-liberation societies. There were independence heroines and martyrs but, except for some communist women, they did not participate in any actual fighting.[9] Hence, women did not gain control of the means of coercion, which, according to Janet Salaff and Judith Merkle, would have guaranteed their power.[10] No specific information is available on communist women's army units during the revolutionary period. However, in a May 1946 speech to the Women's Union, President Kim Il Sung of North Korea maintained that female guerrilla army members "fought arms in hand, for the freedom and independence of their country, the emancipation of Korean women and sex equality."[11] In the Anti-Japanese Guerrilla Army, "the women were completely on an equal footing with men; they all received revolutionary assignments suited to their abilities and aptitudes and carried them out."[12] Later, he praised women's dedication of "the bloom of their youth to the struggle . . . shedding their blood in the alien mountains and wilderness of Manchuria."[13] These statements indicate that some communist women did actually fight.

In an interview with Western scholars, officials of the [North]

Korean Democratic Women's Union emphasized that women contributed greatly to the anti-Japanese movement by participating "in armed struggle like men."[14] North Korea today hails Kim Jong Suk (President Kim's deceased wife and mother of heir-designate, Kim Jong Il) as a revolutionary fighter and a communist leader for women's liberation.[15] At her birth place, Hoeryong, a Hoeryong Revolutionary Site has been set aside where the gun that she used to fight against the Japanese is displayed. Since the late 1960s, North Korea has commemorated her birthday. Her achievements during the revolutionary period have been praised in newspapers, publications by the Democratic Women's Union, commentaries by the Central Broadcasting Station, poems, songs, and slogans such as "Learn from Comrade Kim Jong Suk." The women's magazine, *Choson Yosong (Korean Women)*, has also published numerous articles praising her.[16]

Although the degree of communist women's participation in the revolution, especially in actual armed struggle, may not have been significant enough to affect their status following independence, their participation has been clearly recognized and praised in North Korea. There is no indication of noncommunist women's engagement in actual fighting.

STATUS OF WOMEN IN SOUTH AND NORTH KOREA

The Economic Arena

South Korea. South Korea's primary economic development strategy has been labor-intensive, export-oriented industrialization. Exports surged from $41 million in 1961 to $65 billion in 1990, mostly from manufacturing industries. South Korea's comparative advantage in the world trade system lies in its abundance of low-wage and unskilled labor, mainly young people and women. Their mobilization enabled South Korea to specialize in exporting labor-intensive products. Manufacturing industries account for 83 percent of South Korea's exports, about 25 percent of its GNP, and between 5 and 10 percent of its annual growth.[17] The rapid growth of manufacturing industries is well reflected in the shift in the labor force structure: between 1960 and 1990, the labor force in primary industry dropped from 81 percent to 18 percent, while the distribution for secondary and tertiary industries jumped from 5 to 28 percent and from 14 to 54 percent, respectively.[18]

South Korea's development strategy brought women into the national economy. Between 1963 and 1990, the number of female workers increased fourteen times. The economically active female population fourteen years of age or older increased from two million in 1960 to six million in 1985, faster than male workers,[19] and reached 7.5 million in 1990.[20] The female labor force participation rate rose from 28 percent to 47 percent between 1960 and 1989, while the male rate decreased over that period.[21]

A careful examination of the structure of the labor force suggests that women's participation was crucial to the success of manufacturing industry, the engine of South Korea's economic development (see table 7.1).[22] The rapid increase in the number of female industrial workers has expanded "female manufacturing industries," where women account for more than half of all workers. These include textile and clothing manufacturing, rubber and plastic, electronic goods, shoes, and china and pottery manufacturing.[23] These were responsible for 70 percent of total national export earnings in 1975: about 80 percent of the women in the manufacturing sector produced export-oriented products in the 1970s.[24] Throughout the 1980s, over 70 percent of female industrial wageworkers were employed in the manufacturing sector, accounting for about 40 percent of the work force.[25] These statistics show the extent to which women took a leading role in the industrial frontier and became a crucial force for industrial development.

Despite extensive female participation in economic development, the status of women in the economic arena appears to be far from satisfactory. A great discrepancy exists between women's contributions and their economic rewards. Even a cursory examination suggests that women receive less than half the pay of their male counterparts. Until 1987, the average women's wage was always less than half the wage for male workers. It was only in 1988 that women began to receive at least half the average male wage. Between 1980 and 1988, South Korea recorded the highest wage difference between men and women among the twenty-one countries for which data were available.[26] According to a South Korean Ministry of Labor report on wage levels in industry, the manufacturing industry, where the majority of women are employed, has the lowest wage level, the only one whose wages have always been below the average.[27] Data released by the International Labor Office for 1988 show that the average female wage as a percentage of the average male wage in manufacturing was 67 percent for Costa Rica, 89 for Paraguay, 59 for Cyprus, 68 for Czechoslovakia, 89 for Sri Lanka, 58 for Singapore, and 74 for Hong Kong.[28] Even compared to other Third World countries, South Korea, at 51 percent, shows a large wage differential.

Salary discrepancies occur not only between the wages of male and female industrial workers with low levels of education and skills, but

Table 7.1
Employed Women by Industry (in 1,000 persons, %)

Year	Industry			
	Total Number	Primary	Secondary	Tertiary
1963	2,674	1,837	186	651
	(100.0)	(68.7)	(7.0)	(24.3)
1976	4,820	2,388	1,031	1,401
	(100.0)	(49.5)	(21.4)	(29.1)
1980	5,222	2,034	1,166	2,022
	(100.0)	(39.0)	(22.3)	(38.7)
1985	5,833	1,619	1,356	2,858
	(100.0)	(27.8)	(23.2)	(49.0)
1990	7,341	1,499	2,058	3,785
	(100.0)	(20.4)	(28.0)	(51.6)

Source: Economic Planning Board, Republic of Korea, *Annual Report on the Economically Active Population Survey,* each year.

also between those of workers with higher levels of education. In 1989, the gender differential in wages for college-educated workers was 100 to 68 in favor of men.[29] Wage discrepancy becomes greater as years of employment are accumulated. In 1989, the initial wage difference between men and women was only 100 to 78, while the average wage for all women workers is about half the wage for men. Increasing wage difference according to years of employment is clearly shown in the case of the manufacturing industry. In 1989, the wage difference between men and women employed for less than a year was 100 to 65. The ratio for women steadily decreased to 61, 57, 53, and 51 as the duration of employment increased to 1–2 years, 3–4 years, 5–9 years, and 10–14 years, respectively.[30]

In South Korea, women work more hours than men. In 1983, among the seventeen countries for which data were available, South Korea was the only nation where women worked longer hours than men.[31] In 1988, South Korea was still the only nation where women's working hours were longer than men's among the fifteen countries that released data to the International Labor Office. In manufacturing, women worked an average of 245 hours per month in 1984, four hours more than men.[32] Women worked an average of 9.7 hours a day, more than the legal eight-hour day, compared to nine hours for men. Although this discrepancy decreased in 1989, the same pattern continued.[33]

The traditional gender division of labor also remains unchanged despite the growth in female labor force participation. For example, in 1989, women comprised 1.9 percent of administrators and managers.[34] On the other hand, clerical work is becoming a predominantly female occupation. The percentage of female workers in that field surged from 5.6 percent in 1960 to 36 percent in 1989.[35]

Women's economic equality has yet to be achieved in South Korea. Some even point to sex discrimination as the catalyst of the rapid industrialization of South Korea, providing industries with cheap labor and thus their superior competitive position in the international economic system. It is an irony that discriminatory measures contributed to the country's rapid economic growth, and in turn, growth itself deepened discrimination.

North Korea. Classical Marxist theory posits that sexual equality results from economic liberation. Friedrich Engels argues: "The first requisite for the emancipation of women is that all women participate again in social labor; to achieve this, individual families are required to be no longer the units of the social economy."[36] Kim Il Sung embraced this idea saying: "The women . . . can achieve complete emancipation only if they strive with no less devotion and awareness than men to solve the problems arising on the productive fronts of the factories and countryside."[37] Accordingly, North Korea initiated the "working-classization" of women to enhance their economic independence.

In the late 1950s, the government initiated a mass mobilization campaign called the *Chollima* (flying horse) movement. Its aims were to reach a revolutionary high tide of socialist construction and realize industrialization through the mobilization of the masses. In this campaign, women's policy focused on Engels's "liberation through labor" on the premise that women's emancipation would be achieved only through loyalty to the regime's task of building a socialist Korea. Women were told to turn their energies to productive work to help build socialist Korea. Kim Il Sung made this point clear:[38]

> An important question in Women's Union activities in the past was to wipe out illiteracy and eliminate the feudalistic ideas that oppressed the women. But this work no longer seems to be of major importance in our society. Today, the Women's Union should actively campaign for women's participation in socialist

> construction and bend its efforts to provide conditions that will allow them to work well.

Women were encouraged to act "as one wheel of a wagon in the work of nation-building."

To mobilize women outside the family, the regime advocated the socialization of housework. According to Lenin, although participation in labor is a necessary condition for women's emancipation, real emancipation begins "only where and when an all-out struggle begins against this petty housekeeping."[39] This echoes Engels who said that true equality comes only when "private housekeeping is transformed into a social industry, [and] the care and education of children become a public affair."[40] In 1946, Kim Il Sung urged that the state take steps to rear children under public care to encourage women to take part in public life.[41] In 1970, the Fifth Congress of the Korean Workers' Party (KWP) made freeing women from the heavy burden of the household a major goal of the party. Article 62 of the Socialist Constitution of 1972 provides benefits—including maternity leave with pay, maternity hospitals, free nurseries and kindergartens, and reduced working hours for mothers of large families—to ensure that women participate in public life. The 1976 Law on the Nursing and Upbringing of Children and the 1978 Socialist Labor Law stipulated that women with three or more children under thirteen years of age receive eight hours of pay for six hours of work. Legal provisions stated clearly that it was the responsibility of the state and society to rear children and protect working mothers.

With the launching of the *Chollima* movement, housework began to be socialized through nurseries, kindergartens, laundries, and an efficient food industry. Started with only 12 nurseries and 116 kindergartens in 1949, by 1961 there were 7,600 and 4,500, respectively, caring for 700,000 children.[42] There is also a network of food "take out" services for busy working women. One Women's Union member summarizes the socialization of housework in North Korea:

> Children are brought up at state expense. If there is pressing and ironing [to be done] it goes to the laundries. The foodstuffs industry has been developed, so food can be bought at any time. So what is there left to do in the family?[43]

Although her statement is exaggerated, accounts by defectors from North Korea indicate that various measures for the socialization of housework have begun to be implemented,[44] while women were urged to participate vigorously in the technical revolution by acquiring at least one technical skill in order to free themselves from arduous labor.[45]

All these measures and the *Chollima* mass mobilization campaign greatly expanded women's participation in the labor force. The female labor force, which accounted for only 20 percent of the total in 1956, has steadily increased, and women now constitute about 49 percent of the total labor force.[46] Women play a particularly prominent role in agriculture, light industry, and education.

Recently, North Korea has experienced severe economic difficulty. Due to its increasing trade deficit, foreign debt expanded from $4.7 billion in 1987 to $6.7 billion in 1989, and the annual economic growth rate dropped from 3.3 percent in 1987 to 2.4 percent in 1989. North Korea recorded its first negative growth rate, minus 3 percent, in 1990. Kim Il Sung himself acknowledged that North Korean people are not leading affluent lives.[47] To raise living standards and combat the widespread shortage of food and consumer goods, North Korea declared 1989 to be the year of light industries, and announced a new work-harder campaign, "Speed of the 1990s." As North Korea shifted its emphasis from heavy to light industry, some women were mobilized into household production teams designed to promote sideline production. Women's mobilization based on the new emphasis on light industry and the work-harder campaign is expected to increase because public demand for consumer goods is certain to grow.

Nevertheless, North Korean women can hardly be said to have achieved a level of economic status equal to men's. There are indications that the male and female wage structure is not equitable in North Korea, although no official information on pay scales is available. According to one source, income distribution between a husband and a wife is such that the husband's income is always higher than that of the wife.[48] The husband remains the primary source of income in a typical household and the wife is considered a side-income earner. The wage difference also reflects the unequal representation of women within occupational structures, indicating a gender division of labor. Women are concentrated in low-wage occupations. For example, the monthly salary of an elementary school teacher ranges from 80–120 *won*, but a college professor earns between 100–250 *won*.[49] Women constitute more than 80 percent of elementary school teachers, but only 15 percent of college professors.

Since the late 1980s, women, especially those married to high-income earners, have tended to quit their jobs after marriage.[50] Married women's labor force participation has declined to the point that a majority of married women do not work outside the home.[51] Several factors account for this change. The decline in the national economy reduces economic opportunity, especially for married women who are assumed to be the first ones laid off. In addition, some married women give up their jobs voluntarily because they can generate income working in sideline production teams while staying at home. This reduces their double burdens of housework and economic employment, although it increases their economic dependence. All of this suggests that discrimination against women still exists in North Korea despite socialist ideology and legal provisions mandating equality. North Korean women have been unable to achieve economic equality and recent trends are no grounds for optimism in this alleged paradise where women are presumed to have already achieved liberation.

The Social Arena

South Korea. Following independence, South Korea's 1948 Constitution introduced legal equality between the sexes. Article 8 guaranteed the equality of all citizens and prohibited any political, economic, or social discrimination on account of sex, religion, or social status. Unlike women in the West who had to fight for their rights, Korean women were "given" equality. However, despite the marked improvement in women's participation, especially in educational and economic areas, this constitutional guarantee has not produced enhanced social status.

A case in point is South Korea's 1957 family law which became effective in 1960. It contained many male-dominant provisions regarding marriage, divorce, and inheritance and sparked the formation of the Pan-Women's Society for the Revision of the Family Law by sixty-one women's organizations in 1973. The Society proposed a revision of the family law to the National Assembly in 1975 but opposition to the revised bill by the Confucian community forced the Society to accept much less than it had hoped for. The 1977 version of the family law maintained the patrilineal family system designating the eldest male as the head of the family, *hoju*. The eldest son of a family could not give up his position regardless of his age: even a two-year-old boy could become a *hoju*.[52] The 1977 law included other discriminatory practices, such as different boundaries defining relationships with the husband's and the wife's families, and limited the wife's role in adoption proceedings, parental authority, division of property, and divorce.

The struggle to promote women's rights through revisions in the family law continued, and finally a new family law went into effect in January 1991. It did not completely abolish the controversial family head system, but greatly limited the family head's power and also introduced a succession system. The eldest son may now give up his position and another member of the family can be chosen to succeed to the headship. The new family law also permits a divorcing woman to claim a share of property according to her contribution in gaining the property, and to claim custody of children, formerly awarded automatically to the husband. If a controversy arises over custody upon divorce, it is decided by the courts. The provision defining family membership now includes eighth cousins without differentiating between husbands and wives. The new family law may appear to signify a victory for women, but the nearly three decades of struggle needed to achieve it indicates the persistence of Confucian values which prevents the realization of a fully egalitarian social system. Even the newly amended version of the family law retains clauses which discriminate against women, including the provision that the eldest son is automatically designated the head of household.

North Korea. The communist revolution sought to change the traditional social structure and liberate those oppressed under it. North Korean leaders incorporated this task into the regime formation process. As early as 1946, they launched a series of campaigns and reforms, including family and land reforms and the nationalization of all enterprises that had been owned by Japanese capitalists or Korean collaborators. Concurrently, various laws promoting social change were promulgated by the Provisional People's Committee, such as the law on land reform, the law on sex equality, the labor law, and the law on the nationalization of essential industries.

In March 1946, agrarian reform was instituted with some one million *chongbo* of land confiscated for redistribution gratis among about 724,000 poor and landless peasants. Women were granted equal allotments of land as Kim Il Sung noted: "At the time of the agrarian reform women in the countryside received their share of land on a par with men and became the owners of lands like all the rest of the peasants."[53] The most progressive change in the traditional position of women was the law on sex equality, announced on 30 July 1946. Intended to "transform the old feudal relations of the sexes" and to encourage women to "participate fully in cultural, social, and political life," the law emphasized equal rights in all spheres—the right to free marriage and divorce, and equal rights to inherit property and to share property in case of divorce. It ended arranged marriages, polygamy, concubinage, the buying and selling of women, prostitution, and the professional entertainer system. Thus, for the first time in history, women were legally placed on an equal footing with men.

The North Korean labor law defined women's rights at work. Articles 14 through 17 stipulated the rights of mothers and pregnant women, including seventy-seven days of maternity leave with full pay,[54] paid baby-feeding breaks during work, a prohibition against overtime or night work for pregnant or nursing women, and the transfer of a pregnant woman to lighter work with equal pay. The law on nationalization of essential industries, which began the elimination of private property, weakened the economic power of patriarchs. The transformation of the ownership of the means of production became reality by the end of the 1950s. As Engels had urged, efforts were made to replace individual families with collectives as the units of the social economy. The total collectivization of agriculture and industry which accompanied the *Chollima* movement greatly contributed to the weakening of patriarchal power: elimination of private property led to the demolition of inheritance, destroying the material basis of traditional patriarchy.

In 1946, the mass organization for women, the Democratic Women's Union of North Korea, was established to unite the women's movement under the KWP. The following year, North Korea abolished the family registry system based on male lineage, replacing it with a new citizen registry system. These sweeping changes had a profound impact on traditional patriarchal systems, especially on the family system: clans eventually disappeared, the family lineage-book system was completely destroyed, and a nuclear family system began to emerge. However, granting equal rights in law was not enough to liberate women from patriarchy and the authoritarian culture of the nation rendered the concept of equality alien to both men and women. On the eve of North Korea's first democratic election, men openly opposed women's right to vote and women running for the People's Committee, mobilizing every means (including abstention) to prevent them from being elected. Kim Il Sung responded with an equal rights campaign, delivering numerous speeches, enlarging the Women's Union, and launching an extensive campaign to wipe out illiteracy among women to awaken them to their rights. On the occasion of the democratic elections he pointed out:

> [Some] maintain that women should not be elected to the people's committees and even that they should not be allowed to take part in the elections. This is also wrong thinking. Women account for half of the population. If half of the people do not take part in electing the organ of power or in its work, such power can hardly be called a genuine people's power. Women constitute a great force, and large numbers of them are sharing in the work of

> rehabilitating our country no less creditably than men. In our country women are guaranteed by law equal rights with men in all fields. The Law on Sex Equality, therefore, should be fully enforced in the elections, for only then can they be truly democratic elections.[55]

The emancipation of women from patriarchal family and social systems was strongly emphasized from the start as an integral part of state building by the socialist regime, and impressive institutional mechanisms were created for that purpose. Even so, male domination, firmly entrenched in society, prevented the achievement of gender equality. Women are still expected to follow Confucian virtues by obeying their husbands and sacrificing themselves for men.[56] In the household, the division of labor is still based on gender; almost 80 percent of men regard housework as a woman's job.[57]

The Political Arena

South Korea. The atmosphere surrounding South Korean women is least favorable in the political arena, the most typically male domain. Throughout history, only a handful of women have managed to achieve political positions of any significance. Under Japanese rule, women's political participation originated in the resistance movement where women were active in the effort to realize national independence. Thus, women's first experience in politics is associated with resistance to external domination rather than internally generated change. Three female resistance leaders later became active politicians: Yim Young Shin, Park Soon Chon, and Park Hyun Sook. All imprisoned for their participation in the March First Movement, they became eminent on the political scene in the newly established South Korean government.

Soon after liberation, Yim Young Shin formed the first political party for women, *Taehan Yoja Kukmin-dang* (Korean Women's National Party), in 1945. Park Soon Chon organized *Konguk Bunyo Dongmaeng* (Women's Alliance for Nation Building) to promote participation by women in nation building. She later led *Taehan Buin-hoe* (Korean Women's Association), formed in 1948. Park Hyun Sook organized *Ibuk Yosong Tongi-hoe* (Northern Women's Fellowship Association), working closely with the American military government which later appointed her as one of the four women members in the forty-five-member South Korean Transitional Legislative Assembly.[58] These women made concerted efforts to involve themselves and other women in the political process of nation building. Their resistance against the

Japanese and active involvement in the formation of the first South Korean regime were rewarded politically. Yim was appointed minister of commerce and industry in 1948, and Park Hyun Sook minister without portfolio in 1952 (see table 7.2). Both also served two terms in the National Assembly. Park Soon Chon, who served five terms in the Assembly, became a leading figure in the opposition after she broke her ties with President Rhee Syngman in 1953. She was the only female political survivor of the short-lived Second Republic (1960–1961). Kim Whal Ran, named minister of information in 1950, had been chosen one of the delegates representing South Korea in the U.N. General Assembly in 1948 along with Yim and Mo Yun Sook. They contributed significantly to obtaining U.N. recognition of South Korea as the only legitimate regime on the peninsula. These pioneering female politicians earned their positions based on their uncommon personal merits as independence fighters and political activists. Their credentials enabled them to move into the political arena which had been a taboo for women for centuries. In this sense, these few individuals might be regarded as isolated cases rather than as typical of women in South Korea.

President Rhee included a few women in his administration but in the Third and the Fourth Republics under President Park, no women were brought into the cabinet and no women were elected to the National Assembly from his party. During this period, only Park Soon Chon, Kim Ok Son, and Kim Yun Deuk managed to get elected to the National Assembly (see table 7.3). After the introduction of the proportional representation system, several women were appointed to the legislature as functional representatives. During the last four decades, the total number of women in any National Assembly never exceeded twelve (see table 7.4).[59] The percentage of women has steadily dropped from 5.5 in 1973 to 1.0 in 1992. A total of sixty-four Assembly seats have been occupied by women, but the majority (forty-eight) were appointed through the proportional representation system. Only sixteen female seats were won in elections by only seven different women. Except for Park Hyun Sook, all were reelected for at least one term. Among the appointed members, fewer than 10 percent were reappointed. The declining trend in female representation is reflected in the number of female candidates, which decreased from twenty-two in the first Assembly election to seven in the twelfth.[60] Although fourteen and nineteen women ran for the thirteenth and the fourteenth assemblies, respectively, none was elected. The activities of women who have managed to rise in the power hierarchy, especially those appointed under the proportional representation system, have

Table 7.2
Female Cabinet Members

Date of Appointment	Ministry	Name	Tenure
1948	Minister of Commerce and Industry	Yim Young Shim	10 months
1950	Minister of Information	Kim Whal Ran	4 months
1952	Minister without Portfolio	Park Hyun Sook	2 years
1979	Minister of Education	Kim Ok Gil	5 months
1982	Minister of Health and Social Affairs	Kim Chong Rye	3 years
1988	Minister of the 2nd Ministry of Political Affairs	Cho Kyung Hee	9 months
1988	Minister of the 2nd Ministry of Political Affairs	Kim Young Jung	1 year
1990	Minister of the 2nd Ministry of Political Affairs	Lee Gye Soon	2 years
1991	Minister of the 2nd Ministry of Political Affairs	Kim Kap Hyun	present

generally been confined to women's issues. They participated not as professional politicians but as functional representatives of women, an area that is given low priority in legislative activity. As a result, their power has been relatively insignificant.

As shown in table 7.2, nine women have served in cabinet positions. However, almost a quarter of a century elapsed between the end of Park Hyun Sook's service in 1954 and the appointment of another woman. Half the female ministers served for less than a year. After 1982, none held any office other than the one charged with women's issues, the second ministry of political affairs. No woman has ever occupied the presidency. Park Soon Chon ran for president in 1960, but received only one out of the total of 253 votes cast in the

Table 7.3
Elected Female Legislators (1948–1992)

National Assembly	Name
1st (1948)	Yim Young Shin
2nd (1950)	Park Soon Chon Yim Young Shin
3rd (1954)	Kim Chol An
4th (1958)	Kim Chol An Park Hyun Sook Park Soon Chon
5th (1960)	Park Soon Chon
6th (1963)	Park Soon Chon
7th (1967)	Kim Ok Son
8th (1971)	none
9th (1973)	Kim Ok Son Kim Yun Deuk
10th (1978)	Kim Yun Deuk
11th (1981)	Kim Chong Rye
12th (1985)	Kim Chong Rye Kim Ok Son
13th (1988)	none
14th (1992)	none

indirect election. Yim Young Shin ran for vice president in 1952 and 1960 as a candidate of the Korean Women's National Party, but received only 2.6 and 0.9 percent of the vote in these elections.

In 1983, more than 21 percent of government bureaucracy was staffed by women, up from 16.8 percent in 1978.[61] However, women are virtually absent from high-level positions. In 1983, almost 90 percent of female officials held jobs lower than the sixth grade, and half the total were concentrated in the lowest grade—the ninth.[62] Approximately 1 percent held offices in the top five grades. In 1988, the problem was still evident. Women accounted for 23 percent of public officials, but 92 percent below the sixth grade, and only 1 percent in

Table 7.4
Female Legislators in the National Assembly

	Total	Number of Women	% of Women
Constitutional Assembly (1948)	200	1 (1)	0.5
Second (1950)	210	2 (2)	1.0
Third (1954)	203	1 (1)	0.5
Fourth (1958)	233	3 (3)	1.3
Fifth (1960)	201	1 (1)	0.5
Sixty (1963)	175	2 (1)	1.1
Seventh (1967)	175	3 (1)	1.7
Eighth (1971)	204	5 (0)	2.5
Ninth (1973)	219	12 (2)	5.5
Tenth (1978)	231	8 (1)	3.5
Eleventh (1981)	276	9 (1)	3.3
Twelfth (1985)	276	8 (2)	2.9
Thirteenth (1988)	299	6 (0)	2.0
Fourteenth (1992)	299	3 (0)	1.0
Total	3,201	64 (16)	2.0

Note: Numbers in parentheses are elected legislators.

the top five grades.[63] Women were represented on only 35 of 364 ministerial committees, 156 women out of a total of over 7,000 members.[64] Almost 80 percent were concentrated in ministry of education and ministry of health and social affairs committees. All other ministries had fewer than ten female members on their committees.[65] The same trend is found in party membership. The membership ratio between men and women has increased from 8:2 in the 1970s to 6:4 in 1983. However, women are generally excluded from party governing bodies and are seldom nominated from party strongholds, so their numbers mean little in terms of power. Women are excluded from the nation's policymaking process even though they constitute more than half of the electorate. They hold no power in political structures, and accordingly, have no voice in making decisions about the allocation of values and resources in the society.

North Korea. Compared to their proportion of the population, Kim Il Sung noted only a small number of women cadres, and those few in areas of secondary importance.[66] Women's participation in public affairs was strongly encouraged and, by 1972, women accounted for more than 20 percent of the Supreme People's Assembly (see table 7.5). In local assemblies in provinces, cities, and counties, women have occupied between 20 and 26 percent of the seats since 1956. A 1976 report noted that one-third of all deputies to representative government organizations, ranging from the Supreme People's Assembly (SPA) to local people's assemblies, were women.[67]

Although women occupy about one-third of the representative positions in the lower echelons of power, they are greatly underrepresented at the upper levels, with the exception of the SPA which is not considered a real decision-making center. As one examines the more powerful organizations, such as the Central Committee (CC) and Politburo (Political Committee) of the KWP, and the Administrative Council (the Cabinet), it becomes apparent that very few women have held positions of power. The proportion of female members in the CC has fluctuated between 2.4 percent and 6.9 percent for full members, and from 10 percent to 15.5 percent for candidate members (see table 7.6). Only sixteen different women served the CC as full members, among whom six were reelected. In the highest decision-making body of the KWP, the Politburo, only Pak Chong Ae has served. Chong Kyong Hui was appointed alternate member of the Politburo in the Sixth Congress, later joined by Kim Bok Shin. Thus far, only three women have climbed to the highest level of the power structure. In the Administrative Council, women have filled an average of two positions out of over thirty in each cabinet (see table 7.7). Likewise, North Korean women have not been integrated into the nation's decision-making center although they have been well represented at lower levels of the power hierarchy.

COMPARISON OF WOMEN'S STATUS IN SOUTH AND NORTH KOREA

South and North Korean women experienced radical changes after independence in 1945. Nevertheless, as examined above, neither the socialist revolution in North Korea nor the rapid modernization in South Korea, by themselves, served to liberate women. Both North and South Korean women occupy inferior social positions in patriarchal

Table 7.5
Percentage of Female SPA Members

SPA	Date	%
1st	August 1948	12.1
2nd	August 1957	12.6
3rd	October 1962	9.1
4th	November 1967	16.0
5th	December 1972	21.0
6th	December 1977	20.8
7th	February 1982	15.0
8th	December 1986	21.1
9th	May 1990	20.1

Source: 1st–6th: Dae-Sook Suh, *Korean Communism: 1945–1980* (Honolulu: The University Press of Hawaii, 1981), 442.
7th and 9th: Bong Sook Sohn, "Yosong-kwa Jongchi Chaemyea," in *Bukhan Yosong-ui Siltae* (Seoul, Korea: Second Ministry of Political Affairs, 1990), 227.
8th: *Choson Yosong*, April 1989, 29.

social systems, are subject to many discriminatory measures in the economic arena, and are excluded from the policymaking process. However, the socialist revolution in North Korea seems to have been more effective than the rapid industrialization of South Korea in improving Korean women's position from that of pre-independence days. North Korean leaders were committed to changing traditional family, economic, and social systems and instituted new legal and social arrangements that promoted equal rights. In 1946, North Korean women were guaranteed equal rights to inherit property and to divide property in case of divorce. South Korean women fought for these rights for three decades, finally acquiring them only in 1989. As early as 1947, North Korea eliminated the family registry system based on male lineage. South Korean women have failed to abolish the system in spite of their arduous struggle against it for almost three decades. Clearly, the leaders of North Korea were strongly committed to the abolition of the feudal family system. Kim Il Sung addressed the issue in many speeches promoting equal rights. In South Korea, despite a rhetorical commitment to female equality and the elimination of the

Table 7.6
Female Central Committee Members

Congress	Date	Full Members	%	Candidate Members	%
First	August 1946	Ho Chong Suk* Pak Chong Ae*	4.7	—	—
Second	March 1948	Pak Chong Ae* Ho Chong Suk*	3.0	—	—
Third	April 1956	Pak Chong Ae* Ho Chong Suk*	2.8	—	—
Fourth	September 1961	Pak Chong Ae Kim Ok Sun	2.4	Yi Yang Suk** Hwang Sun Hui* Pak Hyong Suk Yi Yong Sun	10.0
Fifth	November 1970	Chong Kyong Hui* Hwang Sun Hui* Yu Chong Suk* Kim Song Ae* O Suk Hui Yi Son Hwa Yu sun Hui Chon Yong Hui	6.8	Pak Yong Sin Sin Chin Sun** Ho Chang Suk** Wang Ok Hwan** Kim Kum Ok Ho Yon Suk	10.9
Sixth	October 1980	Chong Kyong Hui Yi Son Sil Ho Chong Suk Hwang Sun Hui Han Yong Ok Kim Song Ae Yu Chong Suk Yi Kyong Suk Yi Kyong Son Chon Hui Jong Yi Hwa Yong	6.9	Yi Yang Suk Chae Hui Jong Yun Ki Jong Ok Pong Nin Kim Yu Sun Kim Chu Yong Yi Hwa Son Kil Chae Gyong Sin Chin Sun Kwon Hui Gyong Ho Chang Suk Wang Ok Hwan Yi Ho Hyok Kim Nak Hui Ho Min Son Pak Sol Hui	15.5

*Reelected to full membership

**Reelected to candidate membership

Source: Compiled by the author from Dae-Sook Suh, *Korean Communism: 1945–1980* (Honolulu: University Press of Hawaii, 1981).

Table 7.7
Some Female Members of the Administrative Council

Cabinet	Appointment	Ministry	Name	Tenure
First	1948	Minister of Culture	Ho Chong Suk	9 years
	1957	and Propaganda	Ho Chong Suk	1 month
		Minister of Justice		
Second	1957	Minister of Justice	Ho Chong Suk	1 month
	1961	Minister of Agriculture	Pak Chong Ae	2 years
	1962	Minister of Commerce	Yi Yang Suk	1 year
Third	1966	Minister of Culture	Pak Yong Sin	1 year
	1967	Minister of Foodstuff	Yi Ho Hyok	1 year
		and Daily Necessities		
	1967	Industries	Yi Yang Suk	1 year
		Minister of Textile and		
		Paper Industries		
Fourth	1967	Minister of Foodstuff	Yi Ho Hyok	5 years
		and Daily Necessities		
	1967	Industries	Pak Yong Sin	5 years
	1967	Minister of Culture	Yi Yang Suk	5 years
		Minister of Textile and		
		Paper Industries		
Fifth	1972	None	—	—
Sixth	1980	Minister of Finance	Yun Gi Jong	2 years
	1981	Vice-premier	Kim Bok Sin	1 year
Seventh	1982	Minister of Finance	Yun Gi Jong	4 years
	1982	Vice-premier	Kim Bok Sin	4 years
Eighth	1986	Chair of External	Kim Bok Sin	4 years
		Economic Commission		
		Vice-premier		
	1986	Minister of Finance	Yun Gi Jong	4 years
Ninth	1990	Chair of the Light	Kim Bok Sin	present
		Industry Commission		
		Vice-premier		
	1990	Minister of Finance	Yun Gi Jong	present

1st–6th: Both original and interim appointees
7th–9th: Only original appointees

Source: Compiled by the author from various sources.

traditional family system, the state made no efforts comparable to those made in North Korea to penetrate social and kinship structures. State interference in North Korea in favor of women greatly contributed to enhancing women's lot in that society.

The most remarkable improvements for North Korean women were made in the economic arena. The regime's emphasis on liberation through labor and the abolition of private property led to the decline of the economic power of the patriarch. Women could acquire economic independence through paid labor, which enhanced their status in the family. In addition, the socialization of housework and childrearing greatly relieved working women of the double burdens of family life and outside employment. The economic participation of South Korean women has also grown impressively in the past three decades. Women are well integrated into the modernization process, albeit at the lowest levels. Yet, South Korea appears to be far behind North Korea in freeing women from the heavy burdens of the household. While North Korea admitted almost 100 percent of children into public nurseries and kindergartens in 1976, South Korea did not even establish nurseries until 1990. Both North and South Korean men seem reluctant to share housework. Most North Korean men regard household work as a woman's job, and South Korean men's participation in housework is hardly noticeable.[68] Although household labor remains women's work in both Koreas, North Korea's legal and institutional provisions for socializing housework and protecting working women are more impressive than those of South Korea.

Political opportunities for North Korean women have been greatly expanded, especially at the lower echelons of power, through affirmative measures such as a quota system—not present in South Korea. Women have generally comprised at least 20 percent of local representative bodies since 1972, although their average representation in the CC of the KWP is less than 5 percent. Yet female representation in North Korea is greater than in South Korea where women's average representation in the National Assembly is only 2 percent. Female cabinet members in North Korea also serve longer than those in South Korea. While half the South Korean members held office for less than a year, all of the North Korean members served longer than a year. Except for Pak Chong Ae, who served for a year, three women (Pak Yong Sin, Yi Ho Hyok, and Yi Yang Suk) served for six years and another three (Ho Chong Suk, Yun Gi Jong, and Kim Bok Sin) served more than ten. Except for Pak, all were reappointed—none was reappointed in the South Korean cabinets. Furthermore, four out of nine female South Korean cabinet members were appointed to the office of women's affairs. After 1982, no female minister was appointed to any other cabinet position. Thus, the socialist revolution in North Korea seems to have had a more profound impact on women than the capitalist revolution has had in the South.

PROBLEMS AND PROSPECTS

Gerhard Lenski's theory of social inequality identifies three sources of social power: property, position, and force.[69] As discussed above, neither North nor South Korean women have the power of property completely, despite major advances in this area, and they are far from having the power of position. Furthermore, women's participation in the military, the most significant source of power and leadership in both Koreas, has been virtually nonexistent. When asked the highest rank held by a woman in the military, a representative of the North Korea's Women's Union was unable to answer except to say that some female heads of military hospitals held the rank of colonel.[70] This suggests that North Korean women do not control the means of coercion.

South Korean women also failed to gain the power of force, either during the independence movement or the Korean War. There were independence heroines and fighters, and there is some indication that organized Women's Independence Royal Troops did exist unofficially.[71] However, they did not fight, and neither did they gain control of the means of coercion. The importance of military experience for entering into the power structures of South Korean society explains why the leadership was monopolized by men. In both Koreas, a handful of women played a part in the political leadership hierarchy. But, since women were not organized as women, the result was similar to China's—not the institutionalization of women's power but a "star system."

To draw the China comparison further, in North Korea the problem of organizing women as women stems not only from the traditional culture but also from a basic tenet of Marxist theory which maintains that women will not be fully liberated until communism is fully developed. Thus, the woman question is subsumed under the class question, and any attempt to organize the masses around women's issues is seen as selfish and divisive.

In South Korea, women remain marginal members of society with no access to property, force, or position. What can possibly account for the marginalization of half the population? For one thing, the cultural factor cannot be ignored. The neo-Confucian tradition of male superiority is still very much alive in people's belief systems. Koreans have the highest preference for male births in the world, equal to people in India and Taiwan. A nationwide survey showed that over 90 percent of Korean women still prefer sons.[72] Modernization has had some effect on people's value systems. A recent survey indicates that only 5 percent of men oppose women's employment.[73] However, modernity has not replaced tradition. Another study found that men favor women's working only if they stay home while their children are young.[74] In South Korea, conflicting values coexist, making women's roles far more complicated and precarious.

Cultural characteristics justify discriminatory practices in the recruitment and promotion of working women, and are the basis of women's low level of job consciousness, job security, and company loyalty. Women regard their jobs as temporary because of the retirement at marriage practice. Wage discrimination encourages the view that women's income is only supplementary.[75] This perception deepens the dependency of women on men and reinforces the persistence of male-oriented patriarchal culture.

Despite rapid industrialization, urbanization, the expansion of educational opportunities, and consciousness-raising efforts, die-hard traditional values are still deeply entrenched—promoted by institutional contributions to women's backwardness in South Korea. Major institutions reinforce and perpetuate the notion of inequality between sexes. School curricula offer business and industrial courses for boys and home management courses for girls. Textbooks describe stereotyped sex roles and portray the ideal woman as a "respectful daughter, good mother, sacrificing sister."[76] The family registry system perpetuates traditional patriarchy based on male lineage. The legal system bans women from certain occupations, while the wage system institutionalizes marginal wages for women on the premise that they are supported by male heads of household. Working women do not receive the family, education, and housing allowances commonly given to heads of households.[77] Where male dominance is firmly embedded in major social institutions, efforts to break patriarchy do not bear fruit overnight. The three decades' struggle to eliminate the family-headship system failed because it was feared that it would "shake the roots of the nation itself."[78]

Another problem is the absence of institutional mechanisms to implement legal commitments to sexual equality. The Constitution, as well as recent labor legislation, clearly recognize the principle of gender equality. But the persistence of discriminatory practices reveals that these guarantees hardly function. For instance, the 1989 revisions of the equal employment opportunity act provide for women's equality in recruitment, training, promotion, and retirement, and mandate maternity protection through a one-year child care leave system and a two-month paid leave for pre- and post-natal care. However, to implement the intent of the act, a better child care system is needed.[79] A controversial law establishing nurseries for working mothers was not passed until December 1990. Many women's groups charge that the law does not reflect the interests of poor working mothers. Working women's double burdens necessitate an institutionalized solution even more than an attitudinal change in traditional sex roles.

The marginal status of women in South Korea is also structural. The success of South Korea's labor intensive, export-oriented economy is predicated on low wage, unskilled, young female labor. In the capitalist world economy, the "center" seeks cheap labor for capital accumulation in the "periphery." In South Korea, multinational penetration accelerated rapidly between 1962 and 1974, when the number of multinational corporations (MNCs) increased from 70 to 879.[80] These MNCs concentrated their investment in manufacturing, and accounted for 31.4 percent of Korea's exports through 1974.[81] It is the manufacturing sector where over 70 percent of women wageworkers are employed that has maintained the lowest wage rate among South Korean industries. MNCs that come to peripheral areas such as South Korea profit from existing gender inequalities, exploiting the cheap labor of the "periphery of the periphery." One study found that all MNCs "accept traditional attitudes towards women where they justify giving women lower wages . . . and [expect] greater deference to authority and conscientiousness in work from [women]."[82] Female workers liberated by modern values sought escape from patriarchal oppression by achieving economic independence. Instead, they are subject to new forms of exploitation in multinational employment.

MNCs in South Korea have enjoyed "a virtual extraterritorial privilege" to make economic decisions "free of Korean legal review and interference."[83] The government's overriding concern has been to provide cheap and disciplined labor to facilitate capital accumulation and comply with the structural requirements of "dependent development." This alliance between the state and MNCs led one U.S. MNC executive in South Korea to state that "it is in our own selfish interest to have a strong government that controls . . . labor so everything will blossom and we can continue to make profits."[84] South Korea's peripheral position in the world capitalist economic system imposes the structural constraints that necessitate the exploitation of existing gender inequalities. It is remarkable "how nicely international capitalism collaborated with the traditional patriarchal system to exploit women workers in peripheral economies as that of Korea."[85] Both the domestic and the international capitalist systems are structured to maximize profit using the culturally marginal members of a society, thus making them also economically and politically marginal.

In sum, the backwardness of South Korean women stems not only from a traditional patriarchal culture but also from the institutionalization of those traditional elements coupled to a lack of institutional mechanisms for implementing sexual equality. It is reinforced by the structural characteristics of capitalism. Thus, capitalist patriarchy[86] may be what underlies the marginal status of South Korean women economically, socially, and politically. The backwardness of North Korean women stems mainly from North Korea's adherence to the Marxist perspective that opposes feminism as antithetical to the class struggle. In short, major hurdles to overcome seem to be ideological in North Korea and institutional and structural in South Korea.

NOTES

1. Jon Halliday, "Women in North Korea: An Interview with the Korean Democratic Women's Union," *Bulletin of Concerned Asian Scholars* 17, no. 3 (1985): 50.

2. Yung-Chung Kim, *Women of Korea* (Seoul, Korea: Ewha Woman's University Press, 1976), 37. For a general discussion on Korean women, also see Laurel Kendall and Mark Peterson, eds., *Korean Women: View from the Inner Room* (Cushing: East Rock Press, 1983).

3. Ibid., 52.

4. *Silhak* scholars studied in China during the seventeenth and eighteenth centuries and were introduced to Western ideas. *Tonghak* started with Choe Che-u in strong opposition to *Sohak* (Western learning), Western influence from Catholicism. *Tonghak* stressed nationalism and new social values that would replace traditional values.

5. Kim, *Women of Korea*, 247.

6. Eui-Young Yu, "Women in Traditional and Modern Korea," in *Korean Women in Transition*, ed. Eui-Young Yu and Earl Phillips (Los Angeles: California State University, Los Angeles, Center for Korean-American and Korean Studies, 1987), 20.

7. For example, Buddhist Women's Association (1920), YWCA (1922), *Choson Yosong Dongwoo-hoe* (Korean Women's League) (1924), *Kyungsung Yoja Chongnyon Dongmaeng* (Kyungsung Women's Youth League) (1925), *Yosong Haebang Dongmaeng* (Women's Liberation League) (1925), *Pro Yosong Dongmaeng* (Proletariat Women's League) (1926), and *Kunu-hoe* (1927).

8. See Chang Soon Kim and Jun Yup Kim, *Hankuk Kongsan Jueui Woondong Sa*, vol. 2 (Seoul, Korea: Chyung Kyae Yonkusa, 1986), 153–56.

9. For example, Kim Jong Suk, the deceased wife of President Kim Il Sung, and Kim Whak Sil who was called the "woman general" of the Anti-Japanese Guerrilla Army, participated in actual battles. See *Choson Yosong*, February 1960: 13, and June 1987: 12–37. In addition, *Choson Yosong* carried stories on some women members who participated in armed struggles. For instance, Lim Chul,

"Lee Shin Kum Dongji-e Daihan Hoeisang," December 1960; Pak Kyung Suk, "Chong-eul Chapgi-Kagi," July 1963; and Hwang Sun Hui, "Palchisan-ui Yojangkun, Ho Sung Suk, Dongmu-leul Hoeisang-hayeou," October 1960.

10. Janet Salaff and Judith Merkle, "Women in Revolution: The Lessons of the Soviet Union and China," *Berkeley Journal of Sociology* 15 (1980): 182.

11. His speech addressed the communist workers of the Women's Union, who were scheduled to attend the First Conference of the Democratic Women's Union of North Korea, "On the Future Tasks of the Women's Union," 9 May 1946. *Kim Il Sung Works*, vol. 2 (Pyongyang, DPRK: Foreign Language Publishing House, 1980), 185. A women's detachment consisting of about thirty-two women is mentioned in Dae-Sook Suh, *Kim Il Sung: The North Korean Leader* (New York: Columbia University Press, 1988), 42.

12. "On the Future Tasks," 185.

13. His speech, "Congratulations on the Founding of the Magazine, Korean Women," 6 September 1946, *Kim Works*, 354.

14. Halliday, "Women in North Korea," 55.

15. She is said to have saved Kim Il Sung's life in 1939. Suh, *Kim Il Sung*, 51.

16. The June issue of 1987 contained a twenty-six-page special report, marking her seventieth birthday, and articles on her appeared again in the October and December 1989 issues and the December issue of 1990.

17. Norman Jacobs, *The Korean Road to Modernization and Development* (Urbana: University of Illinois Press, 1985), 159.

18. Economic Planning Board (EPB), Republic of Korea (ROK), *Labor Statistics Annual*, 1961; and *Annual Report on the Economically Active Population Survey*, 1990.

19. See EPB, *Population and Housing Census of Korea*, 1960; and *Annual Report*, 1985. In 1986, the minimum age of fourteen was adjusted to fifteen.

20. EPB, *Annual Report*, 1990.

21. Ibid.

22. As can be seen in table 7.1, the proportions of women employed in the primary, secondary, and tertiary industries in 1963 were 69, 7, and 24 percent, respectively. Over the years, a dramatic shift has occurred in this structure to change the ratios to 20, 28, and 52 percent in 1990. The highest increase was in the secondary sector: the number of employed women increased eleven times, from 186,000 to 2,058,000.

23. Uhn Cho, "Industrialization and Female Labor Absorption in Korea," *Women's Studies Forum* (1985): 84.

24. Ibid.

25. Ministry of Labor, ROK, *Actual Labor Conditions of Establishment Survey*, 1980–1989.

26. International Labor Office (ILO), *Yearbook of Labor Statistics*, 1990.

27. Ministry of Labor, *Report on Occupational Wage Survey*, 1975–1989.

28. ILO, *Yearbook*, 1990.

29. Ministry of Labor, *Report on Occupational Wage*, 1989.

30. Ibid.

31. Women worked an average of 53.7 hours per week while men averaged 51.7. Moreover, between 1975 and 1983, male workers' working hours increased 6.1 percent, while women's jumped by 9.6 percent. Women's working hours were not only longer than men's but also increased at a more rapid rate. See ILO, *Yearbook*, 1984.

32. Ministry of Labor, *Report on Occupational Wage*, 1984.

33. Ibid., 1989.

34. Ibid.

35. Ibid.

36. Phyllis Andors, "Social Revolution and Woman's Emancipation: China During the Great Leap Forward," *Bulletin of Concerned Asian Scholars* 7, no. 1 (January–March 1975): 35.

37. "On the Founding of the Magazine," 354.

38. "The Duty of Mothers in the Education of Children," speech at the National Meeting of Mothers, 16 November 1961. *Kim Il Sung Selected Works*, vol. 3 (Pyongyang, DPRK: Foreign Language Publishing House, 1976), 227.

39. V. Lenin, "A Great Beginning," in *The Emancipation of Women: From the Writings of V.I. Lenin* (New York: International Publishers, 1966), 63–64, in Phyllis Andors, "A Look at the Present Socio-Economic and Political Context of the Changing Role of Women and the Family in China," *The Australian and New Zealand Journal of Sociology* 12, no. 1 (1976): 23.

40. Jane Jaquette, "Women and Modernization Theory: A Decade of Feminist Criticism," *World Politics* 34, no. 2 (1982): 274.

41. "On the Future Tasks," 194.

42. It was reported in 1976 that almost 100 percent of the 3.5 million children could enter more than 60,000 nurseries and kindergartens. Kim Il Sung, "On Further Developing the Nursing and Upbringing of Children," speech delivered at the sixth session of the Fifth Supreme People's Assembly, 29 April 1976.

43. Halliday, "Women in North Korea," 53.

44. However, the variety of food that can be purchased from stores is extremely limited.

45. The technical revolution is one of the programs of the triple revolution of technology, culture, and ideology, which began under the slogan, "Let's meet the requirement of *Juche* (self-reliance) in ideology, technology, and culture." It is regarded as the prerequisite for successful construction of socialism via the *Chollima* movement. For a detailed discussion of the triple revolution and *Juche* ideology, see Kyung Ae Park and Han S. Park, *China and North Korea: Politics of Integration and Modernization* (Hong Kong: Asian Research Service, 1990), chap. 3.

46. The 1980 data show that women occupied 56 percent of the labor force in the agricultural sector, 45 percent in the industrial sector, 20 percent in mining, 30 percent in forestry, 15 percent in heavy industry, and 70 percent in light industry. See Tae Young Lee, *Bukhan Yosong* (Seoul, Korea: Silchon Moonhak Sa, 1988), 194. In education, women accounted for 80 percent of the elementary school teachers, while the figures for middle and high school,

technical school, and college were 35 percent, 30 percent, and 15 percent, respectively. Among professionals and technicians, women accounted for only 14.6 percent in 1963, yet, in 1989, more than 37 percent were women. The number of female professionals and technicians increased 10.6 times between 1963–1989, while that of male increased only 2.5 times. See Ae Sil Kim, "Yosong-ui Kyongje Whaldong," in *Bukhan Yosong-ui Siltae* (Seoul, Korea: Second Ministry of Political Affairs, 1990), 189.

47. In an interview with *Mainichi Shimbun* on 19 April 1991, *North Korea News*, 29 April 1991.

48. Kim, "Kyongje Whaldong," 194.

49. For monthly salaries, see Chae-Jin Lee, "Economic Aspects of Life in North Korea," in C. I. Eugene Kim and B. C. Koh, *Journey to North Korea: Personal Perceptions* (Berkeley: University of California, 1983), 45.

50. About 70 percent of women quit their jobs after marriage. *Hankuk Ilbo*, 7 May 1991.

51. Kim, "Kyongje Whaldong," 187.

52. Ok-Za Yoo, "Korean Women in the Home and Work Place," *Korea and World Affairs* 9, no. 4 (Winter 1985): 833.

53. "On the Future Tasks," 185.

54. It increased later to 150 days. It is said that some women voluntarily give up their long maternity leave to show their loyalty to the country, but it is not known how widely that practice is being held.

55. "On the Eve of the Historic Democratic Elections," speech at a Pyongyang Celebration of the Democratic Elections, 1 November 1946, *Kim Works*, 463.

56. Uhn Cho, "Nambukhan Jumin-ui Euishik Gujobykyo," in *Nambukhan Sawhoi Moonwha Yeukryang Jonghap Pyongga* (Seoul, Korea: National Unification Board, 1990), 162.

57. Ibid., 164.

58. Hyuo-Jae Lee, *Hankuk-ui Yosong Undong* (Seoul, Korea: Jeong Woo Sa, 1989), 240.

59. The highest percentage of women was only 5.5 percent in 1973, and the average representation is only 2 percent (see table 7.4). The percentage of women has steadily dropped from 5.5 in 1973 to 1.0 in 1992.

60. Hoo-Jung Yoon, "Hankuk Yosong-kwa Jungchaek Gyeuljung Chaemyea," *Yosong Yonku* 4, no. 3 (Autumn 1986): 39.

61. Ministry of Government Administration, *Public Official Statistics*, 1984.

62. Ibid.

63. Ibid., 1989. From 1989, recruitment of ninth-grade local public officials is no longer by gender.

64. Yoon, "Hankuk Yosong-kwa Jungchaek Gyeuljung chaemyea," 43.

65. Ibid.

66. "On Revolutionizing and 'Working-Classizing' Women," speech at the Fourth Congress of the Democratic Women's Union of Korea, 7 October 1971, *Kim Selected Works*, vol. 4, 105–26.

67. *Rodong Shinmun*, 3 July 1976.

68. *Korean Women Today* (Summer 1991).

69. Gerhard Lenski, *Power and Privilege: A Theory of Social Stratification* (New York: McGraw-Hill, 1966).

70. Halliday, "Women in North Korea," 54.

71. Lee, *Yosong Undong*, 62–63.

72. Yu, "Women in Traditional and Modern Korea," 24.

73. Yung-Chung Kim, "Future Employment of Female College Graduates," *Women's Studies Forum* (1985): 8.

74. Haejong Cho, "Korean Women in Professions," in Yu and Phillips, *Korean Women in Transition*, 60.

75. In the industrial sector, the average female employment duration rate is only two years. See Hi-Jun Tak, "Hankuk Yosong-kwa Inleuk Whalyong," *Yosong Yonku* 4, no. 3 (Autumn 1986): 98. This phenomenon is compounded by the fact that a predominant portion (90 percent) of the women in light industries are single and under thirty years old.

76. Yu, "Women in Traditional and Modern Korea," 24.

77. Tak, "Hankuk Yosong-kwa Inleuk Whalyong," 89.

78. Yoo, "Korean Women in the Home and Work Place," 830.

79. In a recent survey, 57 percent of married women in industrial areas attributed their unemployment to their child care responsibilities, and 79 percent of women professionals listed child care as the primary difficulty in their lives. Yet, daycare centers began to open only in 1988, and by June 1989, only twelve industries in Seoul and Pusan opened daycare centers in the workplace. See *Korean Women Today* 24 (Autumn 1989): 4–5.

80. Lawrence Alschuler, *Multinationals and Maldevelopment* (New York: St. Martin's Press, 1988), 137.

81. See Stephan Haggard, *Pathways from the Periphery* (Ithaca: Cornell University Press, 1990), 202, table 8.1.

82. Linda Lim, "Women Workers in Multinational Corporations: The Case of the Electronics Industry in Malaysia and Singapore," *Michigan Occasional Papers in Women's Studies* (Ann Arbor: University of Michigan, 1978), 41.

83. Jacobs, *The Korean Road*, 159.

84. "Quote of the Month," *Multinational Monitor*, December 1982: 10, cited in David Kowalewski, "Asian State Repression and Strikes against Transnationals," in *Dependence, Development, and State Repression*, ed. George Lopez and Michael Stohl (New York: Greenwood Press, 1989), 84.

85. Hagen Koo, cited in Yoo, "Korean Women in the Home and Work Place," 847.

86. Socialist feminist Zillah Eisenstein's term denoting "the mutually reinforcing dialectical relationship between capitalist class structure and hierarchical sexual structuring," quoted in Jaquette, "Modernization Theory," 276. For details, see "Developing a Theory of Capitalist Patriarchy and Socialist Feminism," in *Capitalist Patriarchy and the Case for Socialist Feminism*, ed. Zillah Eisenstein (New York: Monthly Review Press, 1979).

Chapter 8

Women and Revolution in Indonesia

Susan MacFarland

The primary motivation behind the Indonesian independence movement was frustration with paternalistic colonial rule. This chapter explores the thesis that Dutch colonial paternalism, oppressive for Indonesian men, was doubly so for women who experienced it in both their public and private lives. That dual oppression motivated zealous participation by women in the movement for Indonesian independence, resulting in independence for the state and an expansion of women's personal and political independence. This exploration of women's involvement in Indonesia's independence movement supports the broader thesis that women are a primary force in the ongoing transformation of contemporary societies, and that progress toward a more egalitarian family system might influence similar progress in the macrosociety.

It is difficult to analyze any particular aspect of Indonesian culture (such as the status of women) in general terms because Indonesia is an extremely diverse multi-cultural nation-state; some two hundred languages are spoken and customs vary considerably within the archipelago. For example, customary laws (*adat*) differ greatly between West Sumatra, a matriarchal culture, and Bali, where women have almost no formal property rights. Indonesia is at once "a very progressive and a very backward state—believing in myths, false messiahs, Marxist prophecy, solid traditional customs, archaic magic, chilling rationality, ultra-futuristic technology."[1] Research problems are compounded by the scarcity of scholarly literature on the status of Indonesian women, while evaluations of the status of both traditional and contemporary women by Indonesians themselves tend to be subjective and difficult to assess.

It is also difficult to evaluate whether and how traditional cultural norms, important at village levels, influence women's national political participation. Women receiving Western education may be more influenced by that education than by tradition. Even though such women are a minority in Indonesia, they may have a more profound influence on politics than their more traditional sisters.[2] While national independence may have changed the lives of some Indonesian women, its influence (whether positive or negative) may not yet have reached many other women. These problems impede the study of women and revolution in any culture, especially those cultures still recovering from generations of colonialism. This is not to say, however, that such studies should be abandoned or disregarded, but rather that more cross-cultural and multi-disciplinary work on women and revolution should be done.

BACKGROUND

Evidence of the earliest stages of human life have been found among the 13,667 islands that make up the Indonesian archipelago. According to Western history, Marco Polo visited the islands in 1292, and he is assumed to be the first European to delight in their wealth and beauty. By the time the Renaissance was pulling Europe out of the Dark Ages, Indonesia had developed an advanced cultural heritage. Buddhism, Hinduism, and Islam contributed to its complex cultural life, and in the seventeenth century Dutch colonizers introduced Christianity. Taking advantage of the region's geographic and cultural fragmentation, the Dutch also established one of the world's richest colonial possessions, the Netherlands East Indies. Dutch economic and political ascendancy, gained through superior weapons (not cultural superiority), arrested Indonesia's development, while Indonesian wealth contributed substantially to the industrialization of the Netherlands. The result was an ever widening gap between colonizers and colony.[3]

Near the end of the nineteenth century, some Dutch colonizers experienced a form of new thinking toward the colonies. *Ethici*, as Dutch humanitarians were called, began to acknowledge and respond to a clearly evident quality-of-life decline among the Indonesian people; they proposed a series of humanitarian reforms to remedy problems. A more pragmatic group agreed that Indonesian poverty had become a Dutch problem because it limited domestic purchasing power, and therefore Dutch profits.[4] In 1901 the Dutch queen, Wilhelmina, supported an Ethical Policy, proposed by the liberal Dutch colonial rulers, that included the recruitment of young Indonesian men into Colonial Services, improved agricultural and communications technology and health and educational opportunities, expanded credit, and decentralized authority from Dutch to indigenous leaders. In return for their self-conscious generosity, the Dutch expected gratitude. Instead, during this progressive period, a new sense of anti-Dutch nationalism began to emerge, a response, in part, to the paternalistic nature of the new policies. New educational policies were to have a particularly significant impact on the growth of nationalism and the move toward independence.

KARTINI

By the late nineteenth century, Dutch colonizers had established modern schools for their own children in Indonesia, but excluded Indonesian children from them. As part of the new thinking and Ethical Policy (and to combat Islam's growing influence) the sons of Indonesian regents (local rulers serving under Dutch superiors) began to be admitted to Dutch schools. One unusually progressive Javanese regent allowed his daughters to attend a Dutch elementary school, for six years, until they were twelve years old. After that, they were to be kept at home in customary fashion until their marriages were arranged.[5]

Raden Adjeng Kartini, the oldest daughter, described her years at home following the years at school as imprisonment. She coped by reading as wide a variety of books as she could and by corresponding extensively with Dutch friends she had met at school. Along with her sister, Kartini began teaching girls in her home, finally convincing her father to let her continue her own studies in Jakarta. At the same time, she developed plans for a school for Indonesian girls. Deciding that the school for girls took priority over her own education, she opted to stay in Djapara, accept an arranged marriage, and work on the girls' school project. In 1904, she died in childbirth at the age of twenty-five. Kartini's letters, collected and published following her death, were critical of traditional Javanese customs, Islamic law, and Dutch colonialism. They became an inspiration to Indonesian revolutionaries.[6] Kartini's letters contain the first articulate expression of nationalism by an Indonesian individual.[7] Translator Agnes L. Symmers said of Kartini:

> The influence of her life and teachings is perhaps greater than that of any other woman of modern times because it reaches all the

> millions of Javanese and extends to some extent throughout the entire East. Therefore, even though she died young, this young woman began the liberation of women and to a great extent pointed the way for their education.[8]

Kartini herself established only one small school for girls in her own home. Following her death, however, Kartini schools were established in her honor by a Dutch foundation, Kartinifonds. The inspiration of C. Th. van Deventer and his wife, who visited Indonesia to study its education system, these schools gradually came to be called "van Deventer schools."[9] Even though there were few of these girls' schools, their students were prominent, becoming important elements in awakening Indonesian women to the possibilities for themselves in a modernizing country. "[I]t was a few individual women, working independently, who roused public opinion and influenced the policy of modern education. . . . [Those who pioneered in the education of Indonesian women were the] precursors of the women's movement."[10]

THE INDEPENDENCE MOVEMENT

During the 1908–1942 period, Indonesian groups organized to promote national unity and independence. Their leadership came primarily from progressive middle-class intellectuals and merchants, supported by peasants who resented both their European exploiters and the Chinese middlemen who worked for the Dutch. The Indonesian independence movement was part of a worldwide reaction to imperialist expansion and penetration. It was strengthened by educational advances that contributed to new awareness, growing frustrations, and rising expectations.[11] By 1912 some of these groups had evolved into what were essentially political parties devoted to independence. The Communist Party of Indonesia (PKI), was formed in 1920. During the 1920s, independence organizations proliferated. In 1927, an "all Indonesia nationalist movement" was organized by youth and women to combat the regionalism beginning to characterize the drive for independence.[12] That same year, the Indonesian Nationalist Party (PNI) was organized by Sukarno and others. Their goal was to adopt a militant policy of noncooperation with the Dutch government and to establish Bahasa Indonesian as the nation's official language. Dutch officials harassed and arrested PKI and PNI leaders, including Sukarno, until the Japanese invasions of 1942.

The Republic of Indonesia was born when the Japanese surrendered on 17 August 1945. Sukarno proclaimed Indonesia's independence and became its first president. It would take five years of fighting, however, before Indonesia was accepted as a member of the international community.[13] Indonesian publications refer to the 1945–1950 period as a War of Independence rather than a revolution. The war was fought by small Indonesian and freedom fighter guerrilla units against Dutch forces, who had returned to regain control of the area with the assistance of British troops. Ostensibly, both Dutch forces and British troops were in Indonesia as representatives of Allied forces assigned to repatriate Allied prisoners of war held by the Japanese. While fighting continued, diplomatic negotiations also were conducted under the auspices of the United Nations. As a result of a December 1949 U.N. conference, the Dutch East Indies ceased to exist and the Republic of Indonesia became a member of the United Nations in 1950.[14]

THE ROLE OF WOMEN IN THE INDEPENDENCE MOVEMENT

The story of Kartini shows that educated women in Indonesia were as ready for a women's movement as women in the West. Indonesian women's organizations, like those in other countries, emerged from the worldwide move toward humanitarianism and equality that began with the American and French revolutions. The Association of Indonesian Women was established in 1912 to strengthen women's positions as mothers and housewives, but the first exclusively women's organizations, extending beyond the home and local community, were organized in the 1920s as part of the nationalist movement. These organizations were generally connected with and subordinate to male organizations. Recognition of that reality and growing dissatisfaction with women's subordination led to the first Congress of Indonesian Women (*Kowani*) in 1928, an event that has been ranked with "the most significant milestones in the history of the Indonesian women's movement."[15] The annual meetings of this coalition of women's groups became institutionalized as the authoritative voice of Indonesia's women's movement, establishing women as integral members of the nationalist movement and legitimate participants in the nation's political processes after independence.[16]

During the Japanese occupation of the Netherlands East Indies, the Japanese attempted to organize native women into a national front in order to serve them. That effort, along with the occupation itself, failed. In anticipation of Japan's approaching defeat in 1945, women and men joined the final phase of the independence movement. These Indonesians knew that the Dutch would use force to re-establish colonial power, and they began spontaneous and strategically planned responses to the threat. Women's revolutionary exploits included spying, establishing defense kitchens to gather combat and hospital supplies, arranging nurseries so mothers could be involved in the revolution, and helping to evacuate battle zones. Women also engaged in actual combat in both guerrilla and regular army units. Women's combined military and community assistance efforts established the necessary mythology for their acceptance into full and equal participation in post-revolutionary Indonesian society.[17]

Women themselves held well-publicized meetings where demands for equality were made based on their wartime activities. One such meeting was held in 1949. At that time it was difficult to travel safely or to find even basic accommodations. Women nevertheless met, at considerable risk, to plan for a unified post-war era characterized by gender equality. An Indonesian newspaper wrote about the event "in terms of a popular legend" describing how the women took a dramatic train ride through occupied territory in order to create unity among women.[18] A primary goal of that 1949 meeting was to impress Indonesian leaders with women's loyalty to a unified Republic. Another goal was to make specific demands for legal, social, economic, and education rights for women. Indonesian feminist groups were not just civic clubs. Generations of tradition that had given women responsibility for maintaining a stable community life for their families also provided the experience to organize for a better life after independence.

INDONESIA'S WOMEN'S MOVEMENT

Indonesian women divide their movement into three periods that indicate the movement's close association with the struggle for independence. These are: the Period of Awakening (1908–1942), the Transitional (Japanese) Period (1942–1945), and the Post-Independence Period (1945–Present).[19] Organizations emerging out of these periods have names such as *Putri Mardiko* (Independent Women), *Keutamaan Isteri* (Accomplishments of Women), *Pawiyatan Wanita* (Educated Women), *Wanita Susilo* (Well-Bred Women), and *Seikat Kaum Ibu Sumatera* (Federation of Women's Associations in Sumatra). Such groups often published magazines dealing with the emancipation of women and improvements in their homes, schools, and work lives.[20]

The 1948 Congress of Indonesian Women (*Kowani*) was convened specifically to bridge the emerging divisions among Indonesian women's groups. The divisions reflected the increasingly divided nationalist movement, as well as the sheer number of women involved in Indonesia's tumultuous political life. In spite of the complexity of the issues and the diversity of strongly held views about them, *Kowani* had developed an effective, federated structure by 1949.[21] Through *Kowani*, women worked as an interest group to modernize marriage laws, improve social welfare programs, and improve their representation in government.[22] In its capacity as an educational, consciousness-raising coalition, *Kowani*'s tactics include networking among member organizations at all levels; this affiliation with international women's organizations kept *Kowani* members informed about international developments pertinent to women.[23]

INDONESIAN WOMEN'S EVOLVING STATUS

While there are substantial variations among communities, most research supports the conclusion that, in general, Southeast Asian women have enjoyed considerable freedom, respect, and equality in traditional settings. Women managed the family economy and participated more actively in the community than men. According to these studies, few limitations were placed on women's opportunities.[24] Reports and studies by the Indonesian government also tend to draw very positive pictures of traditional Indonesian women's lives.[25] Both scholarly and popular assessments acknowledge the existence of other realities, including communities in which girls were bought and sold and in which women had no property rights at all. However, many agree that, for the most part, traditional Indonesian customs provide a foundation for social and political equality and participation among contemporary Indonesian women. "The [customary law or] *adat*, with some exceptions, generally sanctions an egalitarian approach to sex roles."[26]

Reba Lewis, who lived in Indonesia from 1957 to 1960, noted the paradoxical nature of Indonesian women's status before and after Independence. She writes that Hindu and Buddhist influences contributed to tolerant attitudes generally, including acceptance of women's desires for equal rights. Prostitution and illegitimacy are less stigmatized in Indonesia than in the West. A prostitute who marries is accepted as a respectable member of the community. It is the man who refuses to accept responsibility for fatherhood who is stigmatized. According to Lewis, rape was rare. If a man was rejected by one woman, he found another who accepted him. In Indonesia, says Lewis, love is more important than business, politics, or sports.[27] Like other analysts of this complex nation, however, Lewis pointed to the diversity of customs throughout the islands. In northern Sumatra arranged marriages were still common in the 1950s, while in central Sumatra inheritance was through the mother and women occupied a privileged position. Through an intermediary, girls could propose marriage to boys. In Bali, elopement was not uncommon, usually with the full knowledge and complicity of the entire community, including both families. Marriage by request was considered in bad taste. If a boy asked a girl's father for permission to marry, the father was expected to respond that his daughter was a human being, not an animal to be given away as a present.[28] Other research confirms the diversity of influences on gender roles in Indonesian society. Ideological bases of male and female roles in West Sumatra, for example, derive from customs of "separate domains" that assign women to work at home and in their communities (*darat*), while men's domain, which includes politics and the marketplace, lies beyond the village (*rantau*).[29] This separation of domains creates a hierarchical division of labor giving men the influential professional roles in political and economic life while women perform lower status unpaid work. The result is an asymmetrical power relationship between the genders that permeates West Sumatran society. In contrast, Balinese tradition encourages a division of labor that is parallel and complementary rather than hierarchical.[30]

Traditional Javanese theater depicted women exercising power in family, religious, and political situations. Those positive images of women were negatively distorted by Dutch colonial writers who called Indonesian women "exquisite but empty-headed."[31] Dutch rule reduced Minahasa women's independence by imposing Christian marriage laws that mandated female dependency. Changes in property laws and educational opportunities further reduced women's independence and contributed to asymmetrical gender relationships.[32]

Indonesian society is also influenced by *Ibuism*, a tradition deriving from images of motherhood. This tradition allows women to develop networks and move beyond their homes to promote their families' economic and political well being.[33] In 1928, when Sukarno called for a more active political role for women in the nationalist movement, he drew on a long Javanese tradition permitting women to use their authority as mothers to go beyond narrow domestic boundaries to improve family life.[34] Even nonelite women could enhance their status by working in reform movements, as happened with Rahman El Yunisiya, who organized Muslim women to participate in the nationalist movement.[35]

Sukarno himself embodied the ambiguity of Indonesia's attitudes on gender. His blatant womanizing alienated many women yet his public acts and pronouncements gained him support. Sukarno's 1947 treatise on the status of Indonesian women, *Sarinah,* concluded that women were treated unfairly and promised to take steps to put them on an equal footing with men. When his measures were announced, however, they proved to be overwhelmingly symbolic (invitations to participate in dedication ceremonies or diplomatic receptions) and did little to improve women's status or ability to participate in political life. By the end of the Sukarno years in 1965, for example, only four women had held cabinet posts and few others had held high positions in any branch or level of government.[36]

Indonesia's 1945 constitution did guarantee basic rights and equal status to women and men. In 1961, Indonesia ratified the U.N. Convention on the political rights of women to vote, run for election, and hold public office. In 1978, the People's Deliberative Assembly adopted the Guidelines of State Policy which includes a chapter on the role of women in development. It states that women "have the same rights, responsibilities and opportunities as men to fully participate in all development activities."[37] In spite of these official pronouncements, by the 1980s less than 2 percent of all women held policy or decision-making positions, with the majority of them serving in the lower echelons. Increasing numbers of women assuming responsibilities at the village level and their occupation of a wider range of positions at all levels justifies some optimism about future progress, as does the increase in the numbers of women holding responsible positions in universities and research institutions, the judiciary (16 percent of judges in courts of original jurisdiction and courts of appeal were women in 1975), and the civil service.[38]

Post-independence education policy changes included coeducation as a national policy, leading to massive efforts to encourage girls to attend schools and women to enter nontraditional occupations and professions. Primary education is not yet compulsory, however, and less than half (45.9 percent) of all elementary school pupils are female. Literacy rates for rural women improved from 34.1 to 49 percent between 1961 and 1971, and those rates continue to grow.[39] Disproportionate percentages of the unemployed and uneducated continue to be women, however, especially in rural areas. Official publications acknowledge the need to improve education, knowledge, and skill levels among rural women.[40] A national office for the Role of Women in Development headed by an associate minister was created in the 1970s. Illiteracy, health problems, poverty, and gender discrimination were identified as key problems. Proposed solutions included participation by women in all development programs, improved educational opportunities for women, and a continued responsibility to maintain "a happy family" and "guidance of the younger generation."[41]

While post-independence women have become an accepted part of the labor market, men's roles continue to be regarded as more important. Labor legislation ostensibly designed to protect women, for example, by restricting night work, instead benefits men. Generous maternity leave policies justify refusing women responsible positions.[42] Yet in spite of persistent employment problems, the participation of Indonesian women in an integrated work force in both rural and urban areas continues to increase. While women still work most often in agriculture or as unpaid domestic workers, their percentage in the agricultural sector is declining as their participation in the industrial and trade sectors is increasing.[43] Recognition of women's combat participation in the independence movement led to formation of the Women's Corps within the Indonesian Armed Forces and National Police. Women do not hold combat positions, however; "in keeping with their feminine character," they assist the department of defense and security in discharging its tasks.[44]

Considerable education, employment, and political problems persist, then, for Indonesian women as they do for women in most developed and developing nations. That the problems have been acknowledged, that programs are in place to deal with them, and that progress has been made since independence are all signs of hope for the future. They are also evidence that Indonesian women deserve considerable credit for coping in a progressive manner with burdensome traditions.

Cora Vreede-de Stuers, a leading analyst of Indonesian women's lives both before and after independence, reports that traditional Indonesians said of the woman that "her duties were in no way inferior to those of the man." Women are described as independent, active members of their families and communities, respected for their contributions to rural economic life. "All evidence supports the conclusion that the woman's position in traditional Indonesian communities has always been very elevated."[45] Yet Vreede also acknowledges that while in overall terms *adat* has had a positive impact on women's lives, it condoned polygamy, arranged marriages, prostitution, and other forms of women's oppression. Islam and Christianity contain similarly dual influences.[46] The thesis of Vreede's analysis is that "in Indonesia the birth of the feminist movement and the struggle for liberation from the narrow bonds of a traditional society have been intimately allied to the national awakening."[47] Women played a role in the independence movement "equal to that of [men and when it was over] all rights were accorded to [them]."[48] Barriers protecting women that in reality, confined them and separated them from one another, were officially broken down.

Even so, while women were indispensable to the revolution and enjoyed recognition for their contributions to it, once independence was gained and women were given equal political and economic opportunities, men began to view them as competitors. Male resentment, translated into repressive employment practices and regressive policies relating to widows' pensions and to polygamy, contributed to a decline in women's status following the revolution.[49] A new class of working women in Indonesia who cannot afford household help experienced the double-duty problems that working women experience elsewhere in the world. Frustrations in their family and work lives were especially painful for women who had contributed significantly to the revolution. However Vreede was optimistic, in 1960, that Indonesian women would eventually succeed in convincing men that women want to be their partners rather than their rivals.[50]

Other research also challenges the rosy portrait often drawn of both traditional and contemporary Indonesian women. Conducted in the late 1970s, Stephen Douglas's survey supports the thesis that Indonesian women's reputed post-revolutionary high status was more myth than reality. Douglas also asked questions relating to parental attitudes toward sons and daughters in terms of expectations about obedience and education. Here he found that responses were quite similar for parents of boys and of girls. His conclusion was that while equal treatment had not yet been attained in reality, in peoples' minds women and girls were assessed as highly as men and boys.[51] Anne Ruth Willner's studies of post-revolution Javanese women conclude that women's economic roles are "many and pronounced," but their political roles are "fewer and more subdued than those of men." Like Douglas, Willner rejects the notion that even though women seldom hold public office, they do not exert influence on public affairs. Numerous women's organizations exert pressure on public officials and all political parties have active women's auxiliaries. Willner's experience in Jakarta convinced her that individual wives and other women surrounding male leaders do influence the political process, although the extent of that influence is impossible to measure.[52]

Willner explores an interesting thesis relating to the potential for women's progress in Indonesia relative to women in more highly developed regions of the world, including the United States. She suggests that women in less developed regions may have a greater potential for progress than women in technologically advanced areas. Willner admits that her thesis is based not on scientific comparative analysis, but on "impressions of underlying cultural values and attitudes that can influence the success or failure of attempts to change roles and patterns of behavior of and toward women."[53] Among the factors Willner sees as contributing to the likelihood of continued progress for Indonesian women are:

(1) The overt and enthusiastic encouragement women receive from governmental and religious entities. Village families, for example, are exhorted by local government officials to keep daughters as well as sons in school and to get them involved in public projects. Orthodox Islamic leaders who deplore modern sexual mores among young people nevertheless support electing women to parliament.

(2) Many Indonesian women can take advantage of a wide range of choices among work and community activity because of the availability of household help in the form of either servants or relatives. Although daycare centers are neither common nor very much in demand, some male union leaders express interest in their development.

(3) Widows and divorcees (divorce is frequent and accepted) are neither penalized nor isolated as much as they are in other societies. Social life is conducted within extended families or among groups of neighbors rather than on the basis of couples.

(4) Women in traditionally male professions are not made to feel "desexed," less attractive as marriage partners, or that they are emasculating their husbands or colleagues.

(5) Culturally defined categories for evaluating personalities are not divided into masculine and feminine with the positive and negative connotations that go along with those judgments. A woman might be described as logical, strong-willed and outspoken but with no connotation that she is therefore masculine. A man might be considered intuitive or impulsive without being considered feminine.

Willner concludes that the position of women in Java has improved considerably since Kartini's rebellion. She detected neither latent nor overt attitudes opposing a variety of roles for women in Indonesian society, though she warns that Indonesians are extremely polite and are unlikely to express what might be considered distasteful attitudes to an American female political scientist.[54]

Since the late 1980s, European and Indonesian scholars have analyzed the status of Indonesian women from more critical perspectives. In 1988, an international workshop on Indonesian Women as Mediators was held in the Netherlands, and papers that closely examine government policy relating to women were presented at a symposium on poverty and development in Indonesia held at the Hague in 1991. These reports themselves contribute to the already complex realities about the evolving status of women in Indonesia's diverse cultures. For example, in addition to the officially sanctioned *Kowani,* Indonesia's communist party (PKI) developed *Gerwani* (Gerakan Wanita Indonesia, or Indonesia's Women's Movement) which by 1965 had some three million members. *Gerwani* members are now said to have participated in the failed 1965 PKI effort to overthrow Sukarno's regime, which had become increasingly corrupt and inept at controlling either political or economic problems.[55]

As a result of Suharto's intervention, the regime survived the attempted coup (referred to as the 30 September movement). Sukarno, however, did not. He was put under house arrest until his death in 1970. Another immediate casualty of the 1965 tumult was the bloody extermination of Communist Party members by Suharto and his new army. Versions of this episode in Indonesia's history vary both in terms of how many people were killed and who was involved in this effort to exterminate communism and other dissident groups. As many as half a million people may have died by the end of 1965; there was speculation that America's Central Intelligence Agency (CIA) may have been involved.[56]

While the story of the 1965 failed coup is an old one, only with the beginning of contemporary scholarship in the 1980s does mention of women's role in that event begin to emerge. Similarly, descriptions of women's organizations have begun to emerge that differ considerably from either the official accounts or the accounts of earlier analysts. An example is Dharma Pertiwi which, like *Kowani,* is an organization of women created as part of the government's effort to coordinate support for its policies. Formed in 1964, membership consists of the wives of every military man and police officer in the nation. Its purpose is to create a unified support system for the department of defense and security and avenues for women's participation in social development and nation building. Programs include efforts to lower school dropout rates, reduce the number of children per family, promote domestic products, improve health, and increase prosperity and patriotism.[57]

Dharma Wanita, another women's organization, was created in 1974 to coordinate support for the government's development strategies. Members are wives of the Civil Servant Corps (Korpri) at all levels of government. Described as "a dependable entity that will serve as a loyal partner and comrade in arms to the government's Civil Servants' Corps," members work to support a variety of government-sponsored health and education programs.[58] Since persistent ideological dogma specifies that wives are responsible for their husbands' wrongdoing, Dharma Wanita is only ostensibly organized for the benefit of women. In reality, its primary purpose is to organize and control both civil servants and their wives, while it reinforces continuing cultural pressures on wives to obey their husbands (Harus ikut suami).

Another large government-sponsored women's organization is the Family Welfare Movement, which deals with family health and welfare issues at village levels. Contemporary European and Indonesian feminists describe this organization as part of the government's corporatist apparatus for perpetuating its paternalistic system. It parallels and supports the male hierarchy. Created by government, all eligible women are required to participate. Their purpose is to promote the five duties of women according to official policy: to be loyal companions to their husbands, to procreate for the nation, to educate their children, to manage their households, and to be useful members of society.[59]

CONCLUSIONS

The women's movement in Indonesia has many roots but its formal emergence was, in large part, an outgrowth of Indonesia's anti-colonial national independence movement. Indonesian women capitalized on their association with the independence movement. Through *Kowani,* they pushed the new government for better education and employment opportunities and for improved marriage legislation. They demanded greater participation in foreign affairs, and established agencies such as the Women's Cooperative Bank and the Children's Welfare Foundation to pursue their own interests.[60] Although Indonesian women helped to inspire their nation's anti-colonial revolution, participated in it, and benefitted from its success, they also were hurt by a backlash against post-revolution progress. Even so, positive recent developments include the establishment of women's studies programs in some Indonesian universities, and increasing amounts of new research into the real status of Indonesia women by contemporary feminist scholars. A more ambiguous source of future changes for women is the resurgence of Islam, especially in urban areas. Its impact on Indonesian women will need to be a focus for feminist scholars in the years ahead.

The story of Kartini, whose father was progressive enough to give his demanding daughters a nontraditional education, supports the thesis that links exist between families and change in larger social systems. Kartini's story suggests that women and families are potential actors in both evolutionary and revolutionary social change. This link is supported by the work of Stephen Douglas, who sees the larger society in Indonesia as having denied adult women real equality, but Indonesian families as seedbeds for greater gender equality in the future. The case of Indonesia demonstrates that not only can transformation to more egalitarian family systems influence a similar transformation in the larger society, but that any such transformation may have to start there in order to succeed.

NOTES

1. Bill Dalton, *Indonesia Handbook*, 4th ed. (Seattle: Moon Publications, 1988), 17–18.
2. Stephen A. Douglas, "Women in Indonesian Politics: The Myth of Functional Interest," in *Asian Women in Transition*, ed. Sylvia A. Chipp and Justin J. Green (University Park and London: Pennsylvania State University Press, 1980), 152–81.
3. Ailsa Zainu'ddin, *A Short History of Indonesia* (New York and Washington: Praeger Publishers, 1970), 138–39.
4. Ibid., 138–66.
5. Ibid., 147.
6. See Raden Adjeng Kartini, *Letters of a Javanese Princess* (New York: W. W. Norton and Co., 1964).
7. Zainu'ddin, *A Short History of Indonesia*, 174.
8. Ibid., 5.
9. The first school was established in 1913 in Semarang. Others were begun in Solo, Bandung, Djakarta, Malang, Madium, and Bogor. See Cora Vreede-de Stuers, *The Indonesian Woman: Struggles and Achievements* (Hague: Mouton and Co., 1960), 59.
10. Ibid., 57, 59.
11. Ibid., 169.
12. *Indonesia 1989: An Official Handbook* (Jakarta: Department of Information, 1989), 41-47.
13. Ibid., 44–45.

14. Ibid., 47.

15. Douglas, "Women in Indonesian Politics," 160. See also *Indonesia 1988: An Official Handbook*, 190; and Government of Indonesia, *The Women of Indonesia* (Jakarta: Department of Information, 1986), 10.

16. Ibid., 161.

17. Douglas, "Women in Indonesian Politics," 162. See also *The Women of Indonesia*, 12.

18. Vreede-de Stuers, *Indonesian Woman*, 116–17.

19. *The Women of Indonesia*, 8–11.

20. Ibid., 9.

21. Ibid., 163.

22. Ibid., 12–15.

23. Ibid., 23–29.

24. Such positive views of women's lives are depicted in Lucian W. Pye, *Southeast Asia's Political Systems* (Englewood Cliffs: Prentice-Hall, 1967), 16; and in Robbins Burling, *Hill Farms and Padi Fields: Life in Mainland Southeast Asia* (Englewood Cliffs: Prentice-Hall, 1965), 2 and 99. Both are cited and discussed in Douglas, "Women in Indonesian Politics."

25. See, for example, *Indonesia 1989: An Official Handbook*, 189–91.

26. Douglas, "Women in Indonesian Politics," 154.

27. Reba Lewis, *Indonesia: Troubled Paradise* (New York: David McKay, 1962), 53–54.

28. Ibid.

29. Elsbeth Locher-Scholten and Anke Niehof, *Indonesian Women in Focus: Past and Present Notions* (Dordrecht and Providence: Foris Publications, 1987), 231.

30. Ibid., 139.

31. Ibid., 13.

32. Ibid., 181–205.

33. Ibid., 7.

34. Ibid.

35. Ibid., 55.

36. Ibid., 166.

37. Ibid., 65–66.

38. Ibid., 66–67.

39. Ibid., 57.

40. Ibid., 40.

41. Ibid., 23–24.

42. Ibid., 43–44.

43. Ibid., 41.

44. Ibid., 69.

45. Cora Vreede-de Stuers, *The Indonesian Woman: Struggles and Achievements* (The Hague: Mouton and Co., 1960), 44.

46. Ibid., 41.

47. Ibid., 16.

48. Ibid., 163.

49. Ibid., 164.

50. Ibid., 165.

51. Ibid., 156–59. His research surveyed fifteen hundred rural residents in West Java, a region Douglas considers one of the most traditional sectors of Indonesian society.

52. Ann Ruth Willner, "Women's Horizons in Indonesia: Toward Maximum Equality with Minimum Conflict," in *Asian Women in Transition*, 187–88.

53. Ibid., 182.

54. Ibid., 188.

55. M. C. Ricklefs, *A History of Modern Indonesia c. 1300 to the Present* (Bloomington: Indiana University Press, 1981), 244–71.

56. Ibid. See also William McCord, *The Dawn of the Pacific Century: Implications for Three Worlds of Development* (New Brunswick and London: Transaction Publishers, 1991), 64–69; and Frederica M. Bunge, ed., *Indonesia: A Country Study* (Washington, D.C.: American University, U.S. Government Foreign Area Studies Series), 48–55.

57. *The Women of Indonesia*, 31–34.

58. Ibid., 29–30.

59. Diane Lauren Wolf, *Factory Daughters: Gender, Household Dynamics, and Rural Industrialization in Java* (Berkeley: University of California Press, 1992), 65–72, 383 n.17.

60. Douglas, "Women in Indonesian Politics," 163–64.

IV

The Mediterranean and the Islamic World

Chapter 9

Revolution, Islamist Reaction, and Women in Afghanistan

Valentine M. Moghadam

During the 1980s, Afghanistan was the site of a prolonged and bloody battle between government forces, who were assisted by Soviet troops, and an armed tribal-Islamist opposition collectively known as the Mujahideen, which was supported by Pakistan, the United States, Saudi Arabia, and the Islamic Republic of Iran. The geopolitical dimension of the conflict—and international opprobrium for the Soviet military intervention—overshadowed two important issues: (a) the origins of the conflict between tribal-Islamists and the left-wing revolutionary government, and (b) the importance of the woman question to the conflict. It is my contention that the Soviet intervention and world attention to it obscured the essential nature of the conflict: contention between modernizers and traditionalists, and between women's emancipation and patriarchy. It is significant that when the Kabul government fell in April 1992, among the very first acts of the new Mujahideen government was to legislate strict controls on urban women.[1]

This essay was originally prepared for the round table on "Identity Politics and Women," held in Helsinki in October 1990. It uses some material from chapter 7 of my book, *Modernizing Women: Gender and Social Change in the Middle East* (Boulder: Lynne Rienner Publishers, 1993). Another version is forthcoming in *Gender and National Identity: Women and Politics in Muslim Societies*, ed. V. M. Moghadam (London: Zed, 1994).

The focus of this chapter is the conflict over women's rights and women's emancipation, and the importance of gender issues to the revolution and counter-revolution. The chapter surveys the status of Afghan women before and after the Saur Revolution of April 1978, with some comparison of the situation of women under the government in Kabul, drawn from my observations and interviews in early 1989, and under the Mujahideen in the refugee camps of Peshawar, Pakistan, for which I rely on secondary sources. I hope to show that notwithstanding the neglect of the gender dimension in nearly all accounts of Afghanistan, the woman question was an integral part of the conflict between the Mujahideen and the ruling party, the People's Democratic Party of Afghanistan (PDPA).

SOME THEORETICAL ISSUES

Recent feminist scholarship has revealed the gender dynamics of social change, revolution, economic transition, political conflicts, and national identity formation.[2] Women frequently become the sign or marker of political goals and of cultural identity during processes of revolution and state-building, and when power is being contested or reproduced. Representations of women assume political significance, and certain images of women define and demarcate political groups, cultural projects, or ethnic communities. For example, in the history of many Muslim countries, the unveiled modern woman has signified modernity and national progress, while the veiled domesticated woman has symbolized the search for authenticity, cultural revival, and reproduction of the group. Women's behavior and appearance—and the range of their activities—come to be defined by, and frequently are subject to, the political or cultural objectives of political movements, states, and leaderships. In some political projects—such as Turkey under Mustafa Kemal Ataturk, Tunisia under President Habib Bourguiba, South Yemen under Marxist leadership, and Afghanistan under the PDPA—women have been linked to modernization and progress. In other political projects, women have been regarded as central to cultural rejuvenation and religious orthodoxy. Examples are Iran under Ayatollah Ruhollah Khomeini, Pakistan under General Zia ul-Haq, and the Islamic resistance of the Afghan Mujahideen. In patriarchal contexts in particular, where women's reproductive roles are fetishized in the context of kinship-ordered structures, women must also assume the burden of maintaining, representing, and transmitting cultural values and traditions. In such a social-structural context, it becomes difficult to see women in other roles, such as students or as citizens.

This chapter discusses the importance of the issue of women's rights in recent Afghan history, and the battle over the woman question between modernizing revolutionaries on one side, and traditionalists and Islamists on the other. The controversy and conflict over women's rights in Afghanistan did not begin in 1978 with the coming to power of Marxists, but has a long history, nevertheless. Progress on the issue of women's rights historically has been constrained by two factors: (a) the patriarchal nature of gender and social relations, deeply embedded in traditional communities, and (b) the existence of a weak central state, which since at least the beginning of this century has been unable to implement fully modernizing programs and goals. The two are interconnected, for the state's weakness is correlated with a strong (if fragmented) society resistant to state bureaucratic expansion, civil authority, regulation, monopoly of the means of violence, and extraction—the business of modern states. Although many feminists are rightly suspicious of the state and its stance toward women, others have noted the importance of welfare states and legal reforms to women's well-being. State-gender issues need to be examined historically and empirically, with attention to social structure and political conflicts. In the specific case of Afghanistan, efforts to improve the status of women have been constrained by a social structure characterized by patriarchal gender relations, tribal feudalism, and a weak central state.

On one level, the conflict in Afghanistan has been over political power: the prerogatives of the state versus the system of tribal feudalism. The regime that came to power in the Saur Revolution sought to extend central authority in order to develop economically and socially what was one of the poorest and most underdeveloped countries in the world. For the modernizing regime, improving the status of women through a literacy campaign and changes in family law and marriage customs was a part of the program of development and change, and was as integral to the overall project as was land reform. For the traditionalists, both land reform and changes in the gender system threatened the existing power structure in the countryside, and were met with the full fury of mullahs, landlords, and tribes. As Charles Tilly has put it, contenders who are in danger of losing their place in a political or social structure are especially prone to reactive collective action, often taking communal forms.[3]

On another level, the conflict has been over cultural, religious, and national identity, self-definition, and objectives. One may distill the main issues in the form of the following questions: Would Afghanistan become a twentieth-century country with a state whose business it was to develop the economy and society? Or would Afghanistan remain a country fragmented along ethnic and regional lines, replete with tribal fiefdoms that impeded modernizing efforts, including the construction of a railway? Would Afghanistan's women be brought out of the all-enveloping veil and taught to read and write? Or would these women continue to exist under conditions of classic patriarchy, controlled by men and the patriarchal family, and whose status was derived exclusively in terms of the number of sons they bore? Would this state of affairs continue to be justified on religious grounds, with the country's mullahs the most persistent advocates of the status quo? Or would the modernizers and their state be able to redefine Afghan culture and religious practices in a more reformist, liberal, and modern way?

The conflict in Afghanistan over the woman question has parallels with the experience of Bolsheviks in Central Asia whose efforts to emancipate Muslim women were part of their overall program to extend Soviet power and rapidly establish socialist modernization.[4] In much the same way, the question of women was integral to the political-cultural project of the Afghan modernizers, and was an essential component of the identity and social structure of the traditionalists. For the modernizers, the veiled and illiterate woman who was exchanged between men for a brideprice symbolized all that was backward and wrong in Afghan society; she had to be liberated from patriarchal constraints and take part in the development of the country. For the traditionalists, change in women's status would upset the sexual division of labor, the whole rural system of exchange between patriarchs, and masculine honor; under no circumstances could women be freed for education. For the modernizers, women's rights to education, employment, mobility, and choice of spouse was a major objective of the national democratic revolution. For the traditionalists, this was inconceivable.

AFGHAN SOCIAL STRUCTURE, THE PATRIARCHAL HOUSEHOLD, AND ITS IMPLICATIONS FOR WOMEN

Historically, the population of Afghanistan has been fragmented into myriad ethnic, linguistic, religious, kin-based, and regional groupings.[5] Afghan nationalism, properly speaking, is at best incipient because the concept of a nation-state, or of a national identity, is absent for much of the population.[6] Since the nineteenth century, it has been promoted primarily by modernizing elites, as Vartan Gregorian's study shows.[7] During most of the country's recent history, the fragmented groupings composed warring factions. Battles were fought principally over land and water, sometimes over women and honor, usually over sheer power—or what Gregory Massell, writing of early twentieth-century Central Asia, described as primordial cleavages and conflicts.[8] One of the few commonalities in this diverse country is adherence to Hanafi Islam. Afghan Islam is a unique combination of practices and precepts from the *Sharīʿa* (Islamic canon law as delineated in religious texts) and tribal customs, particularly Pushtunwali, the tribal code of the Pushtuns, who comprise over 50 percent of the population. On certain issues, Pushtunwali and Islam disagree. For example, contrary to the Islamic ban on usury, there has been widespread usury which has kept rural households in perpetual indebtedness.[9] Exorbitant expenditure in marriages (*sheer-baha*) has also contributed to the rural household's debt accumulation. The Islamic dower, *mahr*, has been abused as a brideprice. *Mahr*, a payment due from groom to bride, is an essential part of the formal Islamic marriage contract. In the Quran, it is a nominal fee and in many Muslim countries its purpose is to provide a kind of social insurance for the wife in the event of divorce or widowhood. In the Afghan patriarchal context, however, the *mahr* (or *walwar* in Pashtu) is the payment to the bride's father as compensation for the loss of his daughter's labor in the household unit.[10] The absence of inheritance rights for females is also contrary to Islamic law but integral to the complex web of the tribal exchange system.[11]

Afghan rural and poor urban women work extraordinarily hard, but their ability to contribute substantially to household survival or family incomes takes place within a patriarchal context of women's subordination and intra-household inequality. In such a context, a woman's labor power is controlled and allocated by someone other than herself; the products of her labor are managed by others; and she receives no remuneration for work performed. In areas where carpet-making is a commercial enterprise, male kin are able to exploit women's labor without any wage payment, as Haleh Afshar has found for Iran and Günseli Berik has described for Turkey. Behrooz Morvaridi's study of peasant farms in Turkey describes how commercialization of peasant farming increases the intensity of female labor. As Deniz Kandiyoti has argued, in extended patriarchal, patrilineal households, collective (male) interests dictate strict control of female labor deployment throughout a woman's lifetime.[12]

Contemporary Afghanistan is an extreme case of what Kandiyoti has called "classic patriarchy," and what the demographer John Caldwell has termed "the patriarchal belt." This belt stretches from northern Africa across the Middle East to the northern plains of the Indian subcontinent and to parts of China (especially rural China). Here, the patriarchal extended family is the central social unit, in which the senior man has authority over everyone else, including younger men, and women are subject to distinct forms of control and subordination. Young brides marry into large families, gain respect mainly via their sons, and late in life acquire power as mothers-in-law. The social structures in the patriarchal belt are characterized by their institutionalization of extremely restrictive codes of behavior for women, such as the practice of rigid gender segregation and a powerful ideology linking family honor to female virtue. Men are entrusted with safeguarding family honor through their control over female members; they are backed by complex social arrangements which ensure the protection—and dependence—of women. In contemporary Muslim patriarchal societies, such control over women is considered necessary in part because women are regarded as the potential source of social *fitna*, that is, disorder or anarchy.[13]

Women's life-chances are severely circumscribed by patriarchal arrangements that favor men. One typically finds an adverse sex ratio, low female literacy and educational attainment, high fertility rates, high maternal mortality rates, and low female labor force participation in the formal sector. Demographic facts about societies such as Afghanistan, Pakistan, and north India suggest a "culture against women," in which women are socialized to sacrifice their health, survival chances, and life options.[14]

Afghan patriarchy is tied to the prevalence of such forms of subsistence as nomadic pastoralism, herding and farming, and settled agriculture, all organized along patrilineal lines. Historically, Afghan gender roles and women's status have been tied to property relations. Property includes livestock, land, and houses or tents. Women and children tend to be assimilated into the concept of property and to belong to a man. This is particularly the case among Pushtuns, whose tribal culture, Pushtunwali, is highly masculinist. According to anthropologist Nancy Tapper, who has studied the Durrani Pushtuns of north-central Afghanistan: "The members of the community discuss control of all resources—especially labor, land, and woman—in terms of honor."[15] Note that "community" is the community of men, and that "women" are assimilated in the concept of "resources." Gender segregation and female seclusion exist, though they vary by ethnic group, region, mode of subsistence, social class, and family. Inger Boesen reports that women resent male control of their sexuality and they rebel, pursuing extramarital affairs and covering up each other's activities. Such forms of resistance, however, do not change gender status ranking. Men's and women's objectives and lifestyles are in sharp contrast. Although Tapper has stated that a typical Afghan women's wish is for a successful marriage with many sons, Veronica Doubleday's book on women in Herat reveals that women also have other aspirations, but that these are blocked.[16]

In a patriarchal context, marriage and brideprice are a transaction between households, an integral part of property relations, and an indicator of status. In Afghanistan, marriage, forced or voluntary, was a way of ending feuds, cementing a political alliance between families, or increasing the family's prestige. Tapper describes how the exchange of women for brideprice or in compensation for blood maintains a status hierarchy among the households. In the exchange system, men are ranked in the first and highest sphere. Direct exchanges between them include the most honorable and manly of all activities and these activities are prime expressions of status equality: vengeance and feud, political support and hostility, and the practice of sanctuary. Women belong in the second sphere; they are often treated exclusively as reproducers and pawns in economic and political exchanges. There is only one proper conversion between the first two spheres: two or more women can be given in compensation for the killing or injury of one man. Mobility and migration patterns also revolve around the brideprice. For example, men from one region will travel to another to find inexpensive brides, while other men will travel elsewhere to obtain a higher price for their daughters. Tapper's description accords well with Massell's discussion of the importance of *kalym* (brideprice) to overall property relations in early twentieth-century Central Asia.[17]

The seclusion of women (*purdah*) was widespread in Afghanistan, and Inger Boesen has noted a Pushtun saying that "a woman is best either in the house or in the grave."[18] Kathleen Howard-Merriam states that not only do women never ask the men their whereabouts or expect marital fidelity, they are also expected to give all the meat, choicest food, and the best clothing to their husbands, as well as their personal wealth if so demanded. Not surprisingly, maternal mortality has been excessive. Census and surveys undertaken in 1967, 1972–1974, and 1979 have revealed an unusually high ratio of males to females, which exceeds even the expected underreporting of females in a conservative Muslim society.[19]

Doubleday, who lived in Herat on and off between 1972 and 1977, explains in her book that women's complaints focused around two issues, which she came to see as related: sickness and the restrictions imposed by the seclusion. The women complained of backaches, lack of energy, and many other ailments, and said that sometimes their husbands would not let them go to a doctor. Some women complained specifically about their seclusion, which they called *qeit*, or confinement, imprisonment. Doubleday describes how, despite her desire to avoid Western ethnocentrism, she had to conclude that *purdah* was not simply about being segregated and veiled; it meant that men had complete control over the movements of their women, and it gave men ultimate power. She also describes "the deep anxiety women experienced over illness." She writes:

> As mothers and nurturers of the family they had a vital responsibility, and yet they and their children were especially vulnerable since they depended upon their husbands for money for cures. It was iniquitous but true that men could deny women and children recourse to medical help, and it was no wonder that women placed importance upon methods such as divination or diet, which were at least accessible and within their control.[20]

These were among the cultural practices and aspects of the situation of women that were of concern to Afghan reformers and revolutionaries throughout the twentieth century. State initiatives to extend government authority or to establish an infrastructure have frequently resulted in tribal rebellion. Persistent government difficulty in extending education to girls has been noted by many authors; Gregorian describes opposition to the modernizing efforts, including education for girls, of Habibullah Khan (1901–1919) and Amanullah Khan (1919–1929).[21] The existence of a weak state in a predominantly patriarchal and tribal society has had adverse implications for reform and development, as well as for the advancement of women.

THE PDPA AND WOMEN'S RIGHTS

Written in the 1960s, Gregorian's book on Afghanistan frequently refers to the "staggering socio-economic problems" of the country, and to the religio-traditionalist forces who have prevented their resolution. Like many other Third World countries at that time, a modernizing elite, in this case left-wing, organized itself to address the country's problems and to steer Afghanistan away from its dependency on U.S. aid money.

In 1965, a group from the small Afghan intelligentsia formed the

People's Democratic Party of Afghanistan (PDPA). Evoking the Amanullah experiment, the PDPA called for a national democratic government to liberate Afghanistan from backwardness. Among its demands were primary education for all children in their mother tongue and the development of the different languages and cultures of the country. Its social demands included guarantees of the right to work, equal treatment for women, a forty-two-hour week, paid sickness and maternity leave, and a ban on child labor. That same year, six women activists formed the Democratic Organization of Afghan Women (DOAW). The DOAW's main objectives were to eliminate illiteracy among women, forced marriages, and the brideprice. As a result of the activities of the DOAW and the PDPA, and notwithstanding hostility from mullahs and other conservative elements, women won the right to vote, and in the 1970s four women from the DOAW were elected to Parliament. In the years before the Saur Revolution, the DOAW managed to win the legal right of women to study abroad. Another achievement was to win the right of women to work outside the home, previously the privilege of a few women from elite families.[22] Both the PDPA and the DOAW were eager for more profound, extensive, and permanent changes.

Among the most remarkable and influential of the DOAW activists was Anahita Ratebzad. In the 1950s, she studied nursing in the United States, and then returned to Kabul as director and instructor of nursing at the Women's Hospital. Nancy Dupree explains that when the faculty for women at Kabul University was established, she entered the medical college and became a member of its teaching staff upon graduation in 1963. She joined the PDPA in 1965, and along with three other women ran as candidates for parliament. This was the first time liberals and leftists had openly appeared in the political arena, and what they confronted was reaction to female visibility on the part of conservative members of parliament. In 1968, the latter proposed to enact a law prohibiting young women from studying abroad. Hundreds of female students demonstrated in opposition. In 1970, two mullahs protested such public evidence of female liberation as miniskirts, women teachers, and schoolgirls by shooting at the legs of women in Western dress and splashing them with acid. Among those who joined in this action was Gulbeddin Hekmatyar (who went on to be a leading figure in the Mujahideen, one of the "freedom fighters" hailed by President Reagan). This time there was a protest demonstration of five thousand girls.

Modernization, however limited, had created a stratum of men and women eager for further and deeper social change. According to ILO data, Afghanistan in 1979 had a female population of 6.3 million, of whom 313,000 were considered economically active. Of that figure, 85 percent were production-related workers, employed mainly in textiles (clothing and carpets), where they typically did not themselves receive a wage, a pattern also found in Iran and Turkey. The other major category of employed women was "professional, technical, and related workers": thirteen thousand women or 4 percent of the economically active female population. These women were mostly teachers, nurses, and government employees (all high-status occupations), secretaries, hairdressers, entertainers, and two or three parliamentarians: members of the salaried middle class. The salaried middle class, the modern working class, and the female labor force in Afghanistan were all small, but a part of the social fabric, nonetheless.

In April 1978, the PDPA, after having seized power in what came to be called the Saur (April) Revolution, introduced rapid reforms to change the political and social structure of Afghan society, including patterns of land tenure and gender relations. Three decrees—Nos. 6, 7, and 8—were the main planks of the program of social and economic reform. Decree No. 6 was intended to put an end to land mortgage and indebtedness; No. 7 was designed to stop the payment of brideprice and give women more freedom of choice in marriage; No. 8 consisted of rules and regulations for the confiscation and redistribution of land. The three decrees were complementary—particularly Decree No. 6 and Decree No. 7, for, as noted earlier in this chapter, extravagant expenditure on marriage added to or perpetuated rural households' indebtedness. Decree No. 7, however, seems to have been the most controversial, as it was meant to change fundamentally the institution of marriage. The government of President Noor Mohammad Taraki issued the decree with the explicit intention of ensuring equal rights for women, removing patriarchal and feudalistic ties between spouses, and ending the economic exploitation of female labor. It was prohibited to put a price on the bride and the woman's dowry was limited. Forced marriages and the practice of levirate were outlawed and marriage through subterfuge or coercion prohibited. A minimum age of marriage was set for both genders, sixteen years for women and eighteen years for men. In a speech on 4 November 1978, President Taraki declared: "Through the issuance of decrees no. 6 and 7, the hard-working peasants were freed from bonds of oppressors and money-lenders, ending the sale of girls for good as hereafter nobody would be entitled to sell any girl or woman in this country."[23] These decrees are very similar, in both spirit and letter, to the revolutionary decrees in Central Asia that abolished brideprice, polygamy, forced marriage, child marriage, physical segregation, and heavy veils.[24] In both cases, the decrees outlawed traditional cultural practices that were economically significant and integral to property relationships in the countryside.

The six articles of Decree No. 7 were as follows:

> *Article 1*. No one shall engage a girl or give her in marriage in exchange for cash or commodities.
>
> *Article 2*. No one shall compel the bridegroom or his guardians to give holiday presents to the girl or her family.
>
> *Article 3*. The girl or her guardian shall not take cash or commodities in the name of dower [*mahr*] in excess of ten dirham [Arabic coinage] according to Shari^{c}at [Islamic law], which is not more than 300 afs. [about U.S. $10] on the basis of the bank rate of silver.
>
> *Article 4*. Engagements and marriage shall take place with the full consent of the parties involved: (a) No one shall force marriage; (b) No one shall prevent the free marriage of a widow or force her into marriage because of family relationships [the levirate] or patriarchal ties; (c) No one shall prevent legal marriages on the pretext of engagement, forced engagement expenses, or by using force.
>
> *Article 5*. Engagement and marriages for women under sixteen and men under eighteen are not permissible.
>
> *Article 6*. (1) Violators shall be liable to imprisonment from six months to three years; (2) Cash or commodities accepted in violation of the provisions of this decree shall be confiscated.

Along with the promulgation of this audacious decree, the PDPA government embarked upon an aggressive literacy campaign, led by the DOAW, whose task was to educate women, bring them out of seclusion, and initiate social programs.[25] Literacy programs were expanded with the objective of supplying all adult citizens with basic reading and writing skills within a year. Throughout the countryside, PDPA cadre established literacy classes for men, women, and children in villages; by August 1979, the government had established six hundred new schools. The PDPA's rationale for pursuing the rural literacy campaign with some zeal was that all previous reformers had made literacy a matter of choice; male guardians had chosen not to allow their females to be educated; thus 96 percent of all Afghan women were illiterate. It was therefore decided not to allow literacy to remain a matter of (men's) choice, but rather a matter of principle and law.

This was, clearly, a bold program for social change, one aimed at the rapid transformation of a patriarchal society and decentralized power structure based on tribal and landlord authority. Revolutionary change, state-building, and women's rights subsequently went hand-in-hand. The emphasis on women's rights on the part of the PDPA reflected: (a) their socialist/Marxist ideology, (b) their modernizing and egalitarian outlook, (c) their social base and origins: urban middle class, professionals, educated in the United States, the Soviet Union, and western and eastern Europe, and (d) the number and position of women within the PDPA, especially the outspoken and dynamic Anahita Ratebzad.

In 1976, Anahita Ratebzad had been elected to the central committee of the PDPA. Following the Saur Revolution, she was elected to the Revolutionary Council of the Democratic Republic of Afghanistan (DRA) and appointed minister of social affairs. Other influential PDPA women in the Taraki government (April 1978–September 1979) were Sultana Umayd, director of Kabul Girls' School; Soraya, president of the DWOA; Ruhafza Kamyar, principal of the DWOA's Vocational High School; Firouza, director of the Afghan Red Crescent (Red Cross); Dilara Mahak, principal of the Amana Fidawa School; and Professor Mrs. R. S. Siddiqui (who was especially outspoken in her criticism of feudalistic patriarchal relations). In the Amin government (September–December 1979), the following women headed schools and the women's organization, as well as sat on government subcommittees: Fawjiyah Shahsawari, Dr. Aziza, Shirin Afzal, Alamat Tolqun. These were the women who were behind the program for women's rights. Their spirit was reflected in an editorial in the *Kabul Times* (25 May 1978) which asserted: "Privileges which women, by right, must have are equal education, job security, health services, and free time to rear a healthy generation for building the future of this country. Educating and enlightening women is now the subject of close government scrutiny."[26] Their intention was to expand literacy (especially for girls and women), encourage income-generating projects and employment for women, provide health and legal services for women, and eliminate those aspects of Muslim family law which discriminate against women: unilateral male repudiation, father's or patrilineal family's exclusive rights to child custody, unequal inheritance, and male guardianship over women.

INTERNATIONALIZED CIVIL CONFLICT

The Saur Revolution was considered to be not a socialist revolution—which in any event was inconceivable in a tribal-feudalistic society—but a national democratic revolution. President Taraki himself, in his first press conference on 7 May 1978, characterized the new regime as reformist, constructive, and tolerant of Islam. Taraki's conciliatory gestures such as attendance at Friday congregational prayers, and assurances that his government's policies would be consistent with Islamic principles, failed to prevent the mobilization of opposition. In response to the decree of July 1978 on agrarian reform which reduced or cancelled all rural debts prior to 1984 and forbade lenders to collect usury in the future, many angry lenders murdered debtors who refused to pay.[27] There was also universal resistance to the new marriage regulations which, coupled with compulsory education for girls, raised the threat of women refusing to obey and submit to family (male) authority. Believing that women should not appear at public gatherings, villagers often refused to attend classes after the first day. PDPA cadre viewed this attitude as retrograde, and, thus, the cadre resorted to different forms of persuasion, including physical force, to make the villagers return to literacy classes. Often PDPA cadre were either kicked out of the village or murdered. In the summer of 1978, refugees began pouring into Pakistan, giving as their major reason the forceful implementation of the literacy program among their women. In Kandahar, three literacy workers from the women's organization were killed as symbols of the unwanted revolution. Nancy Dupree reports that two men killed all the women in their families to prevent them from dishonor. According to another observer, the reforms "inevitably aroused the opposition of Afghan men, whose male chauvinism is as massive as the mountains of the Hindu Kush."[28]

The content of Decree No. 7 and the coercion of women into education were perceived by some as unbearable interference in domestic life. The prohibition of the brideprice also prevented the traditional transactions and ruined the economy of many households that had counted on this brideprice as convertible capital for the future. Compulsory education was also disliked because the male householder could no longer be in control of the women and their external relations; if women were not in *purdah* then the reputation of the household was at risk. Land reform, cancellation of peasants' debts, and marriage reform threatened vested rural interests and patriarchal structures. The large landowners, the religious establishment, and moneylenders were especially appalled at the prospect of social structural transformation. These kinds of sentiments against the reforms are taken by many observers as the main reason for the early resistance. Reaction was soon to follow. After the announcement of the decree, resistance against the PDPA regime was organized in Paktia and spread rapidly to other areas of east Afghanistan.[29] In the spring of 1979, several armed actions against the government were conducted.

Internal battles within the PDPA (especially between its two wings, Parcham and Khalq) contributed to the government's difficulties. In September 1979, President Taraki was killed on the orders of his deputy, Hafizullah Amin, a ruthless and ambitious man who imprisoned and executed hundreds of his own comrades in addition to alienating the population. The Pakistani regime of General Zia ul-Haq was opposed to Marxists next door, and supported the Mujahideen armed uprising. In December 1979, the Soviet army intervened. Amin was killed and succeeded by Babrak Karmal, who initiated what is called "the second phase" (*marhale-i dovvom*), predicated upon a more gradualist approach to change. Even so, the Mujahideen continued their attacks, encouraged by Pakistan and the United States. In turn, Soviet aircraft carried out bombing raids that resulted in considerable destruction.

It should be noted that not everyone in the PDPA and the DOAW was in favor of the pace of the reforms. According to Soraya, many DOAW activists, including herself, were opposed to the pace and the compulsory nature of the program for land reforms, women's education, and the new family law. As a result of her antagonism toward Hafizullah Amin, Soraya, like many PDPA members of the Parcham wing, was imprisoned, and even endured torture. She, along with the others, was released after the Soviet intervention, the death of Amin, and his replacement by Babrak Karmal.[30]

In 1980, the PDPA slowed down its reform program and announced its intention to eliminate illiteracy in the cities in seven years and in the provinces in ten. In an interview that year, Anahita Ratebzad conceded errors, "in particular the compulsory education of women," to which she added, "the reactionary elements immediately made use of these mistakes to spread discontent among the population."[31] Despite the slowing down of reforms (including concessions such as the restoration of Islamic family law),[32] the opposition movement spread, supported by Pakistan, the United States, China, the Islamic Republic of Iran, and Saudi Arabia.

The literature on Afghanistan has been exceedingly partisan in favor of the Mujahideen and noticeably reluctant to discuss the positive aspects of the PDPA state's social program, especially its policy on women's rights. Mark Urban, however, notes that "one genuine achievement of the revolution has been the emancipation of (mainly urban) women." He continues:

> There is no doubt that thousands of women are committed to the regime, as their prominent participation in Revolutionary Defense Group militias shows. Eyewitnesses stated that militant militiawomen played a key role in defending the besieged town or Urgan in 1983. Four of the seven commanders appointed to the Revolutionary Council in January 1986 were women.[33]

As one enthusiastic teenage girl said to me at a PDPA rally in early 1989: "This revolution was made for women!"

FROM REVOLUTION TO RECONCILIATION

Notwithstanding strong support from urban women and other activists, the Afghan state was unable to impose its will through an extensive administrative and military apparatus. As a result, the program for land redistribution and women's rights faltered. But the DOAW continued its work. In 1986, it was renamed the All-Afghan Women's Council, and also underwent a shift in orientation. It became less radical and more of a service organization providing social and legal services to poor Afghan women. During the late 1980s, the Women's Council was led by Massouma Esmaty Wardak, an early DOAW member and member of parliament, but not a PDPA member.[34] The PDPA's emphasis on the woman question subsided in favor of a concerted effort at national reconciliation, which began in January 1987. In the Constitution of November 1988, the product of a *loya jirga*, or traditional assembly, PDPA members and activists from the Women's Council tried to retain an article stipulating the equality of women with men. This, however, was opposed by the non-PDPA members of the assembly. A compromise was reached in the form of another article which stated that all Afghan citizens, male and female, have equal rights and obligations before the law. According to a PDPA official, this compromise was reached after PDPA members and delegates from the Women's Council failed in their attempts to include a more strongly worded equal rights clause.[35]

Article 38 of the Constitution of the Republic of Afghanistan, ratified in November 1987, stated:

> Citizens of the Republic of Afghanistan, both men and women, have equal rights and duties before the law, irrespective of their

> national, racial, linguistic, tribal, educational and social status, religion, creed, political conviction, occupation, kinship, wealth, and residence. Designation of any illegal privilege of discrimination against rights and duties of citizens is forbidden.[36]

WOMEN IN KABUL AND PESHAWAR: A COMPARISON

During the 1980s in areas under government control, and especially in Kabul, women were present in the different ranks of the Party and the government, with the exception of the council of ministers. The *Loya Jirga* included female delegates: in 1989 the Parliament had seven female members. In 1989, women in prominent positions included Massouma Esmaty Wardak, president of the Women's Council; Shafiqeh Razmandeh, vice president of the Women's Council; Soraya, director of the Afghan Red Crescent Society; Zahereh Dadmal, director of the Kabul Women's Club; Dr. Soheila, chief surgeon of the Military Hospital, who also held the rank of general. The Central Committee of the PDPA had several female members, including Jamila Palwasha and Ruhafza (alternate member), a working-class grandmother and "model worker" at the Kabul Construction Plant where she did electrical wiring.

In Kabul in January–February 1989, I saw women employees in all the government agencies and social organizations I visited. Ariana Airlines employed female as well as male flight attendants. A male employee of the Peace, Solidarity, and Friendship Organization told me that he was thirty-seven, yet had a supervisor who was ten years younger than he and female. There were female radio announcers, and the evening news (whether in Pushtu or Dari) was read by one male and one female announcer. There were female technicians as well as reporters working for radio and television, and in the country's newspapers and magazines. Female workers were present in the binding section of a printer house in Kabul, in the page setting section of the higher and vocational education press house, at the CREPCA state-run carpet company (where young women wove carpets and received a wage), and at the Kabul construction plant (which specialized in housing and pre-fabricated materials). Like their male counterparts, these women were members of the Central Trade Union. I also saw one female employee (and several female volunteer soldiers) at Pol-e Charki prison; she was assigned to the women's section where she oversaw the six remaining female political prisoners, all charged with terrorist acts. I was told that there are female soldiers and officers in the regular armed forces, as well as in the militia and Women's Self Defense (Defense of the Revolution) Units. There were women in security, intelligence, and the police agencies; women involved in logistics in the defense ministry; and even female veterinarians (an occupation usually off limits to women in Muslim countries) and parachutists. In 1989, all female members of the PDPA received military training and arms. These women were prominent at a party rally of some fifty thousand held in Kabul in early February 1989.

Schools were segregated above the primary level, and middle school and secondary school girls could only be taught by female teachers. This was a concession made to the traditionalist elements. In offices and other workplaces, however, there was no segregation. Neither were buses divided into male and female sections.

During the 1980s, there were a number of social organizations with considerable female participants and visibility. Apart from the PDPA itself, they included the Council of Trade Unions, the Democratic Youth Organization, the Peace, Solidarity and Friendship Organization, the Women's Council, and the Red Crescent Society. Two of these organizations were led by women: the Afghan Red Crescent Society and the Afghan Women's Council. In the late 1980s, the Afghan Women's Council (AWC) was run by Massouma Esmaty Wardak and a staff of eight women. (In 1991 she became the minister of education.) Massouma was not a PDPA member, though some of her staff were. A graduate of the Academy of Sciences with a degree in sociology, she had an interest in literature and history, and one of our conversations in her office touched on such topics as early twentieth-century history in Central Asia, the Buddhist influence in Afghanistan, and Persian and Afghan poetry. Among her published works is a book entitled *The Position and Role of Afghan Women in Afghan Society: From the Late 18th to the Late 19th Century*; she also wrote the introduction to a book on Mahmud Tarzi, an early twentieth-century social reformer and women's rights champion.

In discussions with both Massouma and Soraya, I learned that the Women's Council was less political and more social- and service-oriented than it had been in the past. The AWC provided social services to women, such as literacy and vocational training in such fields as secretarial work, hairdressing, and sewing (workshops were located in the complex); organized income-generating activities such as handicraft production (mainly rugs and carpets, as well as sewing); offered assistance to mothers and widows of "martyrs of the Revolution" in the form of pensions and coupons; and provided legal advice, mainly through a network of female lawyers. Some women had "outwork" arrangements with the AWC: "They prefer to work at home; they bring their work to us and we pay them." During two trips to the Women's Council, I was able to observe dozens of women (many of them veiled) entering the grounds to attend a class or to seek advice.

Massouma told me that the AWC had a membership of 150,000 with branches in all provinces except Wardak and Katawaz. The branches organized traditional festivals that included awards for handicraft pieces, and "peace camps" which provided medical care and distributed garments and relief goods free of charge. The branches also assisted women in income-generating activities, such as raising chickens, producing eggs and milk for sale, and sewing and craftwork. The work of the AWC was supported by the government, which provided it with a generous budget.[37]

The principal objectives of the AWC, according to its president, were raising women's social consciousness, making them aware of their rights (particularly their right to literacy and work), and improving women's living conditions and professional skills. She stressed equal pay with men and workplace child care as two important achievements. But customs die hard. There was an ongoing radio and TV campaign against the brideprice, or what she called the buying and selling of girls. The AWC was also trying to change the laws on child custody that favor the father and his agnates.

Like the AWC, the Kabul Women's Club was located on spacious grounds and held two-hour literacy classes daily. It also conducted vocational training and housed employment workshops where women wove rugs and carpets, sewed uniforms, embroidered, and produced handicrafts. The work was entirely waged, and child care and transportation were provided. Courses on house management, health, hairdressing, and typing were offered free of charge. The Women's Club also worked with the public health ministry on mother-and-child issues, such as the prevention of diseases, vaccination of children, breastfeeding, and family planning.[38]

In Kabul, I asked many party members and workers on the Afghan Women's Council if women's rights would be sacrificed on the altar of national reconciliation. All were fervent believers in the party's duty to defend the gains made in women's rights, and in the ability of the women's organizations to stand up for women's rights to education and employment. Among women in the capital, there was considerable hostility toward the Mujahideen, and I was told several times that "the women would not allow" a Mujahideen takeover. I was moved by many things I saw and heard in Kabul, and I was especially impressed by the strong women and girls I met. Being an Iranian, I felt deep affinity with them, and they with me, notwithstanding the Iranian government's support for the Mujahideen, which angered me then and now. Although I had a sense that tragedy loomed for the PDPA and for Afghan women, I wrote a number of articles and letters to the editor, immediately upon my return to the United States, arguing that the PDPA was more popular than it was made out to be, that the Mujahideen were less popular than their many external supporters claimed they were, and that the government and social programs of Dr. Najibullah deserved support.[39]

In Peshawar, the situation of women and the opportunities afforded them were entirely different. Unlike liberation, resistance, and guerrilla movements elsewhere, the Afghan Mujahideen never encouraged the active participation of women. In Cuba, Algeria, Vietnam, China, Eritrea, Oman, Iran, Nicaragua, El Salvador, and Palestine, women were and are active in the front lines, in party politics, and in social services. It is noteworthy that the Mujahideen never had a female spokesperson. Indeed, women in Peshawar who became too visible or vocal were threatened and sometimes killed. The group responsible for most of the intimidation of women was the fundamentalist *Hizb-e Islami*, led by Gulbeddin Hekmatyar, who over the years received substantial military, political, and financial support from the United States, Pakistan, and Saudi Arabia. Furthermore, the educational situation in Peshawar was extremely biased against girls. In 1988, some 104,600 boys were enrolled in schools against 7,800 girls. For boys, there were 486 primary schools, 161 middle schools, and 4 high schools. For girls, there were 76 primary schools, 2 middle schools, and no high schools.[40] A UNICEF study indicated that only 180 Afghan women in the camps had a high school education. This is consistent with the highly patriarchal arrangements among the Mujahideen and in Peshawar.

The subordinate status of women was apparently decried by some in Peshawar. The Revolutionary Association of Women in Afghanistan (RAWA) was founded in 1977 as a Maoist group. It became prominent on 4 February 1987, when its founder, Mina Kishwar Kamal, was killed by Mujahideen in Quetta. On 27 December 1988, RAWA staged a demonstration by women and children in Rawalpindi on the occasion of the ninth anniversary of the Soviet military intervention in Afghanistan. The demonstrators distributed pamphlets attacking the KGB, Khad (the Afghan secret police), and the *Hizb-e Islami* in the strongest terms. They claimed that the majority of Afghans stood for an independent and democratic Afghanistan, where social justice and freedom to women was guaranteed.[41] In a communiqué distributed that day, RAWA deplored "the reactionary fanatics [who] are savagely suppressing our grieved people, specially [sic] the women." It continued:

> Killing the innocent men and women, raping, to marry forcefully young girls and widows, and hostility toward women's literacy and education, are some customary cruelties committed by the fundamentalists who have made the life inside and outside the country bitter and suffocating. In their cheap opinion, the women struggle for any right and freedom is regarded as infidelity which must be suppressed brutaly [sic].

The communiqué decried the "anti-democratic and anti-woman" activities of the fundamentalists and warned of "fundamentalist fascism" replacing the current regime.

Following the withdrawal of Soviet troops in February 1989, there was some hope that a compromise could be reached between the government of President Najibullah and the Mujahideen. To facilitate this, the government revised its ideological and programmatic orientation. Following its congress in Spring 1990, the PDPA changed its name to the *Hizb-e Watan*, or the Homeland Party. Constitutional changes were also made, stressing Islam and nation and dropping altogether references to the equality of men and women. Clearly, a decision had been made that the emancipation of women would have to await peace, stability, reconstruction, and development. But by April 1992, under pressure from the new U.N. Secretary General, Boutros Ghali, and his envoy, Benon Sevan, President Najibullah agreed to give up power. This triggered democratization and desertion in the Afghan military, dissention within the government, and the takeover of Kabul by Mujahideen fighters. Once they came to power, the Mujahideen factions began to fight each other, but the men all agreed on the question of women. Thus the very first order of the new government was that all women should wear veils. As one journalist wrote from Kabul in early May 1992:

> The most visible sign of change on the streets, apart from the guns, is the utter disappearance of women in western clothes. They used to be a common sight. Now women cover up from ankle to throat and hide their hair, or else use the *burqa*, which covers the entire body and has a portcullis-type grill at eye level. Many women are frightened to leave their homes. At the telephone office, 80 percent of the male workers reported for duty on Saturday, and only 20 percent of the females.[42]

SUMMARY AND CONCLUSION

This chapter has underscored the importance of the issue of women's rights in the Afghan revolution and civil conflict. It has also explained the subordinate position of women, the resistance to women's rights (including the right to education), and the inability of the state to implement its reform program in terms of the persistence of patriarchy and the existence of a weak state. Throughout the twentieth century, the Afghan state—small and weak as it was—has been incapable of implementing its program in an effective way. While Afghanistan is not the only patriarchal country in the world, it is an extreme case of classic patriarchy. A rugged terrain and armed tribes have made modernization and centralization a difficult, prolonged, and limited enterprise—as even the Mujahideen government of today is experiencing. This has had serious, and dire, implications for the advancement of women.

There can be no doubt that the manner in which land reform and women's emancipation were implemented immediately after the revolution was seriously flawed and sparked massive flight (mainly to Pakistan but also to Iran) as well as armed resistance. Some of the audacious symbols of the revolution—red flags, the term "comrade," pictures of Lenin and the like—were also ill-advised considering the extremely conservative and patriarchal social structure, and contributed to the hostility. Nevertheless, the conflict in Afghanistan must be understood as contestation over two unalterably opposed political-cultural projects: development and reform on the one hand, tribal authority and patriarchal relations on the other. The government's efforts to raise women's status through legal changes regarding marriage were stymied first by patriarchal structures highly resistant to change, and secondly by an extremely hostile international environment.

In the Afghan case, the woman question assumed huge proportions. One may ask, following Hanna Papanek, "why do regimes raise the Woman Question if it creates so much trouble?"[43] Maxine Molyneux has surveyed the importance of women's rights to socialist societies for both symbolic and mobilizational purposes,[44] and Papanek has noted that movements and regimes use their specific stand on the woman question as a way of signalling their political agenda. In the case of Afghanistan, uncovering versus covering women, liberating women versus keeping them in their place, and other discourses about and plans for women suggested the political, economic, and cultural projects of the contending groups: the modernizers versus the traditionalists, the new middle class versus the tribal-feudalists. In this contention some women were players, but most were pawns.

NOTES

1. Also indicative of the nature of the Mujahideen is that the withdrawal of Soviet troops in 1989 did not lead to a cessation of hostilities on their part, and that the final defeat of the modernizers in April 1992 was followed by renewed fighting between Mujahideen factions which has all but destroyed Kabul.

2. Nira Yuval-Davis and Floya Anthias, eds., *Woman-Nation-State* (London: Macmillan, 1989); V. M. Moghadam, "Revolution, Culture and Gender: Notes on the Woman Question in Revolution," paper presented at the Twelfth World Congress of Sociology, Madrid (July 1990); Deniz Kandiyoti, ed., *Women, State and Islam* (London: Macmillan, 1991); V. M. Moghadam, ed., *Identity Politics and Women: Cultural Reassertions and Feminisms in International Perspective* (Boulder: Westview Press, 1994); V. M. Moghadam, ed., *Gender and National Identity: Women and Politics in Muslim Societies* (London: Zed Books, 1994); and of course all the contributions in this book.

3. See Charles Tilly, *From Mobilization to Revolution* (Reading, Mass.: Addison-Wesley, 1972).

4. This has been described and analyzed in great detail in Gregory Massell's classic study, *The Surrogate Proletariat: Moslem Women and Revolutionary Strategies in Soviet Central Asia, 1919–1929* (Princeton: Princeton University Press, 1974).

5. See Louis Dupree, *Afghanistan* (Princeton: Princeton University Press, 1980); and Olivier Roy, *Islam and Resistance in Afghanistan*, 2nd ed. (Cambridge: Cambridge University Press, 1990), for rich descriptions.

6. Thomas Hammond, *Red Flag Over Afghanistan* (Boulder: Westview, 1984), 5; Mark Urban, *War in Afghanistan* (New York: St. Martins, 1988), 204.

7. Vartan Gregorian, *The Emergence of Modern Afghanistan* (Stanford: Stanford University Press, 1969).

8. Massell, *Surrogate Proletariat*, 9.

9. On Islam as a unifying force in the Afghan resistance, see Eden Naby, "Islam Within the Afghan Resistance," *Third World Quarterly* 10, no. 2: 787–805. On differences between Afghan Islam and the Shariat, especially on usury, see Raja Anwar, *The Tragedy of Afghanistan* (London: Verso, 1988), 133–34. On Pushtunwali and its disagreement with Islam, see Roy, *Islam and Resistance in Afghanistan*, 35–36; John C. Griffiths, *Afghanistan* (Boulder: Westview Press, 1981), 111–12; Beverly Male, *Revolutionary Afghanistan* (New York: St. Martin's Press, 1981); Kathleen Howard-Merriam, "Afghan Refugee Women and their Struggle for Survival," in *Afghan Resistance: The Politics of Survival*, ed. Grant Farr and John Merrian (Boulder: Westview Press, 1987), 103–5; Inger Boesen, "Conflicts of Solidarity in Pushtun Women's Lives," in *Women in Islamic Society*, ed. Bo Utas (Copenhagen: Scandinavian Institute of Asian Studies, 1983), 104–25.

10. See Mohammad Hashim Kamali, *Law in Afghanistan: A Study of the Constitutions, Matrimonial Law, and the Judiciary* (Leiden: E. J. Brill, 1985); Nancy Trapper, "Causes and Consequences of the Abolition of Brideprice in Afghanistan," in *Rebellions and Revolutions in Afghanistan*, ed. Nazif Shahrani and Robert Canfield (Berkeley: University of California International Studies Institute, 1984), 291–305.

11. Kathleen Howard-Merriam, "Afghan Refugee Women," 101–20.

12. Haleh Afshar, "The Position of Women in an Iranian Village," in *Women, Work and Ideology in the Third World*, ed. H. Afshar (London: Tavistock, 1985), especially 75–76; Günseli Berik, *Women Carpet Weavers in Rural Turkey: Patterns of Employment, Earnings and Status* (Geneva: ILO, 1987), especially chap. 4; Behrooz Morvaridi, "Gender Relations in Agriculture: Women in Turkey," *Economic Development and Cultural Change* 40, no. 3 (1992): 567–86; and Deniz Kandiyoti, "Rural Transformation in Turkey and Its Implications for Women's Status," in UNESCO, *Women on the Move* (Paris: UNESCO, 1984), 17–30.

13. On *fitna*, see Fatna Sabbah, *Women in the Muslim Unconscious* (New York: Pergamon Press, 1984); Mai Ghoussoub, "Feminism—or the Eternal Masculine—in the Arab World," *New Left Review* 161 (January/February 1987): 3–13; Naila Kabeer, "Subordination and Struggle: Women in Bangladesh," *New Left Review* 168 (March/April 1988): 95. On patriarchy, see Deniz Kandiyoti, "Bargaining with Patriarchy," *Gender and Society* 2, no. 3 (September 1988): 274–90; and John Caldwell, *Theory of Fertility Decline* (New York: Academic Press, 1982). On the patriarchal family in early twentieth-century central Asia, see Massell, *Surrogate Proletariat*, 65–88.

14. The term "culture against women" is from Hanna Papanek. See her essay, "To Each Less than She Needs, From Each More than She Can Do: Allocations, Entitlements, and Value," in *Persistent Inequalities: Women and World Development*, ed. Irene Tinker (New York: Oxford University Press, 1990), 162–84.

15. On Afghan women as property, see sources cited in n.10. The quote from Tapper appears on 304.

16. Veronica Doubleday, *Three Women of Herat* (Austin: University of Texas Press, 1988). See also Boesen, "Conflicts of Solidarity in Pukhtun Women's Lives," and Tapper, "Causes and Consequences of the Abolition of Brideprice."

17. Tapper, "Causes and Consequences of the Abolition of Brideprice," 304; Massell, *The Surrogate Proletariat*, 160–63.

18. Boesen, "Conflicts of Solidarity in Pushtun Women's Lives."

19. Howard-Merriam, "Afghan Refugee Women." For demographic data on Afghanistan in 1965 and 1979, see Moghadam, *Modernizing Women*, chap. 7, tables 7.1, 7.2, 7.3.

20. Doubleday, *Three Women of Herat*, 149.

21. Gregorian, *Emergence of Modern Afghanistan*. Amanullah Khan, a nationalist and modernizer, initiated many reforms but was deposed in a tribal rebellion with British backing.

22. Interview with Soraya (no last name), a DOAW founder and later director of the Afghan Red Crescent Society, Kabul, 6 February 1989.

23. Tapper, "Causes and Consequences of the Abolition of Brideprice," 291. On Decrees no. 6 and 7 see also Mansoor Akbar, "Revolutionary Changes and Social Resistance in Afghanistan, *Asian Profile* 17, no. 3 (June 1989): 271–81. See also Nancy Hatch Dupree, "Revolutionary Rhetoric and Afghan Women," esp. 322–25, and Hugh Beattie, "Effects of the Saur Revolution in Nahrin," in Shahrani and Canfield, *Rebellions and Revolutions in Afghanistan*, 186.

24. See Massell, *Surrogate Proletariat*, 136.

25. Interview with Massouma Esmaty Wardak, a DOAW founding member, later director of the Afghan Women's Council, and minister of education just prior to the Mujahideen takeover, 1 February 1989, in Kabul.

26. N. H. Dupree, "Revolutionary Rhetoric and Afghan Women," 316.

27. Massell describes a similar outcome in Central Asia. See Massell, *Surrogate Proletariat*, 70.

28. Thomas Hammond, *Red Flag Over Afghanistan*, 71; Nancy Dupree, "Revolutionary Rhetoric," 321.

29. Hanne Christensen, *The Reconstruction of Afghanistan: A Chance for Rural Afghan Women* (Geneva: UNRISD (United Nations Research Institute for Social Development), 1990), 9. See also Hugh Beattie, "Effects of the Saur Revolution in Nahrin." The brief account of the reform of the dowry system by Olivier Roy (*Islam and Resistance in Afghanistan*, 94–95), is incorrect on several counts: it was not dowry but brideprice (or dower) that was being reformed; Decree No. 7 was not, strictly speaking, an affront to Islamic law but rather to customary law; Decree No. 7 provided for not only a ceiling on the brideprice but an end to the levirate, a minimum age of consent, and so on. The reaction to the Decree was, as we have seen, far stronger than Roy suggests in his brief commentary.

30. Interviews with Soraya, in Kabul, 6 February 1989, and Helsinki, 8 October 1990.

31. N. H. Dupree, "Revolutionary Rhetoric and Afghan Women," 330.

32. The formal reinstatement of Muslim family law did not apply to party members. Interview with a PDPA official, New York, 28 October 1986.

33. Urban, *War in Afghanistan*, 209.

34. Interview with Massouma Esmaty Wardak, Kabul, 1 February 1989.

35. Interview with Farid Mazdak, PDPA official, Kabul, 9 February 1989.

36. Constitution of the Republic of Afghanistan, Kabul, 1988.

37. Interview with Massouma Esmaty Wardak, Kabul, 24 January 1989.

38. Interview with Zahereh Dadmal, director of the Kabul Women's Club, Kabul, 8 February 1989.

39. See, for example, "Afghanistan: The Soviets Are All Gone, but the Sky Still Refuses to Fall," commentary in *Providence Journal*, 27 February 1989; "The View from Kabul," *Guardian* (New York), 22 March 1989, 10–11; letter in *The Nation* (New York), 29 May 1989; "Morale in Kabul High," letter, *New York Times*, 18 April 1989.

40. *New York Times*, 2 April 1988, A2.

41. Rahimullh Yusufzai, "Afghanistan: Withdrawal Symptoms," *Herald* (January 1989).

42. Derek Brown, "New Afghanistan Carries on Grisly Game of the Old," *Guardian* (UK), 4 May 1992, 7.

43. Hanna Papanek, "Why Do Regimes Raise the Woman Question Even When It Creates So Much Trouble?" discussant's comments at MIT workshop on Women, the State, and Social Restructuring in Afghanistan, Iran, and Pakistan (Cambridge, Mass., 4 March 1989).

44. Maxine Molyneux, "Socialist Societies: Progress Toward Women's Emancipation?" *Monthly Review* 34, no. 3 (July–August 1982): 2–50.

Chapter 10

Women and Revolution in Yugoslavia (1945-1989)

Obrad Kesić

The Yugoslavian Revolution, like many socialist revolutions, was also a social revolution. In a short period of time, it transformed much of Yugoslavia from a rigid, traditional, mostly rural society into a modern socialist state. Unlike similar movements in other socialist states such as Poland, East Germany and even Vietnam, the Yugoslav social movement faced severe challenges from ethno-regional tensions and extremely uneven patterns of development among its peoples. The former Yugoslavia, like the former Soviet Union, was a multi-ethnic state with traditionally antagonistic ethnic groups; however, unlike those in the Soviet Union, the Yugoslav groups did not have deep-rooted historic ties of empire to bind them.

The social development of Yugoslavia has historically been sporadic and uneven across the regions that formed its republics. The republics of Slovenia and Croatia were dominated and ruled by Austria-Hungary for much of their modern histories. As a result, their political, economic, and social developments paralleled those of the Hapsburg Empire. These two republics were the most economically developed and socially progressive Yugoslav regions. In addition to Austrian political dominance, these societies were also strongly shaped by the Catholic Church. In direct contrast, their southern neighbors, Bosnia-Hercegovina, Serbia, Montenegro, and Macedonia, were comprised predominantly of Orthodox Christians and Muslims. These regions were ruled by the Ottoman Empire for five centuries, and are less developed today in every respect than Slovenia and Croatia.

Each republic and its peoples developed at their own rate and in their own manner. Even when they were united in a post-World War I kingdom, these territories continued to follow separate paths. In modern Yugoslavia, this policy of separate roads towards development has survived—known officially as "separate roads to socialism." A chapter such as this, examining the role of women in Yugoslavia's revolution, has to take into account that national facts and figures are simply averages and that extreme differences in regional (republic) situations often make national averages irrelevant to the real situations in the individual regions. A regional study of the role of women in Yugoslavia is also impractical due to the lack of historical regional data. Given these constraints, this chapter examines the role of women in Yugoslavia's revolution and assesses the outcomes of revolution in regard to women's status and rights by relying primarily on federal data, but also employing regional observations and comparisons wherever possible.

THE STATUS OF WOMEN IN PRE-WORLD WAR II YUGOSLAVIA

The status of women in pre-World War II Yugoslavia was a direct result of the historical development noted above. As a whole, regardless of nationality, women were isolated from political and social institutions. Economically the picture was somewhat different. From 1920 through 1930, women made up over 50 percent of the workers in the agricultural sector and, as a result, greatly contributed to this aspect of pre-war Yugoslavia's economy.[1] Despite their abundant presence in the agricultural sector, however, women's rights to land were severely limited. Few women owned their own land; those who did were usually widows. Women were culturally excluded from the male-dominated inheritance tradition in which a man normally divided his inheritance amongst his sons or his brothers but not his wife or daughters. In the southern territories, this inheritance pattern was more deeply rooted than in the north because, under the Ottoman Empire until the turn of the century, women were legally prohibited from owning land. The northern territories were somewhat more liberal when it came to land ownership, but even there it was rare for a woman to own land.

The northern regions were also more deeply influenced by the industrial revolution. At the turn of the century, more than 80 percent of the south's population lived in the countryside whereas, in the north, roughly 50 percent lived there.[2] It is the industrial revolution that brought significant changes to the role of women in the northern regions, and eventually to the southern ones as well. The growth of industry and the advent of one world war and several regional wars created a demand for female workers to fill both newly created jobs and those left vacant by men going off to fight. This led to the establishment of trade unions in which women gained membership. By 1923, women made up 20 percent of the industrial work force; by 1930, their representation had increased to 25 percent. However, by 1940, their representation had dropped to 19 percent of the entire industrial work force.[3]

In general, the period between 1920 and 1940 was marked by great changes in Yugoslavian society as a whole. The industrial revolution and Western European influences prompted these changes, especially those affecting Yugoslavian women. These influences, however, were not strong enough to ensure that progress with respect to women's issues would continue once statehood had been achieved. For example, in 1921, women made up 16 percent of individuals attending institutions of higher learning. By 1930, that proportion had risen to 22 percent, but by 1939 it had fallen to 19 percent.[4] The percentage of women in government and management positions fluctuated in the same manner, with highs recorded in the late 1920s and early 1930s.[5]

These fluctuations may be explained in part by the coming of age of a new generation of men. World War I had produced massive casualties among Yugoslavia's peoples. The hardest hit were the Serbs, who lost 10 percent of their pre-war population. As in other parts of Europe, women had to step in to fill the void left by heavy male casualties. By the mid-1930s, a new generation of men had emerged to assume the positions that women had been allotted as the result of war. In addition, opportunities for women were severely limited by the Great Depression. Despite the fact that there were no government regulations officially protecting jobs for men, women were systematically pushed aside in order to free up jobs for men. The Balkan mentality as enforced by the politico-economic system of that time held men to be the principal bread-winners in families. Employed women were often officially portrayed as radical troublemakers who posed a challenge to traditional male dominance. This created a sense of frustration among many women. They felt short-changed by the system because they had filled their former positions competently and had shown that women deserved the same opportunities that men enjoyed. As a result, women sought ways to express their frustrations and to promote comprehensive changes in society.

Industrial growth did provide Yugoslavian working women with trade union experience, but this experience was gained in male-dominated organizations; women did not have a trade union organization of their own.[6] The trade union experience was important, however, because it provided the basis for subsequent feminist organizations, as well as for the formation of the Anti-Fascist Front of Women created by the Communist Party of Yugoslavia during World War II. Through their union activities, women gained both valuable experience as organizers and confidence in their own abilities.

The Communist Party of Yugoslavia was quick to see the benefit of supporting organizations that promoted women's issues. The Party's belief in gender equality grew out of three traditions, two of which were ideological and the other political. In terms of ideology the leaders of the Yugoslavian Communist Party, like their Soviet counterparts, characteristically treated gender in the same context that they treated nationality—minimizing differences and stressing the centripetal characteristics of a common worker identity. The foundation of these beliefs, however, developed from another ideological source, one that can be traced to local struggles in the Balkans. Since the nineteenth century, southern Slavic leaders like Svetozar Marković had insisted that the inequality of women directly hindered the development of Slavic society as a whole. The political tradition that supported the Party's formulation of a gender policy grew out of the active involvement of women in all aspects of party work and organization during the underground period, when the party was illegal, and during the liberation movement.[7]

The Party also anticipated benefits from incorporating women into its clandestine operations. The regime did not view female revolutionaries as a major threat and was ill-equipped to deal with them. The prisons and courts were geared towards men. The few women who were prosecuted and imprisoned often received shorter sentences than their male counterparts. This may be explained by the general Balkan belief that, unlike men, women were not likely to be hardened criminals and could be rehabilitated by a good scare and/or a good beating. As a result, whereas male political prisoners were ordinarily separated from the general prison population or sent to special political prisons, female political prisoners, due to the lack of adequate facilities, were routinely thrown in with ordinary criminals.

Immediately preceding World War II, communist women played a primary role in preparing the resistance and revolution because most communist men had been imprisoned under the monarchy. Throughout his memoirs, Milovan Djilas makes reference to the role women played in the Communist Party during the pre-war period. He discusses the assistance the movement received from prominent women of the time, like Smilja Djaković, the owner of the literary magazine *Misao*, and Desanka Maksimović, the well-known Serbian poet, both of whom devoted their talents towards promoting communist ideals through their work.[8] Women participated in all aspects of the communist movement and, as mentioned previously, some like Lidija Sentjukić and Beška Bembaš, even went to jail alongside their male counterparts. Both spent over a year in Yugoslav prisons.[9] Others, like Vukica Mitrović, rose through party ranks to assume important positions as members of local and regional committees. Still others, like Lela Matić and Lola Vuco, were drawn to the party simply because of their husbands' involvement in it.[10]

Eyewitness accounts, such as those of Djilas and Vladimir Dedijer, show that women, regardless of the reasons behind their association with the Party, were instrumental in its ability to survive the intensive crackdowns imposed by the monarchy and to attract widespread popular support during World War II. While most of the Communist Party's men were imprisoned and thus prevented from doing their work, its women were free to pick up the slack and continue the promotion of party policies and programs among the people. Given the extent of women's involvement in the pre-war communist movement, it was only natural that they would assume visible and prominent positions in the Partisans' organizations.

WOMEN IN WAR

The Axis invasion of Yugoslavia in April 1941 caught the Yugoslav Communist Party in a bind. Most of its leadership was either in prison or out of the country. As a result, communists were slow in setting up a resistance movement. Once the uprising began, however, women were quick to join, both as fighters and as support service personnel. Women played a major role in the Partisans—they made up one hundred thousand of the eight hundred thousand armed forces and over two million of the total membership in the Anti-Fascist Council for the liberation of Yugoslavia (AVNOJ).[11] Yugoslavia suffered tremendous casualties during the war—over one-tenth of its population was killed. Yugoslav women comprised many of the casualties—twenty-five thousand were killed and forty thousand were seriously wounded in the Partisan forces: 60 percent of all women in the Liberation Army were either killed or seriously wounded. Of the six hundred thousand women sent to German, Bulgarian, Hungarian, Italian, and Ustaše (Croatian Fascists) concentration camps, 282,000 died.[12] Of those women who perished fighting, the majority were under twenty-five years of age.[13]

In the fight for liberation, women made a fine showing. Their bravery and self-sacrifice were rewarded by officer commissions (two thousand women were given commissions during the war but it should be noted that not a single women was promoted to the rank of general) and by the supreme military award of honor known as National Hero: ninety-one women received this honor.[14] Among them was Marija Bursać, a sapper who bravely attacked bunkers and was killed saving the life of a comrade; and Nada Dimić, who fought in the first Partisan Brigade in Croatia and showed supreme courage in the face of brutal torture after she was captured. She did not reveal even her name to her torturers, providing evidence of the courage of Yugoslav women during the war.

The Partisan women played such an important role in the struggle for liberation that a legend grew up during the war that claimed that Tito was, in fact, a woman.[15] The women of Yugoslavia paved the way toward equality with their blood. Their actions and the mythology that surrounded the partisan movement ensured that women's issues would not be relegated to the back burner during the founding of a new Yugoslavia. As popular folk culture and official communist propaganda spread, the stories of the bravery of men and women alike inspired a new generation of Yugoslavs.

THE STATUS OF WOMEN IN POST-WAR YUGOSLAVIA

Women, Work, and Politics

During the war, AVNOJ passed resolutions that guaranteed equal rights to women and a wide range of regulations designed to protect pregnant women and working mothers. Later these decisions were formally incorporated as amendments to the Constitution. Despite these war-time accomplishments, women soon found themselves losing some of their hard-won gains in post-war Yugoslavia.

Since World War II, indicators of the status of women have risen steadily in some areas but failed to progress in others. The Constitution of 1946 gave all Yugoslav women full political, economic, and social rights, including the rights to equal education, employment, and suffrage. Subsequent constitutions and constitutional amendments consistently upheld these rights. Yet although the Constitution gave women legal rights in the public sector, it did not carry them over to the private, family, and interpersonal, sector.[16] Yugoslavian women faced a different situation than their counterparts in western countries had to deal with—there were no women's policy issues that had to be fought for. Divorce, abortion, and formal equal political rights had all been constitutionally and legally attained. As a result, feminists and women's rights advocates had to focus their activity on raising the consciousness of women and men with respect to gender roles and status.[17] The League of Communists of Yugoslavia (LCY) controlled and set the agenda with respect to public discussion of women's issues. The LCY as the only legal political organization (excluding the Socialist Alliance which it dominated) controlled the policy agenda in all other areas. Consequently, women's issues were dealt with within the guidelines of LCY directives or not at all.

The LCY, like other Marxist groups, placed a greater emphasis on the reform of work relations than of political relations, as a means to change the structure of society.[18] This ideology underpinned the particular LCY emphasis on worker self-management as a means to liberate women. The LCY viewed gender identity as unimportant compared to people's identities as workers. Its leaders claimed that the gender question could be answered by the widespread adoption of a common worker's identity and by each worker exercising greater individual control over the work environment. This perspective depended upon increasing the number of women in the work force, as well as increasing the number of women entrusted with decision-making responsibility in organs of associated labor and in self-managing bodies (both are political economic divisions within the Yugoslavian system).[19]

In the fifteen years following World War II, the proportion of women in the labor force grew to one and a half times what it had been before the war. Furthermore, the proportion of the female population employed outside the home in Yugoslavia rose from 24 percent in 1952 to 39 percent in 1988. The rates in the individual republics also increased significantly (see tables 10.1 and 10.2).[20]

Despite these gains, not all of the news was good. Most women continued to be limited to predominantly local and low-level managerial positions. Furthermore, as in other industrialized states, certain job categories such as public services, public administration, trade, and catering became female ghettoes.[21] It became more and more difficult for women to dispel this occupational typecasting and break into male-dominated higher managerial ranks. What made such a move even more difficult was the prevalence of apathy among Yugoslav women. Most were satisfied with family-oriented lives and few sought further reforms.[22]

Table 10.1
Women as a Percentage of the Total Work Force in Yugoslavia

Year	% Women
1920	14
1930	19
1940	18
1952	24
1960	26
1970	31
1980	36
1988	39

Scholars like Barbara Jancar claim that this apathy reflected "the profound impact Yugoslavia's transformation from a traditional-agrarian society to a modern-industrial one has had on women's lifestyles."[23] In the span of twenty years, 1945 to 1965, the slow-paced, pre-modern lifestyle of Yugoslavs changed to become fast-paced, complex, and modern. Yugoslavia underwent one of the fastest transitions to urbanization in history, causing a sharp disruption in the traditional way of life. The patriarchal family had supposedly given way to a more democratic one, which cast women into a state of economic and social uncertainty. Not only were women, as were all Yugoslavs, affected by a form of culture shock due to rapid urbanization, but they were also forced to deal with a new society that did not conform to the familiar and secure patriarchal pattern. Apathy resulted. It was not only characteristic of Yugoslav women but also of Yugoslav men, and might be better described as a general sense of alienation and frustration affecting the average Yugoslav citizen. The people were torn between a desire for reform and a sense of guilt at their resentment of the authority of the LCY, a group which had previously been perceived as heroic and self-sacrificing. Many retreated into passivity as the result of these cross-pressures.

Soon the LCY's image began to crumble following revelations of corruption and incompetence. Even during the last few years of Tito's life, many people began to experience what could best be described as a spiritual vacuum. Everything that they had been taught to believe in now appeared to be a grand illusion. People began to seek other means of redefining their personal identities and gaining a new sense of self-

Table 10.2
Percentage of Women in the Work Force by Region

	Bosnia & Hercegovina	Montenegro	Croatia	Macedonia
1952	16%	20%	28%	17%
1960	19	22	27	21
1970	25	29	35	25
1980	31	31	39	30
1988	36	39	42	36

	Slovenia	Serbia*	Kosovo	Vojvodina
1952	32%	21%	11%	30%
1960	38	25	13	28
1970	41	29	18	31
1980	44	34	21	36
1988	46	39	23	40

* Figures are for Serbia without its Autonomous Provinces.

Source: *Jugoslavija 1918–1988 Statistički Godišnjak* (Belgrade: Savezni Zavod za Statistiku, 1989), 57–59.

worth. Many found the answer in reasserting an ethnic, pre-Yugoslav identity. Pressure for change increased. Even when the LCY responded, its efforts only led to greater pressures and further instability.

The election of Milka Planinć to the presidency of the LCY presidium in the mid-1980s stimulated calls for greater female representation at all levels of government. In fact, Planinć's rise to political power was a result of the LCY's effort to combat feminist criticism of its record on women's issues and increase the visibility of women at the highest levels of government where they were grossly under-represented (see table 10.3).[24] The LCY's record was marked with successes but also with some glaring failures, due primarily to its inability to assure proportional representation for women in high-level managerial and administrative positions. The proportion of female presidents of workers' councils, for example, ranged from a low of 5 percent in economic enterprises to a high of over 50 percent in social institutions, an area that had become feminized.[25]

Table 10.3
Delegates to Assemblies of Sociopolitical Communities in 1986

	Total	Women	% Women
Federal Assembly	308	48	15.6
Assemblies of the Socialist Republics	1,478	286	19.3
Assemblies of the Socialist Autonomous Provinces	438	106	24.4
Assemblies of Communes	50,743	8,670	17.1

Source: The United Nations Committee on the Elimination of Discrimination Against Women (CEDAW), *Second Periodic Reports of States Parties, Addendum: Yugoslavia* (United Nations Documents, 11 July 1989), 51.

This disparity in representation and other related issues were publicized by both private individuals and the official women's organization, the Conference for the Social Role of Women. A part of the Socialist Alliance, the Council adopted a step-by-step, realistic platform for reform that focused on grassroots activity among women—and men.[26] After the Committee hosted the first feminist conference in Belgrade in 1978, other feminist groups emerged, each dealing with different aspects of women's issues. Some concentrated on research, others on raising public consciousness, and some on solving practical problems.

Women and Family

Perhaps the only entity that in the face of rapid social change continues to be dominated by a patriarchal Balkan mentality is the Yugoslav family unit. The family has traditionally been and continues to be dominated by men. Yugoslav women work and participate in a legally assured equal society only to come home to face extreme inequality, including primary responsibility for performing household duties.[27]

Day-to-day decision-making is dominated by men with little, if any, consultation between husband and wife. It is because of this that Yugoslav women tend to be more vocal than men about equal rights in the family than in public life. Most are quick to refute any doubt as to their equality in public life. They are even quicker to voice dissatisfaction with their private lives. Many are frustrated by the lack of equality they face at home and the double standard of morality and behavior imposed on their private lives. As one female student at Belgrade University put it:

> Husbands work, come home to a cooked meal and a clean house; they eat, and then they disappear to drink with their friends or to pursue mistresses. The wives, on the other hand, work, come home and cook, clean, put the children to bed and wait up for their husbands.[28]

The worst part of this scenario is that the above mentioned behavior is accepted as being normal, but if the roles were reversed it would be unacceptable and the women in question would be labeled "sluts."

In addition and related to this general inequality between men and women in the family, there are serious problems of mental and physical abuse. Although statistics on wife abuse are not available, this is a growing area of concern among feminist groups, and it is becoming apparent, through media coverage, that it is a countrywide problem. There is a definite need for support groups and shelters for abused wives. The government is moving extremely slowly towards meeting this need because of its preoccupation with issues it sees as more pressing, and also because cultural attitudes throughout Yugoslavia have traditionally viewed physical punishment as a man's right to use in maintaining family discipline.

It is painfully clear to most Yugoslav women that victories will continue to be won in the public sector, but that changes in their status within the family will require a long and painful struggle with no indication of victories to come in the near future. The status of women in the family has remained virtually the same as it was in pre-war Yugoslav society. This is especially true in rural areas, where changes have come about extremely slowly, and among Muslim families (especially Albanian), where religious constraints also hinder social reform.

WOMEN AND THE FUTURE: THE CONTINUATION OF THE REVOLUTIONARY TRADITION

Currently as Yugoslavia disintegrates, the political situation is complex and increasingly volatile. The crisis that has led to state disintegration revolves around the competition for political power by nationalities, nationalistic political parties, and specific interest groups. Feminist groups were among those trying to propel their concerns to the forefront of the political agenda in an effort to assure for themselves a slice of the political power pie, now left up for grabs by the dissolution of the LCY and the federal government. Previous efforts at reform led to major changes in Yugoslavia's political and economic systems, but they failed to deal satisfactorily with the pressing economic problems of high inflation and unemployment, and with the resurfaced national question and the ethnic conflicts that have fragmented the state. As the political configuration of competing forces is sorted out and new political entities are created, it is likely that issues (such as women's issues) that are viewed by politicians and the general public as minor will be put aside for later discussion. Meanwhile, as feminist groups vie for political power and influence, they have to take care not to be sucked into the ongoing nationalistic debate. They may have to be content with small collective accomplishments in raising public consciousness, and individual achievements in academic and literary circles. At the same time, they must persuade the public to see the importance of the women's question, and in this way gather enough support to push it to the forefront of public and governmental discussions.

The current crisis has also shown the same revolutionary tradition of World War II characterized by self-sacrifice and heroism on the part of many Yugoslav women. Women are taking active roles in all aspects of current reform movements and have even triggered many reforms on their own. Women made up over 50 percent of the membership of the Slovene Democratic Movement for Pluralism.[29] Women also played primary roles in the budding environmental and peace movements countrywide.

But activism on women's issues has triggered responses that fuel nationalist passions. One of the most notable examples occurred in the autonomous province of Kosovo of the Republic of Serbia, in response to a 1986 statement by Fadil Hoxha, a prominent party official of Albanian nationality. In a conversation with officers of the Yugoslav National Army in Prizren at an official dinner, he said,

> Women from other parts of Yugoslavia should be brought to bars in Kosovo so that the men who enjoy raping women of other nationalities could enjoy themselves; Albanian women don't want to do this, but Serbian women and others would like it, so why don't we let them do this?[30]

The statement was suppressed until ten months later when it was leaked to the press. Needless to say, the statement set off a flood of protest and demonstrations. Thousands of women marched in protest in the Kosovo cities of Pristina, Lipljana, Prizren and even in Belgrade, shouting things such as "We're not sluts, but mothers and sisters of Serbia's and Yugoslavia's sons" and "Hoxha to the gallows."[31] Some feminist groups rushed to their support and the demonstrators received encouragement from others throughout the country. By the time the dust had settled, the women had succeeded in removing Hoxha and other officials from office. Hoxha was also stripped of his party membership (and was later imprisoned for unrelated offenses). The women's movement in Kosovo, however, continued in intensity and grew with nationalistic zeal. The outrage felt over the insult against womanhood gave way to a greater outrage over the insult against their ethnic group, and in this way inadvertently became a political tool for the vocalization of Slobodan Milošević's nationalistic platform.

The incident in Kosovo holds special significance for women in Serbia and Montenegro. Feminism, which had been considered a dirty word in both republics, became respectable in many regions through its association with nationalism. Women such as Mirjana Marković-Milošević, an elected member of the Belgrade Central Presidium and the wife of Serbian strong man, Slobodan Milošević, started calling themselves "communist feminists."[32] Other women throughout the country took notice. Membership in feminist groups has increased noticeably over the past few years. Women have not only organized and marched in demonstrations throughout the country on issues ranging from civil rights to environmental protection, but feminist journals have also been founded as a result of this increased interest and awareness.[33]

Everything accomplished as a result of the Kosovo incident was not positive. The same ethnic nationalism that is pulling Yugoslavia apart as a country also threatens the Yugoslav feminist movement. The Kosovo demonstrations were transformed from occasions to demand women's rights to occasions for promoting Serbian and Montenegrin rights. As a result, feminists of different nationalities became suspicious of Serbian feminists, and some feared that Serbia might use its feminist movement as another tool in its perceived efforts to impose Serbian hegemony on other parts of Yugoslavia. At a time when, and in an area where, unity was needed in order to make substantial, meaningful changes, women's groups found themselves fighting against each other. As environmentalists and human rights advocates have already discovered and feminists are finding out, nationalism in Yugoslavia makes statewide cooperation on any issue nearly impossible. Divided by nationalism, Yugoslavia's feminist groups find themselves swallowed up in the larger ethnic conflicts which, ironically, limits the statewide scope of feminist groups while creating some opportunity for their slight advancement on a regional level.

CONCLUSIONS

Yugoslav women have experienced tremendous changes during the years since the end of World War II. Their lives have changed more rapidly than those of most of their counterparts elsewhere in the industrialized world. This change has paralleled the overall transformation of Yugoslavia from a traditional agricultural society into a modern industrialized one. However, the changes in society and in the status of women have not been experienced evenly, either in public and private life, or geographically. The northern republics of Slovenia and Croatia and, to some extent, the southern republics of Bosnia and Serbia, have consistently seen more rapid and extensive changes. The other southern federal units traditionally lagged behind in all areas of development, including women's rights. However, the Constitution directs all federal units to approach women's rights from the same foundation regardless of history or cultural tradition.

The relatively new Yugoslavian feminist groups strive to ensure that the public will be informed about women's issues, and that women's concerns will not be ignored by national political parties and their leaderships. As the different political groups debate the future of Yugoslavia, it is interesting to note that women, except for a few like Mirjana Marković-Milošević (a leader of the new League of Communists—Movement for Yugoslavia) are noticeably missing among the political elites of every region. As the country's future is being decided through a childish and dangerous game of nationalistic one-upmanship, half the population is not directly represented in these discussions.

In addition to the political questions that remain to be answered, the greatest challenge remaining for women's rights advocates continues to be the need to improve the status of women in the family unit. Despite recent socialist influences on people's thinking, changes in this area will come slowly and will be met with fierce resistance by men reared in the Balkan patriarchy. The reawakening of various nationalisms will generally mean a movement backwards for all aspects of Yugoslav life and society, including family life. In all likelihood, women throughout the country will be forced to give up some of their hard-won gains and assume a more traditional role in the family and in the political life of their individual regions. In fact, this has already occurred to a certain extent as feminist groups assume agendas tainted by nationalistic philosophies.

Further complicating the efforts of women's groups is the desire and necessity to disassociate themselves from their past ties to the LCY. The prevailing anti-communist mood found throughout most of the region threatens the popular support of the women's movement because of its prominence in the success of the socialist revolution. Most people are openly suspicious and hostile to anything that reminds them of the old communist regime and may quickly dismiss many of the feminist demands as being communist-inspired.

There is little doubt that change can be achieved if unity among feminist groups remains intact in the face of growing ethno-regionalism. If ethno-regionalism continues to dominate all aspects of Yugoslavian society, the statewide feminist cause, like other statewide fractional advocacies, will be unsuccessful. Nationalism is dissolving the Yugoslavian federation. In the face of uncertainty and bitter conflict, the importance of issues such as the "women's question" diminish to many Yugoslavs. Feminist groups, like other elements of Yugoslavia's society, are finding that the centripetal forces that have united them are giving way to the stronger centrifugal force of ethnocentrism. As these fragmenting forces grow in intensity, the future of feminist groups, and of Yugoslavia itself, is in such doubt that the advocates of each have little hope. The question today for Yugoslavia's feminist groups is not whether equal rights will be truly attained, but if there will be a Yugoslavia in which to attain them.

NOTES

1. Socijalistička Federativna Republika Jugoslavija (SFRJ) Savezni Zavod za Statistiku, *Jugoslavija 1918–1988 Statistički Godišnjak* (Belgrade: Savezni Zavod za Statistiku, 1989), 39.

2. Gordana Vlajčić, *Jugoslavenska Revolucija i Nacionalno Pitanje 1919/1927* (Zagreb: Globus, 1984), 173.

3. SFRJ Savezni Zavod za Statistiku, 57.

4. Ibid., 363.

5. Ibid., 57.

6. Rada Iveković and Slavenka Drakulić-Ilić, "Yugoslavia: Neofeminism and Its Six Mortal Sins," in *Sisterhood is Global*, ed. Robin Morgan (Garden City, N.Y.: Anchor Books, 1984).

7. Vida Tomšić, *Women in the Development of Socialist Self-Managing Yugoslavia* (Belgrade: Jugoslovenska Stvarnost, 1980); and Maria B. Olujić, "Economic and Demographic Change in Contemporary Yugoslavia: Persistence of Traditional Gender Ideology," *East European Quarterly* 13 (Winter 1989): 477.

8. Milovan Djilas, *Memoir of a Revolutionary* (New York: Harcourt Brace Jovanovich, 1973), 80–81.
9. Ibid., 142–47.
10. Ibid., 252.
11. Richard F. Nyrop, ed., *Yugoslavia: A Country Study* (Washington, D.C.: U.S. Government Printing Office, 1982), 83.
12. Barbara Jancar, "The New Feminism in Yugoslavia," in *Yugoslavia in the 1980s*, ed. Pedro Ramet (Boulder: Westview Press, 1985), 205.
13. Ibid.
14. Ibid.
15. Vladimir Dedijer, *The War Diaries of Vladimir Dedijer: Volume 3 From September 11, 1943, to November 7, 1944* (Ann Arbor: University of Michigan Press, 1990), 197.
16. Rada Iveković and Slavenka Drakulić-Ilić, "Yugoslavia," 735.
17. Ibid.
18. Pedro Ramet, "Women, Work and Self-Management in Yugoslavia," *East European Quarterly* 12 (January 1984): 459.
19. Ibid., 460.
20. SFRJ Savezni Zavod za Statistiku, 59.
21. Barbara Jancar, "New Feminism in Yugoslavia," 203.
22. Ibid., 204.
23. Ibid.
24. Nikola Latin, Administrative Assistant, 5 June 1989, SFRJ Savezni Zavod za Statistiku, Belgrade, Yugoslavia.
25. Rada Iveković and Slavenka Drakulić-Ilić, "Yugoslavia," as well as Barbara Jancar, "New Feminism in Yugoslavia."
26. Rada Iveković and Slavenka Drakulić-Ilić, "Yugoslavia," 735.
27. Barbara Jancar, "New Feminism in Yugoslavia," 204.
28. Slavica Stanković, student, interview, 20 July 1989, University of Belgrade, Belgrade, Yugoslavia.
29. Nikola Latin, interview, 5 June 1989.
30. Darko Hudelist, *Kosovo: Bitka Bez Iluzija* (Zagreb: Biblioteka Dnevnik, 1989), 41–42.
31. Ibid., 42.
32. Milan Andrejevich, "Serbia's First Lady in Politics," *Radio Free Europe/Radio Liberty Situation Report* 12 (October 1989): 31.
33. Nikola Latin, interview, 5 June 1989.

Chapter 11

Sexuality and the Politics of Revolution in Iran

Farideh Farhi

"Iranian women will get it no matter what happens," an exasperated middle-class Iranian woman said to me. This statement was intended not so much as a reflection on the condition of women, but as a commentary on politics in post-revolutionary Iran in general. "On top of the massive setbacks that we have faced in terms of our rights," she continued, "we have to pay with our bodies as various political factions jockey for political power." The power politics of the revolutionary moment was posited by this woman to be the source of continued oppression of women in Iran. Inspired by these comments, let me begin to rehabilitate the politics of revolution in Iran. Rather than discussing the post-revolutionary condition of women in Iran merely in relation to long-term causes, I focus on the ways in which women's bodies were and are used as a contested terrain over which the meaning of the Iranian revolution is inscribed and reinterpreted. It is important to remember that revolutions are world events as much as domestic upheavals. Accordingly, I shall argue that the contests over the ways women should carry or cover their bodies are not only a domestic power claim, but also a product for international consumption. This chapter will trace the historic collusion between

---

An earlier version of this paper was presented at the 1990 meeting of the American Political Science Association in San Francisco. I would like to thank Cindy Kobayashi, Gerry Kosasa-Terry, Marta Savigliano, and Mary Ann Tétreault for helpful comments.

Iranian Islamic revolutionaries and Western eyes in generating images that leave open very few political options for Iranian women.[1]

THE POLITICS OF REVOLUTION

Before discussing sexuality some words are in order about what I mean by the politics of revolution. Much of the literature on various revolutions has focused on origins and outcomes.[2] From this point of view, the revolutionary experience is discussed mostly in relation to its generation from long-term causes and its contribution to outcomes such as class consolidation in a Marxian version or a more bureaucratized state in the Tocquevillian or Weberian version.[3] To be sure, politics is discussed, but the emphasis is on the relationship between a previously existing social base and the specific political and social arrangement that follows from it. The character of politics is explained, therefore, by reference to society, and changes in the political arrangement are traced to prior changes in social relations. Almost all discussion proceeds from the assumption that the essential characteristics of politics can only be explained by their relation to a social ground.[4] This assumption opens the way for the very valid argument that, in relation to long-term outcomes, revolutions typically end up accomplishing different tasks and furthering the consolidation of quite different new regimes from those originally intended by revolutionary participants. Underpinning this line of argument, of course, is the equally valid presupposition that revolutions are not the total breaks in history that they have been advertised to be. Yet explaining revolutions as somewhat clumsy but nevertheless rational instruments of social change leaves a huge hole in the middle of revolutionary drama. Lynn Hunt best expresses the shortcomings by pointing out how "revolutionary innovations in the form and meaning of politics" are often treated as "predetermined or entirely accidental."[5] Having gone back to Iran several times since the revolution, I am convinced that the active creation of a revolutionary culture cannot be ignored, not only because the in-between years affect people in fundamental ways but also because they have long-term effects on the way post-revolutionary society is organized.

Revolutions are those rare moments in the life of a society in which millions of people enter the stage of politics as actors (a people's festival, as Lenin would call it) in order to shape their own future and that of many generations to come. They are also moments when people actually enter an unknown and risky arena by consciously seeking, although perhaps not very successfully, to break with the past and to establish the basis for a new national community. In 1984, when (unlike my more recent trips) people still had vivid memories of their participation in the revolutionary process, they talked about the revolution in precisely those terms. One woman whom I know quite well who had never registered with me as a risk-taker, described how she and her husband, carrying two children on their shoulders, quietly canvassed the streets of Tehran after midnight to post political leaflets. When I asked why, she compared the revolution to a fish passing through the hands of millions. It was too close to ignore, too appealing not to touch, and yet clearly slipping away.

But what makes a revolution to "feel" so close? Surely bad economic conditions or repression are not sufficient explanations. These conditions are simply too prevalent throughout the world to make them useful as explanatory variables. Revolutionary fervor will not spread unless people come to the conclusion either that it is possible (as well as necessary and desirable) to change radically the shape of power itself or impossible to prevent the upcoming change. Much of this conclusion is dependent upon the perceived weakening of the existing power relationships.[6]

But the revolutionary experience is not merely a reaction. The envisioning of a change in the shape of power is an active reading of the context of politics and requires calls for a public togetherness based on new language and symbols.[7] It should not be surprising to discover that the active creation of at least part of this new language in Iran was centered on the woman question. In other words, the woman question, rather than simply becoming a set of issues to be dealt with through appropriate policies, lodged itself into a revolutionary identity ferociously aspiring to become the national identity. It is the dynamics of this process that interests me here. Why did the woman question gain such a prominent place? Where did the energy for maintaining its prominence come from? And how, if at all, did the question become transformed during the revolutionary process?

I am not interested in recounting the narrative of revolutionary events.[8] Neither am I interested in the examination of Islamic ideology—whatever that means. I have always had difficulty with studies that treat politics in terms of competing idea systems invested in political action. I am interested in getting a sense of the emerging strategies for action—with all the coherence and unity within the context of newly defined conflicts and struggles they imply, and figuring out how women's bodies were used in devising such strategies. As François Furet reminds us, one of the most important characteristics of the revolutionary movement is fluidity. With the breakdown of existing structures, opinion becomes the basis of political legitimacy—a legitimacy full of instability, constantly in need of reaffirmation from the supporters of the revolution who, in turn, also need constantly to vow allegiance to the revolution. The fluctuating official ideology adjusts, always frantically, to this instability but, in doing so, risks further revolutionary activity which changes the narrative of the revolution, possibly making previously legitimate positions illegitimate.[9] In what follows I will argue that it is these constant delegitimizing moves and the endless appetite for affirmation that have maintained the centrality of the woman question in Iran. But I must start the story from the beginning.

SEXUALIZED CONTENT OF THE REVOLUTIONARY POLITICAL CULTURE

As is well known, Islamic revolutionaries have shown their sensitivity to the public expression of female sexuality (which they see as expressed through the use of Western clothing) by demanding proper clothing for all women (*hejab-e Islami*). The interesting component of female sexuality, however, is how it becomes connected, implicitly or explicitly, to other issues. For instance, the West German foreign minister's visit to Iran in 1984 resulted in hooligan attacks on women who were presumably improperly dressed. Since 1990, the anniversary of Ayatollah Khomeini's death has been used as an occasion/ritual for early summer campaigns to cleanse the streets by harassing young women or young men who happen to be improperly socializing with them. Most Iranians I talked to agreed that the perceived rapprochement with the West, signalled by the West German minister's visit, or the symbolic reiteration of the solidity of clerical power on the anniversaries of Ayatollah Khomeini's death, better explain attacks on women than an ideological commitment to create more modest female appearance. But this observation still leaves us with the burning question: why are female bodies such important sites of struggle?[10]

The following conversation, overheard in a shopping mall typical of the everyday life in the streets of Tehran in the early 1980s, may give us some clues. This conversation was between a woman, obviously cornered for being improperly dressed, and a female revolutionary guard. The woman apparently was wearing the necessary clothing (*hejab*), but she had chosen to tie her scarf in a way that was deemed seductive by the revolutionary guard. The woman was quite courageous in refusing to accept such a designation, because in those days you could end up in jail for such things. The female revolutionary guard was also quite reasonable given the context. She simply wanted the woman to know the disrespect her disposition showed to the martyrs of the revolution, "our brothers who are fighting to defend the country."

This connection between female modesty and nationalism is not an isolated event. It has been amply reported that the *hejab* was promoted and, to some extent became understood, as a sign of women's political commitment, as women, to the revolution and to its strong anti-imperialist component.[11] With the advent of the Iran-Iraq war, a redefinition was introduced making wearing *hejab* a sign of respect for the martyrs. By this logic, "bare-headed" or improperly dressed women were considered sexually promiscuous—anti-revolutionary as well as traitors. Revolutionary graffiti written all over the walls of Tehran repeatedly bring out the connection to martyrdom (e.g., "Our sisters' *hejab* is the peace of our brothers" or, "Our sisters' *hejab* is our trenches").[12] Recently, the Islamic government has removed thousands of slogans painted on the walls during the period of revolutionary fervor. At the end of the Iran-Iraq War, even the derogatory slogans about Saddam Hussein disappeared. The only set of slogans still untouched are the ones related to female modesty in clothing and behavior. Implicit in these slogans, of course, is the sanctioning of violence against those women who flaunt their sexuality in public.

What do these things mean? One way of interpreting them is to treat the Iranian revolution as a continuity—that is, to refuse to acknowledge novelty. Hence, the sexualized content of politics and the connection between sexuality and violence can be interpreted as part and parcel of the Iranian cultural history. Culture, defined as a set of shared values in this interpretation, becomes yet another set of structures, prisons, from which the Iranians cannot escape: all the revolution did was to make what is normal in Iranian society blatant.[13] This position has been expressed by writers from different political perspectives. For instance, Reza Barahani, the Iranian poet and social critic, lays out the contours of Iranian masculine history in his book, *Crowned Cannibals*, written well before there was any wind of revolution.[14] In this masculine history, massacres, drinking wine in the skulls of enemies, and plucking out the eyes of thousands are presented as common practices of kings or would-be kings. And, within this context, male sexuality (itself the source of male power) is defined by the negation and control of, or doing violence to, everything that is feminine. The content of feminine varies historically, but always includes the female body and women's sexual desires. This eroticism, connected to doing violence to the female (or more accurately feminine) body and desires which, according to Barahani, has its roots in Iranian family structure, becomes the foundation of patriarchal, monarchical, and now presumably clerical politics. Subjugated women themselves participate in this process because "the image of degradation created by men and his [sic] masculine society has now become a part of the psychology of women."[15]

From a different perspective, Iranian feminist Farah Azari delineates how control and subjugation of women within Shiᶜi Islam is intricately linked to the control of women within the family.[16] Azari argues that it is Islam's fear of female sexual forces and its need to control and subjugate them that has caused a direct identification of the woman's being with sex. It is this being, rather than sex itself, that has come under attack because Islam has historically constituted female sexuality as the source of disorder. Hence the woman, seen as *fitna,* a living representative of the dangers of sexuality and its rampant disruptive potential, was and continues to be attacked as a symbol of disorder and the embodiment of destruction.[17] Azari then goes on to examine various practices and institutions within Iranian society—such as the ritual of mourning for the martyrdom of the third Shiᶜi Imam Hussain, *hejab,* virginity, and the institution of the family—in order to lay out some of the ways social institutions have and continue to oppress women sexually, socially, and politically.

Although Azari differs from Barahani by finding the sexual norms and attitudes of Iranian society rooted in Shiᶜism, her analysis ultimately suffers from the same weakness.[18] Simply stated, defining culture as a set of shared values, whether rooted in Shiᶜi or masculine traditions, remaining constant over time undermines the understanding of diversity, resistance, and transformation. This is generally the way outsiders look at sets of practices they do not share. Even if we agree totally with Barahani's observations about Iranian masculine history and the connections this history creates among violence, female sexuality, and politics, or Azari's correlation between women's sexual oppression and their more general oppression in Islamic Iran, there is still a need to understand how the Islamic content of the Iranian revolution shaped, and was shaped by, the forces unleashed during the revolutionary movement.

Hence, two intricately connected questions arise. First, did these actions and practices have mechanisms of coherence and unity even though the revolutionary political culture was always in flux? Second, how are these mechanisms of coherence affected by the resistance and collaboration of those over whose bodies the meaning of the Iranian revolution is being written? I will deal with these two questions in separate sections.

REVOLUTIONARY POLITICAL CULTURE

It is true that the more successful Iranian revolutionaries competing to gain access to state power shared a set of expectations that followed from their desire for Islamic regeneration, however muddled and/or multi-vocal their vision might have been. This desire can only be understood, however, within the context of an organic relationship with their rejection of Western cultural control.[19] And, it is precisely in relation to the rejection of Western cultural control that the question of women's appearance takes such a central role. But, as some observers have pointed out, we should not too readily credit the Islamic activists for connecting the issue of women's appearance to westernization or rejection of it.[20] It was Westerners who first not only insisted that Islam was innately and immutably oppressive to women—a curious blend of colonialism and feminism, as Leila Ahmed convincingly lays out—but also suggested that "the veil and segregation epitomized that oppression and that these customs were fundamental reasons for the general and comprehensive backwardness of Islamic societies."[21] In other words, it was the West who first connected the essence of Islamic culture (which for them was both oppressive to women and backward) to women's appearance by recoding this most visible marker of differentness in ways to reconfirm the superiority of their cultural values as well as practices.

Technically, Iran was never colonized. It was the emerging modern Iranian state under the Pahlavi dynasty which was the agent responsible for actualizing this understanding of veiling. Hence, it should not be surprising that through various ideological and political moves the identity of the modernizing woman (a necessary circumlocution to claim a legitimacy not feasible for a word like "westernizing"), the liberated woman (and let us not forget that there were some women who genuinely felt that way), became forcibly connected to the rejection of veiling.[22]

The Islamic activists clearly objected to this denigrating approach towards veiled women. But their objection never went so far as to question the link between women's appearance and Islamic culture. Their position simply inverted the proposed link by suggesting that veiling was the last bastion of resistance against the encroachment of Western values.[23] If unveiling did indeed open the way for modernizing—westernizing—values, then veiling was simply a logical reactive move to stop the same values which were seen as the source of all social ills.

The development of such a reactive stance can be detected easily in some of the more recent socioreligious texts on the position of women which, as Nahid Yeganeh points out, were produced in rising numbers in the period between 1960s and 1980s, and in the increased discussion occasioned by the participation of women in the revolution itself.[24] These texts and discussions varied in outlook but most of their differences can be explained by the functions they were intended to perform. For instance, Khomeini's initial views on the woman question are primarily located in a treatise providing instructions on bodily, religious, and social functions. Here, sexual intercourse is discussed within the context of a set of instructions for legitimate reproduction.[25] Later on, with revolutionary dynamics in full force, Khomeini's utterances became more political and filled with references to the bitter experience of unveiling and the role veiled women must play in reconstructing a resistive community of anti-Western forces.[26] In his words, unveiling and policies promulgated under the guise of women's liberation victimized women and provided the context for making women the tools for the diffusion of corrupt values. Ultimately, it was these corrupt values that undermined women's humanity and unleashed animal forces that invariably valued the pursuit of raw desires more than human dignity.[27] This is why veiling plays such an indispensable role in assuring the proper control of female sexuality.

Reformist clerics like Ayatollah Motahhari,[28] interested in constructing a rationalized Shiʿi system of the male/female relationship in order to counteract the Western infiltration of Iranian society, did acknowledge the existence of an active sexual instinct in both men and women unconnected to reproduction, but focused on the family as an arena for the proper release of sexual energy. Within this framework, veiling was necessitated by the restriction of eroticism to legal partners in marriage.

The emphasis on the issue of sexual energy should not be considered as surprising. Like most Middle Eastern societies, the Iranian population has been undergoing bewildering and compelling changes affecting economic and sexual identity. As Fatima Mernissi points out in the introduction to the revised edition of her now classic work, *Beyond the Veil*, rapid urbanization and state-funded mass education have had an irreversible impact on the men and women of the Middle East.[29] Both processes invariably brought about profound changes in sex roles and the touchy subject of sexual identity. No matter how often we hear and read of women's marginalization and exclusion from modernity in the Islamic world, the bottom line is that women's roles, both sexually and economically, have changed and they have changed drastically.[30] Attempts by the religious establishment to bring some order to these changes was only expected but, as Mernissi correctly points out, distinction has to be made between actual practices and ideological constructs or justifications about those practices.[31] In terms of practices, it is virtually impossible to put a stop to changes, even by staging a revolution. Hence, it is in the arena of self-representation and identity-formation that attempts are made to impose order on a confusing and shifting reality. The content of this order is dictated by the process of identity formation which has been determined by defining the Islamic identity to and by Western observers.[32] As such, female sexuality offers a fertile ground over which to insist upon the distinctiveness and purity of the Iranian Islamic culture in order to launch a counter-attack. The task is made easier since, as mentioned above, the groundwork for connecting one of the most visible markers of control over female sexuality—the veil—and Islamic culture has already been laid by others.

Of course, the success of this counter-attack depended upon the active creation of an ideal for Muslim women to follow. Ali Shariati perhaps did more in this regard than any other person. Interested in finding a political basis for opposing the Pahlavi regime and its Western supporter, Shariati found a perfect solution in the fusion of the true Muslim woman and the revolutionary and anti-imperialist woman. The result was a woman whose total commitment and love is directed toward Islam. This ideal woman no longer has a sexual instinct. Rather, all her passion is consumed by her love for Islam which, in turn, becomes the basis for her political militancy. Shariati's ideal woman, Fatemeh (Mohammad's daughter), is simple and pure. She is totally dedicated to Islam and the legacy of her father but she is also a true companion to her husband and a dedicated mother to her children. Most importantly, however, she is a militant, challenging political injustice and respecting just authority.[33]

Obviously, this version of the ideal Muslim woman was not simply a creation of Shariati. He presented it to an audience which, like him, was quite cognizant of various critiques of imperialism and Western cultural penetration. Hence, in the midst of revolutionary upheaval, this ideal Muslim woman became not only a symbol of total commitment to the revolutionary cause but also an active fighter against cultural invasion. At that point, the ideal Muslim woman had more tools to fight imperialism than any other member of the society: machine guns as well as the *hejab*, a Che Guevarra, if you will, and more. Standing up as witnesses against what they see as the corrupting influence of the West and capitalism, these "heirs of Zaynab" as they are called, follow the path of Mohammad's granddaughter. Their struggle entails taking up arms in the name of a holy cause and not shrinking from bloodshed. In this process, the Muslim woman, the purest and most dedicated fighter of Islam, becomes both sexually empty and masculinized.[34]

This masculinization of the ideal Muslim woman was indeed very necessary to prevent further penetration of Western culture which presumably always gains access through the acquiescence of the feminine, passive, flexible, and adaptable.[35] To reconstruct the dominated society which gives in through its weak feminine inclinations, the reactive revolutionary culture (so precisely represented by the sternness and austerity of the ideal Muslim woman) calls for a rejection of feminine values. And it should be no surprise that not only the control but the rejection of female sexuality was at the core of this kind of nationalist politics.

But it is also important to point out that this masculinized representation is not without its dilemmas. Women become the defenders of Islamic purity in a hostile global arena but they do so embedded in the context of a well-guarded nuclear family structure. On the one hand, women's roles in the public arena are elevated to utmost importance while, on the other hand, it is only in relation to the way they help to keep the family structure pure through their commitment to Islam that women gain their public prominence. Yet, it is precisely the female role in promoting Islamic purity which introduces a militancy into the family/society dichotomy that may not be easily controllable. The insistence on female purity which is promoted at the societal level reinforces the boundaries of a nuclear family structure which posits the male head of the family as the tempted one and the woman as the morally righteous one. These archetypes combine to create a perfect and presumably harmonious family organism working within and for a perfectly harmonious society. But the ideological move that creates a sexually empty and masculinized woman in the service of a perfect Islamic community threatens the harmony of the family on sexual grounds. Here, it is not only that Iranian men may have a difficult time getting sexual satisfaction within the family,[36] but also that the family guardian of Islamic purity carries a machine gun which may not always be put in the closet once she enters her home. Ultimately, however, it is in the public arena that the lasting effects of this new image will be felt because both the machine gun and the *hejab* undermine the ideological basis for the seclusion of women from the public arena.

Despite the tension, the representation continues. And, I can only assume that the tension as well as the correspondence between a committed revolutionary serving the dictates of the larger society and the committed wife within the family structure will continue to be the terrain upon which the story of the struggles of Iranian women will be written. For now, however, it is still important to ask what is the value of this representation of the veiled woman as the most committed (pure, perfect) revolutionary? Revolutionaries throughout the world have implicitly and explicitly invoked certain ethical values as inspiration for their revolutionary struggle. Usually these values are personified by men and, even in Iran, the most reproduced revolutionary posters depicted male leaders like Khomeini, Montazeri (before he was deposed as Khomeini's replacement), and Khamenehi. But these posters emphasize them as leaders of the revolution. The defense of revolutionary values—purity—ultimately rests on the shoulders of women cloaked in pitch-black veils and carrying machine guns.

This image of the ultimate Iranian revolutionary is extraordinarily useful to ideologues and propagandists pushing radically different interpretations of Iran's revolution. It is useful because the woman who occupies the center is an empty shell. She is there merely to prop up the veil. As such, she can reflect whatever is desired to her audience. For the Islamic revolutionaries, she is simply and exclusively a symbol of rejection, a closed door. After all, Middle Eastern women have played a very important role in Western male fantasies through their constructed participation as exotic sexual objects.[37] Western fantasies of the "Oriental" woman as the embodiment of sexual license have taken different shapes visually and textually throughout the past two centuries but now, as far as the Iranian revolutionaries are concerned, it is time to end that fantasy by destroying the exotic object.[38] The empty female face is also a valued commodity for consumption abroad. In Europe and the United States, it symbolizes the costs of abandoning liberal values, the costs of extremism, and the costs of rejecting modernity. It is a powerful image not only to confirm the superiority of modern ways for the already converted, but also to coax back those who might find the portrayal of female militancy a progressive sign. Indeed, the photograph of a row of women in *hejab* aiming pistols at an unknown target, which is sold as a postcard in New York,[39] is intended to evoke nothing short of "Oh my god!"—despite the fact that none of the women with pistols holds her finger in a proper way on the trigger.

CONFLICTS, RESISTANCE, AND CHOICES

To argue that Iran's revolutionary political culture found the female body to be a fertile ground on which Islamic activists could make a power claim to an internationally contested terrain is not to suggest that the Iranian women do not have an active role in the revolutionary drama or that the representation described above has gone unchallenged. Here, I would like to point out two possible but not exclusive sources of resistance. The first resistive move seems to be generated from within the confines of the revolutionary representation itself. Perhaps the threatening image of a well-armed and determined woman and the exigencies of mobilization for a devastating war worked hand in hand to create another parallel image. This new version of the true Iranian woman also draws from Fatemeh in her role as the primary mourner in the society. She mourns the death or maiming of her men and accuses the world in her sorrow. She is different from the first representation in that, as mother, wife, daughter, and sister, she has regained her feminine and gentle disposition although not her sexuality. Most importantly, however, she is different in her sorrow. The tears she is shedding over the death of a father, brother, husband, or son can also be interpreted as tears for a revolution gone astray.[40]

A second set of resistive moves is generated from among those women generally targeted as the main source of Western penetration—middle-class secular women. Initially, some middle-class women wore the veil to indicate solidarity with their lower middle-class and working-class sisters and to express their opposition to the Shah's close connection to American imperialist policies. The oppositional content of veiling was eclipsed when it became a coercive and institutional mandate. Various middle-class women's organizations at first attempted to oppose this mandate overtly, but their resistance was soon confronted by the revolutionary political culture's portrayal of the ideal Muslim women. This confrontation began quite early, on the first post-revolutionary celebration of International Woman's Day (8 March 1979). The slogans of this day had been carefully selected to emphasize their connection to the culture of revolution. One insisted that "Woman's Day is Neither Eastern nor Western—it is Universal." This kind of universalism, however, was not very appealing to the Islamic revolutionaries who preferred "Neither Western, nor Eastern, but Islamic." The correction came two months later. Speaking on the occasion of Mohammad's daughter's birthday, Khomeini referred to that day as Woman's Day, and this date was officially adopted by the

Islamic Republican Party (IRP) a year later. The choice of Fatemeh, the good daughter of Mohammad, the faithful wife, companion, and exemplary mother, was a logical symbol to counter the image of the westernized woman. But, as mentioned above, there was more. The contemporary Fatemeh, cloaked in a black veil and devoid of sexual desire, is also the defender of revolutionary purity.

With his speech, Khomeini clearly situated the conflict between these two types of women at the center of the revolution. The conflict is no longer merely between traditionalism and modernity, or nationalism and imperialism, but also between revolutionaries and nonrevolutionaries (good and evil). At one pole stand the defenders of revolutionary purity. At the other pole stand those who would corrupt the revolution and the austere committed revolutionaries. There is no doubt that this is a very useful dichotomy for the Islamic leadership, especially because the dichotomy also implicitly and explicitly feeds on a very real division between middle- and working-class women in Iran. Not unexpectedly, however, the dichotomy leaves very little room for the women of either class to maneuver. For middle-class women, for instance, an open protest against *hejab* simply ends up confirming that they are agents of westernization, whores, or deculturated (all in the same breath). But resistance continues. I have already mentioned how changes in the representation of women occasioned by scores of dead and injured men has opened the way for a more critical outlook toward the promises made to defenders of revolutionary purity.

Middle-class women also continue to engage in resistive maneuvers that question the identity imposed on them by authorities. First of all, they continue to occupy the public arena. Second, although they wear the *hejab*, they do not follow it completely (e.g., by showing some hair, wearing makeup). By contesting *hejab* on an everyday basis, these women continue to make a power claim as tempters of the revolution and, of course, continuously risk their bodies. At the same time, by not making *hejab* as such a political issue, while, in effect, acknowledging the way their bodies were used to legitimize the westernizing project of the previous regime, they are attempting to legitimize themselves as members of the new political community. This is, of course, a controversial point. It could be argued easily that middle-class women clearly oppose *hejab* and its material backbone, Islamic patriarchy, but they are justifiably too afraid to organize against it. Certainly this is the most important part of Iranian reality. However, there is more to the story. I began to realize this as the numerous conversations I had with middle-class women revealed that their relationship to *hejab* was at least ambiguous. I was truly astounded when I heard many of these women, who fully reject *hejab* at home, say that they did find some value in wearing it in the streets. Some argued that it made their lives much easier: they did not have to deal with sexual innuendos, pervasive during the Shah's time, or worry about what to wear when they went out. I mention these comments not to create an idealized understanding of the veil, which I find to be truly oppressive, but to remind others that people find ways to live in their oppressive environments. Negotiation, acceptance, resistance, contradictory steps, and so on are simply what most people do to survive. Not to acknowledge this is an idealization of resistive politics as well as a denigration of the subjugated people's will to survive. Put differently, it is true that veiling means acknowledgment of the regime's will to rule, but this acknowledgment in turn may be used to bring about more political control. Should this acquiescence be called female collusion? It is collusion insofar as at least part of the strategy confirms the regime's portrayal of these women as agents of westernization. But this collusion is incomplete and therefore not in opposition to resistance. They work in tandem.

This is by no means to signify that veiling has become a mute issue among secular women with no chance of taking center stage in the future. It is very important to remember that the opening of Iran, and wall advertisements for Dole bananas and Sony televisions replacing revolutionary graffiti, leave forced veiling as the only remaining visual marker of the revolution and the Islamic activists' will to rule. And precisely because veiling is the only visual marker left, any attempt by the government to claim legitimacy among the secular people on the basis of anything other than force must open the question of the veil in the future. Recent government maneuvers on this issue are indeed very interesting but outside the topic of this chapter.

Will the collusion-resistance strategy open the path for such fundamental questioning? Only if it is understood that westernized women are only half of the dichotomy. Westernized women can make headway in changing their situation only if the stereotype of the true revolutionary Muslim woman is also subverted. This is clearly a monumental task which requires not only crossing different practices but also class barriers. The complicating factor is that westernized Iranian women as well as the world community know little about the urban lower middle-class and working-class women who carry this stereotype. They have carried the overwhelming burden of the vicious war with Iraq and their family lives have been most affected by worsening economic conditions due mostly to hyper-inflation and cuts in subsidies.[41]

Given the ignorance, is success possible? I do not know. The question is obviously an important one, not only for researchers but also for political activists. At this point, I feel that the only hope lies in reflecting in collectivities—hence a political project—regarding the full implications that the dichotomization delineated above has for Iranian women. There is no doubt that it is useful to the Islamic regime as well as to many projects and movements in the West, including large parts of Western feminism, which can reaffirm the superiority of their own projects. But it is also clear that the dichotomization is costly to Iranian women on at least two grounds. By making female bodies a contested terrain, it puts them in physical danger. It also does rhetorical violence to the diversity which the category "Iranian women" entails. Whether this violence and the subsequent symbolic and material exploitation it carries can become a source of solidarity will clearly depend on the ability of Iranian women to see themselves in their multiple identities rather than as fragments of a larger whole forcibly constructed by the nationalist Islamic project.

NOTES

1. The category "Iranian women" is obviously quite problematic. Iranian women are differentiated on the basis of class, ethnicity, and region. In what follows, I will not lay out these differences. Rather, I will focus on the images generated by revolutionary conditions that necessarily undermine this diversity.

2. For the best example of this genre, see Theda Skoçpol, *States and Social Revolutions* (Cambridge: Cambridge University Press, 1979). Also see the collections of essays edited by Jack Goldstone, *Revolutions* (San Diego: Harcourt Brace, Jovanovich, 1986). This latter book is intended to be used as a classroom text on revolutions and is organized into sections on causes, processes, and outcomes.

3. For important exceptions to the cause/outcome approaches, see François Furet, *Reinterpreting the French Revolution* (New York: Cambridge University Press, 1981); Lynn Hunt, *Politics, Culture and Class in the French Revolution* (Berkeley: University of California Press, 1985); and Mona Ozouf, *Festivals and the French Revolution* (Cambridge: Harvard University Press, 1988). In what is meant by the politics of revolution, I have benefitted from reading Hunt's book. Although I am not fully convinced of the total incompatibility of the two approaches, I find Hunt's criticism of the cause/outcome approaches as missing the crucial emphasis on the actors and symbols of revolutionary drama to be sound.

4. It is true that recent state-centered analyses allow for the potential autonomy of political structures from dominant classes. But this autonomy is nevertheless discussed within the context of state/class, state/economy, and state/state relations. The active creation of the revolutionary political culture is generally ignored.

5. Hunt, *Politics, Culture, and Class*, 10.

6. Here, I am agreeing with Skoçpol who has convincingly pointed out that it is the crisis centered around the structure and situation of the pre-revolutionary state that launches a revolution. In what happens afterwards, however, Skoçpol mostly focuses on sociological factors. To her, it is the structure of peasant or urban communities that make various kinds of mobilization possible. In this paper, I am focusing less on those sociological factors and more on the formation and mutation of revolutionary culture. For Skoçpol's treatment of the Iranian revolution, see "Rentier State and Shi^ca Islam in the Iranian Revolution," *Theory and Society* 11 (May 1982): 265–304. Also see my *States and Urban-Based Revolutions: Iran and Nicaragua* (Urbana: University of Illinois Press, 1990).

7. By togetherness I do not necessarily mean agreement without conflict, disputes, or struggles. I mean a new basis for the negotiation of meanings. Some now resist, while others search for new possibilities of gaining power and resisting in the new power structure. Hence, this public togetherness is generated within the context of the breakup of the old regime and the buildup of a new one, as various groups and constituencies compete with each other for a better place in the reorganization of power.

8. Books on the Iranian revolution are too many to list. For a thorough synopsis of events leading to the overthrow of the Shah, see E. Abrahamian, *Iran: Between Two Revolutions* (Princeton: Princeton University Press, 1982). For a narrative of events in the immediate post-revolutionary period, see S. Bakhash, *The Reign of the Ayatollahs* (New York: Basic Books, 1984). On the particulars of the clash over women's issues, see H. Afshar, "Women, State and Ideology in Iran," *Third World Quarterly* 7 (1985); and A. Tabari, A. Yeganeh and N. Yeganeh, eds., *In the Shadow of Islam: The Women's Movement in Iran* (London: Zed Press, 1982).

9. Furet, *Reinterpreting the French Revolution.*

10. The temptation here is to use the word vehicle for site. But, as I hope the discussion that follows will show, the woman question, at least up to very recently, has not been used as a trump card to advance the position of a particular group contending for power. In other words, no one person or group has explicitly attempted to engage in power politics with an eye on women as a distinct group with interests emanating from their inferior position in society. However, this may be changing. In the 1992 parliamentary election, the Association of Combatant Clerics, which ran an anti-government slate in Tehran, did try to present itself (if somewhat meekly) as being more liberal in relation to women issues. The newspaper *Salaam*, generally considered to reflect their views, began a weekly page called the Woman's Tribune seriously discussing women's issues. It also called for the election of more women to the parliament. Indeed more women were elected to the parliament (they now number 9 out of 270) but none of them were from the opposition slate. The discussion of the role of women's issues in the recent election requires another paper. For now it is sufficient to say that the possibility of a more liberal position on women by the Association of Combatant Clerics was rendered

politically useless, even among opponents of Islamicization policies, by the portrayal of the Rafsanjani government as the only viable force for economic liberalization.

11. For an analysis of the symbolic use of the veil during the revolution, see N. Yeganeh, "Women's Struggles in the Islamic Republic of Iran," in *In the Shadow of Islam*, ed. A. Tabari and N. Yeganeh (London: Zed Press, 1982), 5–25. For an interesting expression of women's political dilemmas in that early period, see Manny Shirazi, *Siege of Azadi Square: A Novel of Revolutionary Iran* (London: Women's Press, 1991).

12. The focus here on the relationship between sexual modesty and national defense should not overshadow the more traditional themes of male honor. For instance, one very common slogan written on the walls proclaims "death to the woman without *hejab*, and her cowardly husband (*marg bar zan-e bi hejab va shohar bi gheirat-e ou*)." Here, however, I am focusing on the relationship between the national question and *hejab* precisely because the revolution openly posed the male/female dynamic in national terms.

13. Ironically, it would almost flow naturally from this point of view that the forceful reintroduction of the Iranian culture—its becoming blatant—was made necessary by the revolutionary events themselves. There is no doubt in my mind that the Islamic activists were as interested in crushing an *independent* women's *movement* (the key words here are italicized) as "returning to true Islam."

14. Reza Barahani, *Crowned Cannibals* (New York: Vintage, 1977), chap. 3.

15. Ibid., 62.

16. Farah Azari, "Sexuality and Women's Oppression in Iran," in *Women of Iran*, ed. Farah Azari (London: Ithaca Press, 1983).

17. A similar argument about Islam in general has been made by Fatna A. Sabbah, *Woman in the Muslim Unconscious* (New York: Pergamon Press, 1984). She argues that, in Islam, sexuality is not posed as contrary to order; it is considered licit. But its most uncontrollable and versatile human element—desire—is identified as the source and substance of the illicit. Opposite to desire, of course, is the licit reason—the instrument of faith and divine love. The sexual act is threatening to Islam because it threatens the ultimate source of worship—reason. From this comes the necessity to control woman since she is the unique incarnation of desire. Mastering women means mastering desire and the source of disorder.

18. For good criticisms of essentialist approaches to the Iranian culture and Shiʿi Islam, see K. Safa-Isfahani, "Female-Centered World Views in Iranian Culture: Symbolic Representations of Sexuality in Dramatic Games," *Signs* 6, no. 1 (1980): 33–53, and Nahid Yeganeh and Nikkie R. Keddie, "Sexuality and Shiʿi Social Protest in Iran," in *Shiʿism and Social Protest*, ed. Juan R. Cole and Nikkie R. Keddie (New Haven: Yale University Press, 1986), 108–22.

19. In using the term organic, I mean a relationship in which neither of the components can be understood without the other. As such, the particulars of the call for Islamic regeneration must be situated within the context of the rejection of Western cultural control. Islamic regeneration was thus the

symbolic coherence that united the different revolutionary forces facing the West. Of course, the meaning of Islamic regeneration is contested by the different forces so as to represent different things. And, here is where the struggle over the meaning occurs internally and in opposition to the West. From the outside, Islamic regeneration looks coherent; from the insider's point of view, it is a mess (struggles, resistance, and inconsistencies). I would like to thank Marta Savigliano for reminding me how "messy" reality is.

20. See, for instance, the chapter on the "Discourse of the Veil" in Leila Ahmed's recent book, *Women and Gender in Islam* (New Haven: Yale University Press, 1992). On the specifically Iranian context, see Afsaneh Najmabadi, "Hazards of Modernity and Morality: Women, State and Ideology in Contemporary Iran," in *Women, Islam and the State*, ed. Deniz Kandiyoti (Philadelphia: Temple University Press, 1991), 48–68. Najmabadi focuses on the ways the woman question was coopted by the modernizing state.

21. Ahmed, *Women and Gender in Islam*, 152.

22. The attacks on veiling were initiated by Reza Shah who confronted it directly. Mohammad Reza Shah relied mostly on the indirect vehicle of social pressure.

23. According to Ahmed, "the resemblance between the two positions is not coincidental: they are mirror images of each other. The resistance narrative contested the colonial thesis by inverting it—thereby also, ironically, grounding itself in the premises of the colonial thesis." Ahmed, *Women and Gender in Islam*, 166.

24. Nahid Yeganeh, "Sexuality in Contemporary Shiʿi Texts," in *Shiʿism and Social Protest*, eds. Juan Cole and Nikkie R. Keddie (New Haven: Yale University Press, 1986), 122–36.

25. See Ruhollah Khomeini, *Resaleh-e Tauzih Al-Masʾil* (Gom: n.p., n.d.).

26. See *Sima-e Zan Dar kalaam Imam Khomeini* (Tehran: Intesharat-e Vezarat-e Farhang va Ershad Islami, 1369/1990).

27. Ibid., 13. One of the more prominent graffiti in Tehran says: "If lack of veil means civilization, then animals are the most civilized." If unpacked, this statement can explain quite a bit about the Iranian understanding of nature. But, for our purposes, it is important to note that there has been a long tradition in Iran of identifying the animal world as one of uncontrollable emotional/sexual energy. As such, it is understood as inhumane.

28. Morteza Mtahhari, *Mas'aleh-e Hejab* (Tehran: Entesharat Sadra, 1987).

29. Fatima Mernissi, *Beyond the Veil*, rev. ed. (Bloomington: University of Indiana Press, 1987).

30. Despite all their ideological pronouncements, the Iranian post-revolutionary leaders have not been able to alter, for instance, women's labor force participation significantly relative to the pre-revolutionary period. On this see, Val Moghadam, "Women, Work and Ideology in the Islamic Republic of Iran," *International Journal of Middle East Studies* 20 (May 1988): 221–43. This of course does not mean that the Iranian leaders have not tried. For an enumeration of the effects of Islamicization on women, see Val Moghadam, "Revolution, the State, Islam, and Women: Gender Politics in Iran and

Afghanistan," *Social Text* 22 (Spring 1989): 40–61.

31. Of course, ideological constructions are themselves practices. Here, Mernissi is simply making a distinction between what people do and the way they think about their actions.

32. This is, of course, an old story about the operation of colonization. The terms of the anti-colonial struggle are defined by colonialism because it is in opposition to colonialism that the struggle takes shape. In an article on gender and politics in Algeria, Marnia Mazreg nicely lays out this dynamic: "Prior to the French invasion, Algerians had broadly perceived themselves as Muslims in the same sense that the French thought of themselves as Christians. They took their Muslim identity for granted, perceiving themselves, more importantly, in regional, tribal, and family terms. After 1830, however, Islam emerged as the most salient aspect of their identity. A dialectical relationship was thus established between the colonizers and the colonized. The French chose Islam as the Algerians' common denominator and as grounds on which to fight them. Likewise, Algerians responded by making Islam the bastion of their resistance to colonialism." Marnia Lazreg, "Gender and Politics in Algeria: Unraveling the Religious Paradigm," *Signs* 15, no. 4 (Summer 1990): 755–80.

33. Some of the works of Shariati which focus on women and Islam are in the collection, *Zan*, 4th ed. (Tehran: Intesharat-e Chappaksh, 1370/1991).

34. A similar argument has been made by Nayereh Tohidi in her article in Persian on "The Woman Question: Intellectuals and Changes in the Recent Decades," *Nimey-e Degar* 10 (Winter 1368/1990).

35. For the problems some Iranian nationalists have had with the connection between Western penetration and feminine values, see the most famous work of Jalal Al-e Ahmad, *Gharbzadegi* (recently translated as *Occidentosis* but also referred to as *West-Stricken* or *Westoxicated*). Al-Ahmad, who is considered to be one of the most influential thinkers in delimiting the extent and nature of Western penetration, describes a person influenced by the West in the following way: "The Occidentotic is effete. He is effeminate. He attends to his grooming a great deal. He spends much time sprucing himself up. Sometimes he even plucks his eyebrows. He attaches a great deal of importance to his shoes and his wardrobe, and to the furnishings of his home." *Occidentosis*, trans. R. Campbell (Berkeley: Mizan Press, 1984), 97. The scapegoating of the female (or more properly feminine) is also evident in the works of other nationalists. See, for instance, Jose Rizal's *Noli Me Tangere*, trans. León Ma (Hong Kong: Longman, 1961). The manner in which this scapegoating occurs is nicely unpacked in works of writers such as Chinua Achebe (see especially *Things Fall Apart* (London: Heinemann, 1958). For an analysis of Achebe's works see Abdul Jan Muhammad, *Manichaean Esthetics* (Amherst: University of Massachusetts Press, 1984).

36. In fact, the Islamic Republic has gone a long way toward liberalizing sexual relationships by its virtual promotion of temporary marriages. But even this creates problems since, no matter how temporary, these marriages still produce nuclear family structures.

37. On representations of the Middle Eastern women, see Sarah Graham-

Brown, *Images of Women: The Portrayal of Women in Photography of the Middle East, 1860–1950* (New York: Columbia University Press, 1988).

38. An attack on Western orientalism is, of course, a very worthy project but when it is done for the sake of reclaiming native male honor it becomes much more than a mere attack. To be sure, it kills the fantasy, but it also risks killing the one fantasized about if the woman has become fully identified with that fantasy in the minds of native patriarchs.

39. I am thankful to Nancie Caraway for bringing this card to my attention.

40. This sentiment is perhaps best being expressed in some recent novels, movies, and short stories. For instance, see the movie *The Marriage of the Blessed* and the novel *Bagh-e Blour* (The Crystal Garden) (Tehran: Nashr-e Ney, 1368/1989), both by Mohsen Makhmalbaf.

41. Some new works are being generated about working women and veiling in the Arab world that are quite enlightening, most notably, Arlene Elowe McLeod, *Accommodating Protest: Working Women, the New Veiling and Change in Cairo* (New York: Columbia University Press, 1991).

Chapter 12

Women, Revolution, and Israel

Connie Jorgensen

The first Zionist immigration to Palestine in the late nineteenth century began a period known as the Yishuv, literally the community, which continued until the establishment of the state of Israel in 1948.[1] During this period, state structures were formed and a new society created. The Yishuv was characterized by the struggle against the indigenous population and, at times, against the British to create a homeland for the Jewish diaspora. For women, the struggle was also a struggle for equality.

Many of the early Zionist settlers were revolutionaries. In Palestine, they created a new economic system, new social and political institutions, and new educational, cultural, and ideological structures.[2] Palestine was transformed by these idealistic immigrants who dreamed of a homeland for the Jewish diaspora. Many of them had socialist leanings that promised not only a changed Jewish man, but a change in male/female power relations. The need for hard work, dedication, and defense of the settlements created a situation wherein women saw opportunities radically to transform themselves and their relationships with men. The new state promised sexual equality. Even though some women did work side-by-side with their male counterparts to break down sexual barriers, they were the exception, not the rule.

Myths developed about the new Israeli woman: she was strong, independent, and liberated. These myths are still promoted by the state of Israel and accepted as reality by many in the outside world. Unfortunately, despite the promises of Zionism and the hopes of the pioneers, Israeli women never achieved a status close to the myth.

They have not realized equality. In Israel, the predominant focus is on the man; the society is very paternalistic toward women. The Zionist man, or the "new Jew," is strong and stoic; his goal is to conquer the barren earth, creating new life. Reinforcing this masculine perspective is a major focus on the military where, once again, men are primary and women are secondary. This chapter seeks to identify the promises of Zionism and of the Israeli state to women, and to contrast the promises with the reality.

REVOLUTION AND ISRAEL

The creation of Israel does not fit neatly into any one model of revolution. Marx understood revolution as a class-based movement rising out of societies whose different social forces are doomed to conflict. Relationships to property and the mode of production are key ingredients in a Marxist revolution. When the forces of production come into conflict with property relations, a social revolution becomes possible. Increasing class conflicts lead to the rise of a revolutionary class which heads the transition from one mode of production to another. Zionism does not fit the Marxist model very well because Zionism did not rise out of relations to the mode of production. Although Zionist ideology considered the economic position of Jews, economics was not the primary motivation—anti-Semitism was.

Samuel Huntington defines revolution as "a rapid, fundamental and violent domestic change in the dominant values and myths of a society, in its political institutions, social structure, leadership, and government activity and its policies."[3] Huntington notes that "revolution is characteristic of modernization," and that "political modernization involves the extension of political consciousness to new social groups and the mobilization of these groups into politics."[4] Zionism certainly did this. The Jewish population, or a portion of it, became politically active against the existing power structure in Russia and East Europe. However, Zionists chose not to carry out their revolution in Europe but to transplant it to Palestine where they built new power structures. As a result, there is a disjunction between the political and social transformations effected by Zionism.

Theda Skoçpol believes that revolutions should be analyzed from a structural perspective, paying special attention to international contexts and developments that affect the breakdown of old regimes and the creation of new ones. She maintains that in order to explain social revolutions one must identify the emergence of a revolutionary situation within the old regime and then identify the "intermeshing of the various actions of the diversely situated groups"—an intermeshing that shapes the revolutionary process and gives rise to the new regime. The interrelations of groups within the old society must be considered alongside "world-historically developing international structures."[5]

According to Skoçpol, social revolutions change state structures as much if not more than they change class relations, societal values, and social institutions. The class upheaval and socioeconomic transformation associated with social revolutions are closely connected with the collapse of the old state structures.[6] Yet even here, the transplantation of the Zionist revolution to Palestine creates analytical difficulties. Eastern European Jews responded to social conditions in their homelands and created a revolutionary movement—Zionism. But Zionism ultimately changed the state structure of Palestine, not the homelands within which Zionism arose and developed. Indeed, the Zionist revolution in Palestine could not have happened without outside influences such as the U.N. mandate creating Israel.

Even so, the resulting societal changes were revolutionary. The revolution to create a Jewish homeland and a new Jewish person was deliberate and forceful. Its stated goal was to make new structures in society, culture, and state, and to create new relationships between men and women.[7]

BACKGROUND

Modern Zionism was, in large part, a response to the late nineteenth-century rise in European anti-Semitism. Zionist ideology eventually developed into a secular nationalistic movement based not on Judaism but on socialism and a desire to normalize the status of Jews by giving them a homeland. From the beginning, the movement intended women to play an active role. Theodor Herzl, the founder of modern Zionism, speaking at the first Zionist Congress in 1897, said, "A nation striving to be equal among other nations can ill afford not to recognize women as equal to men."[8] As socialism became a part of the Zionist conception of the homeland, the promises of a prominent place for women were reinforced. Women were to be freed from the shackles of childbearing and childrearing and were to work side-by-side with men.

The early Zionists sought to build an egalitarian society based on the concept of working the land collectively. They were committed to the equality of women.[9] It was this group of immigrants to Palestine who were the founders of the kibbutz movement.[10] They, and the members of the second and third immigrant cohort of *Aliyah*[11]

(1905–1914 and 1919–1924), were dedicated to the creation of a secular Jewish community based on self-reliance. Their era is considered to be the formative period of Israeli society during which the dominant values of the state were formed, plans implemented, and major institutional structures developed.[12]

At the end of the nineteenth century, the young Jewish women of Eastern Europe and Russia lived in an era of revolution. They were impressed by the social experiments of the times and the personalities of Russian and Jewish female revolutionaries who then became their role models.[13] Most of these women rejected the example set by their mothers in the shtetl. For them, traditional ideas of family had begun to break down. They saw no reason to follow in their mothers' footsteps, but looked to the Russian revolutionaries for guidance.

The influence of the Russian revolutionaries is evident in the memoirs of the early settlers. We can see that along with a passion for socialism came an awareness of what it means to be Jewish, and that for a Jew, a workers' revolution could only be carried out in Israel. Deborah Dyan, an early settler, describes her decision to emigrate, "And on an unforgettable night I made my decision. . . . The people to whom I have dedicated my life up to now are not my own . . . where are the masses of my own people?"[14] She goes on to say, "in Palestine there are the workers of my people. I will go to them and become one of them."

Although most early pioneers were socialists, after their arrival in Palestine, their focus changed to development of the land and other nationalistic concerns. These concerns still allowed room for women to participate and implied a transformation of "self" and "Jew" into "worker."[15] Members of the first aliyah in the 1880s became gentlemen farmers and hired cheap Arab labor. Jewish women competed with men (both Arab and Jewish) for work. The second aliyah consisted of thirty-five thousand to forty thousand persons primarily from Russian Zionist labor organizations. This group was different from the first aliyah because they did not want to be middle-class landowners. Their ideology had the most effect on ideas about sexual equality,[16] and manual work, physical labor, and defense were strongly emphasized.

The focus on physical labor required changes in the psyche of the traditional Jewish man. The Ashkenazi[17] man had not typically been involved in physical labor or agriculture; Jews in Russia were not allowed to own land. Traditionally, the idealized Jewish man was a scholar, devoted to studying scripture and to the performance of *Mitzvot*, religious commandments. Further, because of intolerance and discrimination against Jews in Europe, Jewish men felt emasculated and powerless.[18] In order to build the Jewish homeland the "new Jew" (the Zionist), had to be strong, masculine, muscled, tan, aggressive, and stoic. Such a radical transformation required a major change in the way Jewish men perceived themselves. In Palestine, they were able to reject traditional values and embrace an ideology of manhood. Zionism became the ultimate male protest against the yoke of oppression that Jews endured in Europe. But while the Zionist men were anxious to develop a new relationship to the land, they were seldom sensitive to those same desires in Zionist women.[19] Although women were supposed to be workers alongside men, the dominant ideology did not include feminine characteristics. To be the ideal pioneer one had to be male.

Most Jewish immigrants to Palestine were young, rebellious, and idealistic. This idealism was smashed when they reached the promised land. Rather than a land of milk and honey, Palestine was a barren land of rocks and thorns. To make matters worse, the neighbors were unfriendly. Walter Lacquer writes, "Everything was strange and unfamiliar. . . . Living conditions were incredibly primitive even by eastern European standards. . . . [The immigrants] had to put up with malaria, snakes, scorpions, various bugs, overseers who made work hell."[20] But these new immigrants felt a zeal to transform both the land and themselves and set to work creating a new Palestine complete with new social relationships, institutions, and myths.

The land became identified with woman, a bride, and a motherly womb.

> Mother Zion, after being made love to by her "homecoming" sons, gave birth to new life. Thus, the children replaced their father, husbanded their mother, and fathered themselves. They, therefore, experienced a Zionist "rebirth" in which they played the new and masterful role of the potent life giver.[21]

Men impregnated the soil and created new life, becoming redeemers of the land. These are intensely masculinist images and they permeated the Jewish psyche. While this mindset had positive effects on men, it placed women in a subordinate role.[22] Women were expected to work in the kitchen while the men went out into the fields. One wrote, "The women were dismayed and disappointed to see the men comrades uniting themselves with the land, and they [the women] though on it, were not part of it."[23] The men were coming together with the earth and the earth was their mistress. Mere women were powerless against her.

The emphasis on masculinity made achievement of sexual equality virtually impossible. Although women were expected to work and contribute to the defense of the settlements, they were effectively excluded from equal participation in the creation of the new society. A prerequisite for women to share in the community was that they first be freed from the "biological tragedy" of childbearing.[24] The term "biological tragedy" indicated that women were shackled by their gender and therefore inherently unable to be equal to men.

In the early twentieth century, as the idea of a Jewish nation became more popular among European Jews, ideas about sexual equality also became stronger. The women who immigrated during this period fully expected to contribute equally to the building of Israel. Their diaries, however, indicate that the reality they encountered was far different from their expectations. They experienced difficulties obtaining jobs in agriculture, construction, and road building. The men tended to treat them contemptuously and did not take their efforts seriously. Many, if not most, found themselves relegated to kitchen work or other traditionally feminine occupations. Sarah Malchin, one of the leaders of the early settlers, wrote, "In Europe we planned and dreamed about our future in Zion; there, there was to be no distinction between men and women. . . . [But when we arrived in Palestine] our beautiful dreams were destroyed by our hostile surroundings. . . . We girls were met with indifference and scorn everywhere."[25] The "girls" were ridiculed by potential employers and felt abandoned by male comrades who still had traditional ideas about the division of labor between the sexes.

> They also considered us absurd. Not only those of us who wanted to break down so-called natural barriers and adopt the difficult occupation of agriculture, but also those of us who engaged in work that women seemed especially suited for—they too were considered absurd.[26]

This attitude toward women and women's desire for equality percolated through all of Palestine's newly created institutions.

WOMEN AND THE KIBBUTZ MOVEMENT

The kibbutz, in theory, is a utopia of sexual equality. It is a socialist community and, as such, its affairs are managed democratically. The means of production are communally owned and operated according to a plan devised by kibbutz members. In order to ensure that the plan is fulfilled, duties are assigned equally among men and women.

Kibbutz ideology emphasizes manual work and physical labor in order that a laboring class be created. Labor becomes a moral and noble endeavor connected to the redemption of the land and working the land becomes a means through which Jews can liberate themselves. The new Jewish people would rise up out of the soil. Self-defense was also an important part of kibbutz ideology. The *Hashomer* (Watchmen), formed in 1909 to guard the settlements, became the earliest heroes of Israel because they were the first professional Jewish warriors in more than two thousand years.[27]

Because of the socialist nature of the kibbutz, all work is theoretically equal in value. If kitchen work is of equal value to work in the fields, there should be no shame for a man to work in the kitchen. Conversely, a woman can fulfill her duty if assigned to manual labor in the field. Further, the upbringing of children is a communal responsibility. Female pioneers expressed their desire to be equal partners by putting themselves alongside men in their visions of the new Jew. This idea was expressed by women workers at Kinneret farm.

> It is our firm opinion that every young man and woman who comes here in the name of the revival of the nation and its spirit, must take the first step in that revival . . . by working in the fields and in the heart of nature; to throw off, once and for all, the habits and ways of life and even thoughts that they brought from the Diaspora.[28]

The kibbutz frees women to work outside the home. Household chores are minimized by communal child care, kitchens, and laundries. Most significantly, since there are no wages on the kibbutz, women do not depend on their husbands' income. Outside the kibbutz, crises such as divorce or widowhood can reduce a woman's standard of living. In the kibbutz, these events have no economic impact.[29] However, despite the sexual equality in theory, the reality of kibbutz life is quite different.

Few women were allowed to join kibbutzim and even fewer were allowed to be agricultural workers. Men feared that women's agricultural skills were inadequate and women's work on the farms was disparaged.[30] Women were typically placed in what are considered to be low-status service roles—women's work. For example, food preparation was women's work even though few of the women knew how to cook and their efforts left the men dissatisfied. The division of labor primarily along gender lines remains the same today. For example, in a study of kibbutz life at Tel Or, Ilea Schuste and Janette Hartz-Karp found 121 women active in the labor force. Of these, sixty-six worked in kitchens, laundries, and children's houses. Nineteen were teachers, and eleven were clerks. The women at Tel Or also had primary responsibility for housework in their private apartments and for the care of their own biological children.[31] Few women held positions of authority; women offered positions such as kibbutz committee chairperson were usually put on committees like education, a traditionally female field.[32]

All community members are expected to donate time to the kibbutz. For men, this involves a token six months to a year in service jobs. For women, it means devoting their entire lives to service occupations.[33] Despite the fact that men are rotated through the kitchens to learn what the job is like and to appreciate it, women often resent kitchen assignments and complain that they get no recognition for the work they do.[34] Golda Meir asked why women find kitchen work so demeaning, noting that the only disgrace is bad food or dirty dishes. This comment brought her instant notoriety and the wrath of other women in the kibbutz.[35] Despite her public image as a woman who stepped outside of traditional roles, in an interview about her life in the kibbutz, Meir emphasized her "feminine" achievements in the kitchen rather than the public jobs she had held.[36] Stereotypes about women's roles in kibbutz society were widespread. Marie Syrkin, a close friend and biographer of Meir, wrote, "Today the early feminist excesses of *halutsa*, the woman pioneer, are a matter of the past. . . . The feminist concept of equality has become less literal and more rational."[37]

Although Syrkin places responsibility for the failure of women to achieve equal rights on early feminist excesses, there seems to be little actual evidence that the women's demands were particularly radical. Obviously, not every woman objected to working in the kitchen, but women did demand that they be allowed to do other work as well, such as raising vegetables and livestock.[38] Kelia Gil'adi, a member of the Sejera collective, said that the wife of a *Shomer* (settlement guard) was a helpmate who carried the full burden of partnership but who performed jobs distinctly different from those of men.[39]

The original plan for the kibbutz, that children be raised communally, was envisioned as relieving women of the burden of childrearing. Marriage was scorned as bourgeois; it seemed claustrophobic, and created only for acquisitive purposes.[40] Couples did come together but did not always call it marriage. The group would recognize the pair as a couple. Eventually children were born of these partnerships, but because kibbutz living had not been planned with children in mind, children often caused conflicts between the family and the group. Still, newborn children were welcomed as new Jews.[41]

It was first assumed that mothers would rear their own children, but this prevented them from fulfilling work obligations to the community, so communal childrearing developed. Even so, the addition of children to the community took more and more women out of agriculture to work in the children's house, the kitchen, and the laundry. The women turned from creating new life from the soil to creating and tending to new Jews. Over the years, women accepted more and more of the responsibility for their own biological children. Today, few children sleep in children's houses, but rather in the apartments of their parents. Because women must combine their responsibilities to the kibbutz with those to their children, their burdens have increased—reinforcing the separation of the sexes along traditional lines.

Many scholars have tried to explain the adherence to traditional roles in the kibbutzim. Some say it is because of biological differences between men and women;[42] others point to the fact that life in the kibbutz has become more routine and say that women themselves initiated the changes;[43] some identify the increased kibbutz birth rate and the subsequent need for child care as the culprit.[44] All of these scholars assume that equality had once been achieved and was then somehow rejected. Yet the evidence shows that gender equality was never realized.

Here again, the obstacle may lie in the image of the transformed Jewish man—the farmer and protector who kept women in traditional roles. Even though women also sought to transform themselves into workers, this was impossible because changes in the male psyche made it unthinkable for men to regress and do woman's work. Therefore, when children came into the commune, it was women who were expected to raise them while men stayed in the fields.[45] As the kibbutz has become more established, women's occupational roles have become specialized. Jobs are assigned along gender lines and the organization has become more structured. Perhaps the most important reason for this is the emergence of the biological family as the primary social institution. Yet, despite evidence to the contrary, members of the kibbutz themselves hang on to the myth of sexual equality. Clinging to this belief provides a sense of unity for the community, support for kibbutz members, and bolsters women's self-esteem.[46]

WOMEN AND RELIGION

Most of the Zionists who settled Palestine were secular. The majority of Orthodox Jews did not accept Zionist ideology because they believed that the Jewish homeland would not be restored until the coming of the Messiah. A few, however, saw Zionism as a means to pave the way for the Messiah. After the 1917 Balfour Declaration, David Ben-Gurion realized the need for unity among world Jewry and began to consider ways to join Orthodox Zionists, non-Zionists, and secular Zionists. In 1947, when Britain announced that the issue was to be turned over to the United Nations, Ben-Gurion sent a letter to a non-Zionist Orthodox group to urge its members to speak at the United Nations in favor of the creation of a Jewish state. As an enticement, Ben-Gurion's letter indicated that the new state of Israel would adopt Orthodox matrimonial law including the prohibition of marriage between Jews and non-Jews, the cleansing of the bride and groom, the *katuba* (contract) agreed to by the bride's father and the groom, the right of a brother-in-law to veto the remarriage of a widow, and the husband's veto power over divorce.[47] The letter created expectations among Orthodox Jews who had overcome their apprehensions about involvement in a pre-messianic state. When a provisional government was established, they were included. Ben-Gurion's letter led to a situation that gave the Orthodox almost total control over women's lives and subjugated women by what has been called the Judaic yoke.

The 1948 Declaration of Independence stated specifically that Israel was to be a Jewish state. The Jewish religion, particularly the Orthodox version, has become the central identifying characteristic of both the people and the state. Orthodox Judaism is paternalistic in nature and considers women to be inferior to men. The identification of Israel with Orthodox Judaism created extremely difficult conditions for Israeli women.

In 1949, Ben-Gurion, still concerned that all Jews participate in the formation of Israel, wrote to the Orthodox leaders insisting upon equal rights for women, yet his letter contained concessions that had the opposite effect. Despite the urging of secular Jews, and Moslems concerned about losing their religious courts, Ben-Gurion agreed that there would be no civil domestic courts in Israel. A law giving control over marriage and divorce to Rabbinical courts was justified as protecting Jewish women from Islamic law, perceived to be more oppressive.[48] Yet, this rationale is difficult to sustain. Although Islamic courts discriminate against women, the Rabbinical courts do so as much or more. For example, women are not allowed to give evidence in Rabbinical courts because they are, as the Talmud says, "temperamentally light-headed."[49] Women may give evidence in Islamic courts, although their testimony is not given the same weight as the testimony of men. Women cannot serve as judges on Rabbinical courts.

Thus, in a forum where matters of marriage and divorce are decided, issues that so intimately affect their lives, women have no institutional status or input. They also have little assurance that those passing judgment are competent. Members of Rabbinical courts are not required to have civil or family law experience. They swear an oath to the state but not to uphold the laws. This gives Rabbinical courts powers beyond any civil court in Israel.

One effect of the law is to reinforce the separation between Jew and non-Jew. Because there is no civil marriage in Israel, marriage between Jews and non-Jews is forbidden. A couple in this situation must leave the country to be married. Their children are considered Jewish only if the mother is Jewish. Even if the partner converts to Judaism, unless that partner is Orthodox, the conversion is not recognized, nor, therefore, is the marriage.

The greatest impact of the Rabbinical courts is in the area of divorce. Because of a literal interpretation of the Biblical statement "a man shall take a woman," and its presumed corollary, if a man takes a woman she can only be released if he so desires, the husband alone decides whether there shall be a divorce. Like a woman whose husband is presumed dead, one whose husband has left her but refuses to grant her a divorce is *aguna*: an abandoned wife anchored to her husband. A wife in that position can request that the Rabbinical court order her husband to grant her a divorce but, as of 1989, only thirty such compulsory divorces had ever been granted.[50]

Ben-Gurion justified his decision to concede control over family law to religious courts: "If we did not establish by statute that marriages must be in accordance with Jewish law, [the Sephardic immigrants, to whom family purity was] holy . . . would have to begin investigating who this young man or woman they are about to marry is."[51] Golda Meir and the Orthodox establishment offered another argument, that civil marriage in Israel might alienate diaspora Jews who wanted to see Orthodoxy enshrined in Israel.[52]

By 1970, Ben-Gurion had changed his tune. "The religious parties misused the law . . . [E]verything done up to now to give legal effect to *halacha* (Jewish law) must be abolished and we must establish that this is a nation of law."[53] But the political clout of the Orthodox prevented fundamental changes. The *halacha* might have been overturned during the National Unity Government (1984 to 1988) when the Labor and Likud coalition formed an absolute majority in the government. Up until this time, the religious parties were the swing votes, and no party could afford to alienate them. But both Labor and Likud, looking toward the government each hoped to create after 1988, were unwilling to take a step that might cost them support later.[54]

WOMEN AND FAMILY

In Israel, the family is the central social institution. The women of the fourth aliyah who fled Nazi Germany and those who followed them were primarily middle class. They were more family oriented and less ideologically oriented than the early pioneers. Family-centeredness increased with the immigration of Jews from paternalistic Arab countries. After the Holocaust, Jewish survival through childbearing became a social and ideological imperative. These changes led Israeli society to back away from women's rights, and shifted its emphasis from the community to the family.[55] The emphasis on family glorifies the role of the mother as opposed to other potential roles for women, reinforcing the traditional male/female division of labor characterized by a rigid distinction between the public and private spheres. Men are in charge of the public, political sphere while women are defined by the private, domestic sphere.[56]

Israel also has a strong pro-natalist domestic policy which makes the decision to have a child almost political. Its roots go back to the 1940s when Ben-Gurion, disturbed at the low Jewish birthrate, called on parents to do their demographic duty. The losses due to the Holocaust, plus the hostility of Israel's Arab neighbors, made this issue one of highest importance. Ben-Gurion stated that an average of 2.2 children per family was required because, with no immigration, the Jewish community in Palestine would otherwise die out.[57] On another occasion he indicated that, without a Jewish majority in Palestine, survival of the Jewish community would be impossible.[58] Even after the state was established and immigration increased, pro-natalist policies continued. One example was a cash prize to be paid to women upon the birth of their tenth child. However, this prize was discontinued in 1959, presumably because it was received by too many Arab women. The religious members of the population were and are pro-natalist because of the biblical injunction that Jews be fruitful and multiply. In 1945, the chief rabbi of Palestine, I. H. Herzog, called on Jews to increase the size of their families, suggesting that family limitation was the worst of sins.[59]

In 1962, a natality committee was established to advise the government on demographic issues. The only recommendation of the heavily pro-natalist committee which was actually implemented was to establish a demographics center within the prime minister's office. His aim was to ensure a favorable psychological climate to increase natality, but the center's effectiveness is in doubt because Israelis have children for reasons that have little to do with government policy. The ultimate result of the natality committee's efforts is likely to be class and ethnic conflicts. The target population—rich, Ashkenazi Jews—do not have large families while poor Sephardic Jews do.[60]

Childbearing is also encouraged through a strong system of pre- and post-natal care for women, the costs of which are borne largely by the state. A well-established health care system is also available for children whose well-being is viewed as the joint responsibility of women and the state. Women are often anxiety-ridden as the result of this responsibility and the pressure they feel to rear a "quality product."[61] Societal pressure makes women feel guilty if they are childless or if they bear children with health problems. The Israeli focus on masculinity makes bearing male children exceedingly important.

The state exhibits little interest in family planning. Sex education is seldom included in school curricula. Information about or access to contraception is very limited, and sterilization is often restricted by hospital policies. Sterilization brings back memories of Nazi experiments; it also conjures up images of Sarah, bitter because of her infertility, and is inconsistent with nationalist images of birth and rebirth.[62] Abortion has been legal in Israel since 1977. Prior to its legalization, abortion was tolerated but extremely expensive and thus available to only a small percentage of women.

Before legalization, Israel was a haven for illegal abortions, about seventy thousand to eighty thousand of which were performed every year.[63] Illegal abortions were available from reputable gynecologists who were not prosecuted unless the abortion caused death or serious damage to the woman. However, the price was very high, the equivalent of a man's average monthly wage—which was far more than a woman's average monthly wage.[64] As a testament to the strength and influence of the religious establishment, Orthodox organizations that opposed abortion were able to prevent the issue from being debated in the Knesset for almost forty years.[65] Legalization was a compromise between free abortion on demand and the status quo. Eligibility was expanded so that legal abortion under regular health care plans was made available to single women and women under social and psychological stress. However, to receive an abortion, a woman's application must be approved by a committee. If she cannot make a case for an abortion, it is still necessary to resort to illegal measures.[66]

The demographic threat was the most frequently used argument against abortion law reform.[67] A woman's prime duty is to have children. Yet one of the major social problems in Israel is that large families (generally Sephardic) tend to be at the bottom of the socioeconomic scale. They are looked down on by other Israelis. The parents are then in a confusing situation. They did their demographic duty, but they get little support from the government and cannot understand society's attitude toward them.

The majority of the population of Israel is not religious, so one cannot automatically assume that Israelis are influenced by the familistic tendencies of Judaism.[68] Typically, ethnic origin is seen as explaining differences in fertility rates. Women from Islamic countries have higher fertility rates than those from European countries.[69] However, Moshe Hartman has shown that religiosity among Jewish women in Israel also affects their pro-natalist tendencies. Religious women tend to marry earlier and have more children. As religiosity increases, women's fertility increases.

Among Israeli women of higher socioeconomic status, the sense that childbearing is a duty tends further to solidify the image of woman's role as mother. This attitude was enunciated and encouraged by Golda Meir when, in an interview with Oriani Fallaci, she called childbirth "the greatest privilege we women have compared to men."[70] It is apparent that Israeli mythology intimately connects a woman and her womb. She must be made aware of the womb's importance to ensure that she does not endanger her most important asset—her ability to have children. Fertility is not important just for women; women must have children for the state and for the Jewish people.

WOMEN, WORK, AND THE LAW

The failure of ideology to bring about equality for women forced Israel to consider the law as the means by which to alter traditional sex roles. However, unless a society agrees on the definition of sexual equality or how much equality to grant, laws may be ambiguous and fail to have the desired effects. In Israel, decisions about the nature of sexual equality in the workplace have been difficult. Laws passed to ensure women's rights often have a negative effect on women because of their ambiguity.

Clause Two of the 1948 Declaration of Independence states that Israel will "ensure absolute equality of social and political rights for all her citizens irrespective of race, religion or sex." and Israel's first government in 1949 upheld the "complete and absolute equality of women."[71] It is significant that this declaration of equality was achieved in the absence of social or legal struggle. However, neither statement has the force of a constitutional legal principle. Equal rights for women failed to become a constitutional premise forcing the legislature to adhere to principles of equality.[72] Even if women's rights were part of the Israeli constitution, Israeli courts cannot declare discriminatory laws to be invalid based on constitutional principles.

The first attempt to guarantee women's equality legally was the 1951 Women's Equal Rights Law (WERL). WERL regulated the actions of the state but had no jurisdiction over private companies, organizations, or individuals. It stated that all laws apply equally to men and women and that any provision of a law that discriminates against women would have no effect.[73] If the law had stopped here it might have been a positive force. Instead, WERL went on to state that "this law shall not affect any legal prohibition or permission relating to marriage or divorce" and "this law shall not derogate from any provision of law protecting women as women." The negative effects of these two clauses quickly became evident when the Rabbinical courts jurisdiction law gave control of marriage and divorce to Orthodox Judaism in 1953 and in 1954 when the employment of women law forbade women to work at night on the grounds that it endangered women's health.[74]

In 1964, Israel's equal pay law guaranteed women an equal wage for the same or generally equivalent job done by men in the same place of work. The law was considered an achievement for women. The fact that it had to be enacted at all indicated a deficiency in women's rights in Israel.[75] Despite its guarantees, the 1978 Commission on Women's Status reported a large disparity between men's and women's wages. Women's wages were lower, not only on average, but also within the same range of academic qualifications, economic branch, and profession or skill.[76] The question of what was generally similar work under the law was not resolved; because the law included no criminal sanction, it was difficult to enforce. Furthermore, until 1988 when it was superseded, it remained unclear whether equal wages also meant equal fringe benefits.

In 1978, Israel's Commission on the Status of Women made several suggestions for legislation designed to affect women. The major result was the equal employment opportunities law of 1981. This law prohibited employers from refusing to hire anyone because of her or his sex, or marital or parental status, unless the nature of the work precluded the employment of a member of a particular sex. It also prohibited advertisements for jobs or vocational training not addressed to both sexes.[77] What this legislation did not do, however, was to define discrimination and the process by which it was to be proven in court. The burden of initiating complaints remained with the individual despite a recommendation of the 1978 Commission that an administrative authority on sex discrimination be established that could initiate legal proceedings. A public council able to make recommendations to the minister of labor was substituted.[78]

The 1988 equal opportunities in employment law replaced the 1951 women's equal rights law, the 1964 equal pay law, and the 1981 equal employment opportunities law—none of which was especially effective in protecting women's rights in employment.[79] This law prohibits discrimination because of sex, marital status, or parenthood in employment conditions, advancement, or dismissal; it establishes the right of both men and women to take maternity leave and time off to care for a sick child, and it establishes sexual harassment as a criminal offense.[80] While the 1988 legislation sounds quite comprehensive and liberal, it is still too early to judge its effectiveness. But despite several attempts to codify women's rights, the family orientation and male domination of Israeli society effectively hold women back. The legislation reviewed here is itself a product of cultural attitudes that strongly encourage motherhood on the one hand and masculinity on the other.

The problems of working women trying to raise families are made worse by the lack of state support for working mothers. Because some elementary schools close as early as noon and daycare facilities are in limited supply, many women are confined to part-time jobs. In 1987 approximately six thousand children who needed day care in Jerusalem and the surrounding area could not be placed due to lack of facilities.[81] The Likud government which came to power in 1977 cut back on building daycare centers and also decreased child care subsidies. In 1984, women were charged 50 percent more for daycare than in 1983. Currently the basis for determining daycare fees is the woman's income. Daycare would be even more expensive if a proposal to use total family income as the basis for setting fees is adopted.[82] For those women who desire a career, the pressure on the family is intense. One study indicated that 45 percent of women working part-time in fact wanted to work full-time, but that full-time workers were less satisfied with their ability to integrate work and family. This same study found that both full-time and part-time workers ranked "satisfaction with opportunity for advancement" lowest or near lowest out of fifteen job characteristics.[83]

Professional women in Israel have different attitudes toward their careers than their American counterparts.[84] The Israeli career woman generally has a family and is the main caregiver in the household. Her emotional support comes from her husband and parents, not from formal women's groups. As a result of the Israeli preoccupation with security and defense, inequality between men and women is accepted as a fact of life and feminism has never achieved the status that it has in America.[85] Women in Israel are less likely to see themselves as discriminated against than their American counterparts and are less personally ambitious. Ambition goes against the prevalent image of woman as nurturing mother and caretaker and the supporter of men who are struggling for national security.[86] These attitudes damage women's competitive positions in the work force.

WOMEN AND DEFENSE

As the third, fourth, and fifth aliyah arrived in Palestine, the ideal of women's equality receded while friction between men and women grew. During this period, the need for defense increased and the settlement movement became more militaristic.[87] National security rose to a top priority for the state of Israel which saw itself as a nation under siege. The new Israeli man, the defender of the state, was afforded privileged status—legitimizing national, ethnic, and gender inequalities.[88]

In the Israeli military, women were trained for combat but, to keep women from competing against men, few were actually assigned to combat units. Men defended the settlements while most women performed service and support tasks. Women did play a larger role in defense during the early days of Palestine. As local resistance to the Zionist settlers grew into a national movement, military affairs became a major preoccupation. In a sense, Israel was always a war society with all its attendant recruitment pressures.[89]

Because the potential for violence existed side-by-side with the ideology of sexual equality, women were included as part of the pool to be drawn upon by the military. Some were assigned to the *Hashomer*, full-time guards hired to defend the settlements. Yet, this group's ideology was a romanticized version of Bedouin life. Women participated marginally in the organization and only a few were allowed to fight. There was also a women's division in the Haganah. Under the British mandate, Haganah women stood watch and taught mothers how to defend themselves and their children. During the ban on bearing arms, women carried concealed weapons, but when the men went out to attack the enemy the majority of women stayed behind to guard the settlement and the children.

The Palmach, Haganah's elite striking arm, had hundreds of women members. Some engaged in activities such as demolition and freeing detained immigrants. Initially these women were trained alongside the men, where they not only had to prove themselves stronger, but also faced great social pressure.[90] In September 1943, women's role in Palmach was redefined as noncombatant. The impetus for this came from Palmach women who recognized that, given the ideology and practice of gender relations in Palestine, identical formal military roles did not in themselves bring about the equality of women's and men's positions.[91]

During World War II, approximately four thousand Jewish women in Palestine joined the Women's Auxiliary Troops of the British Army where they served primarily in noncombat roles.[92] However, twenty-five Israeli men and three Israeli women participated in a secret mission behind enemy lines in Europe to help British captives and Jewish refugees escape. Two of the women, Hannah Senesh and Haviva Reich, and seven of the men were caught, tortured, and executed.[93] The women's experiences form a crucial part of the myth that subsequently developed of the Israeli woman soldier.

Women also participated in the 1948 War of Independence, being most active during the first six months. A few fought alongside the men, but most served in auxiliary roles such as nursing. Women in combat were regarded with ambivalence.[94] On the one hand, they were under pressure to be as good as the men. On the other, when they showed that they were as good as the men, male soldiers said they worried that the women would be captured and raped by the enemy. Abba Eban's autobiography makes no mention of women's contribution in the 1948 war; neither does David Ben-Gurion's.[95]

The 1948 War of Independence laid the foundation for the current policies of the *Zahal* (Israeli Defense Force, IDF). In 1948, a Women's Support Corps was formed to "absorb women into duties and professions which were suited to the women in the army, in order to reinforce the strength of the nation."[96] Recruits wanted to model the Corps after the Palmach and Haganah and fight alongside men; however, the structure that finally developed was similar to the British Corps, where female forces were separate and auxiliary. Women served in battalions designed to aid brigades of men, but they remained part of an independent women's corps. This structure was imposed over the strong objections of the Haganah and Palmach women who argued that women's achievements in the underground organizations had been ignored. Yet women wanted to defend the new state. At the beginning of the first year, 2,659 enlisted in the corps and by the end of the year the number had risen to 12,000.[97] At the end of the 1948 war, military men, but not military women, became national heroes and leaders of the new state.[98] The male veterans of the War of

Independence were admired and almost deified. They became role models for young Israeli boys. All in all, the war caused a society already dominated by images of powerful male figures to become even more male-oriented. Once again women were put in second place.

The status of women in the military also deteriorated, while male dominance increased. At the first Knesset meeting, David Ben-Gurion spoke on the subject of women in the military, arguing that women should be excluded from combat.

> Women have a special mission as mothers. . . . This is woman's task and her blessing. However . . . a woman is not only a woman but a personality in her own right in the same way as a man. As such, she should enjoy the same rights and responsibilities as the man, except where motherhood is concerned. . . . We have no intention of putting women into combat units, though . . . should we be attacked . . . we [might] call in the service of every man and woman . . . we want to give women only the basic military training.[99]

Ben-Gurion's suggestions were adopted and women were kept out of positions of power in the armed forces. In a society in which the military is privileged, this also kept women from progressing in the work world.

In Israel, women are conscripted along with men. However, after conscription the similarity between men and women ends. Women in the IDF belong to a separate women's division called CHEN. The name itself is the result of a compromise. It was suggested initially that the name of the corps be Auxiliary Women Corps (Che'e'n), but Women Corps (Chen) was finally adopted because its initials in Hebrew meant charm—a feminine characteristic emphasized in the corps—and because of the name's more egalitarian connotation. The service requirement only applies to single women without children, although all men are obligated to serve. It is easier for religious women to be exempted from service than religious men. Under the division of labor in the IDF, women are assigned to service jobs and are prohibited from performing jobs that will place them in combat situations.

Most women serve under male officers. Tours of duty for women are only two years compared to three years for men. Men are required to remain in the reserve until the age of fifty-five, women until they are thirty-four. Because women serve less active duty and reserve time, they are offered less training and, therefore, have fewer job opportunities upon discharge than their male counterparts. Israeli female soldiers are urged to emphasize their femininity. The sense is that women are in the military for the sake of the men, to make them happier and to humanize military service.[100] During basic training, women are given guidance in such skills as cosmetics application. In the words of an IDF spokesman, "CHEN adds to the *Zahal*, the grace and charm which makes it also a medium for humanitarian and social values."[101] Since 1948, women have been forbidden to remain at the front once an emergency has been declared. The women who died during the 1973 war, according to the authorities, did so because they remained at the front despite explicit orders. No women died during the Lebanon War.[102]

The IDF establishment does not encourage women, as strongly as men, to make the military a career. Military life and the constant need to prepare for war cultivates such masculine qualities as bravado and toughness.[103] Like Israeli society as a whole, the IDF caters to the new Jewish male, promoting attitudes that effectively exclude women. Psychologically, they inhibit women from advancing in the male military environment and enable male soldiers to hold positions superior to those of female soldiers. Young Israeli boys spend their childhood preparing to become part of the military. Here in the life and death world of war, they can truly test their manhood. The young girl is more likely to see her role as the supportive girlfriend with early marriage as the result. Since in Israel there is a constant threat of annihilation, the desire for children is a prime motivation for these young couples. In this atmosphere, women define themselves as wives and mothers and occupy traditionally female roles.

The 1990–1991 Persian Gulf War was the first time Israeli men were not drafted during wartime. At home, their image as the invincible soldier protecting the homeland was damaged and many men found themselves uncomfortable with this change. Family stress and violence increased as a result. Clearly the image of the male soldier defending the homeland is deeply ingrained in the male psyche. The Israeli man's sexual and national identity have merged.[104]

CONCLUSIONS

Zionism, based on idealistic socialist principles, promised women sexual equality. Influenced by Russian revolutionaries and socialist ideology, women were called to contribute to the movement to create the state of Israel and they responded enthusiastically. Female pioneers arrived in Palestine hoping to work side-by-side with their male counterparts to build a new Jewish homeland and a new Jewish person. However, they found that while men were anxious to develop a new relationship with the land, this relationship was not extended to women. The pre-state structures and attitudes that developed around the love affair between men and the land doomed the liberation of Jewish women. The retreat from the idea of sexual equality began long before 1948. In the new state, women never had a chance.

In Israel, the gap between reality and the ideology of equality is great. This phenomenon is common to revolutionary societies. At the beginning, it is necessary to create new myths and project an attractive image. But the myths of woman's equality and those of the strong male hero contradict one another, not only because both are ideals and neither conforms to reality, but also because an emphasis on masculinity makes sexual equality impossible to achieve.[105] While Zionist women were expected to work and contribute to the defense of the settlements, it was masculinity, not femininity, that was the preferred characteristic, and women were denied the right to equal participation in the new society.

Despite the secular ideology of the early pioneers, religion has an overwhelming influence on daily life of the Israeli citizen today. More so than men, women are controlled by the Judaic yoke. Rabbinical courts have full control over marriage and divorce, leaving women at the mercy of Orthodox Jewish law. Moreover, the Jewish and Israeli emphasis on family has made motherhood a patriotic act and serves to keep women at home bearing and rearing children.

Despite the dreams and hopes of the Zionist pioneers, sexual equality has not been achieved in Israel. War, and the constant preparations for war, reinforce and perpetuate the pervasiveness of male images in Israeli society. At the same time, insecurity idealizes the notion of home life and justifies imposing traditional roles on women. In 1973, Shulamit Aloni, a former member of the Knesset and women's activist, worried that too many Israeli women were happy to have men relieve them of their responsibilities. She wrote that as long as society saw men as dominant and the sole support of women the situation would not change.[106] Today, few are encouraged or even willing to rock the boat and challenge the status quo. The pioneer women dreamed of a new world in which they could be equal partners. Their revolutionary goals were not achieved.

NOTES

1. In this essay, Palestine will be used to denote the state prior to 1948, and Israel will identify the state post-1948.

2. Deborah Bernstein, *The Struggle for Equality: Urban Workers in Prestate Israeli Society* (New York: Praeger, 1987), 2.

3. Samuel Huntington, "Revolution and Political Order," in *Revolutions, Theoretical, Comparatory and Historical Studies*, ed. Jack A. Goldstone (New York: Harcourt, Brace, Jovanovich, 1986), 39.
4. Ibid., 40.
5. Theda Skoçpol, *States and Social Revolutions* (Cambridge: Cambridge University Press, 1979), 18.
6. Ibid., 29.
7. Ibid., 3.
8. Ruth Rosenthal, *Women in the Middle East* (London: Israel Public Affairs Committee, 1985), 5.
9. Natalie Rein, *Daughters of Rachel: Women in Israel* (New York: Penguin Books, 1980), 32.
10. Ibid.
11. Aliyah is a Hebrew word whose literal meaning is "to go up."
12. Dafna N. Izraeli, "The Zionist Women's Movement in Palestine, 1911–1927: A Sociological Analysis," *Signs* 7 (Autumn 1981): 88.
13. Bernstein, *Struggle for Equality*, 3.
14. Zipporah Seid, in *The Plough Woman: Records of the Pioneer Women of Palestine*, ed. Rachel Katznelson-Rubashow (Westport, Conn.: Hyperion Press, 1932), 50.
15. Rochelle Furstenberg, "A Unique Feminism," *Midstream* 28, no. 8 (1982): 35–39.
16. Selma Ross Brandow, "Illusion of Equality: Kibbutz Women and the Ideology of the 'New Jew,'" *International Journal of Women's Studies* 2 (May/June 1979): 271.
17. The Ashkenazi are those Jews who settled in central and eastern Europe after the diaspora and their descendants.
18. Lesley Hazelton, *Israeli Women: The Reality Behind the Myths* (New York: Simon and Schuster, 1971).
19. Furstenberg, "A Unique Feminism," 36.
20. Walter Lacquer, *A History of Zionism* (New York: Weidenfeld and Nicolson, 1972), 281.
21. Hazelton, *Israeli Women*, 93.
22. Ibid., 92–94.
23. Katznelson-Rubashow, *The Plough Woman*, 137.
24. Brandow, "Illusion of Equality," 272.
25. Hazelton, *Israeli Women*, 17.
26. Bernstein, *Struggle for Equality*, 19.
27. Brandow, "Illusion of Equality," 272.
28. Bernstein, *Struggle for Equality*, 18.
29. Dorit Padan-Eisenstalk, "Image and Reality: Women's Status in Israel," in *Women Cross-Culturally: Change and Challenge*, ed. Ruby Rohrlich-Leavitt (Hague: Moriton Publishers, 1973), 504.
30. Margalit Shilo, "The Women's Farm at Kinneret," in *Pioneers and Homemakers*, ed. Deborah S. Bernstein (Albany: SUNY Press, 1992), 139.
31. Ilea Schuster and Janette Hartz-Karp, "Kinder, Kuechi, Kibbutz: Women's

Aggression and Status Quo Maintenance in a Small Scale Community," *Anthropological Quarterly* 59 (October, 1986): 193–94.

32. Ibid., 196.

33. Ibid., 198.

34. Marie Syrkin, "Does Feminism Clash with Jewish National Need?" *Midstream* 31 (June/July 1985): 8.

35. Ibid., 9.

36. Golda Meir, *A Land of Our Own: An Oral Autobiography*, ed. Marie Syrkin (New York: G. P. Putnam's Sons, 1973), 40.

37. Ada Maimon, *Women Build a Land* (New York: Herzl Press, 1962), 3.

38. Bernstein, *Struggle for Equality*, 20.

39. Lionel Tiger and Joseph Shepher, *Women in the Kibbutz* (New York: Harcourt Brace Jovanovich, 1975), 29.

40. Furstenberg, "A Unique Feminism," 38.

41. Ibid.

42. Tiger and Shepher, *Women in the Kibbutz.*

43. Yonina Talmon, *Family and Community in the Kibbutz* (Cambridge, Mass,: Harvard University Press, 1972).

44. Milford E. Spiro, *Kibbutz: Venture into Utopia* (New York: Schocken Books, 1965).

45. Furstenberg, "A Unique Feminism," 38–39.

46. Brandow, "Illusion of Equality," 283.

47. Strum, "Women, Politics, and Religion," 485.

48. Molly Lyons Bar-David, *Women in Israel* (New York: Hadassah Education Department, 1951), 70.

49. Ta'anith 7a.

50. Ibid., 492–93.

51. Philippa Strum, "Women and the Politics of Religion in Israel," *Human Rights Quarterly* 11 (November 1989): 491.

52. Ibid., 488.

53. Ibid.

54. Ibid.

55. Furstenberg, "A Unique Feminism," 39.

56. Simona Sharoni, "Middle East Politics through Feminist Lenses: Toward Theorizing International Relations from Women's Struggles," unpublished draft manuscript.

57. Immigration to Palestine at this time was minimal.

58. Dov Friedlander, "Israel," in *Population Policies in Developed Countries*, ed. Bernard Berelson (New York: McGraw Hill, 1974), 53–54.

59. Ibid.

60. Hazelton, *Israeli Women*, 74.

61. Ellen Boneparth, "In the Land of the Patriarchs: Public Policy on Women in Israel," in *Women in the World: 1975–1985, the Women's Decade*, 2nd ed., ed. Lynne B. Iglitzin and Ruth Ross (Santa Barbara, Calif.: ABC-Clio Press, 1986), 134.

62. Hazelton, *Israeli Women*, 81.

63. Ibid.
64. Ibid.
65. Judith Neulander Elizur, "Women in Israel," *Judaism: A Quarterly Journal* 22 (Spring 1983), 245.
66. Hazelton, *Israeli Women*, 82.
67. Ibid.
68. Moshe Hartman, "Pronatalist Tendencies and Religiosity in Israel," *Sociology and Social Research* 68, no. 2 (January 1984): 248.
69. Friedlander, "Israel."
70. Oriani Fallaci, "Golda," *Ms.* 1 (April 1972): 100.
71. Hazelton, *Israeli Women*, 22.
72. Frances Raday, "Equality of Women Under Israeli Law," *The Jerusalem Quarterly* 27 (Spring 1983): 82.
73. Pnina Lahav, "Raising the Status of Women through Law: The Case of Israel," *Signs* 3 (Autumn 1977): 195.
74. Hazelton, *Israeli Women*, 23.
75. Naava Eisin, *The Working Woman in Israel* (Tel Aviv: Israel Press, 1975), 80.
76. Raday, "Equality of Women," 97.
77. Israel Information Center, *Women in Israel* (Jerusalem: Hamokor Press, 1988), 15.
78. Raday, "Equality of Women," 105.
79. Strum, "Women and the Politics of Religion," 498.
80. Israel Information Center, *Women in Israel*, 15.
81. Ibid., 499.
82. Boneparth, "In the Land of the Patriarchs," 143.
83. Dafna N. Izraeli, "Women and Work: From Collective to Career," in *Calling the Equality Bluff*, ed. Barbara Swirski and Marilyn P. Safir (New York: Pergamon Press, 1991), 175.
84. Alia Lieblich, "Preliminary Comparison of Israeli and American Successful Career Women at Mid-life," *Israel Social Science Research* 5, no. 1–2 (1987): 164–77.
85. For an in-depth discussion of the feminist movement in Israel, see Rein, *Daughters of Rachel*.
86. Lieblich, "Israeli and American Career Women," 174.
87. Ibid., 273.
88. Simona Sharoni, "To Be a Man in the Jewish State: The Sociopolitical Context of Violence and Oppression," *Challenge* 2, no. 5 (Sept./Oct. 1991): 27.
89. Nira Yuval-Davis, "Front and Rear: The Sexual Division of Labor in the Israeli Army," *Feminist Studies* 11, no. 3 (Fall 1985): 654.
90. Yuval-Davis, "Front and Rear," 656.
91. Ibid.
92. Maimon, *Women Build a Land*, 220.
93. Yuval-Davis, "Front and Rear," 658.
94. Ibid.
95. Abba Eban, *My Country: The Story of Modern Israel* (New York: Random

House, 1972), 47–65; David Ben-Gurion, *Israel: Years of Challenge* (New York: Holt, Rinehart, Winston, 1963), 29–45; and David Ben-Gurion, *Israel: A Personal History* (New York: Funk and Wagnalls, 1971), 94–128.

96. Jeff Hirshowitz, "The Women's Corps in the War of Independence," *IDF Journal* 21 (special reprint): 11.

97. Ibid., 12.

98. Rein, *Daughters of Rachel*, 48.

99. David Ben-Gurion, *Israel: A Personal History* (New York: Funk and Wagnalls, 1971), 94–128.

100. Yuval-Davis, "Front and Rear," 663.

101. Ibid., 663.

102. Ibid., 665.

103. Nikki Stiller, "Peace Without Honor: The Battle of the Sexes in Israel," *Midstream* 22 (May 1976): 40.

104. Sharoni, "To Be a Man," 26.

105. Ruth Beizer-Boher, "Images of Women in Israeli Literature: Myth and Reality," *Judaism: A Quarterly Journal* 68, no. 2 (January 1984): 258.

106. Shulamit Aloni, "The Status of Women in Israel," *Judaism: A Quarterly Journal* 22 (Spring 1973): 255.

Chapter 13

Whose Honor? Whose Liberation?

Women and the Reconstruction of Politics in Kuwait

Mary Ann Tétreault

The August 1990 Iraqi invasion and occupation of Kuwait ended seven months later following a war of national liberation involving a multinational force operating under the aegis of the United Nations. While the invasion, occupation, and liberation did not constitute a revolution in the strict sense, they formed a critical chapter in the struggle of the Kuwaiti people to achieve political democracy. Ironically, the success of Kuwaiti opponents of the regime in mobilizing popular support for their pro-democracy movement in 1989–1990 may have lulled Saddam Hussein into thinking that the Iraqi occupation would be welcomed rather than resisted.[1] Instead, the occupation triggered a unity among Kuwaitis that had never been achieved before, and also provided a perverse but effective lesson in democracy. The return of constitutional government to Kuwait in 1992 after more than six years of authoritarian rule was a tribute to the persistence of pro-democracy forces. But the longevity of the restoration is no more guaranteed today than it was when Kuwait's constitution was written in 1962. The ruler of Kuwait twice suspended its civil liberties guarantees and dismissed the parliament it provides for—measures of the tenuous hold of democratic principles and the power of authoritarian practices to reassert themselves. The long-run persistence

---

Research for this chapter was supported by a Fulbright fellowship and grants from the U.S. Institute of Peace and Old Dominion University. None has any responsibility for the content or the analysis.

of democratic forms in Kuwait depends on a fundamental alteration in Kuwaiti principles and practices sufficient to resist authoritarian pressures. In this chapter, I argue that the most promising strategy toward achieving that goal depends upon extending political rights to women.

WOMEN, RELIGION, AND THE STATE IN KUWAIT

Women's rights in Kuwait have a religious as well as a political character because of the role of Islam. Even though Kuwait is technically not an Islamic state,[2] Islam enjoys a preferred status. The pre-invasion population of Kuwait was more than 90 percent Muslim according to government statistics, and the non-Muslim population was nearly all foreign. Thus, Islam is the religion of virtually all Kuwaitis. It is a primary element in Kuwaiti identity, and the state gives it institutional and social support.

Mehdi Mozaffari argues that Islam embodies a theory of authority and a set of practices which include the form of the modern Kuwaiti state, making Kuwait, in this broad sense, an Islamic state.[3] The Islamic quality of Kuwaiti society is not monolithic because, like the other two monotheistic religions originating in the Middle East, its sacred writings convey multiple messages whose interpretations are flexible.[4] Islamism in Kuwait also differs by sect and by the relative fundamentalism of subgroups within each. Kuwait's two Sunni Islamist political groups tend to be more doctrinaire than the Shiʿi political group, reflecting the majority status of the Sunna and the need of the Shiʿa to seek political allies among groups whose philosophies are predominantly secular.

However, the lack of legitimacy characteristic of most modern Arab states encourages an alliance between religious leaders, whom I shall call "the mosque," and the secular—in this case Sunni—leaders of the state. According to Sunni practice as outlined by Ghazali,[5] the mosque in such a state acts like a bridge to link the seat of legitimate power, Islam, and the seat of virtual power, the regime. The two-way traffic over that bridge is legitimate authority: the mosque conveys the authority of Islam to the regime and the authority of the regime to Islam. The regime's political legitimacy is bolstered by Islam, and the state in turn uses its authority to enforce religious practices as defined by the mosque. Article 2 of the Kuwaiti constitution says "the religion of the state is Islam, and the Islamic Shariʿa shall be a main source of legislation." Even non-Muslims are required to observe some Islamic laws, at least in public. For example, all persons entering Kuwait are asked to surrender anything in their luggage containing pork or alcohol, and no one is permitted to eat or drink in public during daylight hours in Ramadan.

Women bear a special burden not imposed on other Kuwaiti citizens because of the role of the mosque in defining women's status. Although the *Qur'an* says that men and women are equal under God,[6] the subjection of women to men on earth is even more authoritatively laid down if length and detail are taken as criteria.[7] Quranic ambiguity on the subject of women gives Islamic sanction to the arguments of feminists as well as masculinists. The Kuwaiti constitution is also ambiguous. Article 29 states that "All people are equal in human dignity, and in public rights and duties before the law," but the constitution also proclaims the family to be "the corner-stone of society . . . founded on religion, morality and patriotism. Law shall preserve the integrity of the family, strengthen its ties and protect under its auspices motherhood and childhood" (Article 9). The family as an institution is defined by cultural tradition, the mosque, and the state. Islam, as an element of each, is understood to be the primary source of legal and social norms governing the regulation of family life in Kuwait. This puts the family and relationships among the persons in the family squarely in the middle of the bridge between Islam and the state in Kuwait.

The constitutional nomination of the family rather than the individual as the basic unit of Kuwaiti society gives legal sanction to a patriarchal order that defines women as inferior, consigns them to the home, and gives male relatives authority over them.[8] Hisham Sharabi says that these values are the foundation of the modern Arab authoritarian state, calling the nested pattern of hierarchy and submission that he identifies "neopatriarchy."[9] Neopatriarchal families are traditional throughout the Arab world. It is important to note that Sharabi sites their historical antecedents in the ethics of desert tribalism, not Islam.

This family form is highly privatized. As a result, the neopatriarchal state is constrained in its ability to intervene in the family and the home is considered a protected space.[10] The state finds support in a privatized family as long as it embodies and reproduces submission to authority as the essence of its social formation. But a privatized family can be a source of danger to the state because families can also deviate from this pattern and produce citizens whose core values are antithetical to neopatriarchy.[11] A second source of danger from a privatized family protected from state penetration is that it allows the home to become a structure within which opposition to the state can organize. In Kuwait, the home is the site of the *diwaniyya*, a meeting of family members and friends that constitutes the only secular protected political space in Kuwaiti society.[12] As a result, there is a community of interest between the authoritarian state and the authoritarian mosque with regard to the control of families, their values, and their behavior.

Kuwaiti social practice regarding marriage and the family reflects Islamic values as well as historical patterns, and varies by individual, sect, and social class.[13] Marriage is commonly arranged by families though a woman can refuse a man chosen by her father or uncles. There is still a preference to marry one's daughter to a relative. If a couple decides together to marry it is socially necessary to get permission from the woman's male relatives. Men customarily pay a bride price (*mahr*) which is specified in the marriage contract. This bride price is divided into a pre-payment which is made to the family of the bride before marriage (in Kuwait, most of it is spent on gold jewelry for the bride) and a post-payment which goes to the wife in the event of divorce. Divorce is available to a wife on carefully circumscribed grounds and to a husband on demand, though family exigencies can, in practice, also constrain the exercise of the man's right. Abortion is illegal in Kuwait although contraception is not. Under the Shiᶜi interpretation of Islam, children belong to their father. The custody of young children following divorce is usually awarded to the mother, but when the children reach the age of nine years they go to their father if he or his family wants them. Sunnis are governed by the 1984 family law which awards custody to the wife or her mother in most cases. Kuwaiti attorney Badria al-Awadhi notes that, within the limits of the family law, Kuwaiti judges favor the child's interests over those of either parent, a practice more consistent with Quranic Islam than either the Shiᶜi or the Malaki (Sunni) interpretation.[14] Yet although Kuwaiti women enjoy the respect of society and the companionship and support of other women, chiefly relatives, their ambitions and behaviors are severely constrained by the demands of family honor.

WOMEN AND FAMILY HONOR

The discrimination against women most frequently mentioned as onerous by Kuwaiti as well as foreign women is the provision under Islamic law that men may have up to four wives simultaneously while a woman may have only one husband at a time.[15] However, another aspect of customary behavior seems much more oppressive to me, especially after the invasion and occupation which subjected an unknown number of Kuwaiti women to sexual assault. The chastity of women in Kuwait, as in other Mediterranean societies, embodies the honor of their families.[16] A woman who is not a virgin at first marriage, or a wife suspected to have had sexual relations with someone other than her husband, brings shame and opprobrium upon her male relatives as long as she lives.

The fetish for virginity and chastity is internalized by women as well as enforced by men. Dr. Marwan al-Mutawa, a Kuwaiti psychologist, sees many sexually dysfunctional patients, some of them war victims.

> Our suffering here, as specialists, is because rape is a social and ethical stigma for the one and for their families. Many families keep their victims locked in the house. Married victims are being divorced. Most rape victims are being treated by traditional methods, reading the Qurʾan, or taking them to special religious people who say verses of Qurʾan over them and give the [holy] water to them. . . . Many cases with reactive anxiety are developing severe psychotic depression—even schizophrenia. . . . Virginity is a very precious concept to a Kuwaiti.[17]

An unchaste woman may be killed by a male relative although the preferred method for dealing with this problem is suicide. Dr. Buthaina al-Muqahawe, a Kuwaiti psychiatrist who has war victims among her patients, sees mostly children with psychological problems resulting from the Iraqi occupation. But three of her patients were rape victims. One was a member of the Resistance who had been raped repeatedly after her capture. She was suicidal and disappeared shortly after seeing the doctor.[18] Dr. Marwan reports a number of suicides among his patients who were rape victims. The daughter of a friend was given a knife to kill herself by her father. However, other cases illustrate the limits of social pressures to internalize misogynist values. For example, another of Dr. Buthaina's patients, a teenaged rape victim, was not only accepted by her family but also received a proposal of marriage, a sign of acceptance by the young man and his family.

THE STATUS OF WOMEN IN PRE-INVASION KUWAIT

Kuwait's first revolution was a state-mediated revolution from above intended to channel the force of modernization to support the traditional regime while weakening traditional elites and their legitimacy to challenge it. Financed by the oil revenues that began pouring into the country in the late 1940s, this revolution altered Kuwait's social structure in unforeseen as well as intended ways. The development that oil money made possible enabled Kuwait's rulers to modernize the economy within a political and social climate discouraging challenges to their authority. Their strategies included reducing the political autonomy of the merchant class and creating a new middle class dependent upon the regime's welfare state for their prosperity and status. The disappearance of traditional industries, pearling and long-distance trading, weakened old class divisions,[19] though other factors maintained and elaborated divisions among Kuwaitis.

In return for their political subordination, the regime supported the merchant elite as a favored economic class, directing substantial financial resources to its members through the Land Acquisition Policy and investment laws requiring foreign firms doing business in Kuwait to have nominal if not actual Kuwaiti partners.[20] At the same time, the decision of the ruler to confer citizenship on large numbers of Bedouin tribesmen accentuated long-standing antagonisms between the *arab dar*, a major component of which were tribesmen, and the *arab hadaar*, the settled community of the city.[21] Another important social division, between the majority Sunni and minority Shiʿi Muslims, was also aggravated by government policy, though the upsurge in sectarianism in Kuwait in the 1980s owed as much to the domestic repercussions of the Iran-Iraq War as to direct government interference.[22] The division between Kuwaitis and non-Kuwaitis, who respectively made up 27 and 73 percent of the population in 1990,[23] grew along with the middle class that depended on the government for its sustenance.[24]

These divisions were reflected in different perceptions of women's roles and the different realities in which women lived. The daughters of the cosmopolitan upper class were the first Kuwaiti women to be educated abroad, mostly in Egypt.[25] They were prominent in the first Kuwaiti women's organization, the Women's Cultural and Social Society (the Society), and today lead the movement to extend full political rights to Kuwaiti women. Other *hadaar* women also enjoyed some independence, but not because they were rich. These were the wives of sailors and pearl divers who, like other navy wives, took over the day-to-day responsibilities of the household when their husbands were out to sea.[26] For the most part, however, the authority of Kuwaiti women born before the oil era was informal and confined to the advancement of their children's interests.[27] It was often opposed by the countervailing and socially sanctioned authority of husbands, fathers, uncles, sons, and brothers.

Limits on the autonomy of nonelite Kuwaiti women diminished as female education became widespread and women began to be employed outside the home. *Hadaar* women were the first to enjoy the benefits of education and outside employment, though far fewer women than men joined the work force. Most *hadaar* women also stopped wearing veils. Bedouin women were physically and socially more isolated than *hadaar* women and educational opportunities came later for them. This accounts for part of the disparity between male and female literacy rates that persisted until the eve of the invasion.[28] The social separation of men and women today is more rigorously observed in Bedouin areas, and Bedouin men are thought to be more likely to have multiple wives than the men of the town.[29] Before the Islamist resurgence that brought the veil back to many young urban women, it would have been safe to assume that most of the veiled women one saw in Kuwait were Bedu.[30]

Differences in the rights and status of women and men in Kuwait are attributed to traditional values which include but are not limited to Islam. Even though education and labor laws guarantee formal gender equality, social practices discriminate against women. Families limit the education of daughters and supervisors deny women jobs that they regard as "unwomanly" even if candidates are qualified.[31] Such problems are not taken to the courts to resolve, although Kuwaiti attorney Hashem al-Saleh has offered to defend women denied their legal rights free of charge.[32] Social pressure also discourages men who desire to challenge formally illegal yet socially accepted practices.[33] But even though female oppression is largely rooted in social practice rather than formal law, legal gender discrimination is a problem as well.

The denial of political rights to Kuwaiti women is a matter of law. The election law, originally written in 1959, has been amended several times but never to include women. A proposal to give women the right to vote was made to the 1981 Majlis al-Umma (parliament) which was dominated by Islamists who constitute the most prominent opponents to women's political rights in Kuwait.[34] The measure was defeated. Even the unconstitutional Majlis al-Watanee (consultative assembly), created in 1990 as a sop to the large numbers of Kuwaitis who had demonstrated for nearly a year for the return of constitutional government—a sop that many rejected—refused to pass a proposal giving women the vote and even refused to recommend that some other institution make this change.[35]

After liberation, the amir made his support of voting rights for women public, leading to speculation that he might change the law to allow women to vote in 1992. As I shall discuss, Kuwaiti Islamists were split on the subject. The occupation experience of those who remained inside Kuwait as well as those who stayed outside added numbers as well as arguments to the feminist side. Yet nearly all Kuwaitis, women as well as men and secularists as well as Islamists, opposed unilateral action by the amir. They ran on platforms or voted for candidates supporting women's political rights, but expected these issues to be dealt with by the Majlis al-Umma rather than by extra-constitutional means. Institutional attempts to give Kuwaiti women political rights have thus come full circle.

EXCEPTIONAL CASES OF DISCRIMINATION AGAINST WOMEN

Other instances of discrimination against Kuwaiti women are confined primarily to cases where they are married to foreigners, yet these laws open a window from which we can view the effects of social practices on all women in Kuwait. Under Kuwaiti law, a wife and children are automatically the same nationality as the husband/father. This results in the loss of citizenship rights both to Kuwaiti women married to non-Kuwaiti men and to their children, and thus the denial of economic benefits that other Kuwaitis, including the children and the non-Kuwaiti wives of Kuwaiti men, enjoy.[36] The far-reaching implications of this social structure and the legal lacunae that allow it to dominate women's lives are evident in the widely publicized abuse of maids in Kuwait.

The relative openness of Kuwaiti society has made an international human rights issue of the mistreatment of household servants in Kuwait.[37] An unknown number of maids, virtually all from south and east Asia, reporting that they suffer physical mistreatment and drastic overwork, have sought refuge in their home countries' embassies.[38] Others register formal complaints at a special police station set aside for this purpose in the Dasma area of the city.[39] A March 1992 visit by U.S. Congresswoman Patricia Schroeder (D-CO) to Kuwait to investigate allegations of human rights abuses of maids produced a number of explanations for the problem from middle-class Kuwaitis, who tended to blame it on Bedouin families with primitive ethics and lifestyles.[40] But Khouloud al-Feeli, a volunteer at the Kuwait Human Rights Center, denies this. "It is not just bedu. Some educated people too are frustrated and take it out on their maids. In bedu areas they would take better care because of their honor."[41] Another human rights activist, Iman al-Bedah, points to culture and class as the problem. "First, it is because they are women, and women are mistreated generally in Kuwait. . . . Second, because they are maids. They are lower-class and people exercise their power over them."[42] A third activist, Ghanim al-Najjar, has another explanation. "The maids issue is mostly a problem of laws. They are not protected under Kuwaiti law. They have no legal contracts. Neither party is protected."[43]

No doubt all three reasons apply, not only to the particular problems of the maids but, by analogy, to the general problem of women in Kuwait. Part of the problem is individual. Some individuals are morally deficient and/or mentally unbalanced and treat people over whom they have power and authority as objects rather than as fellow persons. It is also true that being female and being inferior evoke mistreatment as an epiphenomenon of normality: it is nothing personal—just your lot in life. Finally there is the matter of legal protection. If women live in male custody they are not autonomous persons. Thus, only men need legal protection and they protect their women. In this formulation, women on their own do not constitute a permissible category for analysis: no respectable woman exists on her own. Even though other guest workers have laws that protect their interests to some degree, household workers, nearly all of whom are women, do not. And even though Kuwaiti citizens have many civil and economic rights, including the right to pass their nationality on to their children, Kuwaiti women do not have these rights if they marry non-Kuwaitis—their rights to equal protection under the law cease by virtue of their marriage to a foreigner. As under the Western legal doctrine of coverture, Kuwaiti women are subsumed under the legal personalities of their spouses.[44] There is no clearer denial of the personhood of women than this.

RESISTANCE AND LIBERATION

Stories about the Iraqi occupation feature brave Kuwaitis who risked their lives to care for others; passed information, food, money, and weapons on to those who needed them; and defied occupation forces head-on in demonstrations and armed attacks. Many of these brave Kuwaitis were women. Outside, other Kuwaitis spent the occupation at press conferences, on television and radio, and speaking before hostile and even abusive audiences who did not see any reason why they should be asked to liberate Kuwait. Many of these Kuwaitis were women. The efforts of all these Kuwaiti women and men were instrumental in the eventual liberation of their country. When it was over, women and men actively involved in liberation activities expected that the women's equal part in the resistance would translate into political equality.

I could have written the preceding paragraph using class or sect and it would have been just as true. The occupation reorganized the perceptions of Kuwaitis, especially those who remained inside Kuwait, with regard to the identification of their "tribe."

> The bad thing before the invasion, there was no equality among the Kuwaiti people regarding their loyalty to the country. They are not equal in front of the law. It is a small society and there must be equality among all Kuwaitis here. All mankind. We did not have this before the invasion. But during the invasion we experienced equality and the true spirit of the liberation. . . . When Saddam Hussain came he treated us equally. He did not kill Shi^ca or Sunna: he killed Kuwaitis. He did not kill workers or merchants: he killed Kuwaitis. He did not kill men or women: he killed Kuwaitis.[45]

LIBERATION AND WOMEN'S RIGHTS

The fact that the authoritarian ruling family of Kuwait is the most prominent public institution calling for political rights for women is a signal that what is meant by political rights for women and what these rights imply in the society as a whole should be examined very carefully. The first issue, what do these rights mean, was discussed at some length during the fall 1992 campaign season. The second, what they imply, is not discussed perhaps because, as in other contemporary societies, the connection between family relationships in a society composed of privatized families and political relationships in the public space is invisible. In Kuwait as in other Arab countries, it may also be that the notion of the home as a private space is so pervasive that it is off-limits to discuss it—or that the home as a space under the control of men, the only legally political animals in Kuwait, is off-limits as a space subject to political revision.

Political rights for women in Kuwait are conventionally broken down into three areas. First is the right to vote which, by itself, does not imply a change in the social structure. Like the right to go to school or the right to work outside the home, it can be constrained by customary social practices and informal regulations of female behavior. Before the invasion, Islamists opposed votes for women on precisely these grounds: "they pointed out that under the Sharia law . . . women are weak and incapable of assuming an independent political stand. Hence, if they were enfranchised, they would be liable to manipulation by their husbands."[46] Now secular Kuwaitis are more likely to use this argument, saying that giving voting rights to women would favor conservative candidates because traditionalists have more wives and control them more effectively than liberals do their wives.[47]

The other two areas involve deeper questions of power in Kuwaiti society. One is the right of women to run for office and the other is the right of women to be appointed to ministerial and judicial positions with authority over religious institutions. Khaled Sultan ran for parliament from the third district. He is a Salafi, a member of what is regarded as the more fundamentalist of the two Sunni Islamist political groups fielding candidates in 1992. He discussed his position on women's political rights in an interview at his home in Shuwaikh on 30 September 1992.

> Let's not confuse the rights of women with the right to vote. The rights of women under Islam supersede the rights of women anyplace else. You are specifically referring to the right to vote. The right to vote gives women the right to nominate themselves for parliament. From our religious point of view we cannot allow women to hold political positions. If that right of nomination is separated from the right of voting, and that right to vote would not create—would not have moral consequences on the behavior and the running of the campaign, then we would not object to giving women the right to vote. Women can't come to rallies. . . . If it comes to attending these rallies, then we cannot give women the right to vote.

This position neatly separates the right to vote from the right to participate as an autonomous actor in the political process, either to enter the public space and contend with others for one's own ideas or to achieve a position of leadership and exercise authority over others. According to Khaled Sultan, the entry of women into the public space has moral consequences that are undesirable, justifying their seclusion in the private spaces of their homes—where Islam gives them rights superior to women anyplace else.

What are these moral consequences? First, that women could nominate themselves for political office. If they were to get these offices, they would have authority over men. For members of the relatively liberal Shiʿi political group, the Islamic National Alliance, political authority for women is not a problem but religious authority is.

> In Islam we [hold] that woman is not allowed to be a judge or a ruler so she cannot be a person to be followed as a spiritual leader. She can take part in the election, can participate as a candidate.

> The parliament is a way of organizing the system. The system is to organize the country. Other religious groups look at politics as equivalent to being a spiritual leader. We do not.[48]

Shi^ci liberality in this regard is dictated in part by the minority status of the Shi^ca and it is also a function of Shi^ci practice elsewhere, such as in Iran. A second set of moral consequences revolves around women leaving their homes to attend political rallies. Female occupation of the public space is part of this issue but perhaps more important is the prospect of women's autonomous passage through the boundary separating that public space from the home. The ability to control women is predicated on their incarceration in supervised spaces where they can be observed and restrained. A woman who leaves her home for politics, an arena populated by men who are neither her husband nor relatives forbidden to have sexual relations with her, is a woman who threatens the honor of her family—unless family honor were to be differently defined.

The framing of the issue of political rights for women in this context reflects both the Islamic quality of Kuwaiti society and the regime's alliance with selected Islamist groups to check the secular opposition.[49] Thus, regime and mosque join forces to construct women's rights in a form that satisfies both and has the added attraction of impeaching the cultural legitimacy of the secular opposition. Such a compromise between state and mosque in itself supports the continued framing of political discourse in Kuwait within an ideology enjoining submission to authority as analogous to obedience to God. In this environment, it is not surprising that the movement for women's political rights has been successfully thwarted for so long.

The utility of the woman question in Kuwait to political forces with other agendas to pursue, is made infinitely more complicated to assess by the prominence of Islamists in the Resistance and by the coalition between some Islamists and bedouin tribalists. Islamists are among the most venerated heroes of the occupation. Their personal bravery and their control and utilization of the mosque, the only civil space within which opposition to the Iraqis could be mobilized and coordinated with some security, enhanced their political status enormously following liberation.[50] The 1992 election reflected this, particularly in the districts outside Kuwait City where independent tribal candidates ran on platforms indistinguishable from those of the formal Islamists. Most of the winners from this group were "Friday preachers,"[51] new men whose agendas were more ideological than those of old style tribalist service candidates.[52]

Following the 1992 election, a wave of concern swept across secular Kuwaiti activists at the prospect of a tribalist-Islamist alliance in the parliament that could support an even more fundamentalist application of Islamic principles to Kuwaiti life.[53] But the tribalists have political problems outside their districts and even the image of the Islamists is tarnished in some quarters. Many Kuwaitis remember the behavior of the Bedouins during the crisis as having been cowardly, though members of tribes in the Jahra area were among those most violently brutalized by the occupying forces. However, Kuwaiti Bedouins further south left the country in large numbers before the Iraqis reached their areas. The brunt of the occupation and resistance was borne by *hadaar* Kuwaitis who refused to leave or to leave permanently as long as the Iraqis remained in control of Kuwait. Some Kuwaiti Islamists also came out of the crisis with their reputations soiled, in this case by the actions of fellow Islamists in other countries. The Muslim Brotherhood movement supported the Iraqi invasion, abandoning Kuwaiti members of the Ikhwan spiritually as well as politically. The Kuwaiti Ikhwan disassociated themselves from the international movement, but their group is viewed more skeptically now by their fellow citizens than it was before. Deficiencies in their Resistance credentials put both groups in an inferior position with respect to women, whose performance during the crisis is repeatedly cited as the main justification for the extension of political rights to them.[54]

The nature and character of the Resistance is a critical subject of political manipulation by the regime, and the symbolic devaluation by Kuwait's rulers of the Kuwaitis who stayed at home during the occupation is an ongoing project. Contemporary interpretations of the occupation were dominated by Kuwaitis who, like most of the government, were outside Kuwait. They engaged in propaganda designed to mobilize the coalition forces to liberate Kuwait in part by creating an image of occupied Kuwait that would appeal to foreigners. This portrayal also served the regime's interests after liberation. Kuwaitis who remained dispute the picture of occupied Kuwait that was broadcast by Kuwaitis in exile, especially its dismissal of the Resistance as ineffective, its obsession with rape, and its manufacture of atrocities that made light of the actual atrocities experienced by Kuwaitis.[55]

Reinterpreting the occupation has preoccupied many in authority since liberation. The practical accomplishments of the Resistance were ignored. For example, the government let Kuwaitis go without food and other necessary items rather than utilize the distribution system created during the occupation by the Resistance. The symbolic denigration of those who remained is visible on Kuwait TV where some of the fillers between programs show melodramatic vignettes that invariably portray the Kuwaitis who stayed behind as powerless before the Iraqis. Conflicting estimates of how many Kuwaiti women were actually raped during the occupation is another aspect of post-liberation politics in Kuwait. To nullify Resistance heroism, rumors were spread shortly after liberation implying that every family that had remained in Kuwait during the occupation harbored sexually violated women and therefore was without honor.

The antagonism between those who stayed and those who were outside during the occupation is linked to the resentment by Bedouin men of the movement favoring women's rights. It is demonstrated in the results of student surveys done by political scientist Ma^csuma al-Mubarak at Kuwait University.

> The enthusiasm after liberation is faded now. For a number of years I have been doing a survey of my classes about their attitudes toward political rights for women. In the last four semesters, the first was very strongly in favor, the second less. The third was opposed. They said women did nothing during the occupation. In the fourth semester fewer supported rights for women than had supported them in the second. They said it is still not time. [Was there anything different about the students in the third semester?] They were mostly bedouin in that class and the bedouin were the first to run away.[56]

Both antagonism and distance erode a belief in equal entitlement among contending groups of Kuwaitis, contributing to post-liberation insecurity because Kuwaitis from different groups have begun to hate one another as they did before the invasion.

Yet for some Kuwaiti women, the memories are still vivid and recent enough to inspire a fighting spirit, even among those who were outside during the occupation. Lubna Saif ᶜAbbas ᶜAbdulla was a student at American University who worked as a volunteer with Citizens for a Free Kuwait during much of the occupation. Toward the end, when the Kuwaiti government decided that it would be politically useful to include a handful of women among the Kuwaiti forces participating in the liberation, Lubna was one of nine Kuwaiti female volunteers who successfully made it through basic training at Fort Dix and were then inducted into the army. She worked on war crimes documentation after liberation.

> I get very very angry. You can see how so many people suffered, were executed, and others in this country just don't give a damn. That's why I am so vocal. I never was before but now I feel that if I don't express my views I am just as bad as people who are ambivalent. There are guys who wimped out, who didn't pass the test, yet look how I'm treated as a woman in this society. I don't care if people love me. I want them to treat me equally. I carried an M-16.[57]

CONCLUSIONS

The prospects for democratization in Kuwait are hopeful because Kuwait has a tradition of political participation that has not been successfully erased despite nearly a century of authoritarian rule.[58] The mosque is divided along sectarian lines but the Shiᶜi minority is so large that it cannot be marginalized without threatening the structure of the whole society. This provides opportunities for coalitions between secularists and Islamists that promise stability and a kind of normal politics unusual where Islamist contenders are prominent members of political oppositions. Finally, Kuwaitis' notions of democracy as part of their birthright have been strengthened by what they endured and survived during the horrible experiences of invasion and occupation. Even though there are many who would manipulate the differences between those who lived through this period inside Kuwait and those who lived through it somewhere else, the occupation and its perversely democratic character is a source of unity among all Kuwaitis.

The occupation and the liberation also opened the country and its regime to external observation, and to pressure from the citizens and governments of the members of the coalition that liberated Kuwait. Although the impact of these foreigners is not unidimensional—Saudi Arabia for one is no fan of democratization in Kuwait—the visibility of Kuwaiti domestic politics to interested parties in the international community, coupled to Kuwait's need for continued external security guarantees, creates a climate within which progress toward democratization can be expected—though not expected to be easy.

An important aspect of democratization anywhere is the extension of political rights to women. This is particularly problematic in Arab Islamic countries where colonialism and neocolonialism created and supported authoritarian regimes and dismantled traditional popular checks on political authority. These marginally legitimate regimes exist in a symbiotic relationship with the mosque. Each relies on the other through the medium of Islamic discourse to provide an ideological justification for the authoritarian state which is the mirror image of the authoritarian mosque. Islamic principles can be construed to limit political rights for women just as they can be construed to limit legitimate criticism of the rulers of Islamic states. Consequently, the question of political rights for women in an Islamic state is much more fundamental in its reach and probable impact than the question of political rights for any group of men. Political democratization in Kuwait is thus inextricably linked to the extension of civil rights to women. Without a reordering of the basic social principles that justify state repression and make the notion of a loyal opposition an oxymoron, Kuwait will remain trapped in Arab neopatriarchy. A new notion of honor, based upon trust and legally supported norms of individual responsibility for everyone, is also required for a pluralist society that sustains differences under law.

It is common to throw up one's hands at the prospect of changing a culture and its social practices. Yet the proposition that it is impossible to legislate morality is simply not true. From Hamurabi's code to the drafting of modern constitutions, morality is as it always has been—encoded in laws and made real by their enforcement. Customary social practices do not have lives of their own. They persist because legal systems protect and enforce them. Whether democratization in Kuwait proceeds by granting full political rights to women or by women violating social practices and laws to seize their rights themselves, it will erode the structures and ideologies that support authoritarianism today. If democratization stops where it is, granting formal access to the public space only to men, democracy in Kuwait will remain endangered under a constitution whose ethical principles are not only disdained by authoritarian rulers but are also at odds with the way most Kuwaitis live their lives.

NOTES

1. Mary Ann Tétreault, "Kuwait's Democratic Reform Movement," *Middle East Executive Reports* (October 1990).

2. Arab states are classified in Iliya Harik, "The Origins of the Arab State System," in *The Arab State*, ed. Giacomo Luciani (Berkeley: University of California Press, 1990). Harik calls Kuwait a "traditional secular system [where] authority is vested in a dynasty free from religious attributes" (6).

3. Mehdi Mozaffari, *Authority in Islam*, trans. Michel Vale (London: M. E. Sharpe, 1987), esp. introduction and chap. 2.

4. Fatima Mernissi argues this point in *The Veil and the Male Elite: A Feminist Interpretation of Women's Rights in Islam*, trans. Mary Jo Lakeland (Reading,

Mass.: Addison-Wesley, 1991).

5. Al-Ghazali, cited in ibid., 45.

6. *Qur'an*, Sura 33, verse 35. Sunna make up the majority of Muslims in Kuwait.

7. The position of women under Islam is the subject of a large and growing literature in which the responsibility for female subjection is a major component. See, for example, Mernissi, *The Veil and the Male Elite*, and other works cited below.

8. Fatima Mernissi, *Beyond the Veil: Male-Female Dynamics in Modern Muslim Society*, rev. ed. (Bloomington: Indiana University Press, 1987), chap. 2.

9. Hisham Sharabi, *Neopatriarchy: A Theory of Distorted Change in Arab Society* (New York: Oxford University Press, 1988).

10. Mary Ann Tétreault, "Civil Society in Kuwait: Protected Spaces and Women's Rights," *The Middle East Journal* 47 (Spring 1993): 277.

11. Susan Moller Okin, *Justice, Gender, and the Family* (New York: Basic Books, 1989), makes a similar argument regarding the connection between family practices and social values which is better articulated and more highly nuanced than Sharabi's. Okin's argument is developed further to link religion to definitions of justice in the family by Martha Nussbaum, "Justice for Women!" *The New York Review*, 8 October 1992.

12. Tétreault, "Civil Society in Kuwait," 278–80.

13. Information on Kuwaiti marriage practices came from extensive interviews in Kuwait, especially those conducted in September and October 1992.

14. Interview with Badria al-Awadhi, 28 March 1994, in Kuwait.

15. My nomination of this provision is based on conversations with Kuwaiti women. Although polygyny is not believed to be widespread in Kuwait today, Kuwaiti women talk about it more than its perceived incidence might predict, in part to declare that it is more prevalent than people believe.

16. Nawal El Saadawi, *The Hidden Face of Eve: Women in the Arab World*, trans. Sherif Hetata (London: Zed Press, 1980).

17. Interview, 24 October 1992, in Kuwait.

18. Interview, 28 October 1992, in Kuwait.

19. Jill Crystal, *Kuwait: The Transformation of an Oil State* (Boulder: Westview, 1992), 73.

20. Ghanim al-Najjar, "Decision-making Process in Kuwait: The Land Acquisition Policy as a Case Study," Ph.D. diss., University of Exeter, 1984; Jill Crystal, *Oil and Politics in the Gulf: Rulers and Merchants in Kuwait and Qatar* (Cambridge: Cambridge University Press, 1990), 75–76.

21. These and other divisions in the traditional organization of Kuwaiti society are explored in Nicolas Gavrielides, "Tribal Democracy: The Anatomy of Parliamentary Elections in Kuwait," in *Elections in the Middle East: Implications of Recent Trends*, ed. Linda L. Layne (Boulder: Westview, 1987).

22. Crystal, *Kuwait*, 77.

23. Tétreault, "Kuwait's Democratic Reform Movement," 18.

24. Crystal, *Oil and Politics in the Gulf*, 80. Kuwait University sociologist,

Khaldoun al-Naqeeb, thinks that the state-dependent middle class in Arab states is the primary social support for authoritarianism. Interviews, October 1992.

25. Raymond Bonner, "A Woman's Place," *The New Yorker*, 16 November 1992, 64.

26. Ibid.

27. Kuwait University political scientist Saif ᶜAbbas ᶜAbdulla dedicated his dissertation to his mother, the only member of his family to support his desire to pursue his education. Interviews, September and October 1992, in Kuwait.

28. State of Kuwait, Ministry of Planning, Central Statistical Office, *Statistical Abstract in 25 Years*, special issue, 1990, Table 17.

29. Interviews, September and October 1992, in Kuwait.

30. It could be argued that veiling is a cultural practice rather than a religious practice but, as Farideh Farhi notes in the chapter on Iran in this book, veiling in all its manifestations has been associated with Islamism there, and is also the outfit preferred by the Saudi religious police.

31. Interviews in Kuwait, September–October 1992.

32. Interviews in Kuwait, January–May 1990, March, September–October 1992.

33. Interviews with attorney Mohammad al-Jasim, October 1992, in Kuwait.

34. Kamal Osman Salih, "Kuwait's Parliamentary Elections: 1963–1985," unpublished paper, Kuwait University.

35. Speech by Moudhi al-Hamoud at the campaign *diwaniyya* of Saleh al-Yaseen, 28 September 1992.

36. Interviews in Kuwait, September–October 1992. Also the speech by Badria al-Awadhi at the campaign *diwaniyya* of Saleh al-Yaseen, 28 September 1992.

37. Bonner, "A Woman's Place," 62. Similar abuses of household servants in the more repressive Gulf regimes—or in the United States—do not receive the scrutiny that has become routine for Kuwait.

38. According to ᶜAziz Abu-Hamad, associate director of Middle East Watch, the only embassy still harboring runaway servants is the embassy of the Philippines. The others have responded to pressure from the Kuwaiti government and refuse to accept nationals applying for refuge from abusive employers. Lecture at the Middle East Institute, 11 December 1992.

39. Interviews with Khouloud al-Feeli and Ghanim al-Najjar, two Kuwaiti human rights activists, in Kuwait, 1 October 1992.

40. Interviews in Kuwait, March 1992.

41. Interview, 1 October 1992, in Kuwait.

42. Quoted in Bonner, "A Woman's Place," 62.

43. Interview, 1 October 1992, in Kuwait.

44. For an explanation of coverture, or *feme covert*, in U.S. law, see Marylynn Salmon, "Equality or Submersion? *Feme Covert* Status in Early Pennsylvania," in *Women of America: A History*, ed. Carol Ruth Berkin and Mary Beth Norton (Boston: Houghton Mifflin, 1979).

45. Interview with Saleh al-Hashem, candidate for parliament in the tenth

district, 29 September 1992, at his campaign *diwaniyya.*

46. Kamal Osman Salih, "Kuwait's Parliamentary Elections."

47. Interviews in Kuwait, September–October 1992.

48. Interview with Nasir Sarkhou, candidate for parliament in the thirteenth district, on 2 October 1992, at his campaign *diwaniyya.*

49. Sharabi, *Neopatriarchy,* 35–39; Khaldoun Hasan al-Naqeeb, *Society and State in the Gulf and Arab Peninsula: A Different Perspective,* trans. L. M. Kenny (New York: Routledge, 1990), 108–9, 126–30; Tétreault, "Civil Society in Kuwait."

50. Interviews in Kuwait, September–October 1992. The mosque as a protected space is discussed in Tétreault, "Civil Society in Kuwait."

51. Press conference by [c]Abdullah al-Shayeji, acting chair of the political science department at Kuwait University, 6 October 1992, Meridien Hotel, Kuwait.

52. A service candidate in the Kuwaiti context is one whose *raison d'etre* is to provide benefits to his district and the individuals in it in return for their political support. Such candidates tend to be returned by socially disadvantaged groups such as the Bedouin or the Shi[c]a. Service candidates are supported by the regime (the source of the favors they hand out as elected officials) because they do not care about changing the political order but merely getting a share of the pie for their constituents. Thus, the substitution of tribal Islamists for tribal service candidates may be seen by the regime as netting out at zero if the potential of the Islamists to effect fundamental political change is ignored. The 1992 election was notable for the lack of success of most of the old service candidates.

53. Interviews in Kuwait, October 1992.

54. Interviews in Kuwait, September–October 1992.

55. Interviews in Kuwait, September–October 1992.

56. Interview with Ma[c]suma al-Mubarak, 19 September 1992, in Kuwait.

57. Interview, 17 September 1992, in Kuwait.

58. Mary Ann Tétreault, "Autonomy, Necessity, and the Small State: Ruling Kuwait in the Twentieth Century," *International Organization* 45 (Autumn 1991).

V

The New World

Chapter 14

Women, Adamocracy, and the Bolivian Social Revolution

Gratzia Villarroel Smeall

In 1952, Bolivia underwent one of the most dramatic changes in its history. In less than a year, the populist party, *Movimiento Nacionalista Revolucionario* (Nationalist Revolutionary Movement, MNR), challenged the traditional oligarchic state by securing the support of what, until then, had been neglected groups in Bolivian society. As a result, it established a one-party populist regime and permanently changed the Bolivian social fabric. Until 1952, only white, educated, land-owning males were allowed to vote in national elections, leaving over 70 percent of the population outside the formal political process. Although the Bolivian social revolution is often termed the "failed revolution" or an "unfinished revolution" as compared to other major revolutions in Latin America, it nevertheless unleashed social forces that have since shaped Bolivian political life.[1] Indeed, a massive agrarian reform program, the nationalization of foreign-owned companies, the dissolution of the military forces, and the creation of civilian militias were only some of the populist policies adopted by Victor Paz Estenssoro, the supreme leader of the MNR.[2]

The Chaco War and the MNR were both important agents of change in Bolivian society. The victory of the MNR in 1952 was the culmination of a period of dramatic social change in Bolivian society that was initiated by the loss of the 1935 Chaco War with Paraguay. Not only had young Indian men, mobilized for the war effort, been unwilling to return peacefully to their serf-like pre-war existence, but the emergent middle class and new professional elites had grown resentful of the power held by the traditional elite that had led the country into a useless war. They wanted reform and change and, between 1936 and the 1952 revolution, these newly politicized Bolivians challenged a political system which no longer met their needs.[3] It was the MNR leadership that had the political vision and institutional organization to channel these forces into a successful, multi-class, populist political party. The party sought a series of social reforms which, though vigorously fought by the oligarchy, were responsible for most of the reformist policies implemented in the two decades preceding the 1952 revolution.

Women played an important role in Bolivian society, both before and after the revolution. They were the unintended beneficiaries of the 1952 Universal Vote decree of the MNR which was designed to mobilize the lower classes, primarily the peasants and miners. Nevertheless, the social revolution did little to change women's status as dependents of men.

It has been argued that the sexual subordination of women is a product of culturally created social ideologies as well as the material conditions influencing women's and men's lives. Subordination of women to men persists over and above class, ethnic, and social distinctions.[4] Furthermore, regardless of the existence of legal reform, it is the condition of adamocracy, a situation of male dominance perpetuated through the institutions of the family, polity, and religion, that is responsible for the continued dependent status of women in this society.[5] Even when women do participate in politics, their actions are seen merely as an extension of their motherhood role in the arena of public affairs.[6]

Although structural factors cannot be ignored when studying the subordination of Latin American women, it is the ideological realm that legitimizes these structures. Indeed, as the concept of adamocracy suggests, women's subordination is harder to change within the institutions of the family, religion, and the polity (as opposed to the institutions of education and the work force) because it is in the context of these institutions that the cultural images of women are most strongly reinforced and perpetuated.

In Latin America, the Catholic Church is said to be very important in shaping an authoritarian society in which women occupy a subordinate role. This role is reinforced by women's identification with the suffering and ever-patient Virgin Mary. The term *Marianismo* is used in Latin America to describe religious practices that have produced a standard image of the ideal woman as one with spiritual strength, self-abnegation, and moral superiority. Women are to exhibit self-denial and extreme patience with the men of their world. Although this might permit them to hold indirect power by way of their ability to exploit their moral superiority, it also keeps women on a pedestal isolated in the private realm of the home.[7] Indeed, while the Church is influential in shaping the male-dominated society, it is women that perpetuate, within the family, the ideological and cultural beliefs that keep them subordinated.[8]

The experience of Bolivian women strongly reflects the existence of these conditions. First, women's political participation has been minimal and is characterized merely as an extension of their motherhood roles. Political institutions belong to the public realm, and women are encouraged to remain in the private realm of their homes. Second, even when political parties have incorporated women into their ranks, they usually have used women to further their power and class objectives and not to change women's dependent status. Finally, while female subordination in Bolivia persists across class and ethnic lines, female political participation has usually been guided by class interests as opposed to gender concerns, making it impossible for women to unite across class lines to improve their situations.

BOLIVIAN WOMEN AND TRADITIONAL SOCIETY

From the turn of the century until the 1930s, when Latin American feminism first began influencing the country, Bolivian society was settling into what eventually would be called the oligarchic state. The tin industry had consolidated into a few large firms, owned by tin barons Simon Patiño, Mauricio Hoschild, and Carlos Victor Aramayo, and domestic politics rested primarily upon upper-class white consensus. The frequency of Indian rebellions prompted white and *mestizo* (people from mixed Indian and Spanish heritage) elites to isolate them, deliberately making sure that very few arms ever reached them.[9] It was in this period, one of the most stable and nonmilitary periods of Bolivian history, that the first webs of feminism began to emerge.

The oligarchic state which excluded Indians from the political system also excluded women, even those married to members of the ruling class. At the turn of the century, strong cultural images of "good women" and "bad women" trapped women between being self-sacrificing and self-abnegating followers of the Virgin Mary or being sinful followers of Eve. Good women remained in the domestic realm and fulfilled their moral and religious duties, while bad women were part of the public realm and were not given respect. The limited room women had to express themselves, and the limited educational opportunities open to them, were denounced by the Bolivian writer Alcides Arguedas:

> [The Bolivian woman] has her space for action restricted to the very minimum. Her lot is filled with prejudices from ancient times. It can be said that she still lives in the Middle Ages, and this is true to the point that when one attempts to liberate her from the tyrannies that oppress her, she is the first one to manifest her bewilderment and requests that she be left alone, to live free from the intense struggles that move the souls of other women.[10]

During the early 1920s, most Bolivian women were impervious to the feminist trends that began sweeping the continent, and they preferred to remain that way.

In a society where most Indians, including women, were tied to the land like serfs, and the majority of *cholas*, or urban lower-class women, were excluded from social and political life due to their class and their condition of illiteracy, the few women who did begin to question the system necessarily came from the upper classes.[11] Influenced by poet Adela Zamudio, small groups of women demanding to be accepted as citizens began to emerge throughout the country.[12] In a series of poems signed *Soledad* (Solitude), Adela Zamudio expressed her displeasure with a society which tied women to superficial and defeating roles regardless of their intelligence and capabilities. The controversial poem, *To Be Born A Man* (1887), is her most poignant criticism of the *machismo* of Bolivian society at the time.

Nacer Hombre (1887)
¡Cuánto trabajo ella pasa
Por corregir la torpeza
De su esposo, y en la casa
(Permitidme que me asombre)
Tan inepto como fatuo
Sigue él siendo la cabeza
Porque es hombre!

Si alguna versos escribe
de alguno esos versos son,
Que ella solo los suscribe
(Permitidme que me asombre)
Si ese alguno no es poeta
¿Por qué tal su posición?
¡Porque es hombre!

To Be Born a Man (1887)
How much work she must do
to correct the rudeness
of her husband, and at home,
(Excuse my surprise)
though incompetent and vain,
he continues to be the head
Because he is a man!

If she should write verses
They will surely be called his
As she may only use his name
(Excuse my surprise)
If he is not a poet
Why does he enjoy the fame?
Because he is a man!

Una mujer superior
en elecciones no vota
Y vota el pillo peor
(Permitidme que me asombre)
Con tal que aprenda a firmar
Puede votar un idiota
¡Porque es hombre!

El se abate y bebe o juega
En un revés de la suerte
Ella sufre, lucha y ruega

(Permitidme que me asombre)
Que a ella se le llame
"el ser débil"
Y a él se le llame
"el ser fuerte"
¡Porque es hombre!

Ella debe perdonar
Siéndole su esposo infiel;
Pero él se puede vengar
(Permitidme que me asombre)
En un caso semejante
Hasta puede matar él
¡Porque es hombre!

¡Oh mortal privilegiado
Que de perfecto y cabal
Gozas de seguro renombre!
En todo caso, para esto,
Te ha bastado
Nacer Hombre

A superior woman
in elections cannot vote
yet the worst scoundrel can
(Excuse my surprise)
As long as he can sign
Even an imbecile can vote
Because he is a man!

If he is dejected, he can drink or bet
On one stroke of luck.
She must be patient, struggle and beg

(Excuse my surprise)
That she be called
"the weaker sex"
and he be called
"the stronger sex"
Because he is a man!

She must forgive
If her husband is unfaithful
Yet he can seek revenge
(Excuse my surprise)
In a similar case
He can even kill
Because he is a man!

Oh privileged mortal
So perfect and so correct
You are assured success!
In every case, for this,
It was enough
That you Be Born a Man[13]

Adela Zamudio's rebellion went beyond denouncing gender discrimination. At a time when the power of the Catholic Church was still strong, and conservative upper-class women supported its every activity, she also dared to criticize the luxury, power, and decadence of the Church in her famous poem *Quo Vadis* (1903).[14]

Zamudio's feminism soon inspired other women throughout the country. In Oruro, the *Círculo Artístico e Intelectual de Señoritas* (Intellectual and Artistic Circle of Young Ladies) was founded in 1919. Soon members of that group began to publish the magazine, *Feminiflor*, in which different trends in feminism were frequently discussed.[15] As was acknowledged by Betshabe Salmón de Beltrán, editor of the magazine, Bolivian feminism had been inspired by Zamudio's writings and by reforms indirectly favoring women that were carried out during the progressive administrations of Bautista Saavedra (1920–1925) and Hernando Siles (1926–1930). Their initiatives included making it legal for women to receive higher education and legalizing the eight-hour work shift.[16]

In 1923, the *Ateneo Femenino*, an organization dedicated to the women's intellectual movement and the pursuit of women's rights, was founded in La Paz by Maria Luisa Sánchez Bustamante de Urioste who had been inspired by a similar group in Chile.[17] The *Ateneo Femenino* began to seek alternative spaces for women's development but encountered stiff opposition from those for whom it was inconceivable that women could dedicate their attention to something other than the administration of their homes. One of *Ateneo Femenino's* greatest accomplishments was the organization of the First National Convention of Bolivian Women in 1929. This convention was particularly important because it sought to unify the Bolivian women's movement by including women's organizations from the lower as well as the upper classes—a very progressive stand given the social conditions of the time.[18]

The other important feminist group, founded in the 1930s, was the *Legión Femenina de Educación Popular de America* (Feminine Legion for American Popular Education), organized by Etelvina Villanueva y Saavedra. This group sought to improve the status of women from all social classes by advocating changes in the legal code. In particular, its members sought the recognition of out-of-wedlock children and common-law marriages, and were committed to improving the civil and political rights of women. As did other women of the time, they encountered much opposition from conservative and religious circles. Any attempt at improving women's position in society was ridiculed and attacked:

> **ALARMA**
>
> I am scared, saddened to the extreme of no longer being able to remain silent. You might believe that because I am Spanish, and because there have been massacres in Spain, I am alarmed at the plight of my family. No, thank goodness. Another fear invades me: It is that I have learned about an organization of women that has deathly objectives. You might ask what have I to do with women? Very much for now. It is because this group has for its objective to demoralize, pervert, convert women into lesbians, set them free from their husbands' control, give them all the rights that men have, [indeed, these women] scorn social sanction!

> And do readers really believe that decent young men will be able to fall in love with these manly beings? That instead of gentle looks, sad tears and instances of candor, they will prefer to find themselves with a malicious lawyer- type, who, instead of a smile, shows them the article of a legal code? . . .
>
> Catholic ladies, do not let yourselves be deceived by this feminist society that says it is in favor of improving women's rights. Underneath, their true motives are the most disgraceful moral perversity.
>
> . . . Beware *Señoras and Señoritas.*[19]

The trials suffered by these first feminist groups reflected the limited space women had in Bolivian society. Until new civil and family codes were formulated in 1976, laws affecting women were organized under the Civil Code of 1830 which underwent very few revisions throughout the twentieth century and which stated that women could not engage in contracts of any kind or in judicial activities without authorization of their husbands; they could not control their own assets; and they could not vote. The Civil Code of 1830 also ruled over the private realm of the marriage stating, among other things, that women had the duty of obeying their husbands, of following them wherever they chose to reside, and of having no legal protection if the husbands applied "moderate domestic punishment" when marital problems required it.[20]

The lot of lower-class women of the pre-Chaco War period was even more difficult. Not only did they face gender discrimination but they were also subject to class discrimination. Indian women were bound by the *mita* system by which peasants living in *haciendas* had to serve weekly turns in the land-owner's country home. They were often mistreated and abused, and led slave-like existences. The most visible political activity of women from the popular classes came from urban lower-class women.[21] In the 1930s, several urban women's syndicates were organized in La Paz under the rubric of *Federación Obrera Femenina* (Female Workers' Federation, FOF). Their members were imbued by the *anarquista* (anarchist) thinking of the time. The FOF encouraged the formation of autonomous unions and was particularly popular among the Bolivian working class. It had the strong support of the female vendors and cooks of La Paz. The talents of these women lay in their ability to organize themselves. They demanded a list of concessions to women of their class, at a time when class divisions were deep and upward mobility was extremely limited. These included better working schedules and benefits for *chola* cooks and vendors.

Petronila Infante, one of their most important leaders, even addressed some issues of gender discrimination which illuminate the plight of lower-class urban women of the time:

> The chains of man [are also] ours. But [our sex] is the heaviest and darkest one. . . . Because we are women we are paid less while we have to work more. In the unjust system that rots humanity, the existence of women is a harsh one. Its frontiers are lost in the night of fatigue and hunger, or in the blackness of marriage and prostitution.[22]

In general, however, these groups made few attempts to deal in a comprehensive manner with gender discrimination. They did not join in the demands for female suffrage or cooperate with any other feminist groups of the time. Indeed, they did not feel that they were genuinely welcome in the women's conferences that were organized in the 1920s and 1930s.[23]

Bolivian traditional society was content to limit upper-class women with the "Marian images" of motherhood and marriage while lower-class women remained trapped in the chains of class and gender discrimination. Although the Bolivian social revolution did not intentionally or comprehensively affect the status of women, the series of reforms indirectly affecting women in the 1940s and 1950s had the unplanned effect of politicizing a small sector of the Bolivian female population and mobilizing these women into the formal political structure.

THE CHACO WAR AND THE BOLIVIAN SOCIAL REVOLUTION

The Chaco War (1932–1935), a harsh defeat for Bolivians, was important for having brought soldiers from all classes into the barracks as *compañeros* (comrades) to fight the Paraguayans. It provided the seeds of the destruction of the oligarchic system. The social and political mobilization of the post-war period forever changed the old social structure of Bolivia.

Daniel Salamanca, a popular Republican oligarch, propelled the country into a war that proved to be disastrous. Encouraged by military forces, Bolivia entered the war with several apparent advantages, only to be defeated after three years of useless fighting. In contrast, Paraguay doubled its pre-1932 territory at the expense of the Bolivian Chaco. Salamanca's short-sightedness and petty political squabbles were seen as the primary reasons for the defeat. Salamanca's traditional *Partido Republicano Genuino* (Genuine Republican Party) completely lost its legitimacy, giving way to the dramatic changes of the following two decades.[24]

Although military sectors had inflamed the country and provoked the nationalist fervor that led to the Chaco War, it was the disgruntled Chaco War generation, led by young veterans from middle- and upper-class families, which created a series of new political parties that challenged the oligarchic stronghold of Bolivian pre-war politics. Refusing to support the old regime, the new parties provided for the growth of reformist and radical ideologies, and began expanding at the expense of the traditional oligarchy. When the junior officers of the Chaco generation took office in 1935 after returning from the war, they did so under the rubric of military socialism. Their administration was characterized by extensive reformist activity, and produced the first serious social legislation—including the country's first labor code enacted in Bolivia. The government also promoted the unionization of workers and supported the proliferation of new radical parties which challenged the power of the old oligarchic entities.[25]

In subsequent years, these reforms led to further demands for change by various sectors of the Bolivian population. The Bolivian social fabric had been altered, never to be the same again. Even when reformist regimes were not in power, underground opposition to the traditional oligarchy continued to grow. As Lydia Gueiler, the future president of Bolivia wrote:

> In the mid-1940s, the flaming volcano that was Bolivia was about to explode. For those who have not lived through those glorious stages of titanic struggle of a people against oppression . . . it would be impossible to describe how new political militants were baptized with fire into the underground struggle in an effort to take over the government.[26]

Within the context of social change that culminated in the 1952 revolution, two important developments affected the political status of women in Bolivian society. The first was the struggle for female suffrage which ended unexpectedly with the Universal Vote of 1952. The second was the inclusion of women in political parties, in particular in the new reformist parties created in the post-Chaco War period. Of these parties, the MNR was responsible for the formal organization of a female branch which recruited both upper- and lower-class women. Neither of these developments had the effect, however, of changing the dependent status of Bolivian women. In a sense, female political activity was used to support the higher goals of the state and the revolution. It was not used to change the domestic status of women or to address gender issues. Indeed, Latin American reformist governments have repeatedly used traditional female images to further their own political objectives.[27] This certainly appeared to be the case with the MNR. Even the party's own female militants criticized it for not seriously addressing women's issues.[28]

Female Suffrage

As was the case in other parts of Latin America, the struggle for female suffrage in Bolivia was carried out by a few upper-class women. They had strong intellectual aspirations and were imbued with traditional feminist demands for improving female civil rights. In the years following the Chaco War, the *Ateneo Femenino* and the *Legión Femenina* were in the vanguard of the civil struggle for female suffrage. However, because of strong clerical influences and the religious ideology of Bolivian society which dissuaded women from activities in the public realm, these groups did not find widespread support for their demands among other women of their class. Their struggle was often reduced to personal requests for the female vote through relatives and friends in their social circles. However, in 1936, the *Legión Femenina* finally sent a formal letter to the Bolivian government addressing the role of women:

> The socio-economic evolution that is taking place in the nation proposes in its ideology the coming of equal rights in favor of collective interests. . . . In this context, women can not be ignored since they are the victims of prejudices, humiliations, and inequalities in society. Based on the postulates of equality and justice that the Socialist government proposes, the *Legión Femenina* . . . declares its sincere decision to request of the present government the recognition of the civil and political rights of women.[29]

By 1938, the government was ready to discuss the issue of women's rights within the broader context of "the incorporation of marginalized [social] groups" into the political spectrum. The congressional arguments reflected the social mores of the time, taking as a given that women's ability to participate in politics depended upon their education and intellectual capabilities and was either inhibited or enhanced by their maternal responsibilities. Those who argued in favor of the female vote stated that a feminine touch was needed:

> The female vote will surely bring some advantages for the country . . . politicians never worry about the problems of education of children, protection of mothers, welfare institutions. . . . Women could take their noble aspirations into the political system.[30]

Those opposed to female political participation alluded to the importance of women's motherly and household duties:

> We should not reach the extreme [position] of letting women participate in politics, as [they] would abandon their noble mission of "being women" and educators of their children.[31]
>
> The political rights of women go against the civilization, the progress, and the well-being of the Bolivian home.[32]
>
> Women cannot intervene in politics because this would mean that we [no longer] believe in marriages. . . . We would have converted her into a being that has lost her natural qualities only to acquire an artificial and manly personality.[33]

These and similar arguments were found to be so compelling that women were denied the right to vote by 55 to 31 votes.

The first reformist period did not last long. In 1939, after three years of military rule which culminated in the apparent suicide of a popular Chaco War hero, President Germán Busch, the traditional oligarchic parties came back to power and contained for another decade the forces mobilized by the Chaco War. It has been argued that a lack of unity among the three emerging reformist parties prevented the Bolivian social revolution from taking place in the 1940s. Although the *Partido Obrero Revolucionario* (Revolutionary Labor Party, POR), with close links to unionized miners, the *Partido de la Izquierda Revolucionaria* (Leftist Revolutionary Party, PIR), with powerful support among the middle class, and the MNR, an amalgam of socialist and fascist elements which claimed important middle class support, were all anti-oligarchic, pro-labor, and reformist, their different ideologies prevented their initial coalition into one revolutionary force.[34]

It was not until 1945, with the election of President Gualberto Villarroel, that the reformist parties once again achieved national recognition. This time, the MNR governed along with young military officers who espoused more progressive policies. In 1945, the government voted once again on female suffrage. This time the *Ateneo Femenino* had representatives on the Legislative Commission that was to make recommendations to the Parliament. They sent a delegation to the *Junta de Gobierno* in September 1946 to request that female suffrage be granted. Once again, they mobilized family and social connections to press for their demands.[35]

Within the commission, the debate centered on three points: first, whether women should have the right to universal suffrage or whether female suffrage should be limited to municipal elections; second, whether women should have the right to run for office or only the right to vote; and third, what level of education women should have to be eligible to vote.[36] Despite the opposition of women from conservative circles and thanks to the efforts of feminist groups and a more open climate for social change, women were finally given the right to vote and run for administrative posts in the municipal elections of 1947.[37] The *Ateneo Femenino* strongly supported this decision and immediately encouraged its members to register in political parties and/ or run for office. However, the female turnout in 1947 was very low. Only seventeen hundred women out of twenty thousand potential female voters were registered to vote. There were several reasons for this low turnout. Perhaps the most important was that politics was not seen as an appropriate female activity, and few women really viewed the right to vote as a great accomplishment. Since they had not fought for it, most Bolivian women felt uncomfortable with it. As one female voter commented:

> I have not voted for any of the female candidates because I do not believe that women are capable of dealing with such a delicate matter as politics. Women to your kitchens! That's my slogan, even though I had come to vote cordially invited by my husband.[38]

Once in power, the MNR launched the Universal Vote to incorporate large segments of the Bolivian population into the formal political process.[39] Women benefited from these political turnabouts only indirectly because they were not undertaken with the specific purpose of mobilizing women. Instead, the MNR viewed the Universal Vote as a way of establishing a support base in the countryside. "[Canelas] saw probably correctly—that the Universal Vote was a calculated attempt by the MNR to consolidate its regime by anchoring itself in the countryside."[40] By 1959, Lydia Gueiler decided that the Universal Vote had not been enough: "Despite the universal suffrage and a very limited involvement in affairs of State, I can affirm without fear of being wrong or unjust that, in actuality, the equal opportunity [women] require to fully develop their political abilities and social involvement has not yet been granted [by the MNR]."[41]

The subordination of women was not resolved by giving them the right to vote. While reformist legislation improved women's condition in traditional society, the ideological and institutional framework which kept women in the private realm of their homes had hardly been altered.

Female Participation in Political Parties

The process of change leading to the Bolivian social revolution of 1952 also brought women into the formal political system for the first time. After women were given the right to vote in the 1947 municipal elections, all of the emerging leftist parties incorporated women into their ranks. Some of the most famous and active Bolivian women joined political parties during this period. Agar Peñaranda participated in the POR; Maria Luisa Bustamante de Urioste, along with other members of the *Ateneo Femenino*, soon joined the ranks of the PIR and presented their candidacies for different political offices; and Lydia Gueiler de Tejada was a founding member of the female branch of the MNR in the 1940s.

However, the "Marian image" described above was maintained and promoted as the model for female political participation. Women represented themselves as mothers and wives answering a higher call. When women were involved in clandestine pursuits and underground communication networks (such as hiding potential political prisoners, providing food to those in jail, and providing secretarial services for the party), they were engaged in activities that were an extension of their domestic role. Even women who were more imbued with feminist tendencies were quick to point out their motherly interest in becoming political candidates: "I believe that motherhood is the highest aspiration of women, and for this reason we must dedicate ourselves maternally to the children of our country."[42] Exceptions to the rule were rare and included some of the few militant leaders like the independent Agar Peñaranda, who actively sought and succeeded in achieving inclusion in the decision-making circles of the POR.[43]

By 1946, the MNR emerged as the leading populist party and was given the opportunity to participate in the government of the Villarroel administration. However, Gualberto Villarroel's fall from grace and his lynching by a mob ended its short rule.[44] Again in opposition during the *sexenio* period (the last six years of oligarchic rule preceding the revolution of 1952), the MNR organized a strong female sector to support its underground activities. Originally limited to upper- and middle-class women, many of them the wives and daughters of MNR militants, the party eventually expanded its base of support to include the *cholas*. This was a necessary political move as the MNR aspired to be perceived and accepted as a populist party. In 1947, following a mass commemorating the death of President Villarroel, the newspaper reported that "60 ladies along with a great number of *cholas* were present."[45] The *cholas* were eventually mobilized as the *Barzolas*, the unique grassroots support group sponsored by the MNR.

It was thus the MNR that created the first formal space for female political activity. The female branch of the MNR was hierarchically organized and ultimately responded to the male leadership of the party. It was designed to support the activities of the party by providing traditional female services: taking care of the sick, preparing food, performing administrative activities, supporting electoral activity, and similar tasks. With respect to female activity during this revolutionary period, Lydia Gueiler writes that:

> There was not a minute of rest . . . for any of the militants of the female sector of the MNR. Each groups would organize the attention of the political prisoners. Many of the *compañeras* would stay up nights at a time preparing the food that would be taken the next day to the prisons, the police stations, and the hospitals. No one worried about any other activity that was not dictated by the revolutionary conscience and the instructions of the party.[46]

The MNR never proposed any specific policies to promote the status of women in the party. Thus, they provided the model that has since generally characterized women's role within Bolivian political parties: that of providing support to male politicians. MNR women from more educated groups engaged in administrative, secretarial, and communication activities for the party, but women's issues were never considered important or given specific attention.

After 1952, the MNR began recruiting women from popular sectors to support its political activities. From this new influx of activists, the *Barzolas* was born. Its members were poor, illiterate, urban women—primarily housewives—who needed to supplement their husbands' incomes to support their families. As a group, the *Barzolas* were very controversial. They were believed to have been on the payroll of the MNR, and were involved in the series of corrupt activities that had contributed to the downfall of the social revolution. Unlike other groups of lower-class women who despised the government, the upper classes, and ethnic discrimination, *Barzolas* activities were primarily carried out within the party and their main objective was to guard the revolution.[47]

The *Barzolas* were used by the party to distribute food in neighborhoods during times of scarcity. They were active participants in various labor groups and also members of armed militias. When MNR party leaders realized the usefulness of this newly mobilized group of lower-class women, they formed the *Comando Especial Maria Barzola*—a more select female sector that worked as a secret service agency for the MNR. While this special female commando unit was originally formed in La Paz, it eventually recruited and directed women on a national level. The corrupt activities of this group were the ones that gave all *Barzolas* a bad reputation.

Indeed, as a group, and regardless of any positive contributions, the *Barzolas* were feared by many. They were known for denouncing any anti-governmental activities they spotted in their assigned neighborhoods. The *Barzolas* also recruited as members the *empleadas*—servants—of the old oligarchic society. During a period when class resentments flared in the country, some *empleadas* accused their bosses of reactionary activity. The MNR leadership would then have the accused imprisoned, tortured, and often sent to concentration camps in the eastern part of the country. The *empleadas* probably did not realize the full consequences of their activities but they knew that their valuable information would be rewarded with coupons and bonuses for food, an important privilege during a time of scarcity.

As a result, even though they were extremely loyal to the MNR and contributed greatly to bringing Bolivian women into the political realm, the *Barzolas* were feared and despised by other political sectors.[48] This was specifically true for the women of the *Comités de Amas de Casa,* from the mining districts, and the *Federación Obrera Femenina*—two other important lower-class women's political groups in Bolivia.[49] Members of both groups had very harsh memories of the *Barzolas* whom they believed had betrayed their own class:

> The MNR *Barzolas* sold themselves to serve the party's interests and helped repress the people. They served as an instrument of repression. In La Paz, for example, when people of the working class would make any demands, the *Barzolas* would jump in front of them, brandishing razors, penknives, and whips, attacking people who had gathered in a protest demonstration.[50]

> Those sleazy *Barzolas,* they are shameless, they don't work in anything . . . they live off the "gossip" that they take to the government. I despise them![51]

Even other female members of the MNR were afraid of the *Barzolas* and were constantly asking them to behave themselves more decently and not be so aggressive.[52]

The *Barzolas* were also used in Congress to applaud and favor government representatives and vocally overpower opposition congressmen by booing. They were violent and often attacked men and women whom they believed were against governmental policies. These women were so well known for the *waykillas* (ganging up on a target individual and then assaulting her or him) that they waged that, whenever members of the opposition left the congressional grounds, they did so under protection.[53]

Although they were accused of corruption and of having no ideology because they were on the side of the ruling party, the *Barzolas* had important reasons for supporting the government. They were the wives of MNR militants. They saw the party as truly benefiting their class, the urban popular sectors. However, their organization, modeled in the hierarchical fashion of the ruling party, became a victim of the corruption and violence that characterized the MNR during the second half of the twelve years it ruled the country. The *Barzolas* died with the revolution.

The MNR years witnessed the opening of rural education for the lower classes, including women. Under MNR government, the university increasingly became open to female enrollment. Most important, by providing political legitimacy to marginalized groups such as miners, peasants, and the urban working class, the MNR provided a social and political terrain for the future development of miner and peasant female movements. Still, the MNR did little to improve the status and/or political participation of women in real terms. Women were not included in the decision-making centers of the party. Instead, they were organized and manipulated by the male leadership to support their political objectives. This became increasingly clear in the late 1950s. In 1959, Lydia Gueiler voiced her disillusionment with the party:

> My first disappointment was to realize that, in spite of our revolutionary development, and even with the undeniable aid of holding power in one's hands, the executive leadership had done absolutely nothing to organize MNR women in any responsible or serious manner. If this did not occur within the party, the vanguard of the revolution, we could scarcely demand it of working women or of women in general.[54]

Indeed, women participated in the political system, and rendered invaluable services to the male-dominated political parties, but their concerns were never given the important and unique treatment that would have improved women's status in society. Although female political participation continued to serve the political objectives of the party, the development of a strong Bolivian women's movement continued to be inhibited by ideological and class allegiances.

WOMEN AND THE AFTERMATH OF THE 1952 REVOLUTION

The national revolution incorporated the lower classes into the political spectrum of Bolivian society so thoroughly that they could not be ignored again. But it was soon coopted into the half-way, and uncompleted revolution of the 1960s and 1970s.[55] Indeed, following the influx of massive U.S. foreign aid into the country starting in 1954, the conflict between the right and the left inside the ranks of the MNR shifted to favor the right.[56]

In 1964, the MNR was finally forced to give power back to the military. After having compromised the original ideals of the revolution, there was little it could do to control the political sectors it had mobilized. Once in power, various military governments ruled between 1964 and 1982. Of these, the ones that held power the longest were headed by René Barrientos Ortuño, from 1964 through 1969, and Hugo Banzer Suárez, from 1971 to 1978. Although these regimes were very different in terms of their constituencies and their styles, they had in common the increased violation of human rights that occurred during their terms in office:

> . . . the Barrientos government considerably escalated the level of repression of independent organizations. [Once] [a]gain, worker organizations were the main targets of repression.[57]

> Banzer did not cater to the traditional agricultural areas and their massive peasant populations. . . . The peasants, like labor, were restricted in their organized activities. Restless and neglected peasants were not to remain quiescent. In January 1974, a group of peasants set up roadblocks on arteries leading into Cochabamba in protest of higher food prices. The government, eager to put down this show of opposition, sent in the troops. Firing broke out and an estimated 100 peasants were killed in what was to be known as the Massacre of Tolata.[58]

The repression and torture that characterized military rule from 1964 through 1982 provided for the growth of a strong and cohesive opposition in the country.[59] The POR and the PIR were joined by a new leftist party, the *Movimiento Revolucionario de Izquierda* (Revolutionary Movement of the Left, MRI), which attracted educated middle- and upper-class university students and would become increasingly important in contemporary Bolivian politics.

Few women occupied leadership positions during the years of military power. Instead, most female political activity was reduced to underground opposition and reflected the faces of victims of repression and torture. Although victimizing women for political reasons was not new in Bolivia, this kind of behavior became more prominent and ruthless during the years of military rule. The plight of many Bolivian women is perhaps best reflected in the diary of the female political leader, Domitila Barrios de Chungara.[60] In one of the most dramatic passages of her testimony, Domitila recalls her experience in the hands of government intelligence officers. Nine months pregnant, she was taken prisoner by the government for her leadership role in the *Comite de Amas de Casa*:

> He began kicking me . . . he shouted . . . he called the soldiers and made four of them grab me. He had on one of those big square rings. I don't know what he did with his hand, but he tightened and tightened it [in my stomach] making me scream really loud. And as I screamed he punched me all over my face. And I don't remember anything else.[61]

In self-defense, Domitila bit the man who had been beating her. Unfortunately, he was the son of a higher ranking officer, which only provoked further beatings by his enraged father:

> and he hit me furiously. Then he said: "All right. Luckily you're expecting a baby. We'll take our revenge on your baby" And he took out a knife and began to sharpen it in front of me. And he said that he had enough time to wait until my child was born and that with that knife he was going to make mincemeat out of my baby.[62]

Motherhood and the "Marian image" was used as a tool to exploit women as political prisoners. Politically active women had to decide whether they were going to take their political fight to the last consequences, even if, in the process, they endangered their families.[63]

During the military period, political clientelism was common in the relationship between the government and women's organizations. Nationalist and conservative, the government in power during this period implemented a series of family programs that sought to reproduce the traditional role of women. Indeed, women were seen as a malleable mass that could be sculpted at the will of the government given the appropriate policies.[64] In the end, this was the real legacy of the MNR, which had used women to support party objectives without any consideration for their long-term development as political actors.

CONCLUSIONS

The struggles that Bolivian women underwent in the mid-twentieth century to obtain the right to be accepted as legal citizens and the right to participate in politics reflects the importance of the concepts of adamocracy and *marianismo* in understanding women's subordination. Few brave women struggled to improve the status of women in society and those that did were often ridiculed by both men and women. Social images of women were hard to change and persisted long after the Bolivian social revolution. Women continued to perceive political participation as dangerous and worthless. Even today, the private realm is the preferred area of activity for Bolivian women and, unless they are forced to do so by economic forces or political repression, few of them are willing to risk torture or their lives to participate voluntarily in politics.[65]

Furthermore, both before and after the Bolivian social revolution, women were expected to fulfill the image of the "Marian mother." Sacrifice, self-abnegation, and loyalty were always expected of them, whether they participated in politics or not. Furthermore, while the governments played up the images of motherhood in formal ceremonies, they also tortured and abused women who were on the wrong side of the ideological spectrum. Indeed, there is only a fine line between the veneration of women as pure and sacrificial "Marys" and the exploitation of women as sinful "Eves."

Even the MNR, which was the first Bolivian party to actively recruit women into its ranks, was unwilling to sponsor substantial change in the societal treatment of gender issues. There was no long-term plan for women's permanent political mobilization. While women achieved certain concessions in the economic and educational institutions of society, their subordinate status in relation to men changed very little as a result of the Bolivian social revolution. Even though they were given the vote, they were barred from decision-making circles and were expected to remain loyal and subservient to the male leadership of the various political parties. This trend continued during the years of military rule, as the government forced women to adopt increasingly conservative roles to support their own political objectives.

Finally, ethnic, ideological, and class differences continued to drive Bolivian women apart. In the case of the MNR, the creation of the

Barzolas indirectly contributed to an increased focus on class and ethnic differences among women as opposed to gender identification and solidarity. The political party system and the years of military rule created further ideological divisions among women. During the years of military rule, even upper-class women were divided by ideological differences. These divisions among Bolivian women would persist in future years, inhibiting the development of a comprehensive women's movement in the country. Thus, the few positive benefits women were able to reap from the social revolution did not change their lives in any significant way.

After years of only incremental changes and admirable and heroic efforts by politically active women, Bolivian women today continue to operate at the margins of decision-making circles. While a variety of women's groups dedicated to increasing women's civic and political awareness have emerged in the country, many of the obstacles that Adela Zamudio encountered in her time are still present in Bolivian society. Despite the Universal Vote, the unfinished revolution of 1952 contributed very little to improving gender inequalities, increasing female political participation, or ending ethnic and class differences among women.

NOTES

1. Eduardo A. Gamarra and James M. Malloy, "Bolivia: Revolution and Reaction," in *Latin American Politics and Development*, ed. Howard J. Wiarda and Harvey F. Kline (Boulder: Westview Press, 1991), 366.

2. Victor Paz Estenssoro, considered the father of the Bolivian social revolution, reversed many of these original policies when he was once again elected to office in 1985. He privatized state companies, reduced the national budget, and implemented a series of austerity programs designed to boost the Bolivian economy. In less than thirty years, the MNR had completely shifted its position on the Bolivian ideological spectrum.

3. According to Gamarra and Malloy, "From the Mid-1930s to 1952 Bolivia was in a revolutionary situation in the sense that there was an almost continual open and violent struggle between groups oriented towards substantial change in the existing order and groups defending the status quo." Gamarra and Malloy, "Bolivia: Revolution and Reaction," 365.

4. Susan Bourque and Kay Barbara Warren, *Women of the Andes* (Ann Arbor: University of Michigan Press, 1981).

5. Morris J. Blachman, "Eve in Adamocracy: The Politics of Women in Brazil," Ph.D. diss., New York University, 1976, 63.

6. Elsa Chaney, *Supermadre: Women in Politics in Latin America* (Austin: Institute of Latin American Studies by the University of Texas Press, 1979), 158.

7. Evelyn P. Stevens, "Marianismo: The Other Face of Machismo in Latin America," in *Female and Male in Latin America: Essays*, ed. Ann Pescatello

(Pittsburgh: University of Pittsburgh Press, 1973), 95.

8. Jorge Gissi Bustos, "Mythology About Women, with Special Reference to Chile," in *Sex and Class in Latin America*, ed. June Nash and Helen Safa (New York: Praeger, 1976), 32.

9. Herbert S. Klein, "Bolivia Prior to the 1952 Revolution," in *Modern Day Bolivia*, ed. Jerry R. Ladman (Tempe: Center for Latin American Studies, 1982).

10. *Pueblo Enfermo*, 1910, in Mariano Baptista Gumucio, *El País Machista* (La Paz: Editorial Los Amigos del Libro, 1978). Except where otherwise noted, all translations from Spanish sources cited here were made by the author.

11. The *chola* woman occupies a different position than her Indian counterpart. Not only does the *chola* have greater contact with urban centers and the dominant Spanish culture, but her strong position in controlling the family's financial matters differs from that of women in Indian communities, who are more likely to have complementary roles and, in some cases, subservient roles in relation to their husbands.

12. Adela Zamudio is considered Bolivia's foremost feminist. Born to an upper-class family of Cochabamba, she was an educator, an intellectual, and a writer. She dedicated her life to improve the status of women in Bolivian society despite strong opposition and criticism. She was well respected and admired and her birthdate, 11 October, is celebrated as the "Day of Bolivian Women."

13. Eduardo Ocampo Moscoso, *Adela Zamudio: Una Mujer Admirable* (La Paz: Biblioteca Popular Boliviana de Ultima Hora, 1981).

14. Zamudio's pseudonym, *Soledad* (Solitude) was indeed reflective of a lonely and misunderstood soul who strove for freedom in a very conservative society. *Quo Vadis* caused several ladies from the upper classes and also clerics to turn against her. Animosity against her increased when she decided that she would no longer teach religion in the women's school that she directed. The League of Catholic Women publicly condemned her as did other conservative segments of society. Indeed, her editorial squabbles with Father Pirelli from Tarata caught the attention of national circles of the time. Gratzia V. Smeall, "Catholic and Andean Influences on Bolivian Women's Political Participation," Ph.D. diss.. University of South Carolina, 1990.

15. Luis Ramiro Beltrán, *Feminiflor: Un Hito en el Periodismo Femenino de Bolivia* (La Paz: CIMCA/Circulo de Mujeres Periodistas/CIDEM, 1987).

16. The progressive policies adopted by these two presidents only indirectly benefited women. Bautista Saavedra's administration is historically remembered for its attention to social legislation such as recognizing a worker's right to strike and the eight-hour work day. The administration of Hernando Siles was important for the emphasis it placed on higher education for Bolivian youth. Humberto Vázquez Machicado et al., *Manual de Historia de Bolivia* (La Paz: Gisbert y Compania, 1988), 451–57.

17. Maria Luisa Sánchez Bustamante de Urioste, "Ateneo Femenino: Una Institución que cumple 60 años," *Hoy* (26 April 1983): 3.

18. *Nosotras* (Annual Volumes, Cochabamba, Bolivia), 28 September 1989: 5. Class identification is still evident in Bolivia. Lower-class women view upper-

class women as their oppressors, rarely as their allies. Also, middle- and upper-class men generally feel that they may abuse a lower-class women without fear of being brought to justice. These injustices which mix class, gender, and ethnic oppression make lower-class women view their problems primarily in class terms, and inhibit the possibility of broader gender identification among women (Smeall, "Catholic and Andean Influences").

19. *El Lábaro*, Sucre, 10 September 1936.

20. Mary Loayza Hassenteufel, as cited in Baptista, *El País Machista*, 202.

21. While Indian women were not able to make any demands in Bolivian traditional society, there has been some light shed on the quiet but important role that native women played in Indian rebellions. In particular, it is known that Indian women administered the goods and land obtained during the rebellions, and were instrumental in collecting funds and providing the needed infrastructure to organize Indian uprising in various *haciendas* (Maria Eugenia del Valle de Siles, *Bartolina Sisa y Gregoria Apaza: Dos Heroínas Indígenas* (La Paz: Biblioteca Popular Boliviana de "Ultima Hora," 1981); Jael Bueno, "Mujer en Cochabamba," *Nosotras*, n.d. 1987–B).

22. As cited in Ineke Dibbits et al., *Polleras Libertarias: Federación Obrera Femenina 1926–1965* (La Paz: Tahipamu/HISBOL, 1989), 63–64.

23. While the women from the *Federación Obrera Femenina* were invited to the First National Women's Convention organized in 1929, they were not permitted to present their points of view. The FOF was economically, socially, and ideologically opposed to the upper class female groups that existed at the time. The inauguration of the conference was reflective of the tastes of the upper class elites and included several classical musical numbers. In this context, Petronila Infante, a FOF leader, remembers that "some congratulated us for attending but others were mad at us . . . we, the *cholas*, were there, among all the ladies." The FOF organized a protest march against this convention a few days after it took place (Dibbits et al., *Polleras Libertarias*, 75–79).

24. Vázquez Machicado et al., *Manual de Historia de Bolivia*, 467.

25. Klein, "Bolivia Prior to the 1952 Revolution."

26. Lydia Gueiler de Tejada, *La Mujer y la Revolución* (La Paz: Editorial Los Amigos del Libro, 2nd ed., 1983; 1st ed., 1959), 34. Lydia Gueiler was on of the most important leaders of the female branch of the MNR. Following the revolutionary years, she remained strongly involved in politics. Her career reached a peak when she was elected the first Bolivian female president by Congress in 1980. Unfortunately, her tenure in office only lasted a few months as she was removed by a military coup.

27. Sandra McGee Deutsch, "Gender and Change in Twentieth-Century Latin American Politics," SECOLAS Conference, Charleston, S.C., 13–15 April 1989.

28. Gueiler, *La Mujer y la Revolución*; and Maria Isabel Arauco, *Mujeres en la Revolución Nacional: Las Barzolas* (La Paz: CINCO, 1984).

29. Etelvina Villanueva y Saavedra, *Acción Socialista de la Mujer en Bolivia* (La Paz: Cooperativa de Artes Gráficas E. Burillo Ltda., 1970), 92.

30. Congressman Lanza Solares, as cited by Maria Lourdes Zabala, "Las Madres de la Política," *Nosotras*, 16 June 1987–B.

31. Congressman Arauz as cited in Zabala, "Las Madres de la Política."

32. Congressman Landivar Sambrana as cited in ibid.

33. A. Guzman as cited in ibid.

34. Klein, "Bolivia Prior to the 1952 Revolution."

35. Mery Flores Saavedra, "La Mujer en la Política," *Hoy*, 24 December 1985; and *Nosotras*, 28 July 1987, 5.

36. Zabala, "Las Madres de la Política," 4.

37. Ibid.

38. Ibid.

39. The original five goals of the 1952 revolution affected lower- and upper-class women indirectly. These included universal voting rights aimed at turning Indians into citizens; nationalization of the Big Three tin mining companies intended to make the Bolivians masters of their own political destiny; labor participation in the management of the nationalized mines; land reform aimed at giving the land back to those who worked it; and dissolution of an all-too-often repressive army (Cornelius H. Zondag, "Bolivia's 1952 Revolution: Initial Impact and U.S. Involvement," in *Modern Day Bolivia*.

40. Jerry W. Knudson, *Bolivia: Press and Revolution, 1932–1964* (Lanham: University Press of America, 1986), 217.

41. Gueiler, *La Mujer y la Revolución*, 158.

42. Sánchez Bustamante de Urioste, founder of the *Ateneo Femenino* as cited in Zabala, "Las Madres de la Política."

43. Guillermo Lora, *Agar Peñaranda: La Revolucionaria Ejemplar* (La Paz: Ediciones ISLA, 1979), 32.

44. Gualberto Villarroel, one of the reformist military presidents, was hanged from a lamp post on 21 July 1946, after infuriated mobs captured him in the presidential palace. While Villarroel had been truly committed to the urban working class, his administration's involvement in the murder of several politicians from the oligarchic opposition turned national opinion against him. The regime's legitimacy was further tarnished by its conflict with university students (Vázquez Machicado et al., *Manual de Historia de Bolivia*, 473).

45. Arauco, *Mujeres en la Revolución Nacional*, 54.

46. Gueiler, *La Mujer y la Revolución*, 37.

47. Many people resented that the *Barzolas*, who had such a bad reputation, had taken the name of an Indian heroine, María Barzola, who had been killed in December 1952, while leading a demonstration in the Catavi mining region. The Catavi Massacre became the symbol of the people's struggle against landowner and mine-owner domination (Smeall, "Catholic and Andean Influences").

48. Gloria Ardaya Salinas, feminine supplement of *Hoy*, La Paz, 29 August 1983, 2.

49. While the *Federación Obrera de Mujeres* reached its peak of Syndicalist activity before the 1952 revolution, some of their leaders still had encounters with the *Barzolas* in the early years of the social revolution. The *Comité de Amas*

de Casa of the mining districts became important in the years after the social revolution. Miner women organized themselves to support their husbands as they became increasingly repressed by the MNR in the early 1960s, and by the military governments that subsequently took power.

50. Domitila Barrios de Chungara, leader of the *Comité de Amas de Casa* of the mining districts (with Moema Viezzer), *Let Me Speak!* (New York: Monthly Review Press, 1978).

51. Nicolasa Ibañez, FOF leader, as cited in Dibbits et al., *Polleras Libertarias*, 43.

52. Arauco, *Mujeres en la Revolución Nacional*, 119.

53. Gloria Ardaya, "The Barzolas and the Housewives Committee," in *Women and Change in Latin America* (Massachusetts: Bergin and Garvey Publishers, 1986).

54. Gueiler, *La Mujer y la Revolución*, 149.

55. Zondag, "Bolivia's 1952 Revolution."

56. U.S. foreign aid to Bolivia declined in the first two years of the social revolution. In 1953, president Eisenhower sent his brother Milton, his personal representative in South America, to visit Bolivia. After this visit, the U.S. government became convinced that it could work with the MNR government. The total U.S. outlay came to almost $310 million for the thirteen years during which the MNR governed (James W. Wilkie, "U.S. Foreign Policy and Economic Assistance in Bolivia: 1948–1976," in *Modern Day Bolivia*, ed. Jerry R. Ladman (Tempe: Center for Latin American Studies, 1982), 84).

57. James M. Malloy and Sylvia Borzutsky, "The Praetorianization of the Revolution: 1964–1967," in ibid., 50.

58. Jerry R. Ladman, "The Political Economy of the 'Economic Miracle' of the Banzer Regime," in ibid., 331.

59. While human rights abuses became a rising national and international concern during the years of military rule, the MNR had also committed a series of abuses which directly affected women. Indeed, "in an effort to sustain itself, [the Paz Estenssoro regime] filled the jails as well as its detention camps at Corocoro, Uncia and Curahuara de Caranges with its opponents, including both men and women" (Zondag, "Bolivia's 1952 Revolution," 32). Female relatives of MNR opponents were also subject to sexual abuse when they sought information about their loved ones (author's interviews with female relatives of *Falange Socialista Boliviana* (FSB) leaders in Cochabamba, July 1989).

60. Barrios de Chungara, *Let Me Speak!*

61. Ibid., 145.

62. Ibid., 147.

63. Ibid.; personal interviews with M. J. and A. G., Cochabamba and La Paz, 1989.

64. Maritza Jiménez Bullain, "Contexto de Organización y Participación de la Mujer," conference paper, Tercer Encuentro Nacional sobre la Mujer, Participación Social y Política, La Paz, 8–9 December 1988.

65. Smeall, "Catholic and Andean Influences."

Chapter 15

Gender and the Mexican Revolution

The Intersection of Family, State, and Church

Diane Mitsch Bush
Stephen P. Mumme

> Most movements for self-determination among colonial nations have been far from advocating the liberation of women. On the contrary, women's resistance to male oppression is generally relegated to the margins, separated from class and national struggles, and subordinated to the wider and "higher" cause of national liberation. The issue is often treated as a divisive and distracting self-indulgence, rather than the result of social structures and relations. Thus it is assumed that women can liberate themselves only after liberating all other oppressed sectors of society.[1]

> By and large, however, socialists do not consider fighting women's oppression as a central aspect of the struggle against capitalism itself.[2]

The study of revolution has suffered from the same myopia that has characterized the ideology and organization of many, if not most, social revolutions and wars of national liberation regarding gender as a fundamental feature of inequality. From definitions of the concept of revolution to causal theories about the emergence of revolutions, and theories and findings about mobilization and outcomes, even the most "path-breaking" work on revolution has either included women as an afterthought or ignored gender altogether.[3] As with theory and research in other areas of social life (such as work, stratification, or institutionalized politics), studies of revolution have either assumed that gender is not a feature of social structure and organization or that it is a secondary dimension, relevant only within the family or with regard to women's issues. Those taking the first approach view the exclusion of women from revolutionary organizations and agendas as natural due to their domestic obligations. Those taking the second approach sever the family as an institution from the state when examining revolutions.

Recent theory and research on women and development has sought to remedy the omission of gender as a basic element of social structure.[4] At the same time, feminist theory and research on policy has begun to develop theories of the state that integrate gender with class and status as dimensions which shape state structure and ideology (especially ideology about the category citizen).[5] Simultaneously, theory and research on women, the state, and development have explicitly attempted to integrate feminist theories of the state and theories about women and development.[6]

Yet there is still relatively little research with an explicit focus on gender, the state, and revolution. Judith Stacey[7] and Maxine Molyneux[8] have examined the Chinese and Nicaraguan revolutions, respectively, pointing out the complexities and paradoxes of gendered ideology, movement mobilization, and state structure. Both studies show the uneasy coexistence of traditional ideologies about women's proper place within revolutionary socialist ideologies about women's emancipation. Molyneux shows how the *Frente Sandinista de Liberacion Nacional* (Sandinista National Liberation Front, FSLN) "politicized traditional roles of women, but did not dissolve them."[9] She takes issue with the view that women's interests are simply denied representation or deliberately marginalized in socialist revolutions. Stacey elucidates the reciprocal process whereby family structure and ideology shaped the Chinese revolution and the ideology and structure of the revolution shaped the family as a social institution.[10] Both Molyneux and Stacey reveal the complex, gendered intersection of family, religion, and state in the processes and outcomes of revolutions.

While there is a wide variety of research on the Mexican revolution, very few studies focus on how women participated in and shaped revolutionary ideology and organization or how the ideology and organization of the revolution affected women.[11] None of this research links family, state, and religion as gendered structures which shaped the revolution and were shaped by it. While some studies focus on *marianismo* (the cult of feminine obligation and sacrifice) and *machismo* (the cult of masculinity), these constructions of gender are conceived either as ideological packages internalized by men and women that guide behaviors, or as part of an unchanging Mexican national character or culture that determines political debate and action.

Here we examine the ways in which gender, class, ethnicity, and region intersected in Mexico to create a revolutionary situation shaped by family, church, and state. Our analysis concentrates on how the Mexican revolution had contradictory impacts on family, church, and state and on the systemic relations between them. *Marianismo, machismo,* nationalism, and anti-clericism provided threads which were woven into a multi-textured fabric of revolutionary and counter-revolutionary mobilization grounded in family-church-state relations. We show how the Mexican women's movement and the Mexican revolution meshed and clashed ideologically and organizationally by focusing on the issue of women's suffrage which permeated debate and action for both movements from 1910 to 1953. In sum, our chapter has two purposes: first, to understand better how gender and class structured the Mexican revolution, and second, to elaborate a framework for studying revolution which sees gender as a fundamental feature of social structure underlying the intersection of family, religion, and the state.

REVOLUTION AS PROCESS

If we define revolutions as Theda Skoçpol does—"social revolutions are rapid, basic transformations of a society's state and class structure; they are accompanied and in part carried through by class-based revolts from below"—we are, perhaps implicitly, making two assumptions that impede our understanding of revolutions. Remedying the first assumption is the focus of this book. Skoçpol's definition does not mention, let alone emphasize, how gender and family structure either shape or are changed by revolutions. Rather, the emphasis is on class structure and the state. The second assumption becomes especially clear when considered in light of the first one. Skoçpol, Samuel Huntington, and myriad other theorists of revolution assume successful fundamental change or basic transformation. In fact, the revolutions that these analysts examine were successful at unseating existing regimes and instituting new forms of state organization. Yet to argue that the cases constituted fundamental change in ideology and structure of society is quite different from defining revolution as an attempt to bring about such change. This distinction becomes even more important when we conceive of gender as well as class as a basic feature of social structure. It is one thing for an organization or coalition which is comprised of, or represents, or claims to represent, peasants or the working class to take state power. It is quite another to change the structure of a society. As both Molyneux and Stacey show, revolutions which technically fit Huntington's or Skoçpol's definitions do not necessarily mean a revolution in the social organization of gender.

Our conception of revolution as a process and as an attempt to change the basic ideologies, organizations, and institutions that comprise a society allows us to examine processes and outcomes which are sometimes taken for granted. Central to our inquiry are questions about how church and state intersect with ideology about the family to provide conditions for a revolutionary transformation, and how attempts at such fundamental change have intended and unintended consequences.

Revolutionary ideology and mobilization may refer formally to gender, either in terms of inclusion of both men and women or inclusion of men only, or to ethnicity or class. Our job as analysts is to look for these patterns and to explain their presence and their absence. Instead of assuming success as many definitions of revolution do, we prefer to conceptualize revolution as a process whereby traditionally subordinate groups engage in transforming the culture and structure of power relations within a society. Unlike many analysts of revolution, especially those of the modernization school, we do not assume that revolution necessarily leads to an improvement in women's situation. Rather, we examine how the revolutionary situation and the revolutionary outcome are related to the social organization of gender. Our analysis here will focus on gender as shaping and being shaped by the Mexican revolution within the context of Mexico and within the context of the world system.

SEX-GENDER SYSTEMS AND REVOLUTIONARY PROCESS

Recent studies of revolution have also emphasized their international context, but gender has been ignored in most of these analyses too. This omission is unfortunate, not only because it obscures women's active roles in revolutions, but because it also steers us away from seeing gender inequality as reproduced, even enhanced, by the outcomes of some revolutions. This prevents us from understanding revolutions just as the earlier failure to consider imperialism and the world system as important agents gave us faulty models of causes, mobilization, and outcomes of revolution.

Stacey and Molyneux used frameworks from feminist theory to analyze revolutions just as scholars have used feminist theory to analyze development. This work shows how sex-gender systems intersect with the social organization of production in a capitalist world system to produce specific outcomes for women, families, and states. Gayle Rubin first developed the concept of a sex-gender system to focus attention on the way in which the biological dimorphism of human reproduction becomes socially constructed into gender as a status and therefore as a set of social relationships.[12] This "set of arrangements by which a society transforms biological sexuality into products of human activity and in which these transformed sexual needs are satisfied" can only be understood by examining the interaction of a variety of social institutions, not simply the family, at a specific point in history.[13]

Rubin argues that any sex-gender system constructs two genders by culturally, socially, and politically exaggerating differences between women and men and by suppressing similarities between them. At the same time, similarities among women and among men are exaggerated. Thus, as variation between groups is ideologically maximized, variation within groups is ideologically minimized. This dichotomous construction encourages a gendered division of labor to develop in the family, the economy, and the state. The goal of a sex-gender system is the social control of women's sexuality, especially their biological reproductive capacity. None of the three elements of a sex-gender system necessarily causes the other two. Rather, they are linked reciprocally.

We can incorporate Rubin's conception of sex-gender systems with Michelle Rosaldo's classic analysis of public and domestic spheres to gain a richer picture of the intersection of ideology and structure. Rosaldo argues that cultural placement of the public spheres of economy, state, and church above constructions of the domestic sphere of family provide a basis for stratification, particularly of authority relations.[14] The ideology of separate spheres is a dominant feature of modern Western societies. It is echoed structurally as a greater distance between home and work than existed or was noted in the pre-Renaissance west. However, the concept of sex-gender systems stresses that gender is a fundamental feature of social organization, not simply a biological fact or a dimension of family life. This means that family, economy, and state intersect and interact with each other, both at the macrolevel of institutional life and at the microlevel of face-to-face interaction.[15]

Precisely how family, economy, state, and church actually intersect has been a focus of debate among feminist theorists. Rejecting the modernist view in the social sciences that holds that the family and personal life more generally are distinct and separate from politics and the economy, these debates have focused around whether the mode of production in a given society is causally prior to the social organization of gender.[16] They also consider whether and how states structure sex-gender systems or vice versa,[17] and how capitalism and systems of male domination structure states, economies, and/or families.[18]

These debates parallel the debates about states and capitalism and about states and civil society.[19] Just as Poulantzas's conception of the relative autonomy of the state has proven particularly useful in both theoretical and empirical work,[20] so the conception of the relative autonomy of sex-gender systems from both the state and the economy provides a useful framework for investigating issues ranging from women and development through family leave policy in Western countries, policies dealing with battered women in both Western and Third World countries, and the Chinese revolution.[21] To say that sex-gender systems are relatively autonomous from the mode of production is to argue that the form that a historically specific sex-gender system takes is neither independent of nor completely determined by the specific structure of the economy. Rather the development of each in a given society is related. Likewise, sex-gender systems may be viewed as both shaping and shaped by the history and character of a given state. Thus, to use a framework of relative autonomy is to ask whether and how a historically specific social organization of gender, social organization of production, and social organization of political power are related, rather than to assume that a particular state structure determines family structure or vice versa.

One key question raised by the conception of sex-gender systems and their relative autonomy is that of differences and agency between and within genders. As post-modern feminist philosophers and political theorists point out, there is no such thing as "woman" or even "women's interests" (or "man" or "men's interests").[22] Rather, women's desires, needs, and interests are historically specific and structured by gender, class, race, and position in the world system.[23]

Molyneux uses this insight to distinguish among women's interests, strategic gender interests, and practical gender interests.[24] Women's interests are specific to particular class, ethnic, or age groups within a given society. They are revealed by specifying "how the various categories of women might be affected differently and act differently on account of the particularities of their social positioning and their chosen identities."[25] In contrast, strategic gender interests "are derived

. . . deductively . . . from an analysis of women's subordination and from the formulation of an alternative, more satisfactory set of arrangements."[26] Thus, they often take the form of broad reforms that question the structural basis of gender inequality: suffrage, legal reform of family law, freedom of choice over childbearing, and abolition of the gender division of labor. Practical gender interests are inductively derived and are usually formulated by individuals in concrete positions within the gendered division of labor. Practical gender interests challenge neither the division of labor itself nor gender inequality. For example, if within a given division of labor women are responsible for child nutrition and health, then they may articulate concerns about food subsidies, prenatal care, or immunizations. Policies aimed at these interests may alleviate some of the burden on women but will not question why women and not men are responsible for child care. Molyneux's three-fold distinction makes concrete the issue of reform versus structural change in sex-gender systems, providing one way of analyzing state policy and revolutionary outcomes.

We examine the ideology that underpins the sex-gender system and constitutes its first element—the exaggeration of difference and suppression of similarity. We show that class and regional differences in ideology, interests, and mobilization during and after the Mexican revolution were shaped by the sex-gender system and by conflicts among women's interests and between strategic and practical gender interests. The ideology of separate spheres which took the form of *marianismo* and *machismo* shaped the diversity of women's interests and the deep divisions among them as well as strategic and practical interests. Mobilization processes both reflected and reproduced these divisions, particularly the mobilization around women's suffrage. We focus on suffrage as a key issue and strategic interest.

Feminist political theorists have argued that the instability of the state is linked to perceptions of "women's conservative nature,"[27] leading revolutionary movements to subordinate women's interests and gender interests to broader or basic goals of emancipation. During the period from the 1917 Constitutional Convention to the series of defeats for women's suffrage in the late 1930s and 1940s, shifting alliances, characteristic of a revolutionary situation, emerged in Mexico. Women's suffrage was seen as a direct threat to the power of the ruling party.

This process of strategic maneuvering by the Mexican state in relation to feminist demands for suffrage was a key element in the development of a corporatist state in Mexico. Corporatist states aim explicitly at restricting interest articulation and aggregation in society.[28] While corporatist systems vary in the ways and degrees by which they restrict interest representation, they all set discernable limits on associational life.[29] For example, Philippe Schmitter distinguishes between state corporatist systems which deploy highly restrictive statutory and political sanctions to shape associational behavior, and societal corporatist systems which offer an array of less coercive inducements and constraints to channel interest representation in ways that legitimize the state.

The Mexican corporatist state that emerged during the administration of President Lazaro Cárdenas (1934–1940) is aptly described by Rose Spalding as a variant of state corporatism featuring the following characteristics, "(1) a relatively cohesive and autonomous state apparatus; (2) state creation, differentiation, and orchestration of the organizations for sectoral participation, and (3) state responsibility for pursuing national development goals."[30] Structured as a set of four vertically organized sectoral organizations (the institutionalized military, labor, peasants, and middle-class organizations allied with the state), Mexican state corporatism provided an effective integrating mechanism for channeling political interests and a powerful instrument for executive management of the political system. However, despite feminist demands that women be recognized as a distinct sector within the governing party, and notwithstanding various policy concessions to feminists by the Mexican state, the Cárdenas administration did not accord women such status. Gender and women's interests were subsumed under those of peasants, workers, and middle-class organizations, giving strategic gender interests a lower priority on the state's agenda.

Women's interests, however, were not the only ones subsumed under the official sectoral organizations or excluded from political representation. Big business, particularly foreign investors, and the Catholic Church were also denied formal representation. Within the party, business interests were globally viewed as anti-populist, anti-nationalist, exploitative manipulators of capital requiring the strong regulation of the state. Business interests were incorporated directly in government policymaking, however, through the creation of mandatory commercial and industrial associations licensed by the state.[31] For its part, the Catholic Church was regarded as the institutional defender of the old pre-revolutionary order and an enemy of the secular state. The Mexican revolution's anti-clerical strain was the strongest in Latin America, generating sedition and civil rebellion throughout the 1920s by Catholic ecclesiastics and laypeople opposed to secularizing trends.[32]

Both Jack Goldstone and Skoçpol argue that the major outcome of modern revolutions is the consolidation of the state in a much stronger form.[33] In Mexico, consolidation into a corporatist state meant that the church was less of a threat to state power than during the revolutionary situation. Simultaneously, it appears that many organizations of workers, peasants, and women (and the interests pursued by them), were institutionalized. Thus, by the early 1950s, suffrage for women no longer posed a threat to regime power for the ruling party.

A BRIEF HISTORY OF THE REVOLUTIONARY SITUATION IN MEXICO

The Mexican Civil Code of 1884 so dramatically limited women's rights in the home, employment, and politics that one early Mexican feminist, Genaro García, concluded that Mexican law in the early twentieth century "sustains an almost incredible inequality between the conditions of husband and wife, restricts in an exaggerated and arbitrary manner those rights due the woman, and . . . erases and nullifies her personality."[34] The Civil Code and other manifestations of the sex-gender system which prompted this comment had developed along with class, ethnic, and regional inequalities during the presidency of Porfirio Díaz (1876–1910). During the Porfiriato, modernization took the shape that was to characterize attempts at development in other Latin American countries: economic and political benefits for a small, wealthy elite and a downward spiral of poverty for peasants and workers. Buttressing this uneven development was the ideology of positivism which borrowed from social Darwinism. The positivists, called *científicos* by their critics, saw themselves as natural elites. Allied with the *científicos* were foreign investors and the Catholic Church. Shirlene Soto provides this summary of the consequences of the Díaz regime.

> By 1910, Díaz's three-and-one-half decade rule had resulted in vast differences in personal wealth, a closed political system run by a privileged few, and flagrant favoritism toward foreigners. It had also resulted in the deep alienation of large numbers of Mexican intellectuals, workers, and even some business owners and haciendados (owners of ranches and large estates). Thus, by 1910, there was widespread clamor for change, which led ultimately to the overthrow of Díaz and to the Mexican Revolution.[35]

During the period leading up to Díaz's forced resignation, a variety of women's organizations emerged and played a decisive role in his overthrow. Among the first was *La Siempreviva* founded in 1870 in Merida.[36] *La Siempreviva* published a newspaper by the same name and attempted to increase educational opportunities for women.[37] Also, before the turn of the century, working-class women formed both grassroots and regional associations, usually after participating in strikes. *Hijas de Anáhuac* was founded by female textile workers in 1907.[38] It supported revolution as a vehicle for social change and improved conditions for women. Several feminist organizations, such as *Sociedad Protectorade La Mujer* and *Las Admiradores de Juárez,* appeared in 1904. They promoted women's rights, opposed Díaz, and published many journals and magazines.

In the period between Díaz's forced resignation (1910) and the Constitutional Congress (1917), a wide variety of groups and publications emerged which advocated equality for women as an integral element of the Mexican revolution. The first Feminist Congress was convened in January 1916.[39] It had the full support of former general, then governor of Yucatan, Salvador Alvarado. Debate among factions at the Congress foreshadowed issues that would continue to divide the Mexican women's movement for political and social equality through the 1950s. Three basic ideological positions emerged among the seven hundred delegates: (1) Catholic conservative women wished to maintain traditional wife and mother roles, seeing any threat to the institutional status quo as a threat to women, (2) moderate women saw educational opportunities as the road to political rights and civic participation yet also sought to maintain traditional wife and mother roles, (3) radicals argued that women should be included equally in all areas of social life and should have the same sexual freedom as men.[40] Although moderates and radicals disagreed vehemently on sex education in schools, they concurred in their views that the Civil Code of 1884 should be drastically revised. By the end of the Congress, a consensus supported the opening of all fields of employment to women and the permitting of women to be civically active. After debating whether women were ready for suffrage, and what suffrage would mean for family life, a petition supporting suffrage was passed.[41]

In December 1916, the Constitutional Congress convened in the midst of a three-way civil war among President Venustiano Carranza's constitutionalist coalition, northern populist forces under Francisco (Pancho) Villa, and agrarian reformers led by Emiliano Zapata in the south. Radical delegates, convinced that the Church's influence would be strengthened by giving women the right to vote, opposed suffrage. Conservative delegates supported women's suffrage. In the end, Articles 34 and 35 stipulated that citizenship, suffrage, and holding public office would include only men. However, Article 123 of the Constitution entitled working women to childbirth benefits and obligated employers to provide maternity leave with pay.[42] In April 1917, President Carranza issued the law of family relations to augment his 1914 legalization of divorce. Although the 1917 legislation gave women the right to draw up contracts and provided for equal custody of children, it prevented married women from engaging in a business or profession without their husbands' consent and prohibited unmarried women under the age of thirty from leaving their parents' homes except to marry. For the next thirty years, the issue of suffrage and the relationship between women's rights, family, church, and state dominated the political debate about the strategies and goals of the revolution.

Arguments about women's essentially conservative nature and their strong support of the Church took on added weight during the 1920s. In response to anti-clerical provisions in the 1917 Constitution, the Catholic Church founded the *Unión de Damas Catalieq* in 1920. This organization was intended to provide an alternative to independent feminist organizations and those aligned with unions such as the *Confederación Revolucionario Obrero Mexicano* (CROM), an important labor syndicate. Similarly, *Acción Social Católica* (Catholic Social Action, a coordinating group for Church political activities) organized a separate labor union, *Confederación Nacional Católica de Trabajar* (National Catholic Labor Confederation), in 1922. Together *Unión de Damas* and the *Confederación Nacional Católica de Trabajar* advanced an ideology and social policy which opposed socialism and feminism. Through both organizations, the church crystallized its position: "the woman, from the moment she becomes a worker, ceases to be a woman" but women's political participation could strengthen the home.[43]

In 1926, the conflict between the constitutionalist government and the Church erupted into civil war. The *Cristero* rebellion, which persisted through 1929, pitted radical Catholics in west-central Mexico, particularly in the conservative state of Jalisco, against President Alvaro Obregón and his anti-clerical and secularist reforms. Independent *Brigadas Femininas* (Feminine Brigades) were crucial in sustaining *Cristero* armies in the field.[44] The *Cristero* rebellion inspired Obregón's assassination by a Catholic fanatic in 1928. However, the underlying opposition to feminism, socialism, and secular education, especially sex education, continued to simmer beneath the surface until the late 1930s.[45]

In the wake of the *Cristero* rebellion, the Obregón assassination, and the trials of the accused assassins (one was a Catholic woman), the

Partido Nacional Revolucionario (PNR) was formed in 1929. Its platform included two planks emphasizing women's rights: (1) the full right of women to participate in political life, and (2) full incorporation of peasant women—campesinas—into economic life.

Within the PNR, a separate women's party, the *Partido Feminista Revolucionario,* organized a series of National Women's Congresses. The first Congress of Women Workers and Peasants began on 31 October 1931. Debates among the seven hundred delegates focused on ideology and organization. Some took the position that women needed separate political organizations so that their interests as female workers or peasants would not be neglected by unions or peasant organizations. Others contended that feminism could not achieve its ends without socialist liberation. A proposal for a nationwide women's organization that would include campesinas and workers and would establish formal relations with CROM and another syndicate, the *Confederación General de Trabajo* (CGT), was adopted. The second (1933) and third (1934) National Congresses held debates centering on such issues as minimum wages for women, land reform which would include women, and legal protection for female workers. The issue of suffrage was raised and unanimously supported at each of these congresses.

During the same month and year as the third National Congress of Women Workers and Peasants (September 1934), *Acción Social Católica* organized a mass demonstration of thirty thousand women in Mexico City protesting socialist education and government anti-clerical policies.[46] This demonstration was a reaction to the strategies proposed by Lazaro Cárdenas, the PNR's presidential candidate. Cárdenas had explicitly offered women the prospect of increased political participation and suffrage in exchange for their support of his candidacy.[47]

After he became president, Cárdenas pledged to support a nationwide campaign for women's suffrage. In September 1935, he approved the incorporation of the *Partido Feminista Revolucionaria* into the PNR as a women's wing of the party. Under the new name of *Acción Feminina,* this wing was intended to facilitate the incorporation of women into civil and political life and the attainment of equal rights for women. The first person to head the organization was opposed by leftist women who saw her as unable to represent campesinas and working-class women, so Cárdenas replaced her.[48] Shirlene Soto finds that

> several members of his cabinet were strongly supportive of women's rights. The Ministry of Agriculture (directed by Tomás Garrido Canabal), the Ministry of Communications (directed by

> Francisco Múgica) and the Ministry of Public Education (headed by Gonzálo Vasquez Vela) established women's associations, and women served on the staffs of these ministries.[49]

Outside the PNR and the state, women organized the *Frente Unico Para los Derechos del Mujer* (Sole Front for Women's Rights, FUPDM) in 1935. The FUPDM argued that full suffrage and the right to hold office were only the first steps in a broader quest for female equality. The FUPDM's leaders were associated with Mexico's left. They were supported by such influential socialists as Francisco Múgica, and included María del Refugio (Cuca) García, who had long been a feminist leader whose constituents were campesinas and workers; Soledad Orozco Avila, a participant in the Red Battalions during the civil war phase of the Revolution; and the prominent Mexican artist and feminist, Frida Kahlo. According to Lillian Fisher, by 1939 the FUPDM had "a membership of more than 50,000 women of all social classes, even pure-blooded Indians, and includ[ed] some eight hundred organizations."[50]

Yet by this same year the issue of national women's suffrage appeared to be a lost cause in Mexico. Women had been granted the right to vote in party primaries and in some states (Guanajuato, Puebla, Veracruz, Durango, Tamaulipus, and Hidalgo). But internal PNR power struggles and ramifications of the Spanish Civil War had become central issues for Cárdenas. The experience of the Spanish republic rekindled qualms about women's suffrage. In Spain, the Church literally controlled women's votes in the 1933 election (the first in which women could vote), leading to a serious electoral defeat for the Spanish Socialist Party.

In 1937, Cuca García and Soledad Orozco Avila were selected in PNR primaries as candidates for the chamber of deputies. Both women won. The PNR National Executive Committee subsequently ruled that a constitutional amendment would be required before women could vote or run in national elections.[51] When the chamber of deputies overturned the women's victories, Orozco and García commenced a hunger strike outside Cárdenas's home. In response to the strike and an outpouring of mail, Cárdenas, in November 1937, sent the Senate an amendment to Article 34 which provided for women's suffrage. In his statement, he argued that women would be more susceptible to church influence if they remained outside electoral politics.[52] The Mexican Confederation of Labor (CTM) and feminist organizations strongly supported the bill. However, by December, the chamber of deputies adjourned having taken no action.

Despite this setback, the feminist agenda continued to advance incrementally within the PNR which, in 1938, was reorganized along corporatist lines and renamed the Mexican Revolutionary Party (PRM). Under the new arrangement, *Acción Feminina* was restructured, though retaining its name, as a department within the PRM's new popular sector which catered to middle-class interests.[53] In its new incarnation, *Acción Feminina* also sent delegates to other sectoral organizations representing the military, the campesino, and labor divisions of the PRM. Within the PRM, moreover, women were extended the right to run for office and the right to vote in PRM primary elections—not insignificant considering the PRM's domination of the Mexican electoral process—though the legislature's earlier rejection of the García-Orozco victory clouded the question.[54] The feminist wing of the PRM's popular sector was heavily influenced by the leftist leadership of the FUPDM which continued to lobby vigorously for full suffrage.

In 1938, having consolidated and reorganized the party, Cárdenas nationalized the holdings of seventeen foreign oil companies. This move led to an international crisis which mobilized the Mexican nation to unite behind the president. Soto suggests that women's participation in and contributions to solving the crisis may have led Cárdenas to call a special session of Congress to consider the women's suffrage amendment.[55] Because no one was willing openly to defy the president, the amendment was unanimously approved on 6 July 1938, and referred to the states for ratification. Supporting the amendment, Cárdenas proclaimed to the nation "only the Revolution . . . has achieved for the Mexican woman a complete rescue from her social inferiority, obtaining the constitutional reform necessary to grant her rights and functions of citizenship that put her on the same plane of dignity with man."[56] A majority of states ratified the amendment by the end of the year. But, in May 1939, Congress adjourned having taken no action, even though all twenty-eight states had passed the amendment.

Twice more feminists tried to pressure the PRM and Congress to vote on the amendment. In September, Cárdenas made a speech advocating passage, but still no action was taken. *Acción Feminina* and a coalition of feminist organizations sent Cárdenas a telegram on 24 March 1940, asking him to call a special session of Congress and to designate women's suffrage as the sole issue to be debated. Cárdenas refused to call the session. Shortly thereafter, Mexico turned its attention to World War II. Suffrage was not considered again until 1946 when Mexican women won the right to vote in municipal elections on 31 December. "Seven years later, 31 December 1953, after the church and state had arrived at a *modus vivendi*, and the PRI was firmly in control of Mexican politics, women were granted national suffrage."[57] They first voted in the 1958 presidential election.[58]

Why did the 1939 constitutional initiative fail? It seems clear in retrospect that Cárdenas's initiative to extend the vote to Mexican women was ultimately undone by political infighting and maneuvering associated with the troubled 1940 presidential election. The fledgling PRM was still fragile at the top. Unlike later presidents, who would come to exercise virtually unchallenged authority over the designation of their successors, Cárdenas could scarcely afford to provoke a bitter struggle over the succession among the party's factions. Cárdenas's reforms, in fact, had generated considerable opposition within and beyond the party, particularly among the middle classes.[59] Opposition had increased in the last two years of his presidency, as Nora Hamilton observes,

> taking various forms, including the formation of anti-government groups by old revolutionary generals; the growth of the *Sinarquista* movement—a militant pro-clerical sect—among the peasants of western Mexico; the establishment of the conservative, pro-catholic *Partido de Acción Nacional* (PAN); and finally, the emergence or re-emergence of fascist groups, aided and promoted by German agents and members of the Spanish Falange in Mexico, which added an international dimension to the right-wing offensive.[60]

PRM activists coalesced around the pre-candidacies of two leading party figures, radicals supporting the leftist minister of communications, Francisco Múgica, and party conservatives supporting past-president Emilio Portes Gil. Múgica, a close ally of the president and co-author of several of the 1917 Constitution's most progressive articles, was preferred by many feminists, but he was totally unacceptable to many leading members of the military sector of the PRM. Portes Gil, however, was not committed to Cárdenas's social and political reforms. Thus Cárdenas was persuaded to nominate Manuel Avila Camacho, his secretary of defense, as a national unity candidate capable of assuaging military concerns while simultaneously continuing to support the reform agenda.[61] Of all the various pre-candidates, Avila Camacho was the only one who was not opposed by at least two sectors of the PRM.[62]

Cárdenas's nomination of Avila Camacho notwithstanding, the 1940 presidential election remained contentious. Considerable support within the PRM gravitated towards the candidacy of General Juan Andreu Almazán, political maverick, wealthy landowner, and former commander in the Seventh Military Zone encompassing the northern state of Nuevo Leon.[63] Dissidents on both the right and the left of the party, as well as many Catholics and members of the business community, found refuge in Almazán's *Partido Revolucionaria de Unificación Nacional* (PRUN). At least thirty-four generals took leave to campaign actively for Almazán, indicating strong support for his candidacy within military ranks.[64] A number of leftists, disillusioned by Múgica's unwillingness to mount an independent candidacy, also threw their support to Almazán.[65] Almazán's anti-socialist message also had considerable resonance with women, many of whom joined his banner under the auspices of the *Partido Feminina Idealista* (Feminine Idealist Party) and campaigned actively for his election.[66]

Although the PRM controlled the electoral machinery and the ballot boxes, the military still enjoyed a preponderance of force and party leaders feared a possible coup. In the end, however, the PRM prevailed. Avila Camacho's conservative appeal, his defusing of religious opposition with his famous declaration, "*yo soy creyente*" (I am a believer), his ability to attract substantial military support, and the PRM's mastery over the ballot boxes produced a highly questionable and lopsided victory. Avila Camacho was reported to have garnered 2,265,199 votes to Almazán's 128,574.

Avila Camacho's victory marked the end of an era. With it, the Revolution shifted rightward, away from further socialist reformism. The PRM's triumph, however, provided the political momentum for the consolidation of the institutional changes set in place by Cárdenas and the preservation of key policy reforms. In this context, Cárdenas's unwillingness to push the suffrage amendment through the Mexican Congress in 1939 may plausibly be attributed to his unwillingness to jeopardize the prospects for institutionalizing his reform agenda in the face of conservative reaction and the serious threat of a rupture within the PRM itself.

ANALYSIS AND CONCLUSION

The history of Mexican women's struggle for suffrage during the revolutionary and post-revolutionary eras vividly illustrates the power of the sex-gender system in shaping the revolutionary situation and the revolutionary outcome in Mexican politics.[67] Throughout the revolutionary process, during both its violent and consolidationist phases, women mobilized in support of revolutionary forces and became an important component of the dominant—constitutionalist—governing coalition. While women wrested a variety of reforms which furthered practical gender interests from the dominant party coalition, their demands for basic structural reforms, most particularly their demand for full suffrage at the national level, were denied, even during the most progressive phase of the revolutionary situation—the Cárdenas presidency. The failure of women's demands for suffrage is consistently attributable to a characterization of the masses of women, as compared to the progressive political vanguard of socialist feminist women, as conservative, pro-clerical, and a threat to the consolidation of basic nongendered structural reforms. Political opposition to this perceived threat was institutionalized by the marginalization of women's groups and strategic gender interests in the formation of the corporatist state in Mexico.

Fears in the 1930s that civil war might erupt anew—the Spanish Civil War was a vivid reminder of what might befall—reflected assumptions that women's political positions were inherently conservative and domestically oriented. Divisions within the women's movement itself were seized upon by opponents of suffrage to reinforce these characterizations. As late as the Avila Camacho-Almazán presidential contest in 1940, conservative women were prominent among those opposing Cárdenas's structural reforms. The visibility of church-sponsored conservative women's organizations such as the *Unión de Damas Catalieq*, and those allied with anti-socialist causes and parties like the *Partido Feminina Idealista,* made women appear to be a realistic threat to the PRM. Although *Acción Feminina* and the FUPDM were larger in membership than either the Catholic women's groups or *Feminina Idealista,* the 1938 reorganization of the PNR into the PRM weakened the feminist organizations. *Acción Feminina*'s influence was institutionalized yet simultaneously diluted because it was formally incorporated into only one of the corporatist sectors. In particular, its alliance with the labor and peasant sectors seemed weaker. The FUPDM continued to be a lobbying presence due to its sheer size. However, it was marginalized when its ally Múgica was passed over for the 1940 presidential candidacy and suffrage and women's rights generally were no longer issues embodied in party debates, positions, or platforms.

This case illustrates how a sex-gender system shaped the development of the Mexican revolution and thus the Mexican corporatist state. Constructions of gender as a rigid dichotomy according to which women were defined as fundamentally conservative because of their religiosity and their primary role as mothers cast all women as enemies of change. Such stereotyping and universalizing of woman were remarkably stubborn despite radical women's participation in the revolution and the visibility of the FUPDM. From the Constitutional Congress and the *Cristero* period (whose events added credence to the construction of women as conservative) to the 1930s when various coalitions jockeyed for entry into and control of the state, the social construction of women as highly religious and emotionally tied to the role of mother was a potent force in marginalizing women's groups and strategic gender interests.

The reorganization of the PNR into the PRM in 1938 relegated *Acción Feminina* into a department within the middle-class sector and effectively muted its potential power. Previously, both *Acción Feminina* and the FUPDM had attempted, ideologically and organizationally, to combine the various practical interests of working-class, peasant, and middle-class women into a set of strategic gender interests to be represented in the corporatist state. But the consolidation of the state under Cárdenas subsumed practical and strategic gender interests under the popular (middle-class) sector, consequently marginalizing and further dividing women as an interest group.

These developments during the revolutionary process consolidated corporatist state power as Goldstone would predict. They simultaneously altered and strengthened the existing sex-gender system much as Judith Stacey found in the Chinese case. Materialist ideology, the presumed strong identification of women with family and church, and a presumption of their lack of interest in and knowledge about the economy dovetailed with the need of the PRM to consolidate state power against conservative, church-supported threats. Practical and strategic gender interests were not a footnote to the revolution; rather our examination of them helps illuminate the revolution as a state-making process.

The Mexican case confirms the hypothesis of feminist political theorists that modern revolutionary movements tend to subordinate women's interests to broader or basic emancipatory objectives on the grounds of women's presumed conservatism. The perpetuation of such notions and the force of their appeal even to proponents of structural reforms intended to further the strategic gender interests of women is compelling evidence of the relative autonomy and power of sex-gender systems to shape revolutionary situations. Our analysis of the Mexican case thus lends strong support to the argument that sex-gender systems should be considered an essential object of inquiry as scholars undertake to clarify our understanding of revolution as a modern social, economic, and political phenomenon. Indeed, the social organization of gender played a key role in shaping the ideology and mobilization of the Mexican revolution, just as the revolution reshaped, but did not transform, the social organization of gender in Mexico.

NOTES

1. Edna Acosta-Belen and Christine E. Bose, "From Structural Subordination to Empowerment: Women and Development in Third World Countries," *Gender and Society* 4 (1990): 299–320.

2. Iris Young, "Beyond the Unhappy Marriage: A Critique of the Dual System," in *Women and Revolution: A Discussion of the Unhappy Marriage of Marxism and Feminism*, ed. Lydia Sargent (Boston: South End Press, 1981), 43–70.

3. See, for instance, Jack Goldstone, *Revolutions: Theoretical, Comparative, and Historical Studies* (New York: Harcourt Brace Jovanovich, 1986); Mark Hagopian, *The Phenomenon of Revolution* (New York: Dodd, Mead, 1974); Samuel P. Huntington, *Political Order in Changing Societies* (New Haven: Yale University Press, 1968); Michael Kimmel, *Revolution: A Sociological Interpretation* (Philadelphia: Temple University Press, 1990); Theda Skoçpol, *States and Social Revolutions* (Cambridge: Cambridge University Press, 1979); Charles Tilly, *From Mobilization to Revolution* (Reading, Mass..: Addison Wesley Press, 1978).

4. For example, see Acosta-Belen and Bose, "From Structural Subordination to Empowerment"; Esther Boserup, *Women's Role in Economic Development* (New York: St. Martin's Press, 1970); Maria Mies, *Patriarchy and Accumulation on a World Scale: Women in the International Division of Labor* (London: Zed Press, 1986); Kathryn Ward, ed., *Women Workers and Global Restructuring* (Ithaca: ILO Press, 1990).

5. Zillah Eisenstein, *Feminism and Sexual Equality* (New York: Monthly Review Press, 1984); Linda Gordon, *Women, the State, and Welfare* (Madison: University of Wisconsin Press, 1990); Catherine A MacKinnon, "Feminism, Marxism, Method and the State: Towards a Feminist Jurisprudence," *Signs* 8 (1983): 635–58; Carole Pateman, *The Disorder of Women: Democracy, Feminism, and Political Theory* (Stanford: Stanford University Press, 1989); Mary Ruggie, *The State and Working Women* (Princeton: Princeton University Press, 1984).

6. Sue Ellen M. Charlton, Jana Everett, and Kathleen Staudt, *Women, the State and Development* (Albany: SUNY Press, 1989); Cynthia Enloe, *Bananas, Beaches, and Bases: Making Feminist Sense of International Relations* (Berkeley: University of California Press, 1989); Jane Jaquette, "Female Political Participation in Latin America," in *Sex and Class in Latin America*, ed. Helen Icken Safa (New York: Praeger, 1976); Sheila Rowbatham, *Women, Resistance and Revolution* (New York: Vintage Press, 1972).

7. Judith Stacey, *Patriarchy and Socialist Revolution in China* (Berkeley: University of California Press, 1983).

8. Maxine Molyneux, "Mobilization without Emancipation?" *Feminist Studies* 11 (1985): 227–54.

9. Ibid., 228.

10. Stacey, *Patriarchy and Socialist Revolution in China*, 8, 11, 12, 258.

11. Shirlene Soto, *The Emergence of the Modern Mexican Woman* (Denver: Arden Press, 1990); Anna Macias, *Against All Odds: The Feminist Movement in Mexico to 1940* (Westport, Conn.: Greenwood Press, 1982).

12. Gayle Rubin, "The Traffic in Women: Notes on a Political Economy of Sex," in *Towards an Anthropology of Women*, ed. Rayna Reiter (New York: Monthly Review Press, 1975).

13. Ibid, 159.

14. Michelle Z. Rosaldo, "Women, Culture, and Society: A Theoretical Overview," in *Women, Culture, and Society*, ed. Michelle Z. Rosaldo and Louise Lamphere (Stanford: Stanford University Press, 1974).

15. Feminist theory and research in a multitude of disciplines have used this broad framework implicitly or explicitly to examine how public and domestic spheres are both shaped by gender, class, and ethnicity and how both interact together to produce social order or social change in individuals' lives and in macrolevel patterns. However, Stacey's study of the Chinese revolution is the only study which explicitly uses this framework.

16. Iris Young, "Beyond the Unhappy Marriage"; Heidi Hartmann, "The Unhappy Marriage of Marxism and Feminism," in *Women and Revolution*, 1–42; Michelle Barrett, *Women's Oppression Today: Problems in Marxist Feminist Analysis* (London: New Left Books, 1980).

17. Zillah R. Eisenstein, *Feminism and Sexual Equality* (New York: Monthly Review Press, 1984); MacKinnon, "Feminism, Marxism, Method and the State"; Mies, *Patriarchy and Accumulation on a World Scale.*

18. Rowbatham, *Women, Resistance, and Revolution*; Mies, *Patriarchy and Accumulation on a World Scale*; MacKinnon, "Feminism, Marxism, Method and the State: Towards a Feminist Jurisprudence."

19. Fred Block, "The Ruling Class Does Not Rule," *Socialist Revolution* 33 (1977): 6–28; William G. Domhoff, *The Power Elite and the State: How Policy is Made in America* (New York: Aldine Press, 1990); Erik Olin Wright, *Class, Crisis, and the State* (London: New Left Books, 1978); David Gold, Clarence Y. H. Lo, and Erik Olin Wright, "Recent Developments in Marxist Theory of the State," *Monthly Review* 27 (1975): 36–51.

20. Nicos Poulantzas, *Political Power and Social Classes* (London: New Left Books, 1973). For examples of writings based on this concept, see Domhoff, *The Power Elite and the State*; Block, "The Ruling Class Does Not Rule"; Wright, *Class, Crisis, and the State.*

21. Diane Mitsch Bush, "The Capitalist State and the Social Organization of Gender," paper presented at the annual meeting of the American Sociological Association, Chicago, Ill., 1986; Nancy Chodorow, *The Reproduction of Mothering: Psychoanalysis and the Sociology of Gender* (Berkeley: University of California Press, 1989); Gordon, *Women, the State, and Welfare*; Ruggie, *The State and Working Women*; Ward, *Women Workers and Global Restructuring.*

22. For summaries, see Zillah R. Eisenstein, *The Female Body and the Law* (Berkeley: University of California Press, 1988); Nancy Fraser, *Unruly Practices: Power, Discourse, and Gender in Contemporary Social Theory* (Minneapolis: University of Minnesota Press, 1989); Pateman, *The Disorder of Women*; Linda

Nicholson, *Feminism/Postmodernism* (New York: Routledge Press, 1990).

23. Acosta-Belen and Bose, "From Structural Subordination to Empowerment"; Sargent, ed., *Women and Revolution*; Ward, *Women Workers and Global Restructuring*; Patricia Hill Collins, *Black Feminist Thought* (Boston: Unwin Hyman, 1991); Maxine Baca-Zinn, "Structural Transformation in Minority Families," in *Women Households and the Economy*, Lores Beneria and Catherine Stimpson (New Brunswick: Rutgers University Press, 1987), 155–71.

24. Molyneux, "Mobilization without Emancipation?" 232-33.

25. Ibid., 232.

26. Ibid.

27. See Charlton, *Women the State and Development*; Janet Siltanin and Michell Stanworth, *Women and the Public Sphere: A Critique of Sociology and Politics* (New York: St. Martin's Press, 1984). For further discussion focused on Latin America, see Molyneux, "Mobilization without Emancipation?"; Acosta-Belen and Bose, "From Structural Subordination to Empowerment"; Enloe, *Bananas, Beaches, and Bases*; Margaret E. Leahy, *Development Strategies and the Status of Women: A Comparative Study of the United States, Mexico, the Soviet Union, and Cuba* (Boulder: Lynne Rienner Press, 1986); Linda (Rife) Labao, "Women in Revolutionary Movements: Changing Patterns of Latin American Guerrilla Struggle," in *Women and Social Protest*, ed. Guida West and Rhoda Lois Blumberg (New York: Oxford University Press, 1990), 180–204.

28. On this point see, Phillipe Schmitter, "Still the Century of Corporatism," *Review of Politics* 33, no. 1 (January 1974): 85–131; and Douglas A. Chalmers, "Corporatism and Comparative Politics," in *New Directions in Comparative Politics*, ed. Howard J. Wiarda (Boulder: Westview Press, 1985), 56–79.

29. For discussion of state and societal corporatism, see Schmitter, "Still the Century of Corporatism." On the instruments of corporatist control, see Ruth Berins Collier and David Collier, "Inducements versus Constraints: Disaggregating 'Corporatism,'" *American Political Science Review* 73 (December 1979): 967–86.

30. Rose J. Spalding, "State Power and its Limits," *Comparative Political Studies* 14 (July 1981): 140.

31. On the incorporation of business interests within the state, see Frank Brandenburg, *The Making of Modern Mexico* (Englewood Cliffs, N.J.: Prentice Hall, 1964), 88–89.

32. For discussion, see Michael C. Meyer and William L. Sherman, *The Course of Mexican History* (New York: Oxford University Press, 1983), 587–92.

33. Goldstone, *Revolutions*, 13; Skoçpol, *States and Social Revolutions*.

34. Soto, *The Emergence of the Modern Mexican Woman*, 11.

35. Ibid, 8.

36. Ibid., 67; Janet Saltzman Chafetz, *Female Revolt: Women's Movements in World and Historical Perspective* (Totowa, N.J.: Rowman and Allenheld, 1986).

37. Like women's movements in other North American and Latin American countries in this period and slightly later in India, educational opportunities for middle-class women were an early demand around which pioneering middle-class movement organizations were founded.

38. Soto, *The Emergence of the Modern Mexican Woman*, 15.

39. Lillian Estelle Fisher, "The Influence of the Present Mexican Revolution Upon the Status of Women," *Hispanic American Historical Review* 22 (1942): 215.

40. By way of clarification, it should be noted that the majority of Congress delegates were probably Catholic believers, though many moderate and radical delegates sympathized with anti-clerical views and supported a broad construction of the secular powers of the state against the very narrow construction favored by Catholic conservatives. Differences between pro-clerical and anti-clerical Mexican Catholics was one of the most profound lines of social cleavage during and after the revolutionary era.

41. Soto, *The Emergence of the Modern Mexican Woman*, 70–77. A second Congress was held in November 1916 and was marked by heated debate on suffrage and what it would mean for home life. Delegates to this Congress also approved a petition for suffrage.

42. *Constitución Politica de los Estados Unidos Méxicanos* (Mexico, D.F.: Editorial Olguin, S.A. de C.V.), 134–49.

43. Father Medina, Society of Jesus, as quoted in Soto, *The Emergence of the Modern Mexican Woman*, 114.

44. The *Cristero* movement, whose field armies were no more than forty-five hundred strong by government estimates, nevertheless wrought considerable damage to life and property, provoking similar excesses in response by the government. For the role of women, see Barbara Miller, "Women and Revolution: The Brigadas Femininas and the Mexican Cristero Rebellion, 1926–1929," in *Women and Politics in Twentieth-Century Latin America*, ed. Sandra F. McGee (Williamsburg: Studies in Third World Societies, Department of Anthropology, College of William and Mary, 1981); Elizabeth Salas, *Soldaderas in the Mexican Military* (Austin: University of Texas Press, 1990), 49–50.

45. The *Cristero* rebellion was brutally suppressed by government forces under the direction of Plutarco Elias Calles and had largely subsided by 1930.

46. Soto, *The Emergence of the Modern Mexican Woman*, 111, 128.

47. Ibid, 123.

48. Ibid., 123–24.

49. Ibid., 124.

50. Fisher, "The Influence of the Present Mexican Revolution Upon the Status of Women," 220.

51. Soto, *The Emergence of the Modern Mexican Woman*, 129.

52. Ibid., 130.

53. Nathaniel Weyl and Sylvia Weyl, *The Reconquest of Mexico: The Years of Lazaro Cárdenas* (London: Oxford University Press, 1939). It is possible to view the incorporation of women into the popular sector (National Confederation of Popular Organizations, CNOP) as highly cooptative, actually diminishing their influence and power, certainly their autonomy, in relation to other social formations. Brandenburg, in *The Making of Modern Mexico*, notes that the CNOP was structured as a catch-all category of associations outside the labor and agrarian sectors of the party which was highly manipulable by the president. He says on 94 that the arrangement "offered the president and the state

governors an opportunity to rationalize their handpicked candidates as 'members of the popular sector.'" Nora Hamilton, *The Limits of State Autonomy* (Princeton: Princeton University Press, 1982), 267–70, in a contrasting point of view, sees Cárdenas's reorganization of the party along sectoral lines as a corporatist device which limited the authority of agrarian and labor components of the revolutionary coalition, effectively deradicalizing the revolution. While Brandenburg and Hamilton vary in their emphasis, both agree that the sectoral reform of the party concentrated power in presidential hands and limited the autonomy of constituent organizations. In that sense, just as Hamilton argues with respect to the agrarian and labor sectors, the direction of the women's movement may also have been fundamentally altered by the party's corporatization. It is difficult to argue that their chances for making a successful bid for suffrage would have been even marginally improved outside the party, however.

54. Weyl and Weyl, *The Reconquest of Mexico*, 353.

55. Soto, *The Emergence of the Modern Mexican Woman*, 131.

56. Fisher, "The Influence of the Present Mexican Revolution Upon the Status of Women," 219.

57. Soto, *The Emergence of the Modern Mexican Woman*, 143.

58. See Howard F. Cline, *Revolution to Evolution, 1940–1960* (Oxford: Oxford University Press, 1962), 167. Cline observes that, "contrary to predictions by opponents of the move, the women did not flock to the reactionary, or Church-oriented party, but in the main voted as did the men, supporting the official party, which had expanded its organizations to include their particular interests and had even, in some instances, nominated some women for lesser government posts."

59. Albert L. Michaels, "The Crisis of Cardenismo," *Journal of Latin American Studies* 2 (1970): 51–79; Weyl and Weyl, *The Reconquest of Mexico*, 251.

60. Hamilton, *The Limits of State Autonomy*, 260. On Sinarquismo, see Lesley Byrd Simpson, *Many Mexicos* (Berkeley: University of California Press, 1966), 299–304.

61. Hamilton, *The Limits of State Autonomy*, 260.

62. Edwin Lieuwen, *Mexican Militarism: The Rise and Fall of the Revolutionary Army* (Albuquerque: University of New Mexico Press, 1968), 131.

63. Hamilton, *The Limits of State Autonomy*, 263; Meyer and Sherman, *The Course of Mexican History*, 627.

64. Lieuwen, *Mexican Militarism*, 134.

65. Hamilton, *The Limits of State Autonomy*, 263.

66. Fisher, "The Influence of the Present Mexican Revolution Upon the Status of Women," 222; Soto, *The Emergence of the Modern Mexican Woman*, 132; Michaels, "The Crisis of Cardenismo," 75.

67. For a recent interpretation of the interaction of gender and politics in the active decade of the Mexican Revolution (1910–1920), see Sandra McGee Deutsch, "Gender and Sociopolitical Change in Twentieth-Century Latin America," *Hispanic American Historical Review* 71 (1991): 259–306.

Chapter 16

Remaking the Public Sphere

Women and Revolution in Cuba

Sheryl L. Lutjens

The fate of both the woman question and real women are among the critical issues surfacing in the wake of the unanticipated shifts in the socialist world at the end of the 1980s. Did socialist states fail in their policies for women, as many proclaim, imposing cosmetic change that contributed little to the emancipation of women while adding greatly to their burdens? Will post-socialist reconstruction provide a better route to gender equality, replacing orthodox Marxist strategy with improved possibilities for women? With mounting evidence that transitional turmoil is disrupting the lives of post-socialist women, and much still unexplained about the socialist past, the settling of the woman question has only begun.

This essay uses the case of women and the Cuban revolution to look again at the place of women in the theory and practice of twentieth-century socialism. Cuba has maintained an official

---

This is a greatly revised version of "Women and the Socialist State: Feminist Questions, Cuban Answers," presented at the International Studies Association, Atlanta, 31 March–4 April 1992. It shares that foundation with "Reading Between the Lines: Women, the State, and Rectification in Cuba." I would like to thank Mary Ann Tétreault for her comments and advice in the revision process as well as Joseph Boles, Cathy Small, and Mary Ann Steger for their readings of the original paper. I would also like to acknowledge the institutional support of Northern Arizona University for travel to Cuba between 1989 and 1993.

commitment to socialism within the altered global order of the 1990s—distinguishing the Cuban process of *rectificación* (rectification) from the liberalizing reforms underway elsewhere. This difference, however, makes the Cuban case more, not less, useful. Cuba's ongoing pursuit of socialist goals offers a unique opportunity to examine the results of a traditional strategy that is already part of others' pasts. A closer look at the past gains and current conditions of Cuban women promises more than an inventory of their troubles or of the programmatic failings of socialism, however. Where the present circumstances of Cuban women differ from the worsening conditions of post-socialist women in the East, an analysis of the Cuban case can advance our understanding of the theoretical concerns of women and socialism.

My search for Cuban answers to the classical woman question begins with a mapping of the progress of Cuban women and the problems they face in the period of rectification. As traditional socialist strategy predicts and promotes, Cuban women have moved into the labor force and political life. And while the post-socialist transition quickly reversed other women's formal economic and political gains, the crisis conditions of rectification have not eliminated the state's formal commitment to women's equality in Cuba. Still, long-lived feminist debates about the compatibility of Marxism and feminism have identified practical problems and theoretical dilemmas that confound any simple measure of women's progress within socialism.[1] Criticisms of socialist practice include the top-down imposition of formal equalities, the unequal load borne by socialist women, and the ongoing subordination of women and their interests to the goals of revolutionary development.[2] Growing suspicion of the philosophical foundations of a strategy conceived in the orthodox terms of class and class agency casts more doubt on the possibilities of socialism, linking feminists with others who reject the ontological and epistemological bias of Marxism—and all similarly modernist projects.[3]

If feminist critiques indicate what to look for in the policies and practices of the Cuban revolution, feminist misgivings suggest that how we look at women is a crucial determinant of what we will find. My exploration of the place of women in a socialist Cuba will respond to these empirical and methodological concerns by focusing on the relationship of public and private spheres. Firmly entrenched in modern thinking about the proper organization of social life, the dichotomy between public and private has been crucial in feminist theorizing about women's oppression.[4] Feminists have viewed the public/private dichotomy as the modern expression of the traditional distinction between domestic and public, one that defines the separate and unequal worlds of women and men in societies of all types.[5] Though they criticize the exclusion of women from liberalism's public sphere and have contributed to a widespread rejection of the inclusionary strategies associated with classical Marxist theory, feminists have not abandoned the conceptual and cultural relevance of the categories of public and private.[6] Instead, the dichotomy is used to outline a rich terrain where its explanatory and normative power are both assumed and assailed. Upon this terrain, I will examine the seldom studied construction of a socialist public by focusing on the Cuban case.[7]

An overview of the experiences of Cuban women after 1959 will show what they have gained and where those gains are threatened by the increasing difficulties facing a revolution that remains socialist in a liberal world order. How the relationship of public and private can be used to find and interpret the place of women in Cuban socialism must also be shown, however. Considering the historical, organizational, and international dimensions of the revolutionary reorganization of social life, my analysis challenges prevailing conclusions about a totalizing socialist public sphere and its consequences for women. Formal measures of change in women's lives are therefore a starting point for locating "real" women within socialism. In the end, it is these real women whose actions will provide the best answers to our questions about what the traditional socialist strategy has and has not provided—in Cuba and other once-socialist societies.

REORGANIZING THE PUBLIC SPHERE: FROM REVOLUTION TO RECTIFICATION

In Cuba, what had been a nationalist revolution embraced socialist goals in 1961, formalizing the rejection of liberal democracy and capitalism as they had developed in the pre-revolutionary republic of the twentieth century. The resulting structural and ideological change facilitated significant advances for women. From the idealistic Cuban model of the 1960s to the rectification that began in 1986, women's cumulative gains can be viewed both in terms of the reorganization of the public sphere and in changes and continuities in private life.

Cuban women could claim significant formal equalities within the liberal arrangements of the pre-revolutionary republic, including suffrage and protective labor legislation.[8] The dynamics of neo-colonial society belied the egalitarian ideals of a market economy and liberal democracy, however. Societal norms defined women's place as the house/home (*casa*) and men's as the street (*calle*), though women's subordination and the Cuban tradition of *machismo* interacted with the class, color, and rural/urban differences fomented by dependent capitalist development.[9] Thus, by the 1950s the circumstances of Cuban women reflected marked gender inequalities and equally significant differences among women. The revolution's remedy for women unfolded as the nationalist revolution became socialist in ideology and organization.

Women moved into public life after 1959, in response to the needs and egalitarian ideals of the revolution. The official call for women to work came in the mid-1960s, bringing a group that had been marginal in the pre-revolutionary economy (13.7 percent of the potential female labor force was active in 1953)[10] to make up more than 38 percent of the national workforce in 1990, when almost 45 percent of working-age women were employed (1,381,600).[11] Efforts to provide support for working women began in the 1960s and expanded in the 1970s; and women participated from the beginning in the political arrangements created by the revolution, including the Federation of Cuban Women (FMC) founded in 1960.[12] The path into public life was not smooth, however. Within the economic and political mobilization that characterized the first decade, the traditional division of labor was resilient in law and in practice.[13]

In the institutionalization of the revolution in the 1970s, a new constitution, new legal codes, and a party program formalized the revolution's perspective on gender equality. The Cuban Family Code was enacted in 1975, for example, declaring the equality of spouses and specifying rights and obligations within the family.[14] The 1975 Congress of the Partido Comunista de Cuba (PCC), the first since the party's creation in 1965, produced a Thesis on the Full Equality of Women. The socialist constitution of 1976 proclaimed women's equal rights inside and outside the family and pledged the state's assistance in realizing them. Legal guarantees of equality thus included the home within the purview of the law. Women's activities outside the home expanded as the second decade of the revolution produced the institutional arrangements of a more socialist state.

The reorganization of Cuban society along ideological lines replaced the liberal arrangements of the pre-revolutionary republic with the inclusionary institutions of a socialist state. Reorganization promised a new relationship between public and private. The powerful pre-revolutionary norms of family and femininity had never barred women from entering the public sphere; they were variously present in the public life of the republic, of necessity and by choice.[15] Yet women were far from equal. Bringing them out of the house into a redefined *calle* after 1959 meant challenging the traditional gender practices that ordered Cuban society. The customary conceptions of women and their place in the domestic sphere affected the process of reorganizing social life in several significant ways.

The revolution called for participation in the tasks of socialist development, the creation of a new consciousness and a new socialist man, and women's emancipation. All of these required changes in cultural practices that were neither easy nor automatically produced by official policies. Although Cuban women left their homes to participate in the famous 1961 literacy campaign and myriad other, less spectacular activities, motherhood remained—and remains—at the heart of the official view of women and the Cuban home. Women, according to Fidel Castro's 1974 speech to the second Congress of the FMC, are the "natural workshop where life is created";[16] children and the family are the focus of the Family Code; and the primary responsibility for child care and domestic labor remains with mothers.[17] The circumstances of motherhood and families changed dramatically with the revolution, however. High rates of divorce and low rates of infant mortality (10.7 per thousand births in 1990), for example, affected the dynamics of the still-valued nuclear family in Cuba.[18]

Neither the FMC nor Cuban women have abandoned culturally defined gender differences. Created at Castro's suggestion in August 1960, the FMC's purpose was to consolidate existing women's organizations to support the revolution. It has maintained its character as a female/feminine organization within the revolution. Cuban women have not repudiated motherhood or traditional standards of femininity, though change has occurred. Germaine Greer uses Cuba's Afro-Latin heritage and the ideas of José Martí (a nineteenth-century intellectual and leader in the final war for independence) to explain the roots of the sexual politics of Cuban socialism.[19] Commenting in the mid-1980s on the feminine preoccupations of Cuban women, Greer notes the "pearlised nail polish and lipstick" worn by "women who have been trained to kill," remarking that "heroines of work, who cut cane, go down the mines and drive huge cranes, are depilated, deodorised, and scented." With regard to Cuban *machismo*, she calls adultery the "national sport," but finds that "Cuban men, for all their flirtatiousness, seem to like and respect women."[20] Greer is one among many observers who emphasizes Cuban women's acceptance of the identities defined by home, children, husbands, and lovers.

Cuban socialism entered a third phase of post-revolutionary development in 1986, one marked by the persistence of socialist ideology and organization in a rapidly changing world order. A reform process called the "rectification of errors and negative tendencies" commenced with the objective of resolving the economic, political, and social problems afflicting Cuban development efforts. Identifying both international constraints and domestic mistakes, Cuban reformers reasserted the idealism characteristic of the first Cuban development model to redress problems created by the pragmatism that had been pushed after 1970. Cuban reforms retained the socialist centralization of planning and a vanguard party rather than engaging in the wholesale liberalization that, by the end of the 1980s, undid the Soviet bloc. Instead, rectification revived voluntary labor, reoriented production, and pursued improved performance by all organizations. A socialist commitment to women's equality continues in 1993, though *rectificación* has become increasingly responsive to new international realities.

Survival has replaced the rejuvenation of socialism as the overriding objective of rectification. The decomposition of the Eastern bloc disrupted trade and aid, leading in 1990 to the onset of a second, more austere phase of rectification called the "special period in a time of peace." Current economic strategy emphasizes domestic food production (the food program), tourism to earn hard currency, the promotion of biotechnical and other nontraditional exports, and import substitution. The loss of guaranteed trade with the Eastern bloc—once 85 percent of Cuban trade—and a related 90-percent decline in imports have required ongoing and increasingly painful reductions in consumption.[21] The escalating resource crisis has also led to other changes. In Fall 1991, the much delayed fourth Congress of the Cuban Communist Party (PCC) authorized a wider opening of the economy to foreign investment, as well as a number of political changes including direct elections for national representatives, all of which were given legal status with the National Assembly's July 1992 approval of revisions to the Cuban Constitution. Despite the recent legalization of dollars and limited private enterprise, survival is still defined in socialist terms; a return to liberal democracy and a domestic market economy is not on the formal agenda.

Cuba has, in fact, managed to survive. Tourism and foreign activity in the economy have grown;[22] trade with U.S. third-country subsidiaries rose from $300 million in 1989 to $700 million in 1991;[23] and the 1991–92 sugar harvest produced seven million tons, despite the lack of inputs. Much has changed in public and private life, however, and difficulties escalate. The 50 percent drop in petroleum imports constrains agricultural and industrial production; farmers have turned to oxen for agricultural work and factories have closed. Oil shortages have also restricted public and private transportation. Daily bus trips declined from twenty-nine thousand to eighteen thousand by the end of 1991; hundreds of thousands of imported bicycles are now in use.[24] Blackouts regulate the domestic consumption of electricity and the hours of state offices, while the personal rationbook records the frightening pattern of food shortages in the special period. In 1993, a March storm that caused over one billion dollars in damages and the small four-plus ton sugar harvest present more challenges to survival and the special period.

What are the results of rectification and the special period for Cuban women and their progress? The economic crisis in Cuba clearly affects women, though a closer look at a reorganized public sphere and its relation to private life is needed to explain how this is so.

GENDER IN THE PUBLIC SPHERE

An examination of the organizational dimension of the socialist public sphere sheds useful light on the deeper dynamics of women's place within the goals and policies of the Cuban revolution. The institutional arrangements of socialism and liberal (capitalist) democracy differ substantially, encouraging a closer look at how the public and private were redefined in Cuba. Liberalism and Marxism have traditionally advanced different understandings of the public/private dichotomy. Marxist theory criticized the liberal distinction between public and private on philosophical grounds, arguing for the elimination of a dichotomy rooted in the ideas and institutions of capitalist society.[25] Liberalism, in turn, denounces the elimination by the socialist state of all that it sees as private, claiming that the absence of property rights, markets, and the social and political arrangements of liberal democracy extinguishes the possibility of a meaningful public life.[26] In contrast to the presumed neutrality of liberalism's notion of "public," the sphere that becomes civil society through the interest-based, voluntary association among individuals,[27] modern socialist practice assigns the public sphere an abstract class identity in theory and such specific practical purposes as economic development, social justice, and national defense.

Old and more recent thinking about the public sphere tends to deduce its nature (and goodness) from its organization and goals.[28] Feminist wisdom, however, recommends that the public sphere be considered in terms of the home and the family as the core institutions of what is everywhere private.[29] Thus, feminist theories call attention to the classical neglect of the sexual division of labor that enmeshes the socialist—and the capitalist—home, and they have generated distinctive claims about the organization of public life. Concerned with centralization, hierarchy, and the lack of individual and organizational autonomy, feminists join with others who call for alternative organizational forms, practices, and theories.[30] Where many contemporary feminists share with others an ideal of the public sphere as "public arenas of citizen discourse and association," the specifically feminist critique finds an authoritarian socialist state that is male in personnel, process, and deeper purpose.[31] The problem is more succinctly captured by Maxine Molyneux's claim that socialist policies for women have lacked "strong feminist input into policy—whether from above or below."[32]

The structure and effectiveness of the official commitment to women within the special period can be used to explore the organization, ideology, and gendered content of the socialist public sphere in Cuba. According to Sonia Alvarez, the incorporation of women's organizations and issues led to significant gains for Cuban women; moreover, "gender-specific issues were ideologically politicized as well—the proper role of women in social, economic, and political life became the subject of national debate and the object of legitimate political conflict."[33] For many feminists, including Molyneux and Alvarez, goals and organization are still the crucial concerns. Alvarez defines women's movements in terms of their "claims on cultural and political systems on the basis of women's historically ascribed gender roles." They "constitute deliberate attempts to push, redefine, or reconstitute the boundary between the public and private, the political and the personal, the 'natural' and the 'artificial'—a boundary that is institutionalized by the modern State."[34]

The Federation of Cuban Women is a highly visible symbol of the organization and purposes of the socialist public in Cuba. As a vehicle for mobilizing women since 1960, the FMC is avowedly not a liberation movement in the Western feminist sense. Indeed, these Western feminists criticize it and other socialist women's organizations for their dependence on the state.[35] The FMC has shared the principles of democratic centralism characteristic of all Cuban organizations, as well as a formal commitment to the national goals developed by a predominantly male leadership.[36] The work of the FMC in areas ranging from women's health, education, and political awareness to voluntary and paid work, has undeniably contributed to women's progress. Given widespread suspicions about socialist centralization and the imposition of collective goals, the FMC's role in the rectification period/process is a useful gauge of changes in the public sphere.

The FMC has not assumed an oppositional stance in relation to central goals. Within *rectificación,* the Federation has repeatedly reaffirmed its commitment to prioritizing national economic development/survival and defense of the revolution.[37] Yet, the formal role of the FMC since the mid-1970s has been to represent the interests and worries of women, as well as to fulfill state functions.[38] Among the signs of a stronger and more critical FMC are its advisory relationship to central policymakers, participation in studies of the conditions of Cuban women, and involvement in the implementation of such innovations as the municipal commissions created to coordinate women's employment in the early 1980s.[39] The example of FMC effectiveness cited most often is its successful fight for change in the rule denying men permission to stay with hospitalized family members.

The FMC and state policymakers officially agree that women cannot resolve their problems alone. The Constitution makes the state responsible for providing conditions facilitating women's pursuit of full equality, including child care and maternity leave, while women's attitudes and behavior, as well as men's, have been included among the causes of persistent discrimination. As FMC President Vilma Espín explained in a 1985 interview:

> And we see, moreover, that true discrimination still exists when it is suggested in a work center: "We can't promote Fulana because she has four children and a lot of work at home" and when she discriminates against herself by thinking that she cannot resolve the domestic problems that overburden her; nevertheless her husband also has four children.[40]

A 1990 *Granma* story about the few cases where fathers accompanied hospitalized infants identified the problem as formal rules for securing leave from work that treat women and men differently. It also emphasized women's beliefs that they alone can provide proper care for their children.[41]

The organizational allegiance of the FMC to the current goals of collective survival reflects its acquiescence in putting women's particular issues in second place, precisely what foreign feminists have lamented. The Cuban interpretation of the woman question has in the past led the FMC and its president emphatically to reject the theories and criticisms of "bourgeois feminists."[42] These judgments and FMC's perspective on its own work have changed over time, however.[43] The Federation has shown increased interest in feminist theory and participated in international feminist gatherings.[44] Although there are still no autonomous women's movements competing with the FMC, rectification has called for an organizational renewal that includes more grassroots participation and less top-down control over the active content of the Federation's work. Current changes in the FMC, including a demand for better performance amid recurrent rumors of its demise, reflect the shifting position on women characteristic of rectification policies.[45] The severity of the special period underscores the revolution's continued commitment to women—and the woman question writ large—as well as revealing adjustments and a changing emphasis on private lives and public problems.

The Cuban Family Code continues to be the formal statement of socialist equality in private life. Plans and discussions are underway for revising the Code, although the scheduled legislative debate has been postponed.[46] Families are a crucial focus of current policies and FMC efforts, however. Specific examples include the rejuvenation of commissions for tracking and treating youth with problems. The FMC participates in these commissions. It has also cooperated in the creation of the National Family Group, and the ministry of education's focus on family education and relations between the home and the school. More broadly, the emphasis is on a genuine revolution in the socialist family, one that rejects a traditional caretaker role for the working wife/mother and emphasizes men's participation in the *casa* and shared parental responsibilities. Espín has denied that the Cuban family is in crisis, although its problems remain prominent in the discussion of women's issues.

Early pregnancy and single mothers, both young and old, are also prominent concerns in the current period. High fertility rates among young women continue, combining a legacy of pre-revolutionary customs with post-revolutionary dynamics of sexuality.[47] Concerns with single mothers include the question of paternal support, as well as their psychological and physical well-being.[48] A census of problems with child support done by the FMC and the State Statistical Committee led more than six thousand fathers to start paying.[49] In 1990, Social Assistance provided for 5,443 mothers at a cost of some two-and-a-half million pesos;[50] in 1991, over thirty-four million pesos were spent on social assistance for the old, the infirm, and for single mothers.[51] Concerned with women's reproductive health, the FMC continues its campaign regarding the desirability and health risks of abortion. Despite some decline in abortion rates, nine of every ten pregnancies result in abortion and nearly a third involve teenaged women.[52]

There is also an increased emphasis on issues of sexuality. The educational system has pursued improved sex education since the beginning of rectification, stressing both the quality of school programs and family responsibility. Despite the shift that has occurred in the newer generation's attitudes (toward virginity, for example), sexuality is apparently a neglected topic in many Cuban homes.[53] The private silence contrasts sharply with the ongoing inclusion in the official press of topics ranging from condoms and sexually transmitted disease to women's frigidity.[54] And there is still an official concern with equalizing norms of behavior to realize a socialist sexual morality. Vilma Espín's 1986 article in *Cuba Socialista*, for instance, reiterated the official view on the customary double standard: "what is deemed as immoral for women should be also deemed immoral for men." Further, "account should be taken, in most cases, that intimate situations of a couple which are so-called moral problems, are the sole concern of that woman and not the sphere of attention of organizations and institutions."[55] With regard to another important issue of sexual morality, discrimination against homosexuals appears to have a less secure standing in official debates. It is unclear, writes Midge Quandt, "whether the FMC is willing to discuss this issue publicly."[56]

The significance of refocusing attention on the most intimate conditions of private life becomes clearer in the context of the consuming national concerns of the special period. Repeated calls for fatherly participation or the elimination of stereotypical gender norms are more salient under resource scarcity. Scarcity affects the home and other aspects of women's private lives. Official policies have not ignored the difficult domestic conditions of women.

Women continue to bear the brunt of domestic labor in the Cuban home. Information from the fifth Congress of the FMC in 1990 provides results from several studies that show ongoing inequality in domestic work, as well as the difficulties of changing attitudes about the double shift of women.[57] For example, 91.3 percent of those surveyed in an FMC study believed that men's participation in the home had increased, though 57.2 percent (men and women) thought that marriage changed the wife's life more than her husband's (because she "has to take care of children and housework"); 84 percent believed that women naturally take better care of small children (including 76 percent of young women).[58]

The weight of this burden in the special period is easily seen. The buying and preparation of food are more difficult as supplies grow scarcer and essential ingredients are harder to acquire or missing entirely—for example, cooking oil or meat. More and longer lines to buy what is available are one measure of increasing pressures on women. The current food shortages have another side, however. In the late 1980s, more than a third of Cuban food was imported, much of it from the Eastern Bloc and in already processed form.[59] The drastic reduction in imports helps explain why the food program is so important. It is also related to the mushrooming of family and community gardens. As a recent article in *Cuba Internacional* points out, shifting popular consumption to fresh foods and a diet filled with vegetables will affect the amount of time and work required for food preparation by both women and men.[60] Cooking or otherwise concocting whatever is available is indeed part of a family survival strategy, and recipes are published in the newspapers to provide advice. Adjustment in the mechanisms of distribution have been made, and local innovations such as deliveries to the home have been implemented in some municipalities. Subsidized meals are still available at the workplace and in public institutions; it is hard, but not impossible, to eat out.[61] Perhaps the increase in official attention to breastfeeding is an additional state response to the food crisis during the special period.[62]

Visible centralization and formal inclusionary arrangements continue to characterize the public sphere within which the family and Cuban women are objects of official concern. Women are not overlooked as Cuban policymakers respond to the exigencies of ensuring the survival of all Cubans—and of Cuban socialism. Though feminist observers may find much wanting, it appears that the public sphere has in fact become more feminist. Official policy highlights the gender agenda at this critical point in the Cuban revolution. Moreover, the gendered consequences of the hardships of the special period have been treated publicly. Journalist Mirta Rodríguez Calderón, writing in 1992, identified women's contribution to maintaining the family both physically and psychologically, and noted that the special period is different for women than for men. She also suggested that not enough public attention has been paid to women's contribution, even by the FMC.[63]

The landmarks of the public sphere have also changed. The FMC has participated in the creation of a Women's Studies program at the University of Havana, preceded by the organization of departments for the study of women and social problems in other institutions of higher education. *Casa de la mujer y familia* (women's houses) have been created throughout the island to offer support, advice, and professional assistance for women and families. The official discussion of gender issues has extended horizontally to other mass organizations, such as the Unión de Jóvenes Comunistas, which established a commission for discussing women at its sixth Congress, and the sixteenth Congress of the Confederation of Cuban Labor that in 1989 paid explicit attention to workers' families for the first time. Mass organization has provided the means, and collective national goals the ends, for mobilizing women out of their homes and into public life. How well are real women reflected in the formal reordering of public life?

REAL WOMEN

A focus on formal organizational arrangements leads quite easily to generalizations about the meaning of public and private. International expectations often invoke these generalizations to contrast a totalitarian socialist past with a global democratic future.[64] Socialism has not extinguished private life in Cuba, however, and neither has the state imposed a single set of official interests on Cuban women.[65] To decipher what the inclusionary practices and collective goals of a socialist public do mean, it is necessary to look at Cuban women and their participation in the remaking of a socialist public. Cuban women's travels into the public sphere can help us find and interpret their place—a place that becomes "places" given the differences among them.

Thinking of the relationship of public and private in terms of the boundary between them, Cuban women show how the public and private are enacted—not decreed. Feminist analysis is useful here, though the boundary problem in socialism may be substantially different in terms of organization, goals, and structural conditions. The "boundary between the public and private is not static," according to Alvarez; "[M]asculinity and femininity are socially and historically contingent categories," and "the institutionalized separation between public and private is constantly redefined ideologically and new definitions are coercively enforced by the state."[66] This feminist view fits well with Nancy Fraser's broader claim that, rather than being "straightforward designations of societal spheres," the terms public and private "are cultural classifications and rhetorical labels."[67] Boundary crossings by Cuban women thus demonstrate cultural limits to coercion and the possibilities present in official policies. What boundary crossings best illustrate, however, is where real women are at this point in rectification.

The gender practices of private life have not been eliminated by Cuba's socialist strategy for women. Instead, women's participation carries a variety of traditional identities into the public sphere. Women are mothers, wives, daughters, and grandmothers who express other, newer identities in public life. Women are members of the military. They are party *militantes*, workers, neighbors, and members of the FMC. They are scientific researchers and they are, in many cases, housewives. The idea that women choose from a menu of identities is mistaken, of course. Yet, it is equally wrong to presume that all or any women are coerced into similar places at home and in public life. The range of identities created by women's activities inside and outside the home is visible on the streets, in the workplace, in meetings—everywhere that women go. An official acceptance of women's multiple identities is also visible. Writing about the German Democratic Republic prior to reunification, Maria-Barbara Watson-Francke explains that "women in socialist societies live a double and multiple day; they have added nontraditional activities and skills to their traditional roles as mothers and homemakers." The situation contrasts with working women in nonsocialist settings, though, since "public praise creates a different ideology of the double day than in the West."[68]

Women's participation in voluntary agricultural labor, in the pursuit of such import substituting innovations as herbal medicines, and otherwise making do during the special period, is praised publicly. Forewarning of the move to a special period, Castro also acknowledged women's abiding interest in fashion and beauty at the end of his speech closing the March 1990 fifth Congress of the Federation of Cuban Women.

> I was going to tell you to take care of your clothes for the special period, because at best in the special period we will also have to reduce these articles considerably, we would produce only for children, for newborns, for those who are growing; but with the pretty and elegant clothes that you have, perhaps you have clothes for the special period and won't need a meter of cloth in two, three, four, or five years. I am sure that when we meet after five years of a special period, you will come as elegant and as beautiful as you have come tonight.[69]

The official discussion of women inside Cuba captures much of the daily travels—and travails—of women. There are few representations of women as caricatured workers, selfless revolutionaries, helpless and beleaguered mothers, or cooks. In fact, the Cuban media presents a complex and often contradictory array of images of women, images that reflect boundary-crossing participation.

Rectification targeted the media for improvement, and stories on women both report and support the pushing of boundaries.[70] "Should women lift weights?" is a question posed by the UJC newspaper *Juventud Rebelde*'s invitation to public debate. Or what about women playing *batá*, in which

> everything relates to masculinity, starting from the hide, which cannot come from a female animal (what a sacrilege!) to the *olú-batá*, which have to be men, who must stop playing the drums when they lose their fertility. . . . No woman is allowed to lay a finger on a drum. And the *batá* cannot be kept in a woman's room.

"Men's reproaches don't intimidate them," according to the newspaper account of the *Obiní-batá* group and an "endangered taboo"; the women who play are acting out a "passion for art."[71] The FMC magazine *Mujeres* offers a wealth of insights into the multiple identities of Cuban women. The traditional practice of costly and elaborate *quinces* (celebrations of a girl's fifteenth birthday), for instance, is the subject of a 1991 story that explores change and continuity in parents' and daughters' attitudes about them.

The differences among Cuban women constitute another theme in public commentaries and official policies. Studies of Cuban women document persistent differences among them despite the progress made by women as a whole. Differences between rural and urban women, young and older women, or working women and housewives are identified.[72] Working with these differences is part and parcel of the FMC's current efforts to improve its performance. Rectification calls for less management from the top and more open discussion at the base in order to revitalize mass organizations. The Federation's attention to dissimilar needs and interests among women can therefore be viewed as an official response to real women, their specific problems, and their participation.[73]

The scope of women's participation poses some crucial questions about official policies, public identities, and gender issues. Multiple identities, in other words, are more and less easy to sort out. Thus, it is obvious why the decline of women working in Cuba's agricultural cooperatives has compelled the attention of the FMC, ANAP, and the state.[74] More difficult is the *Playboy* story on Cuba's women published in March 1991. Why would Cuban models pose for *Playboy*? And why was it permitted? Criticized by the FMC as a bureaucratic mistake, the story summons old questions about women dancers in the Tropicana shows and newer questions about the representation of women in the advertisements on tourist TV.[75] A similar problem of interpretation is created by the resurgence of prostitution in Cuba. The tourism strategy for survival has facilitated an illegal market in dollars and goods that also includes the participation of women who sell their time and sometimes their bodies. Of keen interest to foreign journalists and treated publicly by Castro, the resurgence of prostitution is officially explained as a choice, not a necessity, and as something that is therefore different from pre-revolutionary prostitution in scope and dynamics.[76] Whether this or any other public or private identity should be repressed is a matter of interpretation.

The meanings that matter most are those expressed by Cuban women. There is little reason to presume that their public and private lives have a singular, ahistorical meaning. Instead, there is ample reason to acknowledge a multiplicity of gendered identities, as well as the gender issues created and recreated through the activities of real women. Nevertheless, the remaking of the public sphere is more than random boundary-crossings by an infinite variety of dissimilar women. The historical legacy of gender practices, together with the organization, ideology, and goals that characterize the socialist public in Cuba, discipline the dynamics of women's participation in public as well as private life. The most useful conclusions about Cuban women and the reforms of rectification are therefore those informed by a careful look at the places made by real women within a socialist public sphere, a public sphere that has historical, cultural, and ideological meanings.

CONCLUSIONS: THE PERILS OF RE/PRIVATIZATION

While the problems facing Cuban women are in some ways similar to the problems facing post-socialist women, their circumstances are substantially different. Most importantly, Cuban women have not lost the protections of the patriarchal socialist state and its traditional strategy for women. The dismantling of the public sphere elsewhere is rapidly eliminating women's right to work; women are 80 percent of Moscow's unemployed, according to Michael Myerson, "a figure fairly representative of the situation throughout the entire former 'eastern bloc.'"[77] Gone, too, is an assured place in the formal world of politics, exemplified by the decline of women in Poland's lower house from thirty-four to four between 1987 and 1990.[78] According to Katrina vanden Heuvel, the overwhelming number of peddlers on the streets of Moscow are old women and young mothers, suggesting another reality behind the much celebrated return to the home by post-socialist women.[79] A reprivatization of the public sphere inflicts prejudicial outcomes on women, outcomes that are reinforced by the ideology of liberalization. Though Cuban women and those in the East confront a similarly dreadful objective austerity, the subjective circumstances within Cuban socialism are still noticeably different.

What other women are losing, Cuban women maintain, includes employment, affirmative policies, high-level demographic and issue representation, and an official commitment to gender equality. Women are among those displaced by factory closings and the rationalization of employment propelled by the urgent need for efficiency; they are also among the relocated workers. Supports for their double shifts continue.[80] Child care remains in place, for example; with room for only 20 percent of preschool-aged children and an annual cost of eight hundred pesos per child, current plans anticipate an expansion to cover 50 percent by 1995–1996.[81] Indeed, in Cuba the current focus on women includes attention to the pressing practical problems of the home, as well as calls for further public scrutiny of other aspects of private life. And men are formally asked to share the burdens of the special period, an instrumental step toward the shorter- and longer-term goals of Cuban socialism which nevertheless politicizes gender in new ways. What women stand to lose in the event of a collapse of Cuban socialism is obvious.

It is equally clear that the international order contributes to the options and the potential of socialist reforms. The consequences for Cuba of the swift disintegration of the socialist bloc have been dire and direct. With the United States hoping to tighten a three-decades-old embargo, the critical condition of the Cuban economy shows how the international dimension reaches deeply into the everyday worlds of women, families, and the Cuban people. Yet it is often recognized by those anxious to forecast Cuba's future that hostile U.S. policies have in fact preserved and energized the heritage of Cuban nationalism, rather than causing Castro's downfall or the ruin of the revolution. The international context of the 1990s also exhibits the newly rediscovered power of ideas. Economic constraints, an anachronistic U.S. posture in a post-cold war world, and a global rhetoric of markets and liberal democracy all bear on the circumstances of Cuban women.

What seems less clear to many observers is that the future of the Cuban revolution depends on real people, not on abstract arguments about socialism and what it does and does not provide. With regard to *cubanas*, feminist theorizing that offers only abstract or ahistorical perspectives on women can result in the deductive discovery of an essential socialist woman with her categorical interests. A focus on the public and private in socialism that sees women's gains in historical and organizational terms offers better insight into the practical and lived realities of women. Such a focus helps uncover what real women do want, rather than using old and new international measures of what theoretically imagined women should want. With the modest aim of challenging the prevailing conception of a monolithic or totalitarian public sphere, this essay has used the relationship of the public and private to explore the places of real women during the current period of Cuban socialism. Because Cuba clings to socialist goals, what real women believe about socialism, their private lives, and progress and problems in their emancipation calls for more—and more careful—observation. It calls also for further thinking about the public sphere.

In the Cuban case, the public and private are still ordered through socialist organization and ideology. Fidel Castro, the Communist Party, and mass organizations vividly contrast Cuban socialism with the emerging market democracies in the East. Also standing in sharp contrast to the ethnic and nationalist fracturing of these new systems are the nationalist and socialist goals ordering Cuba's quest for survival, as well as the quite limited scope of organized opposition on the island. Important reforms have occurred within the ongoing centralization of the Cuban system, however. The constitutional revisions of July 1992 promise changes in the institutional arrangements of social life. Gone are the definitional agency of the working class, the ideological orthodoxy of Marxism-Leninism, and the irreversible state ownership of the means of production. In their place are a dedication to socialism with roots in Cuban history, a vanguard party to represent the Cuban people, new forms of property compatible with foreign investment, direct elections for the national legislature, and a decentralization of decision-making with the elimination of democratic centralism.[82]

Sweeping conclusions about the failings of socialism tell us little about the future of collective goals, constitutional and more recent reforms, or Cuban women. Foregoing the predetermined judgments that result from seeing only formal arrangements and revolutionary goals, a better look at women can uncover more of the meanings that are needed for building conclusions. The grinding scarcity of such elemental items of daily life as cooking oil or shampoo provides crucial clues about what Cuban women need at this point. What they want may be more complex, however. Women continue to join the Communist Party, for example; *Granma* reported that in 1992 the total number of new members was the highest since 1980.[83] In the elections of December 1992 and February 1993 where voter turnout was more than 97 and 99 percent, respectively, women were 13.6 percent of those elected as local representatives and 23 percent of those directly elected to the National Assembly.[84]* What is a decline in women's percentages may in fact reflect the difficulties of combining public life with the private problems of the special period. The boundary of public and private spheres, however, is not produced, explained, or sustained by the rules and results of elections alone.

It is easy to see where women's gains are threatened by the

international pressures and domestic problems that make survival an overwhelming priority. As they continue to bear the burden of home and family within the complex calculus of daily life in the special period, however, survival may be a public purpose that serves—rather than subordinates—women's gender interests. Though the emphasis here has been on unpacking the gender of the public sphere, much remains to be reconsidered in terms of shared goals, collective identities, and the possibilities for a specifically gendered commitment to the ideals and the reality of the Cuban revolution. Indeed, Cuban women may be unwilling to relinquish their very specific gains, or to trade the Cuban version of the woman question for a reprivatization of public life and a host of new questions with no apparent answers. Ultimately, it is as perilous to presume that meaningful nationalist or socialist commitments are not part of the remaking of a revolutionary public, as it is to posit the generic socialist woman and her relation to an authoritarian public sphere.

NOTES

1. Examples from the Marxism/feminism debate include Michele Barrett, *Women's Oppression Today: The Marxist/Feminist Encounter*, rev. ed. (London: Verso, 1988); Zillah Eisenstein, ed., *Capitalist Patriarchy and the Case for Socialist Feminism* (New York: Monthly Review Press, 1979); and Karen V. Hansen and Ilene J. Philipson, eds., *Women, Class, and the Feminist Imagination: A Socialist-Feminist Reader* (Philadelphia: Temple University Press, 1990). On the classical woman question, see Frederick Engels, *The Origin of the Family, Private Property, and the State* (New York: Pathfinder Press, 1972); and Joan B. Landes, "Marxism and the 'Woman Question,'" in *Promissory Notes: Women in the Transition to Socialism*, ed. Sonia Kruks, Rayna Rapp, and Marilyn B. Young (New York: Monthly Review Press, 1989), 15–28.

2. For early critiques from the vantage of the post-socialist transition, see Maxine Molyneux, "The 'Woman Question' in the Age of *Perestroika*," *New Left Review* 183 (September/October 1990): 23–49; and the essays in "Shifting Territories: Feminism & Europe," *Feminist Review*, special issue, 39 (Winter 1991).

3. See, among others, Alison M. Jaggar, *Feminist Politics and Human Nature* (Sussex: Rowman & Littlefield, 1983); Linda J. Nicholson, ed., *Feminism/Postmodernism* (New York: Routledge, 1990); and the strong statement of the problems of Marxism in Mia Campioni and Elizabeth Grosz, "Love's Labours Lost: Marxism and Feminism," in *A Reader in Feminist Knowledge*, ed. Sneja Gunew (London: Routledge, 1991), 366–97.

4. For an historical review, see John Keane, *Democracy and Civil Society* (London: Verso, 1988); and Norberto Bobbio, *Democracy and Dictatorship: The Nature and Limits of State Power*, trans. Peter Kennedy (Minneapolis: University of Minnesota Press, 1989), esp. 1-21. See also S. I. and G. F. Gaus, eds., *Public*

and Private in Social Life (London: Croom Helm, 1983). Besides the traditional Marxist alternative, the most noted theorizing of the public sphere is by Jürgen Habermas and Hannah Arendt, both of whom have received renewed attention in recent times.

5. The point is made by Linda J. Nicholson, "Feminist Theory: The Private and the Public," in *Beyond Domination: New Perspectives on Women and Philosophy*, ed. Carol C. Gould (Totowa, N.J.: Rowman & Allanheld Publishers, 1983), 221–30. See also the review of the literature offered in Janet Sharistanian, "Bibliographical Essay," in Janet Sharistanian, ed., *Beyond the Public/Private Dichotomy: Contemporary Perspectives on Women's Public Lives* (Westport, Conn.: Greenwood Press, 1987), 185–97.

6. For the critique of liberalism, see among others, Susan Moller Okin, "Gender, the Public and the Private," in David Held, ed., *Political Theory Today* (Stanford: Stanford University Press, 1991), 67–90; Jean Bethke Elshtain, *Public Man, Private Woman: Women in Social and Political Thought* (Princeton: Princeton University Press, 1981); and Carole Pateman, "Feminist Critiques of the Public/Private Dichotomy," in *Public and Private in Social Life*, ed. Benn and Gaus, 281–303. The public and private dichotomy is part of the analysis by Genia Browning, "Soviet Politics—Where are the Women?" in Barbara Holland, ed., *Soviet Sisterhood* (London: Fourth Estate, 1985), 207–36, while its development is treated positively by Maria-Barbara Watson-Franke, "'I Am Somebody'—Women's Changing Sense of Self in the German Democratic Republic," in *Connecting Spheres: Women in the Western World, 1500 to Present*, ed. Marilyn J. Boxer and Jean H. Quartert (New York: Oxford University Press, 1987), 256–66.

7. See the interpretations of Marx and Marxism offered by Nancy L. Schwartz, "Distinction between Public and Private Life: Marx on the *zōon politikon*," *Political Theory* 7, no. 2 (May 1979): 245–66; and Eugene Kamenka, "Public/Private in Marxist Theory and Marxist Practice," in *Public and Private in Social Life*, ed. Benn and Gaus, 267–79.

8. See K. Lynn Stoner, *From the House to the Streets: The Cuban Woman's Movement for Legal Reform, 1898–1940* (Durham: Duke University Press, 1991).

9. In rural Cuba, for example, legal marriage—the foundation of the modern family—was less prevalent and many women lived in common-law unions. On this and other differences, see the report on the 1953 census, María A. Martínez Guayanes, "La Situación de la mujer en Cuba en 1953," *Santiago* 15 (June/September 1974): 195–226. On *machismo*, see Geoffrey E. Fox, "Honor, Shame, and Women's Liberation in Cuba: Views of Working-Class Emigre Men," in *Female and Male in Latin America: Essays*, ed. Ann Pescatello (Pittsburgh: University of Pittsburgh Press, 1973), 273–90. See also the noted historical study, reprinted with a new introduction, Verena Stolcke [Martinez-Alier], *Marriage, Class and Colour in Nineteenth-Century Cuba: A Study of Racial Attitudes and Sexual Values in a Slave Society*, 2d ed. (Ann Arbor: University of Michigan Press, 1989).

10. Of the 16 percent of women employed as professionals, 84 percent were teachers, about 20 percent of working women were employed in manufacturing, and some seventy thousand women worked as unsalaried

domestics. Isabel Larguia and John Dumoulin, "Women's Equality and the Cuban Revolution," in *Women and Change in Latin America*, ed. June Nash and Helen Safa (South Hadley, Mass.: Bergin & Garvey Publishers, 1986), 344–68, esp. 346; Lourdes Casal, "Revolution and 'Conciencia': Women in Cuba," in *Women, War, and Revolution*, ed. Clara Berkin and Clara M. Lovett (New York: Holmes & Meier, 1980), 195–226, esp. 188; and Martínez Guayanes, "La Situación de la mujer," 208, where she notes that 6 percent were employed in agriculture.

11. Federation of Cuban Women, *Proyecto de informe central, V Congreso FMC, 5 al 8 de marzo de 1990* (n.p., n.d.), 8, 7. In the capital, Ciudad de La Habana province, the figure was 43.4 percent (*Proyecto de informe*, 11). The average annual growth in women's employment between 1970 and 1990 was 5.5 percent (United Nations, *The World's Women 1970–1990: Trends and Statistics* (New York: United Nations, 1991), 105).

12. Women participate in the unions and the mass organizations created after 1959, including the National Association of Small Farmers (ANAP), the neighborhood Committees for Defense of the Revolution (CDRs), and student associations at all levels of education. In 1989, nearly 3.4 million women aged fourteen and over belonged to the Federation of Cuban Women. Representative institutions called Poder Popular were inaugurated in 1976 and 8.7 percent of the local level delegates selected in the first nationwide elections were women. By 1989, they constituted 16.7 percent of local delegates, 27.6 percent of indirectly elected provincial delegates, and more than a third of the indirectly elected national deputies (*Mujer y Sociedad*, 91). In 1988, women were 23.9 percent of PCC membership (compared to 15 percent in 1975 and 21.6 percent in 1985) (*Proyecto de informe*, 21). Vilma Espín, president of the FMC and wife of Castro's brother Raúl, has been a member of the political and the central committee.

13. Article 43 of the Cuban Constitution of 1976 guaranteed women equal rights "in the economic, political, social fields as well as in the family," while stipulating that "the state sees to it that they are given jobs in keeping with their physical make-up." For general overviews and the story of labor regulations, see Debra Evensen, "Women's Equality in Cuba: What Difference Does a Revolution Make," *Law & Inequality: A Journal of Theory and Practice* 4 (July 1986): 295–326; and Marifeli Pérez-Stable, "Cuban Women and the Struggle for 'Conciencia,'" *Cuban Studies/Estudios Cubanos* 17 (1987): 51–72. In 1990, women were 84.7 percent of administrative (clerical) workers, 62.5 percent of service workers, and 18.9 percent of laborers. They were 58.3 percent of technical personnel and 26.5 percent of management, however, a change that reflects improved access to secondary and higher education in nontraditional fields. (*Proyecto de informe*, 9; and for figures on the distribution of university graduates, see *Mujer y sociedad en cifras* (Havana: Editorial de la Mujer, 1990), 60.) The best measure of change may be the location of new entrants into the labor force. On this point, see Mariana Ravenet Ramirez, Niurka Pérez Rojas, and Marta Toledo Fraga, *La mujer rural y urbana: estudios de casos* (Havana: Editorial de Ciencias Sociales, 1989), 25–29.

14. According to Article 26, "Both parties must care for the family they have created" and "[t]hey must participate in the running of the home, to the extent of their capacity or possibilities, and cooperate so that it will develop in the best possible way." *Family Code* (Havana: Orbe Editorial, 1975), 20.

15. See Stoner, *From the House to the Streets; mujeres en revolución* (Havana: Editorial de Ciencias Sociales, 1978); and Linda Lobao, "Women in Revolutionary Movements: Changing Patterns of Latin American Guerrilla Struggle," in *Women and Social Protest*, ed. Guida West and Rhoda Lois Blumberg (New York: Oxford University Press, 1990), 180–204.

16. Fidel Castro, "Discurso del Comandante en Jefe Fidel Castro en el Acto de Clausura," in *Memoria: II Congreso Nacional de La Federación de Mujeres Cubanas* (Havana: Editorial Orbe, 1975), 296.

17. A 1975 study of 251 women determined that the woman's work week was 88 hours, *Sobre el pleno ejercio de la igualdad de la mujer; tésis y resolución* (Havana: Departamento de Orientación Revolucionaria, Comité Central, Partido Comunista de Cuba, 1976), 15–16.

18. *Granma Weekly Review*, 10 January 1991, 4. There was a rise in 1985, however, and Villa Clara Province had a low of 6.6 in 1992. (*Granma*, 15 January 1989, 3; *Granma*, 15 January 1993, 2.) See "Woman as Mother," in Margaret Randall, *Women in Cuba: Twenty Years Later* (Brooklyn: Smyrna, 1981), chap. 3. Fertility is not officially regulated in Cuba; defined as births per woman, fertility was 4.3 in 1970 and 1.7 in 1990 (U.N., *The World's Women*, 27), though the pre-revolutionary birthrate was low by Latin American standards.

19. Germaine Greer, "Politics—Cuba," in *Women: A World Report* (New York: Oxford University Press, 1985), 271–91, esp. 282. She refers to matrilineal kinship tendencies and to the bourgeois conception of the feminine as the opposite of the masculine, suggesting that Martí's legacy was to stress the need for feminine traits.

20. Ibid., 282, 280, 281.

21. Elsy Flors, "Actualidad financiera," *Cuba Internacional* 31, no. 7–8 (1993): 5–8, esp. 5. See also Andrew Zimbalist, "Anatomy of the Crisis," *Cuba Update* 13 (August/September 1992): 12–16.

22. In 1991, 424,000 tourists arrived in Cuba and plans are for one million in 1995. (*Granma*, 17 September 1992, 2.) By August 1992, sixty-two economic agreements had been signed and two hundred were under study. (Albert Pozo, "¿Por que confian en nosotros?" *Bohemia* 84 (28 August 1992): B30–B33, esp. B30.)

23. Francisco Forteza, "Looking at Cuba: Investments," *Prisma* 2 (June/July 1992): 42–43, esp. 42.

24. Ramon Pichs, "Problemas y opciones del sector energético en cuba," *Boletín de Información Sobre Economía Cubana* 1 (May 1992): 9–19, esp. 14. Cuban production of bicycles has begun recently.

25. The traditional Marxist classics are one source for the critique, including Lenin's *State and Revolution*. See also Kamenka, "Public/Private in Marxist Theory," in *Public and Private in Social Life*, ed. Benn and Gaus; and Schwartz, "Distinction Between Public and Private Life."

26. A particularly acute example is the statement by Antoni Z. Kaminski,

> It is evident that the sources of the evil were in the "architecture" of the communist order and, probing deeper, in the theoretical design of this order. This proposition should compel us to rethink the basic issues of social order, to re-examine the institutional foundations of human societies. The problem of the *public* and the *private* is at the very center of such concerns. ("The Public and the Private: Introduction," *International Political Science Review* 12 (October 1991): 263–65.)

On the problem of studying the public sphere, see Sheryl L. Lutjens, "Organizing Socialism: The Public and the Private in Cuba," paper presented at the seventeenth Congress, Latin American Studies Association, Los Angeles, Calif., 24–27 September 1992.

27. This is a simple view of civil society, however. For more, see Keane, *Democracy and Civil Society*; or Bobbio, *Democracy and Dictatorship*.

28. This, I believe, applies to Habermas and Arendt whose strong claims for how the public should be organized (or not) make their important concerns about the formation of purposes—(public opinion in Habermas's case—improbable guides for the study of existing socialism. See the collection of essays on Habermas, Craig Calhoun, ed., *Habermas and the Public Sphere* (Cambridge: MIT Press, 1992).

29. Though it is variously conceived in terms of household production, mothering, biological procreation, or social reproduction, the private/domestic world of women is almost always conceived in its relation to the nondomestic, public sphere.

30. Theorizing of nonhierarchical, cooperative, and autonomous organizations has not advanced far, and most calls for alternatives focus on capitalist societies. For feminist examples, see Kathy E. Ferguson, *The Feminist Case Against Bureaucracy* (Philadelphia: Temple University Press, 1984) or Patricia Yancey Martin, "Rethinking Feminist Organizations," *Gender & Society* 4, no. 2 (June 1990): 182–206.

31. Nancy Fraser, "Rethinking the Public Sphere: A Contribution to the Critique of Actually Existing Democracy," in *Habermas and the Public Sphere*, ed. Calhoun, 109–42, esp. 131. She writes:

> Take, for example, the longstanding failure in the dominant wing of the socialist and Marxist tradition to appreciate the full force of the distinction between the apparatuses of the state, on the one hand, and public arenas of citizen discourse and association, on the other. All too often it was assumed in this tradition that to subject the economy to the control of the socialist state was to subject it to the control of the socialist citizenry. Of course that was not so. But the conflation of the state apparatus with the public sphere of discourse and association provided ballast to processes whereby the socialist vision became institutionalized in an authoritarian statist form instead of in a participatory democratic form.

32. Molyneux, "The 'Woman Question,'" 43.

33. Sonia E. Alvarez, *Engendering Democracy in Brazil: Women's Movements in Transition Politics* (Princeton: Princeton University Press, 1990), 21.

34. Ibid., 23–24.

35. Alvarez thus excludes the FMC from her definition of women's movements, ibid., 29 n. 9. Molyneux's criticisms of women's organizations include adherence to the party line (a criticism of the Cuban situation shared by Alvarez), and corruption. "The 'Woman Question,'" 29.

36. For an overview of FMC activities and structure in the 1970s, see Max Azicri, "Women's Development through Revolutionary Mobilization: A Study of the Federation of Cuban Women," *International Journal of Women's Studies* 2 (January–February 1979): 27–50.

37. For example, "Carta de la FMC a Fidel," *Granma*, 3 January 1992, 1.

38. This is formalized by the 1976 Constitution and the party platform.

39. Azicri, "Women's Development," and Evensen, "Women's Equality" make arguments about the FMC that modify conclusions about absolute centralized control.

40. Vilma Espín, "Entrevista concedida a Mirta Rodríguez Calderón, del periódico *Granma*, agosto de 1985," in Vilma Espín, *La mujer en cuba* (Havana: Editora Política, 1990), 37–81, esp. 55.

41. The *Granma* article covered the Cerro Pediatric Hospital which was a pioneering center that had quickly implemented the new program. The story reported that in 9 to 12 percent of the cases, fathers accompanied infants. *Granma*, 18 August 1990, 3.

42. Molyneux concludes that "Cuba's hostility to feminism—expressed in Vilma Espín's regular denunciation of its 'bourgeois' and 'imperialist' character—softened under the impact of changes taking place within socialist movements everywhere." "The 'Woman Question,'" 32. Espín's 1985 explanation of the FMC's unchanging purpose in relation to the language of the classical Marxist woman question reveals the position that feminists so frequently condemn. "In reality, the federation, although it often cited classic texts that spoke in these words, of equality as well as the emancipation or liberation of women, always took great pains not to use them. On the contrary: what we suggested to women was participation; being there for all the tasks of the revolution." "Entrevista . . . Agosto 1985," 62.

43. It is notable that Espín's article evaluating women's progress and the problems of discrimination was published in the mid-1980s, followed in 1990 by three volumes of speeches and interviews. The article appeared in *Cuba Socialista* and was translated as *The Struggle for the Full Exercise of Women's Equality* (Federation of Cuban Women, n.p., n.d.). Vilma Espín Guillois, *La Mujer en cuba: familia y sociedad; discursos, entrevistas, documentos* (Havana: Imprenta Central de las FAR, 1990); Espín, *La Mujer en cuba*; and [Vilma Espín Guillois], *La Gesta revolucionaria: acciones y heroes; Vilma Espín; discursos, entrevistas, documents* (Havana: Editorial de la Mujer, 1990).

44. In a 1989 interview, Espín explained her attitude, using words that reflect central issues in feminist theory.

> Personally, yes, I believe in feminist groups that link the solution

> of the oppression of women, of the liberation of women, with the liberation of all those who are exploited, oppressed, discriminated against, which means approaching present day problems, economic as well as social, political and ideological, through a prism of analysis of classes, of sex, and of race. ("Entrevista concedida a la periodista Griega Elizabeta Popogay, febrero 1989," in Espín Guillois, *La Mujer en cuba: familia y sociedad*, 213–21, esp. 215.)

Molyneux refers to the participation of the FMC in international feminist events, "The 'Woman Question,'" as do Nancy Saporta Sternbach et al., "Feminisms in Latin America: From Bogotá to San Bernardo," in *The Making of Social Movements in Latin America: Identity, Strategy, and Democracy*, ed. Arturo Escobar and Sonia E. Alvarez (Boulder: Westview Press, 1992), 207–39, esp. 224.

45. For more on the FMC in the current period, see Sheryl L. Lutjens, "Reading Between the Lines: Women, the State, and Rectification in Cuba."

46. See Raúl Gómez Treto, "Hacía un Nuevo Código de Familia?" *Revista Cubana de Derecho* 17 (July–September 1988): 31–74. The Family Code was to be discussed in the summer 1990 session of the National Assembly, according to officials of the FMC who were not entirely clear why its consideration was postponed. (Interview, Célia Berges and Ida González, Federation of Cuban Women, Havana, 8 June 1990.) In August 1992, it was still under discussion by the Permanent Commission on Children, Youth, and Women of the National Assembly.

47. In 1975, there were 1,178 births to girls under fifteen years of age and more than 48,000 in the fifteen to nineteen age group; by 1987, the figures were 1,372 and 44,775 respectively, with each reaching a high in 1985. *Mujer y sociedad*, 15.

48. María Isabel Domínguez, "La Maternidad temprana en la Isla de la Juventud: un freno al desarrollo de la personalidad," *Santiago* 62 (March 1986): 83–98; and Marguerite G. Rosenthal, "The Problems of Single Motherhood in Cuba," in *Cuba in Transition: Crisis and Transformation*, ed. Sandor Halebsky and John M. Kirk (Boulder: Westview Press, 1992), 161–75.

49. Aloyma y Maria del Carmen, "¿Y dónde está mi papá," *Mujeres* 30 (December 1991): 6–9, esp. 8.

50. Ibid., 9. Rosenthal cites one report of as many as two hundred thousand single mothers, "The Problems," 166.

51. *Granma*, 30 July 1992, 1.

52. Debra Evensen, "Abortion: Cubans Concerned about High Rates," *Cuba Update* 13 (August/September 1992): 43–44. See the response to "What is the FMC's Position on Family Planning?" in "Conclusiones en la sección 'A Debate' sobre la plena igualdad de la mujer, en el periódico *Juventud Rebelde*, agosto 1984," in Espín Guillois, *La Mujer en cuba*, 49–68, esp. 57–58. Molyneux looks at policies that limit or encourage family expansion as part of the reform process elsewhere in "The 'Woman Question.'"

53. A study done by the Center for the Study of Youth reported that one of the topics never discussed between parents and their children was "doubts and worries" about sexual relations. (*Granma*, 16 August 1990, 2.) See also Aloyma

Ravelo García, *Del amor, hablemos francamente* (Editorial Gente Nueva, 1989); "Dudas sexuales, ¿cómo hablarlas con los padres?" *Mujeres* 30 (April–May 1991): 8; and Lois M. Smith, "Sexuality and Socialism in Cuba," in *Cuba in Transition: Crisis and Transformation*, ed. Sandor Halebsky and John M. Kirk (Boulder: Westview Press, 1992), 177-91.

54. The moral and the medical dimensions of sexuality are addressed in the official press, demonstrating the importance of such themes at a time when severe paper shortages have led to a sharp reduction in publishing. For example, "Sexuality: Neither a Dilemma nor a Sport," *Granma Weekly Review*, 27 January 1991, 3; "Caballo grande, ¿ande o no ande . . .?" *Juventud Rebelde*, 7 January 1990, 13. Cuba has also devoted attention and resources to acquired immune deficiency syndrome (AIDS).

55. Espín offered the unacceptable example of a newspaper advertisement for a course for department store clerks where only female applicants needed to provide a morality certificate (besides being unacceptable, "what body has the authority for issuing such a document?"). Espín, *The Struggle for the Full Exercise*, 41–43.

56. Midge Quandt, "Women's Liberation in Cuba," *Z Magazine* (October 1990): 108–10, esp. 109. See also Laura Gotkowitz and Richard Turits, "Socialist Morality: Sexual Preference, Family, and State Intervention in Cuba," *Socialism and Democracy* 6 (Spring/Summer 1988): 7–29; Smith, "Sexuality and Socialism in Cuba"; and Sonia de Vries, "Thoughts in Flight," *Cuba Update* 14, no. 1–2 (February–March 1993): 19–20.

57. According to the time study of the State Statistical Committee, working women devote more than twenty-two hours to domestic tasks each week, compared to men's four hours and fifty-two minutes; men spend one hour and twenty-two minutes on domestic chores on their days off, while women spend nearly six hours. *Proyecto de informe*, 24.

58. Ibid., 24–25. The study included a 170-question survey of 4,865 persons in nine provinces. Seventy percent thought that cooking, dishes, and cleaning should be done by both men and women, while 61.4 percent considered washing and ironing as tasks for women.

59. See Gail Reed, "Making Do in the Special Period," *Cuba Update* 13 (August/September 1992): 17–19, esp. 17 where she cites a Cuban official's figures of a decline of the imported nutrients in the Cuban diet from 40 percent to 12 percent. By the end of April 1992, there were more than 1.3 million small family or collective plots. Raimundo López, "La Fiebre del huerto," *Cuba Internacional* 31 (July 1992): 41–44, esp. 42

60. López, "La Fiebre del huerto," 42.

61. See Reed, "Making Do"; Esther Mosak, "Coping with the Crunch," *Cuba Update* 13 (August/September 1992): 20-21. Reed provides figures for intake of calories and carbohydrates. López, "La Fiebre," 43, notes the growth of public sales of juice and soups (*caldosas*).

62. According to a recent newspaper article, 62 percent of mothers nurse at birth, although only 5.9 percent breastfeed exclusively for six months. *Granma*, 18 November 1992, 3.

63. Mirta Rodríguez Calderón, "Sin tiempo para el desaliento," *Bohemia* 74 (6 March 1992): 38–42; and "Invitación al Conversáo," *Bohemia* 84 (21 August 1992): B32–B35.

64. There are many examples, but see Habermas's reference to the "totalitarian public sphere." Jürgen Habermas, "Further Reflections on the Public Sphere," in *Habermas and the Public Sphere,* ed. Calhoun, 421–61, esp. 455.

65. See Gotkowitz and Turits, "Socialist Morality," for an innovative view of the relationship of public and private life. Where the recent tendency is to see the extermination of private life by the overweaning public in socialism, Kamenka contrasts Marxist theory with its practice in terms of the accommodation to private life, "Public/Private in Marxist Theory." The question of women's interests is a crucial one, although it will not be explored. See the much referenced distinction between practical and strategic gender interests made by Maxine Molyneux, "Mobilization without Emancipation? Women's Interests, State, and Revolution," in Richard R. Fagen, Carmen Diana Deere, and Jose Luis Coraggio, eds., *Transition and Development: Problems of Third World Socialism* (New York: Monthly Review Press, 1986), 280–302.

66. Alvarez, *Engendering Democracy*, 29.

67. Fraser, "Rethinking the Public Sphere," 131.

68. Watson-Francke, "'I Am Somebody!'" 265.

69. Fidel Castro Ruz, "Discurso pronunciado en la clausura del V Congreso de la Federación de Mujeres Cubanas (FMC), el 7 de marzo de 1990," in Fidel Castro, *En la trinchera de la revolución* (Havana: Editorial Jose Marti, 1992), 131–72, esp. 172.

70. A study of the media at the end of the 1980s found that one woman appeared for every four men—except around the August anniversary of the FMC and International Woman's Day. "Nosotras en la mirilla," *Mujeres* 28 (January 1989): 6–11.

71. *Granma International*, 26 May 1991, 6, citing Fernando Ortiz's essay, "Los tambores bimembranófonos: los batá."

72. Rural and urban women differ along a number of indicators, according to a study of 3,302 women in three characteristic municipalities conducted with the ILO Global Research Project and the help of the FMC in the first part of the 1980s. (S. Catasús et al., *Cuban Women: Changing Roles and Population Trends* (Geneva: International Labour Office, 1988).)

73. A 1991 article in *Mujeres* discussed discrimination in the case of more than one hundred women working on contract farms without maternity leave or vacation (for from one to eleven years). The article offers an intriguing example of recognizing differences. (Isabel Moya, "¿Sin movil aparente?" *Mujeres* 30 (August-September 1991): 2–3.) The problem shared by these women emerged in the first base-level meetings organized to reflect the FMC's new emphasis on bottom-up identification of problems. According to the local FMC secretary, "Look, we have to recognize that for some time we thought that our principal task was fundamentally the housewife, but we have understood that it's necessary to give special attention to the working woman." The farm women are richly described as having "faces marked by the midday sun" and

"frank and direct speech."

74. *Proyecto de informe*, 12, notes that more than 12,000 of the 14,150 women cooperative members were working, but that in 1985 there had been 22,400.

75. The response by the FMC is described in Julien S. Murphy et al., "Feminism in Cuba: Report from the Third Conference of North American and Cuban Philosophers," *Hypatia* 6 (Fall 1991): 227–32, esp. 231.

76. For example, Castro called attention to prostitution in his speech at the sixth Congress of the UJC in the spring of 1992. *Granma*, 7 April 1992, special supplement. The amount of attention devoted by visiting journalists is interesting in its own right; see, for example, Richard McKerrow, "¡Cuba Libre!" *Details* (August 1991): 20–26.

77. Michael Myerson, "Suffer the Little Children & Their Mothers," *On the Issues* 24 (Fall 1992): 36–39, esp. 38.

78. United Nations, *The World's Women*, 33. Poland has recently had a woman prime minister, however.

79. "Women of Russia, Unite!" *New York Times* 12 September 1992, Y13; she cites a poll showing that only 20 percent of Russian women want to stay at home.

80. Figures through June 1991 show women as a quarter of those whose jobs were affected by problems of resources, 54,168 at that point; 86.3 percent of the women were relocated. The figures are different for those whose positions were eliminated for reasons of efficiency. Comité Estatal de Trabajo y Seguridad Social, October 1991, at the Centro de Documentacion y Información de la Mujer.

81. Interview, Dr. Lesbia Cánovas, Director, Instituto Central de Ciencias Pedagógicas, Ministry of Education, Havana, 11 August 1992. In the summer 1991, however, the age of entrance was raised from forty-five days to six months.

82. See the Constitution (and accompanying discussion) published in *Granma*, 22 September 1992, 3–10; and also Hugo Azcuy, Rafael Hernández, and Nelson P. Valdés, eds. "Reforma Constitucional Cubana," *Cuba en el Mes* (Havana: Centrode Estudios sobre America, July 1992).

83. Thirty-five percent of the new members were women: *Granma* reported that the loss of members remained at its historical rate. *Granma*, 7 May 1993, 2.

84. *Granma*, 29 December 1992, 8; *Granma*, 11 March 1993, 5; and Susana Castañeda Donate, ed., "Proceso Electoral Cuban," *Cuba en el Mes* (Havana: Centrode Estudios sobre America, March 1993), 205. The official count showed a decrease in blank or spoiled ballots from 13 percent in December to 7 percent in February (though others have estimated a much higher percentage in December, there has been little comment on the February election). Gail Reed, "Elections: An Unexpected Finish," *Center for Cuban Studies Newsletter* (April 1993): 8.

Chapter 17

Women and the Counter-Revolution in Chile

Joan Supplee

On 11 September 1973, Chile's military establishment under the leadership of General Augusto Pinochet Ugarte ended the oldest democratic tradition in Latin America by overthrowing Salvador Allende's *Unidad Popular* (Popular Unity) government. In the decade of the sixties the Christian Democratic Party, aided by funds from the Alliance for Progress, attempted mild leftist reforms. Such action failed to prevent a socialist victory at the polls in 1970. The threat to Chile's capitalist economy proved stronger than the commitment to democracy. An array of domestic and foreign opponents of Allende joined to overthrow his administration. One of the striking features of this opposition was the prominence of Chilean women in the anti-Allende movement.

For the first time in Chilean history, women took to the streets in huge numbers to demonstrate against the elected government. Middle- and upper-class women joined the campaign against Salvador Allende and his "revolution in the Chilean way." After his defeat, they triumphantly proclaimed, "make no mistake, we organized for the express purpose of helping to overthrow Allende. . . . If it hadn't been for . . . [us], the *Unidad Popular* would probably still be in power today pushing Chile toward Marxism."[1] More surprising than the participation of these women in the anti-Allende movement was the presence of working-class women—women who stood to benefit from Allende's reforms. Some scholars have claimed that these women were "duped" into participating in the anti-Allende movement by their class enemies—the upper and middle classes.[2] This chapter will explore that thesis by examining the way in which Chilean women organized, entered the political arena, and participated in the campaign against the Allende government.

By the close of the nineteenth century, the international capitalist system had penetrated even the remotest areas of Latin America. Their peripheral location in the system did not prevent Latin American nations from undergoing a profound alteration in economic and social structures. The traditional extended patriarchal family structure yielded to a privatized and bourgeois structure which supported and was supported by the state. In Chile, as in other Latin American nations, women were confined to the private sphere, the home, and civil codes and social practice supported this confinement.

This ideal privatized family was breached earlier in Chile than in other areas of Latin America. Women first entered into Chilean public life in the 1870s when they gained admission to institutions of higher learning. By 1968, they comprised 46.1 percent of the student body of the University of Santiago. As a result of their educational achievements, Chilean women joined professional ranks in Chile more frequently and earlier than in the United States; 8.5 percent of all doctors, 32 percent of all dentists, and 10 percent of all lawyers in Chile in the mid-1960s were female. They also out performed U.S. women in holding national office.[3]

While education allowed Chilean women opportunities to expand their horizons beyond the traditional domestic sphere, it did not give them access to positions of authority. The professions they joined did not enjoy the same economic or social status as in the United States. As doctors and dentists for example, they worked long hours for little pay and did not occupy important posts in professional associations. Similarly, their prominence in the judicial system (they held 28 percent of all judgeships) reflected the marginal pay and status of Chilean justices.[4] Elsa Chaney found that "the bulk of women officials either perform the less prestigious judicial chores in the nation's capital or are judges in the provinces."[5] Education provided women with an opportunity to participate in the public life of the nation, but did not grant them equal stature and authority.

Political participation lagged behind educational achievements. The Radical Party first allowed women to attend its meetings in 1888. In 1934, it established a separate women's branch. Women associated with the Communist Party as early as 1911, but were denied access to the party's leadership cadres. When the Socialist Party formed in 1933, it created a women's auxiliary, the *Acción de Mujeres Socialistas*. The Falange, the basis of the Christian Democratic Party, similarly segregated women, as did the Liberal and Conservative parties.[6] The Chilean political system isolated women within party organizations, thereby excluding them from the policymaking process.

To agitate for the franchise and for civil equality, Chilean women organized outside the structure of the traditional parties. Amanda Labarca Hubertson, a Radical Party member and an education activist, formed the Women's Reading Circle in Santiago in 1915 to introduce members to literary and philosophical works. At the same time, upper-class women formed a separate reading group, the *Club de Señoras* (Women's Club). Conservative women and Catholic clergy denounced both clubs for subverting women's primary role as mothers and guardians of the domestic sphere. When club members urged the Conservative Party to support women's suffrage, the church hierarchy threatened them with excommunication. In response, the Reading Circle and *Club de Señoras* united to form the National Council of Women in 1919. This council became the political voice for women's issues in the 1920s. Obtaining the franchise was just one of its goals. The Council also fought to have the civil code revised. Chilean law sustained the *patria potestad* (power of the father) which relegated married women to the same status as children and imbeciles.[7] While some male politicians, such as Pedro Aguirre Cerda and Arturo Alessandri, privately sympathized with the goals of the Council of Women, they took no public action. A more radical group, the *Partido Cívico Femeninio* (Women's Civic Party), also founded in 1919, urged electoral and civil reforms for women and children. It published its own journal, *Acción Feminina,* that reached ten thousand readers.[8] Both of these organizations urged moderate, gradual change and supported limited suffrage (participation in municipal elections) for women as a first step toward full civil rights.

In the 1930s, economic turmoil rent the traditional political structure and afforded Chilean women an opportunity to gain access to positions of power. The Liberals and Conservatives divided over a presidential candidate and lost the election to a socialist coalition in 1931. Although the socialists held power for a scant ten months, they appointed women to higher political offices than their predecessors. Labarca Hubertson assumed the directorship of secondary education and two other women became subsecretaries of education.[9] The economic crisis of the 1930s provided Chilean women a brief opportunity to participate in national politics, but only in areas deemed appropriate for women.

Despite the fact that the political system had accommodated new leftist parties in the 1930s and elevated a few women to positions of power, the majority of male party leaders, particularly those on the left, remained skeptical about extending full voting rights to women. In 1938, President Pedro Aguirre Cerda, a Radical and leader of the Popular Front, expressed doubt that women, "having acquired the vote, would continue along the same line that had brought him to the presidency of the Republic."[10] He feared their defection from the center-left coalition. While women did gain the right to vote in municipal elections in 1931, parties of the center and left considered women more of a burden than an asset in the national electoral struggle with the right.

The final impetus for women's suffrage came from outside established political parties. Several different women's groups emerged in the 1930s to push for enfranchisement. In 1935, *Movimiento Pro Emancipación de la Mujer Chilena* (Organization for the Emancipation of the Chilean Woman, MEMCH), composed of housewives and working women, both professional and working class, appeared. It was associated with the Popular Front and joined a revitalized Women's Civic Party. A National Congress of Women convened in 1944 and inspired the tireless Labarca Hubertson to organize the *Federación Chilena de Instituciones Femeninas* (Chilean Federation of Women's Organizations, FECHIF) to campaign for suffrage. FECHIF's board incorporated women from all political parties. In 1946, María de la Cruz founded the *Partido Femenino Chilena* (Chilean Women's Party, PFCH) to organize women voters. This party attempted to awaken in Chilean women a new political consciousness based on their power at the polls. A year later, the Radical administration organized the *Asociación de Dueñas de Casa* (Housewives' Association) whose primary objective was to teach women of limited resources to be better housewives and, secondly, to prepare them for the polls. According to feminist Julieta Kirkwood, they represented "a conservative response, one which upheld women's sacred traditional place."[11] The Association was organized at the grassroots level by *Centros de Madres* (Mothers' Centers) that operated in most neighborhoods. Each successive regime utilized this organization as a political preserve of motherhood and traditional family values. At this early stage, the Association helped the Radical administration maintain its following among Chilean women and it stood firmly behind FECHIF's actions to secure the vote. When suffrage legislation finally came to a vote in 1949, the newspapers, radio stations, news magazines, and major political parties publicly endorsed the measure. Forty women demonstrated inside the national congress in support of the measure.[12] Their efforts paid off. Chilean women secured complete suffrage, albeit in gender-segregated polling places, on 8 January 1949.

Once the goal of suffrage was reached, both the Federation and the Women's Party dissolved over internal disputes concerning the future direction of the women's movement. The Federation collapsed almost immediately and the Chilean Women's Party did not hold together much longer. In 1952, the PFCH fulfilled Aguirre Cerda's dire prediction when it supported the candidacy of ex-dictator General Carlos Ibáñez, who ran on a reform platform. As a reward for its support, President Ibáñez appointed party members to the ministry of education. The party also managed to elect its president, María de la Cruz, as senator. When the party campaigned for the legalization of divorce, conservative members deserted it. Three women accused Senator de la Cruz of a conflict of interest in front of Congress, and she was removed from office despite her exoneration by a congressional investigating committee. To discredit the group that replaced the party as an enemy of the family, conservative defectors denounced its members as communists, although the group had no ties to the party.[13] Once suffrage had been achieved, both parties organized by and for women lost their raison d'etre and quickly dissolved in the fractious Chilean political scene.

This lack of concern over the impact of women's vote by the major parties of the left and the center troubled women of the left. As early as 1936, when women first participated in municipal elections and supported conservative candidates, the MEMCH publication *La Mujer Nueva* sounded the alarm. An editorial in the June issue warned that the forces on the right would use the women's vote to dilute the power of the rising left. The left was clearly allowing this process to occur because, although its ideology supported women's suffrage, it evinced no firm commitment to the issue. Instead, the left behaved like an ostrich with its head in the sand when it came to women's issues. The editorial concluded by hoping that when the left finally pulled its head out of the sand it would not find women voting with their traditional values intact.[14] By refusing to meet women's issues head-on, the Chilean left abandoned its ideological and moral obligation to a growing segment of Chilean voters.

The impact of women voters became obvious in the presidential elections of 1958. Five candidates ran for president. A coalition of the traditional Liberal and Conservative Parties supported Jorge Alessandri. The Christian Democrats nominated Eduardo Frei Montavo and a united front of Socialists and Communists backed Salvador Allende. The Radicals and an extreme leftist party also sponsored candidates. In the election, Allende polled well in rural areas, but it was the women's precincts—where 35 percent of the votes were cast—which gave

Alessandri the edge over Allende. Of the women who voted, 34.1 percent gave their votes to Alessandri, while only 22.3 percent voted for Allende. Alessandri's coalition included loyal women's sections which focused on social and charity work—traditional and respectable activities for upper-class women. These organizations mobilized for the candidate who shared their conservative values. Their effectiveness cost Salvador Allende the election. Women became known as *hacedoras de presidentes* (president makers) in Chile.[15]

The Christian Democrats were next to capitalize on the perceived power of female voters to make or break presidential candidates. They organized in rural and urban areas to rally women and the working class to their cause. The strategy paid off in the 1964 election. Eduardo Frei Montavo took the election with an absolute majority of the votes, a first in Chilean history.[16] Frei's victory caused parties of the right to redouble their efforts to organize women as a bulwark against the left.

Frei's government, while proclaiming a "revolution in liberty," continued to mobilize women along traditional lines. Renée Viñas Joan, the woman who held the highest political office in the regime, served as the director of primary and teacher education—not much progress since the days of Labarca Hubertson in the 1930s. As one Christian Democratic woman put it:

> There is a great change from ten years ago—when we women used to joke that we were nothing more than the *sandwichero* called in when the men needed refreshments for their meetings. Now we count for more than this, especially since the women's vote is so important in Chile. The party men really court us around election time! . . . But women in our party always continue in the position of incipient leaders, innate leaders . . . women are depreciated, both within our party and in general.[17]

Frei's administration also used traditional models—women's charitable organizations—to respond to the needs of the urban poor. His administration built on the network of Mothers' Centers, begun during the Radical administrations in the 1940s, and created new grassroots organizations, the *juntas de vecinos* (neighborhood councils). Like the neighborhood councils, the Mothers' Centers operated at the community level; middle-class women (party members) met with working-class women to teach them sewing and other domestic activities. Some of the Centers received government contracts for production of uniforms and other goods. In exchange, the working-class women were expected to support the candidates of their middle-class *madrinas* (patrons). The neighborhood councils allowed women to participate in community decision-making directed by the Christian Democrats. The administration oversaw nearly twelve thousand of these organizations, mostly in the capital. They effectively competed with the charity organizations of the right and the attempts of the Marxists to mobilize the urban poor.[18] These activities allowed women to participate in the traditional spheres—education, domestic activities, and charity work—and also perpetuated male models of patronage.

Despite this feverish organization on the part of the Christian Democrats, the women's vote in 1970 could not prevent a socialist victory in the presidential campaign. The reformist program of the Frei regime and the continued growth of the Socialist and Communist parties united the major right-wing parties behind the candidacy of former president Jorge Alessandri. The Christian Democrats and the *Unidad Popular* (Popular Unity coalition, UP) also fielded candidates. The resulting three-way split handed Salvador Allende, the Socialist candidate and head of the UP, his first victory. His coalition consisted of a variety of leftist parties ranging from extreme Marxists to moderate left Christian Democrats. Allende won a plurality of the popular vote, 36.3 percent. Alessandri ran a close second with 34.9 percent, while the Christian Democrats polled 27.8 percent. Broken down by gender, the tallies reveal that women voted against Allende in proportionately greater numbers than men (69 percent versus 58 percent).[19] The Popular Unity coalition, as *La Mujer Nueva* had warned, had organized women less effectively than its opponents to the right and center, and could only win an election when the right and center split.

Allende's electoral victory in September 1970 did not guarantee him control of the presidential palace. Because he did not receive a majority, the election was thrown into the opposition-dominated Congress. Parties of the center, particularly the Christian Democrats, agonized over the decision to relinquish their mandate and confirm Allende's victory. Alessandri's National Party resisted and immediately organized to thwart Allende's ascension to power. Alessandri offered the Christian Democrats a deal. If they would support his candidacy, he would promptly resign and call new elections, restoring the incumbent Christian Democrat Eduardo Frei as a candidate. The Christian Democrats rejected this offer but used it as leverage against Allende to secure his acceptance of a "declaration of democratic guarantees." The declaration promised the opposition that its political liberties would not be restricted and that Allende would not support the formation of a popular militia.[20]

Despite these agreements, the extreme right made one more attempt to stop Allende. On the day before Congress was to confirm his victory, the opposition botched an attempt to kidnap the commander-in-chief of the Armed Forces, resulting in his death. The incident failed to produce chaos and the Congress certified Allende's election at the end of October.[21]

Although he gained the presidency, Allende failed to mobilize women effectively to defend his government. This flaw undermined his subsequent fight for political survival. The Socialists, like other major parties, continued to segregate women within their ranks. The Communist Party, while it had incorporated women, did not accord them positions of power. As a result, the left offered women no alternative to Chile's traditional model of party organization. This shortsightedness seriously undermined the ability of the left to attract women. By casting its appeal in class terms, it ignored gender issues. Allende intended first to change the means of production which, according to Friedrich Engels, would relieve the conditions of women's oppression. He proposed to alter the economy but ignored changes in social relations. His platform called for the expansion of agrarian reform, nationalization of large sectors of the economy, rent reductions based on income, expansion of the cooperative system in the rural areas, and other programs designed to redistribute income in favor of the poorer segments of the population. A minor plank of the platform addressed women's concerns by promising to eliminate the *patria potestad*, remove legal distinctions between legitimate and illegitimate children, and revise divorce legislation. No mention was made of making women equal partners in agrarian reform, in the workplace, or in the political arena. The platform promised civil equality without economic equality, and it undermined the position of women in legitimate unions.[22] Even leading women in the coalition found it difficult to identify with gender over class. In a 1967 interview, a prominent Communist woman admitted that she "couldn't function without the *two* servants she employs."[23] In looking back over the Allende government after the coup, women who worked for the UP discovered "that they had engaged in the struggle of the poor and the working class without recognizing their own oppression as women."[24] The UP did treat women differently than did the traditional parties, but in a negative way. It failed to address any of their specific needs, either in traditional terms used by other parties or in revolutionary terms that one might have expected from a Marxist coalition. As a result, it lost the battle to win their support.

Allende himself did not question the traditional position of women within politics and society. Two vignettes from his household may offer some insight regarding Allende's sensitivity to women's issues.

> In the days when Allende was a Senator, his wife [nicknamed "La Tencha"], did all of the housekeeping herself because his salary of 1,000 dollars was not enough to pay for servants. Once he became president, she was totally liberated from those chores.[25]

> After his 1958 defeat at the hands of women voters, Allende lived with his wife, an unmarried daughter (two others were married), a niece who served as his secretary . . . and a cook. Reportedly, this arrangement made him feel "condemned" to living in a dictatorship. His wife, on the other hand, asserted that democracy reigned in the house . . . it's just that women had more votes.

The traditionalism of his personal views may have contributed to his coalition's failure to mount an effective appeal to women voters, leaving Allende vulnerable to the opposition that did mobilize their support.

Allende's troubles with women began even before he took power. Working for Alessandri's National Party and its right-wing allies, small groups of women dressed in black demonstrated in front of the presidential palace. A petition bearing twenty thousand signatures urged outgoing President Frei "not to give the country away to communism."[26] Wall posters appeared featuring a schoolboy and his shadow image in guerrilla clothing with a gun and the slogan "your child . . . or your enemy? . . . in socialist countries children are forced to spy on their parents."[27] On the day of Allende's confirmation, a group of women staged a mock funeral procession in front of the presidential palace.[28] In defense of traditional values, the right mobilized women in the public sphere.

The UP's campaign rhetoric emphasized the same values as the rhetoric of its opposition, but the UP lacked credibility with a majority of Chilean women. When the women's vote again tipped the balance against the UP in the Valparaíso municipal elections in 1971, Allende made a special appeal to his party.

> We shall fight without rest because the Chilean woman, the proletarian mother, the mother of the people, understands that our struggle benefits them more than anyone else, and when I see, as in the case of Valparaíso, that in an occasional election, in an emotionally charged atmosphere, it is the woman who decides a battle against us. . . . I want to appeal to the conscience of the members of the Popular Unity Parties and their directors: our great task . . . is to make it possible for the Chilean woman—our sister, daughter, mother and friend—to understand that we need her and will fight for her because she is the seed of our future.[29]

Allende's conception of women as the seed of the UP's future refers to their maternal role. Moreover, his appeal to Chilean women as sisters, daughters, mothers, and friends is not far removed from the opposition's appeal to women which appeared in *El Mercurio*, a right-wing newspaper:

> To speak about motherland and family is to speak about women and vice versa. . . . For Marxism, women can only exist in a utilitarian sense, as producing animals, no matter who the father is, as beasts for work and weight-carriers. For Marxism there are no mothers, no wives, no daughters, no sisters. At best, there are only comrades whose functions vary according to the degree of machista hierarchy that is assigned them under the regime of slavery and oppression.[30]

The call to arms for both groups is exactly the same. Women must defend and uphold their traditional roles to preserve Chilean society.

Instability in Allende's ruling coalition also hampered his efforts to rally popular support for his regime. Although he courted Christian Democratic support for his legislative agenda, partisan emotions undermined his efforts. During the municipal elections in April 1971, other members of his coalition stepped up their attacks on the Christian Democrats and the popular Eduardo Frei. In June 1971, an extremist group associated with the UP assassinated Frei's former minister of the interior, Edmundo Pérez Zujovic.[31] The regime denied any connection with the group and ruthlessly pursued the assassins, but the incident dashed Allende's hopes of working with the Christian Democrats. The instability of his coalition, and his inability to prevent extremist groups from damaging the reputation of the UP, cost Allende the support of the Christian Democrats and the Christian Democratic women's organizations.

Those women then joined what had been the right's campaign against Allende. His nationalization programs and his aggressive agrarian reforms hit the middle-class members of the Christian Democrats particularly hard. In late summer 1971, a woman dressed in only a bathing suit traveled from her southern farm to the capital on horseback protesting the government's expropriation of her land.[32] The opposition press gave this incident front-page attention, and used it to damage Allende's image as a responsible patriarch.

Allende's efforts to maintain the support of Christian Democratic women failed. He had appointed Cármen Gloria Aguayo, a former Christian Democrat, to head a commission to draft legislation creating a ministry for the protection of women and the family. The task of the ministry was to coordinate and manage the Mothers' Centers and neighborhood councils created by Frei's government and to supervise the distribution of milk to school children. Aguayo anticipated a government post as reward for her work, but was disappointed when the first female cabinet appointment—minister of labor—went to a member of the Communist Party.[33]

As the Christian Democrats drifted into opposition, female party members took to the streets. The Mothers' Centers became politicized and women acted and spoke out against the government. On 1 December 1971, the Democratic Women's Front, which united women from the National Party and the Christian Democratic Party, held a rally billed as "the march of the empty pots." Demonstrators demanded that Fidel Castro break off a planned visit to Santiago, and that the government lower food prices. The march was well organized and involved about five thousand women. It is unclear how many of the women were working class. Juan de Onís, reporting for the *New York Times*, claimed that there was a significant number, but U.S. Ambassador Nathaniel Davis "suspect[ed] that loyal or gentrified maids from the better suburbs made up more of the 'working class' contingent than women of the shantytowns and poorer districts."[34] The peaceful march turned violent when young UP supporters pelted the demonstrators with rocks. The army restored order and cleared the streets with tear gas. The incident prompted Allende to put Santiago under a curfew. The opposition press had a field day with coverage of the attack on middle-class women of the city. To keep the memory of the debacle fresh, women banged on pots every night between 8 and 10 PM for several months after the march. The UP leaders claimed that these women had two pots—a big one used for hoarding food and a small one with which they demonstrated.[35] The banging of the pots resonated with traditional family values for many Chileans. The opposition kept up the campaign and denounced as fraudulent Allende's professions of concern with the worsening economic plight of the nation.

The women's protest movement became increasingly sophisticated. In 1972, *El Poder Femenino* (Women's Power, EPF) emerged from the street demonstrations. Led by women from the three opposition parties and civic leaders, it took over direction of the women's movement against the Allende regime. It was comprised of female members and wives of members of craft and professional unions and guilds. In April 1972, a communication network, *Solidaridad, Orden, y Libertad* (Solidarity, Order, and Liberty, SOL), organized women in secretive five-person cells. SOL, associated with the extreme right-wing group *Patria y Libertad* (Homeland and Liberty), claimed forty thousand members at the height of its power. Along with the Civic and Family Movement, it produced radio programs unfavorable to the government.[36]

Beyond their own organizations, women also provided essential support for Allende's opponents in the labor movement. In October 1972, the National Truckers Confederation announced a strike to protest the government's proposal to create a state trucking enterprise. The National and Christian Democratic Parties immediately pledged their support to the truckers, and foreign money also filled the strikers' coffers. Transportation workers' wives prepared public soup kitchens on the streets of Santiago to win support for their husbands' cause. EPF members supplied foodstuffs and harbored fugitive strikers. Women occupied radio stations and "assembled home-made stink bombs to drive customers away from non-striking" businesses. They "patrolled the streets, threatening physical violence to strikebreaking merchants, . . . and operated a clandestine plant to manufacture *miguelitos* (sharpened, four-pronged steel devices)" to cut the tires of scab truckers. A new truckers' strike in the winter of 1973 brought the strikers' wives to the presidential palace. When Allende refused them an audience, they occupied the basement of the National Congress. Two days later, middle- and upper-class women and a Christian Democratic congresswoman joined their demonstration.[37]

Women also participated in the campaign to sabotage the UP's economic programs. Using Mothers' Centers in urban districts established during the Frei regime, the women disrupted the UP's rationing programs by setting up alternate distribution networks and harassing workers in the rationing centers. *El Poder Femenino* members formed a stockholders' committee to fight government plans for business expropriations. The committee successfully prevented the government from gaining controlling interest in the Bank of Chile and in the Paper and Carton Company, an important source of newsprint.[38]

The women's press was equally active in the struggle against Allende. EPF members on the staff of *El Mercurio* filled its pages with anti-government features. The director of a middle-class women's magazine, *Eva*, declared war on the UP. "Women must fight; we must help them, stimulate them, mould them."[39] The magazine advised women on how to prepare themselves physically and morally for the effort against Allende. In the cooking section, today's spartan "food for war" recipes were contrasted with sumptuous recipes "from the good old days" before Allende.[40]

Finally, women played an important role in mobilizing the military against the regime. In March 1973, the opposition failed in its bid to win an overwhelming majority against the UP. Frustrated by the voters, the opposition turned to the military. Groups of women started visiting the Military Academy to throw corn—chicken feed—at the soldiers, accusing them of being hens afraid to take action. They also offered to paint the barracks baby blue for the boys. A statement by General Gustavo Leigh reveals the effectiveness of their ridicule: "they said that we were chickens. They left corn at the doors of our houses. They said that we were cowards. Whoever had been in my position on that day would have acted. There was no other way out."[41] Women challenged the military to defend their honor and *machismo*.

Their campaign soon exacted a toll on the nerves of the nation's most important military officer—the commander-in-chief General Carlos Prats González. On his way home from lunch on 27 June he noticed a driver in another car making an obscene gesture at him. He ordered his driver to force the other car off the road. He emerged to confront the offender with his sidearm drawn, but was horrified to discover a woman behind the wheel. A gathering crowd taunted the general for attacking an unarmed housewife. In August, officers' wives delivered a letter to General Prats's wife demanding her husband's resignation. Because of the general's support for Allende, the women claimed that their husbands were ashamed to wear their uniforms in public. On 21 August, several hundred army wives congregated in front of the general's home to shout "*maricon!*" (sissy) and throw corn. When the demonstration turned violent, Prats called for the police. The incident broke him. He said, "I never thought . . . that generals and colonels whom I have known since childhood would hide behind the skirts of their wives. . . . One thing is clear. Unity in the army will not be possible if I remain in the army together with the generals who sent their wives to the door of my house, the house of the commander-in-chief."[42] He resigned on the twenty-third and was replaced by General Augusto Pinochet Ugarte. Women continued their demonstrations against the government until the day of the coup. On 10 September, they gathered in front of the ministry of defense to urge military action. Pinochet moved against Allende the following day.[43]

The military regime that replaced the Allende government proved to be as brutal as any in South America. On taking power, Pinochet promised women representation in the new government and created a national secretariat of women, implicitly acknowledging women's new prominence in national politics. The purpose of the new secretariat, however, was to reestablish the social status quo ante

Allende: it was assigned the task of defending the integrity of the traditional Chilean family and restoring women to the tranquility of the domestic sphere. It used the Mothers' Centers to spread the message at the grassroots level.[44]

But the military, by brutally violating the domestic sphere, insured that women would maintain their organizations in order to survive. Women from all parts of the political spectrum remained active despite Pinochet's attempt to return them to home and hearth. As the dictatorship and the repression continued, only women were permitted to demonstrate. As early as 1978, women who had lost family members during the repression following the coup organized in opposition to the regime. With the support of the Catholic Church, women created and internationally marketed *arpilleras* (embroidered tapestries) which represented family members who had disappeared during the regime. To combat this, Pinochet used the Mothers' Centers. Both sides used the public sphere as the forum in which to defend their families. The regime failed to recognize the danger inherent in allowing women to occupy public space. It was Chilean women who called international attention to the barbarism of the military government and aided human rights organizations in Santiago. Moreover, Chilean women, politicized by the Allende years and the dictatorship, became the electoral majority during Pinochet's rule. Pinochet did retain support from women of all classes, but the majority of Chilean women voted to end his hold on political power in the 1988 plebiscite.[45] Because it operated under a model of strict patriarchy, the Pinochet government underestimated the power women had acquired. Once called to the public sphere, Chilean women remained.

In addition to contributing to the downfall of the dictatorship, Chilean women began assessing the failure of the political left to address their concerns before and after the coup. According to one woman:

> Almost all of the aspects of the junta's policies have been abundantly criticized by the Chilean left. Nevertheless, there has been a curious silence regarding the retrogressive policy of the junta on women [which has contributed to the feminization of poverty in Chile]. What's more, no one has seriously investigated why women were the Achilles heel of the Popular Unity government.[46]

Such an analysis could lead to an understanding of why Chilean women did not support the UP government and may still be reluctant to adhere to parties on the left. Like other political parties, those of the

UP never questioned the traditional methods of political organization of women or acknowledged the sources of female oppression within Chilean society. It offered women nothing revolutionary—no way to break the chain of oppression—and it threatened to disrupt what little security women had within the private sphere. On the eve of the military coup, Salvador Allende warned his supporters that the country had only a three-day reserve of flour, and that meat would be more tightly rationed.[47] Allende's government meant starvation for the Chilean family.

Although it was the economic crisis and opposition of important sectors of the labor movement, the international community, and the military which brought down Allende's government, Chilean women spearheaded the popular opposition. And they did so because in the 1950s and 1960s the Chilean left—the basis of Allende's coalition—exclusively addressed class oppression while ignoring gender oppression. At the same time, parties of the center and right actively moved to organize the new female electorate, albeit along traditional lines. When women took to the streets in response to the economic crisis of the early 1970s, they did so in defense of their families and on behalf of the center and right parties who supported traditional values.

Behind the turmoil in the streets, women's role in Chilean society and politics was changing during the Allende regime. Unable to overcome its own internal divisions, the Popular Unity coalition neglected either to reaffirm women's traditional roles and values or to offer them alternative models. The opposition parties, particularly the Christian Democrats, appealed to and organized women along traditional lines, and then adapted that organization to meet the economic crisis and the changing political order. Allende's inability to control his party and the economy allowed the opposition to activate women from all classes. Allende's coalition failed to offer women the same opportunity. His government, and Chilean democracy, paid the price for that failure during the Pinochet regime. Nevertheless, the activation of women in the public sphere during the Allende government survived the dictatorship and has afforded women the opportunity to participate in the renaissance of Chilean democracy since 1989.

NOTES

1. For more information on the Allende regime and the coup, see María de los Angeles Crummett, "El Poder Femenino: The Mobilization of Women Against Socialism in Chile," *Latin American Perspectives* 4, no. 4 (Fall 1977): 103; Paul E. Sigmund, *The Overthrow of Allende* (Pittsburgh, Pa.: University of

Pittsburgh Press, 1977); Brian Loveman, *Chile: The Legacy of Hispanic Capitalism* (Oxford: Oxford University Press, 1978); Mark Falcoff, *Modern Chile, 1970–1989* (New Brunswick, N.J.: Transaction Publishers, 1989); Arturo Valenzuela, *The Breakdown of Democratic Regimes: Chile* (Baltimore: Johns Hopkins University Press, 1978).

2. An example of this type of scholarship can be found in Michele Mattelart, "The Feminine Version of the Coup D'Etat," in *Sex and Class in Latin America*, ed. June Nash and Helen Icken Safa (New York: J. F. Bergin Publishers, 1976), 279–301.

3. Two women, Isabel Le-Brun and Isabel Tarrago, worked to establish high schools for Chilean girls in the 1870s. The recognition of their efforts came in 1877 when the minister of education allowed their students to qualify for admission into the state university. He also increased national investment in public education and established the first girls' public high school. Elsa Chaney, "Women in Latin American Politics," in *Female and Male in Latin America*, ed. Anne Pescatello (Pittsburgh, Pa.: University of Pittsburgh Press, 1973), 108; Elsa Chaney, *Supermadre: Women in Politics in Latin America* (Austin, University of Texas Press, 1979), 59–60. In 1969, Chilean women occupied 12 out of 147 seats in Chile's lower house and 3 out of 45 Senators were female. In the United States, at the same period, only 10 representatives out of 435 were women and only one Senate seat was held by a female. Michael Francis and Patricia A. Kyle, ed., "Chile: The Power of Women at the Polls," in Patricia A. Kyle, *Reintegrating the Neglected Majority: Government Responses to New Sex Roles* (Brunswick, Ohio: Kings Court Press, 1976), 104.

4. According to Elsa Chaney "the entrance of women into the administration of justice has been facilitated by the disinterest of male lawyers . . . because they are so grossly underpaid." Chaney, "Women in Latin American Politics," 119, 120; Felicitas Klimpel Alvarado, *La mujer chilena: el aporte femenino al progreso de Chile, 1910–1950* (Santiago: Editorial Andrés Bello, 1962), 111.

5. Chaney, "Women in Latin American Politics," 120.

6. Chaney, *Supermadre*, 94.

7. Chaney, *Supermadre*, 74–75; Gabriela Leret de Metheus, *La mujer una incapaz como el demente y el niño* (Mexico: B. Costa-Amic Editor, 1975), 68; Rosa Signorelli de Marti, "Spanish America," in Raphael Patai, ed., *Women in the Modern World* (New York: Free Press 1967), 194.

8. Julieta Kirkwood, *Ser política en Chile* (Santiago: FLASCO, 1986), 107–11.

9. Chaney, *Supermadre*, 70; Chaney, "Women in Latin American Politics," 119; Regis Debray, *Conversations with Allende* (London: Free Press, 1971), 21.

10. Chaney, *Supermadre*, 75. Aguirre Cerda based his fears on women's participation in the municipal elections of 1936 in which the majority of women supported conservative candidates. Kirkwood, *Ser política*, 144; For more evidence on the attitude of political parties toward women's suffrage, see Elena Caffarena and Olga Poblete, "Pioneras de una lucha que renace," in María Angélica Meza, *La otra mitad de Chile* (Santiago: Instituto para el nuevo Chile, 1986), 54–55.

11. Kirkwood, *Ser política*, 130.

12. "El movimiento pro emancipación de la mujer chilena," *Antología una historia del movimiento femenino en Chile* (Santiago: MEMCH, 1982), 2–7; Kirkwood, *Ser política*, 125–36; Chaney, "Women in Latin American Politics," 110; Mattelart, "Chile: The Feminine Version," 292–93.

13. Ibid. The same sort of organizational problems afflicted the women's movement in the United States. For more information, see Eleanor Flexner, *Century of Struggle* (Cambridge: Belknap Press of Harvard University Press, 1959); William L. O'Neill, *Everyone Was Brave: The Rise and Fall of Feminism in America* (Chicago: Quadrangle Books, 1969).

14. MEMCH, *Antología*, 62 (reprint of editorial from *La Mujer Nueva* 1, no. 7, June 1936).

15. For an in-depth analysis of female voting patterns in Chile, see Steven M. Neuse, "Voting in Chile: The Feminine Response," in *Political Participation in Latin America*, vol. 1, *Citizen and State*, ed. John A. Booth and Mitchell A. Seligson (New York: Holmes and Meier, 1978), 129–44; Federico Gil, *The Political System of Chile* (Boston: Houghton Mifflin Co., 1966), 214–15; Loveman, *Chile*, 279; Chaney, "Women in Latin American Politics," 137, n. 38; Jane Jaquette, "Female Political Participation in Latin America," in *Sex and Class in Latin America*, ed. June Nash and Helen Icken Safa (New York: J. F. Bergin Publishers, 1976), 237; Edy Kaufman, *Crisis in Allende's Chile* (New York: Praeger, 1988), 64.

16. Loveman, *Chile*, 297, 303–14; Francisco José Moreno, *Legitimacy and Stability in Latin America* (New York: Crowell Press, 1969), 195.

17. Chaney, "Women in Latin American Politics," 113.

18. Interview with Gladys Zureta, Instituto Nacional de la Mujer, 11 July 1991, Santiago, Chile; Crummett, "El Poder Femenino," 105; Mattelart, "Chile: The Coup," 284; Loveman, *Chile*, 318; Patricia M. Chuchryk, "Feminist Anti-Authoritarian Politics: The Role of Women's Organizations in the Chilean Transition to Democracy," in *The Women's Movement in Latin America*, ed. Jane Jaquette (Boston: Unwin Hyman, 1989), 160; Carol Andreas, "The Chilean Woman: Reform, Reaction, and Resistance," *Latin American Perspectives* 4, no. 4 (Fall 1977): 123.

19. Chile, Ministerio del Interior, *Dirreción del registro electoral* (Santiago, 1971); Kaufman, *Crisis in Allende's Chile*, 64.

20. Paul E. Sigmund, "Chile: Two Years of Popular Unity," *Problems of Communism* 21 (May-June 1971): 39; Paul M. Sweezy and Harry Magdoff, "Peaceful Transition to Socialism?" *Monthly Review* 22 (January 1971): 6, 20; David C. Jordan, "Marxism in Chile: An Interim View of Its Implications for Latin American Policy," *Orbis* 15 (1971): 329–30; L. Whitehead, "The Socialist Experiment in Chile" *Parliamentary Affairs* (Summer 1972): 246.

21. Jordan, "Marxism in Chile," 329–30; Debray, *Conversations with Allende*, 58; Sigmund, *The Overthrow of Allende*, 123.

22. The plank read: "Full civil status of married women will be established (elimination of the *patria potestad*), as will the equal status for all children whether born in or out of wedlock, as well as adequate divorce legislation

which dissolves legal ties and safeguards the woman's and children's rights." J. Ann Zammit, ed., *The Chilean Road to Socialism* (Austin: University of Texas Press, 1973), 271.

23. The importance of this factor in keeping women from organizing across class lines cannot be exaggerated. According to Mattelart, "in 1968, 100 percent of the well-to-do women who had a job also had a housemaid . . . in the petite bourgeoisie, 88 percent of the women who worked were assisted in their domestic chores." Mattelart, "Chile: The Feminine Version," 292. See also Neuse, "Voting in Chile," 136–38; Francis and Kyle attempt to explain the reluctance of Allende to revolutionize gender roles in Francis and Kyle, "Chile: The Power of Women," 111; Chaney, "Women in Latin American Politics," 108.

24. Chuchryk, "Feminist Anti-Authoritarian Politics," 162.

25. Guillermo Ochoa, *Reportaje en Chile* (Mexico: Litográfica Juventud, S.A., 1972), 60–61.

26. Samuel Chavkin, *The Murder of Chile* (Chicago: Lawrence Hill, 1989), 48–49; María Correa Morande, *La guerra de las mujeres* (Santiago: Taller Grafico UTE, 1974), 15–17.

27. Chavkin, *The Murder of Chile*, 49.

28. Correa Morande, *La guerra*, 21–22.

29. Allende's speech is quoted from Kaufman, *Crisis in Allende's Chile*, 64; see also Vania Bambirra, "The Chilean Woman," in North American Conference on Latin America [hereafter NACLA], *New Chile* (Berkeley: Waller Press, 1972), 34–36.

30. *El Mercurio*, 18 August 1973.

31. "VOP—Left Extremism," in NACLA, 32; Sigmund, *The Overthrow of Allende*, 148–49; Kaufman, *Crisis in Allende's Chile*, 62.

32. "A lomo de la protesta," *Ercilla* 1942 (4–10 October 1972): 12; Mattelart, "Chile: The Feminine Version," 282.

33. Kaufman, *Crisis in Allende's Chile*, 64–65; Chaney, "Women in Politics in Latin America," 119.

34. *New York Times*, 2 December 1971; Sigmund, *The Overthrow of Allende*, 162–63; Nathaniel Davis, *The Last Two Years of Salvador Allende* (Ithaca: Cornell University Press, 1985), 47–48; Falcoff, *Modern Chile*, 262–63.

35. According to Soledad Parada, over ninety thousand women were incorporated in the Mothers' Centers which became politicized immediately after Allende's election. Some stayed loyal to the Christian Democrats while others were part of the Popular Unity's support network. Interview with Soledad Parada, director of the Secretaría de la Mujer under Allende, CEPAL, 11 July 1991, Santiago, Chile; Mattelart, "Chile: The Feminine Version," 282, 286.

36. "El nuevo poder," *Ercilla* 1989 (29 August–4 September 1973): 10–13; Kaufman, *Crisis in Allende's Chile*, 66; Crummett, "El Poder Femenino," 103–13.

37. Crummett, "El Poder Femenino," 106.

38. For the campaign against Allende's action against the Carton Company, see *¿Que Pasa?* 48 (March 1972): 53; *¿Que Pasa?* 50 (March 1972): 39; *Ercilla* 1989 (29 August–4 September 1973): 11–12; Carlos Sepúlveda Vergara, "La tentación del papel," *Ercilla* 1892 (20–26 October 1971): 63–65; Mattelart, "Chile: The

Coup," 294–96; Crummett, "El Poder Femenino," 106.

39. Mattelart, "Chile: The Coup," 296–300, Crummett, "El Poder Femenino," 104.

40. Mattelart, "Chile: The Feminine Version," 300. See also "El pan negro cada día," *¿Que pasa?* 83 (November 1972): 13; Carlos Sepúlveda Vergara,"Caldera de tensiones," *Ercilla* 1976 (30 May–5 June 1973): 24–26.

41. Thomas G. Sanders, "Military Government in Chile," in *The Politics of Anti-Politics*, ed. Brian Loveman and Thomas M. Davies, Jr. (Lincoln: University of Nebraska Press, 1978), 272; Mattelart, "Chile: The Feminine Version," 283.

42. Falcoff, *Modern Chile*, 283; Davis, *The Last Two Years of Salvador Allende*, 196–97; see also "El nuevo poder" *Ercilla* 1989 (29 August–4 September 1973): 12–13.

43. Davis, *The Last Two Years of Salvador Allende*, 206–29; Mattelart, "Chile: The Feminine Version," 283.

44. Susana Levy and Norbert Lechner, "CEMA Chile y Secretaría Nacional de la Mujer," in Meza, ed., *La otra mitad de Chile*, 81–99; Giselle Munizaga and Lillian Letelier, "Mujer y regimen militar," in Centro de Estudios de la Mujer, *Mundo de mujer. Continuidad y cambio* (Santiago: Arancibia Hnos y Cia., 1988), 525–62; Ximena Bunster, "Watch Out for the Little Nazi Man that All of Us Have Inside: The Mobilization and Demobilization of Women in Militarized Chile," *Women's Studies International Forum* 11, no. 5 (1988): 485–91; for more information on Pinochet's use of the Mothers' Centers see CEMA-CHILE, *Revista aniversario CEMA-CHILE* (October 1982–1983).

45. Ita Hernández, Servicio Nacional de la Mujer, 12 July 1991, Santiago, Chile; "101 Arrested in Women's Day Demonstrations," Santiago Domestic Service, 11 March 1987, translated in Foreign Broadcast Information Service, vol. 9, *Latin America, Daily Report* (13 March 1987), E1–E9; César N. Caviedes, *Elections in Chile* (Boulder: Lynne Rienner, 1991), 35-54; Instituto Nacional Democrata Para Asuntos Internacionales, *La transición Chilena hacía la democracia* (Washington, D.C.: National Democratic Institute for International Affairs, 1989); "Chileans Vote to Oust Pinochet and Hold Open Elections in '89," *The Ledger Star*, 6 October 1988; Marjorie Agosin, *Scraps of Life: Chilean Arpilleras*, trans. Cola Franzen (Trenton: Red Sea Press, 1987). For more information on the role of women during the Pinochet regime see Patricia M. Chuchryk, "Feminist Anti-Authoritarian Politics," in *The Women's Movement in Latin America*, ed. Jane Jaquette (Boston: Unwin Hyman, 1989), 149–84.

46. Josefina Rossetti, "La mujer y el feminismo" (Santiago: Cuadernos del Círculo, Círculo de Estudios de la Mujer, May 1983), 24 as cited in Patricia M. Chuchryk, "Feminist Anti-Authoritarian Politics," 162.

47. Davis, *The Last Two Years of Salvador Allende*, 214.

VI

Conclusion

Chapter 18

Simultaneous Revolutions and Exits

A Semi-Skeptical Comment

Christine Sylvester

My contribution to this volume is skeptical in only one way, and that is about the generalizability of the Huntington definition of revolution as "a rapid, fundamental and violent domestic change in the . . . social structure."[1] I have no argument with the suggestion that change in gender relations must be factored into the usual notions of revolutionary change; nor am I any more sanguine than other contributors about the degree to which women have benefited from most revolutions.

My semi-skeptical comment derives from observations about revolution in Zimbabwe. I contend that:

> Zimbabwe did not have a revolution which succeeded, failed or changed through difficult circumstances. Rather, it may have experienced four simultaneous revolutions for independence. Each transformed some aspect of consciousness, social structure, state and economy, but none was at the centre of any encompassing historical bloc of change.[2]

This is a departure from the usual ways that analysts understand events framing the independence of Zimbabwe from Rhodesia and Britain. Most studies focus on waves of nationalist sentiment that gave way in the late 1960s to an armed struggle featuring two guerrilla forces, the Zimbabwe African National Liberation Army (ZANLA) and the Zimbabwe People's Revolutionary Army (ZIPRA), arrayed against the Rhodesian military. The war raged until 1979 when a negotiated settlement produced the political discontinuity of independence but set the stage for continuities in economic and social fields—that is, for changes that were far from fundamental. Zimbabwe's revolution, it is often said, became petit bourgeoisified, and vague promises of a scientifically socialist future ended up sharing a diminished amount of political space with less progressive tendencies. This was due to a number of factors: weaknesses in the nationalist leadership, including serious ideological deficiencies and a failure to develop and mobilize the masses; white settler and imperialist intrigues; and the machinations of South Africa.[3]

I argue that we should not think that there was once a revolution in Zimbabwe that, in Andre Astrow's vivid rendering,[4] lost its way. Rather, simultaneous revolutions unfolded from 1945 to 1979 that continue in various forms to affect the political economy of Zimbabwe today, robbing it, so to speak, of a hegemonic core. Indeed, the simultaneities imbue the present with a veritable mish-mash of liberal, Marxist, and authoritarian politics, none of which does justice to people called women.[5]

More generally, I argue that in contexts where anti-colonial or late revolutionary struggles fragment into formidable and semi-permanent blocs of contention—as in Zimbabwe, Angola, Mozambique, and maybe in South Africa—we often find messy revolutions defying our desire for analytical tidiness. Rather than discipline these events by looking for some arbitrary point at which they win or lose, prevail or flounder, change social structure or change leaders, it is more fruitful to look for "transformations of a both-and nature—both successful and unsuccessful, coherent and incoherent, complete and incomplete, complementary and antagonistic, perhaps socialist and non-socialist."[6] Indeed, in some contexts:

> There is no goodness-of-fit to any one ideal-typical model of revolution, nor is one global tendency, class, strategy, or alliance responsible for the disjointed outcomes. Simultaneous revolutions are not teleological, holistic, or binary. They are multicentered and multivectored and, by definition rather than by "mistake," they are un-unified.[7]

One can gauge the degree of simultaneity in a seemingly revolutionary situation by considering the following characteristics of such configurations:

> Simultaneous revolutions require two or more instrumental centres of force, the actions of which have some independent and

> mutually transformative effects on consciousness, state, economy and class structure which may not be intended and are not co-ordinated [and need not be progressive]. Each centre has a primary social base, set of interests, leadership, range of strategies for change and coalition partners locally and in the world system. As well, each has a set of internal contradictions which hamper it from taking the lead in forming an historical bloc, and each operates in a complex field of forces over which it gains only limited control. . . . All centres succeed, in the sense that their actions are responsible for one or more structural discontinuity, and all fail under their own more comprehensive logic of transformation. As a result the uneven and contradictory changes become semi-permanent and cannot be understood in dichotomous terms of revolution/counter-revolution, success/failure, revolution/reform, unity/division, stability/instability.[8]

In elucidating the notion of simultaneous revolutions, I take readers through a set of revisionist interpretations of Zimbabwe's revolution, borrowing along the way from the writings of Antonio Gramsci and others about passive, anti-passive, and council revolutions in post-World War I Italy to help clarify the types of revolutions that have scattered the terrain of Zimbabwean politics. I find that Zimbabwe experienced two passive revolutions—conservative state-centered efforts by ruling classes to stave off crisis by coopting or defeating upcoming class projects. One passive revolution was waged by the (male-led) Rhodesian state between 1945 and 1979 as it struggled to control the forces of nationalism. The other unfolded simultaneously under the leadership of (male) black nationalists as they met Rhodesian calls for racial partnership in a white minority state with similar calls for racial partnership, albeit with eventual majority rule in mind. There was also one anti-passive revolution waged by disgruntled (male) cadres in the nationalist militaries, who tried to jump-start the engines of radical liberationist politics through bold insubordinations against the nationalist forces of passive revolution. And, there was at least one council revolution in the countryside involving a peasant project for land and autonomy, with, as the piece by Sita Ranchod-Nilsson describes, a women's project within it.

Before continuing, it is useful to pull the gendered characteristics of these revolutions out of the shadows, because this is the crux of the issue. The passive revolutions were waged mostly by white and black male leaders of Rhodesia as they jockeyed to give the appearance of being liberal, in the Rhodesian case, and to take advantage, in the nationalist case, of that Rhodesian appearance in order to press for real reforms. The playing field for this mirror-imaged set of revolutionary actions was not entirely devoid of women, but on both sides women's roles were largely of a support nature as local nationalist versions of what Jean Elshtain often refers to as civic cheerleading.[9] Most white women were preoccupied with upholding "white standards" in the face of calls for majority rule, and backed their men in the project to coopt or defeat black nationalism. One of their duties in this effort was to keep alive the memories of pioneer hardships and victories: "intrepid wives of pioneers suffered immeasurable hardships in order to make homes for their menfolk and their children in a wild and often hostile land."[10] Black women were often too bone-wearily busy supporting their families to rise to early nationalist prominence.[11] Joshua Nkomo, the globe-trotting head of the Zimbabwe African People's Union (ZAPU) until 1989, said of his wife:

> My marriage was the best thing I ever did in my whole life. In the thirty-four years of our marriage we have spent less than half the time together, but we have had a perfect understanding all the time. My wife has always borne the main responsibility for such property as we have owned: more, she has kept our family together, because all of us have always been confident that she would be there whatever happened.[12]

There are similar assumptions and silences about women in personal and scholarly accounts of the anti-passive revolutionary attempts by guerrillas to radicalize the civilian nationalist leaderships of the armed struggle. Stories of the Nhari Rebellion among certain ZANLA cadres and the 11 March Movement in ZIPRA are full of the names of heroic men who challenged their bosses ideologically and paid a dear price, even though some of their efforts did result in change.[13] The name of one heroic woman of anti-passive revolution comes readily to mind: Judith Todd, daughter of former Prime Minister Garfield Todd. Todd received widespread personal recognition in this revolutionary center of force because she defied the Rhodesian culture and the politics of race to side with the forces of majority rule.[14] The thousands of black women who joined the male guerrillas in war have their heroines, to be sure (among them, the commander Teurai Ropa Nhongo); the stories of most of them, however, have blended together over time, to constitute a group of anonymous ones.[15]

In the countryside, council-type revolutionary efforts among the peasantry let us see the involvement of many women—dimly. It seems that for a brief time peasant women formed a center of force within a larger rural revolution. Their efforts neither prevailed, leaving behind feted national heroines,[16] nor met total defeat—there have been policy changes in the countryside. It is in the shadowy margins between revolutionary victory and defeat that one finds "women."

THE WAXING AND WANING OF WOMEN'S POWER

Gramsci wrote about council revolutions in the context of worker organizations in Turin that contained germs of a class project for socialism.[17] In the Zimbabwean context there was some classic worker consciousness in the cities and mining towns of Rhodesia following World Wars I and II, but the focal point of council-type organization for change was in the countryside, where peasant farmers were aggravated by a colonial state that interfered with their livelihoods in two ways. First, the state alienated the best tracts of land for whites, thereby releasing black labor for mines and industries. Second, it herded the dispossessed onto Tribal Trust Lands, which soon became overcrowded and inadequate. Against this backdrop, the peasantry, says Terence Ranger, gradually developed a class project to resist what it saw as state efforts to eliminate the peasant option.[18]

Ranger does not emphasize the point that women comprise approximately 70 percent of the permanent rural population in Zimbabwe. He does not conceptualize "women peasants" at all, perhaps because he does not query the gendered content of policies that preserved industrial jobs for true "workers," understood as "men," while also reserving land rights for Tribal Trust "peasants," also "men." It was the rural "woman" who maintained homefires and crops, but who, under Rhodesian law, was a minor for life—unable to negotiate credit, apply for a passport alone, or own property aside from household pots and pans.

Women's plight had not been considerably easier during precolonial times. During much of that long time period, "women" was a designation for biologically sexed females who were assigned responsibility for maintaining men's lineages while suffering the status of "outsiders within" the patrilocal and patrilineal norms guiding most communities (only a small ethnic group called the Tonga have matrilineal practices).[19] The mechanism for producing and reproducing "women," in precolonial Zimbabwe and today, is brideprice, *lobola*. It inscribes the bodies of community members with "truthful" natures and duties according to their sexual characteristics, such that a male-sexed suitor presents "gifts" to the family of a female-sexed person in order to seal a contract that transfers her productive and reproductive capacities to him. The practice establishes "women" as producers of commodities and use-values in society. It also designates as normal that control over "women's" valued production is the purview of a male-sexed person. "Women" are so important it seems, that they must be controlled by someone else.

Norma Kriger maintains that when the nationalist struggle turned militant in the late 1960s, groups that had been oppressed in indigenous societies used the war "to openly express grievances and to manipulate the guerrillas' agenda to their own advantage."[20] Many married women gained some control over their husbands during the early stages of the armed struggle by appealing to the socialist-espousing, or simply new society-envisaging (usually ZANLA), guerrillas who came to their villages to politicize and mobilize the people. For a while, some guerrillas backed the rights of women and openly punished men guilty of wife-beating. As one rural woman recalls, "the young guerrillas tended to trust the mothers in the village, not only because they were women but also because they had been less exposed to the settler regime."[21]

Peasant women, thus empowered, briefly formed the nucleus of a rural center of revolutionary gender force within a larger peasant project and aligned with young, apparently anti-passive revolutionary, men of the guerrilla wings of struggle. The women's efforts were aimed mostly at ending the worst excesses of male dominance in local communities. But the alliance was temporary. Threatened with a backlash from the very men needed for the war effort, guerrilla support for women ebbed until "women" once again reverted to a status of controlled subjects. Thereafter, in account after account, we learn that women became the caretakers of the guerrillas rather than agents of change in their own right:

> In the process of co-operation, we cooked for them, we gave them bread, we killed and cooked chickens to feed them. . . . We carried sadza [the maize staple] to them in buckets. . . . After eating the mothers carried their containers back home. . . . After a long time, when the war was at its peak, [the guerrillas] changed their strategy. They said women should not bring food to their base [because they would be detected by the Rhodesian Forces] and they formed a "base committee" . . . my duty was to supervise the women who prepared the food.[22]

In addition, the guerrillas placed considerable emphasis on maintaining unity in the struggle, and this meant that those who spoke of changing the status of women were accused of being selfish and divisive. The makings of a council-type revolutionary subcenter in the countryside, "manned" by "women" who were simultaneously the prime producers, the majority group, and momentarily victorious against abusive local men, was thereby further diffused by appeals to support the national liberation struggle as defined and led by heroic men. Some younger women—girls really—joined their male counterparts as combatants. But in the words of one female ex-combatant I interviewed in 1988, "the men always told us what we could do and they are still doing that."[23]

Today, in post-independence Zimbabwe, in a country that touts socialism and operates according to the precepts of other ideologies (chiefly a reformist, passive revolutionary liberalism), female peasant farmers can now hold Grain Marketing Board cards in their own name. This means that profits from maize sold to the official government market can now be paid to women rather than to the male head of household only. Yet many a woman has been beaten for failing to turn all profits over to a husband who, as elsewhere in Africa, can often waste those profits:[24]

> The money is spent on drinking, not on us or on the children. We share the work, or do more of it, but he takes all the money telling us it is his—that he earned it. It is a joke.[25]

Now there is a new strategy afoot among the women. Instead of selling all the maize they can to the government parastatal, many women withhold some and sell it privately for higher—and untraceable—sums.[26] With these earnings comes the equivalent of pin money that women use as they see fit, and they often see fit to ensure that female children, who are usually the first to suffer when it gets rough for a family, attend school regularly.[27] In this strategy, we see the resonances of a tendency Kathleen Staudt has alerted us to: women disengage or exit "from conventional politics into more autonomous management of their own affairs to the extent this is still possible with an ever expanding state."[28] In place of the political engagement rural women experienced during the early years of the armed struggle, individual women are walking away from the state. This is not to say that rural Zimbabwean women have completely disengaged from all politics: many are members of the ZANU Women's League, a pro-government civic cheerleading organization, and many vote regularly in local and national elections. Moreover, although there is something of the revolutionary spirit in their specific refusals of gendered Marketing Board rules, the disengagements are not necessarily signs of resistance. There is some powerlessness in the refusals, some acquiescence to old hierarchies. When I asked women in several farming groups in the Murewa area to tell me about the war, many could still remember the days when guerrillas disciplined local male "ne'er do wells." They could still say that "if we had power we would take care of women first because we know how hard we work." But now they said they had no idea how to get what they wanted from the political process.

The irony in all this is that the Zimbabwean state congratulates itself for establishing women's rights; for instance, there is now an Age of Majority Act in effect and this is what entitles women to hold Grain Marketing Board cards in their own names. Like the guerrillas before it, however, the state has been unwilling to stick its neck out too far for women, pulling back whenever a backlash emerges—whenever, that is, the agendas of other ongoing struggles need to be coopted. This behavior by the state is partly explicable by the fact that the council-type revolution in the countryside did not completely prevail and hence many rural voices have not been fully absorbed into the state's agenda. In addition, other revolutionary tendencies in Zimbabwe have also partially prevailed and partially failed, thus bringing contradictory currents to bear on contemporary public policy.[29]

But there is a more "fundamental" problem here and it is this: all the revolutions peppering the Zimbabwe landscape have, at some point in their histories, been masculinized. Women may be incorporated to feed radicals and take care of the properties of petit bourgeois leaders. But "women" are simply evocations of nature in each of Zimbabwe's many revolutions. "Women" are not seen as beings who have certain valued productive assignments that are susceptible to as much change or continuity as "men" experience in the course of living. Nativized in those social roles, "women" are rarely, if at all, able to mount the revolutionary platforms; they are not deemed to be agents in their own right and the fulfillment of their needs is not a local litmus test of revolutionary success.

Naomi Chazan tells us that many people in the African countryside feel that "the state—be it colonial or postcolonial—constitutes an intrusive device from which they can possibly reap benefits, but over which they have little influence."[30] If this is so, had the Zimbabwean state been more bold in its commitment to rural women, this could have been interpreted as yet another form of intrusiveness. But a parallel point worth making is that contemporary states tend to be intrusively *gendered* actors. That is, their intrusions, like those of revolutionary centers of force, have dissimilar consequences for men and women. "For most African women . . . the colonial period was characterized by significant losses in both power and authority," and the promises to women of "economic and political benefits from independence . . . have failed to materialize."[31] Many men also lost ground during the colonial and independence periods. But we cannot ignore the fact that the state is stuffed and bristling with men who can stall changes for and by women under the call of more pressing business.

Are women trapped by the semi-permanent conflicts that characterize situations of simultaneous revolutions? Or are they freed up to find spaces for old and new identities in between cross-cutting trends? Look at Zimbabwe and see that a quick and satisfying answer to that question evades the women who struggle both creatively and desperately to be seen and heard.

NOTES

1. Quoted in Mary Ann Tétreault, "Women and Revolution: A Framework for Analysis," in *Gendered States: Feminist (Re)Visions of International Relations Theory*, ed. V. Spike Peterson (Boulder: Lynne Rienner, 1992), 99.

2. Christine Sylvester, "Simultaneous Revolutions: The Zimbabwean Case," *Journal of Southern African Studies* 16, no. 3 (1990): 453.

3. Andre Astrow, *Zimbabwe: A Revolution that Lost Its Way?* (London: Zed Press, 1983); Ibbo Mandaza, "The State and Politics in the Post-White Settler Colonial Situation," in *Zimbabwe: The Political Economy of Transition, 1980–1986*, ed. I. Mandaza (Dakar: Codesria, 1986); Carol Thompson, *Challenge to Imperialism: The Frontline States and the Liberation of Zimbabwe* (Boulder: Westview, 1985).

4. Astrow, *Zimbabwe.*

5. Christine Sylvester, "'Urban Women Cooperators,' 'Progress,' and 'African Feminism' in Zimbabwe," *Differences* 3, no. 1 (1991): 39–62.

6. Sylvester, "Simultaneous Revolutions," 455.

7. Ibid.

8. Ibid., 453.

9. Jean Elshtain, *Women and War* (New York: Basic Books, 1987).

10. *Profiles of Rhodesia's Women*, quoted in Ruth Weiss, *The Women of Zimbabwe* (London: Kesho, 1986), 56.

11. There were exceptions. One thinks of "Auntie" Jane Ngwenya of ZAPU, who suffered unspeakable conditions of detention for her political activities and has gone on to be a strong defender of women's cooperatives in post-independence Zimbabwe.

12. Joshua Nkomo, *Nkomo: The Story of My Life* (London: Methuen, 1984), 38–39.

13. O. Tshabangu, *The March 11 Movement in ZAPU—Revolution Within the Revolution* (Heslington, 1979); J. Z. Moyo, "Observations on Our Struggle," in

Zimbabwe Independence Movements: Selected Documents, ed. C. Nyangoni and G. Nyandoro (New York: Barnes and Noble, 1979); Phyllis Martin and David Johnson, *The Struggle for Zimbabwe: The Chimurenga War* (Harare: Zimbabwe Publishing House, 1981).

14. Judith Todd, *The Right to Say No: Rhodesia 1972* (Harare: Longman Zimbabwe, 1987); and Judith Todd, *An Act of Treason: Rhodesia 1965* (Harare: Longman, Zimbabwe, 1982).

15. Weiss, *The Women of Zimbabwe*; Kathy Bond-Stewart, *Young Women in the Liberation Struggle: Stories and Poems from Zimbabwe* (Harare: Zimbabwe Publishing House, 1984); and Zimbabwe Project, *Stories and Poems from the Struggle* (Harare: Zimbabwe Project, 1981). Jane Ngwenya claims that ZAPU trained 2,150 women for combat. Since the Zimbabwe African National Union (ZANU) fielded the larger of the two guerrilla armies, it is likely that at least triple that number were among the ZANLA forces. However, the figure of thirty thousand women in the two guerrilla armies has also been bandied about.

16. See Weiss, *Women of Zimbabwe*, and Irene Staunton, *Mothers of the Revolution* (Harare: Baobob, 1990) for the stories of unsung rural women.

17. Antonio Gramsci, *Selections from the Prison Notebooks*, ed. and trans. Quinton Hoare and Geoffrey Nowell Smith (London: Lawrence and Wishart, 1971).

18. Terence Ranger, *Peasant Consciousness and Guerrilla War in Zimbabwe* (Berkeley: University of California Press, 1985).

19. Patricia Hill Collins, "Learning from the Outsider Within: The Sociological Significance of Black Feminist Thought," in Mary Margaret Fonow and Judith A. Cook, *Beyond Methodology: Feminist Scholarship as Lived Research* (Bloomington: Indiana University Press, 1991).

20. Norma Kriger, "Popular Struggles in Zimbabwe's War of National Liberation," paper presented at the Canadian African Studies Association, 1988, 21; and Norma Kriger, "The Zimbabwean War of Liberation: Struggles Within the Struggles," *Journal of Southern African Studies* 14, no. 2 (1988): 304–22.

21. Weiss, *Women of Zimbabwe*, 80.

22. Meggi Zingani, quoted in Staunton, *Women of the Revolution*, 126.

23. Not all women combatants report their war experiences in these terms. Some maintain that they received the same training as men and suffered the same indignities during Rhodesian attacks. Relatively few written reports, however, contain accounts of women actually shooting at the enemy.

24. From my interviews with rural women in Mashonaland in 1988.

25. Quoted in Kathleen Staudt, "Women's Politics, the State, and Capitalist Transformation in Africa," in *Studies in Power and Class in Africa*, ed. Irving Markovitz (New York: Oxford University Press, 1987), 207.

26. From my interviews with peasant women in Mashonaland in 1988.

27. For a moving fictional portrayal of discrimination against school-age girls, see Tsitsi Dangarembga, *Nervous Conditions* (London: Women's Press, 1988).

28. Staudt, "Women's Politics," 207; also Donald Rothchild and Naomi

Chazan, *The Precarious Balance: State and Society in Africa* (Boulder: Westview, 1988).

29. See Christine Sylvester, "Unities and Disunities in Zimbabwe's 1990 Election," *Journal of Modern African Studies* 28, no. 3 (1990): 375–400; also, Christine Sylvester, *Zimbabwe: The Terrain of Contradictory Development* (Boulder: Westview, 1991).

30. Naomi Chazan, "State and Society in Africa: Images and Challenges," in *The Precarious Balance: State and Society in Africa*, ed. Donald Rothchild and Naomi Chazan (Boulder: Westview, 1988), 137.

31. Jane Parpart, "Women and the State in Africa," in ibid., 210, 215.

Chapter 19

Women and Revolution

What Have We Learned?

Mary Ann Tétreault

Our consideration of women and revolution has taken us to many places around the world—despite the title of this volume, even to the fringes of Europe. The cases we have reviewed address a range of issues including changes in property rights and the rise of new classes and new political groups, some that represented the interests or embodied the persons of women. They illustrate how ideology is used as a tool of revolutionary transformation and how complex the layers of ideology are. They show how these layers are manipulated, along with material resources, as a new governing coalition seeks to ensure its dominance, if not its monopoly, over what Michael Walzer calls the spheres of distribution of desirable social goods in a post-revolutionary new regime.[1]

The cases examined here highlight revolutionary social change in all its contradictions. To consider women as a class or social group that does or does not participate in revolution is to consider revolution from the perspective of the individual in politics and society rather than as the success or failure of classes or groups to gain access to state power. The presence of women in nearly every other social class or group, yet seldom as equals or equivalents to the men in them, is a constant reminder of the constraints on liberation embedded in formal and informal institutions and arrangements. When these private relations suddenly enter the realm of public discourse they illuminate the oppression of other groups. A focus on women also shows how social institutions and political economies are mutually conditioned. What constitutes a family and the functions appropriately performed by that family determine and are determined by the relative authority of other social and economic institutions. As a number of authors have noted, when revolutionaries retain or recreate private space as the social and political locus of women and families, they mark off a protected refuge for social forces and production relations that are likely to be antagonistic to their new order.

THE DUAL CHARACTER OF REVOLUTIONS

All the cases we have examined show revolution's dual character. On the one hand, revolutionaries acting together seek to end political regimes they see as oppressive. On the other, revolutionaries compete among themselves to control the outcomes of their revolutions, not only in terms of the designs of new regimes but, perhaps even more, the identity of the individuals and groups who will dominate them. When an old regime falls relatively quickly, this intra-revolutionary conflict may be cut short. Those groups whose pre-revolutionary power was greatest in such a winning coalition—for example, property owners or military officers—also dominate afterwards. Their victories in places like Mexico, Indonesia, and Bolivia changed the cast of characters in ruling elites and altered property and political rights, but they effected few fundamental changes in social organization. Women in these countries, as in every case we present here, were oppressed under old regimes. However, the rapidity with which these old regimes crumbled provided them with little political space to engage and be engaged in the process of transformation. Once the victors had added the resources of the state to their arsenals, they were strong enough to fend off potential rivals with more thoroughgoing social aims. In Theda Skoçpol's terms, this is the outcome of political revolution and it is unlikely to include women *as women* among the victors.

Barrington Moore suggests that social revolutions feature concentrated directed violence that necessarily results in obvious social change because of the relatively rapid selective elimination of particular social groups. This makes the analysis of social revolutions superficially easier than the analysis of political revolutions. The inauguration of a new regime on a vastly different social base almost automatically recreates civil society on new lines. Yet we have seen a number of exceptions, including Afghanistan, Cuba, the North Vietnamese in their 1954 victory against the French, Chile's revolution by election, and Iran, where revolutionaries with ambitious social agendas achieved their victories before this sort of selective elimination had progressed very far. Selective elimination is also retarded when revolutions are the byproduct of external war, as in the case of Yugoslavia, or are derailed by external conflict, as in the case of Kuwait. In these cases, as with the more obviously political revolutions, we should anticipate that domestic politics will continue these internal conflicts by other means.

Other cases, such as China and post-1975 Vietnam, conformed more closely to Moore's notions. Even here, though, what were seen inside and out as victorious conclusions by no means marked the end of domestic conflict to revise the social bases of the revolutions. Chris Sylvester's caution against oversimplifying conceptualizations of revolution alerts us to the complexities of politics and social change among large and diverse casts of characters: revolutions do not begin all at once, or unfold uniformly through time or space, or end on a single beat. They do not produce the same outcome for all survivors. Their conclusion is not the end of history in any sense.

PROMISSORY NOTES[2] AND THE OUTCOMES OF "FEMINIST REVOLUTIONS"

Rapid victories by Marxist coalitions whose ideologies included an explicit commitment to feminist principles touched off or led to the elaboration of policies aimed at freeing women for an independent economic and political existence. But women's status in the longer term depended less on ideology or even its initial implementation as policy and more on the needs of new regimes to fend off counter-revolutionary movements or those elements of the victorious coalitions who were relative losers under the new order. The politics of revolutionary transformation only began rather than ended with the installation of these new regimes. Their public successes and failures in the visible realm of politics and economics were inextricably connected to the often far less visible but still state-mediated politics of family life.

In Afghanistan, feminism constituted more than a component of ideology. The implementation of feminist policies was part of the modernization strategy advocated by Afghan revolutionaries and the new regime they created. One goal was to eliminate the source of counter-revolutionary movements by destroying their traditional base in the countryside. This base rested on the patriarchal family as an economic unit and a tribal structure that utilized women as tokens in the construction of inter-family alliances. The successes of counter-attacks by dissident tribal groups caused the regime to back off from its initial commitments to rural Afghan women in order to pacify externally armed tribal groups and preserve the governing coalition and its governors. These efforts failed. The ongoing internal battles among counter-revolutionaries for control of the Afghan state are also battles for control of Afghan women. The subjection of these women marks the defeat of the socialist revolution and its feminist ideology and also the control of the victors over the successor state and economy.

In Vietnam, the oppression of women under patriarchy was used ideologically as an analogue upon which to build analyses of the oppression of Vietnamese peasants by French and French-allied property owners and the whole Vietnamese people by colonial powers. It also justified the mobilization of individual women to run an economy whose male workers were continually siphoned off by the demands of the revolution, and provided a framework within which these women could identify with the goals of the revolution and claim future rewards in return for their support. But the victorious northern regime faced challenges in the countryside as the result of an ill-conceived land reform policy. As in China, the solution to regime-threatening peasant unrest was found in the reinstatement of rural patriarchy whose effects at first were masked by military demands. The more liberal society of the south was less committed than the north to gender egalitarianism even though women there served in the regular army and participated at higher rates in guerrilla forces. After Vietnam was reintegrated in 1975, women lost formal political power. The return of men to the domestic economy was accompanied by the reintroduction of a gender division of labor reflected in a growing resemblance between the Vietnamese peasant commune and the Israeli kibbutz. Still, the initial commitment to feminism in Vietnam has resulted in a substantial residue of opportunity for the exceptional woman—a variant of the star system—that is not evident in the Israeli case.

In Cuba, socialist feminism provided a means by which an unexpectedly rapid victory by a revolutionary movement that resulted in a profound loss of population, economic resources, and normal external relations with neighbors could compensate for these losses by mobilizing women as integral elements in a new political economy. As in Vietnam and Afghanistan, Cuban women seeking their own liberation via revolutionary transformation became strong partisans of the new regime. They were assisted by the voluntary exile of large numbers of liberals committed to the religiously supported patriarchy of the privatized family. But economic pressures from the collapse of the Soviet Union and increased U.S. efforts to isolate Cuba from the rest of the world opened a chink in Cuba's commitment to feminism, some of which had been articulated during the revolution as the protection of Cuban women's bodies from foreign exploitation. *Playboy*'s Cuban issue and the rise of prostitution for a foreign clientele represent a significant real and symbolic retreat from feminist principles, despite heroic efforts to maintain services that reduce burdens on working wives and mothers.

Socialist ideology by itself cannot mobilize women behind a new regime regardless of the fervor of its profession of feminist values. After Allende's victory in Chile, Chilean women were alienated both by an ideology that exhorted them to do more work and by a regime that failed to reward this work either symbolically or tangibly. Allende's personal insensitivity and patronizing attitude toward women was not only offensive but also prevented him from understanding what he would have to do to build popular support for his regime. The response to his failure to deliver either status or material rewards led crowds of Chilean women to bang pots, throw chicken feed, and taunt military leaders into removing a regime that had left women's power and status unchanged and their economic situations measurably worse. Yet Chilean women do not fit the stereotype that says that women are more conservative than men despite their counter-revolutionary role. Chilean women pressed the civilian case against the military regime, challenging it with their bodies as they mourned, regularly and publicly, for their *desaparacidos*. They shamed the international human rights community to withdraw support for Pinochet just as they had shamed military leaders to overthrow Allende.

Nonsocialist ideologies promising gender egalitarianism are equally unattractive to women in the absence of genuine rewards. Islamist ideology stressing a separate, subordinate, but valued status for women attracted many Iranian women who had presumably been liberated by the Shah's western-style liberalism. But the liberal privatized family is structurally no more advantageous for women than the traditional family form characteristic of the Islamic Middle East. Both inhibit structural changes in gender relations. Meanwhile, other aspects of liberalism in Iran produced political, economic, and social dislocations that had a disproportionate impact on women and families. Increased domestic repression eventually affected nearly every family in the capital. All of these contributed to the disenchantment of Iranian women with the Shah and his regime. Women's continued support for the Islamist regime of post-revolutionary Iran, despite its restrictions on their dress and public behavior, is underpinned by the regime's strengthening of both halves of a gender-divided dual stream of status competition and material rewards and the framing of revolutionary ideology in religious terms.

THE PERSONAL IS POLITICAL—AND ECONOMIC; THE ECONOMY IS POLITICAL—AND PERSONAL

The predominance of patriarchy in post-revolutionary family forms examined here explains some of the failures of revolution to free women and guarantee them equal rights with men. But the predominance of patriarchy itself requires an explanation. In our case studies, we have uncovered repeated and profound resistance to women's liberation by the winners as well as the losers of revolutions. The cause is not so difficult to determine: gains for women are not free. They come at the expense of property rights held by men and policy choices available to states. Including women as autonomous participants in revolutionary movements or post-revolutionary political economies necessarily implies a loss of these property rights and a loss of resources available to leaders who manage post-revolutionary political economies. The prospect and realization of these losses constitute the strongest mutual interest underlying alliances between states and patriarchs to keep women subordinate.

In every case examined here, the systematic gender oppression of women was represented by male customary and/or legal rights to some or all of the labor, bodies, and products of the women in their families. An obvious indicator of men's property rights in women illustrated in these cases is the bride price, a monetary compensation for the women whose productivity and reproductivity are lost to their natal families. Another is child custody rights which are held in most of our cases by fathers or the patrilineal group. From a broader—less obvious—perspective, what Susan Okin has called "vulnerability by marriage"[3]—laws and customs that give men superior property, entry, and exit rights—characterize every case examined in this volume. Under such initial conditions, to confer revolutionary or post-revolutionary agency upon women is to seize the property of men *as men*.

One way of getting around what might be construed as an illegitimate seizure of property rights by revolutionaries who liberate women is to allow women to earn their rights in the new order. They can fight alongside the men during the revolution's violent phases and earn their liberty by spilling their blood. Afterwards, they can demonstrate and stand up for themselves against the various patriarchal orders that oppress them, speak bitterness, and strike back just as peasants or workers or other revolutionary groups have stood and struck against oppressive social and political orders during and after revolutionary conflicts. In every case examined here, though, either the avenues to earn entitlements were blocked or the entitlements earned proved to be acutely vulnerable to erosion.

Avenues are blocked from the top by revolutionaries acting *as men* by excluding women or channeling them into less valued revolutionary roles. In South Korea, Mexico, and Bolivia, women's direct participation was unnecessary to bring about the conclusion of revolutionary conflict. These unmobilized or excluded women were not able to earn equal entitlements and they didn't get them. North Vietnamese, Chinese, and Israeli women were mobilized almost entirely as auxiliaries. The symbolic inferiority of this kind of mobilization was appreciated by Mozambican women who insisted upon equal rights to participate as fighters. Ideological commitments to feminism by socialist North Vietnamese and Chinese were insufficient to override the practical necessity of maintaining an ideological and political alliance between the new regimes and patriarchal peasants, though both also implemented structural changes that added to women's autonomy and enabled female "stars" to rise. Socialist Israelis concentrated on erasing memories that could be used to justify female entitlements. They delegated a large portion of the responsibility for establishing and maintaining structural reforms promoting gender equality on an institution they knew would refuse to do this: the orthodox religious establishment. Some nominally socialist Angolans also forgot women's contributions to their armed struggle, building their nationalist ideology on tribalism and a tradition in which women's place was with children as helpers rather than with men as equal participants in politics, society, and the economy.

Men as men are not the only losers when women obtain equal rights. The leaders of post-revolutionary regimes and political economies are also potential losers. Here a comparison of China and Cuba is instructive. Both post-revolutionary regimes were socialist and explicitly committed to feminist principles. But the social bases of these revolutions differed. The new regime in China depended upon political and economic support from the dominant peasant class, support that was contingent upon the reestablishment of patriarchal relations in the countryside. Still, as long as autonomous women also continued to be political and economic resources, changes in women's status were linked to the economic and political needs of the regime. Women's status alternately rose and declined as the regime balanced the demands of women against the demands of peasant patriarchs. After China became committed to economic liberalization, however, women's status declined steadily along with their value as autonomous workers outside the home.

Throughout the post-revolutionary era in China, declines in women's status enabled state resources that might have provided payments and services to support the families of women working outside the home to be shifted to investment in infrastructure and industry.[4] The huge levels of unemployment produced by the reorganization of the Chinese economy under liberalization were politically easier to manage when women could be saddled with the lion's share of job losses. This was accomplished indirectly. Hiring decisions were left to enterprises that tended to choose men over women to avoid paying for benefits which are collected and accounted for as benefits to female employees rather than as broad-based citizen entitlements.[5] Economic incentives in agriculture were structured to give advantages to family heads commanding large home-based work forces. In China today, women are disproportionately represented in the reserve army of socialism.

In contrast, the post-revolutionary Cuban economy was urban based. Modernization and higher living standards depended upon the economic participation of women working outside the home. The acute need for each worker has been magnified since the Soviet collapse by the embargo which has reduced Cuban labor productivity. The liberalization and capital investment that produced female unemployment in China are foreclosed to Cuba by the policies of the United States, reducing the likelihood of a women's mobilization against Castro analogous to the women's mobilization against Allende.

State economic interests in a patriarchally mediated gender division of labor can be seen most clearly in Kyung Ae Park's detailed analysis of the South Korean economy. There, women who labor under structural disadvantages disguised as cultural constraints on women's liberation are the main attraction for direct foreign investment. Female workers are primary contributors to local economic development via backward and forward linkages, and to the national economy in the form of foreign exchange from exports. What draws outside investment and the local and national economic development it stimulates is the systematic oppression of female workers. Their low wages, long hours, and the social constraints on their behavior that make them such docile, and thus desirable, workers are direct results of gender discrimination. If women were equal to men in South Korea, the country's competitiveness as a source of cheap labor would be significantly reduced.

THE RHETORIC OF REVOLUTION AND THE DISAPPEARANCE OF EARNED ENTITLEMENTS

Paying your dues does not necessarily guarantee permanent membership as an autonomous actor in a post-revolutionary society and political economy. Women's entitlements to freedom and equality can be erased in a number of ways. Structurally, a regime can choose to treat the family rather than the individual as the most fundamental unit of politics, society, the economy, or any combination of these. Customs already reflect status differences between men and women and laws enforce them, even if a state adopts a nominally neutral approach to gender issues. Individual rights to education, to enter and exit marriage, to bear and rear children, and to work and own property, depend upon laws and law enforcement. Even where patriarchy is not formally established as an organizing principle of politics and the economy, failure to guarantee equal rights to women in families and then to preserve those rights through institutions and procedures open to all is effectively to deny equal rights to women and to sanction their economic and sexual exploitation by institutions and procedures already in place and by the men who benefit directly from them. Such sanctified patterns of authoritarianism and exploitation may contradict revolutionary principles. More problematic over the long term, they embed unregulated authority that can be used to challenge the authority of the state in enclaves protected by their locus in the private space.

Symbolically, women's entitlements disappear through gender-selective forgetting of revolutionary experiences. I will never forget how profoundly shocked I was a few years ago when, looking through a book of photographs Hans Namuth had taken in Spain during the Civil War, I saw uniformed women with rifles fighting in the Republican forces. Nothing that I had read about this war before prepared me for those photographs, one of which is reproduced on the dust jacket of this volume. The Museum of the Revolution in Hanoi was similarly shocking but for the opposite reason—because of its omission of representations of what I knew about the activities of women during that period in Vietnam. A more perverse kind of forgetting is institutionalized in Israel, where young women are inducted into the military or join kibbutzim expecting an equal opportunity to serve in any capacity, only to be shunted into decorative and service roles in a way that transforms the responsibility for this political denial of equality into a sense of personal failure. Forgetting may be spearheaded by institutions and groups other than the state, as the Bedouin denial of women's contributions to the liberation of Kuwait has shown. No matter how it comes about, forgetting erodes the legitimacy of women's claims to equality.

Another rhetorical mechanism for erasing equal entitlements is through an ideological emphasis on women's sexual roles. This is evident in "mariolatrous" Catholic cultures like Bolivia's, where the cult of the Virgin Mother with its perfect solution to a man's Oedipal dilemma presents women with an ideal type impossible to aspire to, much less achieve. Gratzia Smeall's description of *Marianismo* is a case example of the Machiavellian double-bind waiting for women who seek a political identity within such an ideological system. If women accept the maternal role and approach politics from a position of moral superiority, men apprehend their actions as those of the "woman experienced by small children as the dangerous mother, who feeds but also dominates and threatens to engulf."[6] If they choose instead the alternative sexualized role and approach politics as an autonomous equal, men become alarmed at "the powers of young women as sex objects [against whom] most of [the] explicit warnings concerning women in politics are directed."[7]

The maternal stereotype is strengthened by the success of mothers as clandestine agents in revolutionary struggles. Zimbabwean mothers carrying guns and food in bundles that look like babies are metaphorically disarming the revolution's enemies. But their power to "unman" remains in the minds of revolutionaries as well. The young women who joined guerrilla units as equals evoked the other fear of the young, sexually powerful woman. The government of Zimbabwe has demonstrated its reactions to both types of ideologically sexualized women in its land-tenure policies which favor rural patriarchs and give them power over the mothers in the countryside, and in its anti-prostitution sweeps which use female sexuality as an excuse to erase the autonomy of urban women. Both are structural responses to the psychological fears engendered by ideological caricatures.

STRUCTURES OF OPPRESSION

States are not alone in their mediation of gender and family roles and responsibilities. Religious institutions have a longer history of entitlement than states do to define and enforce gender roles in society. Synagogue, church, and mosque contest state power in part on the terrain of women's bodies and behavior.[8] Yet to attribute women's continued oppression following revolution to religion alone is to accept the word of the oppressors that what they are doing conforms to religious principles. As Diane Busch and Steve Mumme point out, the ideologies and interests of states and religious bodies must be determined empirically rather than assumed in advance. Sex-gender systems conflate the influence of both on the construction of gender.

The confusion of emotionally charged social practices with religious principles is often deliberate—part of the struggle for resources and power among individuals and groups dedicated to enlarging their own status and authority as well as to different ways of organizing political and social life. The modern gender politics of Protestant and Islamic fundamentalism can usefully be considered in this light. It seeks to admit persons whose legitimacy to rule rests on religious rather than political authority to positions of dominance in what Skoçpol calls the state class. Conflicts of authority between state and church have dominated politics throughout the period of the development of the nation-state. Thomas Hobbes's *Leviathan* warns English kings to beware of challenges to their authority from Rome. Hobbes advises kings to lead their own churches to preserve their supremacy and, under the doctrine of the king's two bodies, that of the state. Following Hobbes, English kings promoted authoritarian Protestant patriarchy to support an authoritarian state.[9] From the other side, Iranian mullahs sanction violence against women to preserve the supremacy of religious leaders in the Iranian state.

The ambiguous role of religion in the persistence of authoritarian forms is considered by Germaine Tillion who finds strong similarities among the structures of female oppression in Jewish, Christian, and Muslim communities in the Mediterranean littoral. These similarities extend to a set of property relations based on endogamy, pronatalism, and territorial expansionism, and are visible to varying degrees not only in the modern societies living in the places formerly occupied by the civilizations of "the Ancient World," but also in the communities descended from their colonies in the western hemisphere and Asia.[10] Analogous survivals of what might loosely be termed "Confucian relations" can be seen in China, Korea, and Vietnam.

Tillion extends the analysis of sex-gender systems by considering explicitly the interdependent contribution of the primordial organizations of family, clan, and community to the construction and reproduction of these systems. She shows how, in communities still identifiably Mediterranean, the influence of authoritarian communal ideologies and structures continues to override contradictory principles espoused by both states and religious bodies. For example, preference for marriage between close relatives has persisted for centuries despite state and religious proscriptions against incest. Her identification of a specific microsocial formation (because of the symbolic and structural role of endogamy in its organization she calls it "the republic of cousins") with an authoritarian, possessive, and expansionist macroculture is a model demonstrating how the survival of oppressive structures in families and communities can become an engine driving their reinstatement in society as a whole.

From this perspective, the greatest failure of the Yugoslav revolution was that it left the republic of cousins virtually intact in communities throughout the country. With some exceptions, most notably urban Bosnia, traditional ethnocentric patriarchy survived throughout Yugoslavia in enclaves protected by the socialist state. When that state dissolved, the dominant ideology and pattern of social order became, by default, the principles and organizations of the republic of cousins. In contrast, urban Bosnian social and family organization was consciously altered to embrace cosmopolitan and exogamous principles. Like similarly organized societies in the so-called primitive periphery, it succumbed to attacks by authoritarians whose ideology of endogamy and possessive individualism is expressed as territorial expansion and ethnic cleansing.[11]

The pivotal role of oppressive families in the expansion and legitimation of larger structures of oppression is masked by political struggles within regimes and between states and institutional competitors for political and economic power. The contenders look for allies in other social groups, including families and communal organizations formed by associations of families such as clans or villages. Traditional family and community heads, whose power would diminish if there were external controls on their deployment of human and other resources, also seek allies to fend off threats to their authority and positions. The community of interests that I have already noted between patriarchs and the leaders of large institutions fosters, if not cooperation, mutual tolerance between them. The low levels of legitimacy characteristic of new states and new regimes may explain why leaders of revolutions decide to privatize the family rather than commit significant resources to regulate its behavior. Another reason is the difficulty of accomplishing structural changes in the family in the absence of alternative institutions and effective mechanisms of enforcement, especially in areas where traditional social organization remains very strong.

These cases also reveal the ambiguity of the state as a structure of oppression, especially where the capacity of a post-revolutionary regime to effect social change is limited by the persistence of local practices which become both the symbolic and the actual means of resisting incorporation into a national society and subordination to a central political authority. Such resistance was clear in Afghanistan and in the African cases where localism is amplified by the multicultural structure of post-colonial states. Where the state is weak, it is unable to effect or protect policies designed to improve both the status and the life chances of women. For example, the Mozambican state party, FRELIMO, was so weak that, in 1989, it actually ignored its own official position condemning polygyny and started recruiting polygynous men to reverse a decline in party membership.

The personal costs to individual women attributed to state weakness is also reflected in the Mozambique case. Participants in local meetings to prepare for a 1984 conference on women in Mozambique rejected FRELIMO's recommendations for improving women's personal lives by abolishing practices such as polygyny, bride prices, and female genital mutilation. Instead, they shaped the discourse on these issues by referring to their own experiences to defend traditional practices. As Kathleen Sheldon has noted, the result was that the final document produced by the November 1984 conference included few recommendations for substantive policy change. Even with regard to female genital mutilation which, because it results in bleeding in virtually every instance of sexual intercourse, is a major vector in the heterosexual spread of AIDS among African women, the document only called for further study of the issue. The fact that women defend practices that result in misery and death for themselves and their daughters is a caution against a too facile an equation between the state and oppression and local control and personal freedom.[12]

WHAT KIND OF REVOLUTION IS BEST FOR WOMEN?

The socialist critique of liberalism rests in part on a criticism of the bourgeois family. The privatization of this family form has led to the development of a personal life which socialists see as a threat to social solidarity, popular political power, and the overthrow of oppressive economic structures.[13] Conservatives also decry personal life as a poor compensation for political or social activism.[14] Yet the personal life that has grown up inside the bourgeois family is a life shared by women and men as equal partners in intimacy.[15] Its internal organization echoes that of the *vita activa* in the early Greek polis, where individuals were mutually and continuously defined by their relative positions in a functionally differentiated formally egalitarian political space.[16] These positions are achieved by individuals deploying resources to assert their individuality in the context of their relationships to others sharing that political space.

The internal configuration of power in any real life example of the bourgeois family is determined by the interactions among individuals and their respective resources.[17] Consequently, a bourgeois family may be oppressive internally just like any other family. What reduces the likelihood that it will be is that the bourgeois family embodies an ideology and a set of social relations antithetic to what I have described as oppressive family structures. The ideology of the bourgeois family, like the ideology of the market, is based upon choice and exchange. What is needed are structures that make the reality of the bourgeois family conform to the principles upon which it is based.

As Karl Polanyi noted in his discussion of market systems, this kind of social organization is not really self-regulating, despite the assertions of liberal ideologues. Rather, it requires extensive external intervention by the state in the form of regulation and the provision of services.[18] The term "private sector" should not be taken to mean a zone of anarchy within a political community. The privacy of the market refers to the autonomy of choice, not to the severance of the market from the rule of law. A similar analysis can be applied to the family. Given the same kind of intervention that is necessary for the operation of markets—in the case of the family, intervention guaranteeing equal rights to entry, exit, property, and protection in marriage—the bourgeois family can achieve high levels of liberty for and equality among its members without impairing its privacy.

The term "bourgeois family" sets up an expectation that such a family form is the natural outcome of political revolutions that replace feudal structures with market relations. However, this is no more accurate than the assumption that a socialist revolution naturally produces an egalitarian family. Revolutions bearing both labels have generated privatized families whose social relations take place inside zones of anarchy relatively unregulated by states. The ideology and construction of privatization are not organized around the principles of individual freedom and equality under law. It is rather ideology and construction that rationalize the dominance of the strong over the weak. Privatization sanctions the surrender of authority to those with power rather than restructuring authority to guarantee freedom and justice for all.[19]

The kind of revolution that is best for women is one that results in a regime based on personal liberty, equal rights for women and men, and laws that are enforced in the home as well as in the street and in the marketplace. Although we can argue about the various meanings of liberty and what constitutes equal rights and how they are defined in constitutions, their practical value in the absence of law and equal protection under that law is worthless. A new regime unwilling or unable to extend equal protection to women and men *in their family lives* as well as in the parts of their lives conventionally viewed as lived in the separate realm of the public space denies them both liberty and equality. There is no private space which is occupied by more than one person. The persistent ideological distinction between public and private is not a wall of separation between politics and nature. It is a means to protect an authoritarian archipelago whose power and resources nurture and model the oppressive governments and regimes of the future.

NOTES

1. Michael Walzer, *Spheres of Justice: A Defense of Pluralism and Equality* (New York: Basic Books, 1983), 10–13.
2. This term comes from Sonia Kruks, Rayna Rapp, and Marilyn B. Young, eds., *Promissory Notes: Women in the Transition to Socialism* (New York: Monthly Review Press, 1989).
3. Susan Moller Okin, *Justice, Gender, and the Family* (New York: Basic Books, 1989), chap. 7.
4. Eli Zaretsky, *Capitalism, The Family, and Personal Life*, rev. ed. (New York: Perennial Library, 1986), 78.
5. Interviews in China, May 1989.
6. Hanna Fenichel Pitkin, *Fortune is a Woman: Gender and Politics in the Thought of Niccolò Machiavelli* (Berkeley: University of California Press, 1984), 136.
7. Ibid., 115.
8. In this context, "synagogue, church, and mosque" refer to the institutional manifestations of Judaism, Christianity, and Islam, respectively, and are analogues to "state" and "class."
9. Lawrence Stone, *The Family, Sex, and Marriage in England, 1500–1800*, abridged ed. (New York: Harper Torchbooks, 1979), 145.
10. Germaine Tillion, *The Republic of Cousins: Women's Oppression in Mediterranean Society*, trans. Quintin Hoare (London: Al Saqi Books, 1983).
11. Ibid., 56–60.
12. See Alice Walker and Pratibha Parmar, *Warrior Marks: Female Genital Mutilation and the Sexual Blinding of Women* (New York: Harcourt Brace, 1993).
13. See, for example, Zaretsky, *Capitalism, the Family, and Personal Life*.
14. For example, Hannah Arendt, *The Human Condition: A Study of the Central Dilemmas Facing Modern Man* (Garden City: Doubleday Anchor, 1959), 35–36, 46–47, 186–88; Robert N. Bellah et al., *Habits of the Heart: Individualism and Commitment in American Life* (New York: Harper Perennial, 1986).
15. Peter Gay, *The Bourgeois Experience Victoria to Freud*, vols. 1 and 2 (New York: Oxford University Press, 1984, 1986).
16. This analysis derives from Arendt's description of the active life in *The*

Human Condition, and from other analyses of autonomy and political identity in ancient Athens, most notably Josiah Ober, *Mass and Elite in Democratic Athens: Rhetoric, Ideology, and the Power of the People* (Princeton: Princeton University Press, 1989) and Cynthia Farrar, *The Origins of Democratic Thinking: The Invention of Politics in Classical Athens* (Cambridge: Cambridge University Press, 1988).

17. Okin, *Justice, Gender, and the Family*, especially chap. 8.

18. Karl Polanyi, *The Great Transformation* (New York: Farrar and Rinehart, 1944), 149.

19. Benjamin Barber, *Strong Democracy: Participatory Politics for a New Age* (Berkeley: University of California Press, 1984), 74.

Contributors

Diane Mitsch Bush is professor of sociology at Colorado Mountain College. She is the author of "Women's Movements and State Policy Reforms Aimed at Domestic Violence Against Women: A Comparison of the Consequences of Movement Mobilization in the United States and India," which appeared in *Gender and Society* in December 1992.

Farideh Farhi is associate professor of political science at the University of Hawaii at Manoa. Her *States and Urban-Based Revolutions: Iran and Nicaragua* was published by the University of Illinois Press.

Connie Jorgensen is a Ph.D. candidate in the Department of Government and Foreign Affairs at the University of Virginia. She is currently doing dissertation research on the Russian Constitutional Court.

Obrad Kesić is a program officer with the International Research and Exchange Board (IREX). His work on the Balkans includes "UN Peacekeeping in Croatia and Bosnia," published in November 1992 in *Balkan Forum*, and "Serbia's Politics of Despair," which appeared in *Current History* in November 1993.

Sheryl L. Lutjens is associate professor of political science at Northern Arizona University. In addition to women and issues of feminist political theory, her research and writing have focused on administration, democracy, and education in Cuba.

Susan MacFarland is associate professor of political science at Wesleyan College, a women's college in Macon, Georgia.

Valentine M. Moghadam is senior research fellow at the World Institute for Development Economics Research of the United Nations University. She is the author of *Modernizing Women: Gender and Social Change in the Middle East*; and editor of *Identity Politics and Women: Cultural Reassertions and Feminisms in International Perspective.*

Stephen P. Mumme is professor of political science at Colorado State University. His research centers on environmental politics and natural resources management in Mexico and Latin America. He is the author of "Clearing the Air: Environmental Reform in Mexico," which appeared in *Environment* in December 1991.

Sita Ranchod-Nilsson is assistant professor of political science and women's studies at Iowa State University. Her chapter "'Educating Eve': The Women's Club Movement and Political Consciousness Among Rural African Women in Southern Rhodesia, 1950–1980" appears in *African Encounters with Domesticity,* ed. Karen Tranberg Hansen.

Kyung Ae Park is research chair of the Institute of Asian Research and assistant professor of political science at the University of British Colombia. she is the coauthor of *China and North Korea: Politics of Integration and Modernization.*

Catherine V. Scott is associate professor of political science at Agnes Scott College and the author of the forthcoming *Gender and Development: Rethinking Modernization and Dependency Theory.*

Kathleen Sheldon is affiliated with the Center for the Study of Women at the University of California at Los Angeles, where she has taught African history and women's studies. She has written a chapter on Mozambique for *Political Parties of Sub-Saharan Africa* and edited a book on urban women in Africa.

Gratzia Villarroel Smeall is assistant professor of political science and director of the international studies program at St. Norbert's College.

Joan Supplee is assistant professor of Latin American history at Baylor University. She is completing a manuscript on regional economic development in Argentina.

Christine Sylvester teaches at Northern Arizona University. She is the author of *Zimbabwe: The Terrain of Contradictory Development* and *Feminist Theory and International Relations in a Postmodern Era.*

Mary Ann Tétreault is professor of political science and director of the Carrie Chapman Catt Center for Women and Politics at Iowa State University. She is the author of "Civil Society in Kuwait: Protected Spaces and Women's Rights," and "The Family Romance of Islam," both published in *The Middle East Journal.*

Index